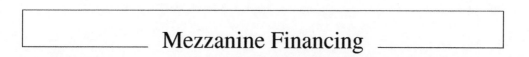

# Mezzanine Financing

For other titles in the Wiley Finance series
please see www.wiley.com/finance

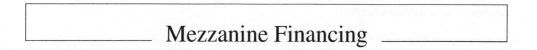

# Mezzanine Financing

## Tools, Applications and Total Performance

### Luc Nijs

# WILEY

Registered office

John Wiley & Sons Ltd, The Atrium, Southern Gate, Chichester, West Sussex, PO19 8SQ, United Kingdom

For details of our global editorial offices, for customer services and for information about how to apply for permission to reuse the copyright material in this book please visit our website at www.wiley.com.

*Library of Congress Cataloging-in-Publication Data*

Nijs, Luc.
    Mezzanine financing : tools, applications and total performance / Luc Nijs.
        pages cm. — (The Wiley finance series)
    Includes index.
        ISBN 978-1-119-94181-1 (hbk)    1. Finance—Management.    2. Risk management.    3. Finance–Law and legislation.    I. Title.
    HG173.N54 2013
    658.15'224–dc23

                                                                                                    2013034153

A catalogue record for this book is available from the British Library.

ISBN 978-1-119-94181-1 (hbk) ISBN 978-1-118-76522-7 (ebk)
ISBN 978-1-118-76520-3 (ebk)

Cover images reproduced by permission of Shutterstock.com

*To my parents.*
*For their relentless support in pretty much everything I do.*
*That they may continue to thrive in good health.*

# Contents

# Preface

For years now, for one and a half decades in fact, I have been engaged in the mezzanine world as an academic, trainer, consultant and as an entrepreneur/investor. Although nothing can replace practice and experience, it is the many students and practitioners I have met in my programs and courses, as well as the many business situations which triggered open-ended questions, that ultimately motivated me to write the book you now have in front of you.

During all those years the mezzanine finance world has changed a lot; it has grown significantly, boundaries have become blurred and financial innovations have made the spectrum more fragmented than before. Not surprisingly, many students and young professionals have wondered if they really understood what was going on, and when it was appropriate to use these products in a variety of situations thrown at them in their professional careers. They wondered which type of product to use and when, what the short and long-term impact would be for their firm, how to legally construct these products and, most importantly, how much risk there would be in each of these products, and therefore what a realistic and meaningful return would be given the risks involved. Some of them ended up in a vicious circle of self-repeating and self-reinforcing questions.

In my students' battle to embrace the dynamics of the product group and assess the adequateness of each product, their eagerness and uncertainty forced me to be clearer and more transparent in the way I communicated about the theme. That clarity is even more important in emerging markets where most of my business engagements are (and also my heart and passion) and where the banking sector has often not yet (fully) commercialized the product group. Sometimes this was because there was no need for the product group, sometimes because overall financial development has not been ongoing at a pace that would justify their introduction, and finally the contractual structure which can, at times, be difficult to understand, and/or difficult to produce, and the position the creditor ends up in when things go wrong, obstructed the introduction of the product group in some of those emerging markets.

This book is written around my experiences during sessions, and is based on years of implementing the product group in many countries, structures and industries while supporting different corporate or entrepreneurial objectives. The book, therefore, has content that can be described as a mix of academic analysis and practical applications for selecting and structuring deals. It is also characterized by a multidisciplinary approach, where economic, legal and financial aspects are intertwined where needed and as deemed appropriate.

I have also included the necessary examples and case studies, as the picture they provide can say more than a thousand words, and will further stimulate those who decide to use the book primarily as a study handbook or guide.

The book's content falls into four major divisions. After an introduction that allows us to look at the mezzanine market and the demarcation of the product group (Chapter 1), the second part of the book will include extensive coverage of the individual products, and contains a list of dos and don'ts for each of them (Chapter 2), the implicit cost of mezzanine products (Chapter 3) and the technicalities with respect to embedded optionalities (Chapter 4) as well as the overall pricing and valuation question. The third part of the book will look at the peculiarities of the product group when applied within certain industries and the implications of highly regulated environments. The banking sector, project finance applications, the real estate sector and private equity settings all pose specific questions and raise individual problems that we need to tackle (Chapters 5–8).

The fourth part of the book will look at the issues of structuring the products, accounting and legal issues, the struggle of rating agencies (Chapter 9) dealing with the product group, cash flow waterfall concerns and, most importantly, the question of an adequate risk–return trade-off for the product group, in particular in distressed situations or issues related to workouts or (outside) courtroom restructuring programs (Chapter 10). I end in Chapter 11 with an outlook for the product group and what innovation has delivered in this field in recent years. The aforementioned case studies and the necessary appendices which primarily contain legal and contractual support documents complete the book.

The book is therefore appropriate for both scholarly and professional purposes. For the academic or student wishing to delve deeper into the specifics of the product group, as well as the practitioner who might be looking for specific answers to the challenges that come with the application of the product group, this book provides the necessary answers and food for thought. The references made in the footnotes facilitate further reading.

The market is continuously in action and financial innovation will, at some point, force this work to be revised. Where possible, I have tried to use foresight to shape the content without leaning towards speculation about certain aspects of the product group's future and its place in the financing spectrum. Where adequate and properly identifiable, I also refer to regional differences in application or pricing levels of the product group. Finally I have tried to anticipate some of the most pressing questions facing the product group, both from a regulatory and a market point of view. No doubt, the future mezzanine market will be shaped in part by how the lending market and the need for credit will evolve into what will still qualify as significantly unstable markets, as well as the impact of Basel III and the wider regulatory reforms on the banking industry, and the further development of the shadow banking system and the regulation it will face. Each of these aspects will have distinct implications that can currently only be vaguely assessed.

Many times during the writing of this book I have had to use discretionary judgment about what to include and in how much detail. Statistically that must mean that, while exercising my discretionary judgment, I have been wrong on a number of occasions when making those decisions, for which I hope you will forgive me.

The mezzanine product group deserves increased attention and I hope this book contributes to that well-justified longevity. Happy reading!

Luc Nijs
February 2013

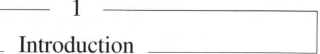

# 1

# Introduction

For as long as some sort of trade-centered economy and society has existed for mankind, people have been financing those activities, either directly or through the sort of intermediaries that we now know as banks or financial institutions. Historically, there have always been two types of financing available for businesses which are trying to raise capital to fund their activities.

That sounds somewhat simplistic but 'debt' and 'equity' have always been the fundamental financing classes tapped into by businesses, despite the many investment vehicles most businesses have access to.

We begin this section by looking at the characteristics of debt and equity and then conclude by defining the scope of the mezzanine product group.

## 1.1 THE BI-POLAR WORLD OF FINANCE

There are many different ways in which businesses can raise money, the primary ones being 'debt' and 'equity.' As I mentioned above, that sounds somewhat basic, and I guess it is, looking at the many product choices firms have these days. However, the two groups point at a fundamental difference as we know it in corporate finance. Let's first look at the characteristics of both groups and then at the individual products that are included in these groups. After that, we will look more closely at the hybrid or mezzanine product group.

Although debt and equity are often characterized by referring to the products that feature their characteristics, i.e., stocks and bonds, the true nature of the difference lies much deeper; in the nature of the cash flow claims of each product.

The first big distinction has to do with the debt claim, which entitles the holder to a contractual set of cash flows to finance the repayment of the principal amount as well as the interests on a period-to-period basis. An equity claim, on the other hand, only holds a residual claim on the cash flows of the firm, i.e., after all expenses and other commitments are honored.

This is the fundamental difference, although the tax code and legal qualifications have contributed to the creation of further distinctive characteristics between both groups.

The second distinction, which can be seen as a direct consequence of the first distinction, is a logical result of the contractual claim that debt holders have versus the residual cash flow claim of equity holders. Debt claims have priority over equity claims, hence the qualification of equity owners as residual cash flow owners. That is true for both the principal amount and interest payments, and is valid until the instrument reaches maturity, even in the case of a bankruptcy or liquidation of the firm (claim by the debt holders on the firm's assets).

The tax laws in most countries make a distinction between the tax treatment of interest versus dividends. Interests paid are tax deductible when paid by the borrowing firm and are therefore cheaper on a net (after tax) basis. Dividends, however, are not tax deductible, as they are considered to be paid out of net cash flows.

Additionally, debt instruments have a fixed maturity, i.e., the principal amount becomes due at a certain point in time, together with the interests which have not yet been paid. (We will ignore, for the time being, perpetual bonds, which are, in essence, 99/100 year renewable instruments). Equity instruments are perpetual or infinite, i.e., they continue to exist until the firm decides to buy them back and retire them, or to liquidate the firm completely.

Lastly, because equity owners are the residual cash flow owners, they are given control over the assets of the firm and its operational direction. Debt investors usually have a more passive role, often with no power of veto over major decisions in the firm. However, in recent years debt owners have done a pretty good job of getting their foot in the door, by using positive and negative covenants in their loan agreements to have (some level of) control over major transactions that would impact their position in the firm, often by making their investment more risky (i.e., due to increased leverage) or by damaging their chances of being repaid.

In short, debt is characterized by a contractual claim on the firm, benefiting from tax-deductible interest payments, with a finite lifetime and a priority claim on cash flows in both going concern situations and bankruptcy or liquidations. Equity, on the other hand, has a residual cash flow claim on the firm, is an infinite security, where dividend payments do not come with tax deductibility, has no priority, but provides control over the management and assets of the firm (in theory). Securities that have characteristics of both are termed hybrid or mezzanine capital, a definition which we will refine later in this chapter.

Figure 1.1a brings the categories and characteristics together but requires some explanation. Starting from the debt and equity positions we have already discussed (which make up boxes 1 and 3), the figure substantiates those two financing classes by indicating which types of instruments can be classified as being either debt or equity and further introduces the hybrid capital category (box 2) with an indicative set of products included.

For the sake of completeness, and to provide a level playing field, I will review most of the products mentioned at this stage. Additionally, all terms are explained in the glossary, which can be found at the end of this book, and which includes a review of all technical terms used in this book, regardless of whether they have already been explained in the core text.

Box 1, which reflects the debt products, includes the following instruments:

(1) Bank debt or loans which are fixed-income instruments with a fixed or floating interest rate and a pre-determined maturity. Often these loans are secured and therefore repayment is secured by collateral.

(2) Leasing, which is a form of asset financing where banks or specialized leasing institutions provide the financing for a specific (im)movable asset. The asset also serves as collateral in case the lessee (the person who has requested the finance) is unable to meet the lease payments. Two main categories exist, i.e., financial (or capital) and operational leases. In an operational lease, the lessor (or owner) transfers only the right to use the property to the lessee. At the end of the lease period, the lessee returns the property to the lessor. In case of a financial lease, the lessee has an option to acquire the asset (often at the end of the lease contract). Technical criteria distinguish operational from financial leases, and there are numerous accounting implications that are beyond the scope of this book. The distinction is also under review by the IASB (accounting body governing IFRS/IAS statements) which has been in its final phase for some time now (at the time of publication). For our purposes the distinction matters less as both types involve the lessee making payments to the lessor, which include a repayment of the loan underlying the asset

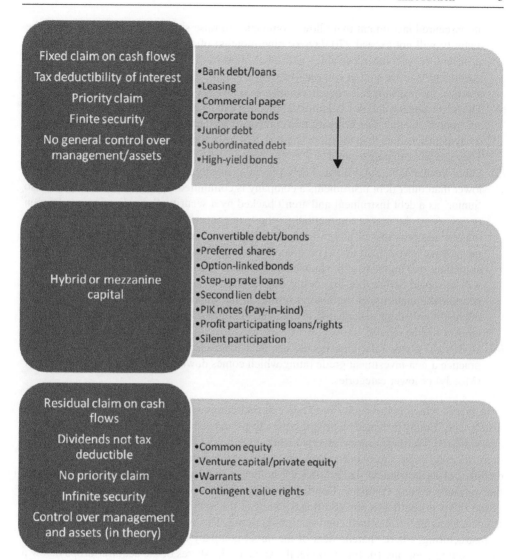

**Figure 1.1a**   The financial spectrum

purchase by the lessor. The lease payments include much more, i.e., insurance, deprecia-
tion, maintenance costs etc.

(3) Commercial paper: when companies want to raise debt they traditionally have two options, they raise bank debt or issue a corporate bond (which can be listed or raised through
a private placement). In both cases the firm will face significant costs, either because of
the fees that come with bank debt or in terms of the capital raising fees it will have to pay
to the investment bankers raising capital for the company. In case of bank debt those expenses can be as significant as 3–6% of the amounts looked for. In the case of a bond this
can be anywhere between 3 and 7% depending on the investment bank one uses, the region where capital is raised and the amount sought. A cheaper alternative for organizations
is to raise debt directly in the market through commercial paper. Commercial paper is

an unsecured instrument that allows companies to raise short-term debt (quite often the maturity will not exceed 270 days or nine months) often to finance current assets such as inventory, account receivables and other short-term liabilities. Because this type of instrument is unsecured, it can only be used by significantly creditworthy companies. In practice, the instrument is open to companies with an A credit rating or higher.

(4)  The next category in box 1 is junior debt, which can be qualified as those instruments that are 'junior' to other debt obligations a company has. That is, they are ranked lower on the repayment schedule than the more 'senior' debt instruments a company has committed to. They are also often unsecured.

(5)  Subordinated debt: Subordinated debt (which is mostly unsecured) is debt that is ranked lower than other debt instruments a company is committed to. In that sense they are also 'junior' as a debt instrument and aren't backed by a security. Subordination can happen in two ways: the first is contractually – the loan contract will explicitly indicate that the interest and principal of this instrument will only be repaid after all other senior instruments have been repaid first. The subordination can also happen structurally – when the conditions and maturity of the loan have been structured in such a way that all other loans will be repaid before the structurally subordinated loan will be repaid. That can happen because the maturity of the loan is further in the future than all other loans and/or the interest is rolled up towards the instrument's maturity. In the meantime, all other senior lenders will be repaid.

(6)  High-yield bonds (aka junk bonds) are debt instruments with a poor credit rating (in practice a non-investment grade rating which comes down to BB+ (S&P and Fitch), Ba1 (Moody) or lower categories.

In box 3, which is the equity box, one can find common equity, the mother of all equity instruments. Equity provided by private equity firms and venture capital firms fits into this category as well. Warrants, once converted, entitle the holder to a certain pre-determined stake, in most cases, in the equity of the firm which issued the warrants. A warrant can therefore be qualified as an instrument that entitles the holder to purchase or receive common equity in the warrant's issuing company. Contingent value rights are like an option where the holder of the rights is entitled to buy additional shares in the issuing company when certain events happen, under pre-determined conditions and pricing. This often happens after an acquisition or restructuring, where shareholders of the target company can acquire additional shares in the acquiring company (if, for example, the value of the shares of the acquirer drops below a certain point before a certain date).

Finally, in category two, the instruments that have characteristics of both debt and equity either simultaneously or subsequently are listed. In Chapter 2 we will discuss extensively each of these instruments and compare their technical characteristics. For now it is sufficient to understand that each of the products included in box 2 will have, with varying degrees of intensity, characteristics of debt and equity and consequently their risk profile will be very different. Some will be hardly any different from a normal debt instrument as included in box 1 and others will show extreme similarities with the equity product group in box 3. What is striking, though, is that almost all are packaged in what qualifies legally as a debt instrument (with the exception of preferred stock), despite their significantly higher risk profile, a risk profile that sometimes hardly differs from an equity instrument.

In the wider context of financing options, mezzanine qualifies as an external source of funding as categorized in Figure 1.1b.

| Forms of financing | | | |
|---|---|---|---|
| **Internal financing** | | **External financing** | |
| **Funds from business activities:**<br><br>•Retained profits<br>•D&A<br>•Reversal of provisions | **Funds from the release of capital:**<br><br>•Sales of assets (divestitures) | **Equity:**<br><br>Capital contribution from existing equity holders<br>Capital contribution from new equity holders<br>Private equity<br>Public equity (IPO, Secondary offering) | **Debt:**<br><br>•Banks (loans)<br>•Capital goods leases<br>•Suppliers (credits)<br>•Customer (advances)<br>•Bonds |
| | | **Mezzanine financing** | |

**Figure 1.1b**   Financing options for companies
*Source:* Credit Suisse economic research

## 1.2  DEMARCATION OF THE PRODUCT GROUP

Now that we have the categories in place, we are left with the grueling task of finding the demarcation line as precisely as possible and defining it as accurately as possible.

We could do that by looking at the reality of how the instruments are used, positioned or otherwise, but that would prove to be a mixed bag as well, and further, would not really help us develop a clearer picture of the product group.

Looking at the legal qualification would force us to drag many hybrid instruments back into either the debt or the equity category, mostly the former, hence the need for a separate category of hybrid capital.

The above issues have left those wishing to define the product group in the difficult position of having to describe the product group by its characteristics. Though I don't want to go out on a limb here, I will take on the challenge of breaking down the individual characteristics, to see where the rough edges are or question marks could be placed.

By looking at the mezzanine product group as a whole, the following characteristics can be identified:

• The individual products *are all unsecured products, i.e., there is no collateral and/or firm lien on some or all assets of the borrowing firm.* Second lien loans are an exception to this criterion, but aren't strictly part of the mezzanine group.
• All the products carry a compensation scheme which includes the provision that *(at least part of) the compensation is dependent on the future profitability of the firm (or, by extension, the return on equity or economic value creation of the firm).* This one raises some additional

questions. Products like junior debt, subordinated debt or unsecured debt all tend to be unsecured in their positions, but otherwise do enjoy the equity kicker that many other mezzanine products do. So some discretionary judgment is needed. On the one hand, these products are legally debt just like most other mezzanine products. On the other hand, they are also unsecured just like all the other mezzanine products. Where they deviate is that they do not directly enjoy the equity uptick that other products have built into their mechanics. It could be argued, however, that the higher spread that is built into the compensation scheme intrinsically includes that equity component. The counterargument is that an increased spread cannot reflect equity performance, it can only reflect higher risk patterns absorbed by the instruments, and in no way can it reflect the potential up- or downside that equity exposure can bring. So you could either argue that they belong to the debt product group (if you overweight the legal debt qualification) or that they are positioned in the outer space of the mezzanine cosmos (if you overweight the unsecured position and the higher overall risk profile they have relative to their peers in the debt group). One could say that there is a difference when defining mezzanine products *sensu lato* and *sensu stricto*.

- *Some products are finite and others are infinite in nature. Besides the perpetual loans and non-redeemable preferred shares, all products are finite in nature.*
- *Most of the products (except for preferred equity) are debt instruments (in their legal qualification)*, which raises the question about the semantics of the term mezzanine capital versus the term mezzanine debt. Nevertheless, most of the products have a risk profile much closer to equity than their legal qualification initially suggests.

So, you can see for yourself that the jury is still out on some of these products in terms of their qualification, or at least that there is a mixed bag of characteristics within the mezzanine product group. An alternative way of looking at the product group is through its risk profile, which we will do in Section 1.4.

The historical distinction between debt and equity doesn't make our life a lot easier. In fact, you might wonder if there is a justification for treating debt and equity in such different ways. In particular, the different tax treatment has raised many questions among scholars, none providing a compelling argument for why the difference emerged, nor for why we should keep the distinction intact, especially since the differences trigger specific behaviors among market participants. Given the (lower) net cost of debt there is an inclination among market agents to use (too) much debt to fund their activities. That in itself is not evil, but raises the fixed cost levels in the firm (as they are fixed commitments). In days of poor economic performance or market volatility, or just lower levels of liquidity in the banking sector, that situation can trigger issues for firms operating high levels of debt, as the 2008 financial crisis demonstrated.

Furthermore, as a country you can wonder if it is so attractive to have a lot of thinly capitalized firms in your economy, as they pose an intrinsic risk to other market participants through enhanced counterparty risk when dealing with them. Many countries have therefore introduced 'thin capitalization rules' in their tax code, which essentially are there to cap the amount of deductible interests a firm can deduct for tax purposes in any given period. The technical way that is determined differs slightly for each country, but the rules either put a nominal cap on the amounts of interests that can be deducted and/or put in place maximum debt/equity relations for any given period. For example, if your debt to equity ratio is higher than 3:1, the interest due on any debt amount above the 3:1 ratio is no longer deductible for tax purposes, making the instrument more expensive on a net basis.

However, only one country in the world went as far as abolishing the distinction between debt and equity for tax purposes. That country is Belgium. In 2007 (yes, before the financial crisis) the Belgian government introduced what is known as the 'notional interest deduction.' The mechanism allows for the tax deductibility of an artificial dividend from the equity side of the financing mix. They don't look at the effective dividends (which are not tax deductible) but at an artificially constructed dividend based on the T-bond rates in that period increased by a certain spread. The level of the spread is then based on certain conditions. This way an equity investment holds the same benefits as a debt investment.

Besides the significant impact the introduction of this rule had on the budget, the government intended to ensure a better capitalized economic environment in the country. That is pretty understandable as the country enjoys major inbound investments every year, and is often the prime location for overseas investors to locate their European holding (and consequently Belgian holdings capitalize many subsidiaries in other European countries). Consequently, the capitalization of that holding determines the economic strength of its subsidiaries in Europe, especially when the economic tide shifts. Since 2007, the rule has been adapted a few times to remove possible abuse situations and non-intended usages within international tax planning schemes.

Going even beyond that, questions can be raised about the true nature of an equity or debt instrument. All too often we look at the legal characteristics of the product to judge its nature. In most cases that is fine, but there are some exceptions that might make you wonder. If one provides a loan (in legal terms) to a firm which is in such a desperate economic state that it almost certainly will not be able to pay back the loan and interests due, one can wonder if the legal qualification is still adequate.

The jurisprudence in many countries has responded to these situations by denying the deduction of the interest, re-qualifying the loan to equity and/or re-qualifying the interest to a 'deemed dividend.' In order to do that, the legal system needs to allow the tax authorities to ignore the legal reality of a business transaction in favor of the economic reality underlying the business transaction.[1] Whether a legal system allows the economic theory doctrine to be applied is often a matter of legal principle in that jurisdiction and the answer often needs to be derived from other parts of the law beyond the tax code. In countries which do not have an economic theory in place, the tax authorities will have to turn to the 'abuse of law' provisions in their tax codes and argue that the participants in the deal were intending a different outcome to the one the legal qualification would normally imply. That is an uphill battle for tax authorities and disputes are therefore mostly settled out of court.

I think it is fair to temporarily conclude that the debt to equity spectrum is a diamond with many angles, which are colored differently depending on your perspective.

## 1.3 POSITIONING AND USE OF MEZZANINE FINANCE

Maybe we will get some further answers when looking at the reason why mezzanine finance exists to begin with and for what purposes it is used. When looking at the transactions for which mezzanine finance is used there is a long list of transactions that keep coming up.

---

[1] In The Netherlands this line of thinking originated from the 'bodemloze put' theory based on a number of historical court cases. It refers to the idea that if you throw money into a bottomless pit you will never see your money again despite the legal claim you might have according to the instrument.

On that list are:

- Funding M&A activity (industry related or not) or funding organic growth and spin-offs.
- Restructuring or reorganization of the business.
- Funding the acquisition of portfolio companies by private equity firms (LBOs or otherwise).
- Management buy-ins/outs.
- Internationalization.
- Succession planning.
- Project finance.
- Change of strategic direction.
- Providing 'bridge' financing to portfolio companies on their way towards an IPO (when owned by a private equity firm).
- Recapitalizations.
- Funding the introduction of new products or service groups, plant expansion or the development of new distribution channels.
- Overall refinancing of activities or financing overall growth ambitions.

It is fair to say that mezzanine financing often comes on the radar for management or business owners if there is no sufficient collateral that would justify bringing in additional senior secured debt, or where the visibility of future cash flows is blurred or prone to many externalities. Added to that list are limited profitability or a deviant corporate risk profile.

It is also fair to say that, given its deviant evolution, mezzanine is looked at differently in the US versus Europe. The US, with its more mature and developed capital markets, has developed a mezzanine group that is seen as a variation on publicly traded bonds (convertibles etc.) and therefore can be called public mezzanine. On the other hand, in Europe, where bank lending has played a more critical role in corporate funding, a private mezzanine market has been developing which tends to be closer to debt financing (subordinated and participating loans etc.). Other critical differences are discussed throughout the book.

First, however, let's consider the life stages of a company and the primary ways of financing in each of the individual stages (Table 1.1).

Firms always have to decide whether they will finance their operations going forward using internal or external sources. Internal financing is often preferred, given the cost of, or access to, external funding, but it is not always realistic given the cash flow generation of the firm or the level of funding needed.

It is fair to say that reality is not as clinical and sharply distinct as reflected in the chart below. Transitions are smoother or less defined and firms may have many ways to reinvent themselves in order to fight off the decline of their product group(s). That can range from introducing new product groups and/or services, to making acquisitions into (un)related industries and offloading certain asset groups that have a higher stand-alone value or are no longer core to the business strategy.

The availability and cost of debt and equity also have an impact on how funding activities will arise. The recent financial crisis of 2008 and the emerging equity gap[2] could push

---

[2] McKinsey Global Institute, 'The emerging equity gap,' October 2011.

**Table 1.1**    Financing the individual life stages of a company

| External funding needs | High, unconstrained | High v-a-v firm value | Moderate v-a-v firm value | Declining v-a-v firm value | Low as opportunities are rare |
|---|---|---|---|---|---|
| **Internal financing** | Low or negative | Low or negative | Low relative to financing needs | High relative to financing needs | Higher than funding needs |
| **External financing** | Owner's equity Bank debt | VC/ Common stock | Common stock, Warrants, Convertibles | Debt | Retire debt, stock buy backs |
| **Growth stage** | Start-up | Expansion | High growth | Mature growth | Decline or re-up |
| | **Venture Capital/ Private Equity** | **Initial Public Offering** | **Ad. Equity** | **Bonds/C. Bonds** | |

the cost of financing up, although some of that will be offset by historically low interest rates applied to the market both in the US and in Europe; interest rates have been hovering around 0–1% for a number of years now and are expected to stay there for at least a few more years, although in early 2013 central banks were starting to prepare the market for the fact that quantitative easing will end at some point. This might happen more unexpectedly than the average market participant would envisage. Pricing in the secondary government bond market already seems to hint that increased interest rates are expected. In emerging markets interest rates are higher, mainly as they are fighting (somewhat) higher levels of inflation, whereas throughout 2011–2012 the main theme was fighting deflation in the US and Europe.

One thing is clear: in cases where senior debt is not an option (or is not sufficient to cover the whole funding need), mezzanine is a plug variable (it plugs the gap between debt and equity). It allows a firm's debt financing to grow, without the owner losing control over company assets. That, however, carries an intrinsic risk, whereby the owner tries to avoid a (further) dilution of their equity stake at any cost, but burdens their company with so many priority debt claims that he or she literally erodes the residual cash flow generating ability of the underlying assets for the equity owners. It is often emotional reasons which make smaller companies turn to mezzanine financing as a less costly (relative to bringing outside equity into the firm) but (partly) fixed cost option, often with no – or only temporary – dilution of their equity stake.

The consequence is that, from a risk perspective, mezzanine products all sit between the layers of senior debt and pure equity. They should therefore, in a risk-return world, trigger higher compensation than senior debt and a lower return than common equity. These often difficult questions about pricing deserve a full chapter later on in the book (Chapter 4).

When mezzanine debt is used in conjunction with senior debt it reduces the amount of equity needed in the business. As equity is the most expensive form of capital and dilutive to existing shareholders, it is common sense for owners or majority stakeholders to aim to create a situation that comes at the lowest cost possible and is least dilutive when the business comes to be expanded.

The following example in Table 1.2 illustrates the latter point:[3]

**Table 1.2**    Reducing the cost of capital

| | Financing structure before mezzanine | | After mezzanine | |
|---|---|---|---|---|
| | US$ | Cost of capital (%)-Assumptions | US$ | Cost of capital (%) |
| (Senior) bank loan | 3 | 5 | 6 | 5 |
| Mezzanine loan | 0 | 0 | 2 | 12 |
| **Debt Capital** | **3** | **5** | **8** | **6.8** |
| **Equity Capital** | **3** | **20** | **3** | **20** |
| **Total Capital** | **6** | **12.5** | **11** | **10.4** |

The advantages and disadvantages of mezzanine finance can be summarized as shown in Table 1.3:[4]

**Table 1.3**    Advantages and disadvantages of using mezzanine finance

| Advantages | Disadvantages |
|---|---|
| • Remedies financial shortfalls and provides capital backing for implementing corporate projects; <br> • Improves balance sheet structure and thus creditworthiness, which can have a positive effect on the company's rating and can widen the room for maneuver as regards financing; <br> • Strengthens economic equity capital without the need to dilute equity holdings or surrender ownership rights; <br> • Tax-deductible interest payments and flexible remuneration structure; <br> • Greater entrepreneurial freedom for the company and limited consultation right for mezzanine investor. | • More expensive than conventional loan financing; <br> • Capital provided for a limited term only, in contrast to pure equity capital; <br> • More stringent transparency requirements. |

## 1.4 THE RISK–RETURN CONUNDRUM

From a balance sheet point of view, mezzanine finance is positioned between senior secured debt and common equity. It is therefore subordinated to senior debt claims but junior to common equity claims, although the latter isn't a claim in the full sense, but only an entitlement to the residual cash flows produced by the firm. Figure 1.2 is a visual representation of the risk–return continuum of the mezzanine space. It is best to ignore the vast variety of instruments listed, but to realize for now that the mezzanine continuum spans the risk–return matrix between senior secured debt and common equity, the two instruments listed at either end of

---

[3] 'Mezzanine finance – A hybrid instrument with a future,' Credit Suisse, Economic briefing, 2006, p.10.
[4] Ibid. p. 9.

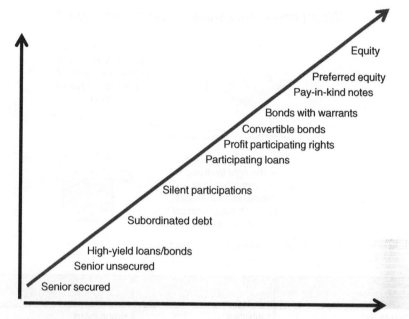

**Figure 1.2**    The risk–return paradigm
*Source:* Adjusted from CS economic research

the risk–return matrix indicated. Also note that the pecking order indicated in Figure 1.2 is essentially a default order. This means that the risk–return order could be altered through the use of covenants in each of the products which would make the product under review less or more risky and consequently change its position in the matrix. As represented here, it reflects the typical risk–return ranking of a plain vanilla product group.

In recent years, mezzanine products have seen increased attention due to the altogether limited availability of credit, the lower valuations attached to certain assets on the balance sheet, or the unwillingness of banks to fund certain current assets with senior debt due to structural weakness in terms of liquidity terms under (dis)stressed situations.

To be more specific:

- Accounts receivable, inventories and even certain fixed assets such as real estate are given a much lower valuation, or not accepted as collateral any longer;
- Lending against goodwill and/or other intangibles is even harder; and
- Banks and other FIs have tighter caps on how much exposure they can tolerate within a specific firm, sector or country (see Figure 1.3a/b).

The question then becomes: 'How much debt is too much before mezzanine emerges as a potential financing tool?' We could opt for a simple pragmatic answer here, but first let's define the parameters of the answer we are looking for. Financial institutions will generally see an end to how far they can travel with a firm in terms of lending. This can be based on bank-specific criteria such as total loan mass (per client or region), total loan mass in a specific industry or maximum loan mass to a specific firm. Most of the time this is a problem only in emerging economies with firms showing high growth prospects and which rely heavily

## When does mezzanine come on the radar?

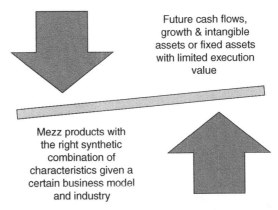

Future cash flows, growth & intangible assets or fixed assets with limited execution value

Mezz products with the right synthetic combination of characteristics given a certain business model and industry

**Figure 1.3a**    When does mezzanine finance come on the radar?

| Company balance sheet | Equity & Liabilities | Financing instruments |
|---|---|---|
| Assets | Liabilities | •Bank loans |
| | Liabilities | •Bonds<br>•Supplier credits<br>•Customer advances |
| | Mezzanine | •Subordinated loans |
| Fixed assets | Mezzanine | •Silent participations<br>•Participating loans/rights<br>•Preferred shares<br>•Convertible bonds with warrants |
| | Equity | •Retained profits |
| | Equity | •Stock<br>•Capital contributions from equity holders<br>•Private equity |

**Figure 1.3b**    Mezzanine capital versus debt and equity

on senior bank debt to execute their business model. However, with Basel III on the horizon (most of it to be implemented by 2019 as it stands in early 2013), and with higher capital ratios included in the rules, banks will have a narrowed platform to provide lending to corporates and the real economy in general. They will most likely channel their funding to government bonds, as they do not require risk capital, in contrast to normal corporate or personal lending loan banks.

On most occasions, however, the problems that arise are firm-specific. Banks and non-bank financial institutions ('NBFIs') are willing to lend to firms and organizations under the condition that they have some sort of guarantee backing their lending arrangement in a structural way, in case of default on the loan. That is easily understood, as it is not much different than you or I buying a house and getting a loan from the bank for which the bank will require a first lien mortgage on the property being financed. However, they are willing to lend in line with the market value of the property, potentially even adding funds to pay for renovations such as a new kitchen or bathroom. The pain is in the word 'potentially,' as most banks in most countries will cap the amount of extra funding they are willing to provide for the simple reason that if you default they will encounter a funding exposure; i.e., they lent you more that the market value of the property, most likely even with the renovations. This is very likely to be true when the costs and transfer duties have been included in the loan amount as well.

Until a few years ago, banks had the benefit of assuming that the value of a house will go up over time. Now that the world has painfully illustrated that this is not necessarily always the case, with varying degrees of intensity across the world I must add, banks have become very conservative in estimating the execution value of the property (i.e., the market value under stress, if you like).

So the market value of assets has become more volatile and insecure in recent years, and from their side banks have become more restrictive in lending terms, unless there are assets with an execution value close to their actual lending exposure providing backing.

Although these numbers, percentages and estimations vary somewhat over time and geography, Figure 1.4 attempts to provide some insight into the parameters that banks use when judging the execution value of an asset.

The figure shows that, just as your bank now requires you to have some money to put down as a deposit when you buy a property (often 20%), the situation is quite similar when you finance assets for a firm. They will consider your actual free cash flow to estimate your ability to repay, and are, to a certain extent, willing to see how your future cash flows will improve and include that information in their calculations. However, even that will reach its limit at some

| Assets | AB lending |
|---|---|
| Cash & securities | 100% |
| Receivables | 70–85% based on quality (backward looking default rates) |
| Inventory | 45–65% of normal liquidation value (NOLV) |
| Equipment & real estate | Lower % NOLV (around 70% of NOLV for equipment and approximately 80% for real estate) |
| Intangibles: patents, etc | Low % of DCF valuation (royalty stream focused) |

**Figure 1.4** Collateral value of assets

point. At that point your banker will tell you that there is very little they can do, unless there is more collateral they can turn to, either within the firm or based on the private wealth of the owner(s). From a market perspective (and driven by regulation) it is clear that banks will only focus on asset-based financing and firms will be in increased need of cash flow-based financing. Intuitively that makes sense, i.e., when you lend capital to a firm they will turn that capital into assets, which will be converted into cash flows at some point, which then will be partly used to repay the interest on and principal of the loan. Nevertheless, finance is not necessarily as rational as you would expect, especially not in cases where you have a regulator breathing down your neck and increasingly regulating how your balance sheet should look, which is the case for most licensed banks these days.

From a balance sheet perspective, Figure 1.5 reflects how that conundrum looks. It should be added here that for specific transactions, like M&A, most banks require an equitable intervention of about 25–30% on behalf of the acquiring firm.

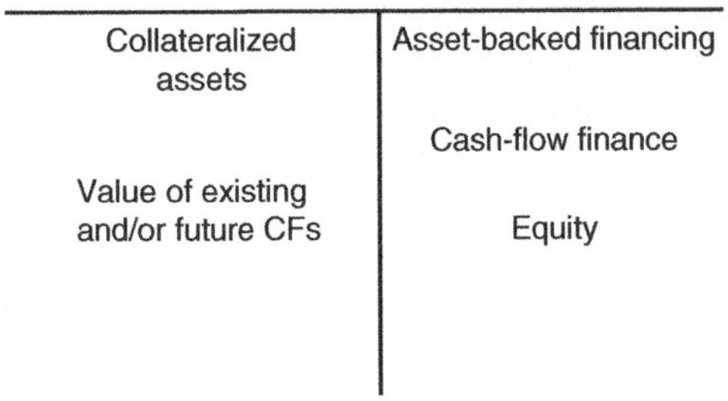

| Collateralized assets | Asset-backed financing |
|---|---|
| | Cash-flow finance |
| Value of existing and/or future CFs | Equity |

**Figure 1.5**   How much debt is too much debt?

Given the banks' position, mezzanine has developed distinct characteristics and is guided by specific features that differentiate the product group from other financial instruments on the balance sheet spectrum. In Table 1.4, I have tried to bring together some of the most important features compared to other financial products. That being said, throughout this book I will pay significant attention to the possible risk profiles, and formulate a structured way of assessing that risk for each of the different positions in which mezzanine finance can be considered. With respect to the criteria included, in particular regarding the pricing components, it needs to be highlighted that those are obviously sensitive to geographically different demand/supply relations and the overall state of the financial markets and interest rates. This helps to explain why some of the bandwidths indicated could appear relatively wide at first glance.

In general terms, it can be stated that the fixed interest component in mezzanine products tends to be larger in the US than in Europe, whereas my market observation is that the equity kicker tends to be larger in Europe than in the US, although total compensation patterns are quite alike across both continents, which has been true across the normal macro-economic cycles. In periods of distress, spikes can be observed in yields. One of the most extreme examples of this phenomenon was in the early days of the 2008 financial crisis when liquidity dried up and available equity was almost non-existent: some mezzanine funds in the CEE region, a region heavily impacted in the early days of the crisis, were able to put their product in the market at yields in the first decile only, and often far above the actual equity return at that point in time. These are usually temporary phenomena. Similar situations have been observed in the past in emerging markets, often also centered around periods of economic distress and/or financial imbalance. It must be said that it is only during the last 10 years

**Table 1.4** The major categories in the debt spectrum

| Feature/Product[5] | Senior secured | Junior secured | High-yield | Mezzanine | Private equity |
|---|---|---|---|---|---|
| **Rank** | Senior | Structural Subordinated | Contractual Subordinated | Structural/Contractual Subordinated | Junior to all other debt/products |
| **Term** | 5–7 years | 5–7 years | Up to 10 years | 5–8 years | N/A |
| **Coupon** | Cash | (Fixed) cash | (Fixed) cash | Cash pay & PIK (fixed) | Dividends |
| **Pricing** | | | | | |
| Upfront fees | 1–2% | 1–2% | None | 2–3% | |
| Interest rate | B+200–300bp | 11–14% | 11–15% | 8–15% | Varies |
| PIK warrants all- | N/A | N/A | N/A | 4–8% | N/A |
| in pricing | B+350–500 bp | 12–15% | 9–11% | 14–25% | 20–25%+ |
| **Covenants** | Extensive | Extensive | Incurrence test | Maintenance, variety of tests, cross defaults with senior lenders | N/A |
| **Security** | 1st lien | 2nd lien | Unsecured | Unsecured/Secured | N/A |
| **Prepayments** | In principle ok, w/o premium | In principle ok w/o premium | Call premium generally very expensive | Expensive call premiums particularly Y1–3 | N/A |
| **Providers** | Banks, NBFIs, asset-based lenders and alternative asset managers | Specialized AB lending firms | Institutional investors, larger FIs | Banks, insurance companies, Mezz funds and PE firms | PE firms, large FIs |

[5] Excluded here are bridge loans. Bridge loans are short-term bridging finance for specific purposes taken out temporarily in anticipation of subsequent definitive (capital market) financing. Once the relevant transaction has been completed with the aid of the bridge loan, the long-term financing is structured using various financing instruments (e.g., bond issue, new stock issue, syndicated loan, etc.). Bridge loans are used most frequently in acquisitions (acquisition bridge financing).

that commercial mezzanine capital has found its way into emerging markets, an area that, until then, was the exclusive territory of development banks or supranational development agencies.

Although it is a rather general statement, it is still fair to say that in most situations I have encountered in practice, the mezzanine lender was exposed to a risk profile much closer to common equity than to senior secured debt. That in itself is probably not shocking, given the fact that many senior lenders have been very liberal in providing finance during the pre-2008 crisis period and, as such, firms considering mezzanine lending often already had steep levels of senior debt on their balance sheets. To provide some indication: the average bank debt/ EBITDA in the US in 1995 was 3.3×, in 2002 2.4× and in 2007 5.1×, while non-bank debt hardly came down from its average 1.5× EBITDA across the last two decades.

What was more remarkable was the fact that when it came to the choice of product, or the way the product or individual components of the compensation were structured, it did not necessarily reflect the often deeply subordinated nature of the position of the mezzanine product used in each case. See Table 1.4.

Now that we are aware of the risk–return structure that comes with a variety of products as discussed, including the wider variety of mezzanine products, high-yield and leveraged loans make the seniority spectrum of the financial instruments look pretty much as shown in Table 1.5:

**Table 1.5**    The risk spectrum for financial products on a balance sheet

| **Highest security** |
| :---: |
| Leveraged (bank) loans |
| (a) Senior secured loans, (b) High-yield bonds (c) unsecured loans |
| Convertible securities |
| Preferred equity |
| Common equity |
| Highest security |
| **Lowest security** |

Somewhat of a maverick product which has not yet been mentioned is the stretched senior, characterized by a partially secured position often with a first lien on specific assets, tight covenants with a fixed coupon based on an adjusted prime rate. Although it is still used it is often pushed out of the market by more recent unitranche products which are faster to execute, less bureaucratic and simpler to use (see also Chapter 11).

That hybrid character of mezzanine finance will stick with us throughout this book. Practically, I have often encountered the difference in perspective between the lender and the borrower with respect to mezzanine products. This distinction often comes back to their individual positions in negotiations. Talking of negotiations, it can be said that every mezzanine book or course should come with a negotiation course, as it is often so crucial to the end result. As mezzanine finance is, in essence, legal or contractual finance (as the covenants are so important, in that they have to reflect the particularities of the case in question), what is agreed upon is often more a reflection of the relative negotiation power and alternatives of each party, rather than the academically most adequate choice of product.

Borrowers often look at mezzanine capital as (expensive) debt (as they are concerned about the extent to which they should charge the free cash flow their firm produces) whereas lenders are often more concerned about the risk to which they expose their capital. There is often a deep rift between the legal qualification of the instrument (as legal debt) and the fact that the risk exposure is often closer to equity risk, given the fact that mezzanine instruments are superseded by a significant amount of senior debt and that they have to agree to contractual subordination. This often leads to the difficult situation that, because of the different appreciation of the same facts, the rift seems deep, sometimes too deep.

In this type of situation, I tend to break down the facts. Rather than looking at the higher total return of the mezzanine product, I break the total cost pattern down. On the one hand, there is the interest income (sometimes limited to the level of interest for a similar debt interest with the equity uptick included). One could argue that this is the firm's cost for bringing mezzanine funding on board. On the other hand, there is the cost to the existing shareholders, which can emerge as a temporary dilution of their shareholding or an additional interest charge (which burdens the existing shareholders' cash flows).

This pattern can then be judged by the owner/shareholders on its pros and cons relative to their (perceived) BATNA or WATNA ('Best or Worst Alternative To a Negotiated Agreement') which is often another mezzanine provider, another attempt to convince bankers to provide an additional layer of senior debt, or on the other side, growing at a slower pace, waiting for the execution of the transaction under review or bringing a full (minority) equity investor on board. Ultimately there will always be a trade-off of some sort. As Stuart Diamond's 2010 book *Getting More*[6] clearly illustrated, it is often better to try to understand each other's position and hammer out a solution based on that understanding and empathy, rather than to push through a solution aggressively which (slightly) benefits one party over the other.

The mezzanine provider, when assessing their risk exposure, will land somewhere between that of senior debt holders and equity owners. They are therefore looking for (total) compensation that is somewhat in line with that risk exposure. Further analysis on this topic will be provided later.

From this perspective, it can be argued that mezzanine finance is like 'borrowed equity.' However, there are two big distinctions to be made. The first one is that there is no loss of control over the firm for existing shareholders. Bringing in new equity owners would change the voting distribution or dilute their existing shares. That dilution can then be limited (and temporary) as the biggest chunk of the returns comes in through interest income. Secondly, most arrangements provide for a buy back (or pre-emption right) of the equity stake obtained by the mezzanine lender in the process of the deal; an arrangement that the lender is also willing to engage in, as they have no intention of looking to become a permanent shareholder. Therefore, they will be looking for either a natural liquidity moment or an artificially created liquidity moment. The interests of the lender and borrower coincide. The only question will be at what cost this needs to happen (see Chapters 3 and 4). Voting rights, if managed incorrectly, can lead to different shareholder coalitions, making this a feature to watch in the overall structuring of the deal. If opponents inexorably stay with their point of view, it is time to run for the exit. Being willing and able to walk away from a deal and straight into the sun is a skill that everybody in this field needs to master.

---

[6] Stuart Diamond, *Getting More: How to negotiate to achieve your goals in the real world*, Crown Business, 2010.

## 1.5  PROVIDERS OF MEZZANINE FINANCE

It can be said that, historically, there have been two categories of mezzanine finance providers developing, known as sponsored and non-sponsored financiers. The *non-sponsored financiers* are banks, financial institutions, institutional investors, endowments and specialized mezzanine boutiques and funds, etc. The *sponsored financiers* are often private equity firms which provide mezzanine finance to their portfolio companies, either to carry out their plans or to bridge the path towards an IPO, hence the wording 'bridge financing.' This distinction has also led to the terms 'sponsored deal' and 'non-sponsored deal,' hinting at their different backgrounds.

In 2013 the market is constructed as shown in Figure 1.6 in terms of market participants. Funds here include both independent providers of mezzanine finance and sponsored funds which provide finance to their portfolio companies.

A special word can be dedicated to the development banks which have been providing equity and quasi-equity capital to firms in emerging countries since long before commercial capital arrived in those countries. They now are often the front runners in the countries included in the OECD category 1 and 2 lists of least developed countries. Commercial capital has arrived in the countries included in categories 3 and 4, although with varying degrees of intensity.

## 1.6  THE MARKET FOR MEZZANINE PRODUCTS

The market for mezzanine providers has known its booms and busts just like the private equity and hedge funds sphere. Mezzanine providers raised $86.4 billion globally between 2005 and 2010, with the majority of the capital raised by US-focused funds and other providers, followed by Europe and Asia. The capital raised stood at $62.5bn, $19.2bn and $4.7bn respectively. 2008 proved to be the most prosperous year in the period for the mezzanine private equity market, during which nearly $31bn was raised. This was largely due to the final closing

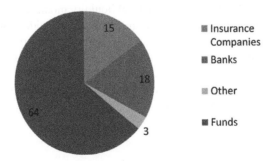

**Figure 1.6**   Number of mezzanine lenders by type
*Source:* Lincoln Partners

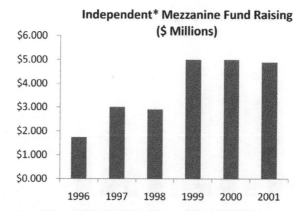

Figure 1.7    Independent mezzanine fundraising
*Source:* Private Equity Analyst

of GS Mezzanine Partners V that year. The fund managed by Goldman Sachs Private Equity Group raised, in total, $20bn of which $13bn was equity commitments and the remaining $7bn leverage.[7]

These are significant numbers, especially when being compared to the fundraising numbers of the period 1996–2001, as shown in Figure 1.7.

The geographical distribution is still somewhat skewed, as 66% of the fund managers in the market with a mezzanine fund are based in North America, 25% in Europe and the remaining 9% across Asia and the Rest of the World.

This situation is mirrored when judging the investment distribution, as 66% of the funds mainly focus their investments in the US, a further 21% focus on Europe and the last 13% primarily target opportunities across Asia and the Rest of the World.[8]

Within the leveraged loan spectrum, which we consider here separately from the pure mezzanine fundraising position, the following picture (see Figure 1.8a and b) has unfolded during the last 10 years; the typical picture of an unstoppable rise until 2007–2008, then a sharp decline, followed by a swift and rapid revival, but with weak intermezzos, as was the case during H2 of 2011. Remarkably enough, the market for leveraged and in particular high-yield ('HY') loans has known a significant renaissance since late 2010. This is particularly due to the fact that investors globally have been looking for investible fixed-income instruments with higher yields than the average government or corporate bond offered. As those investors have been shying away from equities for a long time, despite the massive rally that equities have known since 2009, the place they landed was in the middle, i.e., mezzanine loans and in particular the liquid leveraged and HY loan market.

[7] Preqin 'Funds in Market publication,' 2010.
[8] Preqin 'Funds in Market publication,' 2011.

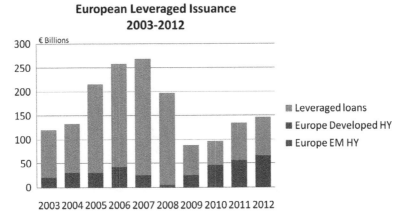

**Figure 1.8a**   European leveraged issuance 2003–2012
*Source:* Dealogic Thomson Reuters LPC, author's own

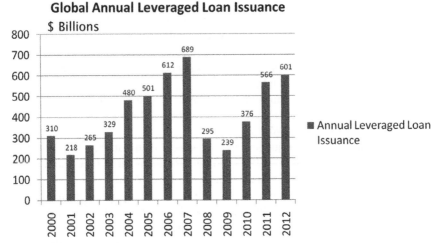

**Figure 1.8b**   Global annual leveraged loan issuance
*Source:* Thomson Reuters LPC, author's own

The more short-term Figure 1.9 represents those dynamics in Europe for the period 2008–2012, and on a global scale in Figure 1.10 for HY loans and Figure 1.11 for all leveraged loans.

What is more frightening, however, is the wall of maturities we are about to witness starting in 2013–2014, as most of the leveraged loans that were issued in the period 2005–2007 are about to mature and therefore need to either be refinanced or repaid. Although 2011 was the most financially stable year since the 2008 crisis, there are still major concerns out there about the ability of the market to facilitate that upcoming period in terms of liquidity. If one embeds the issues in an economic environment that is still very fragile, one can ask questions about the underlying stability of the economic system and the guaranteed availability of a sizeable and stable level of liquidity that such a refinancing operation would require. That is

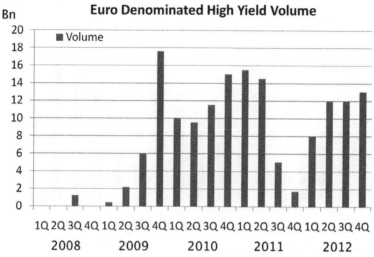

**Figure 1.9** Euro-denominated high-yield volume
*Source:* Thomson Reuters LPC, author's own

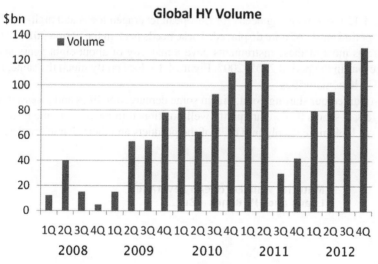

**Figure 1.10** Global high-yield volume
*Source:* Thomson Reuters LPC, author's own

certainly the situation we find ourselves in now; where banks and companies prefer to park billions of Euros at the ECB rather than lend them out to customers or make them available in the interbanking markets, and where at the same time close to a trillion Euros was taken out in the period 2011–2012 via the two long-term refinancing operation ('LTRO') facilities that the ECB made available.

This book's purpose is not to evaluate the policy mistakes that potentially have been or are being made by governments and banks, nor is it the ambition to re-digest everything (and that is a lot) that has been said on this front since 2008, so let's stick to the facts, and what we can observe about that upcoming refinancing wall.

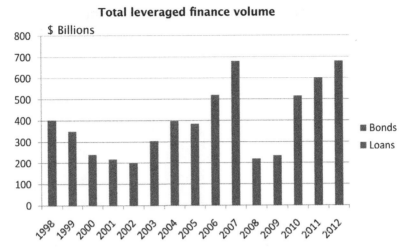

**Figure 1.11**    Total leveraged finance volume
*Source:* Standard & Poor's LCD, author's own

In Figure 1.12 the refinancing needs for European leveraged loans and high-yield loans per year for the period until 2021 are displayed. These needs peak in the period 2014–2016, which makes sense as most of these instruments have a maturity of about eight years and most of the issuance was in the period 2005–2007. Figure 1.13 does pretty much the same, but for the upcoming US loan maturities.

Having solidified our starting point, drawn some demarcation lines and assessed the market and its players, it seems that we are pretty well positioned to move on to the next chapter, in which we will look more deeply into each of the products and their characteristics.

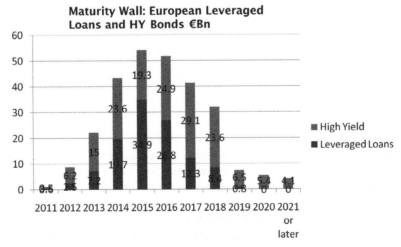

**Figure 1.12**    Maturity wall: European leveraged loans and HY bonds
*Source:* Lipper

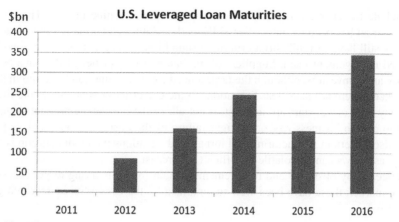

**Figure 1.13**   US leveraged loan maturities
*Source:* Bloomberg LP

In Chapter 3, I will also have to touch on issues that deal with modern financial theory and more specifically the funding cost of each product and the implications it has for the borrower, i.e., the cost of capital for the company and the impact of choosing a mezzanine product. Obviously, the fact that most compensation structures are made up of an equity component on the one hand and a debt component on the other will make our analysis somewhat more complicated. Nevertheless, it is one of the most important features when considering mezzanine as a funding tool, both as a lender and as a borrower.

This is especially true given what I mentioned before: that often the compensation structure and total compensation levels are not in sync with the product's risk exposure given its position on the balance sheet and the volume of senior debt already in place. At the risk of jumping the gun here, my observation is often that, because most professionals who are dealing with this have a debt capital markets ('DCM') or lending background, the inclination is to build a mezzanine product out of a senior lending template, which forces you to start off on the wrong foot. This invariably implies that the compensation is structured as a bottom-up process, built on the basis of a base rate (often the cost of funding or an interbanking rate of some sort). This does not necessarily provide a compensation structure and level reflecting the actual risk that the mezzanine product absorbs, as I will go into in more detail later. This partly has to do with the fact that mezzanine risk is much wider in its intrinsic DNA than typical lending risk. Whereas typical lending risk is all about the risk linked to the ability of the borrower to repay, mezzanine risk also absorbs certain risks that we can consider to be equity risk (or equitable risk) which requires us to think about the operational, business and strategic risks that are inherent to the business we intend to invest in. It is very difficult, if not impossible, to reflect those risks as a spread on a base rate. It also leaves an open question about the total return target one needs to aim for given the risk profile. What that risk profile is will be determined by your cash flow waterfall on the one hand but also the equity structure you intend to use on the other. A top-down approach therefore seems more appropriate than a bottom-up approach with respect to return modeling for mezzanine products. I will flesh this out a little further in the next two chapters. The next chapter will foremost be devoted to an extensive review of the product group, the dos and don'ts of each product and some of the contractual or legal aspects that are worth focusing on when considering a mezzanine investment.

To conclude the chapter, a last few words about the mezzanine market. The traditional investible market has been the upper-tier SME market. Although normally highly rated companies, they still have to fulfill strict criteria: a sound track record, stable cash flows and an experienced management team. Suppliers of mezzanine to lower-tier SMEs have been predominantly angel investors, although the largest need for mezzanine can be found in that part of the market.[9] There are also clear limitations to the use of mezzanine due to the life phase the company is in (seed, start-up) as most, if not all, of the mezzanine product group is not equipped to absorb business risk or outright failure of the business model and its product/services. Also in certain restructuring and turnaround situations the product group is less adequate, as cash flows can be volatile or difficult to forecast.

In practice, many obstacles and requirements remain for firms trying to get access to the mezzanine market; these have been well summarized by the Credit Suisse research group – see Table 1.6.[10]

**Table 1.6**   Requirements and obstacles for mezzanine financing

| Requirements | Obstacles |
| --- | --- |
| • Possibilities for funding from own resources have been exhausted and loan financing is either insufficient or not available;<br>• Strong market position based on products/technology and market shares;<br>• Healthy financial position and good earning power with steady profit growth where possible;<br>• Focused business strategy and positive long-term development prospects;<br>• Positive, stable cash flows that can be forecasted reliably;<br>• Appropriate finance and accounting function, and open information policy;<br>• Quality and continuity of corporate management. | • Inadequate earnings/cash flow;<br>• High leverage;<br>• Low equity resources;<br>• Volatile business performance;<br>• Weak market position and negative development prospects;<br>• Restrictive information policy;<br>• Inadequate finance and accounting function;<br>• Start-up/little business experience;<br>• Quality and experience of management inadequate. |

---

[9] See further: 'Mezzanine finance; final report,' Roundtable between bankers and SMEs, EC, Enterprise Publications, 2010.

[10] 'Mezzanine finance – A hybrid instrument with a future,' Credit Suisse, Economic briefing, 2006, p. 11.

# 2

# The Mezzanine Product Group

This chapter will essentially help us to get familiar with the mechanics of each of the products in the mezzanine group. What is key in understanding the product group is the fact that you have five original product groups. You could call them the parent categories, which each include a plain vanilla product model. They include (1) subordinated debt ('subdebt') with step-up rates or PIK (payment-in-kind) rates; (2) subdebt with profit participation; (3) subdebt with warrants; (4) convertible loans; and (5) preferred equity. Following on from that list, a wide variety of more exotic models has been generated by practice, when tailoring these basic product categories to the needs of businesses as and when they emerged. I have tried to structure the review of each product category consistently, but only partly succeeded as I prioritized demonstrating the essence and techniques of each of the basic products, which are very different in nature. Nevertheless, this overview will serve well for those looking for a review outlining the mezzanine product group along with the practicalities and flexibility each of the original product groups demonstrates. It includes a technical description of the most important features within each product group, an example to demonstrate the flexibility of the product group in practical terms and, where needed, some details with respect to the contractual aspects of the product group. It further includes the most important and most frequently recommended dos and don'ts for each product group. In Chapters 3 and 4 respectively I will deal with the cost of funding the product group as well as the particularly interesting topic of embedded optionality in some of the mezzanine products.

## 2.1 CATEGORIZATION OF THE MEZZANINE PRODUCT GROUP

One observation when reviewing the mezzanine product group is that, besides the typical 'basic debt product plus equity kicker of some sort' characteristic, they have very little in common. You could say that, judging by their characteristics, it is a category that is scrambled together as a default group between 'debt' and 'equity,' and this is relatively close to the truth.

So I thought it best to give it another try, to see if we could create a more systematic categorization based on the mechanics and characteristics of the products in the mezzanine group.

The basic product group consists of the following product (categories):

- Subordinated debt with step-up rates.
- Subordinated debt with PIK interest.
- Subordinated debt with a profit participation scheme attached.
- Subordinated debt with warrants.
- Convertible loans.
- Preferred shares.

There are a few more at the outer ends of the spectrum as mentioned before, i.e., plain vanilla subordinated debt ('subdebt') and high-yield bonds. We will get back to those a little later.

It is fair to conclude that, looking at the individual products, a possible further categorization of the product group can be built around the mechanism of the equity kicker and how that is structured. Some products will look for equity exposure through an effective stock participation of some sort, i.e., either common stock or preferred stock. Convertible loans, subdebt with warrants and preferred shares are part of that category.

On the other hand, there are those products which create exposure to the equitable uptick the firm might experience. This is done through a mechanism which tries to reflect a possible uptick without creating an effective legal or economic exposure to the equity portion of the firm's balance sheet. Into that category fall subdebt with step-up rates, subdebt with PIK interest and subdebt with profit participation schemes attached.

| Products with equitable compensation mechanics but no effective equity exposure | Products with (ultimately) effective equity exposure |
| --- | --- |
| Subdebt with step-up rates; Subdebt with PIK interest; Subdebt with profit participation schemes. | Subdebt with warrants; Convertible loans; Preferred shares. |

What follows is an analysis of each of the products, a review of the dos and don'ts of each of the product groups, and an analysis of their mechanics. To complement the analysis, I've included a model contract for each of the products discussed (Appendix 1) which provides further information about the legal mechanics of the product. The relevant provisions in each of the contracts will be highlighted in each product review.

## 2.1.1 Subordinated debt with step-up rates

Subordinated debt with step-up rates is used in situations where existing cash flows are mainly consumed by senior debt and plain vanilla subordinated debt, and consequently there is very little room for an additional debt product with a fixed compensation mechanism attached to it, especially not on a subordinated level, which would trigger higher interest rates. Subdebt with step-up rates allows for an additional layer of subdebt which is adjustable to the firm's projected ability to service the increasing level of interest charged throughout the product's lifetime. Obviously, this does require an estimation of the expected incremental cash flow payments the firm will produce over the next few years. This will be derived either from additional sales and enhanced net margins, or cash flows that are freed up throughout the product's lifetime due to senior debt and other subdebt claims that will mature earlier than your subdebt with step-up product.

The step-up rate, which implies that interest will be charged at an increasing interest rate as the product matures, will be modeled in stages. How those stages are modeled is very fact sensitive and can be 'time-based' or 'criteria-based.' Note that the underlying basic product is plain vanilla subdebt which has been combined with a flexible compensation model. It can therefore be used in situations where incremental cash flows are very likely but difficult to model (due to new market, new product/service group, acquisition pay-off and timing etc.).

Let's take an example. A client of yours is looking for subdebt and has currently no (or insufficient) cash flows to service that debt, particularly due to high levels of senior debt they took on in prior years before considering adding an additional layer of subdebt to their balance sheet. They are looking for a product with a tenor (the initial term length of the loan) of eight years and, if possible, a grace period of two years (an initial period during which no interest payments are due). The grace period in itself will already solve some of the problems the firm is facing, by creating no additional cash outflows from day one. Let's assume the loan will be arranged and effective January 1, 2013. You can offer your client the following scheduled step-up mechanism:

| | |
|---|---|
| 2013 | Grace period |
| 2014 | Grace period |
| 2015 | 4% |
| 2016 | 5% |
| 2017 | 7% |
| 2018 | 9% |
| 2019 | 10% |
| 2020 | 11% + principal |

By doing so, you basically increase the interest payments towards the end of the loan, thereby assuming that by then the firm will have realized incremental sales and better margins, and have paid off senior debt (or other subdebt they have on their books) which will mature before our loan. There is obviously no guarantee that the firm will indeed have created additional (and sufficient) cash flows to service our debt in the years we increase the interest rate. In a way, the schedule is somewhat arbitrary, as the change in interest rate is linked to how the business performs in subsequent years, and requires us to rely on the visibility (if any) of cash flow growth, as well as the sensitivity of the business and its cash flows to macro-economic trends, inflation and competition.

An alternative could therefore be to make the scheduled increase criteria linked, dependent on the performance of the firm, i.e., its ability to effectively meet those increasing cash flow payments.

The schedule then would, for example, look like this:

| | | |
|---|---|---|
| 2013 | Grace period | |
| 2014 | Grace period | |
| 2015 | 4% | Interest coverage ratio >1.5 |
| 2016 | 5% | Interest coverage ratio >1.7 |
| 2017 | 7% | Interest coverage ratio >1.9 |
| 2018 | 9% | Interest coverage ratio >2.2 |
| 2019 | 10% | Interest coverage ratio >2.5 |
| 2020 | 11% | Interest coverage ratio >3 |

I used the criterion 'interest coverage ratio' as an example, as it directly relates to the firm's ability to service its existing debt. One can, however, use any criterion which would point to an increased level of cash flow generation relative to existing interest payments and current ability to generate cash flows, for example, this can be growth in net earnings/EBIT(DA), or free cash flows to the firm (FCFF) among others.

This scenario would be ideal from a firm's perspective, as it is positioned in such a way that a default can be prevented at any point in time. The synthetic nature of the debt allows the instrument to move with the firm's business dynamics, reflected by their ability to serve debt or generate cash flows. Or, put differently, it would make the return on the product too equity-like relative to what the mezzanine lender is comfortable with. From their position, at any given point in time they will want to secure an adequate return, dampening the true variability of an equity return. This can only be achieved by using objective criteria, where interest payments do not effectively swing up and down with the economic performance and cash flow generation of the firm, but without putting the firm on such a short leash that it would be irreparably damaged due to defaulting on a debt product although economically in no distress. In this sense, every debt provider wants to ensure that a company which raises debt feels sufficiently disciplined and will manage the firm in such a way that repayment of the debt can be guaranteed.

The distinction between economic and financial distress is important here. Essentially, financial distress occurs when one defaults on a debt instrument one holds. Economic distress occurs when, due to a variety of reasons, the existing business model, strategy and/or execution is no longer in line with what the market is looking for, and doesn't allow the firm to compete profitably in the market going forward. Only a change in strategic and operational direction can help a firm in economic distress. What one wants to avoid at all times is to push a firm into financial distress without that being caused by economic distress within the firm, but merely by a badly constructed debt instrument, especially when that could trigger a 'cross holding default' (a technique which results in a company being considered to have defaulted on all the debt it owes if it defaults on just one debt instrument – this can even be judged on a group level) and consequently acceleration of repayment of other debt instruments the firm holds, which is often included in debt contracts these days.

There is no 'one size fits all' here, and the right criteria will depend on the firm's business area and the existing pallet of senior debt and other mezzanine or subordinated debt that the firm has on its balance sheet.

It is clear that this product fits situations where the instrument is deeply subordinated or where the company risk requires and/or justifies (relatively) high returns (compared to equity), but where a standard high interest rate is not possible or recommendable given the existing senior debt service obligations the firm is exposed to. It also fits situations where pure equity positions are either not possible or undesirable, or where, over time, the necessary liquidity positions justified by a pure equity position are not available and cannot be artificially created.

Since the interest payments start at a later time, and the biggest chunk of the total return is placed towards the instrument's maturity, this product is not recommended for use in situations where the visibility regarding future cash flow is so low or volatile that an excess of interest payments towards maturity (or a rolling up towards the end of some sort of interest payments, i.e., bullet payment), including a principal repayment at the end, would be considered imprudent from the debt holder's perspective.

On a different note, the product can also be used at HoldCo level, where the operational company incurs the senior debt supported by the firm's operational cash flows. The mezzanine debt, often as part of acquisition finance, is incurred at HoldCo level. This raises the additional complication that one needs to ensure that the HoldCo, which in principle does not produce any cash flows itself (or very reduced), can rely on a mechanism which would allow the OpCo to upstream a certain level of cash flows to service the unsecured debt engaged in at HoldCo level. This mechanism will be extensively discussed in the chapter on leveraged acquisitions (Chapter 8).

The bottom line question is often how to price the product from a risk–return adjusted perspective. The increasing scale of interest rates should deliver an overall 'average' return which respects the risk the debt instrument is exposed to. That question goes hand in hand with the question of the instrument's position in case of a breach of covenants or wider default of some sort. Some sort of hybrid model is often experienced in practice, whereby a certain level of interest is fixed and is due whatever the actual performance of the firm (i.e., a kind of floor is built into the compensation model), combined with an additional layer of interest payments which are then dependent on certain qualitative criteria, as agreed between lender and borrower. As I've already mentioned, every mezzanine course, book or document should come with a negotiation course, as the outcome in practice is often more determined by the relative bargaining position of each party, their negotiation skills, and the direct alternatives both parties have to fund activities or put a certain amount of capital to work within a certain risk bandwidth. A possible outcome could be:

| 2013 | Grace period | |
| 2014 | Grace period | |
| 2015 | 3% | 1% in case ICR(*) > 1.5 |
| 2016 | 4% | 1% in case ICR > 1.7 |
| 2017 | 5% | 2% in case ICR > 1.9 |
| 2018 | 6% | 3% in case ICR > 2.2 |
| 2019 | 7% | 3% in case ICR > 2.5 |
| 2020 | 8% | 3% in case ICR > 3 |

(*) Interest Coverage Ratio or any other adequate or agreed criterion or criteria.

The level and depth of subordination and position in distressed and restructuring situations is directly related to the question of the instrument's overall position in the total debt structure, the maturity of each layer and the nature of the products in each layer. The cash flow waterfall will then – often combined with some sort of sensitivity analysis – provide us with some answers to that question. I've included some examples and case studies at the end of the chapter to illustrate those positions. The specific, and somewhat more complicated, issues of restructuring or default and/or a new inter-creditor agreement will be dealt with in Chapter 10.

## 2.1.2  Subordinated debt with PIK interest

A PIK (payment-in-kind) loan is a (mostly) subordinated debt instrument which does not yield any interest (or principal repayment) for the lender between the moment of drawdown and the moment of maturity or the refinance date (no interim interest payments). One could say that it is an instrument where both principal and interest payments become due in one balloon or bullet payment at the maturity date. The interest payments accrue until maturity or refinancing.

The implied mechanics make it a high-risk, often deeply subordinated instrument which, because of the high risk profile, comes with a considerable price tag.

The instruments are either unsecured or deeply subordinated (sometimes a third lien is foreseen[1]). Not infrequently, the instrument is accompanied by warrants, i.e., instruments which include the right to purchase a certain amount of stock, shares or bonds at a given price for a certain period of time. It then falls into the category of actual equity exposure, which we will deal with later.

---

[1] A third lien indicates that the lender is ranked third in the collateral ranking on some or all assets that the firm has put up as collateral. A third lien, however, tends to be so weak that it is considered equal to a subordinated position where there is no actual collateral available.

Just like the subdebt with step-up rates these instruments are often used at HoldCo level especially in situations of acquisition finance or wider M&A applications.

The PIK lender takes on considerable amounts of risk and will be looking for a certain minimum IRR. The lender basically has three sources of income: the arrangement and/or commitment fee (although this often covers only admin expenses), the compounded interest, and sometimes the 'ticking fee', which is a fee paid to a lender by a borrower to compensate for the time lag between the commitment allocation on a loan and the actual funding. This type of fee could be considered a relationship fee. Borrowers want to keep lenders content while the remaining details of a deal are worked out. Once a bank or fund commits to a deal, capital is allocated. The bank (or other capital provider) wants to start earning a return on its investment. Lenders cannot easily walk away from a deal once the documentation is complete, and it would be difficult to trade out of it in the secondary market. For the lender, even the receipt of such a fee may not be enough to compensate for the risk associated with a credit, because the bank still owns the risk. The ticking fee can range from a basic 50 bp up to a level similar to the spread on the loan itself (200–350 bp) depending on the situation both the lender and borrower are in.

Refinancing of a PIK loan is often only possible after several years (contractually defined), and often completely impossible or significantly restricted in the first 1–2 years, i.e., prepayment protection. PIK loans have a maturity of at least five years and can go all the way to 10 years although the most conventional timeframe is about 7–8 years. Besides the risks that come with subordination, bullet repayments at the end and accruing interest until maturity, PIK loans are often exposed to refinancing risk, i.e., often the borrower is not expected to generate sufficient incremental cash flows during the repayment period to pay off both the principal amount and accrued interest once the instrument has reached maturity. Consequently, lenders will often assess the material growth potential of the firm being financed in order to reduce the nominal refinancing exposure. Although true for most mezzanine instruments, the PIK loan has an advantage, in that it can be freely structured and arranged to accommodate certain situations or client-specific positions.

In addition, both the step-up rates and accrued (i.e., compounded) interest payments are tax deductible in most countries, providing the lender with a significant tax shield.

PIK toggle notes or bonds are a rather specific variant. The toggle note has a specific feature which the borrower can decide on, i.e., to pay the interest (partly or in full) in each period, or to accrue a part or the whole interest payment due. Often, the loan documentation will stipulate that if the borrower uses a certain discretion in doing so (i.e., paying part or nothing at all), the overall interest rate will increase according to certain basis points which are often between 25–100 bp. These contracts often include certain cash flow triggers that would effectively trigger payment of the interest component during a certain period. The discretion of the borrower then comes at the cost of an increased spread.

In contracts where the borrower's discretion is the standard arrangement, the borrower can independently decide how much interest they want to pay and when in any given period. Often, these are known as 'PIYW' and 'PIYC' clauses ('Pay if you want' and 'Pay if you can' clauses), referring to the discretionary judgment of the borrower and the cash flow criteria that are used to determine when interest payments should be made.

This product is often used in LBOs, and is then generally junior relative to any other instrument available, those being senior debt, (other) junior debt, other mezzanine products and second lien loans. This increases the exposure of the product to such a degree that compensation is often above 20% on an annualized basis. This has often raised the question – not least during the 2008 financial crisis – of whether the high compensation will erode the equity return the corporation or PE firm intends or expects to make on its investment.

I guess it is plain financial logic which comes into play here. If an organization shifts such a tremendous amount of company-specific risk out to a third party, the third party incurs significant risk. For example, in the case of the toggle bond holder, where the risk profile is not limited to their ability to repay the principal and interests, but due to the very deep subordination (and aligned limited visibility due to 8–10-year tenors) of the product, the lender incurs a true entrepreneurial and equitable risk that requires adequate compensation. Often not hindered by the actual or expected ROE (return on equity) the firm is yielding or will yield, the extreme levels of compensation might make the investment unattractive unless structured otherwise.

Just like for step-up rate loans, the repayment ballooning in the far future makes the product unattractive if visibility is too low or future performance too uncertain. Nevertheless, many banks have been playing ball with PE firms over the last decade, up until 2008, and this market has come back relatively quickly in 2010–2012 but never with the same size and magnitude as before 2008. The high risk profiles combined with often very light covenants (cov-lite), especially in the case of syndicated loans, have caused defaults, write-offs and often loss of control by the PE over the portfolio company. A very visible and unfortunate example of this is the loss of control by Terra Firma, a UK private equity group, over EMI, an icon in the music industry, to Citigroup who provided a significant chunk of the mezzanine financing for the acquisition which happened at the top of the market in 2007. Most likely aggressive pricing for the firm, easy access to mezzanine financing with light covenants, and the firm's deteriorating performance after acquisition due to the economic crisis, as well as the deteriorating position of music label companies in the music business (something that could have been anticipated) have led to the demise of the firm.[2]

In the period before 2008, several LBOs saw some secured second lien term bank loans coming with PIK or, more often, toggle features, in order to support the firm's ability to cover cash interest during the initial period after the LBO. If the acquired company performed well, the PIK toggle feature allowed the equity sponsor to avoid giving extraordinary (or excessive) returns to the PIK debt holder, which might have happened if the debt was strictly PIK. Since 2008, PIK toggle instruments have vanished to a large degree.

In recent times, when a bond pays in kind (PIK), it means that the interest on the bond is paid other than in cash. The most common form of this is for the principal owed to the bond holder to be increased by the amount of current interest. In case of partial payment of interests due, that can be considered as a form of negative amortization. Often seen in mortgage loans, negative amortization occurs when the payments made by the borrower are less than the accrued interest and the difference is added to the loan balance.

Let's take a mortgage loan example as a comparative case study.

The monthly mortgage payment on a 30-year fixed-rate loan of US$100,000 at 6% is US$600. In the first month, the interest due to the lender is US$500, which leaves US$100 for amortization. The remaining balance at the end of month one would be US$99,900.

---

[2] The firm was then, in November 2011, ultimately split in two, whereby the record business was bought by Vivendi-owned Universal Music Group for US$1.2 billion and the publishing unit of EMI was sold for GBP 1.4 billion to a Sony-led consortium, versus the purchase price of GBP 4.5 billion that Terra Firma paid in 2007 when they put up GBP 2 billion of their own equity.

Because a payment of US$600 a month maintained over 30 years would just pay off the balance, assuming no change in the interest rate, it is said to be a fully amortizing payment. A payment greater than US$600 would pay off the loan in less than 30 years. A payment less than US$600 would leave a balance at the end of 30 years.

Suppose you made a payment of US$550, for example. Then only US$50 would be available to reduce the balance. Amortization would still occur, but it would be smaller and not sufficient to reduce the balance to zero over the term of the loan. US$550 is therefore a partially amortizing payment.

Next, suppose you pay only US$500. Since this just covers the interest, there would be no amortization, and the balance would remain at US$100,000. The monthly payment is interest-only. In the early part of the last century, interest-only loans usually ran for the term of the loan, so that the borrower owed as much at the end of the term as at the beginning. Unless the house was sold during the period, the borrower would have to refinance the loan at term.

In more recent times, some loans are interest-only for a number of years at the beginning, but then the payment is raised to the fully-amortizing level. For example, if the loan referred to above was interest-only for the first five years, at the end of that period the payment would be raised to US$644. This is the fully-amortizing payment when there are only 25 years left to go.

Finally, suppose that for some reason, your mortgage payment in the first month was only US$400. Then there would be a shortfall in the interest payment, which would be added to the loan balance. At the end of month one you would owe US$100,100. In effect, the lender has made an additional loan of US$100, which is added to the amount you already owe (you basically issued an additional IOU to your lender). When a payment does not cover the interest, the resulting increase in the loan balance is negative amortization. The same methodology is applied to some of the PIK loans described, which have partial interest coverage during the instrument's lifetime. Now, everybody understands what these negative amortization mechanisms try to do, and that is to reduce the mortgage payment at the beginning of the loan contract. Alternatively, the argument can be to reduce the potential for payment shock, a very large increase in the mortgage payment associated with an increase in the adjustable mortgage interest rate. The downside of negative amortization is that the payment must be increased later in the life of the mortgage. The larger the amount of negative amortization and the longer the period over which it occurs, the larger the increase in the payment that will be needed later on to fully amortize the loan.

Other forms of PIK arrangements are also available, such as paying (transferring to) the bond holder an amount of stock (most often in the company issuing the bond) with value equal to the current interest due.

It makes sense that when lenders provide instruments to the market that are deeply subordinated, even to the extent that the distinction with pure equity risk becomes a very fine line, they would protect their debt instrument as a typical lender would do. For example, to assess your position in the repayment schedule, one would at least want to be able to decide the level of additional debt (of whatever sort) that the firm you financed would bring on board after you agreed to finance it. This would simply allow you to understand where you are in the cash flow waterfall and which additional debt with a shorter maturity would push you further down the repayment spectrum. Even senior debt holders require this these days, on top of all the information covenants which are included in a contract.

PIK and toggle notes often come with light covenants. Beside light covenants they often allow the borrower to not report the normal financial matrices included in the agreement, as there are loan-to-value ratios, gearing, EBITDA ratios and the like; further characteristics often encompassed include:

- Restrictions on other third party debt brought in after the deal is closed.
- Events of default relating to 'material adverse change' of the position of the borrower.
- Restrictions on negative pledges.
- Requirement to deliver annual accounts to the bank.
- Requirements for bank approval to change the form of the debtor group's business.

These loans were also a major part of the loan portfolios included in ABS (Asset-backed securities), RMBS (Residential mortgage-backed securities), CMBS (Commercial Mortgage-backed securities), CDOs (Collateralized debt obligations), CFOs (Collateralized fund obligations) and CMOs (Collateralized mortgage obligations) of different sorts. They are potentially intrinsically more risky products, despite the safe outlook that was given by ratings agencies and the issuers of these products.

However, covenants were eroded and became a part of everyday life, especially for syndicated banks. This was, until it abruptly ended in 2008, partly due to the easy availability of mezzanine loans and the level of competition among providers, and partly due to banks not putting all their available capital to work in their normal corporate loan program.

## 2.1.3 Subordinated debt with profit participation

For those situations where subordination is too deep and/or visibility regarding cash flows is too troublesome to even consider step-up rates or PIK loan applications, one needs to consider which mechanism will provide the debt–equity risk balance mezzanine providers are characterized by. Or, put differently, the challenge becomes to develop a mechanism which will provide for sufficient downside protection, and at the same time provide for an adequate way to participate in upside momentum, despite the lack of transparency regarding how and when that momentum will occur.

A possible mechanism which is often considered is to use some sort of profit participation scheme (PPS), which then (partially) replaces the fixed and/or variable loan mechanism used in straightforward senior and plain vanilla subdebt applications. These loans are then known as PPLs (Profit Participating Loans) and are often, but not necessarily, provided by a syndication of FIs or banks.

This has implications. The fact that a part of the interest pool will be dependent on the actual performance of the organization being financed has the direct implication that the owner or management of the business adding additional debt doesn't directly result in an increase of the Fixed Cost/Total Cost ratio of the firm. Traditionally, enhanced leverage resulted in an increased Fixed Cost/Total Cost ratio, and therefore implicitly enhanced the inherent (perceived) risk of the firm.

In a public equity context the explanation would be as follows: as the beta reflects the relative riskiness (volatility) of the firm observed, relative to the defined market of an investor, that beta has three fundamental drivers. While being the result of a statistical analysis (regression), the beta of a firm has three implicit drivers:

- **The nature of the product(s)/service(s) the firm produces or distributes and the industry/industries the firm is active in.** Within this framework discretionary goods are considered more risky than non-discretionary goods (staples/utilities) and cyclical companies more risky than defensive (or non-cyclical) ones. The assessment can be dependent on which country one performs the analysis in, and will evolve over time.

- **The operational leverage of an organization. This is related to the question of how much of the firm's cost structure is fixed in total.** The question is obviously relevant as the higher a firm's Fixed Cost to Total Cost ratio is, the more vulnerable the firm will be when a recession kicks in, or the market is characterized by lower levels of liquidity. A higher FC/TC ratio will invariably lead to higher earnings variability, which will, in its turn, lead to a higher beta. This phenomenon can be monitored. However, as the nature of fixed and variable costs is often hard to obtain, the nature and intensity of the phenomenon are measured using the EBIT Variability Measure which can be equated as follows:

EBIT Variability Measure = % Change in EBIT/% Change in Revenues

This ratio measures how quickly earnings before interest and taxes change as revenue changes. The higher this number, the greater the operating leverage. It can be concluded that, in an industry like aviation where pretty much all your operational costs are fixed, the operational leverage and EBIT variability is high:

- Plane leases, employee costs, fuel costs, gate licenses at airports and attractive time slots, expensive jet engines, airport handling service providers etc. are all fixed, i.e., those costs are there regardless of how many people fly in that plane. Turning cost structures around is often like moving an oil tanker; it takes quite some effort, as well as patience, before the initiative pays off.
- A consulting or law firm with an office, desk and IT infrastructure needs lower levels of investment, and can naturally react more quickly to any upticks or downswings in economic activity when servicing its clients, due to a flexible cost structure.
- **The financial leverage of the firm.** As we will see later on, the use of leverage in a firm has distinct financial or strategic advantages. We will also conclude at some point that the biggest issue with debt is that it increases the FC/TC burden a company faces. Not surprisingly it is those firms with an operationally high level of FC/TC (due to the high levels of fixed operational assets needed) which often rely heavily on leverage to operate their business models. This constitutes a double whammy: high operational leverage combined with high levels of financial leverage. The aviation and automotive industries are two of the more obvious poster children of this phenomenon which, on top of many strategic mistakes made over the years, accounts for the many bankruptcies and work-outs observed in these industries.

So, going back to our PPLs, they have the benefit of (partially) taking out the downside of enhanced leverage by turning the compensation structure into a flexible mechanism which will move with the profitability of the firm over the macro-economic cycles.

Let's break the product down further in terms of its characteristics:

- The loan and the PPS can be detachable (but don't have to be). This means they don't have to be chronologically in sync until the fixed-income instrument reaches maturity.
- The PPS can outlive the loan or bond underlying the debt instrument. This can take many forms:
  - A loan of 10 years can have a PPS of 15 years and will therefore outlive the debt instruments by five years.

- A loan of 10 years which has a PPS of 10 years which will only start halfway through the loan's lifetime will outlive the loan by five years.
- Ultimately, the idea is to structure the PPS in such a way that it covers the period in which the value the underlying loan is expected to create will show up and can be benefited from by the lender. In extremis, this can imply that the PPS will only come into effect after the maturity of the loan.
- One of the most critical terms is obviously how the profit sharing is constructed. It is often done on a % basis, and the basis on which it can be applied can be revenues/EBIT(DA)/earnings on a projected or actual basis for the validity period of the PPS.
- The most adequate level depends on the health of the firm, the industry it is in, the purpose of taking on a PPL (and how the financial results of that transaction are going to show up) and the existing structure of the balance sheet when going in. It needs to be stressed that each of these criteria is an accounting standard, and is therefore affected by the respective principle, whether that is US GAAP, IFRS or a local GAAP. The consequence is that the deeper the criterion is on a typical P&L, the more it is going to be impacted by accounting standards, and therefore the less it will reflect the enhanced profitability of value created by offering the PPL to the firm. The same argument can also be used to shy away from PPS mechanisms linked to a criterion which is judged at group level or HoldCo level (in particular in multi-industry firms).
  - Let me illustrate this with a real-life example. Winston Groom is the author of the novel on which the movie *Forrest Gump* is based. The deal Groom made with Paramount was that he would receive US$350,000 for the rights to his book as well as 3% of the film's total box office gross. Unfortunately, the producers and movie studio did not end up paying Groom anything. The reason for this was because of a technique called 'Hollywood accounting' which conned Groom out of his money by saying that the film lost money. It effectively did (in accounting terms), because under Hollywood accounting rules it was possible to deduct a 40% provision for (future) movies which may turn sour. It is a given that about 9 out of 10 movies produced don't go anywhere. The provision can be claimed from the profits of blockbuster movies which go well. It was said that both Tom Hanks and director Robert Zemeckis earned US$40 million from percentages in box office receipts. Because of this incident, Groom refused to allow Hollywood to turn *Forrest Gump*'s sequel, *Gump and Co.*, into a movie.
- The profit participating loan differs from a silent participation particularly in the fact that the lender does not hold a stake or share in the company. They cannot influence the company's business (although they can protect themselves through a set of negative covenants – see Chapter 10 – and will then not participate in the company's losses).
- The profit participating loan has an advantage over other methods of investment, in that it can be sold publicly without a formal sales prospectus. Therefore, the company seeking capital does not have to put up with delays caused by the preparation of the prospectus and the subsequent admission procedure of the local financial supervisor. The profit participating loan is an investment model with a simple structure which can be implemented in a quick and cost-efficient way. It is therefore also suitable as bridge financing for an intended IPO.
- The compensation mechanism can also be extended with a cap and a floor, i.e., there will always be a minimum level of compensation due, regardless of the performance of the firm, and a maximum, therefore not letting the PPS have its full effect.

---

### EXAMPLE: COMBINED PROFIT PARTICIPATING MODEL

**Input data**

- €10 mil. PP loan starting 1.1.2013
- PPS: 3% EBIT
- Tenor: 10 years
- Principal repayment at maturity
- Floor: €150,000 annually
- Cap: €230,000 annually

| 000s | 2013 | 2014 | 2015 | 2016 | 2017 | 2018 | 2019 | 2020 | 2021 | 2022 |
|------|------|------|------|------|------|------|------|------|------|------|
| **Sales** | 10,000 | 12,000 | 14,000 | 16,000 | 18,000 | 20,000 | 22,000 | 24,000 | 24,000 | 25,000 |
| **EBIT** | 4,000 | 4,500 | 5,300 | 6,000 | 6,100 | 6,900 | 7,300 | 8,200 | 9,000 | 9,700 |
| **PPS** | 120 | 135 | 159 | 180 | 183 | 207 | 219 | 246 | 270 | 291 |
| **Cap** | 120 | 135 | 159 | 180 | 183 | 207 | 219 | **230** | **230** | **230** |
| **Floor** | **150** | **150** | 159 | 180 | 183 | 207 | 219 | 246 | 270 | 291 |

---

- The floor and cap can obviously be expressed as a % on EBIT, or even a different criterion than that in which the compensation mechanism is constructed. For example, it can be agreed that the floor is an annualized yield of 4% IRR and the cap 7%.
- The PPS can, as is often the case in practice, have a decreasing scale towards its later years.
- An element which always needs to be fleshed out contractually is whether the PPS is cumulative or not. A firm can decide not to pay PPS when, although there is a positive EBIT at the firm (and therefore profit participating payments are due), net earnings are negative or cash flows can't cover operational needs. The question then becomes whether the unpaid sum can roll over to future years or is lost forever. It seems recommendable to agree on what conditions can trigger a temporary or permanent withholding of PPS-related payments (and, if temporary, which conditions need to be fulfilled to restart payments, beginning with the ones due from previous years).
- Another related question that needs to be covered in the contract is if there will be the option for either the borrower or lender to withdraw or sell back the instrument, i.e., whether there will be a put and call option included in the document. The put option allows the lender to sell the instrument back to the borrower if he believes he can get a better deal elsewhere or when it seems that the instrument will yield no further income until maturity (this would require clarification on whether the lender can accelerate repayment of the principal amount, as there is no real breach of covenants in this case). The call option allows the borrower to withdraw the instrument if he can refinance under better conditions or otherwise. The ability to do so can be linked to certain dates or periods and restricted in other periods (for example not in the first two years and set-up of the contract).
- An element which needs validation before even considering using the instrument is the tax status of profit-linked interest payments. First of all, it is not the case that because the payments are profit or performance driven, they no longer qualify as interest. The payments are based on an instrument which has the legal qualification of a loan or bond, and consequently most legal systems qualify the payments as tax deductible interests, even if

the levels of payout are driven by performance or profit levels. Some tax authorities have seen some products as a form of informal capital, and re-qualified interest payments into deemed dividends as a consequence. A question which arises here is obviously how that relates to the freedom to take out contracts as you see fit (the tax authorities can never walk in the shoes of the manager or entrepreneur). There are still many jurisdictions where the tax authorities, to determine whether 'interest' is really interest in a tax sense, are not allowed to use an economic analysis, but have to treat the loan in the same way it is treated for commercial accounting and/or legal purposes. A reclassification of interest into a deemed dividend will not easily occur there. However, in The Netherlands and a few other countries the tax authorities, either by law (written) or by jurisprudence (court decisions), are allowed to follow an economic approach. The most far-reaching tax test would be 'could the subsidiary have obtained this loan from a bank?' and if not, the loan is no longer a loan for corporate income tax purposes and the interest thereon is deemed a dividend distribution (non-deductible for corporate income tax and perhaps even subject to a dividend withholding tax). This is the approach in the UK including for transfer pricing purposes.

Digesting the jurisprudence on intercompany profit-participating loans, the following picture can be drawn:

1. That primarily the legal denomination (i.e., the denomination under accounting law) of a loan will determine its tax consequences, but that
2. if the loan is granted under such conditions that the creditor, to a certain extent, participates in the business of the subsidiary, the tax treatment of the loan may require reclassification as the hidden provision of informal capital. The interest payments therefore no longer qualify as such for tax purposes but become deemed dividend income or expense, which is true if the following three criteria have been met simultaneously:
   a. The loan has a maturity date of 50 years or more.
   b. The interest is highly dependent on the future profitability of the debtor.
   c. The 'loan' is subordinated to all other debts of the subsidiary.

This Dutch Supreme Court verdict was rendered in the case of a French loan which is commonly known in France as a 'Prêt participatif.' Interestingly, this PPL contained a clause on an early repayment possibility (which at first sight seems to conflict with requirement (a), though this did not bring the judges to a different verdict).

Beyond this, many Corporate Income Tax Codes in the world contain a special provision which made PPL interest income taxable unless the tax payer could prove that the interest was not tax-deductible abroad. Often, this principle is embedded in wider anti-abuse provisions in the tax codes.

The dos and don'ts of profit participating loans can be summarized as follows:

- One of the benefits of a PPL is that ultimately the instrument matures and consequently there is no liquidity needed to monetize the profit-driven dynamics of the instrument.
- The same is applicable to situations where there are restrictions on equity or warrants, or more generally any instrument which has the potential to further dilute the equity stake of existing shareholders.
- As indicated earlier in this chapter, the product tends to work well in cases where there are relatively stable and transparent cash flow projections.

- When accounting standards are weak and/or corporate governance standards non-existent or ineffective, risks are included due to the profit-driven and therefore accounting-based performance mechanism.
- It is less adequate as a product for high-growth companies or companies with large and repeated capex needs, as any cash flow created should be used towards growing the business.
- Companies with complex transfer pricing structures pose an inherent risk to themselves. Intercompany transfer pricing has come into the limelight as globalization kicked in during the last two decades. This mainly happened from a tax point of view, although historically the term originates from the cost accounting and management control sphere. 'Intercompany' usually means that there is some level of ownership or control by one party over the other (individuals or corporations), or at least that they act in some level of concert due to aligned interests. The whole conceptual mechanics behind transfer pricing is that multinational companies have the benefit of engaging in business with each other (by providing goods and services, making intellectual property available or providing loans and guarantees) under conditions which would not be applied if the counterparty were a third party to the firm ('at arm's length principle'). This leads to situations where multinational companies can charge prices for these goods and services in such a way that most of the profits at group level are allocated to those entities in the group that enjoy the lowest effective tax rate. This leads to an overall reduction of the global effective tax rate of the firm, particularly in situations where one could shift functions and risks among group entities to justify the adverse pricing mechanisms for these goods and services. This might be an attractive idea in itself, were it not for the fact that taxation, from a sovereign perspective, is a national affair and therefore the national tax authorities are eager to assess if the revenue, and more importantly profit level generation, is in line with the actual functions and risks performed by the respective group company located in that country. This is done through extensive benchmarking with third party data, and often includes the ability to conclude APAs (Advanced Pricing Agreements) to provide certainty about the tax treatment of certain transactions pertaining to pricing/cost levels and structures, or the entire spectrum of intercompany mechanisms in place. Going back to our PPL, this includes some inherent risk for PPL holders, as obscure transfer pricing mechanisms can blur the visibility or erode the actual financial end result of a group company. This will then lead to a reduced credibility or at least a reduction of the ability to repay the principal and interests due. Depending on the transaction analyzed, the impact can be on EBIT level (as it impacted the cost of sales of the company) or on EBIT/earnings level when the transactions involved overhead-related goods or services or were of a financial nature.
- The above risk becomes even more pertinent if the PPL was provided to a HoldCo in the group. As holding companies often do not yield any operational income themselves, they are therefore dependent on dividend or cash flow upstreams from any of the operational companies to satisfy the liabilities due under the PPL. It might seem contradictory to provide a PPL, a loan characterized by profit participating compensation mechanisms, to a HoldCo whose essential nature is that it does not produce any income or cash flows itself (or at least, that is not its primary nature). In itself and on a stand-alone basis, that is a valid question and could nullify the issues were it not for situations in which providing the loan to the operational company is impossible. Two situations are envisaged here: the first is a private equity owned company where the acquisition finance flows through an SPV (Special Purpose Vehicle) which does not yield any income either, and which serves the purpose of being the acquisition holding (see Chapter 8). The other situation is where the operational

company has maxed out its senior debt levels within the firm and the PPL provider therefore feels more comfortable providing the PPL at HoldCo level. This ensures that other operational companies for which the PPL was provided can contribute, in case the original OpCo defaults on its commitments or experiences deteriorating performance throughout the PPL's lifetime. This could also be orchestrated by making the PPS dependent not only on the performance of the company to which the PPL is provided, but also (partly) dependent on the performance of other group companies, though the PPL legally is being provided to the PPL-seeking group entity (rather than the parent holding).

The legal position and interest of the lender in a PPL is quite different even compared with normal subordinated debt providers, as the entire (or at least some of the) compensation for the PPL is based on the economic performance of the company. One could argue that every lender is dependent on the performance of the firms to which it lends, and consequently there is counterparty risk even in the most risk-free loan or bond one can imagine. That is very much true and experience shows that some AAA-rated instruments, whether sovereign bonds or structured products, all rely on the cash-generating capacity of the underlying assets or economy of a firm or sovereign being lent to.[3] One could say we learned that the hard way during the 2008 crisis.

The big difference in the case of a PPL is that the compensation is not fixed and therefore entirely dependent on the firm's effective profit levels before any payout will occur, which is different to any other mezzanine instrument. Consequently, PPL investors tend to be looking for a more stringent set of covenants. The following elements will invariably play a critical role in shaping those covenants. PPL investors will be looking for a veto, co-decision process or qualified/simple majority for a number of critical decisions. These critical decisions will obviously all relate to the potential impact they might have on the future cash flow generating capacity of the firm and its asset base. This position can be approached from a positive or negative point of view.

From a negative point of view it means that, as in the case of many subordinated debt covenants, and given the often deep subordination, the borrower is not in a position to add more debt to their balance sheet after the PPL investor has stepped in, or to provide a second lien or negative pledge on any of the firm's existing assets. The PPL lender will be looking for similar rights when it comes to decisions which impact the future strategic direction of the firm or the sell-off of certain strategic assets, business units or complete subsidiaries.

Given the fact that (almost) all of the lender's compensation is linked to actual performance without having the protection of control (like normal shareholders), they will be looking for control or at least the ability to terminate or accelerate repayment of the PPL in the case of a change of control of ownership in the firm. Normal shareholders would have either tag- or drag-along rights, or at least pre-emption rights to protect themselves against other shareholders leaving or majority owners deciding to sell their stake in the firm.

The question then becomes what happens in the case of any of these events occurring? I hinted already at a possible acceleration of repayment a little earlier on, but that could deliver suboptimal results, harm the firm (even further), or would leave the PPL holder without any meaningful compensation. Therefore it tends to happen more frequently that a number of exit situations which would lead to termination of the PPL are specifically contractually listed, along with the

---

[3] Aswath Damodaran, 'Into the abyss: what if nothing is risk-free?' Working Paper Series, NY University, Stern School of Business, 2010.

consequences of any of these conditions, should they occur. Often a provision will be included, which will allow the PPL holder to receive the NPV (net present value) of the future PPS at the moment of exit as a kind of penalty, or to compensate for the missed business opportunity and the potential risk of having to invest at lower compensation levels in the market at that point in time.

Obviously the question arises of how one can determine the NPV of future compensation if that compensation is dependent on the future financial performance of the firm. Most often, a model is included which assumes a certain percentage growth trajectory based on the profit-linked criterion in the year of exit. Alternatively, one can use an (adjusted) average growth rate going forward similar to the one observed during the previous years of the PPL.

As indicated earlier in this chapter, banks and FIs have often constructed these PPLs as syndicated loans. These participations in the loan were then sold by the lead bank to other banks. A separate contract called a loan participation agreement is normally structured and agreed among the banks. Loan participations between those banks can be made either on a *pari passu* basis (this term refers to two or more loans, bonds or classes of shares having equal payment rights or level of seniority), with equal risk sharing for all loan participants, or on a senior/subordinated basis, where the senior lender is paid first and the subordinate loan participant paid only if there are sufficient funds left over to make the payments. Such senior/subordinated loan participations can be structured either on a LIFO (Last In First Out) or FIFO (First In First Out) basis, which often refers to the valuation techniques for inventory under US GAAP and IFRS standards although LIFO is not permitted under IFRS standards.

The most common reasons for financial institutions to engage in participation loans are the following:

- Buying participation loans is a way for banks to diversify their assets. By investing a variety of loans in different locales, they reduce their risk and exposure to potential losses if a calamity, such as a natural disaster or severe economic depression, were to strike their particular community.
- Banks which buy loan participations share in the profits of the lead bank. If a lending institution isn't doing much business on its own, or is in a slow market, it can team up with a profitable 'lead bank' in a healthier market to generate more lending income.
- Selling loan participations allows the lead bank to originate an exceptionally large loan that would otherwise be too large for it to handle by itself. By engaging other banks as participants, the lead bank can remain within its own legal lending limits and still come up with sufficient cash for funding.
- Selling loan participations allows a bank to reduce its credit risk to a customer or specific community which would usually have a greater than average risk profile.
- Selling participation loans allows the lead bank to keep (more) control of important customer relationships with their large corporate customers, instead of sharing the relationship with other competing banks.

## 2.1.4 Subordinated debt with warrants

It is perfectly imaginable that a firm looking for additional financing has already accumulated such a pallet of existing senior and subordinated debt that it becomes very difficult to assess the implicit risk that the loan sought will be exposed to. Combined with limited visibility on cash flows and their timing going forward, the lender might conclude that none of the products mentioned so far are adequate given their mechanisms, or at least that the compensation mechanisms of enhanced spreads (over and beyond senior lending) do not capture the full risk, or are not sufficient to reflect those enhanced risk patterns.

There is clearly a theoretical argument to be made here for this line of thinking. The deeper the subordination, the more the mezzanine lender's risk profile will shift in nature from the criterion of 'creditworthiness' to entrepreneurial/business risk. This undoubtedly raises the question of the extent to which, and the way in which, this different risk dynamic needs to be reflected, and whether the additional risk can be captured by an increased spread on the principal amount. Or, put differently, is it fair to approach entrepreneurial risk with a lender's way of thinking, and what are the possible consequences of doing so? I mentioned earlier that high-yield bonds which carry an annual compensation higher than the ROE of the shareholders of the firm in which the loan was invested will trigger refinancing or worse.

Let's make a comparison: you want to buy a house, but don't have the money to do so. In fact, you don't have any money to spend, not even 10% or so of the purchase price. So you want to buy that house without putting any money down. Surprisingly enough, there are some banks in some parts of the world which, until recently, were willing to consider financing this. For others (the European readers) this might all sound a bit off the wall. But let's assume the bank plays ball and finances the full amount of the negotiated price, the expenses which come with the transfer and potential renovations (i.e., a new larger kitchen etc.) you want to complete before moving in. So the bank is financing you for an amount equal to 120% of your property's purchase price (and assuming that the purchase price is somewhere close to fair value at the moment of the transaction). Beside the brutal repayments which will be due over the next 20–30 years, it is also clear that, if a situation occurs where you become unable to repay the monthly or quarterly payments, you will be tempted to drop the house keys at the bank and walk off into the sunset rather than refinancing or taking out further loans, all driven by the fact that you yourself don't have any equity in the house. Or, to put it in insurance terms, you don't have any insurable interest, or only interest which will grow very slowly over the next 20–30 years.

Going back to our original position, the mezzanine lender is now looking at a risk exposure which requires an almost entire equity exposure to the firm to justify taking on the risk which comes with the investment. However, as the entrepreneur/management looks at this as a debt instrument, they will therefore exclude the possibility of the lender participating in the equity of the firm directly to avoid them enjoying the equity uptick based on value created before they invested in the firm. The lender therefore needs to look for an instrument which will allow them to benefit from the equitable upside in the firm but which is created (or at least shows up) after their investment in the firm. The lender basically takes out an option on the future, assuming that their contribution will allow for the firm to advance given the business plan it is about to roll out, which might include organic growth, restructuring, acquisitions, etc.

The instrument which does all that for the lender is what is known as a 'warrant.' A warrant can be defined as a security which entitles the holder to buy (in most cases) the underlying stock of the issuing company at a fixed exercise price until the expiry date. The word warrant means to 'endow with the right.' Warrants are frequently attached to bonds/loans or even preferred stock as a sweetener, i.e., the investor will potentially derive an additional income from the warrant once exercised on top of the interest (or fixed dividend in case of a preferred shareholding). This often implies that the borrower will pay a (significantly) lower interest rate, at least compared to subordinated debt of a similar risk profile with no warrants attached to the loan (or warrants which are negotiated with the loan but detached from it and therefore can be independently sold on). Thus, the lender may exercise the warrant but not redeem the bond. They can further be used to enhance the yield of the bond, and make them more attractive to potential buyers. Warrants can also be used in private equity deals (see Chapter 8) as part of the mezzanine mix.

In the case of warrants issued together with preferred stocks, stockholders may need to detach and sell the warrant before they can receive dividend payments. It is therefore sometimes beneficial to detach and sell a warrant as soon as possible (early after being issued or granted) so the investor can earn (fixed) dividends. Detachable warrants can be actively traded in some financial markets. The most dominant ones are the Deutsche Börse (Germany) and Hong Kong exchange.

There is a lot of substance to this product which we need to flesh out before we can critically position the instrument in the wider mezzanine spectrum. To begin with, the warrant does not dilute the value of existing shareholders at the moment of issue. In this sense it is similar to the options issues top managers receive, or those within the framework of an ESOP (Employee Stock Option Plan). However, the moment that these options are exercised, the issuing firm will have to issue new common stock which, at that point in time, will dilute the existing shareholder holdings (and consequently the EPS (Earnings per Share) of the firm). This is also true for the embedded optionality in a convertible loan and convertible preferred shares. Therefore, the financial documents of a firm always indicate, at the bottom of the P&L, the normal EPS and the EPS on a fully diluted basis, so that potential investors in the firm can assess the impact of all embedded options which will be exercised at some point in the future, and which will then impact their shareholding. One can therefore question the accounting rules that allow options to be recorded in the accounting books at cost (of issuance) rather than at real economic cost to the firm, something Warren Buffett has repeatedly brought up in the past (for the accounting treatment of warrants and other mezzanine products, see Chapter 9).

One of the issues which makes this product different from others within the mezzanine group is the fact that it will ultimately provide a lender or investor (not necessarily the first investor as he could have sold the warrants on unless they were restricted) with effective equity in the firm. This raises an avalanche of questions and issues we need to address. Some of them deal with the valuation of the warrants, which we will deal with later; others are centered around the liquidity needed to monetize the common stock once the warrants are exercised. It raises questions about the liquidity of the stock in which one invests, particularly when investing in a closely-held firm.

Two situations can be distinguished here:

1. There is likely an upcoming natural liquidity element in which the investor can participate. This natural liquidity moment can be a merger or acquisition, an IPO, a sale by the majority owner, a consolidation in the industry that is upcoming or ongoing, or the activation of a stock buy-back program by the firm. All situations will lead to the equity owner being able to monetize their position. That will always be the investor's starting position, i.e., that they want to monetize their stake in the firm as there was no intention of becoming a permanent (or sizeable) shareholder. If that had been the objective of the investor, other instruments would have been more adequate.
2. An artificial liquidity moment needs to be created or contracted. These are usually contractually defined. The first option is 'drag-along rights,' which will allow the minority owner (the former warrant owner) to drag the majority owner(s) into selling their stake to a third party (assuming they can get the third party to extend their agreed conditions to the majority owners). An alternative is to write a put option into the contract which will allow the investor to sell their stake back to the entrepreneur or (other) shareholders. The put option will allow the investor to sell back their stake within a certain period or at/after a specific

date. This period or date will fall after the full vesting and exercise period of the warrants has terminated, which is known upfront.

The last situation does raise some pertinent questions. Assuming that such a clause has been agreed on and, at a certain date or during a certain period, the investor is looking to exercise the put option, a certain number of situations can occur:

1. The majority owner(s) buy back the equity owned by the investor.
2. The majority shareholder(s) wants to buy back but doesn't have the liquidity (any more). This might occur if a sizeable chunk of the owner's wealth is tied up in the firm.
3. The majority owner(s) can buy back the shares but for whatever reason has no intention of doing so, despite the clause in the contract.

Cases two and three might lead to legal repercussions initiated by the investor.

In these situations one might want to consider the following option. If the investor wants a clause in the contract saying that the shares can be sold back to the majority owners, the majority owners will most likely want two things in exchange. Firstly, they will be looking for a call option, i.e., the right to buy back the shares from investors within a certain period of time or on a specific date. Secondly, when they accept the put option, they most likely will not be able (or, in fact, willing) to buy the shares back at fair market price when the buy back comes around. They will want to see a discount on the market value of the shares. This makes sense; the majority owners provide the service of liquidity, and that comes at a cost. Invariably, this will lead to discussion about how to contractualize the negotiations on the price or discount at which the shares need to be bought back. The reverse is true for situations where the majority owners want to buy the shares back based on the call option mentioned.

It is not uncommon for investors and existing shareholders to agree on a certain guaranteed annualized IRR, which can be at instrument level or at warrant level, if the shares are bought/sold back through the execution of the call or put option. To actively support the buy-back of the shares, the majority owners can consider offering a decreasing IRR scale to investors, and the investors can offer an increasing IRR scale to majority owners if the buy/sell back of shares does not happen in line with the timeline initially agreed. For example, the investors were looking to yield an average IRR on the shares of 15%, given the interest levels they receive on the loan or bond and the strike date of the call option. The investors have negotiated a call option on the shares as well.

## EXAMPLE

The investor provides a seven-year loan with a fixed interest rate of 4%. Given the risk involved, the investor is looking for an average annualized yield of 12% on the shares they intend to receive when executing the warrants they negotiated. The loan date commences on 1.1.2013 and runs until 12.31.2019. The warrants provided can be exercised in return for 100 shares in common stock/equity in the firm. Although in most mezzanine positions the warrants come at no cost to the investor, it is not unthinkable that the majority owners would want to negotiate a certain price for the warrants. That price may even be the market value of the underlying shares at the moment the warrants are issued (i.e., the embedded option is 'at' the money). It will require the investor to think about how many shares they need, and at what price: to get that additional 12% average annualized yield they need to get a total return (including the 4% and the loan or bond) adequate for the risk they are exposed to. The market price of the shares on 12.31.2012, assuming that is the date the contract is signed, is €14. The current return on equity is 18% and that is expected to stay constant, on average, over the next 10 years or so. The investor can buy the warrants at €14. As mentioned before, this is unusual in a mezzanine position.

Now let's assume the warrants are issued at 1.1.2013 as well. The contract states that the warrants may be exercised either at a specific point in time, or as of a certain date for a specific period of time. The difference between the two situations is linked to the difference between European and US option contracts. The key difference between American and European options relates to when the options can be exercised:

- A European option may be exercised only at the expiration date of the option, i.e., at a single pre-defined point in time.
- An American option, on the other hand, may be exercised at any time before the expiry date.
- A third option is the Asian option (aka the average value option), which is a special type of option contract. In the case of Asian options, the payoff is determined by the average underlying price over some pre-set period of time. This is clearly different compared to the usual European and American options, where the payoff of the option contract depends on the price of the underlying instrument at exercise; Asian options are therefore often considered exotic options compared to the European and US ones, which are considered plain vanilla options.
- One advantage of Asian options is that these reduce the risk of market manipulation of the underlying instrument at maturity. Because of the averaging feature, Asian options reduce the volatility inherent in the option; therefore, Asian options are typically cheaper (relative cost) than European or American options.

Now let's say that the exercise date or period ends at maturity of the loan (i.e., 12.31.2019). From there onwards, and except for a restricted period, the call and put options can be put in place. In this case, let's assume a restricted period of two years. This implies that the call and put options can be put in place as of 1.1.2021. Obviously, the strike date of the call and strike date of the put option don't have to fall together and normally do not.

In order to provide an incentive to both parties, the following schedule could be agreed upon. As the market price of the shares at the strike date of the call and put option is the benchmark here, there is a likely chance that we will be somewhat wrong in the effective estimation of the capital gain which will be realized on these shares.

|  | 1.1.2021 | 1.1.2022 | 1.1.2023 | 1.1.2024 | 1.1.2025 | 1.1.2026 |
|---|---|---|---|---|---|---|
| **Call option (discount to market value) IRR** | 17% | 15% | 13% | 12% | 11% | 9% |
| **Put option IRR** | 9% | 12% | 15% | 17% | 20% | 25% |
| **Historical cost (Euro)** | 14 | 14 | 14 | 14 | 14 | 14 |

Given the 12% target yield on the warrant the investor is looking for, and the existing and expected constant ROE at 18%, the investor will have an incentive to use their put option as of 2022 and the company will be inclined to use its call option pretty much from day one, if that would be contractually possible. The threshold on the call option could also have been expressed as well as an average IRR which would have shown a decreasing level in percentage terms as time progressed.

A product of this nature obviously comes with a set of covenants. They are, however, somewhat more relaxed relative to senior loan covenants. One of the main hurdles is still the inability of the borrower to take on board additional (senior) debt, although existing (senior) debt can be refinanced at a later date without prior consent of the subordinated lender.

Another feature, which is particularly important when the loan is provided to a HoldCo, is a share pledge of the HoldCo shares to ensure repayment of the subdebt and interest, even though the HoldCo in itself does not yield any cash flows. This also often happens if a particular part of the business is being financed and the HoldCo shares are pledged as a security, but also to access (although indirectly) the cash flow generating capacity of the other business activities. Direct pledges of the OpCo of other business units (sometimes with better margins, more FCF and/or lower debt levels) held by the same HoldCo are extremely difficult to negotiate.

As the compensation on the debt loan can be structured as a normal monthly or quarterly interest payment or alternatively as a PIK loan, a 'cash sweep provision' can be considered for inclusion, which would ensure that the cash generated by an asset sale or sale of a set of assets (e.g., business unit) will be used as a cash sweep for the subordinated debt, in particular when a PIK loan (or toggle loan) is involved. Although there can be a direct relation between (a pool of) assets[4] earmarked for the cash sweep operation, the subdebt holders get no first or second lien on that asset or asset pool. The loan is ultimately structurally subordinated. The choice between normal subdebt and a PIK loan will depend on the actual D/E position of the firm when investing, and the actual debt capacity available to service any intermediate interest components.

Prepayment of the loan is normally made possible under certain conditions (i.e., not in the early years) and the warrants should always outlive the prepayments. The prepayment penalty is normally 1–5% of the loan's (remaining) principal.

Although warrants usually mature on a specified date, some are perpetual. A warrant holder may exercise it by purchasing the stock, may sell it on the market to other investors, or may continue to hold it. The company cannot force the exercise of a warrant. If agreeable, the company may have the exercise price of the warrant change over time (e.g., increase each year). If a stock split or stock dividend is issued before the warrant is exercised, the option price of the warrant will be adjusted for it.

---

[4] The cash sweep can also refer to incremental cash flows generated in future years about a pre-determined level.

### The embedded option in a warrant contract

I'm sure it was already made quite clear earlier on in the section on warrants that the embedded option in a warrant contract looks very similar to other equity derivatives. Before we dive into the valuation and financial mechanics of options, which we will do in Chapter 4, we will first review some of the characteristics, similarities and differences.

Just like an option, the warrant contract states as key aspects:

- The exercise date/period (although they can be perpetual).
- The restriction period (during which the warrants cannot be exercised).
- Expiration date: This is the date the warrant expires. The warrant must be exercised before this date. The more time remaining until expiry, the more time for the underlying security to appreciate, which will support the increase of the warrant's price (unless it depreciates i.e., the price of the option goes down). Therefore, the expiry date is the date on which the right to exercise ceases to exist.
- Gearing (leverage): The gearing indicates how much exposure you have to the underlying shares (using the warrant) relative to the exposure you would have if you bought shares through the market.
- Restrictions (on the ability to exercise): I have already mentioned the different exercise types associated with warrants such as American style (holder can exercise any time before expiration) or European style (holder can only exercise on expiration date).
- Potentially, the restrictions on buying and selling activities after conversion into common equity.
- Premium: The 'premium' represents how much extra you have to pay for your shares when buying them through the warrant as compared to buying them in the regular way.
- Conversion ratio: How many shares (common stock) will be acquired after exercising the warrant.
- Exercise price (or strike price) of the warrant: Essentially, the cost at which the warrant holder obtains the document. Theoretically, that can be at a price below, par to or above the market price of the underlying shares at the moment the warrants are issued. The embedded option will show whether it is respectively out, at, or in the money, and in the last case only, the option will have an intrinsic value from the moment of issuance of the warrant (see Figure 2.1).

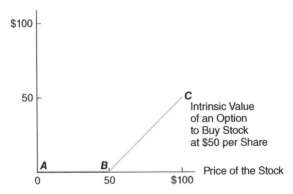

**Figure 2.1** The relationship between the price of a stock and the intrinsic value of a call to buy the stock at US$50 a share

- Vesting period: We already mentioned the fact that the warrant holder can be restricted from exercising the convertibility option based on the criteria included in the US or European option-style contract, which can be a specific date, or during the entire period until maturity. On top of this, it can be agreed that the option cannot be exercised during the first *x* years after the shares are issued. On top of both of these mechanisms, there is often a vesting period agreed, i.e., a period during which the ownership of the warrant gradually transfers to the subdebt lender. This is admittedly used more often in ESOPs (Employee Stock Option Plans) than in mezzanine lending situations (as the performance by the lender is known (i.e., they will provide a certain volume of subdebt for a certain period of time)). As the lender has been holding their part of the deal in the air by making their cash available, the vesting clause is less common in mezzanine positions, unless the lender has agreed on additional duties (i.e., additional to providing subdebt) which can be of a financial, business, strategic or legal nature (see Figure 2.2).

The contractual freedom *inter partes* allows the parties to basically agree on anything they want, and has therefore led to the growth of many different types (and features) of warrants, of which a non-exhaustive list is given below.

- The typical equity warrants: Equity warrants can be call and put warrants (or a combination):
  - Callable warrants: Callable warrants give the company the right to force the warrant holder to exercise the warrants into their pre-determined number of shares at a pre-determined price (or using a pre-determined price formula) after certain contractual conditions are met.
  - Puttable warrants: Puttable warrants give the warrant holder the right to force the company to issue the underlying securities at a pre-determined price after certain contractual conditions are met (see Figure 2.3).

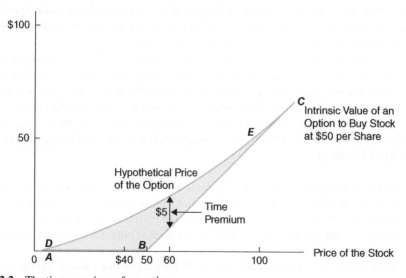

**Figure 2.2**    The time premium of an option

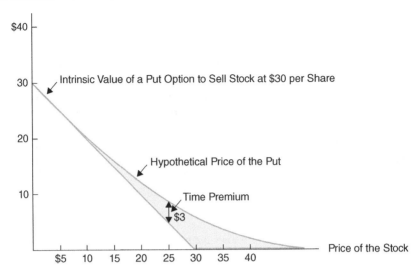

**Figure 2.3**  Put option

- Covered warrants: A covered warrant is a warrant which has some underlying backing, for example; the issuer will purchase the stock beforehand or will use other instruments to cover the option. In many ways it has all the features of a normal warrant, i.e., it allows the holder to buy or sell a specific amount of equities, currency or other financial instruments from the issuer at a specified price at a pre-determined date. However, in contrast to normal warrants, they are usually issued by financial institutions instead of normal (share issuing) companies and are often listed as fully tradable securities on a number of stock exchanges. They can also have a wide variety of underlying instruments, not just equities, and may allow the holder to both buy and sell the underlying asset. These attributes make it possible to use covered warrants as a tool to speculate on financial markets. That in itself puts this topic somewhat beyond the boundaries of the scope of this book.
- Turbo warrants: Turbo warrants are options of the barrier type (where their existence is extinguished in the event of the underlying asset's price breaching a barrier), and specifically of the 'down and out' type (the spot price starts above the barrier level and has to move down for the option to become null and void). It is similar to a plain vanilla option contract, but with two additional features: it has a low vega, meaning that the option price is much less affected by the implied volatility of the stock market, and it is highly geared due to the possibility of knockout.

The strike price of the option is generally the same as the barrier: if the stock hits the barrier, the option expires and becomes worthless. Variations on turbo options include forms where the strike and barrier are not identical; forms where the barrier is only active at, for example, the close of business but the strike is continuously monitored (smart turbo options); and forms with no fixed maturity (minis).

On a comparative note, a regular call option will have a positive value at expiry whenever the spot price settles above the strike price. A turbo will have a positive value at expiry when the spot settles above the strike and the spot has never fallen below the strike during the option's lifetime (if it had done so the option would have crossed the barrier (strike) and would have become worthless).

- Basket warrants: As with a regular equity index, warrants can be classified at, for example, an industry level. Thus, it mirrors the performance of the industry.
- Index warrants: Index warrants use an index as the underlying asset. Your risk is dispersed – using index call and index put warrants – just as is the case with regular equity indexes. It should be noted that they are priced using index points, i.e., you deal with cash, not directly with shares.
- Wedding warrants: these are attached to the subdebt and can be exercised only if the host debentures are surrendered.
- Detachable warrants: the warrant portion of the security can be detached from the debenture and traded separately.
- Naked warrants: these are issued without an accompanying bond.

Warrants, just like options, are most often used by investors to protect their portfolio from falling in price terms.

Although tradable, most warrants trade OTC (over-the-counter, i.e., in the private market). This is because most of them are tailor-made contracts and not standardized like option contracts; in order to be traded on an exchange, you must be able to properly assess counterparty risk, which is exactly why these contracts are standardized.

Warrants are also often longer-term contracts (at least compared to option contracts). The Black–Scholes option valuation methodology, the commonly accepted but not completely untainted valuation methodology for options, is the default valuation model to value warrants. The Black–Scholes model shows quite a few inaccuracies when dealing with option contracts which mature far in the future, something Warren Buffett alluded to in his annual letter to shareholders for 2008.[5]

In his letter to shareholders for 2008, he even devotes some time to providing examples of the wildly inaccurate valuations for long-dated option contracts. An excerpt for fans and enthusiasts:

> The Black–Scholes formula has approached the status of holy writ in finance, and we use it when valuing our equity put options for financial statement purposes. Key inputs to the calculation include a contract's maturity and strike price, as well as the analyst's expectations for volatility, interest rates and dividends.

> If the formula is applied to extended time periods, however, it can produce absurd results. In fairness, Black and Scholes almost certainly understood this point well. But their devoted followers may be ignoring whatever caveats the two men attached when they first unveiled the formula.

> It's often useful in testing a theory to push it to extremes. So let's postulate that we sell a 100-year US$1 billion put option on the S&P 500 at a strike price of 903 (the index's level on 12/31/08). Using the implied volatility assumption for long-dated contracts that we do, and combining that with appropriate interest and dividend assumptions, we would find the 'proper' Black–Scholes premium for this contract to be US$2.5 million.

---

[5] Warren Buffett, 'Annual letter to shareholders 2008,' p. 21. The full text is available at http://www .berkshirehathaway.com/letters/2008ltr.pdf. Reproduced with permission of the author.

To judge the rationality of that premium, we need to assess whether the S&P will be valued a century from now at less than today. Certainly the dollar will then be worth a small fraction of its present value (at only 2% inflation it will be worth roughly 14¢). So that will be a factor pushing the stated value of the index higher.

Far more important, however, is that one hundred years of retained earnings will hugely increase the value of most of the companies in the index. In the 20th Century, the Dow-Jones Industrial Average increased by about 175-fold, mainly because of this retained-earnings factor.

Considering everything, I believe the probability of a decline in the index over a one-hundred-year period to be far less than 1%. But let's use that figure and also assume that the most likely decline – should one occur – is 50%. Under these assumptions, the mathematical expectation of loss on our contract would be US$5 million (US$1 billion x 1% x 50%).

But if we had received our theoretical premium of US$2.5 million up front, we would have only had to invest it at 0.7% compounded annually to cover this loss expectancy. Everything earned above that would have been profit. Would you like to borrow money for 100 years at a 0.7% rate? Let's look at my example from a worst-case standpoint. Remember that 99% of the time we would pay nothing if my assumptions are correct. But even in the worst case among the remaining 1% of possibilities – that is, one assuming a total loss of US$1 billion – our borrowing cost would come to only 6.2%. Clearly, either my assumptions are crazy or the formula is inappropriate.

The ridiculous premium that Black–Scholes dictates in my extreme example is caused by the inclusion of volatility in the formula and by the fact that volatility is determined by how much stocks have moved around in some past period of days, months or years. This metric is simply irrelevant in estimating the probability weighted range of values of American business 100 years from now. (Imagine, if you will, getting a quote every day on a farm from a manic-depressive neighbor and then using the volatility calculated from these changing quotes as an important ingredient in an equation that predicts a probability-weighted range of values for the farm a century from now.) Though historical volatility is a useful – but far from foolproof – concept in valuing short-term options, its utility diminishes rapidly as the duration of the option lengthens. In my opinion, the valuations that the Black–Scholes formula now place on our long-term put options overstate our liability, though the overstatement will diminish as the contracts approach maturity.

Even so, we will continue to use Black–Scholes when we are estimating our financial-statement liability for long-term equity puts. The formula represents conventional wisdom and any substitute that I might offer would engender extreme skepticism. That would be perfectly understandable: CEOs who have concocted their own valuations for esoteric financial instruments have seldom erred on the side of conservatism. That club of optimists is one that Charlie and I have no desire to join.

Most warrants are not traded and are issued by private firms. The secondary market for these instruments therefore is limited. This implies that the pricing of these products is often less obvious.

### Comparing options and warrants
There are many similarities between options and warrants, and I have already named a few. Despite this, there are some key differences. Hereafter, I try to be a bit more exhaustive in my analysis.

- Warrants are (often) issued by private companies, most often the corporation on which a warrant is based, rather than a public options exchange.

- Warrants issued by the company itself are dilutive. When a warrant issued by a company is exercised, the company issues new shares of stock, so the number of outstanding shares increases. When a call option is exercised, the owner of the call option receives an existing share from an assigned call writer (except in the case of employee stock options, where new shares are created and issued by the company upon exercise; this is also true for convertible loans and convertible preferred shares upon conversion). Unlike common stock shares outstanding, warrants do not have voting rights.

- Warrants are considered over-the-counter instruments, and thus are usually only traded by financial institutions with the capacity to settle and clear these types of transactions. More and more, however, I am seeing investors using the instrument in emerging markets to create an equity kicker in illiquid investments, rather than for trading purposes (which would likely be extremely limited given the often severe illiquidity). I have encountered many situations where the investor, after exercising the warrant, would be left with common stock in such volumes that, even despite the fact that the company was listed (in an African country), it would still take them three years and the total trading volume per year for those three years to monetize on the entire stake. This obviously increases the carrying cost of the instrument (plus a significant bid–ask fork), which unfortunately is not always priced (correctly or at all) in the product.

- A warrant's lifetime is measured in years, while options are typically measured in months, or, put differently, warrants are longer dated (on average) than options. Even LEAPS (long-term equity anticipation securities), the longest stock options available, tend to expire within two or three years. Upon expiration, the warrants are worthless unless the price of the common stock is greater than the exercise price.

- Warrants are not standardized like exchange-listed options. While investors can write stock options on pretty much any exchange, they are not permitted to do so with listed warrants, since only companies can issue warrants. Also, while each option contract is over a certain amount of the underlying ordinary shares, the number of warrants which must be exercised by the holder to buy the underlying asset depends on the conversion ratio set out in the offer documentation for the warrant issue.

## 2.1.5  Convertible loans

### Convertible security fundamentals[6]

Let's move on to our next product group; the convertible loan group. Whereas warrants are separate and detachable from the subdebt, the convertible loan group has the option of embedding the warrant in the subdebt itself. Or, put differently, the fixed-income instrument can be exchanged for a certain (pre-determined) number of common shares in the issuing firm (based on conditions described in the indenture). The product can therefore change nature during its lifetime, from a fixed-income instrument into common equity (i.e., it is an option, although in some cases the conversion is mandatory, see later in this chapter). It will, at the moment of conversion, dilute the existing position of the common shareholders. It can have other embedded options included (call or put, soft or hard, protection, etc.).

---

[6] For a more detailed overview, see F.J. Fabozzi and S.V. Mann, *The Handbook of Fixed Income Securities*, 2011, 8th edn, Chapter 59: 'Convertible securities and their investment characteristics.'

A convertible bond is therefore very similar to a straight bond with an embedded warrant. Table 2.1 gives a comparison of the characteristics and mechanics of straight and convertible bonds:

**Table 2.1**   Financial dynamics of straight versus convertible bonds

| Straight corporate bond | | Convertible bond |
| --- | --- | --- |
| • Coupon | **Common characteristics** | • Coupon |
| • Maturity | | • Maturity |
| • Call provision | | • Call provision (interest rate) |
| • Put provision | | • Put provision |
| • Business risk | ◄── **Assessment of capital structure** ──► | • Business risk |
| • (Credit rating) | **Evaluation of cash flows** | • (Credit rating) |
| • Covenants | **Volatility of earnings** | • Covenants |
| • Liquidity | **Growth of prospects** | • Liquidity |
| | | Plus (+) |
| | | **Warrant on the equity** |
| | | – Conversion price |
| | **Sophisticated financial** ──► | – Dividend assumption |
| | **modeling** | – Time to expiration |
| | | – Expected volatility |
| | | – Borrow rate |

A convertible bond is consequently a bond with an option for the holder to exchange the bond into 'new' (although technically they can come out of Treasury stock as well) shares of common stock for the issuing company under specified terms and conditions. These include (amongst others) the conversion period and the conversion ratio. The conversion period is the period during which the bond may be converted into shares. The conversion ratio is the number of shares received per converted amount. The conversion price, which is the effective price paid for the common stock, is the ratio of the face value of the convertible to the conversion ratio. Convertibles almost always have a call provision built in. The yield at issuance of convertible bonds is lower than the yield on the same issuer's more senior debt (reflecting the conversion privilege via the cumulative sacrificed yield).

Convertible securities have evolved significantly in recent times due to an overall sophistication of the market in terms of analytics, trading and attention to risk dynamics. Although convertible securities always try to strike a balance between common stock and straight debt attributes, some will end up close to common stock in terms of their risk profile and others will be more skewed towards straight debt. Maturity can range from three years to perpetual instruments where the issuer is not even required to repay the par or the principal amount of the security. Also, over time the risk dynamics of a convertible product can change. A product which started out as very close to straight debt might end up close to common stock owing to price appreciation in the common stock into which it is convertible (the reverse is also true).

Essential features,[7] some of which have been mentioned, are:

• Convertibility date or period before maturity (often with an initial non-conversion period). In recent times, sometimes contingent conversion clauses are included.

---

[7] For a full review of the product group and its characteristics see also Fabozzi and Mann, *The Handbook of Fixed Income Securities*, McGraw-Hill, 2011, 8th edn and in particular Chapter 60: 'Convertible securities and their valuation.'

- Convertibles are convertible in the shares of the issuing firm. Sometimes convertibility occurs in the shares of another traded entity (i.e., exchangeables).
- Conversion right is with the holder and optional (unless defined otherwise, i.e., mandatorily convertible).
- In most cases a redemption feature for the issuer is included.
- Most conversion is forced by an issuer call with a number of exceptions to this general rule.
- In most cases the settlement upon conversion is in stock but can be in cash when the prospectus allows (cash settle option) which normally yields a slightly lower return than a physical settlement.
- A convertible's current yield, yield-to-maturity or yield-to-first-put usually exceeds the dividend yield of the underlying stock.
- Convertibles have a fixed maturity with the exception of mandatory convertibles which can be extended by a period of 1 to 30 years.
- Convertibles have a fixed conversion ratio. Exceptions occur when the conversion ratio is a function of the underlying share price on the settlement date. Maximum and minimum limits are normally defined. Another exception is in the case of a reset/refix clause, whereby the conversion ratio is reset if the underlying stock price does not exceed certain predefined trigger prices.
- The price of the convertible is at least equal to the value of the shares into which it is convertible, with some exceptions.
- Convertibles are subject to duration risk and convexity just like any fixed income security; an active CDS market has therefore developed.
- Convertibles are normally subordinated debentures (but can also be senior subordinated and senior unsubordinated debentures).

The convertibles market was viewed, until recently, as a source of funds for firms with marginal credit quality which were often unable to access the public debt markets but has expanded rapidly over the last decade to also cover firms with investment grade status.

The convertibles market is essentially formed of four areas:

1. Publicly issued convertibles.
2. Small and micro-cap convertibles.
3. Highly structured and individually negotiated transactions (private investments) often with very specific conditions attached.
4. Privately placed equity-linked products (and restricted stock situations).

The product group can be categorized as follows. It would take us too long to discuss each product in detail but there is value in understanding how the product group can be structured – although there is no exclusivity on how the product group has to be structured. Also, in the next subsection 'Alternative forms of convertible financing' we will shed some light on the largest categories mentioned in the overview. Towards the end of the overview you can see the preferred shares category is included. Although they are not technically part of the convertible loan spectrum, they share similar characteristics and build a bridge towards hybrid convertible bonds (which are included as the last category in the review).

- Convertible debt products.
    - Traditional convertible debt.
    - Zero-coupon convertible debt (LYONs, see below).

- Original issue discount convertible debt.
- Premium redemption convertible debt.
- Step-up convertible debt (PIK lookalike).
- Contingent convertible and contingent payable puttable bonds.
- Negative yield convertible debt.
- Convertible preferred products (mandatory or not).
  - Non-mandatorily convertible preferred shares.
    - Perpetual maturity convertible preferred shares.
    - Dated convertible preferred.
    - Step-up convertible preferred.
  - Mandatorily convertible preferred shares.
    - Capped common.
    - Modified capped common.
    - Traditional mandatorily convertible preferred.
    - Modified mandatorily convertible preferred.
- Hybrid products (preferred shares but structured so as to be tax-deductible).
  - Trust non-mandatory preferred.
  - Trust mandatory debt.
  - Zero-premium exchangeable debt.

Special types of convertibles are: mandatory convertible bonds, exchangeable bonds and liquid yield option notes (LYONs – see further in this chapter).

A convertible is much like a bond with a warrant attached. However, from a valuation point of view, we are looking at quite a different situation, given that the option is embedded in the fixed-income product. An important problem is that the exercise price of the warrant (the conversion price) is paid by surrendering the accompanying bond, therefore the exercise price changes through time. The fact that most convertibles are callable creates another valuation problem.[8] For a full review of the valuation topic for convertibles see Chapter 4.

The issuer of a convertible bond taps into two distinct advantages: a lower interest cost and less restrictive covenants relative to non-convertible bonds. The investor pays for the right to participate in future favorable price changes in the underlying common stock, accepting a lower yield and less restrictive covenants (risk of expropriation which comes with the issuance of additional new debt). The investor receives the advantage of more senior security through a safety of principal and relative income stability (plus increased bond value if the underlying value of the shares rises). It is therefore an attractive instrument for those investors who face discrete equity market risk allocation constraints.

*Why use convertible loans/bonds?*     Motives for the issuance of convertibles can be divided into traditional and modern motives.

Traditional motives are that convertibles are:

- A deferred sale of stock at an attractive price; and
- A cheap form of capital.[9]

---

[8] See further: M.J. Brennan and E.S. Schwartz, 'Analyzing convertible bonds' (1980) *Journal of Financial and Quantitative Analysis* **4**:907–929.

[9] E.F. Brigham (1966) 'An analysis of convertible debentures: theory and some empirical evidence, (1966) *The Journal of Finance* **21**:35–54.

These motives were criticized by Brennan and Schwartz.[10] The first motive is based on the fact that the conversion price is normally above the market price of the underlying stock at the issuance date.

However, it makes a lot of sense for the conversion price to be compared to the underlying stock price at the exercise date:

- If the underlying stock price is higher than the conversion price, the company suffers an opportunity loss.
- If it is lower than the conversion price, the conversion right will not be exercised.

The second argument is based on the fact that the coupon rate of a convertible is lower than the coupon rate of an ordinary bond. However, if the cost of the conversion right is taken into account, it can be demonstrated that the cost of convertibles is relatively high.

The cost of convertibles is neither a reason to issue, nor a reason to refrain from issuing convertibles. Its cost is just an adequate compensation for the risk involved in its investment.

*More contemporary reasons for using convertibles*    Modigliani and Miller have demonstrated that in perfect markets the financing decisions of a firm are irrelevant to its market value. Therefore, modern arguments for the issuance of convertibles are based on market imperfections. The aforementioned Brennan and Schwartz argue that convertibles are relatively insensitive to the risk of the issuing company. If the risk increases, the value of the bond part decreases, but the value of the warrant part increases, because the value of a warrant is an increasing function of the underlying stock or security's volatility. This evens the level playing field somewhat for bond issuers and purchasers, and helps them come to terms when they disagree about the riskiness of the firm.

Because of the insensitivity towards risk, convertibles may result in lower agency costs between share and bond holders. Bond holders are less concerned about the possibility that shareholders attract risky projects. Because of their conversion right they also participate in the value created if risky projects are undertaken.[11]

Other arguments, based on the same imperfection theme, include the reduction of flotation costs compared to when a firm raises debt now and equity later, and the possibility to 'polish' the company's financial accounts by recording the convertible as debt on the balance sheet.[12]

With regard to the optimal moment to call convertibles, some authors have demonstrated that this moment occurs when the conversion value – this is the value of the common stock to be received in the conversion exchange – equals the call price. However, in an empirical study one author finds that in practice the calls show a delay. On average, the conversion value of the bonds was 43.9% above the call price.[13] Although the study is somewhat dated, observations in the markets over the last couple of years point in the same direction, although the average premium might be lower than indicated in the study.

[10] M.J. Brennan and E.S. Schwartz, 'Analyzing convertible bonds' (1980) *Journal of Financial and Quantitative Analysis* **4**:907–929. and M.J. Brennan and E.S. Schwartz, 'The case for convertibles' (Summer 1988) *Journal of Applied Corporate Finance* **80**:55–64.

[11] R.C. Green 'Investment incentives, debt, and warrants' (1984) 13 *Journal of Financial Economics* 115–136.

[12] C. Veld, *Analysis of Equity Warrants as Investment and Finance Instruments*, Tilburg, Netherlands, Tilburg University Press, 1992.

[13] J. Ingersoll, 'An examination of corporate call policies on convertible securities' (1977) *The Journal of Finance* **32**:463–478.

## Alternative forms of convertible financing

The following table[14] demonstrates six convertible types (all of which can be traced back to the overview in the previous subsection) and how they differ from traditional convertibles, demonstrating a wide variety of alternatives feeding different portfolio and situational objectives.

| Convertible structure | Distinctive characteristics |
| --- | --- |
| High coupon | Premium greater<br>Income greater<br>More bond-like<br>Sacrificing equity participation |
| Puttable securities | Reduce credit risk<br>Shorten bond life<br>Sacrifice yield |
| Callable securities | Forced conversion<br>Reduce effective option period due to either changes in interest rates or changes in the stock price |
| Exchangeable securities | Bond of an issuing company exchangeable into the equity of another company<br>Permit exchange of credit risk with equity risk |
| Zero coupon | Greater credit risk<br>More interest rate exposure per maturity<br>Lower premium<br>Lower bond floor |
| Premium redemption price | Advertised yield-to-maturity realized only if bond held to maturity |

Additionally, the following exotic convertible models can be signaled:

Exchangeable Bonds

An exchangeable bond may be converted into existing shares of the same or an alternative company. It is much like a convertible, except that in a convertible, the bond may be converted into 'new' shares. In parallel, the conversion right of an exchangeable bond is equivalent to a covered warrant.[15]

Liquid Yield Option Notes (LYONs)

Liquid yield option notes (LYONs) are zero-coupon, callable, puttable convertibles. This security was created by Merrill Lynch in 1985. It was first issued by Waste Management Inc. in spring 1985. A number of subsequent issues were made in the United States. Two authors developed a valuation model, shortly after the introduction of the product, which takes all the abovementioned characteristics of LYONs into account.[16]

---

[14] Source: ibid. note 8.

[15] C. Ghosh, R. Varma and J.R. Woolridge, 'An analysis of exchangeable debt offers' (1990) *Journal of Financial Economics* **19**:251–263.

[16] For more on this, see: J.J. McConnell and E.S. Schwartz, 'LYON taming' (1986) *The Journal of Finance* **41**:561–576.

Mandatory Convertible Bonds

Mandatory convertible bonds may be converted during the conversion period, and are automatically converted at the end of the conversion period. The holder has effectively no choice here as is the case with a real option, as their instrument will be converted into common stock at the end of the conversion period. They can, as a consequence, not effectively retire the product as a fixed-income instrument (loss of principal amount for the benefit of (a pre-determined amount of) common stock).

A number of more specific features for convertible loans as a mezzanine product group, which can be added to the list provided at the beginning of this subchapter, should be re-iterated here:

- Given the embedded option, most (if not all) convertible loans carry an interest rate (well) below (often in the range from 1–6%) that of subordinated debt with the same risk profile without the embedded option. The embedded option is there to lift total compensation above (or at least on par with) that of normal compensation levels in similar risk-profiled subdebt.
- Partial or full conversion, mandatory conversion or not, are all possible conversion mechanics.
- Call option (normally not allowed in initial period after issuance, but afterwards): For example, if the share price rises by $x\%$. This essentially allows for an acceleration of the effective conversion by the holder with a view to being called upon and collecting the NPV of the fixed income instrument (eventually added with a prepayment penalty).

*Adequacy of the product:*   It should be stressed upfront that this product, as is the case with warrants, will effectively lead to an actual shareholding in the firm. The product is a bit like dating. You see what is on the table in the first instance. If you like what you see (and think there is an upside to all this), you push through and move on to the next phase (by converting your loan/bond into equity). If you don't like what you see or are not convinced, you take your money off the table and run for the exit (by letting the product retire as a fixed-income instrument). In case of doubt, one could make the convertibility dependent on meeting certain business or financial criteria.

This requires us to think about exit liquidity as, like most lenders, we are not looking to become long-term equity holders. The public capital markets guys would argue here that if one isn't looking to become a long-term shareholder, it would be better not to exercise the conversion option, but to sell the product on in the market and capture the market value of the embedded option (or something close to that) through the enhanced yield to maturity on the instrument. Although thorough, in many markets and situations this is not a realistic option, and so the liquidity question stays intact in many situations.

Ideal as a pre-IPO financing instrument, other situations are more cumbersome from a liquidity point of view. The liquidity in question can occur in a traditional sense. e.g., a sale by the majority shareholder, an ongoing or expected consolidation within the industry, a trade sale, a recapitalization with change of equity owner (second (partial) buy-out) or otherwise. For those cases where no natural liquidity is expected, a combination of put and call options can be a (partial) solution.

In cases where there is too little visibility, or in cases where the post-conversion holding is too high for the investor's liking, the instrument would not be the preferred tool.

The most frequently cited reason to invest in convertibles is that they provide upside participation with downside protection. That is only partly true for mandatory securities, where the holder retains the stock's downside risk. Nevertheless, one can argue that the dominant investment objective is to obtain equity exposure with portfolio volatility lower than that of common stock.

The price behavior of a convertible security is determined by its debt and equity components, and shows characteristics strongly similar to option valuation models.

The four stages of a convertible security based on valuation economics (see Chapter 4) can be categorized (with no distinct boundaries, however) as:

1. **Balanced converts:** Convertibles with a conversion premium of between 25–40% and investment premium of 15–25% either on issuance or subsequently as a result of stock price appreciation;
2. **Equity substitute converts:** Where stock price is above fixed conversion with less than 25% conversion premium and 40%+ investment premium (convert is in-the-money). The more in-the-money, the more its risk/return dynamics mimic those of the underlying shares;
3. **Busted converts:** When a conversion option is deep-out-of-the-money (due to declining share price) with a conversion premium larger than 50% (up to 200%) and the investment premium less than 15%. The convertible bond value approaches the value of the bond as non-convertible debt;
4. **Distressed converts:** (Subset of busted converts) where share price has dropped so significantly that there is a material probability of default. Normally only a market for distress or vulture funds.

As I have previously said, there are no distinct boundaries as convertibles are not static, in that their price response changes, and therefore they may become more equity or straight debt-like, which corresponds with the risk/return profile. Investment selection of convertibles needs to be done based on investment premium criteria (rather than conversion premium) using analytical tools for valuing fixed-income securities and derivatives.

When analyzing convertible securities, five distinct factors need to be distinguished:[17]

1. The appreciation in price of the common stock which is required before conversion could become attractive as measured by the conversion premium.
2. The prospects for growth in the price of the underlying stock.
3. The downside price risk in the event that the conversion privilege proves valueless. The ultimate credit quality of the issuer helps define the stability of the bond floor.
4. The probability of greater than anticipated volatility in the price of the underlying common stock.
5. Special provisions and covenants.

## 2.1.6 Preferred shares[18]

The preferred share type is that outer spectrum of the mezzanine group, with distinct characteristics compared to the rest of the mezzanine family. They are the closest to common equity

---

[17] Source: ibid. note 8.

[18] See more extensively: Fabozzi and Mann, *The Handbook of Fixed Income Securities*, McGraw-Hill, 2011, 8th edn, in particular Chapter 59: 'Non-convertible preferred stock.'

in the firm, and therefore the most like common shareholders to the actual business and financial risks of the firm.

The preferred share instrument has garnered quite some public attention in the last couple of years. This was due in a large part to three remarkable transactions entered into by Warren Buffett's Berkshire Hathaway. The first one is the US$5 billion investment in preferred shares in Goldman Sachs, the US banking giant. That happened in September 2008, in the midst of the financial crisis unfolding, when the capital markets were literally closed for firms like GS given their involvement in many now questionable fixed-income markets, as well as the fact that the financial industry was center-stage among the principal drivers behind the crisis. Berkshire negotiated a 10% fixed dividend on the instrument (or US$500 million in annual dividends). Additionally, Berkshire negotiated the right to buy US$5 billion of Goldman Sachs common stock at US$115 per share (or 43.5 million shares) through October 1, 2013.

Goldman Sachs called the preferred stock for redemption on April 18, 2011 at a premium of 10% over par value, plus accrued and unpaid dividends. As a result, Berkshire Hathaway earned approximately US$1.75 billion (US$1.25 billion in dividends plus a redemption premium of US$500 million) in 2½ years on its investment of US$5 billion. This represents a return of 35% over this time period from the preferred stock alone. In that same period they also invested US$3 billion (under similar terms) in General Electric in preferred shares and warrants.

In late March 2013 Goldman Sachs and Berkshire Hathaway agreed on trading those remaining warrants for shares worth the equivalent of the capital Berkshire Hathaway would receive from exercising those warrants without any further cash outlay (calculated using the average price on the 10 trading days before October 1, 2013). Or, put differently: (average closing price/share − US$ 115/share) × 45.5 million shares = $ value of the shares received.

In August 2011, Berkshire entered into a similar transaction when investing in Bank of America. It was a vote of confidence for the beleaguered financial firm, which was still suffering from the aftermath of the financial crisis, implications of undercapitalization and engagement in law suits with respect to its mortgage-backed securities business.

Under the terms of the deal, Berkshire bought US$5 billion of preferred stock that pay a 6% annual dividend, and receive warrants for 700 million shares, which it can exercise over the next 10 years. Bank of America has the option to buy back the preferred shares at any time for a 5% premium.

Buffett was a known quantity at BoA as he had been a shareholder there before. In the midst of the subprime crisis in 2007, Berkshire bought 8.7 million shares, quickly increasing the stake to 9.1 million shares. He hasn't always been happy with BoA though. He told the Financial Crisis Inquiry Commission that Bank of America paid a 'crazy price' to acquire Merrill Lynch in the midst of the disaster. Mr Buffett sold off his remaining shares in Bank of America at the end of 2010.

Let's first review some of the product characteristics. Preferred shares are the most subordinated product there is. They are more junior, or subordinated if you want, than all other subdebt or mezzanine products. In fact, they are positioned right before the common equity holders.

They carry a fixed dividend. They are therefore not dependent on what the board of directors (BoD) decides regarding how much they are going to pay in dividends for any given year. Having said that, they are dependent on the BoD to decide whether or not there will be a dividend payment that year. There is no payout of the fixed dividend if the BoD decides not to pay the dividend in any given year.

In this sense, the preferred shareholder is also a residual cash flow owner. There is no event or default if the dividend payment is missed. Having said that, if the preferred shares are cumulative, the missed dividend payment goes into arrears. If a corporation fails to declare the preferred dividend, those dividends are said to be in arrears. The dividends in arrears must be disclosed in the notes (footnotes) to the financial statements. Cumulative preferred stock requires that any past, omitted dividends must be paid to the preferred stockholders before the common stockholders will be paid any dividend.

Those fixed dividends do have a sort of actual seniority over normal dividends to common equity owners. This is also true in cases of insolvency and liquidation (Chapters 7 and 11 of Title 11 in the US Bankruptcy Code) where the preferred shareholders have priority over common shareholders. Having said that, failure to make dividend payments may trigger certain restrictions on the issuer's management. For example, if dividends are in arrears, preferred shareholders may be granted voting rights to elect some members to the issuer's board of directors. This feature is called contingent voting because the voting is contingent on a missed dividend payment. This is in contrast to blank check preferred dividends which contain a provision that gives voting rights to approved preference shareholders as protection against a hostile takeover attempt.

Cumulative preferred stock also has debt-like features: (1) cash flows promised to preferred shareholders are fixed, and (2) preferred shareholders have priority over common shareholders with respect to dividend payments and distributions of assets in the case of bankruptcy (see above), in which the position of non-cumulative shareholders is considerably weaker. When there are multiple layers of preferred equity owners on the equity part of the balance sheet, the first preferred claims to dividends and assets have priority over other preferred stock. A ranking between the different layers occurs.

Almost all types of preferred stock have a sinking fund provision, structured along the lines of corporate bond provisions. A sinking fund provision is a provision allowing for the preferred stock's periodic retirement over its life span, mostly meaning that periodically a specific number of shares or a certain percentage of the original issues is retired, usually on an annualized basis. Payments can be satisfied in cash or by calling the required number of shares or delivering shares purchased in the open market.

As is shown in the overview hereafter, the product can have either no maturity or can be redeemable at a specific point in time or as of a certain date for a certain period of time. Often, the fixed dividend increases after a certain date, to move towards ROE or even higher, in order for the issuer to have sufficient incentive. The step-up dividend encourages the issuer to redeem the instrument at some point in time by eating away at the ROE of common shareholders, just like when an increasing IRR is agreed on a subdebt with warrants, as discussed earlier in this chapter (see above, Section 2.1.4).

Preferred shares carry no voting rights, which makes them an economic ownership instrument rather than a legal ownership instrument (see Table 2.2).

### Types of preferred shares[19]
Essentially, there are three types of preferred stock:

1. Fixed-rate preferred stock.
2. Adjustable-rate preferred stock (ARPS), whereby the dividend rate is reset quarterly based on a pre-determined spread from the highest three points on the Treasury yield curve (dividend reset spread). The reset spread is added to or subtracted from the benchmark rate

---

[19] Based on and see for wider coverage, ibid source, note 20.

**Table 2.2**  Characteristics of the preferred share category

| Preferred share criteria | Main characteristics |
| --- | --- |
| Legal qualification | Equity |
| Economic qualification | Debt-like |
| Convertible | Yes/No |
| Cumulative | Yes/No |
| Priority | Over common shareholders |
| | In case of liquidation or bankruptcy |
| Dividend | Fixed/Resettable |
| Call or Put option | Allowed (potentially with a restriction period) |
| Premium when called | Yes (often 10–45% over nominal value) |
| Can be combined with other instruments | Yes, typically warrants |
| Voting rights | No, but with significant exceptions possible |
| Additional profit participation | Possible, *pari passu* with common equity |
| | holders after fixed dividend has been paid |

determined from the yield curve. The three points on the yield curve are (1) 3-month T-bill rate, (2) 10-year T-bond rate and (3) 30-year T-bond rate (or local equivalents). The reset spread is often expressed as a percentage of the benchmark rate. There is often a cap and a floor on the dividend rate. Popularity is often low, as the ARPS can trade below par after issuance if the spread demanded by the market as compensation for the risk of the security is greater than the dividend reset spread (often when the credit risk of the issuer deteriorates).

3. Auction rate and remarketed preferred stock: Like ARPS the divined rate is reset periodically but the dividend rate is established through a Dutch auction process. Participants in the auction are current preference shareholders as well as potential buyers. The dividend rate reflects current market conditions whereby commercial paper often serves as a benchmark. In the case of remarketed preference stock, the dividend rate is reset periodically by a remarketing agent who resets the dividend rate so that any preference stock can be tendered at par and be resold at the original offering price. Resetting happens every 7 or 49 days.

Preferred stock allows the holder to have rights not available to common stockholders. One important right is a preference to dividends expressed as a percentage of par values if the preferred stock is issued with a par value or as a specific dollar amount if the preferred stock is a no-par preferred stock.

Cumulative Preferred Stock
Holders of cumulative preferred stocks are owed dividend in arrears for years the dividend is not declared. For example: holders of 5,000 shares of 10%, €100 par cumulative preferred stocks are entitled to a €10 annual dividend per share. If the dividend is passed for 2 years, the preferred shareholders are entitled to dividends in arrears of €100,000 (€10 x 5,000 shares x 2 years) and €50,000 for the third year. The amount paid in the third year is €150,000.

Participating Preferred Stock
Holders of participating preferred stock are entitled to share either fully (fully participating preferred stock) or partially (partially participating preferred stock) in any dividend available after the preferred stockholders have been paid at a rate equal to that paid

for preferred stock. If preferred stock is paid at 10%, any amount in excess of 10% paid to common shareholders is shared between the preferred and common stockholders.

Convertible Preferred Stock

Holders of convertible preferred stock have the option to exchange their preferred shares for a specified amount of common stock. The redeemable convertible preferred equity instrument therefore becomes very similar to a convertible loan instrument.

Callable Preferred Stock

Callable preferred stock allows the corporation to call or redeem at its option the outstanding preferred shares under conditions specified by the stock contract. At issuance of the callable preferred stock, the difference between the market and par value is credited to the additional paid-in-capital on preferred stock.

The difference is not treated as a gain or loss and two situations arise:

- **Case 1:** If the call price exceeds the contributed capital (preferred stock plus additional paid-in-capital associated with the recalled preferred stock), the difference or 'loss' is debited to retained earnings like a dividend distribution.
- **Case 2:** If the call price is less than the contributed capital, the difference or 'gain' is credited to additional paid-in-capital from recall of preferred stock.

---

### EXAMPLE

Let's assume that the XYZ Corporation has 5,000 shares of €100 par callable preferred stock issued at €120 per share. I decided to enter some accounting features as they are so intrinsically linked with the features of the preferred share classifications. Other accounting-related issues will be dealt with in Chapter 9.

Assuming a call price of €130, the following entry is made accounting-wise at the recall:

[Debit] Preferred Stock (€100 par × 5,000) = 500,000
[Debit] Additional Paid-in-Capital or Preferred Stock = 100,000
[Debit] Retained Earnings (€650,000 − €600,000) = 50,000
[Credit] Cash (€130 × 5,000) = 650,000

Assuming a call price of €110, the following entry is made at recall:

[Debit] Preferred Stock, €100 par = 500,000
[Debit] Additional Paid-in-Capital on Preferred Stock = 100,000
[Credit] Cash (€110 × 5,000) = 550,000
[Credit] Additional Paid-in-Capital from Recall of Preferred Stock (€600,000 − €550,000) = 50,000

---

Preferred Stock with Stock Warrants

Preferred stocks may be issued with stock warrants offering the holder not only preference as to dividends, but also rights to purchase additional shares of common stock at a specified price over some future period. Given these dual rights, the proceeds from the issuance of preferred stock with attachable warrants are to be allocated to both preferred stockholders' and common stockholders' equity, on the basis of the relative fair values of the two securities at the time of issuance.

## EXAMPLE

Let's say that the XYZ Company issues 5,000 shares of €100 par value preferred stock at a price of €130 per share with a detachable warrant which allows the holder to purchase for each preferred share one share of €20 par common stock at €50 per share. Following the issuance, the preferred stock was selling ex-rights (without the warrants) at a market price of €120, while the warrants were selling for €8 each. The following calculations are required:

- Market Value of Preferred Stock: (€120 × 5,000) = €600,000
- Market Value of Warrants: (€8 × 5,000) = €40,000
- Total Market Value: (€600,000 + 40,000) = €640,000
- Issuance Value (€130 × 5,000) = €650,000
- Allocation to Preferred Stock: €650,000 × [€600,000/€640,000] = €609,375
- Allocation to Warrants: €650,000 × [€40,000/€640,000] = €40,625

At the time of issuance the following entry should be made:

[Debit] Cash (€130 × 5,000) = €650,000
[Credit] Preferred Stock, €100 par (5,000 × €100) = €500,000
[Credit] Additional Paid-in-Capital on Preferred Stock = €109,375
[Credit] Common Stock Warrants = €40,625

When the warrants are exercised, the following entry is made:

[Debit] Cash (€5,000 × €50) = €250,000
[Debit] Common Stock Warrants = €40,625
[Credit] Common Stock, €20 par = €100,000
[Credit] Additional Paid-in-Capital on Common Stock = €190,625

## Dos and don'ts

One of the features which need to be checked is the accounting and tax classification of the instrument. Often, it will be seen as an equity instrument despite its fixed dividend. The consequence is that the dividend is not tax-deductible (as discussed in the introduction), just like the dividends paid to common shareholders. This makes it a significantly expensive instrument compared to the others in the mezzanine group.

## 2.1.7 The wider space of hybrid instruments[20]

Financial innovation has not left a single opportunity to create products which have a hybrid character. Whether mezzanine products and hybrid products are equal in terms of definition and scoping of products is more a question of semantics than a practical definition.

It can be indicated here that there has been a wide range of products emerging which are in a way a derivative or second generation product group, related to the primary group discussed in this chapter.

Part of this group is formed by the reverse convertibles, ELKS, DECS index-linked notes and LYONs. Each of those products comes with an exotic variety of features and variations, such as reset clauses (adjusting interest rate at different intervals throughout lifetime of bond), negative pledge provisions (not creating a security interest over pre-identified assets), screw* clauses (or interest forfeiture clauses) and forced (i.e., mandatory) conversion clauses, as well as step-up coupons, call schedules, call options with soft and hard protection (hard protection means a fixed level of capital protection, but only at maturity of the product), regardless of asset class performance. With soft protection, the protection falls away (even at maturity) if the asset value breaks a given pre-determined barrier (known as the 'knock-in barrier,' which is often set at 50%). For example, a 40% soft protection means that the value of the underlying asset can drop 60% with no protection for the part with soft protection. Soft-protection bonds trigger a higher compensation due to the embedded equity risk, etc; the list is pretty much endless. If the barrier is breached, an investor's return of capital at maturity will reflect any negative performance of the underlying asset on a 1:1 basis. The group is known as SCARPS (Structured Capital-At-Risk Products).

(*) Screw clauses can be invoked legally to deny investors in convertibles an entire interest payment, which can mean as much as half a year's interest. The screw clause has historically been somewhat mis-defined. It was constructed as a clause that states the expiration of the conversion privilege prior to the redemption date. Early expiration only equates to a screw clause, or interest-forfeiture provision, in cases where a bond or preferred holder would be forced to convert prior to the interest- or dividend-payable date during the call-protection period. After the call protection expires, however, issuers of all callable convertibles can redeem the securities so as to deprive holders of interest and dividends which accrued during the period in which the call occurs. For example: in the case of debentures called for redemption, the conversion rights will expire at the close of business on the fifth business day prior to the redemption date.

Let me qualify the aforementioned reverse convertibles:

1. **Reverse convertible bonds:** Tend to be short-term bonds which are linked to a specific underlying stock or index, or a basket of stock or indexes. They pay a high coupon, which is interesting in times of inflation or low interest rates. At maturity the holder receives back the principal amount (in cash) or, if the value of the shares dropped (below a certain pre-determined threshold), a pre-determined number of shares. It therefore is the issuer (through a clause) who determines whether there will be a conversion or not. Considerable risk and loss of capital is often part of the equation as the repayment will be determined by the underlying security's share price at maturity of the bond. If the price of the stock or

---

[20] For a more detailed analysis of the product group and features, see: Israel Nelken and Izzy Nelken, *Handbook of Hybrid Instruments*, John Wiley & Sons, 2000.

index drops, the issuing firm will convert and the holder will get back less than the principal amount.

2. **ELKS (Equity-linked securities):** Are hybrid debt securities whose return is connected to an underlying equity (usually a stock). ELKS pay a higher yield than the underlying security and generally mature in one year. At maturity, these securities will pay back the original principal, or if the linked equity has fallen below a pre-determined price, then the ELKS will convert into shares of the underlying security.

One of the most distinguishing ELKS characteristics is that the size and nature of the principal repayment is determined by the linked stock's price. For example, if Company ABC's stock was €10 per share when the ELKS were issued, then ELKS investors will receive their principal back in cash only if Company ABC's stock price stays above, say, 80% of €10 per share (or €8 in this case) while the ELKS are outstanding. If the price of Company ABC's stock goes below €8 at any time during the life of the ELKS, then the investors receive a pre-determined number of Company ABC's shares (say, a quarter of a share of Company ABC for every ELKS they hold) rather than cash when ELKS mature. The value of ABC shares the investor receives at maturity could be worth more or less than what they initially invested. Income investors like ELKS due to the large distributions they make compared to the underlying security. The securities usually make two pre-determined payments before their maturity. ELKS can be listed and are tradable.

Like convertible bonds they share the characteristics of both stocks and bonds. With a convertible bond, however, the bond holders can participate in the company's stock price appreciation because the higher the market value of the underlying shares goes, the more the bond trades like a stock. However, this upside is limited with ELKS; the investor instead simply collects their interest payments and gets the privilege of receiving their principal back in cash when the ELKS mature. Thus, their return is limited to the coupon rate.

Likewise, convertible bond holders are somewhat protected from steep stock price declines: during those times, they still receive their interest and principal payments and have priority over the company's stockholders. However, ELKS do not offer this principal protection. If the price of the underlying stock declines, the investor could theoretically receive a pile of worthless stock instead of a cash principal repayment.

3. **DECS (Dividend-enhanced convertible stock):** A debt instrument which provides the holder with coupon payments in addition to an embedded short put option and a long call on the issuing company's stock. DECS instruments provide the holder with the right to convert the security into the underlying company's common stock. Or, put differently, preferred stock entitling the holder to guaranteed dividends and to which a put option and a call option are attached. Therefore, if the stock declines in price the holder of DECS may sell it for the stated strike price. Likewise if the stock increases in price, the holder may exercise the call and buy more stock for a discount. DECS also have a convertible option allowing the holder to exchange the DECS for common stock.

PRIDES (Preferred Redeemable Increased Dividend Equity Security) are an example of a DECS. PRIDES are synthetic securities consisting of a forward contract to purchase the issuer's underlying security and an interest-bearing deposit. Interest payments are made at regular intervals, and conversion into the underlying security is mandatory at maturity. Just like the LYONs they were first introduced by Merrill Lynch, now part of BAML. Similar to convertible securities, PRIDES allow investors to earn stable cash flows while still participating in the capital gains of an underlying stock. This is possible because these products are valued along the same lines as the underlying security.

4. **Index-linked notes (ILN) or Equity-linked notes (ELN):** An Equity- or Index-Linked Note is a debt instrument which differs from a standard fixed-income security in that the final return is based on the return of the underlying equity, which can be a single stock, basket of stocks, or an equity index to which the bond is linked. A typical ELN is principal-protected, i.e., the investor is guaranteed to receive 100% of the original amount invested at maturity but receives no interest, which sets it apart from the products described under point 1 which don't carry the principal protection.

   The final return is the amount invested, times the gain in the underlying stock or index times a note-specific participation rate. So let's say that the underlying equity gains 75% during the investment period and the participation rate is 70%; the investor receives €1.525 for each Euro invested. If the equity remains unchanged or declines, the investor still receives one Euro per Euro invested unless the issuer defaults. Generally, the participation rate is better in longer maturity notes, since the total amount of interest given up by the investor is higher.

   Equity/Index-linked notes can be thought of as a combination of a zero-coupon bond and an equity option. In most cases the issuer of the bond typically covers the equity payout liability by acquiring an identical option. In some equity-linked notes, the payout structure is more complicated, reflecting an embedded exotic option. Equity/Index-linked notes belong to the structured product family.

   Most equity-linked notes are not actively traded on the secondary market and are essentially designed to be kept to maturity. However, the issuer or arranger of the notes may offer to buy them back. In contrast to the maturity payout, the buy-back price before maturity may be below the amount invested in the first place.

5. **LYONs (Liquid yield option notes):** A convertible, callable and puttable zero-coupon (no interest accrues) bond. A LYON is a bond which is convertible to common stock and may be bought or sold as an option, but which does not pay interest. Because it pays no interest, it is issued at a considerable discount from par value of the bond. This guarantees a positive return to the investor, as long as they wait until such time as it becomes profitable for them to put the bond back to the issuing company for an amount over the issue price. Generally, the total return on a LYON is less than that of the company's common stock, assuming the company performs.

6. **Zero-coupon convertible bonds or optional convertible notes (OCN):** A fixed-income instrument which is a combination of a zero-coupon bond and a convertible bond. Due to the zero-coupon feature, the bond pays no interest and is issued at a discount to par value, while the convertible feature means that the bond is convertible into common stock of the issuer at a certain conversion price. The zero-coupon and convertible features offset each other in terms of the yield required by investors. Zero-coupon bonds are often the most volatile fixed-income investments because they have no periodic interest payments to mitigate the risk of holding them; as a result, investors demand a slightly higher yield to hold them. On the other hand, convertibles pay a lower yield compared to other bonds of the same maturity and quality because investors are willing to pay a premium for the convertible feature.

   When they are issued at a discount to par, they exhibit an implicit yield and trade essentially as coupon convertibles. Similarly, if they are issued at par but redeemed at a stated price above par, an implicit coupon is paid and so again these bonds trade in similar fashion to coupon convertibles. A zero-coupon bond issued at par and redeemed at par is a slightly different instrument for investors to consider. With these products, the buyer is looking for equity exposure compared to conventional OCNs, but with an element of capital protection retained.

A buyer of a par-priced zero-coupon OCN will take the position that the underlying equity has high upside potential. However, the stock will have high volatility, so the OCN route is still lower risk than pure equity exposure. The investor pays an opportunity cost in terms of interest foregone in order to retain greater safety compared to pure equity. The soft call option is often built in so that the issuer can force conversion if the equity has performed as expected, which caps the investor's upside.

In many cases, zero-coupon OCNs are issued in one currency but reference shares denominated in another (less liquid) currency, so that investors can have exposure to an equity without having to hold assets in the less liquid currency. Buyers often focus on price volatility, rather than price *per se*, and the value of the note will increase if volatility increases. In other cases, the volatility trade is put on as an arbitrage; that is, a simultaneous position in which the trader is:

- long the OCN bond, and
- short the underlying equity.

In such a trade the investor benefits if volatility increases. For issuers, the advantage of zero-coupon par-priced OCNs is even greater than that afforded by conventional OCNs: they receive no-cost funding compared to a normal bond or loan. In return they are selling (for them) a cheap route to their equity should the share price perform.[21]

Finally, the most recent kid on the block is the CoCo-bond, or contingent convertible bond. As the bond is mostly issued by financial institutions, I will deal with the product in the chapter on financial institutions (Chapter 5).

## 2.2 CASE STUDY: THE KRATOS COMPANY – MERGER FINANCE

In fall 2012, the Kratos company ('Kratos') was considering the acquisition of Odin Inc. ('Odin') from Castor global holdings ('Castor'). The acquisition would be a firm statement to the market that Kratos had every intention of staying a market leader in its industry, on top of the fact that the merger would deliver over 160 years of operational and industry expertise. Both companies, although they had many clients in common, had very few products in common. One of the areas to focus on would be the joint servicing of customers through a unified sales-rep. structure. The ability to streamline manufacturing activities and processes should deliver an estimated $80 million in cost savings. Paying too high a price would make all these synergies move to the shareholders of Castor.

There was also another concern going on. Given the size of the acquisition, Kratos was quite concerned about the impact on its balance sheet given the already 'decent' amount of debt it had. Depending on whether the deal would be (partly) financed by the issuance of new debt or not (assuming that Castor's shareholders would be looking for at least a partly cash deal), the increased leverage on its balance sheet would invariably lead to a downgrade of its rating by the rating agencies. This would also lead to the firm losing its investment-grade rating which would then lead to future inflexibility within finance operations, on top of the fact that the total debt

---

[21] For further insights and examples, see: Moorad Choudhry, 'Zero-coupon convertible bonds,' yieldCurve .com (2006).

volume would potentially be unsustainable given the margin squeeze the industry was experiencing. The management team at Kratos was concerned about their ability to meet interest payments in the years to come given the additional debt load and wondered if they should be looking at a different financing package, which could not include a vast dilution of existing shareholders.

Bearing products come in a wide variety of shapes and sizes and have made their way into a wide variety of industries and product groups ranging from household to aerospace, medical devices, computer disk drives and automobiles. In the US in 2012, the industry employed about 30,000 people, mainly in ball- and roller bearing manufacturing facilities.[22]

The bearing industry was and is an endless list of complex issues. Being close to the steel industry, it is clear that policies which favor the steel industry have not always been in the interest of the bearing industry. However, as producers of (or contributors to) secondary steel products, they were pretty much in the middle of the production chain, leaving them very little wiggle room. Also, the US government has been a large consumer of this product. It can be found in components of military and civilian equipment and machinery.

However, globalization kicked in here as well, and US market share has been lost to foreign competitors who were and are able to produce the same sort of quality at much lower prices. Things became so bad that some US manufacturers filed charges against foreign companies related to illegal dumping practices. Some of these high-profile cases were won by US firms. The response, however, from foreign firms was that they either turned around and left the US market, or alternatively, that they moved ahead in the US markets and bought local competitors in the US to supply the US market.

Shipments of ball- and roller bearings grew at very decent levels throughout the 90s. Since the late 90s, demand has been firm but flattened out, and during the 2008 crisis the demand dropped significantly. It is fair to say that during the 2000s, the eroding of margins continued. Combined with the 2001 and 2008 economic recessions, drop in demand for cars and the economic instability following the 2008 crisis, this has led to limited aggregate demand in the US. Besides the fact that it is a cyclical industry, it has been in a steady trough for quite a while now.

The bearings industry on a global scale was in much better shape. The industry has grown at an average rate of 5.5% for the last couple of years, to a large degree driven by the Chinese car bonanza which has been going on for some years now. Ever since late 2011 but definitely during 2012, there was the question of whether China was facing (or about to face) a hard or a soft economic landing and whether the party was able to turn the country from an export-led economy to a consumer giant the world so badly needed. The answer to that question remains somewhat unanswered but even if affirmative, it will take more time than the difficult market conditions could justify.

Having said that, supply levels have been growing with total demand, in fact they have been front-running demand significantly, but overall prices have been able to stick at a certain level in the marketplace. Quite a bit of the Chinese production came into the US, and the US government decided to levy import duties on the products from which Kratos had been benefiting for some years.

Kratos was considered among the market leaders together with ABC Corps and SwedCo, a Stockholm-based producer. Together they controlled about 25% of the market, more than twice the amount held by their direct competitors. Kratos had about $6 billion in sales, up about 15% in 2011 due to improving market conditions. However, it was still recovering from the 2007–2009 period during which it went through a near-dead experience. Major industries it serviced were still automotive, electronics and the IT sector. Further financial details can be found in

---

[22] KPMG industry report 2011, sector analysis Chapter 5.

Dataset 1. Two-thirds of its sales came from bearings and about 20% of sales came from outside the US. It had facilities and operations in about 25 countries and about 19,000 employees.

## 2.2.1 Kratos Inc. – A closer look

The firm was founded by Henri Kratos in 1890 when he patented a design for tapered roller bearings. Over the generations, the firm emerged as a global producer of highly engineered bearings, alloy and specialty steel and a wide array of components.

The company listed in 1924, while World War II increased demand for most of its products. In the 60s it started its overseas expansion. In 1981, it suffered its first loss since the Depression due to increased competition coming from Europe and Japan. During the years that followed, the firm engaged in joint ventures, alliances and acquisitions in the US as well as overseas including the UK, Europe, India, China etc. Just before the turn of the millennium, the firm cut global production back to around 85% and started a consolidation process, remodeling the firm in different business units. The implications were plant closures, lay-offs and outsourcing of distribution functions across the world. In the process it trimmed about 10% of its workforce, a process that went on during the initial years of the new millennium, through the recession which kicked in after the internet bubble burst. In fact, looking with hindsight, the process has continued, all the way through to 2012. As mentioned, it experienced a near-death experience in 2008–2009 as it had to cut even deeper than it did 10 years earlier. The long-term dynamics of the firm and the industry didn't really alter over time.

**Structure of the firm[23]**

The firm currently operates three units: the automotive, the steel and the industrial group. The automotive and industrial group designed, produced and distributed a range of bearings (tapered roller bearing made up of different parts) and related products and services. Customers of the automotive group include the OEM ('Original Equipment Manufacturers') of passenger cars and trucks including light-, medium- and heavy-duty trucks. Industrial group customers included both OEMs and distributors for a diverse set of industries including agriculture, mining, construction and energy. The concept was the same: the components (which come in different shapes and sizes) have to carry weight, causing a minimum of rolling resistance. The same concept was advanced to be applied in more sophisticated environments (custom designed) such as the aerospace sector (extreme speed and weather conditions) and other high-accuracy environments (medical, dental, IT,…). Competition in this space comes from both domestic and foreign companies. The steel division designed, manufactured and distributed different alloys in both solid and tubular sections as well as custom-made steel products for both automotive and industrial applications including bearings.

**Castor**

Castor was an US$11 billion global diversified manufacturer of industrial and commercial equipment and components. Its early years go back to 1874 when its founder patented a steam-powered rock drill, a watershed event which led to the formation of the Castor company. In 1879, the first rand drill air compressor was introduced. In 1885 the Sergeant drill company was formed by a former employee of Castor company. Both companies merged in 1888. The combined firm merged in 1905 with the Rand Drill Company. That delivered the firm as we know it today, headquartered in NY.

---

[23] Source datasets: company website and analyst coverage (Credit Suisse).

They made quite a few acquisitions in the 60s including Odin, the bearing division of Textron. They made Castor the largest US bearing producer. They continued to make acquisitions in the 70s and 80s. In 2012, the firm was built around four divisions: (1) Climate Control: accounting for over ¼ of their sales and which produced portable temperature units, heating ventilation and air-conditioning systems for a variety of applications (e.g. trucks, buses, etc.), (2) Infrastructure: accounted for another ¼ of their sales. They produced a variety of equipment for public and private sector works in the area of construction, renovation and repair, (3) Security and Safety: producing close to 12% of sales and the product group of which included steel doors, electronic access systems and staff attendance systems for both the residential and professional market and (4) Industrial Solutions: accounting for over 1/3 of total sales. Products included motion control devices, gas and other compressors. Further, it included a wide product range for the oil, gas and chemical industry.

In early 2012, Castor decided to divest the Odin engineering segment. Strategically, that decision appeared to be consistent with the company's desire to allocate capital to higher potential growth and higher return service businesses. Castor could not justify allocating substantial capital resources to maintain a leading competitive position in a consolidating, relatively slow-growth industry. In 2012, Castor reported a loss of US$173.5 million on sales of US$8.9 billion (Dataset 2) and assets of US$10.8 billion (Dataset 3).

Odin started as a company specializing in the production of sewing machine needles. Late in the 19th century, they were the first to produce them in a uniform way based on a novel technique. That concept has then been taken to different industries and applications around the world, although ¾ of their business was coming from Northern America, even at the moment of the intended transaction. In 2012, revenues and operating income for Castor's Odin Division were US$1.204 billion and US$85.2 million (Dataset 4). They were servicing many different industries including industrial, automotive, consumer, natural resources and agricultural.

**Kratos's financial strategy**

In 2012, Kratos was involved in a company-wide restructuring, which included consolidating operations into global business units to reduce costs and to set the stage for international growth, part of it through acquisitions like the one under consideration. In addition, Kratos was planning to add new products to its portfolio to become more than a supplier of bearings. Within the industry, this strategy was called 'bundling'. This was mainly to escape the eroding margins in the mainstream commoditizing part of the industry and avoid pure price comparability on the side of the (potential) customer. Foreign competitors were making simple products at substantially lower costs than US companies could produce them. To differentiate their products and command higher margins, Kratos and other companies had begun to enhance their basic product with additional components in order to more precisely meet customers' needs with a higher-value-added product. They accomplished this by offering complementary products and add-on features, added to a number of standard parts combined with maintenance and installation services and other integrated systems (for example, pre-assembled bearing packages for car producers). They also reduced the number of suppliers and made a significant reduction in routine labor, or they would replace them with advanced technologies for production purposes. That was in line with a long-lasting trend whereby customers were not only looking for low(er) prices, but companies were also wanting their suppliers to handle an increasing number of (integrated) tasks.

Over the past 10 years, Kratos experienced significant variation in its financial performance. Earnings per share (EPS) topped US$2.73 in 2007, but had hit a low in 2011, with a loss of

US$0.69 per share. Dividends had steadily increased until 2008, when they remained flat until the loss in 2011 led to the dividends being cut to US$0.52 in 2012. With 2012 EPS at US$0.63, Kratos's dividend payout had risen to 85%. At the same time, Kratos's leverage, as measured by total debt-to-capital, had steadily risen from a low of 21.5% in 2005 to a high of 44.1% in 2012. The trend of increasing leverage had prompted the rating agencies to place Kratos's BBB rating on review. Kratos considered it a priority to carry an investment-grade debt rating in order to maintain access to the public debt markets at reasonable interest rates.

### Odin as a potential acquisition

Leaving the operational dynamics behind in terms of what the acquisition could produce regarding world leadership in the bearings industry, and the potential complementary products it could develop with limited amount of overlap with their current product groups while serving the same customers in the market, at least to a large degree (+80%), Kratos was convinced that it would give them a position (through higher penetration and a larger, more diversified, customer base which would lead to more end-customers and cross-selling opportunities) in the market (and in particular from foreign competitors) that would allow them to distinguish the company through added-value products, and could create margin expansion (or at least get out of the race-to-the-bottom margins that have been prevalent in the industry in recent years). Hopefully, it would also give them more leverage in negotiations with suppliers and, likewise, with customers. Of particular interest to Kratos were the expected annual cost savings of US$80 million by the end of 2017. That would come from both reducing the combined sales forces, and giving much larger volume to a reduced list of suppliers in exchange for price reductions. Before the $80 million in cost savings could be realized, however, certain other costs associated with integrating the two companies were likely to be incurred. Those integration costs were estimated at a total $130 million over the first couple of years following the merger.

Regardless of the price paid for Odin, Kratos would face significant challenges regarding the financing of the deal. Two credit rating agencies had placed Kratos's ratings of Baa1/BBB on review. In view of Odin's size, Kratos knew it would be very difficult to raise the required cash without significantly raising the level of debt on its books. For example, if Castor agreed to sell Odin for $800 million (a somewhat estimated value of the company) and Kratos raised the entire amount with a debt offering, Kratos's leverage ratios would suffer enough to virtually guarantee that Kratos would lose its investment-grade rating (see Dataset 4). This was particularly problematic, not only because Kratos would be forced to borrow the money at 'higher-yielding' rates, but also because the availability of future funds could become limited for companies carrying non-investment-grade ratings (capital rationing).

Given the size of the transaction, Kratos concluded that the ideal capital structure needed to be a combination of debt and equity financing. Kratos could do this by issuing shares to the public to raise cash and/or by issuing shares directly to Castor as consideration for Odin. Over previous years, Kratos had relied solely on debt to raise US$140 million for refunding existing debt and for investment purposes, which would partly explain the indebtedness on its books. With the company's stock currently trading around US$19 a share, it would require a significant amount of share issuance to finance the deal in a reasonable and balanced way, and in a way that would also be sustainable over time. Information on bearing-industry companies is reported in Dataset 5.

The Kratos management team was now taking things forward and looking to finance the deal in a way which would limit or even avoid a possible downgrade of its credit rating, while ending up with a balance sheet which would avoid financial distress in the coming years by avoiding interest volumes rising beyond what the margins in the business could tolerate. They also wanted to isolate, where possible, the existing shareholders of the firm from dilution, given its already very low share price.

The management team was also considering the use of mezzanine products to push out debt and interest payments in the future. The team understood that there were a variety of products out there in this field, with each having varying characteristics and therefore a different impact on the balance sheet and repayment issues as mentioned. Some seem to have the ability to push out interest payments toward maturity of the debt instrument, but don't have the ability to change a lot when it comes to avoiding a potential downgrade. Others seem to have that ability but then trigger relatively hefty payments in the earlier stages after the acquisition, and might create financial inflexibility over time. Also the question arose of how investors would respond to the idea of bringing these products on board. Maybe a mix of different products and/or an equity issuance could have helped the situation forward.

## 2.2.2 Case guidance

1. This is clearly not a straightforward situation, and therefore potentially requires a combination of both mezzanine products and/or equity issuance. The first question is obviously whether this is a good deal, and whether the synergies identified are strong and sizeable enough to justify the deal (and buy Odin in full rather than the division as it was initially intended).
2. What the additional debt products would mean in terms of the firm's ability to repay interest payments and principal amounts in the years post acquisition needs to be quantified. The debt capacity of Kratos is center stage here.
3. Further, there is the impact on the rating based on the selection of financial instruments. What are the implications when deciding a certain mix of products?
4. In addition to this, the question emerges of what the cost is or should be for any of the products considered.

   To provide a bit of a benchmark, I have indicated the yields on government (US) and industrial corporate bonds in March 2012.

| Government Y | Yield |
|---|---|
| Short-Term (6 month) | 0.14% |
| Intermediate (2 year) | 0.36% |
| Long-Term (10 year) | 2.2% |

| Industrials | Yield (2/10y) |
|---|---|
| AAA | –/3.14% |
| AA | 0.76/3.37% |
| A | 1.11/3.43% |
| BBB | 1.89/5.43% |
| BB | 3.39/9.76% |
| B | 4.79/11.6% |

5. Finally, should the management team be bothered with the potential negative response of shareholders to a possible dilution of their stake in the firm (given the level of its existing share price)? Should the preference be to issue new equity to Castor or to the public, and use the proceeds to pay off castor at the moment of transaction?

## 2.2.3 Datasets[24]

DATASET 1: INCOME STATEMENTS 2011–2012 KRATOS INC.

| | 2011 | 2012 | 2011 | 2012 |
|---|---|---|---|---|
| Total operating revenue | 2, 447.2 | 2,550.1 | 100% | 100% |
| Cost of goods sold | (2,046.5) | (2,080.5) | | |
| Gross profit | 400.7 | 469.6 | 16.4% | 18.4% |
| S, G &A expenses | (363.7) | (358.9) | | |
| Operating income | (54.7) | (32.1) | | |
| Net interest expense (net of interest income) | (17.7) | 78.6 | −0.7% | 3.1% |
| Receipt of continued dumping & subsidy | (31.3) | (29.9) | | |
| Offset act payment | 29.5 | 50.2 | | |
| Other non-operating expenses | (7.5) | (13.4) | | |
| Income before tax | (27.0) | 85.5 | | |
| Income tax | (14.8) | (34.1) | | |
| Net income before cumulative effect of accounting change | (41.7) | 51.4 | | |
| Cumulative effect of accounting change | 0 | (12.7) | −1.7% | 2.0% |
| Net income | (41.7) | 38.73 | | |

### 5-YEAR SUMMARY 2008–2012

| | 2008 | 2009 | 2010 | 2011 | 2012 |
|---|---|---|---|---|---|
| Net sales | 2,679.8 | 2,495 | 2,643 | 2,447.2 | 2,550.1 |
| EBIT | 225 | 132.8 | 105.6 | (17.7) | 78.6 |
| EBIT (before non-recurring) | 225 | 132.8 | 133.4 | 37.0 | 110.7 |
| Depreciation | 139.8 | 150 | 151 | 152.5 | 146.5 |
| Capital expenditures | 258.6 | 173.2 | 162.7 | 102.3 | 90.7 |

### KRATOS'S BALANCE SHEET (IN MILLIONS OF $)

| Assets | 2011 | 2012 |
|---|---|---|
| Cash | 33.4 | 82.1 |
| Receivables | 307.8 | 361.3 |
| Inventory | 429.2 | 488.9 |
| Other current assets | 58.0 | 36.0 |
| **Total current assets** | **828.4** | **968.3** |
| Net PPE | 1,305.3 | 1,226.2 |
| Other assets | 399.4 | 553.9 |
| **Total assets** | **2,533.1** | **2,748.4** |

*(continued)*

---

[24] Source datasets 1–3: respective company websites.

| Assets | 2011 | 2012 |
|---|---|---|
| **Liabilities** | | |
| AP | 258 | 296.5 |
| Current portion of LT debt | 42.4 | 111.1 |
| Notes payable | 2.0 | 0 |
| Other current liabilities | 338.8 | 226.5 |
| **Total current liabilities** | **641.2** | **634.1** |
| LT debt | 368.2 | 350.1 |
| Deferred tax liability | 742.0 | 1,155.1 |
| **Total liabilities** | **1,751.3** | **2,139.3** |
| Shareholders' equity | 781.7 | 609.1 |
| **Total liabilities & owners' equity** | **2,533.1** | **2,748.4** |

## DATASETS 2 AND 3: CASTOR HOLDINGS AND ODIN INCOME STATEMENTS 2011–2012

### CASTOR HOLDINGS

| | 2011 | 2012 | 2011 | 2012 |
|---|---|---|---|---|
| Total operating revenue | 9,682 | 8,951.3 | 100% | 100% |
| Cost of goods sold | (7,611.5) | (6,826.5) | 21.4% | 23.7% |
| Gross profit | 2,070.5 | 2,124.8 | | |
| S,G &A expenses | (1,454.2) | (1,481.7) | | |
| Restructuring charges | (6.8) | (10.7) | | |
| Operating profit | 496.3 | 618 | 5.1% | 6.9% |
| Net interest expense | (253) | (230.3) | | |
| (net of interest income) | | | | |
| Income before tax | 243.3 | 387.7 | | |
| Income tax | 2.9 | (20.3) | | |
| Minority interest | (20.1) | (14.4) | | |
| Discontinued operations | | 93.6 | | |
| Effect of accounting | | (634.5) | | |
| changes | | | | |
| Net income | 246.2 | (173.5) | 2.55 | −1.9% |

*Odin*

| | 2011 | 2012 | 2011 | 2012 |
|---|---|---|---|---|
| Sales | 1,077.8 | 1,203.75 | 100% | 100% |
| Operating income | 78 | 85.15 | 7.2% | 7.1% |

# CASTOR HOLDINGS BALANCE SHEET (IN MILLIONS OF $)

| Assets | 2011 | 2012 |
|---|---|---|
| Cash | 114 | 342.2 |
| Receivables | 1,359.8 | 1,405.3 |
| Inventory | 1,143.9 | 1,983.8 |
| Deferred tax assets | 321.2 | 0 |
| Other current assets | 760.2 | 381.1 |
| **Total current assets** | **3,699.1** | **4,112.4** |
| Net PPE | 1,289.5 | 1,279.4 |
| Goodwill | 4,807.5 | 4,005.5 |
| Intangible assets | 848.1 | 890.9 |
| Other assets | 489.6 | 520.9 |
| **Total assets** | **11,133.8** | **10,809.6** |
| **Liabilities** | | |
| AP | 701.6 | 2,347.4 |
| Accrued expenses | 1,470.7 | 1,155.5 |
| Short-term debt | 569.1 | 0 |
| Other current liabilities | 249.3 | 295.2 |
| **Total current liabilities** | **2,983.5** | **3,798.1** |
| LT debt | 2,900.7 | 2,092.1 |
| Minority interest | 107.6 | 115.1 |
| Other non-current liabilities | 1,225.4 | 1,326.1 |
| **Total liabilities** | **7,217.2** | **7,331.4** |
| Shareholders' equity | 3,916.6 | 3,478.2 |
| **Total liabilities & owners' equity** | **11,133.8** | **10,809.6** |

# ODIN FINANCIAL SUMMARY AND PROJECTIONS 2008–2017

| | 2008 | 2009 | 2010 | 2011 | 2012 | 2013E | 2014E | 2015E | 2016E | 2017E |
|---|---|---|---|---|---|---|---|---|---|---|
| **Net sales** | 1,239.5 | 1,239.5 | 1,161 | 1,004.3 | 1,204 | 1,282 | 1,365.3 | 1,454.1 | 1,548.6 | 1,649.2 |
| **Operating income** | 137.2 | 145.7 | 172.6 | 102.1 | 85.2 | 90.7 | 96.6 | 102.9 | 109.5 | 116.7 |
| **Capex** | 36.7 | 30.1 | 25.2 | 23.4 | 23.8 | 25.3 | 26.9 | 28.7 | 30.6 | 32.5 |
| **Depreciation expense** | 28.6 | 25.2 | 21.8 | 19.3 | 21.0 | 21.8 | 23.2 | 25.6 | 28.8 | 32.9 |

## DATASET 4: SELECTED FINANCIAL RATIOS BY S&P CREDIT-RATING CATEGORIES (FOR INDUSTRIAL COMPANIES 2010–2012)

|  | AAA | AA | A | BBB | BB | B | CCC |
|---|---|---|---|---|---|---|---|
| **EBIT interest coverage (x)** | 23.4 | 13.3 | 6.3 | 3.9 | 2.2 | 1 | 0.1 |
| **EBITDA interest coverage (x)** | 25.3 | 16.9 | 8.5 | 5.4 | 3.2 | 1.7 | 0.7 |
| **EBITDA/sales (%)** | 23.4 | 24 | 18.1 | 15.5 | 15.4 | 14.7 | 8.8 |
| **Total debt/capital (%)** | 5.0 | 35.9 | 42.6 | 47.0 | 57.7 | 75.1 | 91.7 |

## DATASET 5: FINANCIAL DATA ON COMPANIES IN THE BEARING INDUSTRY (* $ IN MILLIONS)[25]

| Companies | Beta | Debt* | Sales* | EBITDA* | Net Income* | EBITDA Interest coverage | EBITDA/ Sales (%) | Enterprise value/ EBITDA | Debt rating |
|---|---|---|---|---|---|---|---|---|---|
| CQS Corp. | 1.25 | 72.4 | 279.4 | 60.1 | 25.4 | 3.6 | 21.5 | 11.3 | |
| Deviant Inc. | 0.85 | 53.1 | 180.2 | 26.2 | 4.7 | 6.5 | 14.5 | 7.5 | |
| Kratos | 1.1 | 373.9 | 2,550.1 | 275.7 | 51.5 | 4.3 | 10.8 | 5.2 | BBB |
| Commercial Metals | 0.63 | 255.6 | 2,441.5 | 138.2 | 40.5 | 5.2 | 5.7 | 5.5 | BB |
| Metals for all Inc. | 0.38 | 128.7 | 943.7 | 4.0 | 48.8 | 0.2 | 0.4 | – | |
| Thyssen Industries | 1.08 | 18.2 | 955.3 | 123.9 | 71.2 | 84.9 | 13.0 | 7.3 | BBB |
| LinkParc Corp. | 1.1 | 612.4 | 2,117.2 | 389.6 | 159.4 | 6.2 | 18.4 | 4.5 | |
| Adetex | 0.75 | 75.6 | 994.4 | 127.0 | 55.5 | 5.2 | 12.8 | 5.1 | |
| Hot Metals | 0.49 | 290.9 | 2,219.9 | 188.0 | 75.2 | 2.4 | 8.5 | 10.1 | BBB |

---

[25] Source: analyst coverage Credit Suisse, Unicredit, Barclays, Morgan Stanley.

# 3

# The Implicit Cost of Mezzanine Products

We already concluded in Chapter 1 that in terms of a risk profile, the mezzanine product group fits nicely between the debt product group and the equity area. As this is valid in terms of product characteristics and risk being absorbed by the respective product groups, it makes sense to assume that from a 'cost of capital' perspective the product group also sits comfortably in the middle. At least, if we are willing to assume that we live in a risk–return world, and if we are also able to reflect these ideas in a theory which makes these assumptions applicable across the board for the product group, thereby creating uniformity in the way risk is measured. Although there are a number of theories around which claim to do this, we will focus on the one theory which, despite the large number of issues and defaults that have been revealed ever since the theory came to light decades ago, is still the dominant default theory when considering risk in modern finance. It is fair to say that at this point I don't share many of the views and assumptions the theory makes. Where needed I will provide my humble opinion on where the theory's weak spots are. It is fair to say that, when it comes to measuring the risk of an equity security, I am very much in the Buffett camp. I will clarify that later, when focusing on specific aspects of the theory.

## 3.1 MEASURING RISK

When trying to come up with a theory to measure risk 'tabula rasa,' we would probably have to agree that such a theory has to:

1. Define what risk it measures.
2. Standardize the way it measures risk.
3. Be applicable across asset classes and situations to allow for comparison.
4. Have a forward-looking dynamic (a certain predictive level), although the theory itself will necessarily be based on historical data to validate its existence and premises.
5. Allow that measure of risk to be translated into a way to determine the level of return needed to justify the risk being absorbed by an investor. The latter implies that we would have to complement it with market data to provide the background against which we can judge the findings.

### 3.1.1 Risk and return expectations

We need to take a couple of steps before we can talk about the actual theory. We will do so, however, in a somewhat advanced mode, as it is rather supportive to the discussion about mezzanine products.

(1) We need to define risk in terms of the distribution of actual returns around the expected return of a certain investor; (2) we need to differentiate between risk which is specific for

an investment or a few investments, and risk which affects a much wider cross-section of investments. We will argue that when the marginal investor is well diversified, it is only the latter risk, called market risk, which will be rewarded; (3) we need to know what the alternative models for measuring market risk and the expected returns are.

### 3.1.2 How do you measure risk?

A tough one, as risk and risk levels can mean different things to different people at the same point in time, and different things to the same people at different points in time. Investors who buy an asset expect to make a return over the time horizon for which they plan to hold the asset. The actual return that they make over this holding period may be very different from the expected return, and this is where risk comes in. Consider an investor with a 2-year time horizon buying a 2-year Treasury bill (or any other default-free one-year bond) with a 2% expected return. At the end of the 2-year holding period, the actual return that this investor would have on this investment will always be 2%, which is equal to the expected return. So that makes it a riskless investment, though in nominal terms because inflation will kick in, for which normal bonds provide no protection (TIPS or inflation-linked bonds do, however).

On the other hand, consider an investor who invests in Apple. This investor expects, for example, to make a return of 20% on Apple over a 1-year holding period. The actual return over this period will almost certainly not be equal to 20%; it will be much greater or much lower. Apparently the investor needs to worry about more here, i.e., the spread of the actual returns around the expected return, rather than whether or not they will make 20% on the investment in the next year. This is captured by the variance, or standard deviation, of the distribution; the greater the deviation of the actual returns from expected returns, the greater the variance. Also, the bias towards positive or negative returns is captured by the skewness of the distribution.

Figure 3.1 demonstrates a normal distribution as well as a positive and a negative one. When the distribution is positively or negatively skewed, it indicates that there are more extreme returns extending to the right (positively skewed) or to the left (negatively skewed). Skewness therefore provides information about the shape, location and variability of the (expected) return distribution.

Additionally, the kurtosis provides extra information about the shape of the return attribution. More specifically, it measures the weight of returns in the tails of the distribution relative to the standard deviation, but is more often associated as a measure of flatness or peakedness of the return distribution. Or, put differently, it measures how risk is hidden in the tail end of

Normal Curve          Positive Skew          Negative Skew

**Figure 3.1**   Different forms of skew

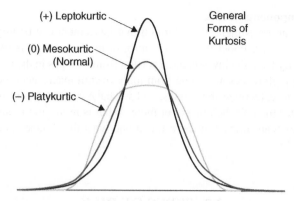

**Figure 3.2**   General forms of kurtosis

the distribution – or as Nassim Taleb[1] has coined it, Black Swans. They are extreme events which are highly unlikely to happen, but when they occur, tend to come unexpectedly (hence tail risk) and cause disproportionately large amounts of damage to returns and portfolios. He reiterates the understanding that our quantitative models of measuring risk tend to work well when measuring mainstream (normal) risk, but tend to underperform when abnormal or unlikely risk requires assessment.

In the investment world, the kurtosis captures (or tries to) the inclination of the price of a particular investment to invariably move in either direction (see Figure 3.2). When skewness is absent, investments can be measured on only two dimensions: (1) the expected return on the investment and (2) the variance in anticipated returns comprising the risk on the investment.

An investor with a choice between two investments with the same standard deviation but different expected returns will always pick the one with the higher expected return. Even when distributions (between different investment options) are neither symmetric nor normal, very often investors still choose between investments on the basis of only the expected return and the variance. Purely technically, they prefer positively skewed distributions over negatively skewed ones, and distributions with a lower kurtosis over those with a higher kurtosis.

The model which we will look at (the capital asset pricing model or CAPM) explicitly requires that those choices be made, but only in terms of expected returns and variances. It ignores kurtosis completely.

One final note: the assumption being made is that, by using historical variances, past return distributions are good references for future returns and their distributions.

### 3.1.3 What risks do we compensate for?

Risk arises from the deviation of actual returns from expected returns. This deviation, however, can occur due to a number of reasons, and these reasons can be classified into two categories: those which are specific to the investment being considered (called firm-specific risks), and those which have widespread availability across investments and markets (market risks).

---

[1] Nassim N. Taleb, *Black Swans: The impact of the highly improbable*, Random House Trade Paperbacks, 2010, 2nd edn.

**The individual components of risk**

When a firm makes an investment, the return on that investment can be impacted by several elements. Whether they are under the direct control of the firm or not is irrelevant. Some of the risk comes directly from the investment, a portion from changes in the industry, some from changing consumer preferences and some from more overall macro-economic factors. There are countless ways to categorize these risks, and we have no pretension to assume that our classification is better than all the others out there. What is more important is to understand these risks, how they (can) impact the investment and what the (financial and structural) impact will be if they do.

## 3.2  TYPES OF RISK

1. Investment/firm-specific risks.
2. Changes in industry dynamics (competition risk).
3. Industry-specific risk.
4. Macro-economic risks.

(1) An individual project or company as a bundle of projects may have higher or lower cash flows than expected, either because the firm mis-estimated the cash flows for that project or because factors specific to that project made it very difficult to estimate the cash flows properly. A bundle of projects should diversify certain specific risks but not necessarily; it will ultimately all depend on the type of risks, how they interact, the sources of those risks and how their occurrence correlates.

(2) The second source of risk is changes in industry dynamics; a big chunk of this translates into competition risk, whereby the overall performance of a firm is affected by the actions taken by competitors. Although economic theories and foresight help to interpret and predict competitors' behavior, competitive pressure is hard to model as it has many sources and ways in which it can impact a business, especially in a time when globalization has created a level playing field for competitors from different industries competing across sectors through innovation and leveraging on multi-industry operational skills.

(3) The third element of risk is industry-specific risk, i.e., those factors which impact the earnings and cash flows of a specific industry as a whole. There are, broadly speaking, four sources of industry-specific risk. The first is technology risk, which reflects the effects of technologies which change or evolve in ways different from those expected when a project was originally analyzed. The second source is legal risk, which reflects the effect of changing laws and regulations. The third is commodity risk, which reflects the effects of price changes in commodities and services which are used or produced disproportionately by a specific industry. The fourth dynamic is the shift in consumer preferences and the impact of scarcity, which forces businesses to revisit their business models, the way they finance themselves and the way they produce and market their products and services.

(4) The fourth element of risk is macro-economic risk. A firm experiences this risk as earnings and cash flows will be affected by macro-economic factors which affect essentially all companies and all projects, but in varying degrees. This can range from changes in interest rates which will affect the value of current and future projects, exchange rate exposures, the term structure of fixed-income instruments, the risk preferences of investors,

inflation and economic growth, political risk and central monetary policy. Some of this risk may be diversified away by the firm in the normal course of business by investing in projects in different countries whose currencies may not all move in the same direction, or reducing their exposure to the exchange rate component of this risk by borrowing in the local currency to fund projects. Other options are to contractually shift certain risks away to other parties better equipped to deal with them, or who can offset them with matching counter-risk positions. Overall, investors with an international dynamic in their portfolio should be able to reduce their exposure to these risks by diversifying regionally and/or globally.

## 3.2.1 Diversification as a rule reduces or eliminates firm-typical risk

Risk which affects one or a few firms, i.e., firm-specific risk, can be reduced or even eliminated by investors as they hold more diversified portfolios.

Each investment in a diversified portfolio is a much smaller percentage of that portfolio. Thus, any risk which increases or reduces the value of only that investment or a small group of investments will have only a small impact on the overall portfolio.

The effects of firm-specific actions on the prices of individual assets in a portfolio can be offset (because they can be either positive or negative for each asset in any given period). Theoretically, in large portfolios, it can be reasonably assumed that this risk will balance out and therefore won't impact the overall value of the portfolio. However, risk which impacts most assets in the market will continue to exist even in large and diversified portfolios. It is therefore too ambitious to think that one can steer away from this risk through natural hedging of those risks, especially as most risks tend to ride the wave of increasing correlation between asset prices globally, and monetary policy by central banks drives, to a large degree, the pricing of assets in the market. That is the natural consequence of turning most assets in this world liquid; they lose their ability to naturally hedge against certain market risks and become prone to dollarization or Euro-ization, thereby becoming hostages of central bank policies. Some level of illiquidity might be good for the stability of asset prices in general.

Whilst intuitively speaking, the case for diversification is simple, the benefits of diversification can also be measured. That is done through statistics, and in particular the concept of 'standard deviation' as the measure of risk in an investment. When you combine two investments which do not move together in a portfolio, the standard deviation of that portfolio can be lower than the standard deviation of the individual stocks in the portfolio, because of certain risk exposures' offsetting counter-dynamics.

## 3.2.2 Modern financial theory is eyeing a certain type of investor

Every investor has certain characteristics, i.e., it is the investor, while executing their strategy, who has the most influence on the pricing of their equity positions. It is not so much a certain profile of investor that modern financial theory eyes, but the investor who meets certain criteria. It ultimately comes down to those investors who hold a significant portion of (different) stock in one or more firms and trade those securities on a regular basis.

Why do we care about this profile of investors? Well, since they are assumed to set prices, their assessments of risk should govern how the market as a whole thinks about risk. Thus, if those profiles' investors are diversified, the only risk that they see in a company is the risk that they cannot diversify away. If they are undiversified parties, they will care about all risk in a company.

Thus we assume that they are diversified. Does that matter? It does. Because when they are considered diversified, the only risk that will be priced in is the risk as perceived by that particular investor profile. The risk in an investment will always be perceived to be higher for an undiversified investor than a diversified one, since the latter does not consider any firm-specific risk while the former does. Consequently, the diversified investor will be willing to pay a higher price for that asset because of their risk perceptions. Consequently, the asset, over time, will end up being held by diversified investors because of that natural pricing dynamic.

The end-game is that the market only compensates for systemic risk (non-diversifiable risk), because it assumes that market participants are diversified (or at least can be diversified) for non-diversifiable risk, i.e., risk that cannot be diversified away and which will come naturally when investing in the market, rather than putting their wealth in a risk-free (?) bank account or sovereign security.

Diversification does not mean that investors have to give up their ambition for higher returns. Investors can be diversified and try to beat the market at the same time. The problem is, however, that when you are very diversified (and have reduced specific risks to a minimum), your portfolio will start to mirror the market. Under those circumstances it will be difficult to beat the market in return terms. More focused portfolios are the only way to beat the market, assuming you underwrite the idea that it is a market of stocks out there and not a stock market.

It is only now that we are getting closer to what we really need to discuss, and that is how we are going to measure market risk which cannot be diversified away. We need a theory which we can use in a consistent way across the board and which can equally consistently measure that risk.

This is where the CAPM theory comes onto the radar.

### 3.2.3  Measuring market risk: the CAPM (capital asset pricing model) theory

In a risk–return world, most investors tend to agree that risk comes from the distribution of actual returns around the expected return, and that risk should be measured from the perspective of a marginal investor who is well diversified. They seem to fall out, however, when it comes down to how to measure non-diversifiable market risk.

There are, in essence, four basic models circulating: the capital asset pricing model (CAPM), the arbitrage pricing model (APM), the proxy models and the multi-factor models. Observe the word models in the last two categories, as each model often breaks down into different sub-models which developed over time. I will only elaborate on the first as it is, despite all its assumptions and flaws, still after so many years the default model when it comes to pricing market risk.

### 3.2.4  The capital asset pricing model

What are the assumptions underlying this model?

While the benefits of diversification are clear, most investors don't fully diversify. There are two reasons for this: the first is that the marginal benefits of diversification become smaller as their portfolio gets more diversified. The cost of adding an additional security might outstrip the benefits of diversification. The second reason is that many investors are only willing to hold stocks below their intrinsic value (and assume they can identify them at all times).

The capital asset pricing model assumes that there are no transaction costs, that there is no private information (i.e., not known to the public in general) and that investors therefore cannot find under- or over-valued assets in the marketplace. By making these assumptions, it takes away the factors which, in reality, cause investors to stop diversifying. Without those real boundaries, every investor would hold a piece of each traded stock in their portfolios.

If every investor in the market constructed the portfolio just described, how would they make allocation decisions to reflect their understanding of risk which would be implied in a certain asset vis-à-vis the risk-free benchmark? This seems to assume that there is something like a risk-free asset. For a long time, and with a little help from the global rating agencies, the world was able to convince itself that there was something like a risk-free asset. It was to be found in sovereign bonds and structured fixed-income products. No doubt, the last couple of years evidenced that that assumption was maybe a little ambitious (or naïve might be the better word here).[2]

Let me briefly comment on this. Whether you put your money into a bank account, a T-bond or equities, you are engaging in the business of lending money to each other (under certain conditions). There will always be some sort of compensation for making that money available, sometimes that will be fixed sometimes not (as is the case in equities). Whatever the situation, there will always be a counterparty that needs to produce returns to pay you back, including the compensation. If they don't, they will default in a way, i.e., by defaulting on the loan or by not providing you with sufficient return to justify the risks absorbed while investing in equities. It can therefore be concluded that, since there is a counterparty who has to deliver on something, there is not really such a thing as a risk-free asset, as it always requires a counterparty delivering on something in the future. It can be argued that governments, because of their license to print new money, will always be in a position to pay off their debt and therefore are essentially risk-free. That is only partly true, since printing that extra money will cause the money you lend them to became worthless over time (through inflation) and therefore they can still default on you (in inflation-adjusted terms). In 2012, central banks understood very well that inflating their sovereigns out of their debt position might be the only way to rebalance the budgets and debt positions of many sovereigns without causing massive deflationary pressures.

The risk of any asset to an investor is the risk added, by that asset, to the investor's overall portfolio. In the CAPM theory, the risk of an individual asset to an investor will be the risk that this asset adds to the market portfolio. Assets which move more with the market portfolio are considered riskier than assets which move less, since movements which are unrelated to the market portfolio will not affect the overall value of the portfolio when that asset is added to it. Statistically, this added risk is measured by the covariance of the asset with the market portfolio. The covariance is a non-standardized measure of market risk; the fact that the covariance of company $x$ with the market portfolio is 50% does not provide much insight as to

---

[2] See further: A. Damodaran, 'Into the Abyss: What if nothing is risk-free?' Working Paper, July 2010, NY Stern School of Business.

whether that firm is riskier or not relative to the average asset. We therefore standardize the risk measure by dividing the covariance of each asset with the market portfolio by the variance of the market portfolio. This yields what we know as the beta of the asset:

Beta of asset $x$ = covariance of asset $x$ with portfolio/variance of the market portfolio

Since the covariance of the market portfolio with itself is its variance, the beta of the market portfolio, and further, the average asset underlying, is one. Assets which are riskier than average, using this measurement method, will have betas higher than one, and assets which are safer than average will have betas lower than one.

Now, we said before that a useful theory would be one which has the ability to consistently convert a certain risk measurement into a return expectation. The expected return on an asset is linearly related to the beta of the asset. The expected return on an asset can therefore be expressed as a function of the risk-free rate and the beta of that asset.

Expected return on asset $x$:

$$ER_x = rf + \beta_x * (k_{em} - rf)$$
$$= \text{Risk-free rate} + \text{Beta of asset } x * (\text{Risk premium on market portfolio})$$

Where:   $ER_x$ = Expected return on asset $x$
         $rf$ = Risk-free rate
         $k_{em}$ = Expected return on market portfolio
         $\beta_x$ = Beta of asset $x$.

We need three inputs in order to properly use the capital asset pricing model:

- The riskless asset is defined as an asset where the investor knows the expected return with certainty for a specific time horizon (so there is no default risk or re-investment rate risk). Consequently, the riskless rate used will vary depending upon whether the time period for the expected return is 1, 5 or 10 years.
- The market risk premium is the premium required by investors for investing in the market portfolio, which includes all risky assets in the market, instead of investing in a riskless asset. Thus, it does not relate to any individual risky asset but to risky assets as a group (class).
- The beta, which we defined as the covariance of the asset divided by the market portfolio, is the only firm-specific input in this equation. In other words, the only reason two investments have different expected returns in the capital asset pricing model is because they have different betas.

In the capital asset pricing model all of the market risk is captured in one beta, measured relative to a market portfolio, which at least in theory should include all traded assets in the market place held in proportion to their market value.

I mentioned earlier that I had some concerns about the way modern financial theory measures risk, i.e., through volatility around a market portfolio. Hereunder are my concerns (and as said, I'm deep in the Buffett camp on this one).

When it comes to conventional portfolio theory, Buffett disagrees with the popular notion of diversification in investing, arguing instead that investors should focus on what they understand, and by doing that limit the universe of stocks they consider investing in. He considers the overuse of 'betas' as measures of risk in stock purchasing ridiculous, since it is precisely the volatility of stocks which provides opportunities for investors who've taken the trouble to determine the intrinsic value of companies.[3] Volatility does not measure risk. The problem is that the people who have written and taught about risk do not know how to measure it. Beta is the preferred concept because it is mathematical and easy to calculate, but it is wrong – past volatility does not determine investment risk.[4]

---

[3] Warren Buffett and Lawrence Cunningham (eds), 'The Essays of Warren Buffett: Lessons for corporate America,' (1998) *Cardozo Law Review*.

[4] Michael Keppler, 'Risk is not the same as volatility' (November 1990) *Die Bank* **11**:610–614. See also: Shailesh Kumar, 'Beta of a stock is a meaningless measure,' Valuestockguide.com, March 1, 2012. Copyright © Value Stock Guide 2010–2013. An excerpt:

'For most investors who have grown up on the diet of high beta = high risk, this statement will come as a surprise. Beta means nothing for a stock. And beta explains nothing about the investment merits of a stock.

Let me start with two thought experiments to drive this point home.

Scenario 1: Let's say you are interested in a stock that has declined significantly in the recent months. So much so that at this time, after you have done your research and due diligence, you come to a conclusion that the stock presents a compelling value. In fact, you conclude that this investment is as sure a bet as any one is ever likely to get. The market has overdone its selling, as it generally does when there is an investor panic.

Let's also spice it up a little and inject some specifics. This company, even though its stock has taken a beating, continues to generate more in free cash flow per year than its entire market value, even after servicing its debt. You look deeper and find that after you clear away all the accounting clutter and GAAP mandated nonsense, the stock is priced at about 1 times net earnings per share.

In short, this is a bargain unlike any other.

Heck, if this level of undervaluation continues, the company can just decide to buy itself out and go private. That would be a very wise decision on their part. Alternatively, it is a very good acquisition for a smart corporate buyer. There is no way this kind of undervaluation will be allowed to continue. Sanity eventually returns.

Now the question is, if you decide to invest in this stock, are you taking enormous amounts of risk? The market thinks you are. The recent falling over the cliff of the stock price has pushed the stock's beta to beyond the threshold a rational investor would contemplate investing at. When the price starts moving up, it is likely going to be very volatile as well.

But you know that the risk here is close to zero. Just like Buffett thought the risk of investing in Washington Post was close to zero.

Scenario 2: Let's say you found a stock that no one cares about. It is a small company in the middle of nowhere in a boring industry. There is no analyst coverage, they have never been part of the Inc 500 and the CEO owns so much of the company stock that it is almost like his family business. Which it was at one time.

In a quaint departure from the norm, the company management makes decisions that are decidedly long term. Some of these decisions involve capital expenses that will kill their next quarter's earnings, were it not for the fact that they do not worry about issuing guidance and there is no analyst breathing down their necks.

The company's balance sheet is like Fort Knox. Their margins lead the industry. It is a real gem. And the dividend is to die for. The management takes care of its shareholders.

You realize that the stock price today is much below where it ought to be given the company fundamentals. It is a great buy. And when some of the past capital investments start paying off, the company and the stock will be noticed. For the past few years, though, the stock has stayed sleepy and its beta is less than half of the market.

The reason the capital asset pricing model has survived as the default model in modern finance is primarily due to the failure of more complex models to deliver significant improvement in terms of expected returns. Volatility is a measure for price variation in a financial instrument over time. Volatility does not measure the direction of price changes, merely their dispersion. Risk is (1) the size of a potential loss and (2) the probability of its occurrence. These are losses of a permanent nature (not volatility-related). Risk is a function of time. Volatility is constant;[5] the difference between price and value underlies this misconception.

---

footnote (*continued*)

So you buy the stock.

You know your risk is low, and the beta is low, so it all matches up. Right? But that is not why you bought the stock. You bought this stock because you expect the stock to provide a return that is significantly better than the market. And as the stock gets discovered, this return will come to you in fits and starts. The price may become volatile, but you know in the long run you will make handsome profits.

You bought the stock because you know you are buying it at a low and your downside is protected, but you want the beta to be high on the upside and you want to capture that upside.

Just to rile up the Efficient Market Hypothesis proponents a little more, I will lay out the two key rules of investing. Especially value investing.

1. Price =/= Value, and
2. Volatility (beta) =/= Risk

Besides, stock prices over the short term are essentially random and over the long term are dictated by the fundamentals and the company performance in the future. The beta measures the past volatility of the stock and has no bearing on what the stock does in the future. A stock is not born with a beta assigned to it. Every stock moves through periods of high beta and low beta. The trick is to focus on the business fundamentals and find great opportunities to invest.

As Warren Buffett points out, cash and other 'currency' investments are some of the lowest beta investments available, and they are the riskiest ones for preserving or enhancing your future purchasing power. What is more important is to judge the risk of capital loss before making any investment.

[5] Let's say you're saving up money for a down-payment on a home. You expect to need the money sometime within the next 3–5 years. Common sense tells us that the stock market is probably a poor place to invest that money. Over any 3-year period, there's no telling what the stock market might do. (It is, after all, quite *volatile*.) It could be much lower in 3 years than it is now. Investing your downpayment money in the stock market would be quite *risky*.

Now, let's say you're also saving up money for retirement, and you know that you're not going to need this money for *at least* 20 years. Conventional wisdom tells us (correctly) that the stock market is a great place for this money. It's a practical certainty that the stock market will be much higher 20 years from now than it is today. Suddenly, despite the fact that the stock market is still *volatile*, it's no longer *risky* in this particular situation.

What's the difference? The timeframe. What do we learn? An investment class's volatility is constant. Stocks will be volatile throughout a 1-year period, a 5-year period or a 50-year period. Stocks never move up in a straight line. Risk, however, is not constant. It's a function of time. For stocks, time and risk are inversely related. (That is, the longer you have for your money to grow, the less risky stocks become.)

So what's the value of this distinction? The way I see it, the value is this: Understanding that an investment can be volatile *without being risky* should give us courage. Hopefully, it will give us the courage to put more of our money into those investments which will provide us with the most growth between now and the time we need the money. Hopefully, it will give us the courage to understand that declines in the market do not mean stocks are unsafe. They simply mean that stocks are volatile. (And we already knew that, now didn't we?)

## 3.3  EQUITY RISK VERSUS THE RISK OF BORROWING: DEFAULT RISK AND THE COST OF DEBT

When you, as an investor, lend to a firm, there is the possibility that the borrower may default on interest and/or principal repayments. This possibility of default is what we call 'default risk.' From a risk–return perspective, borrowers with higher default risk should pay higher interest rates on their borrowing than those with lower default risk. We need to figure out a way to measure the level of default risk, and the relationship between default risk and the interest rates on lending products.

Contrary to the general risk and return models for equity, which evaluate the effects of market risk on expected returns, models of default risk measure the consequences of firm-specific default risk on promised returns. Or, put differently, they look only at your expected ability to repay the lender, and in doing so the analysis is limited to borrower-specific features. No externalities are or need to be considered. Diversification doesn't really play a role, as fixed-income instruments have limited upside; that is, their compensation is fixed no matter how successful, or not, the firm is. Consequently, the expected return on a corporate bond is likely to reflect the firm-specific default risk of the firm issuing the bond.

### 3.3.1  What are the drivers behind default risk?

The default risk of a firm is a function of both its capacity to generate cash flows from operations and its financial obligations. It is also a function of how liquid a firm's assets are, since firms with more liquid assets should have an easier time liquidating them, in a crisis, to meet debt obligations.

Consequently, the following propositions relate to default risk:

- Firms which generate high cash flows relative to their financial obligations have lower default risk than do firms which generate low cash flows relative to obligations. Or, firms with significant current investments which generate high cash flows will have lower default risk than will firms which do not.
- The more stable the cash flows, the lower the firm's default risk will be. Firms which operate in predictable and stable businesses will have lower default risk than will otherwise similar firms which operate in cyclical and/or volatile businesses, for the same level of indebtedness.
- The more liquid a firm's assets, for any given level of operating cash flows and financial obligations, the less default risk in the firm.

Assessments of default risk have been based on financial ratios which measure the cash flow coverage and control for industry effects, to capture the variability in cash flows and the liquidity of assets.

As financial markets deepened over the last couple of decades, banks, and later on rating agencies, started to develop their own proprietary models to assess default rates of loans, bonds and sovereign as well as structured papers. These models use the same financial ratios as have always been used, and complemented these with qualitative criteria with respect to the business, countries etc. the borrower is active in. The same happened for sovereign borrowers, although the models obviously reflect the different position sovereigns are in vis-à-vis corporate borrowers.

The interest rate on a corporate bond (and other fixed-income products) should be a function of its default risk. If the rating is a good measure of the default risk, higher-rated bonds should be priced to yield lower interest rates than lower-rated bonds. The difference between the interest rate on a bond with default risk and a default-free government bond is called the default spread. This default spread will vary by maturity of the bond and can also change from period to period, depending on economic conditions. The rating tables as we now know them are then used to set interest rates on products relative to the underlying risk, using spreads (default spread) per rating rank which are then added to the cost of funding for the lender (Libor, Euribor or otherwise). The practical implication of this phenomenon is that default spreads for bonds have to be re-estimated at regular intervals, especially if the economy shifts from low to high growth or vice versa.

A final point worth making here is that everything which has been said about the relationship between interest rates and bond ratings is pretty much valid more generally for interest rates and default risk. The existence of ratings is a convenience which makes the assessment of default risk a little easier for us when analyzing companies.

This status quo raises the question about what to do when assets don't have a rating. That is pretty much true for all non-listed assets and instruments, and about 70–90% of the real economy is still not listed (varying depending on where you are in the world). We'll get back to this later in the chapter.

So, now we need to focus on how to measure that market risk through the parameters defined as included in the CAPM model. It will ultimately allow us to determine some sort of hurdle rate for the debt and equity used by a corporation, and how mezzanine plays out, ultimately sitting somewhere in the middle.

**The parameters within the cost of equity**
The cost of equity is the rate of return which investors require to invest in the equity of a firm. The CAPM discussed needs a risk-free rate and a risk premium. We'll look at these first and then at the estimation of risk parameters.

## 3.3.2  The risk-free rate

What is needed here is the expected return on the type of asset which qualifies as the risk-free rate. The expected returns on risky investments are then measured relative to the risk-free rate, with the risk creating an additional risk premium that is added on to the base rate.

We need to define risk-free first. We can define a risk-free asset as one for which the investor knows the expected returns with absolute certainty. It requires two conditions to be met:

- There has to be no default risk, which generally implies that the security has to be issued by a government. This implies that the sovereign has a AAA rating, if not it is not risk-free in its own right. If it is not risk-free, it requires you to take into account a default spread, as mentioned before, to account for the differential.
- There is no reinvestment rate exposure. Or, put differently, the maturity on the risk-free instrument needs to be the same as the one under review. If not, there is an implicit reinvestment risk.

An additional element could be that there is a need for a currency match (between the risk-free instrument and the one reviewed) to account properly for expected inflation, or in cases where different currencies are used, an adjustment to reflect the differential in terms of expected inflation, assuming the analysis is done in nominal terms.

### The risk premium dissected

The first question here probably is what do we try to measure? The risk premium in the CAPM measures the extra return that would be demanded by investors for investing their money in the market, rather than leaving it in risk-free investments. Two elements play a role here:

1. Risk perception/aversion of investors: As investors become more risk-averse, they will demand a larger risk premium for putting their money to work in the market. That risk perception, although always there in an implicit way, will vary with the economy and the analysis of which risks are on the horizon. Recent experiences, like in 2008, keep risk premiums higher for extended periods of time. When the market is doing well, risk premiums will be lower than when the economic outlook is turning south.
2. The intrinsic riskiness of the average risky investment: As the riskiness of the average risk investment increases, so should the premium. This will depend on which firms are actually traded in the market, their economic fundamentals and how involved they are in managing risk.

Each investor assesses those risks in a different way, so we are looking for a market average of that risk assessment.

Those risk premiums can be assessed in three different ways.

1. Survey-based premiums:
   This is done by estimating the premium through a survey of investors about their expectations for the future. Obviously these surveys, which are not used a lot in practice, carry their own intrinsic flaws.
2. Historical premiums:
   The most common approach to estimating the risk premium(s) used in financial asset pricing models is to base it on historical data. In the CAPM, the premium is defined as the difference between average returns on stocks and average returns on risk-free securities over an extended period of history.
3. The third method, which is the only forward-looking methodology, is the implied equity premium method. This is when value can be considered the equivalent of the expected dividends in the future (Required ROE – expected dividend growth rate) or, put differently, the present value of dividends growing at a constant rate. Except for the required rate of return, all inputs are observable. Solving the equation and deducting the risk-free rate will provide the implied equity premium or the equity premium embedded in any given level an index is trading at. Besides the fact that the model doesn't require any historical data or assume that the future will look like the past, it is a forward-looking model by using the actual level of an index as a starting point for defining the actual risk premium embedded in a market at any given point in time.

Also here there are some implicit assumptions:

1. The risk aversion of investors has not changed in a systematic way across time.
2. The average riskiness in the market has not changed in a systematic way across time.

Given the large number of estimations and technical criteria one has to decide on (e.g., arithmetic or geometric averages), the potential margin of error is significant. Nevertheless, the method is often used in practice. Another complication is often centered around emerging market applications of this method, the lack of data when going back for longer periods of time and the need to stay consistent if one cannot define a risk-free rate in those currencies. The time and space needed to elaborate on most of these issues makes them beyond the natural scope of the book.

## 3.4 PUTTING IT ALL TOGETHER

The two components of every balance sheet debt can be technically framed as:

Cost of Debt = Risk-free rate + default rate
Cost of Equity = Risk-free rate + (beta * market risk premium)

Those two components then will have to be weighted, based on how much of total funding they provide for an organization. So our weighted 'average cost of capital' will be read as:

WACC = (Cost of Debt * Debt/Debt + Equity) + (Cost of equity * Equity/Debt + Equity)

For the purposes of calculating the WACC, market values of debt and equity should be used. Although conservatism could lead you to use the more stable accounting values, it is the worst thing to do. This is for the simple reason that the difference between the accounting and market value of debt is rather modest, and is driven by the interest rate in the market. On the other hand, the difference between the accounting and market value of equity can be significant, both on the up- and downside, and therefore using accounting values will, under normal circumstances, lead to an under-weighting of equity when calculating the cost of capital. As it is the most expensive part of our funding structure, we therefore under-weight the most expensive part and therefore will end up with a lower WACC. This will lead to all sorts of dysfunctional decision making at the firm involved, as well as leaving investors with an inadequate view of the risk included in the firm (once again, this is all judged within the framework of the CAPM). It can be added that, for calculating the cost of equity, all outstanding shares should be included as well as any equity options out there including convertible loans, convertible preference shares or ESOP, or management option plans or warrants issued together with subdebt.

Now that we are clear on which values should be used, we can move on to see what it means at the level of the balance sheet. Using too little debt basically makes the firm too expensive, as one uses more equity than necessary. It also could make your firm more vulnerable to (hostile) takeovers, as a potential acquirer will be able to buy you by lending money against your own assets.

On the other hand, using too much debt creates too high a level of fixed-cost burdens and inherently increases the risk of the firm, just like a business with a high fixed-cost burden will be more risky than one with a naturally lower average fixed-cost burden. This is then reflected in the beta. The latter is operational leverage, the former financial leverage.

This means that with 0% debt and 100% equity, your WACC is higher and will come down when you start using debt. The WACC will come down until it reaches a certain level at which it will stagnate (indicating the optimal capital structure), and will then reverse when more debt is added to the balance sheet. Table 3.1 represents a textbook example (cost of equity and after-tax cost of debt assumed, and firm value for illustration purposes only):

**Table 3.1**   Relationship between cost of funding and firm value

| D/(D+E) | Cost of equity | After-tax cost of debt | Cost of capital | Firm value |
|---------|----------------|------------------------|-----------------|------------|
| 0       | 10.50%         | 4.80%                  | 10.50%          | $2,747     |
| 10%     | 11.00%         | 5.10%                  | 10.41%          | $2,780     |
| 20%     | 11.60%         | 5.40%                  | 10.36%          | $2,799     |
| 30%     | 12.30%         | 5.52%                  | 10.27%          | $2,835     |
| 40%     | 13.10%         | 5.70%                  | 10.14%          | $2,885     |
| 50%     | 14.50%         | 6.10%                  | 10.30%          | $2,822     |
| 60%     | 15.00%         | 7.20%                  | 10.32%          | $2,814     |
| 70%     | 16.10%         | 8.10%                  | 10.50%          | $2,747     |
| 80%     | 17.20%         | 9.00%                  | 10.64%          | $2,696     |
| 90%     | 18.40%         | 10.20%                 | 11.02%          | $2,569     |
| 100%    | 19.70%         | 11.40%                 | 11.40%          | $2,452     |

The WACC will stagnate at a certain level taking into account the risk-free rate in the market, the maturity of the debt taken on board, the maturity of the business, the business your firm is in etc. Although there are some (but few) exceptions to the rule, most firms will find their optimal capital structure somewhere in the ballpark range of 30–45% debt (and so 55–70% equity). Note that the WACC is directly correlated to the firm's value and both functions are inversely related, since the WACC functions as the discount factor to judge the firm's future cash flows, or the firm's aggregate value.

The fact that the WACC will be higher after that optimal point is due to:

1. Lenders understanding that there is limited or no collateral and/or no existing cash flow at the firm to serve its debt, making it implicitly or explicitly junior and subordinated to senior debt holders. This happens the moment the WACC turns around and starts sloping upwards.
2. As residual cash flow holders, equity holders realize that piling up fixed costs even further will leave very little room for an adequate return on their investment, and will adjust their risk premium for investing in that firm, thereby pushing the WACC up even further as more debt is taken on board.

For mezzanine products this has the following implications:

Cost of debt → Cost of mezzanine → Cost of equity

This seems to make sense. If the risk profile of mezzanine products lies between a senior debt product and equity, the cost will mirror that, at least in a CAPM and risk–return-driven world.

### 3.5  HOW MUCH RISK IS THERE IN A MEZZANINE PRODUCT?

This is a very general question which requires a very specific and fact-dependent answer.

Ratings will be used to assess the (financial) risk, or used as a benchmark against firm-specific methods of analysis. At the end of the day, that is also what rating agencies do when rating a company or specific financial instrument (rating methodology), although in a somewhat more complex way – combining qualitative and quantitative arguments – see Chapter 9 for an in-depth evaluation of the methodology for mezzanine instruments.

Most senior lenders will start this process looking at their cost of funding, whether that is Libor or Euribor or any other interbanking lending rate. Following that, it will add spreads to reflect the inherent risks and current and expected performance of the business, the strength and volume of the collateral (whereby fixed assets are preferred and inventory and A/P less so) and the amount and maturity of the existing debt already committed to by the firm.

For mezzanine products, there is no collateral (except for those products with a second or third lien); existing debt levels and products are known. So, two real questions remain:

1. What is my level of subordination? Given the structuring and maturity of existing debt, what is the level of financial distress during the lifetime of my mezzanine products, given the expected performance of the firm?
2. What is the reasonably expected growth in free cash flows during the next couple of years? The first is a question of forecasting and normalization of earnings over longer periods of time. It requires you to think hard about the dynamics of the industry, the competitive forces and rivalry in this line of business and the intrinsic strengths of the particular firm you intend to finance. Although the cash flows are quantifiable, the judgments driven by the shape of those cash flows are all qualitative in nature.

With respect to the first element, which is a pure quantifiable metric, a rating agency will tell you it uses many different formulas which all stress-test the ability of a firm to repay, the D/E relationship in a variety of ways and the growth of free cash flows etc. Although useful, there are two different objectives here: (1) the level of subordination and (2) the issues impacting the pattern of your free cash flows. This pattern can be impacted by the market or industry outlook, determined by firm-specific features, sensitivity to inflation, evolution of certain currency crosses or overall GDP, as well as regulatory features etc. In my understanding, these issues are, and should be, tackled at the level of forecasting. Or, put differently, the level of subordination can be measured solely based on a metric as simple as the times interest earned ratio (TIER), also known as the interest coverage ratio (IC ratio).

$$TIER = EBIT(DA)/Interest\ paid$$

This will also provide a good understanding of where and when any potential financial distress will occur. Aswath Damodaran did the full exercise by matching the TIER levels with the appropriate rating quotation as we know them from S&P. Table 3.2 provides an excerpt of his findings:[6]

---

[6] Please visit this website for further information: www.damodaran.com – lecture notes valuation class.

**Table 3.2**   Relationship between the S&P rating categories and TIER results

| Rating | IC Ratio (large caps i.e. > 5 Bio. USD in revenues) | IC (small cap) |
|---|:---:|:---:|
| AAA | >8.5 | >12.5 |
| AA | 6.5–8.5 | 9.5–12.5 |
| A+ | 5.5–6.5 | 7.5–9.5 |
| A | 4.25–5.5 | 6.0–7.5 |
| A– | 3.0–4.25 | 4.5–6.0 |
| BBB | 2.5–3.0 | 4.0–4.5 |
| BB+ | 2.05–2.5 | 3.5–4.0 |
| BB | 1.9–2.05 | 3.0–3.5 |
| B+ | 1.75–1.9 | 2.5–3.0 |
| B | 1.5–1.75 | 2.0–2.5 |
| B– | 1.25–1.5 | 1.5–2.0 |
| CCC | 0.8–1.25 | 1.25–1.5 |
| CC | 0.65–0.8 | 0.8–1.25 |
| C | 0.2–0.65 | 0.6–0.8 |
| D | <0.2 | <0.65 |

We can, however, take this whole thing up one notch and ask ourselves to what extent can a risk analysis be performed based on the transaction being financed? Although the answer is, to a certain degree, that forecasting will deal with most of it, there is most likely value in us reflecting a little further on the topic. In the end it is undeniably true that financing a merger or acquisition is quite different from financing an LBO or MBO ('leveraged buy-out' and 'management buy-out') or financing an internationalization or the launch of a new product line.

Besides the quantitative hoops we have to jump through, defining risk from a qualitative point of view requires us to think about the dynamics and magnitude of risk included in certain transactions.

Figure 3.3 reflects a possible way of classifying risk. The stress should be on 'possible' as there are dozens of equally valid classifications of risk.

What is important to consider is how certain types of risk affect a certain business and its ability to generate profitable sales. The task here doesn't end with identifying and classifying risk and its patterns, but brings up the more relevant question of how the emergence of these risks economically impacts a business and its outlook. Is the impact temporary or permanent? How does it show and does it impact competitors the same way? If not, what are the key sensitivities? How does it impact our competitive position over time? And how does it impact the relationship with our suppliers and clients? Can we protect ourselves (partly) against some risks and at what cost? Will it impact our ability to innovate or overall impact our agility within the marketplace and constrain our ability to take on new opportunities? Will there be new regulation impacting our business? Will there be a toughening or liberalization of the marketplace?

Many of these questions sound logical but are often hard to estimate or quantify, especially when certain transactions span 5–8 years or longer, which is often the case in LBO/MBO, M&A or recapitalization situations.

Another related question is how the balance sheet structure will change after you invest as a mezzanine investor. Take, for example, a commercial bank which wants to strengthen the tier

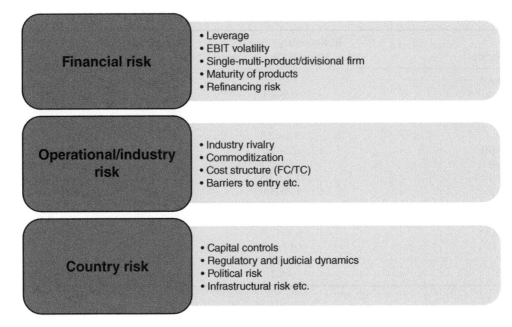

**Figure 3.3**   Risk categories a company is or can be exposed to

1/2 part of its balance sheet to expand the business. This will invariably imply that there will be a new wave of senior debt coming in after you invest. Ultimately, the commercial bank has artificially expanded its capital structure with quasi-equity (being cheaper than a new rights issue). That extra quasi-equity will free up balance sheet space to bring on board new senior debt (which wasn't possible before) to complement the mezzanine lending facility. Part of this will directly feed into the covenants a mezzanine investor needs to put in place, but one can only do so after one understands the dynamics of those risks.

## 3.6  COST VERSUS RETURN DYNAMICS FOR MEZZANINE PRODUCTS

I mentioned in the introduction that we would be coming back to return dynamics for mezzanine products, and it is a somewhat tough question. It is not as structured as a pure lending product, where spreads are added on top of base funding costs based on risks identified in the borrower's business or transaction. Nevertheless, I see in practice that many mezzanine lending contracts are built off a normal lending contract which implicitly feeds through those structural ways of thinking into the mezzanine space. Ultimately we accept that we will incur some sort of equity-like risk and that needs to show. This means we need to think about the true earning potential of assets rather than the ability to repay us kind-of-approach. Let me conceptualize it:

Senior lenders work from the bottom up when determining their compensation for a product.

This is fine, but if you decide to apply this approach consistently for mezzanine products, you will run into trouble for two reasons:

1. You will run into risks which you cannot accurately quantify when turning them into spreads.
2. You might end up with a total return on the product that, although technically correct and reflecting all the risks you identified accurately, becomes inadequate or might even harm the firm financially, and most likely will be higher than the forward-looking ROE which common shareholders will receive.

It is therefore my approach, and you don't have to agree, to work with a 'top down' and 'bottom up' approach simultaneously in the return modeling process. This has two clear advantages:

1. One can still accurately define the traditional risks of a lending product through spread over base funding cost (bottom up).
2. Starting from the (expected) ROE, one can define a realistic approach towards return modeling for the product (top down). In most cases, the mezzanine lender will go home with compensation (somewhat) lower than the ROE given their risk exposure versus common shareholders. That will leave you as follows:

| ROE-adjusted return for mezzanine holders | ↓ |
| Return gap | |
| Base funding cost + spreads | ↑ |

We now know what our return gap is in terms of magnitude and dynamics. Based on that knowledge, it might become easier to model the equity kicker in a certain product, or even step back and wonder if the chosen product is the best given the return dynamics and the possible complications it brings. Potentially, there are better products in the mezzanine range (or a better combination of products), which might suit the firm better, reduce risk (which in itself enhances returns) and provide better visibility for the mezzanine investor regarding how returns will be generated. Mezzanine returns which compromise or structurally exceed the ROE for shareholders will lead to all sorts of complications (particularly in project finance situations), ranging from recurring repayment issues, cash flow drains, inability to finance new assets and projects, to equity investors cutting their losses and abandoning the project.

We are now good to move on and focus on some of the specifics and complications of mezzanine finance due to regulation, industry characteristics, insolvency and bankruptcy positions, and there are many of them.

# 4

# The 'Pricing' Question and Further Financial Dynamics of Convertible Loans and Preferred Convertible Shares[1]

The first part of this chapter will be devoted to the question of the mezzanine product group's pricing: we will build further on the discussion we started at the end of Chapter 3. The second part will be devoted to some of the intrinsic complexities of embedded optionalities as they can be found in convertible loans and preferred convertible shares.

## 4.1 PRICING GRID FOR MEZZANINE PRODUCTS

As indicated earlier, the pricing of these products is very fact dependent. However, basic logic with respect to debt pricing and the underlying debt still applies. As the creditworthiness of a firm deteriorates, the pricing of the instrument will go up. Often this process is, to a large degree, linked to the firm's credit rating which takes into account the subordination of the debtholders, the amount of (expected) FCF etc. For non-listed instruments or companies this is much more complicated.[2] In these situations there are basically two options with respect to structuring the pricing of subdebt, regardless of the category in which they fall.

**The first option** is to create a synthetic credit rating for the firm or instrument. The Damodaran chart below – which is taken from Chapter 3 – reflects the correlation between the S&P credit rating and the Interest Coverage ratio. The outcome can then be used to substantiate the spreads added to the basic funding cost. The chart indicates the ranking for both Large-Caps and Small/Midcaps. What that means depends on the country. For the USA, however, the tipping point between two categories is US$5 billion in annual revenues.

---

[1] For more extensive coverage of the topic, see: F.J. Fabozzi and S.V. Mann, *The Handbook of Fixed Income Securities*, McGraw-Hill, 2011, 8th edn, and in particular the chapters 'Convertible securities and their valuation,' 'Convertible securities and their investment characteristics' and 'Valuations of bonds with embedded options'.

[2] Most rating agencies also developed a rating methodology for private companies. The one for Moody's can be found here: https://riskcalc.moodysrms.com/us/research/crm/56402.pdf.

| S&P rating | IC ratio (large cap) | IC ratio (small/mid cap) |
|---|---|---|
| AAA | >8.5 | >12.5 |
| AA | 6.5–8.5 | 9.5–12.5 |
| A+ | 5.5–6.5 | 7.5–9.5 |
| A | 4.25–5.5 | 6.0–7.5 |
| A– | 3.0–4.25 | 4.5–6.0 |
| BBB | 2.5–3.0 | 4.0–4.5 |
| BB+ | 2.05–2.5 | 3.5–4.0 |
| BB | 1.9–2.05 | 3.0–3.5 |
| B+ | 1.75–1.9 | 2.5–3.0 |
| B | 1.5–1.75 | 2.0–2.5 |
| B– | 1.25–1.5 | 1.5–2.0 |
| CCC | 0.8–1.25 | 1.25–1.5 |
| CC | 0.65–0.8 | 0.8–1.25 |
| C | 0.2–0.65 | 0.5–0.8 |
| D | <0.2 | <0.65 |

**The second option** is to link your additional spreads (above Libor, Euribor etc. as a base lending rate) to the default and recovery rates of each instrument. Geography will also play a role here, as well as the credit rating of the company the debt is provided to and the maturity of the loan provided. For example, credit rating firm Fitch produces default and recovery tables on a regular basis for all categories of subordinated debt ranked based on the credit rating of the underlying firm. A spread model can be built based on the likelihood of default on the product provided.

In more specific cases, for example, mezzanine investment in financial institutions/insurance firms, an additional criterion could be the amount of economic capital required. In the case of investments in financial institutions/microfinance, an additional question will be what the additional finance will serve to do. How much additional wholesale funding will be added after the investment? Will the amount be used for raising new deposits or organic or acquisition growth? These qualitative arguments will all color the risk dynamics of the investment. For more information on this see Chapter 5.

Whatever method you choose (or combination of methods), the pricing grid will never be as systematic as for senior secured debt, and the pricing from different providers for the same instrument will differ much more than offers for the same senior debt. This has to do with the fact that not only credit risk needs to be appreciated, but also the (level of) equity risk in the instrument. A further complication is the fact that, dependent on the chosen product, there will be multiple streams of income besides the base interest of dividend payment. In most cases that will be either a profit-dependent interest rate, or alternatively a potential equity appreciation of the stocks obtained directly or after conversion of the fixed-income product. Appreciation of that portion of the risk can differ significantly per provider. A total return picture therefore needs to be drawn, referring back to the top down and bottom up approach suggested in Chapter 3. In this sense, pricing and covenants for mezzanine products are truly 'negotiated positions.'

## 4.2  FINANCIAL DYNAMICS OF CONVERTIBILITY IN CONVERTIBLE LOANS AND PREFERRED CONVERTIBLE SHARES

Both products have something in common; they enjoy an embedded option in what is, essentially, a fixed-income driven product (interest or dividend-based). In this section we will consider some of the features and valuation aspects of these products. It could be argued that warrants would fit in here as well; in a way this is true, and we discussed the specifics in Chapter 2. One thing, however, sets warrants apart; a warrant has no underlying fixed-income instrument, or more broadly no income-generating instrument. A warrant, essentially, only reflects the right of the holder to exchange the warrant for a certain number of shares. The difference with the price paid for those warrants then qualifies as the economic return generated through these warrants.

### 4.2.1  Convertible bonds

We already concluded that convertible bonds are essentially debentures (i.e., unsecured debt instruments), which may be converted (often) by the option's holder into the underlying company's stock. For technical details on the product, refer back to Chapter 2. Because of the fact that the firm granted the holder the right to convert the bonds, these bonds are subordinate to the firm's other debt. Due to the embedded option, they also carry a lower interest rate than is available on non-convertible debt with a similar risk profile. The conversion option allows the firm to issue lower-grade debt at a low(er) interest rate. Investors considering investing in these products will do so and accept the lower interest rate, due to the fact that the bond will become worth more when the price of the stock rises. They are exchanging part of the interest income for possible (higher) capital gains (when converting the instrument).

Convertible bonds have all the typical characteristics of a normal bond instrument. They are therefore characterized by (1) a principal amount, (2) a maturity date and (3) a coupon rate which is paid semi-annually (or otherwise) and often has a sinking fund requirement. The latter happens when, rather than the issuer repaying the entire principal of a bond issue on the maturity date, another company buys back a portion of the issue annually, usually at a fixed par value or at the current market value of the bonds, whichever is less. Should interest rates decline following a bond issue, sinking-fund provisions allow a firm to lessen the interest rate risk of its bonds, as it essentially replaces a portion of existing debt with lower-yielding bonds.

From the investor's point of view, a sinking fund adds safety to a corporate bond issue: with it, the issuing company is less likely to default on the repayment of the remaining principal upon maturity, since the final repayment amount is substantially less. This added safety affects the interest rate at which the company is able to offer bonds in the marketplace.

After conversion, all these features become meaningless. Convertible bonds are also (always) callable. In a way, the issuer forces the holder through the call to exercise the option and convert the bond. If the bond is not converted, the incremental value following an increase in the firm's stock value will be lost. The benefit for the firm is that, after conversion, interest is no longer due on top of the fixed repayment of the principal amount at maturity.

Some convertible bonds also have a put option included, which will allow the bond holder to sell it back to the issuer. This can happen under certain pre-determined conditions, or within certain time frames after issuance of the instrument. Playing around with the timelines between call and put options can be part of the issuer's strategy to force a certain behavior on the other party when certain conditions materialize either in the market or at firm level, and/or create an exit when interest rates in the market change dramatically during the lifetime of the instrument before conversion. The choice of the conversion date or period within the timeline of the underlying debt instrument is a strategic choice in itself. Conversion options which can be converted at a later date, close to maturity of the underlying debt instrument, will increase the time value of the embedded option. However, they also pose risks on price movements in the issuing firm's stock price (particularly when the firm is listed), or structural dynamics in pricing levels of the market as a whole, especially in this day and age where volatility can spike almost at random and change price actions for protracted periods of time in the market.

Nevertheless, convertible bonds are attractive to certain investors because of the debt-related features of the instruments. Ultimately, if the bond is not converted, it will retire at maturity and the principal amount will be returned to the issuer at that time. Since there is no obligation to convert, an investor can hide in the shadow of the debt instrument characteristics. Having said that, due to the lower interest rate a convertible bond carries, it is fair to assume that in cases where the investor retires the instrument without converting, they will walk away with compensation which, on a risk-adjusted basis, is not sufficient vis-à-vis other options available in the marketplace.

The interest rate, however, is normally higher than the dividend yield when buying stock in the issuing company, something which might prevail as an argument for income-seeking retail and institutional investors. So, it comes down to the safety of debt combined with the potential of equitable upside. It is, however, subordinated debt and therefore inherently more risky compared to senior debt or debt with collateral.

More importantly, because of the embedded option reflecting the stock price evolution, the value of a convertible bond will change over time. Fluctuations in the stock price will cause changes in the price of convertible bonds. These changes come on top of those due to movements of interest rates in the markets, the primary driver of changes in the market value of debt instruments. When interest rates are rising, convertible bonds are particularly badly off, as their already reduced interest rate causes the price of the instrument to drop proportionately more than that of non-convertible debt with higher interest rates. On top of this, if interest rates in the market rise, the equity markets normally retreat (it becomes relatively more interesting to invest in fixed-income instruments) which will reduce the intrinsic value of the embedded option which is directly linked to the stock price of the issuing firm.

**Valuation aspects which relate to convertible bonds**
In terms of convertible bond valuation, there are two key elements: (1) the value of the stocks into which the bond can be converted and (2) the value of the bond as a debt instrument. The third could be how (1) and (2) come together in a hybrid instrument.

**The conversion value**
The conversion value is the value of a convertible bond in terms of the stock value (CV). Its value is dependent on (1) the face value or principal value of the bond (FV), (2) the conversion price of the bond (CP) and (3) the market price of the common stock (MP). The face value divided by the conversion price of the bond gives the number of shares into which the bond may be converted. If a bond of €2,000 can be converted at €20 per share, then the bond will be converted into 100 shares (2,000/20). The number of shares multiplied by the market price of

a share gives the market value of the bond in stock terms. So, for example, if the market price is €25 then the bond value in stock terms is 100 * €25 = €2,500.

The conversion ratio is therefore: FV/ CP
The conversion value is the product of: CV = FV/CP * MP or CV = FV/conversion ratio

Let's take our example a bit further. In Table 4.1, the left side is the actual market price at different times, the middle column is the shares into which the bonds can be converted, and on the right is the value of the bond in stock value terms.

The relationship between the price of the stock and the conversion value of the bond is illustrated in Figure 4.1. The stock price and the conversion value of the bond are given. As the price of the stock rises, the conversion value of the bond increases. The line represents the intrinsic value of the bond in stock terms. When the stock has a market value of €20, the market price equals the exercise price and the bond, in stock terms, has the same value as the principal amount of the underlying debt instrument. In cases where the stock price rises above the exercise price, the bond's value in stock terms will exceed the principal value of the underlying debt instrument.

Therefore, the market value of a convertible bond cannot be lower than the bond's conversion value. If that happened, an opportunity to arbitrage would exist. The investors would sell the stock short, buy the convertible bond, exercise the conversion feature and use the shares to cover the short sale position. Their gain would be the difference between the price of the convertible bond and its conversion value. In our example, let's say our bond was selling at €1,500 when the stock sold for €20 per share. At €20 per share, the bond is worth €2,000 in terms of the stock (€20 * 100). The investors would sell 100 shares short for €2,000, buy the bond for €1,500 and convert the bond (i.e., exercise the option). After the shares were acquired, they would cover the short position and earn themselves €500. This phenomenon will drive up the price of the bond and the pricing wedge will disappear. This would happen if the price of the bond as a debt instrument became equal to or higher than the bond's value in stock value terms. The market price of the convertible bond, on the other hand, is rarely equal or even close to the conversion value of the bond. Often, the convertible bond is valued above its conversion value (embedded option is 'in the money').

**The convertible debt as a fixed-income instrument**
The fixed-income value (FIV) of a convertible bond is driven by the principal aspects of every debt instrument: (1) the semi-annual interest payment ($i$), (2) current interest rate on the

**Table 4.1**  Relationship between the stock price and the value of the bond in equity terms based on the conversion rate

| Stock price (Euro) | Shares in which the instrument can be converted | Value of the bond in stock terms (Euro) |
|---|---|---|
| 0 | 100 | 0 |
| 3 | 100 | 300 |
| 10 | 100 | 1,000 |
| 15 | 100 | 1,500 |
| 20 | 100 | 2,000 |
| 25 | 100 | 2,500 |
| 30 | 100 | 3,000 |

market of comparable debt ($mi$) and (3) retirement of principal amount (FV) at maturity (assuming the bond is not converted).

The fixed-income value of the convertible debt is:

$$FIV = i/(1 + mi)1 + i/(1 + mi)2 + \ldots + i/(1 + mi)n + FV/(1 + mi)n$$

Or, put simply, it is the current price of any (non-convertible) bond.

Let's go back to our example. Let's say it is a 10-year bond and pays a 5% interest rate annually. Non-convertible debt with the same risk profile currently yields 8% in the market. The investment value of the bond as non-convertible debt then would become:

$$FIV = €100/(1 + 0.08)1 + €100/(1 + 0.08)2 + \ldots €100/(1 + 0.08)10 + €2,000/(1 + 0.08)10$$
$$FIV = €100 (6.710) + €2,000 (0.463) = €1,597$$

Using the present value tables, the equation can be solved.

## Discount Factors

**Present value of \$1, discounted to the $n$th year**

| n | 0% | 1% | 2% | 3% | 4% | 5% | 6% | 7% | 8% | 9% | 10% |
|---|------|--------|--------|--------|--------|--------|--------|--------|--------|--------|--------|
| 1 | 1.0000 | 0.9901 | 0.9804 | 0.9709 | 0.9615 | 0.9524 | 0.9434 | 0.9346 | 0.9259 | 0.9174 | 0.9091 |
| 2 | 1.0000 | 0.9803 | 0.9612 | 0.9426 | 0.9246 | 0.9070 | 0.8900 | 0.8734 | 0.8573 | 0.8417 | 0.8264 |
| 3 | 1.0000 | 0.9706 | 0.9423 | 0.9151 | 0.8890 | 0.8638 | 0.8396 | 0.8163 | 0.7938 | 0.7722 | 0.7513 |
| 4 | 1.0000 | 0.9610 | 0.9238 | 0.8885 | 0.8548 | 0.8227 | 0.7921 | 0.7629 | 0.7350 | 0.7084 | 0.6830 |
| 5 | 1.0000 | 0.9515 | 0.9057 | 0.8626 | 0.8219 | 0.7835 | 0.7473 | 0.7130 | 0.6806 | 0.6499 | 0.6209 |
| 6 | 1.0000 | 0.9420 | 0.8880 | 0.8375 | 0.7903 | 0.7462 | 0.7050 | 0.6663 | 0.6302 | 0.5963 | 0.5645 |
| 7 | 1.0000 | 0.9327 | 0.8706 | 0.8131 | 0.7599 | 0.7107 | 0.6651 | 0.6227 | 0.5835 | 0.5470 | 0.5132 |
| 8 | 1.0000 | 0.9235 | 0.8535 | 0.7894 | 0.7307 | 0.6768 | 0.6274 | 0.5820 | 0.5403 | 0.5019 | 0.4665 |
| 9 | 1.0000 | 0.9143 | 0.8368 | 0.7664 | 0.7026 | 0.6446 | 0.5919 | 0.5439 | 0.5002 | 0.4604 | 0.4241 |
| 10 | 1.0000 | 0.9053 | 0.8203 | 0.7441 | 0.6756 | 0.6139 | 0.5584 | 0.5083 | 0.4632 | 0.4224 | 0.3855 |
| 11 | 1.0000 | 0.8963 | 0.8043 | 0.7224 | 0.6496 | 0.5847 | 0.5268 | 0.4751 | 0.4289 | 0.3875 | 0.3505 |
| 12 | 1.0000 | 0.8874 | 0.7885 | 0.7014 | 0.6246 | 0.5568 | 0.4970 | 0.4440 | 0.3971 | 0.3555 | 0.3186 |
| 13 | 1.0000 | 0.8787 | 0.7730 | 0.6810 | 0.6006 | 0.5303 | 0.4688 | 0.4150 | 0.3677 | 0.3262 | 0.2897 |
| 14 | 1.0000 | 0.8700 | 0.7579 | 0.6611 | 0.5775 | 0.5051 | 0.4423 | 0.3878 | 0.3405 | 0.2992 | 0.2633 |
| 15 | 1.0000 | 0.8613 | 0.7430 | 0.6419 | 0.5553 | 0.4810 | 0.4173 | 0.3624 | 0.3152 | 0.2745 | 0.2394 |
| 16 | 1.0000 | 0.8528 | 0.7284 | 0.6232 | 0.5339 | 0.4581 | 0.3936 | 0.3387 | 0.2919 | 0.2519 | 0.2176 |
| 17 | 1.0000 | 0.8444 | 0.7142 | 0.6050 | 0.5134 | 0.4363 | 0.3714 | 0.3166 | 0.2703 | 0.2311 | 0.1978 |
| 18 | 1.0000 | 0.8360 | 0.7002 | 0.5874 | 0.4936 | 0.4155 | 0.3503 | 0.2959 | 0.2502 | 0.2120 | 0.1799 |
| 19 | 1.0000 | 0.8277 | 0.6864 | 0.5703 | 0.4746 | 0.3957 | 0.3305 | 0.2765 | 0.2317 | 0.1945 | 0.1635 |
| 20 | 1.0000 | 0.8195 | 0.6730 | 0.5537 | 0.4564 | 0.3769 | 0.3118 | 0.2584 | 0.2145 | 0.1784 | 0.1486 |
| 21 | 1.0000 | 0.8114 | 0.6598 | 0.5375 | 0.4388 | 0.3589 | 0.2942 | 0.2415 | 0.1987 | 0.1637 | 0.1351 |
| 22 | 1.0000 | 0.8034 | 0.6468 | 0.5219 | 0.4220 | 0.3418 | 0.2775 | 0.2257 | 0.1839 | 0.1502 | 0.1228 |
| 23 | 1.0000 | 0.7954 | 0.6342 | 0.5067 | 0.4057 | 0.3256 | 0.2618 | 0.2109 | 0.1703 | 0.1378 | 0.1117 |
| 24 | 1.0000 | 0.7876 | 0.6217 | 0.4919 | 0.3901 | 0.3101 | 0.2470 | 0.1971 | 0.1577 | 0.1264 | 0.1015 |
| 25 | 1.0000 | 0.7798 | 0.6095 | 0.4776 | 0.3751 | 0.2953 | 0.2330 | 0.1842 | 0.1460 | 0.1160 | 0.0923 |

To be attractive to investors relative to non-convertible debt in the market, the bond would have to sell at €1,597. The relationship between the price of the common stock and the value of the bond as non-convertible debt is illustrated in Figure 4.1. The horizontal line shows the

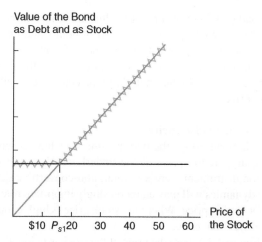

**Figure 4.1** The actual minimum price of a convertible bond

price of the bond if it were non-convertible to equity (€1,597). The principal amount of the bond is also indicated (€2,000). The principal amount is higher than the value of the bond as a fixed-income instrument since it has to trade at a discount to be equally attractive to investors (see Tables 4.2 and 4.3).

As indicated, the value of the bond varies with interest rates in the market. And since the interest rate on the bond is fixed, the value of the bond as fixed-income instrument varies accordingly. As the interest rate goes up, the value will fall and vice versa. This relationship is indicated in Table 4.2. The first column indicates the market interest rate, the second the fixed interest rate on the product, and the column on the right shows the value of the bond as a fixed-income instrument (FI instrument). It is assumed that the interest on the instrument is paid annually.

The value of the bond as non-convertible debt is the minimum value that the bond will carry in the market. It competes at that level with other non-convertible debt in the market with the same maturity and risk profile. If the bond sold below this level, it would become attractive relative to other similar debt and investors would buy into the instrument to get access to a higher than risk-adjusted yield. By doing so they would help elevate the price of the bond until it was on par with other non-convertible debt with similar characteristics. The bond's value as non-convertible debt is the floor for the price in the market. Even if the underlying stock value price dropped significantly, it would be halted by this bottom value. The curve reflects the

**Table 4.2** Relationship between interest rates and bond values

| Market interest rate (%) | Coupon rate (%) | Convertible bond valued as FI instrument (Euro, rounded off) |
| --- | --- | --- |
| 3 | 5 | 2,341 |
| 4 | 5 | 2,163 |
| 5 | 5 | 2,000 |
| 6 | 5 | 1,852 |
| 7 | 5 | 1,718 |
| 8 | 5 | 1,597 |
| 10 | 5 | 1,386 |
| 12 | 5 | 1,209 |

value of a convertible bond both in terms of its FI value and of its underlying stock value. The value will always be higher than or equal to the higher of both valuations. If not, arbitrageurs or investors will step in, and by doing so will correct the differential.

Ultimately, when stock prices are low (below $P_{s1}$ in the chart) the minimum price will be the bond's value as debt. For prices higher than $P_{s1}$ in the chart, the bond's value as stock will determine the minimum price.

**The convertible bond as a hybrid security**

The value of a convertible bond brings the two dynamics we have discussed together (valuation as debt and as equity). If the price of the underlying shares drops significantly, the valuation will be as if the instrument were a normal, non-convertible debt. If the stock rises significantly, the equity dynamics will play an increasingly important role in the determination of the convertible bond's market price. Where the stock price is high enough, the market price will match that of the conversion value.

This is illustrated in Figure 4.2, where the price of the stock is below $P_{s1}$, the market value of the CD is equal to similar non-convertible debt. Above $P_{s2}$ levels, the value of the CD is equal to that of the underlying stock price valuation. At the extremes, it will become pure debt or equity in terms of its valuation. For price points between $P_{s1}$ and $P_{s2}$, the market value will be influenced by both the value of debt and equity. Depending on where the price point is on the continuum between $P_{s1}$ and $P_{s2}$, the dominant dynamic in valuation terms will be either that of non-convertible debt or equity.

Valuation of a CD can therefore be approached from the perspective of the premium the CD is valued at versus its valuation level as non-convertible debt or equity. This would allow for comparison between CD and similar characteristics, and might trigger buying or selling of certain instruments.

The premium dynamic is summarized in Table 4.3. It brings together previous tables and adds the premium analysis. From the left column to the right, the following items are reflected: (1) Price of the equity (€), (2) Number of shares into which the CD can be converted, (3) Conversion value of CD in equity terms (€), (4) Value of CD as non-convertible debt (€), (5) Market price of the convertible bond €), (6) Premium vis-à-vis the value in equity terms (€) and (7) Premium vis-à-vis the value as non-convertible debt (€).

For clarification purposes: column 6 equals column 5 (market price bond) minus column 3 (conversion value as stock), and column 7 equals column 5 (market price bond) minus column 4

**Table 4.3**  Summary of premium dynamic

| Price of the equity instrument (€) | Number of shares into which the CD can be converted | Conversion value of CD in equity terms (€) | Value of CD as non-convertible debt (€) | Market price of the convertible bond (€) | Premium vis-à-vis the value in equity terms (€) | Premium vis-à-vis the value as non-convertible debt (€) |
|---|---|---|---|---|---|---|
| 0 | 100 | 0 | 1,597 | 1,597 | 1,597 | 0 |
| 3 | 100 | 300 | 1,597 | 1,597 | 1,297 | 0 |
| 10 | 100 | 1,000 | 1,597 | 1,597 | 597 | 0 |
| 15 | 100 | 1,500 | 1,597 | 1,850 | 350 | 253 |
| 20 | 100 | 2,000 | 1,597 | 2,200 | 200 | 603 |
| 25 | 100 | 2,500 | 1,597 | 2,600 | 100 | 1,003 |
| 30 | 100 | 3,000 | 1,597 | 3,000 | 0 | 1,403 |

(value as non-convertible debt). A comparison of columns 6 and 7 demonstrates the inverse relationship between both premiums. Figure 4.2 below also shows where the market price of the CD, the value in stock terms and the value in non-convertible debt terms are brought together.

What the figure shows us makes sense: when the price of the stock is low, and therefore the bond is trading close to the value of the CD as non-convertible debt, the premium above the intrinsic value of the CD as stock is substantial, but the premium above the bond's value of debt is minimal. The other way around is true too. The conclusion, therefore, can be that the premium paid for the bond over its value as equity declines as the price of the stock increases. The decline in value of the premium is due to the impact of the conversion value on the CD's market price (and also the decreasing impact of the debt element). When the stock's price rises, the safety feature of the debt instrument loses value. In cases where this happens in a significant way, the risk that the bond will be called also increases.

Despite the safety feature combined with the equity upside, CDs are often an inferior investment. In cases where the stock price rises, the stock itself is a better investment as it will yield larger capital appreciation than the rise in market value of the CD. This is because the CD investor paid a premium to get insurance and downside protection. The other way around, when the stock price goes down, a normal non-convertible loan will yield a larger interest income for the investor relative to a CD. So what makes it strong (safety plus upside) are also its weaknesses (inferior growth relative to stock and lower interest income compared to non-convertible debt with similar characteristics).

On top of all that, in cases where the debt was bought at a premium above its debt value, there is a substantial risk of loss if the stock price comes down (although the loss on the bond will be smaller than the loss on the underlying stock). This happens without interest rates in the market moving.

As a final note, we have approached this topic from the perspective of the value of the bond as stock or as non-convertible debt. One could turn it around and express the value of the stock in terms of the bond's pricing, i.e., conversion parity.

Conversion parity = Market price of the bond/conversion ratio

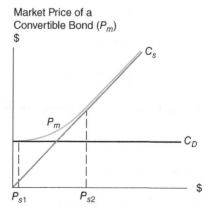

**Figure 4.2**    Market price of a convertible bond

Let's assume:

- Price of the bond = €1,000
- FV of the bond = €1,500
- Conversion rate = 1/30 (the bond is convertible into 50 shares of €20 each)
- Conversion parity: 1,000/(1,500/20) = 13.33
- The value of the stock in bond terms is €13.33. The stock can trade at a premium or discount relative to this value. It is therefore an alternative way to determine the premium paid for a convertible.

## Convertible bonds – application

*Convertible bond features*

| | |
|---|---|
| • Issuer: | Anglo-American plc |
| • Settlement date: | September 24, 2002 |
| • Issue date: | April 17, 2002 |
| • Redemption date: | April 17, 2007 |
| • Issue price: | 100 |
| • Redemption price (at maturity): | 100 |
| • Currency: | USD |
| • Denominations: | 10,000 |
| • Coupon: | $3\frac{3}{8}\%$ |
| • Yield to maturity: | 4.85% |
| • Coupon frequency: | Semi-annually (April & October 17) |
| • Day basis: | Actual/Actual |
| • Conversion ratio per 10,000: | 432.5259 |
| • Initial exchange rate: | £1 = $1.4333 |
| • Conversion start: | March 28, 2002 |
| • Conversion end: | April 3, 2007 |
| • Issuer call start date: | May 9, 2005 |
| • Call trigger price: | 130% |
| • Redemption value (if called): | Par |
| • Current convertible price: | 101.00 |
| • Current share price: | £8.45 |
| • Dividend yield: | 4.00% |
| • Historical volatility: | 35% |
| • Current exchange rate: | £1 = $1.5659 |

*Related Questions*    Calculate the following making sure you have taken into account the exchange rate where appropriate.

1. The conversion price (in GBP).
2. Parity (as a % of the USD bond's nominal).
3. Conversion premium.
4. The investment floor (using a yield to maturity of 4.85%).
5. The investment /risk premium.

*Solutions*
1. (410,000/1.4333)/432.5259 = £16.13
2. (£8.45 × 432.5259 × 1.5659) = 5,723.12 per $10,000 nominal, so 57.23 per $100
3. (101.00 − 57.23)/57.23 = 76.48%
4. 94.02
5. (101−94.02/94.02)x100 = 7.42%

## 4.2.2 Convertible preferred stock (CPS)

As the name implies, this stock may be converted into common stock of the issuing firm. The product shows many similarities with CDs, but also a number of noteworthy differences. The differences can be defined along the lines of the differences between preferred convertibles and non-convertible debt. The former is considered equity – so there is no obligation to pay a dividend – and can be perpetual unlike debt. Many convertible preferred stocks have a sinking fund requirement and are callable.

The value of CPS is related to the price of the stock into which it may be converted and to the value of competing non-convertible preferred stock. These values, as is the case with CDs, set floors on the valuation of the instrument. It therefore cannot trade below its value as common stock, as it would trigger investors stepping in and buying the price up.

The minimum value of CPS will be equal to the conversion value (CV) of the stock:

CV = market price of stock into which CPS can be converted multiplied by
the number of shares obtained after conversion.

The CPS value as non-convertible preferred stock (perpetual) is a function of the dividend it pays and an appropriate discount factor, which is the return on alternative non-convertible preferred stocks or:

CPS value as non-CPS = dividends/yield on alternative non-CPS.

That is pretty much in line with what we discussed regarding CDs, with the exception that there is no maturity here. However, it sets a pricing floor as, at this level, it is equally attractive relative to non-CPS.

As it is a hybrid security, its value will be dependent on the value of common stock as well as the value of non-CPS. It can be noted, though, that the premium the instrument carries over non-CPS is smaller than with the premium carried by CDs (relative to non-CD). The reason for this is that the dynamics of the CPS instrument are pretty close to that of common stock and therefore lack the safety of a debt instrument, therefore the premium over its value as common stock is more modest.

Just like with CDs, the product can have many different features attached. One particular instrument is the 'convertible exchangeable preferred stock,' which includes two options. The holder may convert the shares into the firm's common stock, or the company may force the holder to convert the instrument into the firm's bonds. The exchange option gives the firm more control over the preferred stock, as it can force retirement of the shares without any cash outflow if the value of the common stock goes up or down. If the value goes up, the investor will convert the PS. If the firm uses the option to exchange bonds for the PS, the investor will convert or face a loss in capital appreciation. If the value of the common stock should decline, no one would convert. Without the exchange option, the firm would be without options. Now, with this option it can force the preferred shareholder to exchange the shares for debt.

An alternative instrument in this category is the 'preferred equity redemption cumulative stock' (PERCS). This is a preferred stock but with options embedded. It has, however, the built-in feature that the instrument will be redeemed (exchanged) at a certain point in the future, into the firm's common (thereby generating upside equity potential for the investor). The redemption feature can have conditions attached; for example, the redemption can only take place if the value of the CS is at a certain level.

### Embedded call options[3]

The benefit of an embedded option in hybrid products is the issuer's ability to force the holder to convert into stock (and save on interest payments or fixed dividends). It can also be done if the firm believes that it can refinance itself at a lower cost (although the cost of calling might come close to equaling the NPV lost by the current holder until the instrument reaches maturity). Forced conversion also improves the firm's balance sheet, with less debt and more equity. The reduction in leverage has been achieved without any (further) cash outflows.

To ensure that enforcement of conversion will happen, management will wait until the price has sufficiently risen to ensure that once the call is out, the stock price cannot drop below the exercise price (which would lead to investors not converting their instruments but accepting the call).

### Embedded put options

The put bond permits the holder to sell the instrument back to the issuer. The firm must therefore redeem the bond at a specific date for its entire principal amount. The potential loss for investors (or the opportunity elsewhere) due to interest rate changes in the market has triggered put bonds to emerge. This is particularly true if investors have to commit funding for extended periods of time. So, if interest rates drop they sit tight or sell the convertible instrument at a premium. If interest rates rise in the market, the investor exercises the put option and re-invests at a higher rate in the market. Long-term borrowers engage in this, given the lower interest charge, despite the possible refinancing risk down the road. The put option comes at a cost to investors, i.e., the premium of the option comes in through a reduced interest rate on the instrument. The impact of the put on the valuation of the

---

[3] See further: Qi-yuan Zhou, Chong-feng Wu, Yun Feng 'Decomposing and valuing the callable convertible bonds,' Financial Engineering Research Center, Shanghai Jiao Tong University (2009). Also: Robert L. Navin, 'Convertible Bond Valuation: 20 Out Of 30 Day Soft-call,' *Quantitative Analysis and Quantitative Trading Strategy*, Highbridge Capital Management, LLC (1999) and Dr Russell Grimwood and Prof. Stewart Hodges, 'The Valuation of Convertible Bonds: A Study of Alternative Pricing Models,' Working Paper (2002) Warwick University. And further: Andreas J. Grau, Peter A. Forsyth and Kenneth R. Vetzal, 'Convertible Bonds with Call Notice Periods,' School of Computer Science, University of Waterloo, Canada (2003) and Stéphane Crépey, Abdallah Rahal, 'Pricing Convertible Bonds with Call Protection,' Équipe Analyze et Probabilité, Université d'Évry Val d'Essonne' (Winter 2011/12) *The Journal of Computational Finance* **15**(2):37–75.

instrument when interest rates change can be better understood by analyzing the following example:

---

## EXAMPLE

A company issues a bond (€1,000) with a 20-year maturity and 7% coupon. At the end of year 5 investors can redeem the bond at par. In cases where the option is not exercised, the product matures 15 years later. There is only one exercise date for the put option (in practice there might be more dates). Let's say the current interest rate is 5%. The value of the bond, then, is:

$$€70 * (12.46) + €1,000 * (0.377) = €1,248.2$$

The interest factors are the annuities at 5% for 20 years – that is the appropriate number of years, as the investor will not redeem the bond and the option will not impact on the price of the bond.

If the current interest rate were 10%, the current value of the bond would be:

$$€70 * (3.791) + €1,000 * (0.621) = €886.37$$

In this case, the interest factor is only at 10% for five years. Five years is the appropriate time as the investor will exercise the option and redeem the bond.

By comparing this value and the bond's value without the option (that is, at 10% for 20 years, because the bond has no put option), the value of the bond would be:

$$€70 * (8.514) + €1,000 * (0.149) = €744.98$$

The option increases the value of the bond by €886.37 – €744.98 = €141.39

The option impacts the value of the bond if interest rates rise. It reduces the amount by which the bond's price will fall, because the expected life of the instrument is until the redemption date and not the initial maturity date.

So, if interest rates stay stable from issuance, the issuer will benefit as they issue LT bonds at a lower than normal market price given the risk profile. If the interest rate rises, the holder benefits, because they can exit the investment and reinvest at higher rates. With inflation expectations going forward (medium to longer term) and consequently higher interest rates, this might be an attractive alternative to other types of LT debt instruments.

---

## Conclusion

Whichever way you take it, somebody pays the piper for having the option included in the instrument. The put option favors the investor and therefore interest rates are lower. The cost is the lost interest. The call feature favors the issuing firm and therefore the interest rate should be higher. The difference is the cost to get out via the call option. On the public side, it is noteworthy that trading volumes in these securities are much lower than in the underlying stocks of the issuing firms, and bid–ask spreads tend to be larger vis-à-vis the underlying stock.

The valuation of bonds with embedded options proceeds in the same fashion as in the case of an option-free bond. The complexity comes in when the cash flows have to be adjusted to reflect the embedded option. This will be based on how the option is structured, and the conditions and timing under which the put and call option can take place. The traditional valuation method is based on the idea that buying a convertible instrument is similar to buying common stock at a premium, with the premium recouped over time from the difference between the higher income from the convertible coupon and the lower dividend of the underlying stock. The payback vs. break-even period determines the attractiveness of buying the convertible versus buying the common stock; the shorter that payback period, the more attractive the convertible, especially when the payback is shorter than the call protection period. All valuation models used in practice can, in some way or the other, be brought back to the contingent claim (option pricing) analysis as discussed in Chapter 1. The only differences between the models used come down to the number of stochastic variables used in the construction of the model. The one-factor models assume that the stock return is the only stochastic variable. Therefore the valuation model breaks down, in terms of inputs, into:

- Descriptors and variables (which are either known or can be estimated, although with estimation errors): spot price of the underlying security, dividend yield of security, coupon, issuer redemption, maturity, investor put and liquidity and hedging costs.
- Stochastic variables: stock returns, interest rates, credit spreads and exchange rates.

The valuation of the embedded option, in conjunction with the fundamental equity analysis of the underlying security, will drive the holistic valuation process.

### 4.2.3 Valuation and pricing of (embedded) options

Before diving into the technicalities of the Black–Scholes Model, it might be wise to first have a look at how the model has been developed historically.

**The Black–Scholes Model – some history**

The Black–Scholes Model was first discussed in 1973 by Fischer Black and Myron Scholes, and then further developed by Robert Merton. It was for the development of the Black–Scholes Model that Scholes and Merton received the Nobel Prize for Economics in 1997. The idea of the Black–Scholes Model was first published in 'The Pricing of Options and Corporate Liabilities' in the *Journal of Political Economy*, by Fischer Black and Myron Scholes, and then elaborated in *Theory of Rational Option Pricing* by Robert Merton in 1973.

The Black–Scholes Model creators were academics; Myron Scholes was then the professor of finance at Stanford University, Robert Merton was an economist with Harvard University and Fischer Black was a mathematical physicist with a doctorate from Harvard. When Myron Scholes and Fischer Black tried to publish their idea of the Black–Scholes Model in 1970, Chicago University's *Journal of Political Economy* and Harvard's *Review of Economics and Statistics* both rejected the paper. It was only in 1973, after some influential members of the Chicago faculty put pressure on the journal editors, that the *Journal of Political Economy* published the Black–Scholes Model paper. Within six months of the article's publication, Texas Instruments had incorporated the Black–Scholes Model into its calculator, announcing the new feature with a half-page ad in *The Wall Street Journal*.

The three young Black–Scholes Model researchers – who were still in their twenties – set about trying to find an answer to derivative pricing using mathematics, exactly the way a physicist or an engineer approaches a problem. However, few thought that their approach would work, because options trading was very new and highly volatile (the CBOE opened in April 1973, just one month prior to the release of the Black–Scholes Model paper.) Mathematics could be applied using a little-known technique called stochastic differential equations, and that discovery led to the development of the Black–Scholes Model as we know it today.

The Black–Scholes Model has become a tool for equity options pricing. Prior to the development of the Black–Scholes Model, there was no standard options pricing method and nobody could put a fair price on options. The Black–Scholes Model turned that guessing game into a mathematical science which helped develop the options market into the lucrative industry it is today. Options traders compare the prevailing option price in the exchange against the theoretical value derived by the Black–Scholes Model in order to determine if a particular option contract is over- or under-valued, which assists them in their options trading decision. The Black–Scholes Model was originally created for the pricing and hedging of European call and put options as the American Options market, the CBOE, started only one month before the creation of the Black–Scholes Model. The difference in the pricing of European options and American options is that European options pricing does not take into consideration the possibility of early exercising (as discussed earlier). American options therefore command a higher price than European options, due to the flexibility to exercise the option at any time. The classic Black–Scholes Model does not take this extra value into consideration in its calculations.

### Black–Scholes Model inputs

The Black–Scholes model takes as input (1) current equity price, (2) the option's strike price, (3) length of time until the option expires worthless, (4) an estimate of future volatility known as implied volatility, and (5) risk-free rate of return, generally defined as the interest rate of short-term US treasury notes. The Black–Scholes Model also works in reverse: instead of calculating a price, an implied volatility for a given price can be calculated (see Figure 4.3).

Implied volatility is commonly calculated using the Black–Scholes Model in order to plot the volatility skew, which is the difference in implied volatility between out-of-the-money, at-the-money and in-the-money options.

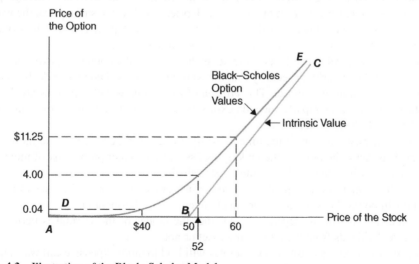

**Figure 4.3**   Illustration of the Black–Scholes Model

The mathematical characteristics of the Black–Scholes Model are named after five Greek letters, which are used to represent them in equations: Delta, Gamma, Vega, Theta and Rho. These are now passionately known to option traders as the 'Greeks.'

### The Black–Scholes Model – underlying assumptions

There are several assumptions underlying the Black–Scholes Model of calculating options pricing. The most significant is that volatility, a measure of how much a stock can be expected to move in the near term, is a constant over time. The Black–Scholes Model also assumes stocks move in a manner referred to as a random walk; at any given moment, they are as likely to move up as they are to move down.

The six assumptions that the Black–Scholes Model makes are:

1. Stock pays no dividends.
2. Option can only be exercised upon expiration.
3. Market direction cannot be predicted, hence the 'random walk' hypothesis.
4. No commissions are charged in the transaction.
5. Interest rates remain constant.
6. Stock returns are normally distributed, thus volatility is constant over time.

It goes without saying that the validity of many of these assumptions is questionable or invalid, resulting in theoretical values which are not always accurate. Hence, theoretical values derived from the Black–Scholes Model are only good as a guide for relative comparison and are not an exact indication to the over- or under-priced nature of a stock option, and by extension, of warrants.

However, it is important to have some understanding of the various influences on warrant prices. The market value of a warrant (as well as of an option) can be divided into two components:

- **Intrinsic value:** This is simply the difference between the exercise (strike) price and the underlying stock price. Warrants are also referred to as in-the-money or out-of-the-money, depending on where the current asset price is in relation to the warrant's exercise price. Thus, for example, for call warrants, if the stock price is below the strike price, the warrant has no intrinsic value (only time value, see below). If the stock price is above the strike, the warrant has intrinsic value and is said to be in-the-money.
- **Time value:** Time value can be considered as the value of the continuing exposure to the movement in the underlying security that the warrant provides. Time value declines as the expiry of the warrant gets closer. This erosion of time value is called time decay. It is not constant, but increases rapidly towards expiry (see below). A warrant's time value is affected by the following factors:
  - Time to expiry: The longer the time to expiry, the greater the time value of the warrant. This is because the price of the underlying asset has a greater probability of moving in-the-money which makes the warrant more valuable.
  - Volatility: The more volatile the underlying instrument, the higher the price of the warrant will be (as the warrant is more likely to end up in-the-money).
  - Dividends: This factor depends on whether the holder of the warrant is permitted to receive dividends from the underlying asset or not.
  - Interest rates: An increase in interest rates will lead to more expensive call warrants and cheaper put warrants. The level of interest rates reflects the opportunity cost of capital.

Warrants do not have an investment value because there is no interest, dividends, or voting rights. Therefore, the market value of a warrant is only attributable to its convertibility feature into common stock. However, the market price of a warrant is typically more than its theoretical value, which is referred to as the premium on the warrant. The lowest amount which a warrant will sell for is its theoretical value.

Warrants are thus, as discussed in Chapter 2, call options issued by (mainly private) firms, which give the holder the right to purchase shares at a fixed price from the firm. The main difference between a warrant and a standard call option is the fact that the firm is the writer of the warrant and issues new shares if the warrant is exercised by the holder. Exercising the warrant means that the firm receives cash equal to the exercise price and issues a new share to the holder. This means that at exercise, there are more shares outstanding. As such, the choice of exercising depends on what the stock price will be with the new shares outstanding, and the way to view a warrant is as an option on the firm's equity, not on a share of stock.

In order to see how this works we can use some simple notation:

$E$ is the value of the firm's equity at time $t$,
$S$ is the common share price of the outstanding shares at time $t$,
$N$ is the number of old common shares outstanding prior to any exercise of the warrants,
$W$ is the value of the warrant at time $t$,
$M$ is the number of warrants.
$X$ is the exercise price of the warrants.

The choice of whether to exercise a warrant at maturity is based on the following criteria: Exercise if

$$X < E + M*X/N + M$$

where    $E + M*X/N + M$ is the per share price if all the warrants are exercised.

If the stock price after all the warrants are exercised is greater than the warrant's exercise price, all holders of the warrants will exercise. Hence the payoff of a warrant at maturity is:

$$Max\ ((E + M*X/N + M) - X,0)$$

This is quite different to the payoff of a regular call option in that the payoff depends on the number of warrants outstanding. For regular call options the number of options outstanding does not affect the payoff, since in that case the exercise of the option does not change the number of shares outstanding.

This means that the payoff on the warrant depends on the value of equity at maturity and the value of the warrant is the usual value of a call option with an exercise price of $X$, a time to maturity of $T$, volatility, risk-free rate and an underlying asset of $E/N$. The underlying asset value is the value of $E/T$ today or $Et/N$. Hence the value of the warrant today must depend on the value of call option adjusted for the dilution effects of the warrants, or:

Warrant value $= N/N + M *$ Call (given that:    UAV $= Et/N$
                                                  Maturity $= T$
                                                  Rf $=$ Volatility $= \delta$ and exercise $= X$)

Usually, if I ask the question 'what is the value of equity?' the response is that it is current common share price times the number of shares outstanding. However, the real definition of the value of equity is:

$$\text{Value of Asset} - \text{Value of Liabilities (Debt)} = \text{Value of Equity}$$

If there are warrants outstanding, these, along with the common stock, represent a claim on the value of the firm's equity. As such, the value of equity at time 0, $Et$, is:

$$\textbf{Et} = \textbf{\# of common shares} \times \textbf{Common stock price} + \textbf{\# of warrants} \times \textbf{warrant price}$$
$$Et = N * St + M$$

The underlying asset value (UAV) is:

$$\textbf{UAV} = Et/N = N * St + M * Wt/N = St + M/N * Wt$$

And the value of the warrant then is

$$Wt = nN/M + N * \text{Call}$$

given that     $UAV = St + M/N * Wt$
Maturity: $T$
Exercise price: $X$
Risk-free rate: Rf
Volatility: $\delta$

What is somewhat awkward about this is that the value of the warrant depends on the value of the warrant. Consider the following example. A firm has issued 1 million warrants, with an exercise price of €20 and a maturity of two years. There are 22 million common shares outstanding with a current price of €15 per share. The continuously compounded 2-year risk-free rate is 4%, and the volatility estimate of the stock is .35. The value of the warrants would be:

$$Wt = 22/22 + 1 * \text{Call (BS model) given that}$$

UAV = 15 + 1/22 * $Wt$
Maturity = 2 years
Exercise price = 20
Risk-free rate = 4%
Volatility $\delta$ = .35

In order to solve for the warrant value we need to arbitrarily assume some warrant value. Let's assume that $Wt$ = €5.00. This would yield the following

$$Wt = 22/22 + 1 * \text{Call (BS model) given that}$$

UAV = 15 + 1/22 * 5 = 15.23
Maturity = 2 years

Exercise price = 20
Risk-free rate = 4%
Volatility $\delta$ = .35

A call with these attributes has a value of €1.92. With the dilution of .9565 (22/23 = .9565), the estimated warrant value is €1.83. This is not the $Wt$ = €5.00 that we started with. If we start with a warrant price of €1.83, going through all the steps yields a warrant price of €1.77. If we now start with €1.77, we end up with €1.77. This is the warrant price.

Now, reality is often not as simple as this. Often, the warrant is made dependent on multiple stocks, or there are warrants dependent on only one stock, but whose value is dependent on other securities. As this is somewhat (or even quite a lot) outside the scope of this book, I will not go into the specifics in detail here.[4] For those looking for some more details on warrants from a public markets and trading perspective, refer to the introductory but still read-worthy brochure issued by the Australian Securities Exchange in 2007.[5]

Before looking at the Black–Scholes Model, it needs to be mentioned that whereas the Black–Scholes Model values warrants using the entry equity price of the underlying asset, reality will often dictate that you go away with the actual value of the equity after you convert the warrants into common stock and/or sell your common stock, if those two moments in time are not the same (this is shown in the JJ Bars & Restaurants case study later in this chapter too). The Black–Scholes and exit valuation methodology can yield significantly different valuations simply based on an entry or exit valuation mechanism.

**Known problems of the Black–Scholes Model**
Now, I mentioned before that there are some issues with the BS model. In fact, it has often been stated that the demise of the hedge fund Long-Term Capital Management was due to some intrinsic faults in the model. Two of the three 'creators' (Merton and Scholes) worked at the indicated hedge fund, which went under in 1998.

First, the Black–Scholes Model assumes that the risk-free rate and the stock's volatility are constant. This is obviously wrong, as risk-free rate and volatility fluctuate according to market conditions. The longer the strike date, the more this becomes a problem.

Second, the Black–Scholes Model assumes that stock prices are continuous and that large changes (such as those seen after a merger announcement) don't occur.

Third, the Black–Scholes Model assumes a stock pays no dividends until after expiration.

Fourth, analysts can only estimate a stock's volatility instead of directly observing it, as they can for the other inputs.

Fifth, the Black–Scholes Model tends to overvalue far out-of-the-money calls and undervalue deep in-the-money calls.

Sixth, the Black–Scholes Model tends to misprice options which involve high-dividend stocks (as it assumes that stocks don't pay dividends, see above).

To deal with these limitations, a Black–Scholes Model variant known as ARCH, Autoregressive Conditional Heteroskedasticity, was developed. This variant replaces constant volatility with stochastic (random) volatility. A number of different models were developed after this, like the GARCH, E-GARCH, N-GARCH, H-GARCH, etc., all incorporating ever more

---

[4] Please refer to the excellent reading of Kian-Guan Lim and Eric Terry, 'The valuation of multiple stock warrants,' School of Business, Singapore Management University, Working Paper Series, 2009.
[5] Australian Securities Exchange, 'Warrants: Understanding trading and investment warrants,' 2007.

complex models of volatility. However, despite these known limitations, the classic Black–Scholes Model is still the most popular with options traders today due to its simplicity.

### Alternative to the Black–Scholes Model

As the Black–Scholes Model does not take into consideration dividend payments as well as the possibilities of early exercising, it frequently under-values American-style options. Let's remember that the Black–Scholes Model was initially invented for the purpose of pricing European-style options. As such, a new options pricing model called the Cox–Rubinstein binomial model was introduced (see below). It is commonly known as the Binomial Option Pricing Model or, simply, the Binomial Model, and was invented in 1979. This options pricing model is more appropriate for American-style options as it allows for the possibility of early exercise.

In summary of the above, and to contrast with the binomial option, the Black–Scholes Model can be represented as:

$$C_0 = S_0 N^{(d_1)} - Xe\text{-}rTN^{(d_2)}$$

Where: $d_1 = [\ln(S_0/X) + (r + \sigma^2/2)T]/ \sigma \sqrt{T}$

And: $d_2 = d_1 - \sigma \sqrt{T}$

And where:
$C_0$ = current option value
$S_0$ = current stock price
$N(d)$ = the probability that a random draw from a standard normal distribution will be less than $(d)$.
$X$ = exercise price
$e$ = 2.71828, the base of the natural log function
$r$ = risk-free interest rate (annualized continuously compounded rate on a safe asset with the same maturity as the expiration of the option; usually the money market rate for a maturity equal to the option's maturity).
$T$ = time to option's maturity, in years
$\ln$ = natural logarithm function
$\sigma$ = standard deviation of the annualized continuously compounded rate of return on the stock.

Even though, as mentioned before, the original Black–Scholes Model does not take dividends into consideration, an extension of the Black–Scholes Model proposed by Merton in 1973 alters it in order to take annual dividend yield into consideration. This model is not as widely used as the original, as not every company pays dividends.

Here's the Black–Scholes Model for Dividend Stocks formula:

$$C_0 = Se\text{-}dTN^{(d_1)} - Xe\text{-}rTN^{(d_2)}$$

Where: $d_1 = [\ln(S_0/X) + (r - d + \sigma^2/2)T]/ \sigma \sqrt{T}$

And: $d_2 = d_1 - \sigma \sqrt{T}$

### The alternative model[6]

The Binomial Option Pricing Model (BOPM) was invented by Cox–Rubinstein in 1979. It was originally invented as a tool to explain the Black–Scholes Model to Cox's students.

---

[6] Many more details can be found in Simon Benninga, *Financial Modeling*, MIT Press, 2008, 3rd edn.

However, it soon became apparent that the Binomial Model was a more accurate pricing model for American-style options. The Binomial Model is thus named as it returns two possibilities at any given time. Therefore, instead of assuming that an option trader will hold an option contract all the way to expiration like in the Black–Scholes Model, it calculates the value of the trader exercising their option, including possible future movement of the underlying asset, reflecting its effects on the present value of that option, thus giving a more accurate theoretical price of an American-style option.

The Binomial Model produces a binomial distribution of all the possible paths which a stock price could take during the life of the option. A binomial distribution, or what is simply known as a 'Binomial Tree,' assumes that a stock can only increase or decrease in price until the option expires, and then maps it out in a 'tree.' Here is a simplified version of a binomial distribution just for illustrative purposes.[7]

The following inputs were used:

- Two dates are used, date 0 is now and date 1 is one year from now.
- There are two assets in play, a stock and a bond. There is also a call option written into the stock.
- The stock price today is €50. At date 1 it will go up by 10% or down by 3%.
- The interest rate in the period is 6%.
- The call option matures at date 1 and has an exercise price $X = €50$.

This is the result when applying the BOPM model:

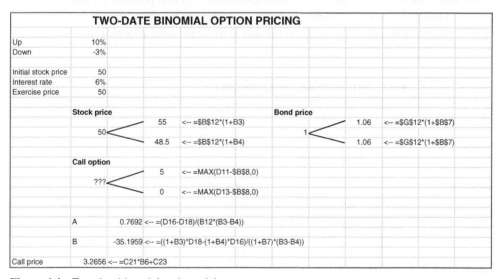

**Figure 4.4**  Two-date binomial option pricing

---

[7] Further information can be found at Darden School of Business, University of Virginia, 'Binomial option pricing note,' UVA-F 0943, http://faculty.darden.virginia.edu/conroyb/derivatives/binomial%20option%20pricing%20_f-0943_.pdf.

**TWO-DATE BINOMIAL OPTION PRICING WITH STATE PRICES**

| | | | | |
|---|---|---|---|---|
| Up | 10% | **State prices** | | |
| Down | -3% | $q_u$ | 0.6531 | <-- =(B7-B4)/((1+B7)*(B3-B4)) |
| | | $q_d$ | 0.2903 | <-- =(B3-B7)/((1+B7)*(B3-B4)) |
| Initial stock price | 50 | | | |
| Interest rate | 6% | | | |
| Exercise price | 50 | | | |
| **Call payoff** | | | | |
| In up state | 5 | <-- =MAX($B$6*(1+B3)-$B$8,0) | | |
| In down state | 0 | <-- =MAX($B$6*(1+B4)-$B$8,0) | | |
| Call price | 3.2656 | <-- =$E$4*B11+$E$5*B12 | | |
| **Put payoff** | | | | |
| In up state | 0 | <-- =MAX($B$8-(1+B3)*$B$6,0) | | |
| In down state | 1.5 | <-- =MAX($B$8-(1+B4)*$B$6,0) | | |
| Put price | 0.4354 | <-- =$E$4*B16+$E$5*B17 | | |
| **Put-call parity** | | | | |
| Stock + put | 50.4354 | <-- =B6+B18 | | |
| Call + PV(X) | 50.4354 | <-- =B13+B8/(1+B7) | | |

**Figure 4.5**  Two-date binomial option pricing with state prices

After having stated prices, and based on our previous analysis, this gives the results shown in Figure 4.5.

The Binomial Model can easily be extended to more than two periods. We can extend the previous two-period model to a three-period model, whereby the prices of the stock can go up by 10% and down by 3% in every period compared to the previous period. That gives:

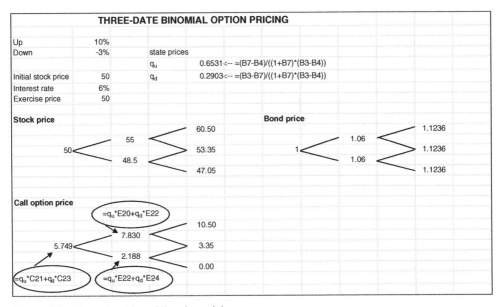

**Figure 4.6**  Three-date binomial option pricing

It then fills in the theoretical value of that stock's options at each time step from the very bottom of the binomial tree all the way to the top where the final, present, theoretical value of a stock option is arrived at. Any adjustments to stock prices at an ex-dividend date, or option prices as a result of early exercise of American options, are worked into the calculations at each specific time step.

The advantage of the Binomial Option Pricing Model is that it can more accurately price American-style options than the Black–Scholes Model, as it takes into consideration the possibilities of early exercise and other factors like dividends.

The main disadvantage of the Binomial Option Pricing Model is that it is much more complex than the Black–Scholes Model; it is slow in its roll-out and not useful for calculating thousands of option prices quickly.

### The Black–Scholes Model in Excel

The Black–Scholes Model can easily be calculated using Excel functions.

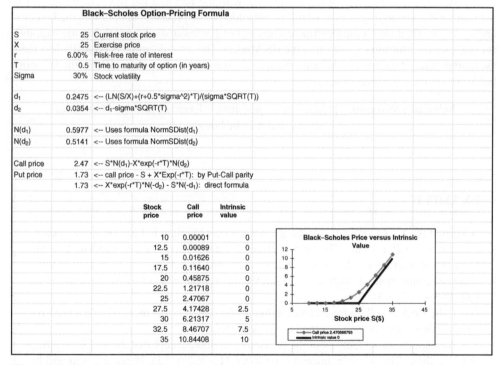

**Figure 4.7**    Black–Scholes option-pricing formula

### Valuing warrants issued by private firms

Quite a few of the inputs to the Black–Scholes Model are hard to identify when a private firm issued the warrants. The most difficult aspect is probably the volatility of the underlying stock for which the warrants can be exchanged. An easy way out would be to look at the volatility of peer firms which are listed. This practice triggers many arbitrary decisions about the comparability of the peer firms vis-à-vis the private firm in terms of size, country focus, where listed, and in terms of activities and whether that can be judged in an out of the ordinary way, i.e., thinking outside the box.

The simple alternative approach, as suggested by certain professionals, is to take the intrinsic in-the-money value – say Fair Market Value (FMV) price of the share as determined by the last financing round (in case of a VC backed firm, or a stand-alone valuation of the firm at the moment a valuation is needed, i.e., annual audit purposes) less the exercise price – of the warrants.

A potentially problematic feature is liquidity as, essentially, nobody would ever actually pay the intrinsic value as there is no market for the warrants, and in many private companies, there will be no natural liquidity event upcoming. This would, in itself, lead to an overvaluation of the warrants. However, it can be noted that the liquidity discount should already be priced into the FMV price of the private company shares, just like it is in a DCF valuation model, either through the discount rate or through an illiquidity discount at the end of the valuation.

*The valuation end-game*    We are now familiar with the fact that the theoretical value of a warrant (or the underlying option which is embedded to be precise, the option is the holder's ability to convert it into a pre-determined amount of common stock underlying the warrant) is computed by a formula (most often the BS Model). The formula value is typically less than the market price of the warrant because the speculative nature of a warrant allows the investor/holder to obtain some level of leverage:

**Value of a Warrant** = [Market price per share – Exercise price] × Number of shares that may be bought

---

### EXAMPLE

A warrant for XYZ Company's stock gives the owner the right to buy one share of common stock at €25 a share. The market price of the common stock is €53. The formula price of the warrant is €28 ((€53 – €25) × 1). If the owner had the right to buy three shares of common stock with one warrant, the theoretical value of the warrant would be €84 (€53 – €25) × 3).

If the stock is selling for an amount below the option price, there will be a negative value. A zero value is then assigned to the warrants.

Assume the same facts as in the previous example, except that the stock is selling at €21 a share. The formula amount is –€4((=€ 21 – € 25) × 1). However, zero will be assigned.

The value of a warrant depends (as mentioned before) on the remaining life of the option, dividend payments on the common stock, the fluctuation in price of the common stock, whether the warrant is listed on the exchange, and the investor's opportunity. There is a higher price for a warrant when its life is long, the dividend payment on common stock is small, the stock price is volatile, it is listed on the exchange, and the value of funds to the investor is great (because the warrant requires a lesser investment).

---

## (ANOTHER) EXAMPLE

XYZ stock has a market value of €50. The exercise price of the warrant is also €50. Thus, the theoretical value of the warrant is €0. However, the warrant will sell at a premium (positive price) if there is the possibility that the market price of the common stock will exceed €50 prior to the expiration date of the warrant. The more distant the expiration date, the greater the premium will be, since there is a longer period for possible price appreciation. The lower the market price relative to the exercise price, the less the premium will be.

Assume the same facts as in the previous example, except that the current market price of the stock is €35. In this case, the warrant's premium will be much lower since it would take longer for the stock's price to increase above €50 a share. If investors expect that the stock price would not increase above €50 at a later date, the value of the warrant would be €0.

If the market price of XYZ stock rises above €50, the market price of the warrant will increase and the premium will decrease.

Or, to wrap things up, when the stock price exceeds the exercise price, the market price of the warrant approximately equals the theoretical value so the premium disappears. The reduction in the premium arises because the advantage of owning the warrant compared to exercising it lessens.

---

## 4.3  CASE STUDY: JJ BARS & RESTAURANTS – MEZZANINE FOR EXPANSION

Dana Rosenzweig, an MD at Europewide Capital Partners (ECP), overlooks the city of Amsterdam from her corner office located next to the Vondelpark on November 18, 2011. Fall has been mild in 2011, but the temperature is heating up even more inside the office, as later that day there is an investment committee meeting and one of her proposals is included. The heat is on, because informal contacts with members of the committee have shown that this is not yet a done deal.

Dana's team has proposed a €20 million mezzanine investment in JJ Bars & Restaurants (JJ), a chain of restaurants in The Netherlands with significant growth potential. Dana was aware of the fact that some committee members were skeptical about investments in the restaurant or wining and dining industry altogether. Despite the growth of the industry, individual chains are exposed to risks which are out of the firm's control. An additional issue here was that, just because the chain was successful in The Netherlands, that didn't mean it would be able to roll out that success in other European countries. The question on the table was whether the brand was strong enough to travel across European countries which were, when it came to wining and dining, each characterized by their own preferences and tastes, and built around their own gastronomic heritage. Even if it were strong enough to travel across Europe and become a pan-European brand, the question remained whether it would provide adequate returns for the given investment and accompanying risk pattern.

Mezzanine investments were typically there to fill the gap between senior debt and equity, and consequently had characteristics of both. It also justified why the returns on mezzanine investments were somewhere between those on senior debt and common equity. Mezzanine investors were concerned about preserving capital (i.e., credit approach) as well as structuring the deal so that they could maximally benefit from the equity uptick (equity position).

Firms were often interested in mezzanine capital when senior debt was not available and they didn't want to dilute the equity stake of existing shareholders. Because the structuring of the deal and product choice could benefit both the firm and investors, mezzanine products were often used in a variety of situations.

Most products were structured in a way that included a coupon payment of some sort (i.e., debt feature) and an equity kicker. The product range could include profit-participating loans, convertible bonds, preferred shares, junior debt etc.

## 4.3.1 Europewide Capital Partners

ECP had a strong track record in Europe. The firm was founded in 1950 and had been working through a number of highly successful decades of providing debt, equity and equity-like solutions to firms across Europe with emphasis on the midcap sector. The company had performed well since inception and had earned 19.5% return for its investors over the years and across the funds. With more than €3 billion in assets, and having invested in over 250 companies over the years, ECP was a well-established household name in the investment world.

ECP focused on businesses in less cyclical companies, which included business services and consumer products to a large extent. It had considered investments across the transaction spectrum including buy-outs, acquisitions, growth capital and recapitalizations. Debt investments have traditionally ranged between €10–200 million; equity investments between €50–400 million.

## 4.3.2 The Dutch and European restaurant industry

In 2011, the European restaurant industry accounted for about 5% of European GDP, with about €400 billion in sales. Nominal sales growth was at around 8% per annum for the period 1980–2010. Sales were expected to grow at a compounded rate of about 3% per annum going forward, which was lower than in the years before the financial crisis of 2008, but that growth wasn't evenly spread across the different segments of the wining and dining industry (W&D). During the financial crisis the W&D market grew by a meager 0.5 and 1% in 2008–2009. It has somewhat recovered since then but, as mentioned, unevenly across sectors.

In fact, the industry only experienced negative sales growth during three years in the period 1980–2011 (see Dataset 1). The limited number of negative sales growth years was mainly due to the baby boomers who were aging and willing to spend, as well as a growing number of dual-income households and increased consumers for more convenience. The restaurant sector, ever since the early 2000s, had managed to take more share of the total food Euros spent. Outside-home spending had grown to 53% of total food expenditure in 2011 (it was only 25% in 1980 and 45% in 2000).

### 4.3.3 Industry segments

For the purposes of this transaction, ECP divided the restaurant business into three main categories: (1) quick-service restaurants, (2) family dining and (3) casual dining. The casual dining segment outpaced the other two in the period 2009–2011 in terms of growth, with an average 6% growth.

Quick-service restaurants (QSR) were fast-food restaurants which mainly competed on price and the speed of service. The average ticket per person was €4–8. Traditional quick-service restaurants included McDonalds, Burger King, Quick and the like. In recent years, a sub-segment had emerged called the 'fast casual.' The recipe was the higher quality food normally associated with casual dining, combined with the convenience of quick-service restaurants. The segment has been eating market share away from the QSR segment.

Family dining was known for its consistency, value and variety. The average ticket per person was €9–15. This segment was the most mature and losing steam, which mainly benefited the casual dining segment.

The casual dining segment was highly fragmented and accounted for about a third of total sales and growing. The segment had two sub-segments: the 'mid-end' and 'high-end.' This segmentation also characterized the newer and older concepts known in this part of the market. The mid-end segment had an average ticket per person of about €12–19, and the high-end from €16–30. Historically, this part of the segment was dominated by independent operators, but in recent years resto-chains have also maneuvered themselves into the market. The high-end market segment also experienced higher alcohol sales than all of the other segments mentioned. Dataset 2 gives a comparison.

The high-end casual sub-segment had been experiencing rapid growth, and some of the chains had managed to turn themselves into household names. In 2011, the median enterprise multiple was about 9 x EBITDA (that is after pre-opening expenses), with the best-known chain showing multiples of up to 18x EBITDA. Dataset 3 provides some further details.

### 4.3.4 JJ Bars & Restaurants

**Company information**

JJ was headquartered in Amsterdam, The Netherlands, and consisted of 10 locations (casual dining) across The Netherlands, mainly in the larger cities. The African-themed full-service restaurant served lunches and dinners, seven days a week. It offered an ethnically diverse menu, while blending some European-style features and entrées like fish, pasta, salads etc. Most of the entrées were priced below €10 and the average total ticket per person was €15–25. They served significant portions per person, enhancing the value proposition towards clients. Menus for lunch and dinner were the same and the offering was similar across all locations.

JJ focused more on the lunch segment relative to other restaurants, and there was a good reason for that. One of the key success factors in this industry was the ability to attract and retain top-talent managers. JJ decided that in order to make that happen, they should focus on offering the managers a good quality of life through their work–life balance. By focusing on lunch customers they were able to close at 11.00 pm during the weekends and 10.00 pm on weekdays (in comparison to the 2.00 am average across other restaurants). By focusing on lunches and offering the same menu, they leveraged on fixed costs. About 40% of their business came from lunches and about 25% (of overall sales) came from alcohol sales.

The first location was opened by Cornelis Claassen (who was born in South Africa and emigrated to The Netherlands in 1988 at the age of 21) in 1990, and the chain has been growing ever since, although most growth was experienced in the first decade of the 2000s. That, not surprisingly, coincides with the time when the management team was reshuffled and the concept redesigned. By doing so, they created a more relaxed atmosphere in their locations and a more standardized approach to their store set-up. The first four stores were opened in the 1990s and the other six after the turn of the century. Dataset 4 provides details on store openings and Dataset 5 on how the new concept locations outperformed the older ones.

The new concept locations accentuated the African theme much more. Each location had a large bar in the front of the restaurant with tables in the back and middle. Wherever possible, there was also an outdoor terrace or patio where African outdoor living was accentuated. The bar was appreciated by customers as it made the location more dynamic, waiters could oversee the restaurant better and could move around more easily. There were around 200 seats inside, plus another 100 at the bar and about 70 outdoors (on average). There was also consistently a look-through kitchen which enhanced transparency and reliability. The walls were painted with African themes from safaris to tribes to outdoor living. All finishes were in line with the African theme: dark wood, stripes, spotted carpets, bamboo fans, tropical plants and palms as well as a waterfall or other symbol of the African way of living, or natural dynamics of the Southern hemisphere, where possible. The client mix was made up of locals, expats and tourists in a 50/30/20% mix.

**Cost structure of the business**
The two important matrices in the restaurant business are the food cost to sales and the labor cost to sales ratios. The food to sales ratio is around 30%. Given their relatively small size (10 restaurants), they could not maximize their purchasing efficiencies, which left them in the middle of the industry range. Dataset 6 shows the comparison of cost dynamics with its peers. Other firms had advantages in their menu mix, such as serving less meat and therefore having lower overall costs, or serving more high-margin desserts. JJ was actively looking to decrease its costs levels, primarily by using a new point-of-sale system (POS – an IT system that basically tracked costs per store and made communication with headquarters more efficient and streamlined). For the foreseeable future, however, they would be too small to be eligible for a national or international distribution contract, and so working on the menu was the only way to further decrease the business's food cost.

Having all of its locations in urbanized areas in The Netherlands made its employee cost significantly higher than those chains located in other countries or with diversifiable business across the region. Minimum wages combined with social security contributions and very high payroll taxes delivered a comparative disadvantage.

Another disadvantage with respect to employee costs was the fact that in the new concept, a relatively high number of employees were put to work in each location, particularly in the first few months when the firm tried to identify traffic patterns so that it could adjust its headcount accordingly (see further details in Dataset 6). As the number of locations increased, and locations became more geographically dispersed, it took more managers and travel time to oversee operations and keep tight control over activities.

**Maintenance, remodeling and other costs**
Maintenance and remodeling (M&R) costs were always higher than expected and requiring investments that dampened returns. ECP was aware of this as it had previous experience on

this front. It was a critical cost, though, as JJ wanted to ensure that all locations looked fresh and comfortable at any given point in time. You can only make a first impression one time. Cornelis, however, considered that because most locations were relatively new, the cost for M&R would be moderate. On top of that, the good news was that JJ had a policy where each restaurant manager each year set aside €60,000 for cosmetic operations as a kind of reserve for future expenditures. Spending about €150,000 every five years per restaurant, that reserve had usually, in previous years, taken the issues off the table, and the group never experienced a slow-down in traffic in any of its locations due to a run-down look and feel.

The firm had always been frugal when it came to general and administrative (G&A) expenditures, but, as indicated, the need for new hires and increasing training costs for the new locations always made the exercise a challenge.

### Cornelis and his team
Cornelis (who was the founder and CEO) started this business in 1990. JJ was a concept which he tried in South Africa during his time there. He sold the few stores he had in the mid-1980s before moving back to The Netherlands. In that sense he hit the ground running when he started operations in The Netherlands. Back in South Africa he operated the few stores as part of a larger chain operated by his family. His strength was clearly innovative concept design and the impact it had on menu and other related choices. His creativity led often to unusual dishes and ingredient choices. He also hired his right-hand, Truus Berkhout, who was hired as COO after a 15-year stint in an independent family-operated chain of only three – but top-rated – restaurants in the south of the country. This allowed Cornelis to work more on strategy, cost-cutting and the necessary visionary activities. The rest of the team were all seasoned individuals with at least 15 years in the profession.

Cornelis owned 25% of the firm and the rest of the management team accounted for an additional 15%. He wanted to see the next move forward happen without any further dilution of the existing shareholders' equity stake. His large equity position undoubtedly contributed to him being able to put pressure on private equity firms to consider financing the next expansion round through mezzanine debt rather than equity, which theoretically would be the most appropriate financing tool for an expansion of this nature.

### The majority equity owner
The rest of the equity stake in the firm was owned by ROJ, a private equity player who, through a recapitalization in 2000, got their hands on the majority stake. Back then, they paid about €15.5 million or €2.50 per share. The transaction provided some liquidity to Cornelis and sufficient fuel for growth which, as previously mentioned, accelerated after 2000 (six out of 10 stores opened after 2000). The firm had a long history of investing in restaurant and related businesses and stayed confident about the outlook for JJ and its growth prospects.

### The path and strategy to growth
As previously mentioned, all 10 locations were in The Netherlands and performance had been good even in less urbanized or less cosmopolitan environments than Amsterdam, where it all started. The Netherlands had been keeping the balls in the air pretty well during the recent and, in fact, still ongoing financial crisis. Their experience outside the capital, Amsterdam, led them to believe that there were larger opportunities abroad and particularly in the neighboring

countries. They therefore planned to open another four stores in 2012–2013 – two in Belgium and two in Germany – to increase the company's diversification profile. If things went well they wanted to increase that number in the period 2014–2015 and further diversify into other countries. Cornelis noticed many Belgian and German visitors in locations close to the Dutch border with those countries. Additionally, the economy of these countries was very interwoven with that of The Netherlands and Cornelis was therefore very positive about the diversification and expansion plans, although the chain had no presence and was not known in Belgium or Germany.

**Geographical distribution of locations**

|                        | 2011 | 2012 | 2013 | 2014 | 2015 |
|------------------------|------|------|------|------|------|
| **Total stores**       | 10   | 12   | 14   | 16   | 19   |
| **Total non-Dutch stores** | 0    | 2    | 4    | 6    | 9    |

The expansion envisaged after 2013 was made dependent on the success of the roll-out in 2012–2013. The diversification was also driven by the fact that there was not only national concentration, but also concentration in revenue terms, as five stores accounted for about 70% of total revenue. The newer stores were doing well in terms of profits and cash flows but were less consistent than the older ones which had lower, but more consistent, profit and cash flow generating capability.

Cornelis and his team had been extensively studying the expansion plans. Their experience was that the new locations always followed a certain pattern in terms of performance. Revenues geared up in the first year to stabilize towards the end of that first year. From year two onwards, sales normally pitched at about 90% and then grew at a certain level going forward. Locations were profitable often from month two onwards after operations commenced.

Their choice to be in urbanized areas had everything to do with the fact that they focused on lunch customers and therefore always looked for locations where, within a certain radius, there was a high concentration of employees (a median of about 30,000 in a 5 km radius). Their choices in Belgium were Antwerp and Ghent, and in Germany, Cologne and Düsseldorf for the same effect. They often looked for locations which were free-standing, with good visibility and with decent car traffic (about 50,000 cars per day) on the neighboring streets. They tried to be close to malls or other concentrations of wining and dining outlets. With their value proposition they appealed most to middle-income earners, who were in fact their target audience.

The cash investment was relatively low compared to the rest of the market and was about €2 million per location. That is about a third less than the €3 million median in the industry.

ROJ had contacted ECP during 2011 to discuss the proposed transaction. ROJ and ECP had worked successfully in the past on similar deals in the restaurant industry. Given the aggressive expansion plans to increase the capacity of the group by 40% in two years' time, there was no doubt that the group needed the additional capital. After talks between ROJ and ECP, they decided to make the investment capital available in stages. They also decided that a subordinated note (secured by a second lien) for the aggregate value of €20 million was the most appropriate instrument which would mature five years after closing. The investment would pay a 10% interest rate and a 4% PIK (paid-in-kind) interest. There was senior debt provided by Rabobank secured on the assets of the existing stores, but ECP would have a first lien on the assets of the new stores. Datasets 7 and 8 provide further deal terms and historical financial statements.

JJ would have, due to its aggressive growth strategy, negative cash flows for quite a number of years, and would therefore not be able to pay off debt during that period. Equity instruments were most common to fund operations in situations like this, both ROJ and ECP agreed, but Cornelis was convinced that given the intrinsic strength of the group it could meet any interest payments which would come with a mezzanine investment. Given the risk that came (and the longer-term upside) with such investments, ECP had tentatively been talking to Cornelis about receiving a 3% equity stake through warrants which were to be issued at the time the first €5 million was drawn.

## The investment committee and its decision

Before going into the meeting Dana was aware that at least one committee member was skeptical (to say the least) about the deal. Part of it had to do with him not liking the 'look and feel' of the locations, and wondering why the Belgians, with their rather Latin/German oriented and excellent home-grown cuisine (which was known as 'French quality, German quantity'), would be attracted to the concept. Also the Germans with their typical German-style food – were they really looking for what he considered a rather kitschy concept? Even if the concept would travel abroad, would the menu do the same? The diversified menu, with any ingredients used in one dish often only being used in that one dish, only served to raise concerns with the committee members about the chain's ability to capture economies of scale.

To make things worse, a few weeks previously, one of their locations had been impacted by a case of food infected by the q-fever bacterium. As it was unclear at this point in time if there would be an impact on customers, this could have turned into a massive PR disaster for the firm. This all points back to those uncontrollable risks mentioned at the beginning of the case study.

In order to gain approval, the proposal had to meet a certain IRR (internal rate of return) threshold. Given the uncertainties about growth prospects, sales projections and appetite for the concept abroad, some committee members saw this as an equity project with equity-like risks. Only when Dana was able to convince them that a target IRR of 17–18% was realistic on top of a 1.5x to 2x (invested) cash back, did the whole thing start to look appealing, rather than dead in the water.

Cornelis and his team had been looking at the numbers and future performance. Their findings can be found in Dataset 9. In Dataset 10, Dana and her team have remodeled these numbers into a base-case scenario, assuming that management's assumptions are often too optimistic. The main differences between the two models are a lower level of sales and somewhat lower levels of expected cost-cutting, which would increase the use of the debt facilities available. The question here was how returns should look if management could not realize their projections. Given the increased risk, some committee members would argue for the adequateness of the warrant coverage (or possible expansion of the warrant program relative to what was initially discussed).

If things went well, however, opportunities would be endless. However, as a mezzanine investor, ECP was clearly more concerned with protecting its downside against the loss of principal rather than the equity uptick, which it only saw as adequate given the risk profile the instrument was exposed to.

## 4.3.5  Datasets

DATASET 1: EUROPEAN RESTAURANT INDUSTRY 1980–2011
(REAL SALES GROWTH IN %, POSITIVE UNLESS INDICATED)

| | | | |
|---|---|---|---|
| 1980 | −0.1 | 2003 | 2.1 |
| 1981 | 1.2 | 2004 | 3.2 |
| 1982 | 1.4 | 2005 | 4.3 |
| 1983 | 3.8 | 2006 | 5.7 |
| 1984 | 4.2 | 2007 | 5.4 |
| 1985 | 4 | 2008 | 3.1 |
| 1986 | 4.4 | 2009 | −0.9 |
| 1987 | 3.5 | 2010 | 1.5 |
| 1988 | 3.7 | 2011 | 2.9 |
| 1989 | 1.1 | | |
| 1990 | 0.4 | | |
| 1991 | −0.4 | | |
| 1992 | 2 | | |
| 1993 | 2.5 | | |
| 1994 | 3.1 | | |
| 1995 | 2.6 | | |
| 1996 | 2.5 | | |
| 1997 | 3.1 | | |
| 1998 | 2.1 | | |
| 1999 | 2.9 | | |
| 2000 | 3.2 | | |
| 2001 | 0.5 | | |
| 2002 | 1.1 | | |

DATASET 2: (SELECTED) HIGH-END CASUAL DINING
COMPARABLES

| | |
|---|---|
| Average | 19.5 |
| X | 29.5 |
| Y | 25.9 |
| Z | 18.4 |
| JJ | 20.1 |
| A | 15.9 |
| B | 26.6 |

## NUMBER OF OUTLETS

| | |
|---|---|
| A | 49 |
| B | 53 |
| C | 250 |
| X | 390 |
| Y | 120 |
| JJ | 10 |
| Average | 255 |

## SALES PER SQUARE METER (IN 000'S OF EURO)

| | |
|---|---|
| A | 90 |
| B | 60 |
| C | 50 |
| X | 55 |
| Y | 45 |
| JJ | 65 |
| Average | 50 |

## AVERAGE SALES PER UNIT (IN 000'S OF EURO)

| | |
|---|---|
| X | 10,000 |
| Y | 8,500 |
| Z | 7,000 |
| A | 6,500 |
| B | 4,000 |
| JJ | 5,500 |
| Average | 3,000 |

## EBITDA MARGIN (IN %)

| | |
|---|---|
| A | 23.5 |
| B | 20 |
| C | 15 |
| X | 13 |
| Y | 18 |
| JJ | 22.5% |
| Average | 18.5 |

## DATASET 3: HIGH-END CASUAL DINING SEGMENT

| Company | EBITDA Multiple | Volatility | Beta |
|---|---|---|---|
| A | 18.2 | 62% | 1.37 |
| B | 18 | 38% | 1.28 |
| C | 10 | 45% | 1.12 |
| X | 8.7 | N/A | N/A |
| Y | 7.3 | 31% | 1.01 |
| Z | 7.3 | 45% | 0.97 |
| All comparables | | | |
| Mean | 11.6 | 45% | 1.15 |
| Median | 9.4 | 45% | 1.12 |
| Dutch Treasury rates | November 2011 | | |
| 1-year | 0.8% | | |
| 5-year | 1.7% | | |
| 10-year | 2.1% | | |

## DATASET 4: HISTORY OF STORE OPENINGS

| Year | Location |
|---|---|
| 1991 | Amsterdam |
| 1996 | Rotterdam |
| 1998 | Eindhoven |
| 1999 | Utrecht |
| 2001 | Maastricht |
| 2003 | The Hague |
| 2005 | Tilburg |
| 2007 | Groningen |
| 2009 | Almere |
| 2011 | Nijmegen |

## DATASET 5: STORE CASH FLOW OLD VERSUS NEW CONCEPT LOCATIONS (IN 000'S OF EURO)

| Year | Old | New |
|---|---|---|
| 2002 | 400 | 850 |
| 2005 | 350 | 800 |
| 2008 | 300 | 900 |
| 2010 | 250 | 850 |
| 2011 | 200 | 800 |

## DATASET 6

### Food cost comparison

| Company | Food cost as a % of sales | 2009 | 2010 | 2011 |
|---------|---------------------------|------|------|------|
| X | | 25.4 | 26.9 | 23.5 |
| Y | | 27.4 | 28.4 | 29.3 |
| Z | | 32.2 | 33.4 | 34.6 |
| A | | 36.9 | 38.9 | 37.6 |
| B | | 25.9 | 27.7 | 29.9 |
| **JJ** | | **29.4** | **30.5** | **29.7** |

### Labor cost comparison

| Company | Labor cost as a % of sales | 2009 | 2010 | 2011 |
|---------|----------------------------|------|------|------|
| X | | 23.5 | 25.4 | 24.5 |
| Y | | 27.5 | 28.4 | 29.6 |
| Z | | 25.4 | 23.2 | 29.3 |
| A | | 30.2 | 32.5 | 33.5 |
| B | | 33.9 | 34.6 | 35 |
| **JJ** | | **35.5** | **36.5** | **36** |

## DATASET 7

### Deal structure & term sheet

| | |
|---|---|
| **Structure** | Senior subordinated loan/second lien |
| **Commitment amount** | 20 Million Euro |
| **Minimum initial draw** | 5 Million Euro |
| **Future draws** | Minimum of 2.5 Million Euro after leverage test |
| **Maturity** | 5 years from close |
| **Coupon** | 10% interest and 4% PIK |
| **Warrant** | 3% equity stake issued in full upon drawing the first 5 million Euro |
| **Amortization** | Bullit at maturity |
| **Prepayment penalty** | |
| **Fees** | 2.5% (1.0% commitment fee and 1.5% drawdown fees) |

# DATASET 8

## Historical performance

| Assets | 2011 (till end 11/2011) | 2010 |
|---|---|---|
| **Current assets** | | |
| Cash and equivalents | 1,376,600 | 3,810,300 |
| Receivables | 375,100 | 138,600 |
| Inventory | 418,500 | 377,500 |
| Prepaids and other current assets | 449,000 | 190,100 |
| **Total current assets** | 2,619,200 | 4,516,500 |
| PPE net | 19,618,900 | 14,357,400 |
| Goodwill net | 990,200 | 1,071,400 |
| Deferred tax assets | 495,200 | 509,200 |
| Loans to shareholders | 194,900 | |
| other | 655,600 | 597,500 |
| **Total assets** | 24,574,000 | 21,052,000 |

| Liabilities | 2011 (till end of 11/2011) | 2010 |
|---|---|---|
| **Current liabilities** | | |
| A/P and accrued expenses | 4,012,600 | 3,137,500 |
| Accrued construction payables | 641,700 | 168,500 |
| Income tax payable | 71,400 | 54,900 |
| Others | 1,480,700 | 810,000 |
| **Total current liabilities** | 6,206,400 | 4,170,900 |
| LT debt and capital lease less current portion | 610,100 | 1,119,600 |
| Deferred rent | 3,589,800 | 2,090,300 |
| **Total liabilities** | 10,406,300 | 7,380,800 |
| **Equity** | | |
| Series A convertible preferred, no par value | 18,027,900 | 15,906,800 |
| 1,000 shares authorized, 62,000 issues and outstanding | | |
| Accumulated deficit | -3,860,200 | -2,235,600 |
| Total stockholders equity | 14,167,700 | 13,671,200 |
| **Total liabilities and equity** | 24,574,000 | 21,052,000 |

| Income statement | 2011 (till end 11/2011) | 2010 |
|---|---|---|
| Revenues | 2,098,000 | 45,093,900 |
| Restaurant cost and expenses | | |
| Cost of sales | 5,120,800 | 13,420,600 |
| Labor | 18,730,300 | 15,704,500 |
| Operating | 7,117,900 | 6,263,900 |
| Occupancy | 3,438,800 | 3,008,500 |
| **Total restaurant costs** | 44,497,800 | 38,397,500 |
| | | |
| G&A | 4,572,800 | 3,478,300 |
| D&A | 1,768,900 | 1,288,000 |
| Pre-opening costs | 350,350 | 504,200 |
| Income from operations | 908,000 | 1,425,900 |
| Interest income | 94,900 | 109,300 |
| Interest expense | −148,800 | −202,600 |
| Loss on disposal of P&E | −2,200 | −97,500 |
| Minority interest | | −258,200 |
| Income before income tax provision | 851,900 | 976,900 |
| Provision for income tax | 355,400 | 279,000 |
| Net income | 496,500 | 697,900 |

## DATASET 9

| Financial projections | Management case |
|---|---|
| **Financing conditions** | |
| 20 Million Euro Interest | 10% |
| 5 year maturity | 4% PIK |
| | |
| **Fees** | |
| Commitment fee | 1% |
| Drawdowns fee | 1.50% |
| Warrant | 3% |

(*Continued*)

| P&L (in 000's of Euro) | 2012 | 2013 | 2014 | 2015 | 2016 | 2017 |
|---|---|---|---|---|---|---|
| **Sales** | 87,653 | 13,338 | 183,492 | 233,892 | 269,592 | 290,592 |
| Less G&A of running locations | −74,877 | −110,358 | −154,104 | −195,055 | −224,919 | −241,996 |
| **Store cash flow** | 12,776 | 19,980 | 29,388 | 38,837 | 44,673 | 48,596 |
| Corporate G&A | −7,202 | −9,384 | −12,844 | −16,372 | −18,871 | −20,341 |
| Legal expense | 143 | | | | | |
| EBITDA | 5,717 | 10,596 | 16,544 | 22,465 | 25,802 | 28,255 |
| Pre-opening expenses | −2,458 | −2,541 | −3,013 | −2,946 | −1,250 | −1,250 |
| EBITDA post-opening exp. | 3,259 | 8,055 | 13,531 | 19,519 | 24,552 | 27,005 |
| Amortization | −176 | −300 | −334 | −334 | −334 | −334 |
| Depreciation | −2,809 | −5,049 | −8,171 | −10,528 | −10,370 | −10,370 |
| EBIT | 274 | 2,706 | 5,026 | 8,657 | 13,848 | 16,301 |
| Interest income | | | | | | |
| Other income | | | | | | |
| ROJ fee | −152 | −150 | −150 | −150 | −150 | −150 |
| **Interest expense** | | | | | | |
| Existing debt | −74 | −79 | | | | |
| Revolver | | | −99 | −339 | −375 | −265 |
| Seasonal interest | | | | | | |
| Rabobank loan | −150 | −609 | −624 | −602 | −626 | −523 |
| Term loan | | | | | | |
| Capital lease | −183 | −133 | −92 | −47 | −14 | −4 |
| Subordinated note | | −2,625 | −3,053 | −3,114 | −3,176 | −3,239 |
| **Total interest expense** | −407 | −3,446 | −3,868 | −4,102 | −4,191 | −4,031 |
| Pre-tax income | −285 | −890 | 1,009 | 4,405 | 9,507 | 12,120 |
| Tax provision | 284 | −100 | −363 | −1,540 | −3,336 | −4,250 |
| **Net income** | −1 | −990 | 646 | 2,865 | 6,171 | 7,870 |

| Balance sheet (in 000's of Euro) | 2012 | 2013 | 2014 | 2015 | 2016 | 2017 |
|---|---|---|---|---|---|---|
| **Assets** | | | | | | |
| Operating cash | 4,017 | 2,217 | | | | |
| Excess cash | | | | | | |
| Accounts receivable | | | | | | |
| Inventory | | | | | | |
| Prepaid expenses & other | | | | | | |
| Other current | 1,573 | 2,319 | 3,065 | 3,811 | 4,062 | 4,379 |
| **Total operating expenses** | 5,590 | 4,536 | 3,065 | 3,811 | 4,062 | 4,379 |
| Fixed assets | 54,079 | 72,452 | 100,194 | 125,470 | 137,184 | 148,898 |
| Accumulated depreciation | −10,357 | 15,470 | 23,521 | 38,891 | 44,261 | 54,631 |
| **Fixed assets net** | 43,722 | 56,982 | 76,673 | 91,579 | 92,923 | 94,276 |
| Deferred tax assets | 247 | 247 | 247 | 247 | 247 | 247 |
| Shareholders loans | 195 | 195 | 195 | 195 | 195 | 195 |
| Other assets | 1,620 | 2,388 | 3,157 | 3,926 | 4,223 | 4,520 |
| Capitalized transaction costs | 516 | 580 | 460 | 302 | 302 | 302 |
| Existing goodwill | 990 | 990 | 990 | 990 | 990 | 990 |
| New goodwill | | | | | | |
| **Total assets** | 52,880 | 65,918 | 84,787 | 101,050 | 102,942 | 104,900 |
| **Liabilities & Equity** | | | | | | |
| Accounts payable | 4,770 | 7,033 | 9,297 | 11,560 | 12,435 | 13,310 |
| Accrued expenses | 3,733 | 5,505 | 7,276 | 9,048 | 9,643 | 10,394 |
| Other current liabilities | 455 | 671 | 887 | 1,103 | 1,176 | 1,267 |
| **Total current liabilities** | 8,958 | 13,209 | 17,460 | 21,711 | 23,254 | 24,791 |
| Deferred rent | 6,240 | 6,327 | 6,408 | 6,488 | 6,979 | 7,470 |
| Deferred compensation | 30 | 30 | 30 | 30 | 30 | 30 |
| Existing debt | 7,000 | | | | | |
| Revolver | | | 12,124 | 21,999 | 17,446 | 10,483 |
| Rabobank loan | 8,666 | 12,304 | 11,905 | 11,469 | 9,735 | 8,002 |
| Term B loan | | | | | | |
| Capital leases | 2,974 | 2,199 | 1,357 | 21,999 | 17,446 | 10,483 |
| Subordinated note | 17,500 | 20,350 | 20,757 | 21,172 | 21,596 | 22,027 |
| **Total debt** | 36,140 | 34,853 | 46,143 | 55,111 | 48,777 | 40,636 |
| **Total liabilities** | 51,368 | 54,419 | 70,041 | 83,340 | 79,040 | 73,107 |
| **Sponsors preferred equity** | 21,095 | 21,095 | 21,095 | 21,095 | 21,095 | 21,095 |
| Retained earnings | −7,086 | −6,941 | −6,189 | −3,226 | 2,969 | 10,862 |
| Total equity | 14,009 | 14,154 | 14,906 | 17,869 | 24,064 | 31,957 |
| **Total liabilities & equity** | 65,377 | 68,573 | 84,947 | 101,209 | 103,104 | 105,064 |

Rounding errors might occur

## DATASET 10

| Financial projections | Reworked case by ECP |
|---|---|

**Financing conditions**

| 20 Million Euro Interest | 10% |
|---|---|
| 5 year maturity | 4% PIK |

**Fees**

| Commitment fee | 1% |
|---|---|
| Drawdowns fee | 1.50% |
| Warrant | 3% |

| P&L (in 000's of Euro) | 2012 | 2013 | 2014 | 2015 | 2016 | 2017 |
|---|---|---|---|---|---|---|
| **Sales** | 87,653 | 128,747 | 178,751 | 228,793 | 264,493 | 285,493 |
| Less G&A of running locations | −74,877 | −109,519 | −151,806 | −193,460 | −223,474 | −240,550 |
| **Store cash flow** | 12,776 | 19,228 | 26,945 | 35,333 | 41,019 | 44,943 |
| Corporate G&A | −7,202 | −10,300 | −14,300 | −18,303 | −21,159 | −22,839 |
| Legal expense | 143 | | | | | |
| **EBITDA** | 5,717 | 8,928 | 12,645 | 17,030 | 19,860 | 22,104 |
| Pre-opening expenses | −2,458 | −2,541 | −3,013 | −2,946 | −1,250 | −1,250 |
| EBITDA post-opening exp. | 3,259 | 6,387 | 9,632 | 14,084 | 18,610 | 20,854 |
| Amortization | −176 | −300 | −334 | −334 | −334 | −334 |
| Depreciation | −2,809 | −5,049 | −8,171 | −10,528 | −10,370 | −10,370 |
| **EBIT** | 274 | 1,038 | 1,127 | 3,222 | 7,906 | 10,150 |
| Interest income | | | | | | |
| Other income | | | | | | |
| ROJ fee | 152 | 150 | 150 | 150 | 150 | 150 |
| **Interest expense** | | | | | | |
| Existing debt | −74 | −79 | | | | |
| Revolver | | −139 | −442 | −549 | −515 | |
| Seasonal interest | | | | | | |
| Rabobank loan | −150 | −609 | −624 | −602 | −626 | −523 |
| Term loan | | | | | | |
| Capital lease | −183 | −133 | −92 | −47 | −14 | −4 |
| Subordinated note | | | | | | |
| Total interest expense | −407 | −821 | −855 | −1,091 | −1,189 | −1,042 |
| Pre-tax income | −285 | 67 | 122 | 1,981 | 6,567 | 8,958 |
| Tax provision | 284 | 482 | 1,016 | 398 | −1,195 | −2,010 |
| **Net income** | −1 | 549 | 1,138 | 2,379 | 5,372 | 6,948 |

| Balance sheet (in 000's of Euro) | 2012 | 2013 | 2014 | 2015 | 2016 | 2017 |
|---|---|---|---|---|---|---|
| **Assets** | | | | | | |
| Operating cash | 4,017 | 1,133 | | | | |
| Excess cash | | | | | | |
| Accounts receivable | | | | | | |
| Inventory | | | | | | |
| Prepaid expenses & other | | | | | | |
| Other current | 1,573 | 2,319 | 3,065 | 3,811 | 4,067 | 4,390 |
| **Total operating expenses** | 5,590 | 3,452 | 3,065 | 3,811 | 4,067 | 4,390 |
| Fixed assets | 54,087 | 72,452 | 100,194 | 125,470 | 137,184 | 148,898 |
| Accumulated depreciation | −10,357 | −15,470 | −23,521 | −33,891 | −44,261 | −54,631 |
| **Fixed assets net** | 43,721 | 56,982 | 76,673 | 91,579 | 92,923 | 94,267 |
| Deferred tax assets | 247 | 247 | 247 | 247 | 247 | 247 |
| Shareholders loans | 195 | 195 | 195 | 195 | 195 | 195 |
| Other assets | 1,620 | 2,388 | 3,157 | 3,926 | 4,248 | 4,571 |
| Capitalized transaction costs | 516 | 580 | 460 | 302 | 302 | 302 |
| Existing goodwill | 990 | 990 | 990 | 990 | 990 | 990 |
| New goodwill | | | | | | |
| **Total assets** | 52,879 | 64,834 | 84,787 | 101,050 | 102,972 | 104,962 |
| **Liabilities & Equity** | | | | | | |
| Accounts payable | 4,770 | 7,033 | 9,297 | 11,560 | 12,511 | 13,462 |
| Accrued expenses | 3,733 | 5,505 | 7,276 | 9,048 | 9,656 | 10,422 |
| Other current liabilities | 455 | 671 | 887 | 1,103 | 1,177 | 1,271 |
| **Total current liabilities** | 8,958 | 13,209 | 17,460 | 21,711 | 23,344 | 25,155 |
| Deferred rent | | | | | | |
| Deferred compensation | 6,240 | 6,327 | 6,408 | 6,488 | 7,021 | 7,555 |
| Existing debt | 7,000 | | | | | |
| Revolver | | | 15,768 | 29,244 | 28,565 | 25,659 |
| Rabobank loan | 8,666 | 12,304 | 11,905 | 11,469 | 9,735 | 8,002 |
| Term B loan | | | | | | |
| Capital leases | 2,974 | 2,199 | 1,357 | 471 | | 124 |
| Subordinated note | 17,500 | 20,350 | 20,757 | 21,172 | 21,596 | 22,027 |
| **Total debt** | 36,140 | 34,853 | 49,787 | 62,356 | 59,896 | 55,812 |
| **Total liabilities** | 51,368 | 54,419 | 73,685 | 90,585 | 90,291 | 88,552 |
| **Sponsors preferred equity** | 21,095 | 21,095 | 21,095 | 21,095 | 21,095 | 21,095 |
| Retained earnings | −7,086 | −8,025 | −9,834 | −10,471 | −8,251 | −4,519 |
| Total equity | 14,009 | 13,070 | 11,261 | 10,624 | 12,844 | 16,576 |
| **Total liabilities & equity** | 65,377 | 67,489 | 84,946 | 101,209 | 103,135 | 105,128 |
| Rounding errors might occur | | | | | | |

### 4.3.6 Questions: JJ Bars & Restaurants

1. Is the restaurant industry an attractive industry to invest in? Is JJ a star performer in the industry? (A SWOT analysis of some sort would do the trick).
2. What are the risks of a mezzanine investment in a growth company? How does ECP propose transactions to mitigate this risk? Think like an equity investor not like a banker!
3. What internal rate of return can ECP expect under the case developed by the management and the redesigned case they developed themselves (i.e., Dana and her team)? And what about the 'times money back' multiple?
4. Where needed, how can ECP alter the deal structure and terms to attain its target returns?
5. How will these returns vary based on the multiple at exit? What will drive ECP's ability to capture 'multiple arbitrage' (i.e., exiting at a higher multiple than the purchase price multiple)? Building some sort of return sensitivity matrix (to EBITDA multiple at exit) should do the trick.
6. A member of ECP's investment committee (probably the same guy as mentioned in the case) worries that this transaction will offer mezzanine returns for equity-like risks. Do you believe these concerns are justified and why?
7. Should ECP undertake the investment in JJ Bars & Restaurants?
8. Would you have considered this product or suggested a different one? If so, which one?

# 5

# The Mezzanine Product Group and the Financial Industry

So far we have been looking at mezzanine applications in corporations where our concern was related to the dynamics of the product, the return target and the intrinsic risk embodied in the level of subordination of the mezzanine product and/or the risk nature of the transaction being financed, whether that was an acquisition, recapitalization, internationalization or otherwise. Our understanding of risk and corporate governance did the trick.

There are, however, industries where the regulator doesn't leave it completely up to the shareholders or management team to decide how the activities of the firm need to be financed. This often happens because the regulator considers that the public deserves protection when engaging with these firms and the claims they potentially have against the firms (as these firms have built up a liability towards that public). Many types of legislation try (and some manage to a certain degree) to protect the audience against potential issues which might arise at these firms.

We are talking here about the financial sector, and to a large degree as well about the insurance sector. Since they either raise raw material (deposits) from the public or insure them against certain risks and agree to provide a payment in case that risk materializes, the regulator thought it was wise to regulate how the structure of the balance sheet of those institutions should look given the type of risk they are exposed to, with a view to protecting the public in their dealings with these institutions.

It is beyond the scope of this book to provide a full overview of all the initiatives the regulators have taken in this respect. It is also outside of this book to drill deep into the experiences and policy responses the 2008–2009 financial crisis has triggered, and how the understanding of whether the rules in place were solid enough to protect against certain types of systemic market risks has changed. Finally, it is also outside the scope of this book to judge or evaluate the new rules which have been put in place and to what extent they will prove to be a more solid framework against future risks. Besides the many technical discussions, it is clear that regulators are often behind the curve in solving issues in legislation, and bringing them in line with reality. They, at least, have a bad track record of mending issues in rapidly evolving industries in a society which also moves at an increasingly rapid pace. Think about the Sarbanes–Oxley rules after Enron and Worldcom etc; the regulator always tries to mend the rules with too much focus on the case that revealed a weakness in the legislation, known in many law schools as 'bad cases make bad laws.' Unfortunately, the next crisis will show up in different ways and with different characteristics, and therefore there is the need to fight the undercurrent rather than the symptoms.

In a globalized world, policy initiatives don't mean a lot unless you can implement them in a coordinated action on a global scale, and to avoid unfair competition among global competitors just based on where they are located or headquartered. It also discourages regulatory arbitrage among global players.

I'm definitely not in a position to advocate that things are looking picture perfect as it stands in 2013, but at least we have something of a standard in the financial industry with some level of moral authority. The global standards with respect to the banking industry and the capital requirements of those institutions are in the hands of the Basel Committee, a committee of global central bankers which meets in the city of Basel, Switzerland, on a regular basis. They have been doing so for many years. The decisions they deliver are known as the Basel standards, which are updated or changed on a regular basis. This happened very recently in a very extensive manner, following the financial crisis.

In this chapter we will focus on the Basel rules specifically geared towards capital rules and capital definitions, in order for us to assess the impact of the rules and constraints on bringing in mezzanine products as a way to finance financial and insurance operations.

First, we will go through a short history of the Basel rules, before we focus on the capital rules and definitions, how they have evolved over time and, most importantly, the impact of the most recent Basel III rules issued in 2010–2012.

## 5.1 THE BASEL COMMITTEE AND FRAMEWORK

The Basel Committee on Banking Supervision is a committee of banking supervisory authorities which was established by the central bank governors of the Group of Ten countries in 1974. It provides a forum for regular cooperation on banking supervisory matters. Its objective is to enhance understanding of key supervisory issues and improve the quality of banking supervision worldwide. The Committee also frames guidelines and standards in different areas – some of the better known among them are the international standards on capital adequacy, the Core Principles for Effective Banking Supervision and the Concordat on cross-border banking supervision.

The Committee's members come from Argentina, Australia, Belgium, Brazil, Canada, China, France, Germany, Hong Kong SAR, India, Indonesia, Italy, Japan, Korea, Luxembourg, Mexico, The Netherlands, Russia, Saudi Arabia, Singapore, South Africa, Spain, Sweden, Switzerland, Turkey, the United Kingdom and the United States. The Committee's Secretariat is located at the Bank for International Settlements (BIS) in Basel, Switzerland. However, the BIS and the Basel Committee remain two distinct entities.

The Basel Committee formulates broad supervisory standards and guidelines and recommends statements of best practice in banking supervision in the expectation that member authorities and other nations' authorities will take steps to implement them through their own national systems, whether in statutory form or otherwise.

The purpose of the committee is to encourage convergence toward common approaches and standards. The Committee is not a classical multilateral organization, in part because it has no founding treaty. BCBS does not issue binding regulation; rather, it functions as an informal forum in which policy solutions and standards are developed.

## 5.2 THE EVOLUTION OF THE BASEL RULES (BASEL I AND II)

In 1988 the first set of rules for the banking sector was published and enforced by the G10. They are, by current standards, considered very basic, as the financial industry, risk management techniques and financial innovation have evolved tremendously since then. The triggering event for the rules to be developed was the messy wind-up of a German bank in 1974 (Herstatt bank).

Basel I's framework primarily focused on credit risk. Assets of banks were classified and grouped in five categories according to credit risk, carrying risk weights of zero (for example home country sovereign debt), 10, 20, 50, and up to 100% (this category has, as an example, the most corporate debt). Banks with international presence were required to hold capital equal to 8% of the risk-weighted assets. So, very soon the world understood there was a need for a Basel II, although it took until 2004 to get Basel II in place. It has been updated very often ever since. Basel II in its new format was intended to create an international standard for banking regulators to control how much capital banks need to put aside to guard against the types of financial and operational risks banks (and the whole economy) face. Basel II attempted to accomplish this by setting up risk and capital management requirements designed to ensure that a bank has adequate capital for the risk the bank exposes itself to through its lending and investment practices. Bottom line, these rules mean that the greater risk to which the bank is exposed, the greater the amount of capital the bank needs to hold to safeguard its solvency and overall economic stability. It was only after the crisis of 2008 that the world got serious about implementing those rules in the Basel III format negotiated in the aftermath of the financial crisis.

Basel II took Basel I quite a large step further by building a three-pillar structure, particularly by expanding the risk dynamics and variety in pillar 1. A short review of the three pillars follows.

Basel II uses a 'three pillars' concept – (1) minimum capital requirements (addressing risk), (2) supervisory review and (3) market discipline.

The Basel I accord dealt with only parts of each of these pillars.

## 5.2.1 The first pillar

The first pillar deals with maintenance of regulatory capital calculated for three major components of risk that a bank faces: credit risk, operational risk and market risk. Other risks are not considered fully quantifiable.

The credit risk component can be calculated in three different ways of varying sophistication, namely the standardized approach, the Foundation Internal Rating-Based Approach (IRB) and the Advanced IRB.

The standardized approach sets out specific risk weights for certain types of credit risk. The standard risk weight categories used under Basel I were 0% for government bonds, 20% for exposures to OECD banks, 50% for first line residential mortgages and 100% weighting on consumer loans and unsecured commercial loans. Basel II introduced a new 150% weighting for borrowers with lower credit ratings. The minimum capital required remained at 8% of risk-weighted assets, with Tier 1 capital making up not less than half of this amount.

Banks which decide to adopt the standardized ratings approach must rely on the ratings generated by external agencies. Certain banks used the IRB approach as a result.

For operational risk, there are three different approaches: the basic indicator approach, the standardized approach and the internal measurement approach (advanced measurement approach or AMA).

For market risk the preferred approach is VaR (value at risk).

## 5.2.2 The second pillar

The second pillar deals with the regulatory response to the first pillar, giving regulators a variety of improved techniques. It also provides a framework for dealing with all the other risks a bank may face, such as systemic risk, pension risk, concentration risk, strategic risk, reputational risk, liquidity risk and legal risk, which the accord combines under the title of residual risk. It gives banks power to review their risk management system. The Internal Capital Adequacy Assessment Process (ICAAP) is the endgame of Pillar II.

## 5.2.3 The third pillar

This pillar aims to complement the minimum capital requirements and supervisory review process by developing a set of disclosure requirements which will allow the market participants to gauge the capital adequacy of an institution.

## 5.2.4 Capital definitions under Basel II

Pillar 1 of the Basel II framework addresses the total minimum capital requirements for credit, market and operational risks. The capital ratio is calculated using the definition of regulatory capital and risk-weighted assets. The total capital must be no lower than 8%, which means a bank may lose at least 8% of its assets (mostly loans) without becoming insolvent. This ratio is used to protect depositors and promote the stability and efficiency of financial systems around the world.

**What is a Capital Ratio?**
A Capital Ratio or Capital Adequacy Ratio (CAR) or Capital to Risk-Weighted Assets Ratio (CRAR) is a measure of a bank's capital expressed as:

$$\text{CAR/CRAR} = \text{Tier 1 Capital} + \text{Tier 2 Capital} / \text{Risk-Weighted Assets}$$

So to compute CAR/CRAR, we need to figure out Tier 1 and Tier 2 capital in the numerator and the Risk-Weighted Assets in the denominator.

**What is capital?**
Capital is the funds, a mix of equity and debt that publicly traded companies hold to support their businesses. For regulatory purposes, Basel II has divided banks' capital base into three tiers:

**Tier 1 capital**
Tier 1 capital is the highest quality form of capital which is permanently and freely available to absorb unanticipated losses without the bank being obliged to cease trading. It consists of core capital and other instruments, sometimes called innovative Tier 1.

Core Tier 1 capital consists largely of shareholders' equity and includes:

- Common stock holders' equity: common stock/ordinary shares/equity capital/paid up share capital are all the same things.
- Disclosed reserves: created or increased by appropriations of retained earnings or other surplus, e.g., share premiums, retained profit, general reserves and legal reserves.

Other instruments (innovative Tier 1) may include:

- Irredeemable/perpetual non-cumulative preferred stocks.
- Qualifying mandatorily redeemable securities of subsidiary trusts.
- Minority/non-controlling interest in consolidated subsidiaries.
- Statutory reserves: state regulated reserve requirements which must be held as either cash or marketable investments.
- Innovative perpetual debt instruments (limited to 15% of total Tier 1 capital).

### Tier 2 (supplementary capital)

Temporary capital which can absorb losses in the event of a winding-up, and so provides a lesser degree of protection to depositors. Tier 2 capital can be divided into upper and lower Tier 2 capital upon the discretion of the national regulatory authority.

Upper Tier 2 includes:

- Perpetual deferrable subordinated debt (including debt convertible into equity).
- Revaluation reserves from fixed asset.
- Fixed asset investments.
- General provisions for doubtful debts/general loan loss reserves up to 1.25% of risk-adjusted asset if the bank is using the standardized approach to credit risk or 0.6% of credit risk-weighted assets if the bank is using the IRB approach for credit risk.
- Hybrid debt/equity capital instruments.
- Undisclosed reserves: not identified in the published balance sheet but have the same high quality and character as a disclosed capital reserve.
- Unrealized marketable equity securities gain (up to 45% of pretax net unrealized holding gains on available for sale equity securities with readily determinable fair values).
- Foreign currency translation adjustment.

Lower Tier 2 includes:

- Subordinated term debt not exceeding 50% of Tier 1 capital.
- Limited life redeemable preference shares.
- Any other similar limited life capital instruments.
- Unrealized gains from fair value of equity securities.
- Collective impairment provision.

### Tier 3 capital

Tier 3 capital is solely for the purpose of market risks and may be used only at the discretion of the national regulator. It consists of only short-term subordinated debt which satisfies the following conditions:

- Unsecured, subordinated and fully paid up.
- Has an original maturity of at least two years.
- Is subject to a lock-in clause which stipulates that neither interest nor principal may be paid (even when due at maturity) if the bank is below its minimum capital requirement or if such payment makes the bank go below the minimum capital requirement.

**Deductions from the capital base (Tier 1, Tier 2 and Tier 3 capital)**
The following deductions should be made from the total capital base and should not be included for the purpose of calculating the risk-weighted capital ratio.

- Net unrealized gains and losses on debt securities available for sale.
- Net unrealized holding losses on available for sale equity securities with readily determinable fair values, net of tax.
- Accumulated net gains on cash flow hedges, net of tax.
- Intangible assets such as goodwill and other disallowed intangible assets/investments.
- Investments in unconsolidated banking and finance subsidiary companies (50% from Tier 1 and 2 capital each).
- Significant minority investments in banking, securities and other financial entities.
- Investments in the capital of other deposit-taking institutions (at the discretion of national authorities).

Limits and restrictions:

- At least 50% of a bank's total capital base to consist of equity capital and published reserves from post-tax retained earnings (Tier 1).
- Tier 2 is limited to 100% of Tier 1, in other words Tier 2 capital cannot exceed Tier 1 capital.
- Only 25% of a bank's total capital can be lower Tier 2.
- Tier 3 capital can only be used to support market risk capital requirements, and is limited to 250% of Tier 1 capital being applied to market risk exposures. If Tier 3 capital is used for capital adequacy, then any Tier 2 capital used for the same purpose counts towards this 250% limit. For example, if US$100 is the Tier 1 capital available for market risk, then the maximum Tier 3 capital (including any Tier 2 elements substituted for Tier 3) can be 250% × $100 = $250. The total capital available, then, is US$350, of which US$100 is Tier 1. Thus, the minimum Tier 1 capital needed for market risk ends up being about 28.5% ($100/$350).

The sum of Tier 1, Tier 2 and Tier 3 capital constitutes the total capital base.

## 5.3  OBJECTIVES OF BASEL III AND THE CENTRAL THEMES

Despite the fact that the Basel Committee has been trying to tackle multiple issues following the 2008–2009 financial crisis, the one that is most important here is 'improving the quality, consistency and transparency of the capital base.'

This is what they had to say about the topic: 'It is critical that banks' risk exposures are backed by a high quality capital base. The crisis demonstrated that credit losses and write-downs come out of retained earnings, which is part of banks' tangible common equity base. It also revealed the inconsistency in the definition of capital across jurisdictions and the lack of disclosure that would have enabled the market to fully assess and compare the quality of capital between institutions.

To this end, the predominant form of Tier 1 capital must be common shares and retained earnings. This standard is reinforced through a set of principles that also can be tailored to the context of non-joint stock companies to ensure they hold comparable levels of high quality Tier 1 capital. Deductions from capital and prudential filters have been harmonized internationally and generally applied at the level of common equity or its equivalent in the case of non-joint stock companies. The remainder of the Tier 1 capital base must be comprised of instruments that are subordinated, have fully discretionary non-cumulative dividends or coupons and have neither a maturity date nor an incentive to redeem. Innovative hybrid capital instruments with an incentive to redeem through features such as step-up clauses, currently limited to 15% of the Tier 1 capital base, will be phased out. In addition, Tier 2 capital instruments will be harmonized and so-called Tier 3 capital instruments, which were only available to cover market risks, eliminated. Finally, to improve market discipline, the transparency of the capital base will be improved, with all elements of capital required to be disclosed along with a detailed reconciliation to the reported accounts.

The Committee is introducing these changes in a manner that minimizes the disruption to capital instruments that are currently outstanding. It also continues to review the role that contingent capital should play in the regulatory capital framework.'[1]

## 5.3.1 Capital definitions under Basel III

The Basel III rules have consequently and significantly altered the definitions of capital under the Basel rules. Hereafter you can find the new capital rules (and where possible, summaries) as they were published in their most recent edition[2] – I maintained the original numbering of the paragraphs. At the end of the chapter I conclude with the impact these new rules have on the individual mezzanine products. They are part of the revised rules to strengthen the global capital structure of banks and financial institutions:

---

### PART 1: MINIMUM CAPITAL REQUIREMENTS AND BUFFERS

48. The global banking system entered the crisis with an insufficient level of high quality capital. The crisis also revealed the inconsistency in the definition of capital across jurisdictions and the lack of disclosure that would have enabled the market to fully assess and compare the quality of capital across jurisdictions. A key element of the new definition of capital is the greater focus on common equity, the highest quality component of a bank's capital.

### I. DEFINITION OF CAPITAL

### A. Components of capital

**Elements of capital**
49. Total regulatory capital will consist of the sum of the following elements:

**1. Tier 1 Capital (going-concern capital)**
   a. Common Equity Tier 1
   b. Additional Tier 1

---

[1] Basel III: A global regulatory framework for more resilient banks and banking systems – revised version June 2011. The earlier edition was published in December 2010. Basel Commission on banking supervision (BIS), pp. 2–3.

[2] That is the edition of June 2011, Basel III: A global regulatory framework for more resilient banks and banking systems – revised version June 2011. The earlier edition was published in December 2010. Basel Commission on banking supervision (BIS).

**2. Tier 2 Capital (gone-concern capital)**

For each of the three categories above (1a, 1b and 2) there is a single set of criteria that instruments are required to meet before inclusion in the relevant category.[3]

**Limits and minima**

50. All elements above are net of the associated regulatory adjustments and are subject to the following restrictions:

- Common Equity Tier 1 must be at least 4.5% of risk-weighted assets at all times.
- Tier 1 Capital must be at least 6.0% of risk-weighted assets at all times.
- Total Capital (Tier 1 Capital plus Tier 2 Capital) must be at least 8.0% of risk-weighted assets at all times.

## B. Detailed proposal

51. Throughout this section the term 'bank' is used to mean bank, banking group or other entity (e.g. holding company) whose capital is being measured.

### 1. Common Equity Tier 1

52. Common Equity Tier 1 capital consists of the sum of the following elements:

- Common shares issued by the bank that meet the criteria for classification as common shares for regulatory purposes (or the equivalent for non-joint stock companies).
- Stock surplus (share premium) resulting from the issue of instruments included in Common Equity Tier 1.
- Retained earnings.
- Accumulated other comprehensive income and other disclosed reserves.[4]
- Common shares issued by consolidated subsidiaries of the bank and held by third parties (i.e. minority interest) that meet the criteria for inclusion in Common Equity Tier 1 capital. See section 4 for the relevant criteria; and
- Regulatory adjustments applied in the calculation of Common Equity Tier 1

Retained earnings and other comprehensive income include interim profit or loss. National authorities may consider appropriate audit, verification or review procedures. Dividends are removed from Common Equity Tier 1 in accordance with applicable accounting standards. The treatment of minority interest and the regulatory adjustments applied in the calculation of Common Equity Tier 1 are addressed in separate sections.

---

[3] As set out in the Committee's August 2010 consultative document, Proposal to ensure the loss absorbency of regulatory capital at the point of non-viability, and as stated in the Committee's October 19, 2010 and December 1, 2010 press releases, the Committee is finalizing additional entry criteria for Additional Tier 1 and Tier 2 capital. Once finalized, the additional criteria will be added to this regulatory framework.

[4] There is no adjustment applied to remove unrealized gains or losses recognized on the balance sheet from Common Equity Tier 1. Unrealized losses are subject to the transitional arrangements set out in paragraph 94 (c) and (d). The Committee will continue to review the appropriate treatment of unrealized gains, taking into account the evolution of the accounting framework.

*Common shares issued by the bank*

53. For an instrument to be included in Common Equity Tier 1 capital it must meet all of the criteria that follow. The vast majority of internationally active banks are structured as joint stock companies[5] and for these banks the criteria must be met solely with common shares. In the rare cases where banks need to issue non-voting common shares as part of Common Equity Tier 1, they must be identical to voting common shares of the issuing bank in all respects except the absence of voting rights.

## Criteria for classification as common shares for regulatory capital purposes[6]

1. Represents the most subordinated claim in liquidation of the bank.
2. Entitled to a claim on the residual assets that is proportional with its share of issued capital, after all senior claims have been repaid in liquidation (i.e. has an unlimited and variable claim, not a fixed or capped claim).
3. Principal is perpetual and never repaid outside of liquidation (setting aside discretionary repurchases or other means of effectively reducing capital in a discretionary manner that is allowable under relevant law).
4. The bank does nothing to create an expectation at issuance that the instrument will be bought back, redeemed or cancelled nor do the statutory or contractual terms provide any feature which might give rise to such an expectation.
5. Distributions are paid out of distributable items (retained earnings included). The level of distributions is not in any way tied or linked to the amount paid in at issuance and is not subject to a contractual cap (except to the extent that a bank is unable to pay distributions that exceed the level of distributable items).
6. There are no circumstances under which the distributions are obligatory. Non-payment is therefore not an event of default.
7. Distributions are paid only after all legal and contractual obligations have been met and payments on more senior capital instruments have been made. This means that there are no preferential distributions, including in respect of other elements classified as the highest quality issued capital.
8. It is the issued capital that takes the first and proportionately greatest share of any losses as they occur.[7] Within the highest quality capital, each instrument absorbs losses on a going concern basis proportionately and *pari passu* with all the others.

---

[5] Joint stock companies are defined as companies that have issued common shares, irrespective of whether these shares are held privately or publicly. These will represent the vast majority of internationally active banks.

[6] The criteria also apply to non-joint stock companies, such as mutuals, cooperatives or savings institutions, taking into account their specific constitution and legal structure. The application of the criteria should preserve the instruments' quality by requiring that they are deemed fully equivalent to common shares in terms of their capital quality as regards loss absorption, and do not possess features which could cause the condition of the bank to be weakened as a going concern during periods of market stress. Supervisors will exchange information on how they apply the criteria to non-joint stock companies in order to ensure consistent implementation.

[7] In cases where capital instruments have a permanent write-down feature, this criterion is still deemed to be met by common shares.

9. The paid in amount is recognized as equity capital (i.e. not recognized as a liability) for determining balance sheet insolvency.
10. The paid in amount is classified as equity under the relevant accounting standards.
11. It is directly issued and paid in and the bank cannot directly or indirectly have funded the purchase of the instrument.
12. The paid in amount is neither secured nor covered by a guarantee of the issuer or related entity[8] or subject to any other arrangement that legally or economically enhances the seniority of the claim.
13. It is only issued with the approval of the owners of the issuing bank, either given directly by the owners or, if permitted by applicable law, given by the Board of Directors or by other persons duly authorized by the owners.
14. It is clearly and separately disclosed on the bank's balance sheet.

**2. Additional Tier 1 Capital**
54. Additional Tier 1 Capital consists of the sum of the following elements:

- Instruments issued by the bank that meet the criteria for inclusion in Additional Tier 1 Capital (and are not included in Common Equity Tier 1).
- Stock surplus (share premium) resulting from the issue of instruments included in Additional Tier 1 Capital.
- Instruments issued by consolidated subsidiaries of the bank and held by third parties that meet the criteria for inclusion in Additional Tier 1 Capital and are not included in Common Equity Tier 1. See section 4 for the relevant criteria; and
- Regulatory adjustments applied in the calculation of Additional Tier 1 Capital.

The treatment of instruments issued out of consolidated subsidiaries of the bank and the regulatory adjustments applied in the calculation of Additional Tier 1 Capital are addressed in separate sections.

*Instruments issued by the bank that meet the Additional Tier 1 criteria*
55. The following box sets out the minimum set of criteria for an instrument issued by the bank to meet or exceed in order for it to be included in Additional Tier 1 Capital.

# Criteria for inclusion in Additional Tier 1 Capital

1. Issued and paid in.
2. Subordinated to depositors, general creditors and subordinated debt of the bank.
3. Is neither secured nor covered by a guarantee of the issuer or related entity or other arrangement that legally or economically enhances the seniority of the claim vis-à-vis bank creditors.
4. Is perpetual, i.e. there is no maturity date and there are no step-ups or other incentives to redeem.

---

[8] A related entity can include a parent company, a sister company, a subsidiary or any other affiliate. A holding company is a related entity irrespective of whether it forms part of the consolidated banking group.

5. May be callable at the initiative of the issuer only after a minimum of five years:
   a. To exercise a call option a bank must receive prior supervisory approval; and
   b. A bank must not do anything which creates an expectation that the call will be exercised; and
   c. Banks must not exercise a call unless:
      i. They replace the called instrument with capital of the same or better quality and the replacement of this capital is done at conditions which are sustainable for the income capacity of the bank;[9] or
      ii. The bank demonstrates that its capital position is well above the minimum capital requirements after the call option is exercised.[10]
6. Any repayment of principal (e.g. through repurchase or redemption) must be with prior supervisory approval and banks should not assume or create market expectations that supervisory approval will be given.
7. Dividend/coupon discretion:
   a. The bank must have full discretion at all times to cancel distributions/payments.[11]
   b. Cancellation of discretionary payments must not be an event of default.
   c. Banks must have full access to cancelled payments to meet obligations as they fall due.
   d. Cancellation of distributions/payments must not impose restrictions on the bank except in relation to distributions to common stockholders.
8. Dividends/coupons must be paid out of distributable items.
9. The instrument cannot have a credit sensitive dividend feature, that is a dividend/coupon that is reset periodically based in whole or in part on the banking organisation's credit standing.
10. The instrument cannot contribute to liabilities exceeding assets if such a balance sheet test forms part of national insolvency law.
11. Instruments classified as liabilities for accounting purposes must have principal loss absorption through either (i) conversion to common shares at an objective pre-specified trigger point or (ii) a write-down mechanism which allocates losses to the instrument at a pre-specified trigger point. The write-down will have the following effects:
    a. Reduce the claim of the instrument in liquidation;
    b. Reduce the amount re-paid when a call is exercised; and
    c. Partially or fully reduce coupon/dividend payments on the instrument.
12. Neither the bank nor a related party over which the bank exercises control or significant influence can have purchased the instrument, nor can the bank directly or indirectly have funded the purchase of the instrument.

---

[9] Replacement issues can be concurrent with, but not after, the instrument is called.

[10] Minimum refers to the regulator's prescribed minimum requirement, which may be higher than the Basel III Pillar 1 minimum requirement.

[11] A consequence of full discretion at all times to cancel distributions/payments is that 'dividend pushers' are prohibited. An instrument with a dividend pusher obliges the issuing bank to make a dividend/coupon payment on the instrument if it has made a payment on another (typically more junior) capital instrument or share. This obligation is inconsistent with the requirement for full discretion at all times. Furthermore, the term 'cancel distributions/payments' means extinguish these payments. It does not permit features which require the bank to make distributions/payments in kind.

13. The instrument cannot have any features that hinder recapitalisation, such as provisions that require the issuer to compensate investors if a new instrument is issued at a lower price during a specified time frame.
14. If the instrument is not issued out of an operating entity or the holding company in the consolidated group (e.g. a special purpose vehicle – 'SPV'), proceeds must be immediately available without limitation to an operating entity or the holding company in the consolidated group in a form which meets or exceeds all of the other criteria for inclusion in Additional Tier 1 Capital

*Stock surplus (share premium) resulting from the issue of instruments included in Additional Tier 1 Capital*
56. Stock surplus (i.e. share premium) that is not eligible for inclusion in Common Equity Tier 1, will only be permitted to be included in Additional Tier 1 Capital if the shares giving rise to the stock surplus are permitted to be included in Additional Tier 1 Capital.

**3. Tier 2 Capital**
57. Tier 2 Capital consists of the sum of the following elements:

- Instruments issued by the bank that meet the criteria for inclusion in Tier 2 Capital (and are not included in Tier 1 Capital).
- Stock surplus (share premium) resulting from the issue of instruments included in Tier 2 Capital.
- Instruments issued by consolidated subsidiaries of the bank and held by third parties that meet the criteria for inclusion in Tier 2 Capital and are not included in Tier 1 Capital. See section 4 for the relevant criteria.
- Certain loan loss provisions as specified in paragraphs 60 and 61; and
- Regulatory adjustments applied in the calculation of Tier 2 Capital.[12]

The treatment of instruments issued out of consolidated subsidiaries of the bank and the regulatory adjustments applied in the calculation of Tier 2 Capital are addressed in separate sections.

*Instruments issued by the bank that meet the Tier 2 criteria*
58. The objective of Tier 2 is to provide loss absorption on a going-concern basis. Based on this objective, the following box sets out the minimum set of criteria for an instrument to meet or exceed in order for it to be included in Tier 2 Capital.

## Criteria for inclusion in Tier 2 Capital

1. Issued and paid in.
2. Subordinated to depositors and general creditors of the bank.
3. Is neither secured nor covered by a guarantee of the issuer or related entity or other arrangement that legally or economically enhances the seniority of the claim vis-à-vis depositors and general bank creditors.

---
[12] An operating entity is an entity set up to conduct business with clients with the intention of earning a profit in its own right.

4. Maturity:
   a. Minimum original maturity of at least five years.
   b. Recognition in regulatory capital in the remaining five years before maturity will be amortized on a straight line basis.
   c. There are no step-ups or other incentives to redeem.
5. May be callable at the initiative of the issuer only after a minimum of five years:
   a. To exercise a call option a bank must receive prior supervisory approval.
   b. A bank must not do anything that creates an expectation that the call will be exercised;[13] and
   c. Banks must not exercise a call unless:
      i. They replace the called instrument with capital of the same or better quality and the replacement of this capital is done at conditions which are sustainable for the income capacity of the bank;[14] or
      ii. The bank demonstrates that its capital position is well above the minimum capital requirements after the call option is exercised.[15]
6. The investor must have no rights to accelerate the repayment of future scheduled payments (coupon or principal), except in bankruptcy and liquidation.
7. The instrument cannot have a credit sensitive dividend feature, that is a dividend/coupon that is reset periodically based in whole or in part on the banking organisation's credit standing.
8. Neither the bank nor a related party over which the bank exercises control or significant influence can have purchased the instrument, nor can the bank directly or indirectly have funded the purchase of the instrument.
9. If the instrument is not issued out of an operating entity or the holding company in the consolidated group (e.g. a special purpose vehicle – 'SPV'), proceeds must be immediately available without limitation to an operating entity[16] or the holding company in the consolidated group in a form which meets or exceeds all of the other criteria for inclusion in Tier 2 Capital.

*Stock surplus (share premium) resulting from the issue of instruments included in Tier 2 Capital;*
59. Stock surplus (i.e. share premium) that is not eligible for inclusion in Tier 1, will only be permitted to be included in Tier 2 Capital if the shares giving rise to the stock surplus are permitted to be included in Tier 2 Capital.

*General provisions/general loan-loss reserves (for banks using the Standardized Approach for credit risk)*
60. Provisions or loan-loss reserves held against future, presently unidentified losses are freely available to meet losses which subsequently materialize and therefore qualify for inclusion within Tier 2. Provisions ascribed to identified deterioration of particular

---

[13] An option to call the instrument after five years, but prior to the start of the amortization period, will not be viewed as an incentive to redeem as long as the bank does not do anything which creates an expectation that the call will be exercised at this point.

[14] Replacement issues can be concurrent with, but not after, the instrument is called.

[15] Ibid. note 10.

[16] Ibid. note 12.

assets or known liabilities, whether individual or grouped, should be excluded. Furthermore, general provisions/general loan-loss reserves eligible for inclusion in Tier 2 will be limited to a maximum of 1.25 percentage points of credit risk-weighted risk assets calculated under the standardized approach.

*Excess of total eligible provisions under the Internal Ratings-based Approach*
61. Where the total expected loss amount is less than total eligible provisions, as explained in paragraphs 380 to 383 of the June 2006 Comprehensive version of Basel II, banks may recognize the difference in Tier 2 Capital up to a maximum of 0.6% of credit risk-weighted assets calculated under the IRB approach. At national discretion, a limit lower than 0.6% may be applied.

### 4. Minority interest (ie non-controlling interest) and other capital issued out of consolidated subsidiaries that is held by third parties

*Common shares issued by consolidated subsidiaries*
62. Minority interest arising from the issue of common shares by a fully consolidated subsidiary of the bank may receive recognition in Common Equity Tier 1 only if: (1) the instrument giving rise to the minority interest would, if issued by the bank, meet all of the criteria for classification as common shares for regulatory capital purposes; and (2) the subsidiary that issued the instrument is itself a bank.[17,18] The amount of minority interest meeting the criteria above that will be recognized in consolidated Common Equity Tier 1 will be calculated as follows:

- Total minority interest meeting the two criteria above minus the amount of the surplus Common Equity Tier 1 of the subsidiary attributable to the minority shareholders.
- Surplus Common Equity Tier 1 of the subsidiary is calculated as the Common Equity Tier 1 of the subsidiary minus the lower of: (1) the minimum Common Equity Tier 1 requirement of the subsidiary plus the capital conservation buffer (i.e. 7.0% of risk-weighted assets) and (2) the portion of the consolidated minimum Common Equity Tier 1 requirement plus the capital conservation buffer (i.e. 7.0% of consolidated risk-weighted assets) that relates to the subsidiary.
- The amount of the surplus Common Equity Tier 1 that is attributable to the minority shareholders is calculated by multiplying the surplus Common Equity Tier 1 by the percentage of Common Equity Tier 1 that is held by minority shareholders.

*Tier 1 qualifying capital issued by consolidated subsidiaries*
63. Tier 1 Capital instruments issued by a fully consolidated subsidiary of the bank to third party investors (including amounts under paragraph 62) may receive recognition in Tier 1 Capital only if the instruments would, if issued by the bank, meet all of the criteria

---

[17] For the purposes of this paragraph, any institution which is subject to the same minimum prudential standards and level of supervision as a bank may be considered to be a bank.

[18] Minority interest in a subsidiary which is a bank is strictly excluded from the parent bank's common equity if the parent bank or affiliate has entered into any arrangements to fund, directly or indirectly, minority investment in the subsidiary whether through an SPV or through another vehicle or arrangement. The treatment outlined above, thus, is strictly available where all minority investments in the bank subsidiary solely represent genuine third party common equity contributions to the subsidiary.

for classification as Tier 1 Capital. The amount of this capital that will be recognized in Tier 1 will be calculated as follows:

- Total Tier 1 of the subsidiary issued to third parties minus the amount of the surplus Tier 1 of the subsidiary attributable to the third party investors.
- Surplus Tier 1 of the subsidiary is calculated as the Tier 1 of the subsidiary minus the lower of: (1) the minimum Tier 1 requirement of the subsidiary plus the capital conservation buffer (i.e. 8.5% of risk-weighted assets) and (2) the portion of the consolidated minimum Tier 1 requirement plus the capital conservation buffer (i.e. 8.5% of consolidated risk-weighted assets) that relates to the subsidiary.
- The amount of the surplus Tier 1 that is attributable to the third party investors is calculated by multiplying the surplus Tier 1 by the percentage of Tier 1 that is held by third party investors.

The amount of this Tier 1 Capital that will be recognized in Additional Tier 1 will exclude amounts recognized in Common Equity Tier 1 under paragraph 62.

*Tier 1 and Tier 2 qualifying capital issued by consolidated subsidiaries*
64. Total capital instruments (i.e. Tier 1 and Tier 2 Capital instruments) issued by a fully consolidated subsidiary of the bank to third party investors (including amounts under paragraphs 62 and 63) may receive recognition in Total Capital only if the instruments would, if issued by the bank, meet all of the criteria for classification as Tier 1 or Tier 2 Capital. The amount of this capital that will be recognized in consolidated Total Capital will be calculated as follows:

- Total Capital instruments of the subsidiary issued to third parties minus the amount of the surplus Total Capital of the subsidiary attributable to the third party investors.
- Surplus Total Capital of the subsidiary is calculated as the Total Capital of the subsidiary minus the lower of: (1) the minimum Total Capital requirement of the subsidiary plus the capital conservation buffer (i.e. 10.5% of risk-weighted assets) and (2) the portion of the consolidated minimum Total Capital requirement plus the capital conservation buffer (i.e. 10.5% of consolidated risk-weighted assets) that relates to the subsidiary.
- The amount of the surplus Total Capital that is attributable to the third party investors is calculated by multiplying the surplus Total Capital by the percentage of Total Capital that is held by third party investors. The amount of this Total Capital that will be recognized in Tier 2 will exclude amounts recognized in Common Equity Tier 1 under paragraph 62 and amounts recognized in Additional Tier 1 under paragraph 63.

65. Where capital has been issued to third parties out of a special purpose vehicle (SPV), none of this capital can be included in Common Equity Tier 1. However, such capital can be included in consolidated Additional Tier 1 or Tier 2 and treated as if the bank itself had issued the capital directly to the third parties only if it meets all the relevant entry criteria and the only asset of the SPV is its investment in the capital of the bank in a form that meets or exceeds all the relevant entry criteria[19] (as required by criterion 14 for Additional Tier 1 and criterion 9 for Tier 2). In cases where the capital has been issued to

---

[19] Assets which relate to the operation of the SPV may be excluded from this assessment if they are *de minimis*.

third parties through an SPV via a fully consolidated subsidiary of the bank, such capital may, subject to the requirements of this paragraph, be treated as if the subsidiary itself had issued it directly to the third parties and may be included in the bank's consolidated Additional Tier 1 or Tier 2 in accordance with the treatment outlined in paragraphs 63 and 64.

## 5. Regulatory adjustments

66. This section sets out the regulatory adjustments to be applied to regulatory capital.

In most cases these adjustments are applied in the calculation of Common Equity Tier 1.

*Goodwill and other intangibles (except mortgage servicing rights)*

67. Goodwill and all other intangibles must be deducted in the calculation of Common Equity Tier 1, including any goodwill included in the valuation of significant investments in the capital of banking, financial and insurance entities that are outside the scope of regulatory consolidation. With the exception of mortgage servicing rights, the full amount is to be deducted net of any associated deferred tax liability which would be extinguished if the intangible assets become impaired or derecognized under the relevant accounting standards. The amount to be deducted in respect of mortgage servicing rights is set out in the threshold deductions section below.

68. Subject to prior supervisory approval, banks that report under local GAAP may use the IFRS definition of intangible assets to determine which assets are classified as intangible and are thus required to be deducted.

*Deferred tax assets*

69. Deferred tax assets (DTAs) that rely on future profitability of the bank to be realized are to be deducted in the calculation of Common Equity Tier 1. Deferred tax assets may be netted with associated deferred tax liabilities (DTLs) only if the DTAs and DTLs relate to taxes levied by the same taxation authority and offsetting is permitted by the relevant taxation authority. Where these DTAs relate to temporary differences (e.g. allowance for credit losses) the amount to be deducted is set out in the 'threshold deductions' section below. All other such assets, e.g. those relating to operating losses, such as the carry forward of unused tax losses, or unused tax credits, are to be deducted in full net of deferred tax liabilities as described above. The DTLs permitted to be netted against DTAs must exclude amounts that have been netted against the deduction of goodwill, intangibles and defined benefit pension assets, and must be allocated on a pro rata basis between DTAs subject to the threshold deduction treatment and DTAs that are to be deducted in full.

70. An over-installment of tax or, in some jurisdictions, current year tax losses carried back to prior years may give rise to a claim or receivable from the government or local tax authority. Such amounts are typically classified as current tax assets for accounting purposes. The recovery of such a claim or receivable would not rely on the future profitability of the bank and would be assigned the relevant sovereign risk weighting.

*Cash flow hedge reserve*

71. The amount of the cash flow hedge reserve that relates to the hedging of items that are not fair valued on the balance sheet (including projected cash flows) should be derecognized in the calculation of Common Equity Tier 1. This means that positive amounts should be deducted and negative amounts should be added back.

72. This treatment specifically identifies the element of the cash flow hedge reserve that is to be derecognized for prudential purposes. It removes the element that gives rise to artificial volatility in common equity, as in this case the reserve only reflects one half of the picture (the fair value of the derivative, but not the changes in fair value of the hedged future cash flow).

*Shortfall of the stock of provisions to expected losses*
73. The deduction from capital in respect of a shortfall of the stock of provisions to expected losses under the IRB approach should be made in the calculation of Common Equity Tier 1. The full amount is to be deducted and should not be reduced by any tax effects that could be expected to occur if provisions were to rise to the level of expected losses.

*Gain on sale related to securitisation transactions*
74. Derecognize in the calculation of Common Equity Tier 1 any increase in equity capital resulting from a securitisation transaction, such as that associated with expected future margin income (FMI) resulting in a gain-on-sale.

*Cumulative gains and losses due to changes in own credit risk on fair valued financial liabilities*
75. Derecognize in the calculation of Common Equity Tier 1 all unrealized gains and losses that have resulted from changes in the fair value of liabilities that are due to changes in the bank's own credit risk.

*Defined benefit pension fund assets and liabilities*
76. Defined benefit pension fund liabilities, as included on the balance sheet, must be fully recognized in the calculation of Common Equity Tier 1 (i.e. Common Equity Tier 1 cannot be increased through derecognising these liabilities). For each defined benefit pension fund that is an asset on the balance sheet, the asset should be deducted in the calculation of Common Equity Tier 1 net of any associated deferred tax liability which would be extinguished if the asset should become impaired or derecognized under the relevant accounting standards. Assets in the fund to which the bank has unrestricted and unfettered access can, with supervisory approval, offset the deduction. Such offsetting assets should be given the risk weight they would receive if they were owned directly by the bank.

77. This treatment addresses the concern that assets arising from pension funds may not be capable of being withdrawn and used for the protection of depositors and other creditors of a bank. The concern is that their only value stems from a reduction in future payments into the fund. The treatment allows for banks to reduce the deduction of the asset if they can address these concerns and show that the assets can be easily and promptly withdrawn from the fund.

*Investments in own shares (treasury stock)*
78. All of a bank's investments in its own common shares, whether held directly or indirectly, will be deducted in the calculation of Common Equity Tier 1 (unless already derecognized under the relevant accounting standards). In addition, any own stock which the bank could be contractually obliged to purchase should be deducted in the calculation of Common Equity Tier 1. The treatment described will apply irrespective of the location of the exposure in the banking book or the trading book. In addition:

- Gross long positions may be deducted net of short positions in the same underlying exposure only if the short positions involve no counterparty risk.

- Banks should look through holdings of index securities to deduct exposures to own shares. However, gross long positions in own shares resulting from holdings of index securities may be netted against short positions in own shares resulting from short positions in the same underlying index. In such cases the short positions may involve counterparty risk (which will be subject to the relevant counterparty credit risk charge).

This deduction is necessary to avoid the double counting of a bank's own capital. Certain accounting regimes do not permit the recognition of treasury stock and so this deduction is only relevant where recognition on the balance sheet is permitted. The treatment seeks to remove the double counting that arises from direct holdings, indirect holdings via index funds and potential future holdings as a result of contractual obligations to purchase own shares.

Following the same approach outlined above, banks must deduct investments in their own Additional Tier 1 in the calculation of their Additional Tier 1 Capital and must deduct investments in their own Tier 2 in the calculation of their Tier 2 Capital.

*Reciprocal cross holdings in the capital of banking, financial and insurance entities*
79. Reciprocal cross holdings of capital that are designed to artificially inflate the capital position of banks will be deducted in full. Banks must apply a 'corresponding deduction approach' to such investments in the capital of other banks, other financial institutions and insurance entities. This means the deduction should be applied to the same component of capital for which the capital would qualify if it was issued by the bank itself.

*Investments in the capital of banking, financial and insurance entities that are outside the scope of regulatory consolidation and where the bank does not own more than 10% of the issued common share capital of the entity.*
80. The regulatory adjustment described in this section applies to investments in the capital of banking, financial and insurance entities that are outside the scope of regulatory consolidation and where the bank does not own more than 10% of the issued common share capital of the entity. In addition:

- Investments include direct, indirect[20] and synthetic holdings of capital instruments. For example, banks should look through holdings of index securities to determine their underlying holdings of capital.[21]
- Holdings in both the banking book and trading book are to be included. Capital includes common stock and all other types of cash and synthetic capital instruments (e.g. subordinated debt). It is the net long position that is to be included (i.e. the gross long position net of short positions in the same underlying exposure where the maturity of the short position either matches the maturity of the long position or has a residual maturity of at least one year).

---

[20] Indirect holdings are exposures or parts of exposures which, if a direct holding loses its value, will result in a loss to the bank which is substantially equivalent to the loss in value of the direct holding.

[21] If banks find it operationally burdensome to look through and monitor their exact exposure to the capital of other financial institutions as a result of their holdings of index securities, national authorities may permit banks, subject to prior supervisory approval, to use a conservative estimate.

- Underwriting positions held for five working days or less can be excluded. Underwriting positions held for longer than five working days must be included.
- If the capital instrument of the entity in which the bank has invested does not meet the criteria for Common Equity Tier 1, Additional Tier 1, or Tier 2 Capital of the bank, the capital is to be considered common shares for the purposes of this regulatory adjustment.[22]
- National discretion applies to allow banks, with prior supervisory approval, to exclude temporarily certain investments where these have been made in the context of resolving or providing financial assistance to reorganize a distressed institution.

81. If the total of all holdings listed above in aggregate exceeds 10% of the bank's common equity (after applying all other regulatory adjustments in full listed prior to this one) then the amount above 10% is required to be deducted, applying a corresponding deduction approach. This means the deduction should be applied to the same component of capital for which the capital would qualify if it was issued by the bank itself. Accordingly, the amount to be deducted from common equity should be calculated as the total of all holdings which in aggregate exceed 10% of the bank's common equity (as per above) multiplied by the common equity holdings as a percentage of the total capital holdings. This would result in a common equity deduction which corresponds to the proportion of total capital holdings held in common equity. Similarly, the amount to be deducted from Additional Tier 1 Capital should be calculated as the total of all holdings which in aggregate exceed 10% of the bank's common equity (as per above) multiplied by the Additional Tier 1 Capital holdings as a percentage of the total capital holdings. The amount to be deducted from Tier 2 Capital should be calculated as the total of all holdings which in aggregate exceed 10% of the bank's common equity (as per above) multiplied by the Tier 2 Capital holdings as a percentage of the total capital holdings.

82. If, under the corresponding deduction approach, a bank is required to make a deduction from a particular tier of capital and it does not have enough of that tier of capital to satisfy that deduction, the shortfall will be deducted from the next higher tier of capital (e.g. if a bank does not have enough Additional Tier 1 Capital to satisfy the deduction, the shortfall will be deducted from Common Equity Tier 1).

83. Amounts below the threshold, which are not deducted, will continue to be risk weighted. Thus, instruments in the trading book will be treated as per the market risk rules and instruments in the banking book should be treated as per the internal ratings-based approach or the standardized approach (as applicable). For the application of risk weighting the amount of the holdings must be allocated on a pro rata basis between those below and those above the threshold.

*Significant investments in the capital of banking, financial and insurance entities that are outside the scope of regulatory consolidation.*[23]

84. The regulatory adjustment described in this section applies to investments in the capital of banking, financial and insurance entities that are outside the scope of regulatory

---

[22] If the investment is issued out of a regulated financial entity and not included as regulatory capital in the relevant sector of the financial entity, it is not required to be deducted.

[23] Investments in entities which are outside the scope of regulatory consolidation refers to investments in entities which have not been consolidated at all, or have not been consolidated in such a way as to result in their assets being included in the calculation of the group's consolidated risk-weighted assets.

consolidation where the bank owns more than 10% of the issued common share capital of the issuing entity or where the entity is an affiliate[24] of the bank. In addition:

- Investments include direct, indirect and synthetic holdings of capital instruments. For example, banks should look through holdings of index securities to determine their underlying holdings of capital.[25]
- Holdings in both the banking book and trading book are to be included. Capital includes common stock and all other types of cash and synthetic capital instruments (e.g. subordinated debt). It is the net long position that is to be included (i.e. the gross long position net of short positions in the same underlying exposure where the maturity of the short position either matches the maturity of the long position or has a residual maturity of at least one year).
- Underwriting positions held for five working days or less can be excluded. Underwriting positions held for longer than five working days must be included.
- If the capital instrument of the entity in which the bank has invested does not meet the criteria for Common Equity Tier 1, Additional Tier 1, or Tier 2 Capital of the bank, the capital is to be considered common shares for the purposes of this regulatory adjustment.[26]
- National discretion applies to allow banks, with prior supervisory approval, to exclude temporarily certain investments where these have been made in the context of resolving or providing financial assistance to reorganize a distressed institution.

85. All investments included above that are not common shares must be fully deducted following a corresponding deduction approach. This means the deduction should be applied to the same tier of capital for which the capital would qualify if it was issued by the bank itself. If the bank is required to make a deduction from a particular tier of capital and it does not have enough of that tier of capital to satisfy that deduction, the shortfall will be deducted from the next higher tier of capital (e.g. if a bank does not have enough Additional Tier 1 Capital to satisfy the deduction, the shortfall will be deducted from Common Equity Tier 1).

86. Investments included above that are common shares will be subject to the threshold treatment described in the next section.

*Threshold deductions*
87. Instead of a full deduction, the following items may each receive limited recognition when calculating Common Equity Tier 1, with recognition capped at 10% of the bank's common equity (after the application of all regulatory adjustments set out in paragraphs 67 to 85):

- Significant investments in the common shares of unconsolidated financial institutions (banks, insurance and other financial entities) as referred to in paragraph 84.
- Mortgage servicing rights (MSRs); and
- DTAs that arise from temporary differences.

---

[24] An affiliate of a bank is defined as a company which controls, or is controlled by, or is under common control with, the bank. Control of a company is defined as (1) ownership, control, or holding (for example, a participation in voting rights not representing ownership) as of 20% for any given class of securities the firm has issued (20% in one class is sufficient); or (2) consolidation of the company for financial reporting purposes.

[25] Ibid. note 21.

[26] Ibid. note 22.

88. On 1 January 2013, a bank must deduct the amount by which the aggregate of the three items above exceeds 15% of its common equity component of Tier 1 (calculated prior to the deduction of these items but after application of all other regulatory adjustments applied in the calculation of Common Equity Tier 1). The items included in the 15% aggregate limit are subject to full disclosure. As of 1 January 2018, the calculation of the 15% limit will be subject to the following treatment: the amount of the three items that remains recognized after the application of all regulatory adjustments must not exceed 15% of the Common Equity Tier 1 capital, calculated after all regulatory adjustments. See Annex 2 for an example.

---

## ANNEX 2

### The 15% of common equity limit on specified items

1. This annex is meant to clarify the calculation of the 15% limit on significant investments in the common shares of unconsolidated financial institutions (banks, insurance and other financial entities); mortgage servicing rights, and deferred tax assets arising from temporary differences (collectively referred to as specified items).
2. The recognition of these specified items will be limited to 15% of Common Equity Tier 1 (CET1) capital, after the application of all deductions. To determine the maximum amount of the specified items that can be recognized*, banks and supervisors should multiply the amount of CET1** (after all deductions, including after the deduction of the specified items in full) by 17.65%. This number is derived from the proportion of 15% to 85% (i.e. 15%/85% = 17.65%).
3. As an example, take a bank with €85 of common equity (calculated net of all deductions, including after the deduction of the specified items in full).
4. The maximum amount of specified items that can be recognized by this bank in its calculation of CET1 capital is €85 × 17.65% = €15. Any excess above €15 must be deducted from CET1. If the bank has specified items (excluding amounts deducted after applying the individual 10% limits) that in aggregate sum up to the 15% limit, CET1, after inclusion of the specified items, will amount to €85 + €15 = €100. The percentage of specified items to total CET1 would equal 15%.

*The actual amount that will be recognized may be lower than this maximum, either because the sum of the three specified items is below the 15% limit set out in this annex, or due to the application of the 10% limit applied to each item.
** At this point this is a 'hypothetical' amount of CET1 in that it is used only for the purposes of determining the deduction of the specified items.

---

89. The amount of the three items that are not deducted in the calculation of Common Equity Tier 1 will be risk weighted at 250%.

*Former deductions from capital*   90. The following items, which under Basel II were deducted 50% from Tier 1 and 50% from Tier 2 (or had the option of being deducted or risk weighted), will receive a 1250% risk weight:

• Certain securitisation exposures.
• Certain equity exposures under the PD/LGD approach.

- Non-payment/delivery on non-DvP and non-PvP transactions; and
- Significant investments in commercial entities.

**6. Disclosure requirements**

91. To help improve transparency of regulatory capital and improve market discipline, banks are required to disclose the following:

- A full reconciliation of all regulatory capital elements back to the balance sheet in the audited financial statements.
- Separate disclosure of all regulatory adjustments and the items not deducted from Common Equity Tier 1 according to paragraphs 87 and 88.
- A description of all limits and minima, identifying the positive and negative elements of capital to which the limits and minima apply.
- A description of the main features of capital instruments issued.
- Banks which disclose ratios involving components of regulatory capital (e.g. 'Equity Tier 1', 'Core Tier 1' or 'Tangible Common Equity' ratios) must accompany such disclosures with a comprehensive explanation of how these ratios are calculated.

92. Banks are also required to make available on their websites the full terms and conditions of all instruments included in regulatory capital. The Basel Committee will issue more detailed Pillar 3 disclosure requirements in 2011.

93. During the transition phase banks are required to disclose the specific components of capital, including capital instruments and regulatory adjustments that are benefiting from the transitional provisions.

## C. Transitional arrangements

94. The transitional arrangements for implementing the new standards will help to ensure that the banking sector can meet the higher capital standards through reasonable earnings retention and capital raising, while still supporting lending to the economy. The transitional arrangements include:

(a) National implementation by member countries will begin on 1 January 2013. Member countries must translate the rules into national laws and regulations before this date. As of 1 January 2013, banks will be required to meet the following new minimum requirements in relation to risk-weighted assets (RWAs):
  - 3.5% Common Equity Tier 1/RWAs.
  - 4.5% Tier 1 Capital/RWAs; and
  - 8.0% Total Capital/RWAs.
(b) The minimum Common Equity Tier 1 and Tier 1 requirements will be phased in between 1 January 2013 and 1 January 2015. On 1 January 2013, the minimum Common Equity Tier 1 requirement will rise from the current 2% level to 3.5%. The Tier 1 Capital requirement will rise from 4% to 4.5%. On 1 January 2014, banks will have to meet a 4% minimum Common Equity Tier 1 requirement and a Tier 1 requirement of 5.5%. On 1 January 2015, banks will have to meet the 4.5% Common Equity Tier 1 and the 6% Tier 1 requirements. The Total Capital requirement remains at the existing level of 8.0% and so does not need to be phased in. The difference

between the Total Capital requirement of 8.0% and the Tier 1 requirement can be met with Tier 2 and higher forms of capital.

(c) The regulatory adjustments (i.e. deductions and prudential filters), including amounts above the aggregate 15% limit for significant investments in financial institutions, mortgage servicing rights, and deferred tax assets from temporary differences, would be fully deducted from Common Equity Tier 1 by 1 January 2018.

(d) In particular, the regulatory adjustments will begin at 20% of the required adjustments to Common Equity Tier 1 on 1 January 2014, 40% on 1 January 2015, 60% on 1 January 2016, 80% on 1 January 2017, and reach 100% on 1 January 2018. During this transition period, the remainder not deducted from Common Equity Tier 1 will continue to be subject to existing national treatments. The same transition approach will apply to deductions from Additional Tier 1 and Tier 2 Capital. Specifically, the regulatory adjustments to Additional Tier 1 and Tier 2 Capital will begin at 20% of the required deductions on 1 January 2014, 40% on 1 January 2015, 60% on 1 January 2016, 80% on 1 January 2017, and reach 100% on 1 January 2018. During this transition period, the remainder not deducted from capital will continue to be subject to existing national treatments.

(e) The treatment of capital issued out of subsidiaries and held by third parties (e.g. minority interest) will also be phased in. Where such capital is eligible for inclusion in one of the three components of capital according to paragraphs 63 to 65, it can be included from 1 January 2013. Where such capital is not eligible for inclusion in one of the three components of capital but is included under the existing national treatment, 20% of this amount should be excluded from the relevant component of capital on 1 January 2014, 40% on 1 January 2015, 60% on 1 January 2016, 80% on 1 January 2017, and reach 100% on 1 January 2018.

(f) Existing public sector capital injections will be grandfathered until 1 January 2018.

(g) Capital instruments that no longer qualify as non-common equity Tier 1 Capital or Tier 2 Capital will be phased out beginning 1 January 2013. Fixing the base at the nominal amount of such instruments outstanding on 1 January 2013, their recognition will be capped at 90% from 1 January 2013, with the cap reducing by 10 percentage points in each subsequent year. This cap will be applied to Additional Tier 1 and Tier 2 separately and refers to the total amount of instruments outstanding that no longer meet the relevant entry criteria. To the extent an instrument is redeemed, or its recognition in capital is amortized, after 1 January 2013, the nominal amount serving as the base is not reduced. In addition, instruments with an incentive to be redeemed will be treated as follows:

- For an instrument that has a call and a step-up prior to 1 January 2013 (or another incentive to be redeemed), if the instrument is not called at its effective maturity date and on a forward-looking basis will meet the new criteria for inclusion in Tier 1 or Tier 2, it will continue to be recognized in that tier of capital.
- For an instrument that has a call and a step-up on or after 1 January 2013 (or another incentive to be redeemed), if the instrument is not called at its effective maturity date and on a forward-looking basis will meet the new criteria for inclusion in Tier 1 or Tier 2, it will continue to be recognized in that tier of capital. Prior to the effective maturity date, the instrument would be considered an

'instrument that no longer qualifies as Additional Tier 1 or Tier 2' and will therefore be phased out from 1 January 2013.

- For an instrument that has a call and a step-up between 12 September 2010 and 1 January 2013 (or another incentive to be redeemed), if the instrument is not called at its effective maturity date and on a forward-looking basis does not meet the new criteria for inclusion in Tier 1 or Tier 2, it will be fully derecognized in that tier of regulatory capital from 1 January 2013.
- For an instrument that has a call and a step-up on or after 1 January 2013 (or another incentive to be redeemed), if the instrument is not called at its effective maturity date and on a forward-looking basis does not meet the new criteria for inclusion in Tier 1 or Tier 2, it will be derecognized in that tier of regulatory capital from the effective maturity date. Prior to the effective maturity date, the instrument would be considered an 'instrument that no longer qualifies as Additional Tier 1 or Tier 2' and will therefore be phased out from 1 January 2013.
- For an instrument that had a call and a step-up on or prior to 12 September 2010 (or another incentive to be redeemed), if the instrument was not called at its effective maturity date and on a forward-looking basis does not meet the new criteria for inclusion in Tier 1 or Tier 2, it will be considered an 'instrument that no longer qualifies as Additional Tier 1 or Tier 2' and will therefore be phased out from 1 January 2013.

95. Capital instruments that do not meet the criteria for inclusion in Common Equity Tier 1 will be excluded from Common Equity Tier 1 as of 1 January 2013. However, instruments meeting the following three conditions will be phased out over the same horizon described in paragraph 94(g): (1) they are issued by a non-joint stock company;[27] (2) they are treated as equity under the prevailing accounting standards; and (3) they receive unlimited recognition as part of Tier 1 Capital under current national banking law.

96. Only those instruments issued before 12 September 2010 qualify for the above transition arrangements.

As you most probably have experienced while reading, this really doesn't make you happy. If you experienced issues understanding some (or all) of what they tried to say while reading, I have good news for you: you weren't alone. Therefore, the same Basel Committee issued a Frequently Asked Questions (FAQ) document elaborating on some of the issues discussed in the main document, specifically on the topic of the capital base.[28] I'm not going to terrorize you once again by displaying their writings, but will provide a reference to where the document can be consulted. It does, however, make an interesting read as it at least tries to explain some of the notions mentioned in the main text.

---

[27] Non-joint stock companies were not addressed in the Basel Committee's 1998 agreement on instruments eligible for inclusion in Tier 1 capital, as they do not issue voting common shares.

[28] The document is called: 'Basel Committee on Banking Supervision: Basel III Definition of capital, FAQ,' December 2011 and can be found here: http://www.bis.org/publ/bcbs211.pdf.

## 5.4  IMPACT ON THE USE OF MEZZANINE PRODUCTS IN THE FINANCIAL SECTOR

One thing is clear: a central theme of Basel III, beyond creating a uniform definition for capital in the banking sector, is to ensure that capital is more loss absorbing, especially in times of distress. That undeniably has an impact on the qualification of mezzanine products. Minimum maturities, loss-absorption guarantees and no incentives to accelerate repayment are all part of that initiative. Overall, it can be concluded that Basel III will make the application of many mezzanine products either impossible or more expensive and in any case, fewer mezzanine products will qualify for inclusion in Tier 1 or 2.

The ultimate answer will depend on the covenants and structuring of the individual financial products. Undeniably, certain interpretative issues will occur going forward. For example, the 'incentive to accelerate repayment' can be explained *sensu lato* and *stricto* and can possibly be explained in different ways depending on the context of application. Also, newer products (like the CoCo bond – see further in this chapter) will be tested and will trigger application and interpretative issues.

For convenience purposes, I have attached a summary chart at the end of this chapter reflecting the different technical criteria to be observed when implementing mezzanine products while complying with Basel III.

## 5.5  REGULATION IN THE INSURANCE SECTOR IMPACTING THE USE OF MEZZANINE PRODUCTS

For quite some time now, the European Commission has been looking at introducing pretty similar rules to those for financial institutions in the insurance sector, driven by the same argument of protecting the consumer and the public. Also in the proposed rules, the discussion on regulated capital is center stage. A full discussion of this topic is somewhat outside the scope of this book, in particular as the rules are still somewhat in the making, although as of early 2013 it seems to be the case that the proposed rules will take partial effect on January 1, 2014. It is unclear, however, to what extent last-minute changes to the rules can be expected throughout 2013. Full implementation is only expected by 2016 given the many regulatory hurdles which are still ahead – to such an extent that some national regulators are thinking of implementing part of the Solvency II rules ahead of the official Solvency II Directive coming into effect. Or, put differently, the insurance lobby groups are still putting pressure on the Commission to alter what has become known as the 'Solvency II rules' on a number of critical items. Not without some success, as it turns out at the moment this book was drafted.[29] The process will lead to a delay in implementation, and future changes have not been taken off the table. It is therefore, to a large degree, a question of when and what final rules will come into place and need to be implemented. Therefore, hereafter only an overview of how regulatory capital will be regulated based on the draft rules as they were at the date of closing the manuscript is provided – after an initial (short) introduction to Solvency II.

---

[29] Alistair Gray, 'Insurers wary after EU compromise on new rules,' *Financial Times*, 3/22/2012.

## 5.5.1 Solvency II

The Solvency II Directive[30] is part of a wider set of regulations from European level trying to codify and harmonize the insurance regulation in Europe, and at the same time trying to enhance consumer protection. This is a process which has been going on since the early 70s when Solvency I was introduced. Ever since the introduction of Solvency I in 1973,[31] the industry has been in constant evolution, and our understanding of risk management systems has also improved. The reason why Solvency II gets so much attention is that this time around the rules deal with the level of capital needed, given the risks absorbed. That is going to hurt the bottom line, to the extent that some insurers have already threatened to leave Europe for that reason alone. We are used to statements like that: during the drafting (or should I say negotiations) of Basel III, bankers across the world were warning about the impact of Basel III ranging from shortage of liquidity to more expensive credit across the board and yes, even a 0.3% drop in global GDP growth if the Committee powers through with those rules. They ultimately did, in a somewhat watered-down version. In my earlier writings I have already shared some of my views regarding the EU's regulatory hell, and consequently there is no need to repeat that here.[32] Solvency II, therefore, has a much wider scope.

The Solvency capital requirements serve the following purposes:

- To reduce the risk that an insurer would be unable to meet claims.
- To reduce the losses suffered by policyholders in the event that a firm is unable to meet all claims fully.
- To provide early warning to supervisors so that they can intervene promptly if capital falls below the required level; and
- To promote confidence in the financial stability of the insurance sector.

Therefore, they are often called 'Basel for insurers.' Solvency II is indeed somewhat similar to the banking regulations of Basel II. The proposed Solvency II framework has three main pillars:

- Pillar 1 consists of the quantitative requirements (for example, the amount of capital an insurer should hold).
- Pillar 2 sets out requirements for the governance and risk management of insurers, as well as for the effective supervision of insurers.
- Pillar 3 focuses on disclosure and transparency requirements.

Chapter 6 in particular interests us from a capital perspective. Chapter 6 deals with 'rules relating to the valuation of assets and liabilities, technical provisions, own funds, solvency capital requirement, minimum capital requirement and investment rules.'

---

[30] Directive 2009/138/EC of the European Parliament and of the Council of 25 November 2009 on the taking-up and pursuit of the business of Insurance and Reinsurance (Solvency II) Text with EEA relevance. Official Journal L335, 17/12/2009 p. 0001–0155.

[31] First Council Directive 73/239/EEC of 24 July 1973 on the coordination of laws, regulations and administrative provisions relating to the taking-up and pursuit of the business of direct insurance other than life assurance. Official Journal L228, 16/08/1973 p. 0003–0019.

[32] Luc Nijs, 'Shaping Tomorrow's Marketplace: Investment philosophies for emerging markets and a semi-globalized world,' *Euromoney*, 2011.

The capital framework set out qualitative and quantitative requirements for calculation of technical provisions and Solvency Capital Requirement (SCR) using either a standard formula given by the regulators, or an internal model developed by the (re)insurance company. Technical provisions comprise two components: the best estimate of the liabilities (i.e., the central actuarial estimate) plus a risk margin. Technical provisions are intended to represent the current amount the (re)insurance company would have to pay for an immediate transfer of its obligations to a third party. The SCR is the capital required to ensure that the (re)insurance company will be able to meet its obligations over the next 12 months with a probability of at least 99.5%. In addition to the SCR capital, a Minimum Capital Requirement (MCR) must be calculated, which represents the threshold below which the national supervisor (regulator) would intervene. The MCR is intended to correspond to an 85% probability of adequacy over a one-year period and is bounded between 25% and 45% of the SCR.

For supervisory purposes, the SCR and MCR can be regarded as 'soft' and 'hard' floors respectively. That is, a regulatory ladder of intervention applies once the capital holding of the (re) insurance undertaking falls below the SCR, with the intervention becoming progressively more intense as the capital holding approaches the MCR. The Solvency II Directive provides regional supervisors with a certain amount of discretion to address breaches of the MCR, including the withdrawal of authorization from selling new business and the winding up of the company.

## 5.5.2 Regulated capital under Solvency II

The specifics on capital requirements can be found in Section 6.5. They discuss the issue starting from a required minimum level of capital. Section 6.4 deals with the technical way of calculating the Solvency capital requirement (Articles 100–127) and Section 6.3 determines what qualifies as own funds (Articles 87–99).

The regulation recognizes two distinct types of own funds:

---

1. Own funds (Articles 87–88)

    Own funds shall comprise the sum of basic own funds, referred to in Article 88 and ancillary own funds referred to in Article 89.

    Basic own funds shall consist of the following items:

    (1) The excess of assets over liabilities, valued in accordance with Article 75 and Section 2.

    (2) Subordinated liabilities.

    The excess amount referred to in point (1) shall be reduced by the amount of own shares held by the insurance or reinsurance undertaking.

2. Basic own funds (Article 89)

    Ancillary own funds shall consist of items other than basic own funds which can be called up to absorb losses.

    Ancillary own funds may comprise the following items to the extent that they are not basic own-fund items:

    (a) Unpaid share capital or initial fund that has not been called up.

    (b) Letters of credit and guarantees.

    (c) Any other legally binding commitments received by insurance and reinsurance undertakings.

In the case of a mutual or mutual-type association with variable contributions, ancillary own funds may also comprise any future claims which that association may have against its members by way of a call for supplementary contribution, within the following 12 months.

Where an ancillary own-fund item has been paid in or called up, it shall be treated as an asset and cease to form part of ancillary own-fund items.

There is also a third category defined as:

---

## ARTICLE 91

### SURPLUS FUNDS

Surplus funds shall be deemed to be accumulated profits which have not been made available for distribution to policy holders and beneficiaries.

Insofar as authorized under national law, surplus funds shall not be considered as insurance and reinsurance liabilities to the extent that they fulfil the criteria set out in Article 94(1).

---

Articles 93–99 deal with the tiering structure (just like Basel does) of the capital base and the eligibility of the own funds to be categorized in one of them.

Although technical, a few snapshots are given regarding the classification and its criteria:

---

## ARTICLE 93

### Characteristics and features used to classify own funds into tiers

1. Own-fund items shall be classified into three tiers. The classification of those items shall depend upon whether they are basic own-fund or ancillary own-fund items and the extent to which they possess the following characteristics:
   (a) The item is available, or can be called up on demand, to fully absorb losses on a going-concern basis, as well as in the case of winding up (permanent availability).
   (b) In the case of winding up, the total amount of the item is available to absorb losses and the repayment of the item is refused to its holder until all other obligations, including insurance and reinsurance obligations towards policy holders and beneficiaries of insurance and reinsurance contracts, have been met (subordination).
2. When assessing the extent to which own-fund items possess the characteristics set out in points (a) and (b) of paragraph 1, currently and in the future, due consideration shall be given to the duration of the item, in particular whether the item is dated or not. Where an own-fund item is dated, the relative duration of the item as compared to the duration of the insurance and reinsurance obligations of the undertaking shall be considered (sufficient duration).
   In addition, the following features shall be considered:
   (a) Whether the item is free from requirements or incentives to redeem the nominal sum (absence of incentives to redeem).
   (b) Whether the item is free from mandatory fixed charges (absence of mandatory servicing costs).
   (c) Whether the item is clear of encumbrances (absence of encumbrances).

---

# ARTICLE 94

## Main criteria for the classification into tiers

1. Basic own-fund items shall be classified in Tier 1 where they substantially possess the characteristics set out in Article 93(1)(a) and (b), taking into consideration the features set out in Article 93(2).
2. Basic own-fund items shall be classified in Tier 2 where they substantially possess the characteristic set out in Article 93(1)(b), taking into consideration the features set out in Article 93(2).

   Ancillary own-fund items shall be classified in Tier 2 where they substantially possess the characteristics set out in Article 93(1)(a) and (b), taking into consideration the features set out in Article 93(2).
3. Any basic and ancillary own-fund items which do not fall under paragraphs 1 and 2 shall be classified in Tier 3.

# ARTICLE 95

## Classification of own funds into tiers

Member States shall ensure that insurance and reinsurance undertakings classify their own-fund items on the basis of the criteria laid down in Article 94.

For that purpose, insurance and reinsurance undertakings shall refer to the list of own-fund items referred to in Article 97(1)(a), where applicable.

Where an own-fund item is not covered by that list, it shall be assessed and classified by insurance and reinsurance undertakings, in accordance with the first paragraph. That classification shall be subject to approval by the supervisory authority.

# ARTICLE 96

## Classification of specific insurance own-fund items

Without prejudice to Article 95 and Article 97(1)(a) for the purposes of this Directive the following classifications shall be applied:

(1) Surplus funds falling under Article 91(2) shall be classified in Tier 1.
(2) Letters of credit and guarantees which are held in trust for the benefit of insurance creditors by an independent trustee and provided by credit institutions authorized in accordance with Directive 2006/48/EC shall be classified in Tier 2.
(3) Any future claims which mutual or mutual-type associations of shipowners with variable contributions solely insuring risks listed in classes 6, 12 and 17 in Part A of Annex I may have against their members by way of a call for supplementary contributions, within the following 12 months, shall be classified in Tier 2.

In accordance with the second subparagraph of Article 94(2), any future claims which mutual or mutual-type associations with variable contributions may have against their members by way of a call for supplementary contributions, within the following 12 months, not falling under point (3) of the first subparagraph shall be classified in Tier 2 where they substantially possess the characteristics set out in Article 93(1)(a) and (b), taking into consideration the features set out in Article 93(2).

# ARTICLE 97

## Implementing measures

1. The Commission shall adopt implementing measures laying down the following:
   (a) A list of own-fund items, including those referred to in Article 96, deemed to fulfil the criteria, set out in Article 94, which contains for each own-fund item a precise description of the features which determined its classification.
   (b) The methods to be used by supervisory authorities when approving the assessment and classification of own-fund items which are not covered by the list referred to in point (a).

   Those measures, designed to amend non-essential elements of this Directive by supplementing it, shall be adopted in accordance with the regulatory procedure with scrutiny referred to in Article 301(3).

2. The Commission shall regularly review and, where appropriate, update the list referred to in paragraph 1(a) in the light of market developments.

# SUBSECTION 3

## Eligibility of own funds

# ARTICLE 98

## Eligibility and limits applicable to Tiers 1, 2 and 3.

1. As far as the compliance with the Solvency Capital Requirement is concerned, the eligible amounts of Tier 2 and Tier 3 items shall be subject to quantitative limits. Those limits shall be such as to ensure that at least the following conditions are met:
   (a) The proportion of Tier 1 items in the eligible own funds is higher than one third of the total amount of eligible own funds.
   (b) The eligible amount of Tier 3 items is less than one third of the total amount of eligible own funds.
2. As far as compliance with the Minimum Capital Requirement is concerned, the amount of basic own-fund items eligible to cover the Minimum Capital Requirement which are classified in Tier 2 shall be subject to quantitative limits. Those limits shall be such as to ensure, as a minimum, that the proportion of Tier 1 items in the eligible basic own funds is higher than one half of the total amount of eligible basic own funds.
3. The eligible amount of own funds to cover the Solvency Capital Requirement set out in Article 100 shall be equal to the sum of the amount of Tier 1, the eligible amount of Tier 2 and the eligible amount of Tier 3.
4. The eligible amount of basic own funds to cover the Minimum Capital Requirement set out in Article 128 shall be equal to the sum of the amount of Tier 1 and the eligible amount of basic own-fund items classified in Tier 2.

Section 5 then goes on and deals with the minimum capital requirements by stating:

# ARTICLE 128

## General provisions

Member States shall require that insurance and reinsurance undertakings hold eligible basic own funds, to cover the Minimum Capital Requirement.

# ARTICLE 129

## Calculation of the Minimum Capital Requirement

1. The Minimum Capital Requirement shall be calculated in accordance with the following principles:
   (a) It shall be calculated in a clear and simple manner, and in such a way as to ensure that the calculation can be audited.
   (b) It shall correspond to an amount of eligible basic own funds below which policy holders and beneficiaries are exposed to an unacceptable level of risk were insurance and reinsurance undertakings allowed to continue their operations.
   (c) The linear function referred to in paragraph 2 used to calculate the Minimum Capital Requirement shall be calibrated to the Value-at-Risk of the basic own funds of an insurance or reinsurance undertaking subject to a confidence level of 85% over a one-year period.
   (d) It shall have an absolute floor of:
      (i) EUR 2,200,000 for non-life insurance undertakings, including captive insurance undertakings, save in the case where all or some of the risks included in one of the classes 10 to 15 listed in Part A of Annex 1 are covered, in which case it shall be no less than EUR 3,200,000.
      (ii) EUR 3,200,000 for life insurance undertakings, including captive insurance undertakings.
      (iii) EUR 3,200,000 for reinsurance undertakings, except in the case of captive reinsurance undertakings, in which case the Minimum Capital Requirement shall be no less than EUR 1,000,000.
      (iv) the sum of the amounts set out in points (i) and (ii) for insurance undertakings as referred to in Article 73(5).
2. Subject to paragraph 3, the Minimum Capital Requirement shall be calculated as a linear function of a set or sub-set of the following variables: the undertaking's technical provisions, written premiums, capital-at-risk, deferred tax and administrative expenses. The variables used shall be measured net of reinsurance.
3. Without prejudice to paragraph 1(d), the Minimum Capital Requirement shall neither fall below 25% nor exceed 45% of the undertaking's Solvency Capital Requirement, calculated in accordance with Chapter VI, Section 4, Subsections 2 or 3, and including any capital add-on imposed in accordance with Article 37.

Member States shall allow their supervisory authorities, for a period ending no later than 31 October 2014, to require an insurance or reinsurance undertaking to apply the percentages referred to in the first subparagraph exclusively to the undertaking's Solvency Capital Requirement calculated in accordance with Chapter VI, Section 4, Subsection 2.4.

4. Insurance and reinsurance undertakings shall calculate the Minimum Capital Requirement at least quarterly and report the results of that calculation to supervisory authorities.

Where either of the limits referred to in paragraph 3 determines an undertaking's Minimum Capital Requirement, the undertaking shall provide to the supervisory authority information allowing a proper understanding of the reasons therefore.

5. The Commission shall submit to the European Parliament and the European Insurance and Occupational Pensions Committee established by Commission Decision 2004/9/EC(1) OJ L 3, 7.1.2004, p. 34. (1), by 31 October 2017, a report on Member States' rules and supervisory authorities' practices adopted pursuant to paragraphs 1 to 4.

That report shall address, in particular, the use and level of the cap and the floor set out in paragraph 3 as well as any problems faced by supervisory authorities and by undertakings in the application of this Article.

# ARTICLE 130

## Implementing measures

The Commission shall adopt implementing measures specifying the calculation of the Minimum Capital Requirement, referred to in Articles 128 and 129.

Those measures, designed to amend non-essential elements of this Directive, by supplementing it, shall be adopted in accordance with the regulatory procedure with scrutiny referred to in Article 301(3).

# ARTICLE 131

## Transitional arrangements regarding compliance with the Minimum Capital Requirement

By way of derogation from Articles 139 and 144, where insurance and reinsurance undertakings comply with the Required Solvency Margin referred to in Article 28 of Directive 2002/83/EC, Article 16a of Directive 73/239/EEC or Article 37, 38 or 39 of Directive 2005/68/EC respectively on 31 October 2012 but do not hold sufficient eligible basic own funds to cover the Minimum Capital Requirement, the undertakings concerned shall comply with Article 128 by 31 October 2013.

Where the undertaking concerned fails to comply with Article 128 within the period set out in the first paragraph, the authorisation of the undertaking shall be withdrawn, subject to the applicable processes provided for in the national legislation.

# 5.6  COCO BONDS – CONTINGENT CONVERTIBLE BONDS

Although described as new kids on the block in terms of their inclusion as mezzanine capital, the bonds with features which include a forced conversion have been around for at least two decades, and are not therefore particularly new. It is likely that the (intended) use of the product to shore up their balance sheet (or compensate executives through CoCo-bonuses) by the likes of Credit Suisse, Barclays and Lloyds,[33] at a time when the discussion about the definition of capital under Basel III heated up in the aftermath of the financial crisis gave it more attention than it deserves based on its technical features.

**Definition of contingent capital:**[34] Essentially, the term contingent capital is used very generally to describe a kind of put option enabling the issuer to issue new equity at pre-negotiated terms. As a rule, issuance is triggered by the occurrence of certain risk-based events defined ex ante in the contract conditions. Many constructions and terminologies currently in circulation can be subsumed under the heading contingent capital; CoCo bonds are also a variant. Often, however, constructions resembling contingent convertibles and called CoCo bonds prove, on closer inspection, not to qualify as such, although they are a type of contingent capital:

- Write-down bonds: write-down instead of conversion

  Write-down bonds are a market-based financing instrument. Rather than being converted, as is the case with CoCo bonds, their value is written down instead. The difference is that no additional capital is made available; the liabilities are simply reduced as a result of the valuation adjustment. So, while the company's financial position looks better on paper, equity is created only to the extent of the write-down made, since release of the liabilities generates exceptional gains which can be allocated to retained earnings.

- Temporary write-down bonds

  Temporary write-down bonds – also known as step-up, step-down bonds – are debt instruments which, on the one hand, can have their liabilities reduced once a pre-determined trigger event occurs but, on the other hand, also have upside potential. In other words, a valuation adjustment can also step up their value proportionately, meaning that the bonds are written down only temporarily. Bonds structured this way already exist in the marketplace. So far, however, accounting regulations have prevented bonds of this kind from being counted towards regulatory capital ratios. Rather, the Basel proposal provides for permanent, partial loss absorption, which is not the case with temporary write-down bonds.

---

[33] Hereunder, the specifics of the most visible deals up till now (source: Contingent Convertible Bonds and the Impact of Basel III, December 20, 2011, Cadwalader, Wickersham & Taft LLP. Reproduced by permission of A. Duncan, A. Prentice and A. Maginness) – in all cases triggers were capital ratio-based:

**Lloyds Banking Group**
In November 2009, Lloyds offered Enhanced Capital Notes (ECNs) in exchange for existing hybrid bonds. Holders of specified Tier 1 and Upper Tier 2 instruments were invited to exchange such instruments for ECNs or an amount payable in new and/or existing shares, or cash. The ECNs are capable of qualifying as Lower or Upper Tier 2 Capital, and will convert into new and/or existing ordinary shares in Lloyds if the Lloyds Core Tier 1 ratio falls below 5%. The conversion rate is pre-determined, based on the observed share price, and is to be adjusted in certain circumstances. The ECNs have maturities of between 10 and 15 years, and the coupon is set between 1.5% and 2.5%. As Lloyds had been partly nationalized at the time of the exchange offer, it could neither redeem bonds nor pay interest, as a result, the exchange was an attractive offer as the ECNs carried a higher coupon and could be sold upon conversion.

footnote (*continued*)

### Rabobank

In March 2010, Coöperatieve Centrale Raiffeisen-Boerenleenbank B.A. (Rabobank Nederland) issued €1,250 billion of Senior Contingent Notes ('SCN'). The coupon was set at 6.875%. These notes are contingent, but not convertible. If the Rabobank Group Equity Capital Ratio, defined as retained earnings and member certificates relative to risk-weighted assets, falls below 7% before the notes mature, the par-amount and unpaid coupons will be written down by 25% and investors will immediately be repaid at this redemption price. Unless previously redeemed or purchased and canceled, the SCN will be redeemed at 100% of their principal amount on March 19, 2020. As the write down of Rabobank Nederland's notes does not meet the requirements of Basel III, the notes do not, therefore, count towards regulatory capital. This issuance was designed to further enhance triple A rated Rabobank's creditworthiness.

In November 2011, Rabobank Nederland issued $2 billion Hybrid Tier 1 Notes. The notes have a perpetual maturity with a call after 5.5 years. The coupon was set at 8.4% and is fully discretionary, with no link between payments and dividends. If Rabobank's Equity Capital Ratio falls or is expected to fall below 8%, the notes will absorb losses pro rata with equity capital and other loss-absorbing instruments. The issuer or the regulator can also trigger the write down. The notes were designed to comply with Dutch and European capital requirements (CRD II) and incorporate provisions to address the guidelines issued to date for the upcoming CRD IV regulatory requirements, and to strengthen Rabobank's capital base ahead of the upcoming Basel III implementation.

Rabobank also issued $2 billion hybrid notes in January 2011. These notes were Hybrid Tier 1 Perpetual Notes, callable at 5.5 years, with a coupon set at 8.375% and a write-down trigger if equity capital ratio falls below 8%. The Rabobank issuances are unusual for a number of reasons: (i) Rabobank is unlisted, making it the only private sector bank with a triple A credit rating; (ii) Rabobank is mutually owned and therefore cannot convert bonds into equity; and (iii) Rabobank's current Equity Capital Ratio (July 2011) is 14%, providing a substantial capital buffer (approximately €12.3 billion) before its contingent debt can be written down.

### Credit Suisse

In February 2011, Credit Suisse Group (Guernsey) I Limited issued $2 billion Tier 2 Buffer Capital Notes (Tier 2 BCNs). The coupon was set at an initial rate of 7.875% per annum, and thereafter at a rate, to be reset every five years, based on the mid-market swap rate plus 5.22%.

In this issuance, the conversion trigger was linked to the occurrence of either a contingency event or a viability event. In summary, a contingency event will occur if the Credit Suisse Group's (Credit Suisse) Common Equity Tier 1 ratio falls below 7%, and a viability event will occur if: (i) FINMA is of the opinion that Credit Suisse would reach the point of non-viability without conversion of the debt into equity, or (ii) if Credit Suisse receives a promise of State-aided support without which it would become non-viable. If either event should materialize, the Tier 2 BCNs will, subject to certain conditions, mandatorily convert into ordinary shares. Unless previously redeemed or purchased and canceled, the Tier 2 BCNs will be redeemed at 100% of their principal amount on February 24, 2041. Credit Suisse also issued SFr6 billion of Tier 1 Buffer Notes Capital Notes (Tier 1 BCNs). Similar to the Tier 2 BCNs, a contingency event and viability event trigger applies to the notes, with the contingency event trigger threshold set at 7%. Again, if the Credit Suisse Common Equity Tier 1 ratio falls below this threshold, the Tier 1 BCNs will convert into Credit Suisse ordinary shares.

### Bank of Cyprus

In April 2011, the Bank of Cyprus offered €1,342,422.297 of perpetual Convertible Enhanced Capital Securities (CECS) to existing shareholders in the ratio of €3 CECS for every two shares held. The coupon was set at an initial fixed rate of 6.5% until June 30, 2016 and thereafter, at a floating rate of Euribor plus 3%. The CECS will be mandatorily converted into ordinary shares at a mandatory conversion price on the occurrence of a contingency event or a viability event. Similar to the Credit Suisse issuance, a contingency event will occur if the bank's Common Equity Tier 1 Ratio falls below 5%, and a viability event will be deemed to occur if the Central Bank of Cyprus determines that either the conversion of CECS is necessary to ensure the bank's viability or the bank requires extraordinary public sector support to prevent non-viability.

[34] Deutsche Bank research, EU Monitor 79, March 2011.

- Call Option Enhanced Reversible Convertibles (COERCs)

So far this is nothing more than a theoretical proposition describing a bond which is automatically converted when a pre-determined trigger is met. The conversion rate is below the price which triggers conversion and the bonds feature a buy-back option for existing shareholders, i.e., a kind of subscription right. To what extent instruments of this kind are fit for purpose is an open issue, nor is their regulatory recognition clear.

**Definition of a CoCo bond:** Historically, a CoCo bond is a convertible bond in which the price of the underlying stock must reach a certain level before conversion is allowed. Contingent convertible bonds define a stock price (higher than the strike price) which the underlying stock must meet before a bond holder is allowed to convert. For example, the conversion price for a convertible bond may be $10 per share, but if the stock price is below $20 per share, the investor may not convert the bond (aka upside contingency). However, in more recent times, CoCo bonds come with different features; for example, if the issuer is a bank the condition may be that it will convert to equity if the issuer's Tier 1 capital (or its credit rating or certain core capital ratios) falls below a certain pre-determined limit. The automatic conversion will then re-capitalize the bank. The issuance of bank CoCo bonds, in the aftermath of the financial crisis, in order to provide extra Tier 1 capital in times of stress has become widespread (to replace the discredited hybrid securities they used before).

Figure 5.1 illustrates the implication on a bank's balance sheet in a 'before' and 'after conversion' scenario.[35]

It is important here to differentiate between liquidity and capital: CoCos do not introduce new capital into the firm after conversion, but transform a debt component into new common stock, enabling better absorption of future losses (and avoiding interest payments on the debt instrument).

However, in 2011 the Basel Committee somewhat took the punch bowl away regarding the development of this product, after it significantly blocked the use of the product to shore up Tier 1 capital at financial institutions (see further in this chapter). The Committee basically addressed the issue by stating that the higher (core) Tier 1 levels under Basel III need to come from common

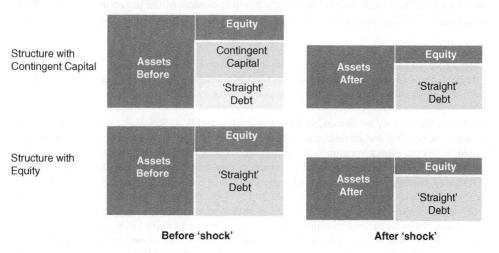

**Figure 5.1**    Comparing contingent capital (CoCo) to equity

[35] Source: Prof. Anat Admati (2011) Stanford Graduate School of Business.

equity or other core reserves (common shares and retained earnings) and not from CoCo bonds. However, national regulators are free to include them in any separate requirements they impose.

Others qualified the instruments as 'equity time bombs,'[36] as they would further dilute the EPS after automatic conversion (by broadening the firm's equity base), and consequently would put even more stress on the already stressed stock price at that point.

The attractiveness of the product obviously lies in its cheaper costs, and the non-convertibility lock-in during 'normal periods' in business versus expanding its equity base through a new rights issue.

It requires very little empathy to understand the viewpoint of financial institution investors after the 2008–2009 events and the losses they took in that period. What the product has working in its favor is its loss-absorbing capacity in times of stress, something the Basel Committee stressed when creating Basel III. The question, however, is at what cost that loss-absorbing capacity comes if one converts after stress has already kicked in. The conversion event then becomes destabilizing for the bank in cases where there is too much contingent capital versus real equity.

Comparisons were made with the 'death spiral bonds' which were commonplace in the 90s. Death spiral convertible bonds differ from normal convertible bonds in the sense that instead of having a pre-determined, fixed conversion ratio, death spirals have a floating conversion ratio in which the holder receives a discount for converting shares. They support large drops in share prices and stimulate short selling indirectly.

Banks may still use CoCo bonds to meet capital requirements imposed by national regulators above the 7% core Tier 1 minimum set by Basel III, but need to use common equity for their Tier 1 capital levels. Banks are also permitted under Basel III to hold 1.5% of their risk-weighted assets in non-core Tier 1 and 2% in Tier 2 capital, principally subordinated bonds. Under Basel II, non-core Tier 1 capital included hybrid instruments, securities that won't be permissible under Basel III, as we reviewed earlier in this chapter.

It would probably be beyond the scope of this book to fully flesh out all the details of this specific product – there are others who do that for us.[37] There is one document which brings together a lot of analysis on the product and particularly analysis of the trigger events for the CoCo bonds to automatically convert. The IMF paper,[38] and in particular Appendix 2, provides a well-structured approach with respect to the possible content of the triggering clauses (which can be bank or market specific or a combination, see further in this chapter and its implications,

---

[36] Anousha Sakoui and Patrick Jenkins, 'Stability concerns over coco bonds,' *Financial Times*, November 5, 2009. For a more comprehensive review, see Michel Goyer, *Contingent Capital: Short-term Investors and the Evolution of Corporate Governance in France and Germany*, Oxford University Press, 2012, 224 pages.

[37] The following is highly recommended: Jan de Spiegeleer and Wim Schoutens, 'Contingent Convertible Notes: Structuring and pricing,' Euromoney Books, 2011; and from a more generic perspective: Craig M. Lewis and Patrick Verwijmeren, 'Convertible Security Design and Contract Innovation,' Owen Graduate School of Management, Vanderbilt University, Research Paper 2010, and Charles W. Calomiris and Richard J. Herring, 'Why and How to Design a Contingent Convertible Debt Requirement,' Working Paper, revised 2011, Columbia Business School, and National Bureau of Economic Research & Wharton School, University of Pennsylvania. These last authors claim that to be maximally effective: (a) a large amount of CoCos (relative to common equity) would be required, (b) CoCo conversion should be based on a market value trigger, defined using a moving average of a 'quasi market value of equity ratio' (QMVER), (c) all CoCos should convert if conversion is triggered, and (d) the conversion ratio should be dilutive of preexisting equity holders.

[38] Ceyla Pazarbasioglu, Jianping Zhou, Vanessa Le Leslé and Michael Moore, 'Contingent Capital: Economic Rationale and Design Feature,' IMF staff discussion note, January 25, 2011 SDN/11/01.

good and bad). What sets it apart from typical hybrid debt is the fact that it provides loss-absorbing capital in times of stress in contrast to typical hybrid debt where the holder wouldn't convert in times of stress as there would be no equity to be captured. That benefit needs to be weighted with the implication of an equity dilution at a moment characterized by enhanced stress levels.

There are three different measurements on which triggers for conversion are generally based:

- Capital-based triggers which rely on accounting measures of capital adequacy.
- Regulatory discretion-based triggers which allow regulators to mandate conversion of CoCo bonds into common equity during a banking crisis; and
- Market-based triggers which use declines in stock prices or increases in the premiums of credit default swaps.

Quite a lot of critique can be defined with respect to the intrinsic quality of these triggering events:

- With respect to capital triggers which rely on accounting measures, criticism can be built around the timing/delay in responding to a situation of distress, since financial reporting only happens on a quarterly basis. This could mean that, in practice, the CoCo bond cannot properly perform its primary function, that is, to act as an effective loss-absorber, as it would only be triggered at the end of an accounting period.
- Regulatory-based measures have the potential of leading to uncertainty (for investors), as they are often ad hoc decisions. The discretion being in the hands of the regulator makes it difficult for investors and rating agencies to assess the probability of conversion.
- Market-based triggers, such as share price, are subject to stock market volatility and possible stock price manipulation. Further, a market-based trigger may be activated by market events which are completely unrelated to the financial situation the bank is in.

With respect to the valuation of those products, many things have been said in the last couple of years. Most authors refer back to an equity-derivative (option) type of approach,[39] as is the case for most debt instruments with a convertibility feature attached. The feature additionally built into the model is obviously the value of the option and how it changes when markets evolve and/or the financial position of the issuing firm.

As previously mentioned, the instrument has received quite a lot of attention in recent years, particularly in the context of financial institutions using the product, although its use is definitely not limited to those situations. The instrument could also be interesting for corporations within the context of the traditional corporate finance sphere, and particularly the balance sheet structure and optimal capital structure and valuation decisions.[40]

---

[39] See extensively: Henrik Teneberg, 'Pricing Contingent Convertibles using an Equity Derivatives Jump Diffusion Approach,' 2012, Working Paper. He favors the equity derivatives approach, by letting the underlying asset follow a jump-diffusion process instead of a standard Geometrical Brownian Motion. Issues might arise, such as that prices need to be followed in the market and data absence or disparity may limit its effective use. Also: Jan De Spiegeleer and Wim Schoutens, 'Pricing Contingent Convertibles: A Derivatives Approach,' 2011, Working Paper Series, KU Leuven Belgium – included in their book mentioned under note 35, and Jan De Spiegeleer, Wim Schoutens, Albert Ferreiro-Castilla *et al.* 'Efficient Pricing of Contingent Convertibles under Smile Conform Models,' 2011, Working Paper – they look at the problem of pricing CoCo bonds where the underlying risky asset dynamics are given by a smile conform model, more precisely an exponential Levy process incorporating jumps and heavy tails.
[40] See, for example: Boris Albul, Dwight M. Jaffee and Alexei Tchistyi, 'Contingent Convertible Bonds and Capital Structure Decisions,' Working Paper, 2010, Haas School of Business, University of California at Berkeley.

## 5.6.1  Outlook for the product[41]

As mentioned before, the Basel Committee didn't want to play ball regarding the qualification of the product. That, however, doesn't make it dead in the water, but its success will be highly dependent on the reasons behind using the product, and the structuring of the product.

The choice of conversion trigger and the terms on which a CoCo bond is converted are essential in any discussion about the outlook of the product group. Tailoring of the conditions to fit the situation will be essential.

As a final note, the following critical elements should be considered:

- **Trigger levels:** Are they used as catastrophe bonds providing capital insurance (low trigger) or as a more permanent pre-emptive buffer (high trigger)? The higher the trigger, the more expensive the CoCo from an investor point of view, which is expected to be around 8–9%. Alternative triggers could be based on (or a combination of):
  - Book values/balance sheet values (but data reported only quarterly).
  - Risk-weighted assets/capital ratios (also reported only at end of each quarter).
  - Market prices/share prices (most market-driven but also subject to market volatility).

    The trigger criteria determine the loss absorption capacity and could, within the Basel framework, replace the hybrid capital position. There seems to be a consensus that leaving the conversion decision to regulators creates too much uncertainty in the default probability.
- **Conversion rate:** Conversion at par value seems to be advisable as a conversion rate above par could trigger a greater incentive for the issuing bank to avoid conversion by taking corrective action.
- **Maturities:** Although the average bond investor expects a maturity of 3–7 years, the IIF already indicated that when CoCos want to play a meaningful LT role on a bank's balance sheet, longer maturities of up to even 30 years should be considered. A system of different layers of maturities/triggers is probably the direction in which reality is going.
- **Pricing:** Since contingent convertibles convert automatically once the trigger is met, investors bear the risk of becoming shareholders at a very inconvenient time. It may be assumed that CoCos will, in general, carry a higher coupon than traditional bank bonds. Drivers of the coupon are the trigger point and the conversion risk associated with it. The higher the conversion risk, the higher the premium. If the coupon is too close to the cost of equity, the CoCos obviously lose their value for the issuer. Drivers of the conversion risk are: (1) FI's business model and expected volatility in earnings, (2) level of Tier 1 capital (the lower the more likely the conversion), (3) degree of probability of conversion (including the discretionary intervention rights which national authorities hold, who can step in very early), (4) impact of CoCo issue on cost of senior debt for issuer (lower default risk).
- **Rating of the instrument.**
- **Regulatory intervention (under distress):** New regulatory acts across countries all include the authorities' ability to intervene, and quite often allow them to waive lenders' rights. These interventions (which are ex-post) are separate from CoCo conversion (which are ex-ante) but can impact the CoCo investor in their position.

---

[41] See further: Contingent Convertibles: Banks take on a new look, May 2011, Deutsche Bank Research.

# 5.7 ANNEX I – SUMMARY BASEL III

**Redefining Tier 1 & 2 Capital**

- Under Basel III: Instruments qualifying for recognition as Tier 1 or Tier 2 capital will be restricted substantially.
- Distinction between upper Tier 2 and lower Tier 2 will be eliminated.
- Tier 3 capital will be eliminated.

In summary, in order to qualify, new non-common equity Tier 1 and Tier 2 instruments must:

- Be more loss-absorbing.
- Not contain incentives to redeem prior to their stated maturity.
- Be written off or converted to equity when the relevant supervisor determines that either the bank will not be viable without the write-off, or a public sector capital injection is to be made.
- Changes render ineligible a wide range of outstanding upper Tier 1 and Tier 2 instruments. Most ineligible instruments (e.g., innovative hybrid capital instruments with incentives to redeem), formerly limited to 15% of T1 capital base, will be phased out or even fully derecognized from 2013.

**Components Common Equity Tier 1**

Common shares issued by bank:

- Stock surplus (share premium).
- Retained earnings (including interim profit or loss).
- Accumulated other comprehensive income and other disclosed reserves.
- Common shares issued by consolidated subsidiaries of the bank and held by third parties (i.e., minority interest) which meet criteria for CET 1 (subject to additional conditions below).
- Regulatory deductions (see above).
- Dividends removed from CET 1 in accordance with applicable accounting standards.

**Components of additional Tier 1**

Instruments meeting criteria for inclusion:

- Stock surplus (share premium) resulting from instruments included in AT 1.
- Instruments issued by consolidated subsidiaries of the bank and held by third parties (i.e., minority interest) which meet criteria for AT 1 (subject to additional conditions below).

**Components of Tier 2 Capital**

Instruments meeting criteria for inclusion:

- Stock surplus (share premium) resulting from instruments included in T2.
- Instruments issued by consolidated subsidiaries of the bank and held by third parties (i.e., minority interest) which meet criteria for T2 (subject to additional conditions below).

   Certain loan loss provisions or reserves.

   Standardized banks: loan loss provisions or reserves held against future, presently unidentifiable losses which are freely available to meet losses, limited to 1.25% of risk-weighted assets.

   IRB banks: excess (if any) of total eligible provisions (as provided in Basel II) over total expected loss amounts, limited to 0.60% of risk-weighted assets.

- Regulatory deductions.

## 5.8 ANNEX II – BASEL III – SPECIFIC FEATURES

| Contractual Feature | Tier 1 Common Equity | Tier 1 Additional going-concern capital | Tier 2 Capital |
|---|---|---|---|
| **General** | Perpetual | • Perpetual.<br>• No step-ups or other incentives to redeem. | • Minimum original maturity of at least five years.<br>• Recognition in regulatory capital in remaining five years before maturity amortized on straight line basis.<br>• No step-ups or other incentives to redeem (an option to call after five years but prior to start of amortization period, without creating expectation of call, is not incentive to redeem). |
| **Redemption/ Repayment** | • Principal perpetual and never repaid outside of liquidation.<br>• Discretionary repurchases and other discretionary means of effectively reducing capital permitted if allowable under national law. | • Repayment of principal (e.g., through repurchase or redemption) only with prior supervisory approval.<br>• Instrument cannot have features hindering recapitalization, such as provisions requiring issuer to compensate investors if new instrument issued at lower price during specified time frame. | Investor must have no rights to accelerate repayment of future scheduled payments (coupon or principal), except in bankruptcy and liquidation. |
| **Call** | | • Callable at initiative of issuer only after minimum of five years:<br>(a) To exercise call option bank must receive prior supervisory approval; and<br>(b) Bank must not do anything creating expectation that call will be exercised; and | • Callable at initiative of issuer only after minimum of five years:<br>(a) To exercise call option bank must receive prior supervisory approval; and<br>(b) Bank must not do anything creating expectation that call will be exercised; and |

| Contractual Feature | Tier 1 Common Equity | Tier 1 Additional going-concern capital | Tier 2 Capital |
|---|---|---|---|
| | | (c) Bank must not exercise call unless:<br>i. bank replaces called instrument with capital of same or better quality and replacement done at conditions sustainable for income capacity of bank (replacement must be concurrent with call, not after); or<br>ii. bank demonstrates that capital position well above minimum capital requirement after call exercised ('minimum' requirement refers to national law, not Basel III rules). | (c) Bank must not exercise call unless:<br>i. bank replaces called instrument with capital of same or better quality and replacement done at conditions sustainable for income capacity of bank (replacement must be concurrent with call, not after); or<br>ii. bank demonstrates that capital position well above minimum capital requirement after call exercised ('minimum' requirement refers to national law, not Basel III rules). |
| No Expectation | Bank does nothing to create expectation at issuance that instrument will be bought back, redeemed or canceled, nor do statutory or contractual terms provide any feature which might give rise to such expectation. | Bank should not assume or create market expectation that supervisory approval for repayment of principal will be given. | Bank must not do anything which creates expectation that call will be exercised. |
| **Distributions/Coupons** | | | |
| Source | • Distributions paid out of distributable items (retained earnings included).<br>• Level of distributions not in any way tied or linked to amount paid in at issuance and not subject to cap (except to extent bank unable to pay distributions exceeding level of distributable items). | Dividends/coupons paid out of distributable items. | |

(continued)

| Contractual Feature | Tier 1 Common Equity | Tier 1 Additional going-concern capital | Tier 2 Capital |
|---|---|---|---|
| **No obligation** | • No circumstances under which distributions obligatory.<br>• Non-payment not event of default. | Dividend/coupon discretion:<br>(a) Bank must have full discretion at all times to cancel distributions/ payments ('dividend pushers' and requirement to pay distribution/ payment in kind both explicitly prohibited);<br>(b) Cancellation of discretionary payments must not be event of default.<br>(c) Banks must have full access to canceled payments to meet obligations as they fall due.<br>(d) Cancellation of distributions/payments must not impose restrictions on bank except in relation to distributions to common stockholders. | Investor must have no rights to accelerate repayment of future scheduled payments (coupon or principal), except in bankruptcy and liquidation. |
| **Priority** | • Distributions paid only after all legal and contractual obligations met and payments on more senior capital instruments made.<br>• No preferential distributions, including in respect of other elements classified as highest quality issued capital. | | |
| **Margin adjustment** | | Instrument may not have a credit-sensitive dividend feature, i.e., dividend/coupon reset periodically based in whole or part on bank's current credit standing. | Instrument may not have a credit-sensitive dividend feature, i.e., dividend/ coupon reset periodically based in whole or part on bank's current credit standing. |

| Contractual Feature | Tier 1 Common Equity | Tier 1 Additional going-concern capital | Tier 2 Capital |
|---|---|---|---|
| **Subordination** | | | |
| **Priority** | • Represents most subordinated claim in liquidation of bank.<br>• Entitled to claim of residual assets proportional to share of issued capital after all senior claims repaid in liquidation (i.e., unlimited and variable claim, not fixed or capped claim). | Subordinated to depositors, general creditors and subordinated debt of bank. | Subordinated to depositors and general creditors of bank. |
| **Loss absorbency** | • Takes first and proportionately greatest share of any losses as occur.<br>• Within highest quality capital; absorbs losses on going-concern basis proportionately and *pari passu* with all others. | • Instruments classified as liabilities must have principal loss absorption through either:<br>  (a) Conversion to common shares at objective pre-specified trigger point; or<br>  (b) Write-down mechanism allocating losses to instrument at pre-specified trigger point.<br>• Write-down will have following effects:<br>  (a) Reduce claim of instrument in liquidation.<br>  (b) Reduce amount repaid when call is exercised; and<br>  (c) Partially or fully reduce coupon/dividend payments on instrument. | |
| **Equity-like nature** | • Paid-in amount recognized as equity capital (i.e., not recognized as liability) for determining balance sheet insolvency.<br>• Paid-in amount classified as equity under relevant accounting standards. | Instrument cannot contribute to liabilities exceeding assets if balance sheet test forms part of national insolvency law. | |
| **Security** | Neither secured nor covered by guarantee of issuer or related entity or subject to other arrangement legally or economically enhancing seniority of claim. | Neither secured nor covered by guarantee of issuer or related entity or other arrangement legally or economically enhancing seniority of claim vis-à-vis bank creditors. | Neither secured nor covered by guarantee of issuer or related entity or other arrangement legally or economically enhancing seniority of claim vis-à-vis depositors and general bank creditors. |

## 5.9  CASE STUDY POSITIONS: MEZZANINE FINANCING FOR FINANCIAL INSTITUTIONS

The following three case study positions are put in place to illustrate the different rationales for using mezzanine within an FI's balance sheet, the drivers behind the choice and, ultimately, the implications of doing so. This requires us to reflect on the intrinsic risk which is included in the underlying business transaction which will rely on the mezzanine funding. Although cases, in reality, come with much larger and often more confusing datasets, I have tried to limit the data provided to the key essentials for decision making, rather than for number crunching.

## 5.10  CASE STUDY 1: FINANCING THE FUTURE OF BANK ALHANBRA

Bank Alhanbra, established in 1990, is active in one of the smaller South-East Asian countries. The bank holds third position in the national leagues with a 15% market share. The bank is family owned. Total assets at the end of 2012 are about US$1 billion and it has an equity position of US$60 million. Traditionally, it positioned itself as a traditional corporate bank. It has, however, entered the retail segment successfully, and makes up about half of its business in terms of its loan portfolio. It wants to (1) focus on strengthening its retail and corporate banking position through organic and acquisition growth, (2) enhance its syndicated loan position, (3) build a trade finance platform and (4) offer factoring and other corporate and retail services on a fee basis.

This should allow it to become the number two or even one in the next few years. The family is considering its long-term options and how to see a way to monetize their investment a few years down the road, as there is an intensifying wave of consolidation going on in the region and the industry. This is particularly driven by regional players such as CIMB and global players such as Citigroup and JPMorgan working their way into the region, trying to benefit from the (sometimes slow and volatile but) steady growth the region's economies are experiencing. Although the LT outlook is definitely good, they realize that the tide can turn quickly, and that instability in the regional and global banking sector and the undigested impact of new regulation including Basel III could end the consolidation wave and close the exit door for the family and other investors in the firm. Also, politically, the country seems to be in good and stable shape. Nevertheless, regional economic instability coming from Thailand, Pakistan and/or Afghanistan might (temporarily) impact the country and its sovereign structure.

Due to the existing growth and their expected growth plans, both in terms of its existing and new business operations, the bank's Tier 1 capital base has become somewhat tight. They are looking at about US$40 million in additional capital which will be used for the purposes mentioned above. Basel requirements are either not at all or not fully implemented, and can therefore be ignored in this case. (This is a frequent thing in emerging markets, which can simplify or indeed complicate even further the implication of capital requirements relative to the Basel conditions – under Basel II or III the options in terms of a product would be very limited, i.e., the only mezzanine product eligible for Tier 1 would be non-redeemable non-cumulative preferred shares.)

The country is in the process of implementing IFRS statements and plans to complete that process by 2016. There is an existing stock exchange which originally planned to open in 2009, but ultimately did in 2011. There are only three stocks listed (partial listings of SOEs through partial privatization) and liquidity is very low. Market capitalization is unlikely to increase significantly over the next couple of years.

The bank has a good relationship with its central bank. The central bank's balance sheet is very limited; in distress it might not play the lender-of-last-resort role. You can ignore any currency issues which might arise. The following dataset was made available:

| Millions USD | 2009 | 2010 | 2011 | 2012 | 2013 Est. |
|---|---|---|---|---|---|
| Total assets | 605 | 759 | 865 | 987 | 1109 |
| Net loans | 360 | 430 | 450 | 490 | 520 |
| Deposits | 410 | 450 | 510 | 550 | 610 |
| Equity | 40 | 45 | 65 | 70 | 80 |
| Equity/TA (%) | 6.61 | 5.9 | 7.51 | 7.09 | 7.21 |
| BIS-ratio (%) | 11.0 | 12.0 | 11.5 | 12.5 | 12.9 |
| Interest income | 40.6 | 49.6 | 52.4 | 55.7 | 72.9 |
| Interest expense | 21.2 | 26.7 | 27.9 | 30.5 | 40.6 |
| Other income | 20.3 | 27.9 | 30.6 | 34.9 | 40.6 |
| Loan loss provisions | 3.0 | 3.9 | 4.9 | 5.1 | 5.4 |
| Net income | 5.9 | 6.7 | 7.9 | 10.9 | 15.9 |
| Asset growth (%) | N/A | 25 | 14 | 14 | 12 |
| Net interest margin (%) | 4.3 | 4.9 | 5.1 | 5.5 | 5.1 |
| NPL > 90 days (%) | 3.1 | 2.9 | 2.1 | 2.5 | 2.4 |
| Cost to income ratio (%) | 81.4 | 75.3 | 60.5 | 65.4 | 59.3 |
| RoAA (%) | 0.8 | 1.4 | 1.9 | 1.7 | 2.0 |
| RoAE (%) | 14 | 18 | 29 | 23 | 25 |

## 5.10.1  Case guidance

Besides the question of product choice, the case requires you to think about the implications of using mezzanine products in this case. The deposit base will expand significantly and so will its debt ratios. Another feature to consider is how to structure the product of choice to arm it against a possible evaporation of a natural liquidity event (acquisition by foreign players who are looking to enter the market), or if the family changes its mind about selling the business. What if a formal put option is not acceptable for the family? Are there other ways via which we can incentivize the family to use their call option beyond a certain point in time in the future? Is intermittent liquidity provided by a product an absolute necessity in this case, or just an interesting add-on feature? Would your assessment be different if the growth were gained through the acquisition of the number four or five player in the market, rather than through organic growth? How would your risk assessment be different, and what would the impact be on the health of the balance sheet after acquisition?

The other question that will come up is about the pricing of the instrument, which will obviously depend, in terms of its structuring, on the choice of mezzanine instrument. The average forward-looking P/B and P/E in the region at the moment of the transaction in the sector are respectively 3.1 and 15.6. If call and put options will be used, the question arises as to whether it makes sense to apply a top-down IRR approach to determine the total return on the product required, given the level of risk it is exposed to.

## 5.11  CASE STUDY 2: GROWING THE BRAZILIAN MARKET

Alegria Bank Lda. is a mid-tier bank located in Aracuja in the north of Brazil (in the state Sergipe, the smallest state of the Brazilian federation with just over 2 million inhabitants), with an estimated 600,000 inhabitants and about 10 million inhabitants in the wider economically relevant region. It focuses on retail and SME finance in the city/state and is planning on continuing to do so. It has been going through a phase of rapid growth in the last couple of years, both based on increased consumer and SME activity and equally due to the development of mainly coastal real estate.

The plan is to grow the bank's position in the retail and SME space both in the state and in the neighboring states, where they expect to improve the market share. They are uncertain as to what extent the real estate sector will contribute to future growth, both because the sector is looking at sourcing subordinated debt rather than senior debt, and the bank capped its position in subordinated products to about 15% of its total loan portfolio. The other reason is linked to the overall performance of the real estate sector, the uncertainty about American consumers who still account for a big chunk of both rentals and acquisitions of real estate, and the questionable loan-to-value relationship of some recent projects. The bank already, as a strategy, only finances projects which are 80% pre-sold. Real estate financing accounts for about 30% of its total loan portfolio, that is not including retail mortgage loans.

The break-down of loan allocation is:

- 30% real estate (residential, office and resorts combined).
- 15% retail mortgage.
- 30% senior loans to SMEs.
- 15% subordinated facilities to SMEs (often part of a unitranche arrangement and sometimes with second lien facilities).
- 5% personal loans.
- 5% leasing facilities.

Overall economic activity in the region is driven by the industrial and service sectors, accounting for 52% and 41% respectively.

Part of the growth strategy is to contribute to the development of small and medium-sized cities in the state, but even more in its neighboring states (Alagoas, Parnambuco, Paraiba and the much larger state of Bahia), where it sees significant opportunities, and to provide a broad range of high quality services to families and SMEs in a variety of sectors.

Its strategic benefits are the fact that it is a strong brand with high brand awareness in the market, a complete pallet of products, a wide network of branches (120) and sophisticated IT platform to serve both individuals and businesses. It is governed by the central bank of Brazil and has an A-rating provided by S&P. It has relatively limited competition, as the larger national players focus more on the larger states and centers of interest.

It is owned by its two founders (33.33% respectively) and one third is owned by a Rio de Janeiro-based investment firm which bought into the bank in an earlier stage of growth finance in 2006.

They are looking for a 10-year subordinated loan facility with a bullet structure and a call option after five years. Preferably, they would like to source the facility in local currency, the real. The real has appreciated significantly in recent years, particularly against the USD, but hedging facilities for extended periods of time would be either unavailable or too costly to justify the action. Uncertainty about where the latest rounds of global quantitative easing in the USA will lead, and the heated debates Brazilian president Mrs Dilma Rousseff has publicly engaged in, referring to currency wars and currency manipulation on the part of developed nations by deflating their currencies (the West, Japan, Eurozone), stresses the relevance of sourcing a real-denominated facility.

The following dataset was made available:

| Real '000 | 2010 | 2011 | 2012 |
|---|---|---|---|
| Total assets | 220,454 | 476,000 | 698,765 |
| Net loan portfolio | 120,867 | 354,098 | 490,074 |
| Deposits | 56,076 | 130,765 | 240,756 |
| Equity | 40,876 | 89,098 | 121,098 |
| Solvency (Eq./TA)(%) | 18.54 | 18.71 | 17.33 |
| CAR (%) | 24.9 | 19.4 | 13.5 |
| NIM (%) | 6.5 | 7.9 | 9.6 |
| Provision/Net interest income (%) | 3.7 | 14.5 | 19.6 |
| Net profits | 4,546 | 7,655 | 9,634 |
| Cost-to-income ratio (%) | 43.3 | 78.9 | 67.9 |
| RoAA (%) | 2.4 | 2.1 | 1.9 |
| RoAE (%) | 19.6 | 20.4 | 20.7 |

Its capital adequacy ratio is acceptable to good, but has deteriorated in recent years. The bank is suffering from the phenomenon which most retail-focused banks are suffering from and that is high capital level needs due to its large branch network which is, for the largest part, rents (65%) unless it is more economically reasonable to buy.

The investment firm re-capitalized the bank when it entered years ago through equity and a subordinated loan (that loan will mature in 2014 – tenor: eight years). Although they re-invest much of their earnings, that no longer seems efficient, and additional capital will be needed. The other elements are the increasing concern of the real estate portfolio, the strength of the borrower and the market value of the underlying collateral. The bank realizes that real estate prices in the region have gone against the flow, increasing even in recent turbulent years in international real estate. However, it also realizes that there is no guarantee whatsoever that this phenomenon will continue going forward. It has, in recent years, increased the provisioning for bad loans quite significantly to soften a downfall in this part of the business.

2012 has seen slower growth for the Brazilian economy, and the international dynamics are far from optimal either. That has not translated into the 2012 numbers, but during early 2013 that economic trend might start to show up in its numbers, as SMEs and families start feeling the pinch of the slowdown.

Its portfolio quality is pretty decent and its deposit base has grown significantly:

| Criteria | 2011 | 2012 |
|---|---|---|
| Non-performing loans (NPL)(%) | 3.9 | 7.2 |
| Loan loss reserve (LLR)(%) | 5.5 | 7.9 |
| LLR/NPL (%) | 141% | 109.7 |
| Write off (%) | 1.4 | 1.9 |

In terms of its A/L management, it has positive mismatches on all the maturity baskets, ranging from less than one month to more than one year.

## 5.11.1  Case guidance

Is the subordinated loan with bullet payment suggested by the bank the right instrument for its strategy, given its current financial position and its outlook? Why or why not? If not, what alternative do you have in mind? Is it possible that the level of subordination will deteriorate, even after the 2006 subordinated loan provided by the investment matures? What will trigger that event? Can we structure the product in such a way that we are sheltered from that event happening?

## 5.12  CASE STUDY 3: FINANCING A SOUTH AFRICAN FI WHICH IS PART OF A LARGER CONGLOMERATE PRIOR TO AN IPO

The FI under review is part of a private family conglomerate based in Cape Town, South Africa. The conglomerate has been in operation for over 100 years, and is now run by the third generation. The last couple of years have been very good for the firm, both on the FI as well as the non-FI side. They have significant expansion plans and realize that an IPO will become unavoidable going forward. The decision was made to list part of the FI rather than the holding's shares. They do, however, understand that despite the fact that South Africa and Africa as a continent have not been suffering as much as other parts of the world from the economic recession and financial crisis, they are impacted indirectly through more volatile FDI flows, uncertain portfolio flows and the fact that long-term equity is still in limited supply on the continent. The longer term outlook is good and SA's role as FDI location to access the wider Sub-Saharan Africa region is validated, although Nigeria will gain an increasingly important role, and both countries together account for slightly over 50% of the continent's GDP. Unemployment as a lagging indicator is causing concern as the ANC doesn't seem to be able to tackle a stubbornly high unemployment rate which, in 2012, hovered around 24% with significantly higher youth unemployment, which in some parts of the country went up to 45%. The firm seems well insulated from the direct impact of all that, but is slightly concerned with the collateral effects. Its NPL has gone up but is still at reasonable levels.

Some selected data regarding the FI arm were provided (in USD rather than SA Rand):

| USD '000 | 2010 | 2011 | 2012 |
|---|---|---|---|
| Total assets | 967,067 | 1,456,867 | 2,756,878 |
| Loan portfolio | 450,776 | 870,989 | 1,768,576 |
| Equity | 87,787 | 120,767 | 198,787 |
| Equity/TA (%) | 9.07 | 8.28 | 7.21 |
| Net profit | 25,737 | 29,787 | 46,745 |
| RoAE (%) | 29.6 | 27.6 | 30.5 |
| NPL (%) | 2.1 | 2.6 | 2.9 |
| LLR/NPL (%) | 130.43 | 104.54 | 108.56 |

The other part of the conglomerate is involved in the consumer goods industry, building materials, insurance, mining and transport. There are significant intercompany transactions between the banking side of the conglomerate and the rest of the firm. Its local rating (holding level) is A2 (Moody's).

The family is somewhat in doubt about how to structure the US$20 million in financing it needs. If the loan were provided to the bank arm directly, it would have to be in the form of a subordinated loan with a significant grace period versus its tenor, and potentially with a cash sweep clause included (which would allow for the free cash flow above a certain level to be directed towards repayment of the investor's subdebt, and potentially accelerate the repayment). In two years' time another existing subdebt provided by Absa Bank will mature and a large part of the funding will be available to replace that instrument. The instrument would have to carry a tenor of about 5–7 years in case either the IPO window stayed shut for longer periods of time, or the valuation of the company would not incentivize listing the FI in the short to medium term. If the loan were provided at holding level, it could be a senior loan with similar characteristics in terms of tenor, but with a fixed spread of 400 bps over JIBAR. With JIBAR standing at around 6% that comes close to a 10% interest rate. The loan would then be used to capitalize the banking arm.

## 5.12.1 Case guidance

To possibly bring the interest rate down (a bit), the investor is considering providing an alternative compensation schedule through a profit participating scheme and/or detachable warrants. If they were to engage in the financing of this transaction this way, they would be looking for a security that would be accompanied by a pledge on the holding's shares (or would it be better to do so at the level or the FI? – what would the pros and cons for each of the options be?). Should they look for a floor in the profit participating scheme? Should the profit participating scheme be at a holding level or FI level – what are the pros and cons of each of the options?

Is the pledge a real security, or just to provide peace of mind? What would happen if the pledge were executed and the investor became an ultimate minority owner in the holding; illiquidity and very little leverage towards the family? Should they negotiate a put option in case the pledge is executed? The same story would occur if they were to exercise the warrants which come with the subdebt. Would the same solution work for more or less the same problem?

From a general perspective: What are the benefits and detriments of providing financing at holding level versus providing that financing at FI level? Would the answer in this case be different if the plan were to list the conglomerate rather than the FI?

# 6

# Mezzanine and Project Finance

Very often I have been asked to define or demarcate project finance, and very often I have done so by defining it in contrast to corporate finance.[1] However, ultimately one could argue that corporate finance is a bundling of many project finances put together and run through one balance sheet. I don't object to that approach. It is not possible, nor is it my intention, to be fully comprehensive when it comes to the fundamentals and techniques of project finance in this chapter. That would not be in line with the objectives of this chapter, nor the book in general for that matter. What I'll try to do is provide the components of the framework within which project finance is active, in order to better understand the role mezzanine products can play (or not). As a starter, let's (try to) agree on the following features for each of the techniques (see Table 6.1):

**Table 6.1** Corporate versus project finance

|  | Corporate finance | Project finance |
|---|---|---|
| Capital formation | Will impact debt capacity | Will not impact debt capacity, because it is off balance sheet |
| Risk exposure | Could impact overall cost structure and cost of funding | Limited |
| Tax shield | Hard to take advantage of | Easier to bundle |
| Cash flow | Subject to corporate policy on dividend (corporate treasury) | Directly to the investor |
| Cost of project financing | None | High due to setting up cost |
| Capital cost | Companies' track records | High due to no history |
| Oversight by the sponsors | None | Very demanding |

The essence of project finance is that all the parties involved basically judge the financial viability of the project based on the projected cash flows which relate to the project, rather than looking at the balance sheet of the parties involved in the deal. Since pretty much all project finance deals are long term, the use of projected cash flows can mean you will end up being terribly wrong. Nevertheless, the use of project finance has only increased over the last two decades. There are very few firms, if any, whose balance sheet can tolerate accumulating project by project for decades and then wait to get a payoff over the next 15–25 years. It would

---

[1] See Krishnamurthy Subramanian, Frederick Tung and Xue Wang, 'Project finance versus corporate finance,' Goizueta Business School, Working Paper Series, 2007.

make the firm unworkable, external financiers would become worried and the firm would start to move like an oil tanker while trying to take on board new opportunities.

Although project finance can serve a variety of purposes, it is well known in the context of real estate projects (see Chapter 7) and infrastructure projects, either on a private basis or on a PPP basis (public–private partnerships) where the public sector works together with private companies in achieving certain public objectives. That can be hard infrastructure like toll roads and bridges, mining, telecoms, power plants, waterways, ports (air and maritime) or it can be soft infrastructure like schools, hospitals, sports facilities, cultural centers etc. The decision to use a project finance structure is often to bring together parties in an orderly fashion, to reduce risk, but is often also economically driven.[2] It has become widespread as a concept and used pretty much all over the world, sometimes with a local flavor attached to it (i.e., Islamic project finance in the Middle East). The role of project finance and infrastructure projects cannot be overestimated, in particular in developing nations[3] where they can act as a catalyst in getting local economies going, as well as in Western countries where societies are facing dilapidated infrastructure and growing structural levels of unemployment in the real estate and construction sector.

Although most project finance structures are engineered to suit the individual needs and facts of a particular project, one could say that there is something which looks like a standard (BOT) project finance structure (see Figure 6.1).

Every project finance deal has a number of parties involved:

1. Project company (SPV) which will hold the project assets.
2. (Equity) sponsors.
3. Government/grantor (in PPP deals).
4. Banks/lender (or syndication of banks/lenders).
5. Technical adviser.
6. (Sub)contractors.
7. Lawyer, accountants etc.
8. External equity investors.
9. Regulatory agencies.
10. Multilateral agencies.
11. …

Since the focus is on the project's cash flows (only), and the only thing that binds the parties together is a set of contracts, it is also often called contractual finance. Both returns and risk allocation are done contractually, and are therefore critical in every project finance position. It not only determines the ultimate return for parties (and their position if things change along the way) but also co-determines the behavior of parties (e.g.,

---

[2] B. Esty, 'The economic reasons for using project finance,' HBS Working Paper series, 2002.

[3] See, for example: Stefanie Kleimeier and Roald Versteeg, 'Project Finance as a Driver of Economic Growth in Low-Income Countries,' Working Paper, Maastricht University, 2008; also: Vikas Srivastava and Ashish Kumar, 'Financing Infrastructure Projects in India from Corporate Finance to Project Finance,' *International Research Journal of Finance and Economics*, Issue 55 (2010) and Benjamin C. Esty, 'Why Study Large Projects? An Introduction to Research on Project Finance' (2004) *European Financial Management* **10**(2):213–224.

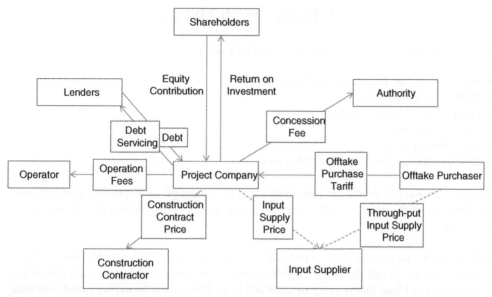

**Figure 6.1**  Funding for a BOT project

incentivizing subcontractors; are lenders sufficiently awarded for the risk they take? How do we avoid the project sponsor walking away if the project turns south? How do we properly lock in guarantees provided by government or development banks etc?). It is often difficult to over-estimate the complexity of the deals and the potential situations which contracts have to foresee. More and more, the market experience is that lenders are looking for fallback guarantees for the sponsors and/or external equity investors (or other critical parties like governments etc.). Those fallback guarantees go back to the balance sheet of the underlying companies (sponsors) involved in the deal. Most of it is beyond the scope of this book.

To get the picture right, and before talking about mezzanine finance in this context, I want to point out that the identification and allocation of risk[4] is an integrated part of what are called the project delivery methods and the contractual arrangements surrounding each of them.[5]

[4] See Corene Crossin and Jessie Banfield, 'Conflict and Project Finance: exploring options for better management of conflict risk,' Background paper, January 2006.
[5] For a comprehensive review of the topic, see, amongst others: Barbara Weber, *Infrastructure as an Asset Class: Investment strategy, project finance and PPP*, John Wiley & Sons, 2010; Neil Grigg, *Infrastructure Finance: The business of infrastructure for a sustainable future*, John Wiley & Sons, 2010; Michael Underhill, *The Handbook of Infrastructure Investing*, Wiley Finance, 2010; Rajeev Sawant, *Infrastructure Investing: Managing risks and rewards for pensions, insurance companies and endowments*, Wiley Finance, 2010; Willie Tan, *Principles of Project and Infrastructure Finance*, Routledge, 2010; Jeffrey Delmon, *Private Sector Investment in Infrastructure: Project finance, PPP projects and risks*, Kluwer Law International, 2008; Benjamin Esty, *Modern Project Finance: A casebook*, John Wiley & Sons, 2003; Henry Davis, *Infrastructure Finance: Trends and techniques*, Euromoney Books, 2010.

# 6.1 TYPES OF PROJECTS

The most commonly used project delivery methods are:

- B(O)OT – Build-(Own)-Operate-Transfer.
- DBB – Design-Bid-Build.
- DAB – Design-Award-Build.
- DB – Design Build.
- DC – Design Construct.
- DBOM – Design-Build-Operate-Maintain.

The project model ultimately determines the identification and quantification of risk, the duration of the projects and how risks should be allocated. This makes sense. A few examples:

- If you build and operate a power plant, the government will ultimately determine the price at which you can sell the energy. Before commencing, you would want some sort of understanding of how that is going to work and how changes will be implemented over time (off-take and supply agreement). The same goes for mining and telecom infrastructure projects.
- Will ownership of a sports stadium, railway or airport be transferred to the government after completion or not? Who will operate (and maintain) the infrastructure?
- If you need a concession from the government: for how long and under what conditions? What might trigger a change in the contractual conditions? (Concession agreement.)
- Does the infrastructure just need to be built or also maintained (O&M contract – operation and maintenance)?
- Inter-creditor agreement: How will the lenders engage in the deal, and what will happen in case of a default? Who will be repaid and in what order? etc.
- In cases with multiple shareholders: Who will incur what risk and under what conditions? (Joint-venture contract.)
- Other contracts involved will be (EPC – engineering, procurement and construction) loan agreements between SPV and (syndication of) banks and potentially insurance firms etc.

Project finance is also widely used outside the infrastructure space. Examples here are aircraft and maritime finance, as well as more specialized forms of asset finance.

A big chunk of the financing for these projects comes from debt products. Since we are talking about infrastructure and the returns come from the cash flows of the project (only), financial modeling is a critical decision-maker in this respect. Scenario modeling and measuring the impact of intermediate changes in input levels are key to understanding and allocating risks. That can be a sensitivity to macro-economic variables, interest rates, inflation, GDP, consumer spending and purchasing power, cultural aspects (are consumers willing to pay for a toll road or would they still prefer to line up in the congested secondary roads?), timing sensitivity (how quickly does volume of output grow, for example in mining or power stations?), pricing levels of the product or service, especially when prices are dictated (or at least capped) by governments and/or regulators (energy, healthcare, sports facilities etc.), currency issues, and all other non-quantifiable risks (earthquake, tsunami, or political risk;

can my concession or licenses be revoked or pricing agreement be unilaterally changed if the administration changes?).

Allocation of risk and return on a contractual basis is not only there to guarantee a stable project despite the headwinds every project will experience (somewhere down the road), but also to keep the overall cost of funding as low as possible given the inherent risks in the project. Risk identification and allocation therefore also contribute to a lower WACC. Why? If you allocate a specific risk to the party which is best positioned to deal with that risk, it will also be able to deal with that risk at the lowest cost of all the parties involved. That will ultimately feed into a lower WACC, as return expectations will end up in line with that understanding of the parties incurring that risk.

If parties come to the conclusion that potential returns are structurally not in line with risk levels, the project becomes un-financeable. Then, additional guarantees, heavy involvement of development banks (although they are commercial in mindset as well these days) or the government taking the project further and financing it completely themselves are the only remaining options on the table.

## 6.2 FINANCING ASPECTS

Much of the total funding need in project finance comes, as previously mentioned, from debt products. On average, only 20–25% of the project ends up being equity financed by the sponsors and/or external equity investors.[6] This means foremost that in project finance a considerable amount of risk is borne by the lenders, rather than the equity owners.[7] It will also mean that purely static 15- or 20-year loans will become problematic, as it would push the fixed cost/total cost ratio too high for it to be financially feasible, and drain the young project of cash flows too early due to heavy early interest payments.

Lenders (often in syndication) are willing to step in with senior debt (non-recourse loans) to the extent the asset base of the project can justify. Those loans are secured by all assets of the project (and revenue-generating contracts, for example supply or off-take contracts), rather than the assets or creditworthiness of the sponsors. However, the funding needs are more significant than just the cost of the assets developed. They have a first lien on all assets and contracts, and therefore can assume control of the project in the case that the project turns sour. That is the downside of asking lenders to absorb significant amounts of risk on these projects.

Riskier projects or projects with large amounts of non-asset investments or expenditures will have to turn to alternative ways of financing part of their funding needs. That can go two ways: either by taking on board limited recourse financing with an appropriate collateral or surety from the sponsors and/or via mezzanine products. That will often be combined with securitization, options (derivatives), (war) insurance provisions, or other

---

[6] Antonio Vives and Paulina Beato, 'How much equity is enough in project financing?' Working Paper, Inter-American Development Bank, 2007.
[7] See extensively: Marco Sorge, 'The nature of credit risk in project finance' (2004) *B.I.S. Quarterly Review*.

types of collateral enhancement to make the financial model work or enhance the credit-worthiness of the project to bring down the cost of funding. Sometimes things will become complicated, particularly when the sponsor intends to use off-balance-sheet financing. In parallel or on top of the funding needs, often an insurance firm will issue a performance bond (secured bond) to guarantee that the contractors complete the project on time (it also often guarantees completion by another firm in the case that the contractor or subcontractors go bankrupt in the process). Besides financial guarantees provided by the government or other public bodies, they can also engage in non-financial guarantees like the guarantee of a certain minimum price for the product or service and/or certain volumes (which are not necessarily guaranteed by off-take agreements), as normally the market fundamentals can run free there.

What also occurs a lot is the introduction of staged financing. This can be done with the original set of lenders or a different set. What happens is that the lenders originally agree to finance the development of the project up to a certain degree (dependent on what the project is about, building facilities etc.). Only when certain milestones are completed will the financing for further stages become available. Often this is arranged with lenders upfront and in one holistic proposal, as no sponsor will take the risk of the project falling apart halfway due to a lack of funding for the next stages. The benefit is that, when the project advances, the inherent risks of the project also come down, which should make the following tranches of financing less expensive. Often the same result is achieved through securitization, where parts of the debt financing are offloaded to free up the balance sheet and improve financial ratios like the DSCR (debt service coverage ratio) and LLCR (loan life coverage ratio) as well as a wide range of project-specific financial ratios which will undoubtedly relate to performance, liquidity and profitability (i.e., asset utilization ratio, gross rent multiplier (GRM) or (combined) loan-to-value ((C)LTV) ratio in real estate).

As everything in project finance is linked to the specifics of the case, I would like to illustrate some of the aforementioned specifics through two case studies; one which deals with the building of a toll highway, and the other which deals with the building of a windfarm. Both can be found later in the chapter.

It is advisable to keep the following framework and dynamics in mind. Given the difference between financial and economic insolvency as discussed in Chapter 1, the structure for a project should allow it to flourish and not strangle a perfectly economically sound project by piling up maturities too close to each other, or providing loans with a maturity mismatch relative to the earn back period or economic lifetime of the project. It should also be noted that using larger amounts of equity (beyond 20–30%) in much of the project finance world, would make the project uninteresting for the sponsors or external investors compared to other alternatives there are in the market.[8]

---

[8] D.P. Goldman, J.J. McKenna and L.M. Murphy, 'Financing Projects That Use Clean-Energy Technologies: An Overview of Barriers and Opportunities,' National Renewable Energy Laboratory, 2005; J.P. Harper, M.D. Karcher and M. Bolinger, 'Wind Project Financing Structures: A Review & Comparative Analysis,' Ernest Orlando Lawrence Berkeley National Laboratory, 2007.

## 6.3  SECURITIZING PROJECT LOANS

There are a number of ways, but principally two, to securitize project finance loans. The first mechanic is for the holders of such loans, which can be a pool of loans with different characteristics, to sell those loans to an SPE, which will obtain the funds to make such a purchase by issuing debt or equity securities to (often) long-term institutional investors. The second way is for long-term investors to accept new loans being issued in order to refinance the original, which were issued to finance one project or different projects (which would diversify the project-specific risks). Such refinancing mechanisms, especially if they involve more than one project, may utilize an SPE, owned by the project entities, as the new borrower and issuer of the debt securities.

This process is often not without complications. The most common issues are:

- Estimating the **risk of loss** is often complicated because of uncertainties as to the credit quality of the borrower. Also when the size of the loan volume increases, predicting default becomes problematic due to its technical nature. This problem may be mitigated by having a large pool of loans, although that brings in other complications, i.e., they will involve different industries, different economic issues and contractual structures. In general it can be argued that there is a relatively clear view on the actual risk of loss, either because there is a supply or off-take agreement, or because there are demographic and other studies to support the (WTP) willingness to pay for the goods or service of future customers (see case study later in the chapter). Others risks, such as construction risks, are covered by lump-sum guaranteed turnkey completion contracts or otherwise.
- **Completion of construction and performance of project facility.** Only a problem when the loans are securitized before the completion of the construction and the beginning of the loans' performance.
- **Rating agency criteria.**[9] In general rating agencies assess, besides financial risk on the one hand, completion, operation, revenue and macro risks on the other hand. Despite the fact that most rating agencies did not only issue criteria for assessing project finance in recent years, but also for specific industries, it is fair to state that most of the models are inherently vague in nature as often the ultimate assessment is subject to specific facts in a case, and so strong theoretical modeling or methodological formulation is difficult and therefore skewed.

The most commonly used techniques in securitization are:

- Warranties.
- Credit enhancement (by protecting against certain basic risks).
- Issuance of junior notes (which bear a higher risk in the project – tranching).
- Discount sales.

---

[9] See extensively: Fitch Rating Research, 'Rating Criteria for Infrastructure and Project Finance,' Global Master Criteria Report, 2009.

- Cross-collateralization.
- Third party credit enhancement (i.e., insurance bond).
- Spread account (in case the interest on the project loans is higher than the yield on the securitized instrument(s)).

## 6.4  CASE STUDY 1: DEVELOPING A TOLL ROAD IN POLAND (A2)

Caveat: although I will try as much as possible to reflect the situations as they would be in real life, thereby honoring the role of the case studies and the space they can justify within the context of this book, it needs to be stressed that the actual situations are often characterized by a more complex array of features and issues coming together, as well as being subject to a more complicated structure of legal relations, as are many projects in reality. Certain factual patterns might, therefore, be condensed or omitted due to the focus on those aspects which directly relate to the mezzanine finance-related features of the case.

At the end of the nineties, after Poland emerged as an independent country and was preparing to enter the EU, which it would do in 2004, it was faced with a huge problem, a problem known to many emerging economies. That is, the dilapidated road infrastructure and its potential to hamper trade with the rest of Europe and dampen economic growth in the country.

In fact, Poland had the potential to act as a transit country for exports from the EU, and in particular Germany and the Benelux, to Russia, a very important trading partner of the EU. The actual situation was, however, less promising. From west to east through Poland, there was no single mile of highway which could facilitate international or transit cargo, or passenger transport for that matter. In order to contribute to that objective, the A2 project was developed. Autostrada Wielkopolska SA (AW), a special-purpose consortium of Polish (ownership 77%, including firms from the hotel, tourism, insurance, PE and power industries) and European firms (ownership 23%, predominantly heavy construction firms such as Strabag) won the concession to build and operate a significant portion of the A2, the first toll road in Poland. A syndication of banks was involved, led by Crédit Lyonnais (CL) and Commerzbank. The total project costs were estimated at €934 million (for the first phase of the project), of which €242 million was earmarked to come from senior loans. It would become the first Paris all-the-way-to-Moscow transit corridor and part of the Trans-European network linking EU countries. On the A2, an 'open toll' system would be applied, meaning that the tollhouses would be located along the route.

The main relationships in the project structure are:[10]

- The Polish government providing a guarantee and the concession agreement to AWSA.
- Loan agreement provided to AWSA by senior lenders (syndicate).
- An O&M agreement between the operating company and AWSA.

---

[10]Based on ibid. note 11. See also for complete project structure.

- Design and construction contract between the development company and AWSA.
- Engineering agreement between AWSA and independent engineering firms.
- Insurance contracts between independent insurance firms and AWSA.
- Shareholder and shareholder (subordinated) loan agreements between owners and AWSA.
- Bond agreement between bondholders and AWSA (indirectly through internal finance company).

The financial picture was designed as shown in Table CS6.1:[11]

**Table CS6.1**   Project balance sheet

| Funding Req. | Euro (Mn) | Zloty (Mn) | % in total | Funding Req. | Euro (Mn) | Zloty (Mn) | % in total |
|---|---|---|---|---|---|---|---|
| Construction cost | 622 | 2,804 | 66.5 | Equity | 108 | 461 | 10.9 |
| Design cost | 16 | 69 | 1.6 | Shareholder loan A | 73 | 327 | 7.8 |
| Owners and other costs | 63 | 269 | 6.4 | Shareholder loan B | 53 | 239 | 5.7 |
| Pre-operating costs | 3 | 13 | 0.3 | **Shareholder funds** | **235** | **1,027** | **24.4** |
| Concession costs | 10 | 37 | 0.9 | Senior debt | 242 | 1,100 | 26.1 |
| **Project cost** | **713** | **3,192** | **75.7** | Bonds (3 tranches) | 266 | 1,196 | 28.4 |
| Loan fees | 9 | 38 | 0.9 | Bond interest, f/x losses | 135 | 630 | 14.9 |
| Interest roll-up | 182 | 852 | 20.2 | **Debt funds** | 643 | 2,926 | 69.4 |
| Capital reserve account | 11 | 52 | 1.2 | **Total capital** | 878 | 3,953 | 938 |
| O&M during construction | 15 | 73 | 1.7 | Early toll revenues | 34 | 164 | 3.9 |
| Taxes | 2 | 8 | 0.2 | Interest on cash balance | 22 | 100 | 2.4 |
| Working capital | (2) | (4) | (0.1) | | | | |
| Cash | 4 | 5 | 0.1 | | | | |
| **Total requirements** | **934** | **4,217** | **100.0** | **Total sources** | **934** | **4,217** | **100** |

The projected daily traffic and toll rates were estimated as shown in Table CS6.2.[12]

The financial estimations are illustrated in Table CS6.3[12].

And in Table CS6.4[12], the heat map in terms of debt service sensitivities and rate of return.

---

[11] Deutsche Bank AG, 'A2 motorway – Poland – Information memorandum, November, 1999, containing all tables reflected.

[12] Adjusted from ibid. note 11 and working documents Commerzbank/CL regarding this project.

**Table CS6.2** Projected daily traffic and toll rates

| | H2 2002 Average daily traffic (ADT) | H2 2002 Charge per vehicle | H2 2002 Expected semi-annual cash flow (millions in Zloty) | H2 2005 Average daily traffic (ADT) | H2 2005 Charge per vehicle | H2 2005 Expected semi-annual cash flow (millions in Zloty) | H2 2007 Average daily traffic (ADT) | H2 2007 Charge per vehicle | H2 2007 Expected semi-annual cash flow (millions in Zloty) | H2 2012 Average daily traffic (ADT) | H2 2012 Charge per vehicle | H2 2012 Expected semi-annual cash flow (millions in Zloty) |
|---|---|---|---|---|---|---|---|---|---|---|---|---|
| **Type of vehicle** | | | | | | | | | | | | |
| Passenger | 3,500 | 9.48 | 3,600 | 14,900 | 12.53 | 32,500 | 16,000 | 15.04 | 44,000 | 21,000 | 20.80 | 79,000 |
| Commercial type 1 | 1,600 | 14.22 | 2,600 | 6,000 | 20.14 | 22,600 | 7,000 | 23.97 | 30,000 | 9,000 | 34.32 | 54,000 |
| Commercial type 2 | 700 | 21.33 | 1,600 | 2,700 | 30.25 | 14,500 | 3,000 | 35.91 | 18,000 | 3,000 | 51.48 | 30,000 |
| Commercial type 3 | 1,850 | 33.18 | 6,600 | 6,600 | 46.99 | 56,500 | 7,000 | 55.93 | 73,000 | 9,000 | 80.08 | 131,000 |
| Total | 7,650 | | 14,400 | 30,200 | | 126,100 | 33,000 | | 165,000 | 42,000 | | 294,000 |
| Operating & maintenance costs | | | 8,000 | | | 29,000 | | | 34,000 | | | 42,000 |
| **Operating profit** | | | 6,400 | | | 97,100 | | | 131,000 | | | 252,000 |
| +/- Net WC | | | 0 | | | 22,000 | | | 0 | | | 0 |
| Tax flows | | | 0 | | | 0 | | | 0 | | | 0 |
| Free cash flow | | | 6,400 | | | 75,100 | | | 131,000 | | | 252,000 |
| **Senior debt payments** | | | | | | | | | | | | |
| Interest | | | 0 | | | 40,000 | | | 36,000 | | | 9,000 |
| Principal | | | 0 | | | 39,000 | | | 42,000 | | | 149,000 |
| **Total** | | | 0 | | | 79,000 | | | 78,000 | | | 155,000 |

**Table CS6.3** Financial estimations

| Project year | Calendar year | Construction, design, fees and WC (in Zloty) | Toll & other revenues | Operating costs | Taxes | Senior debt Principal | Senior debt Interest | Bonds/ mezz debt Principal | Bonds/ mezz debt Interest | Refin. Principal | Refin. Interest | Shareholder payout on subdebt and equity |
|---|---|---|---|---|---|---|---|---|---|---|---|---|
| 1 | 2000 | (852) | 0 | 0 | 0 | 243 | 6 | 1,147 | 63 | | | 372 |
| 2 | 2001 | (746) | 0 | 0 | 0 | 203 | 23 | | 104 | | | 232 |
| 3 | 2002 | (583) | 21 | (12) | 0 | 183 | 40 | | 116 | | | 175 |
| 4 | 2003 | (433) | 36 | (18) | 0 | 159 | 51 | | 128 | | | 126 |
| 5 | 2004 | (297) | 57 | (26) | 0 | 47 | 65 | | 142 | | | 83 |
| 6 | 2005 | (98) | 175 | (42) | 0 | (64) | (3) | | 157 | | | 41 |
| 7 | 2006 | | 278 | (55) | 0 | (78) | (78) | | 171 | | | 0 |
| 8 | 2007 | | 318 | (74) | 0 | (115) | (73) | | 187 | | | 0 |
| 9 | 2008 | | 358 | (75) | 0 | (143) | (68) | | 203 | | | 0 |
| 10 | 2009 | | 402 | (82) | 0 | (200) | (60) | | 219 | | | 0 |
| 11 | 2010 | | 451 | (72) | 0 | (240) | (49) | | 237 | | | 0 |
| 12 | 2011 | | 506 | (186) | 0 | (301) | (35) | | 257 | | | 0 |
| 13 | 2012 | | 562 | (81) | 0 | (39) | (17) | (1,300) | 232 | 734 | (19) | 0 |
| 14 | 2013 | | 605 | (89) | 0 | | (1) | (1,210) | 148 | 842 | (60) | 0 |
| 15 | 2014 | | 652 | (199) | 0 | | | (1,191) | 51 | 542 | (102) | 0 |
| 16 | 2015 | | 705 | (210) | 0 | | | | | (500) | (106) | 0 |
| 17 | 2016 | | 761 | (107) | 0 | | | | | (588) | (77) | 0 |
| 18 | 2017 | | 821 | (97) | 0 | | | | | (688) | (45) | 0 |
| 19 | 2018 | | 890 | (96) | 0 | | | | | (342) | (9) | (451) |
| 20 | 2019 | | 864 | (92) | 0 | | | | | | | (880) |
| 21 | 2020 | | 1,045 | (89) | (13) | | | | | | | (952) |
| 22 | 2021 | | 1,132 | (177) | (49) | | | | | | | (908) |
| 23 | 2022 | | 1,218 | (87) | (61) | | | | | | | (1,086) |
| 24 | 2023 | | 1,282 | (88) | (113) | | | | | | | (1,090) |
| 25 | 2024 | | 1,350 | (187) | (144) | | | | | | | (1,018) |
| 26 | 2025 | | 1,421 | (211) | (156) | | | | | | | (1,061) |

**Table CS6.4** Debt service sensitivities and rate of return

| | DSCR (annualized) for senior debt | DSCR (annualized) for senior debt | Interest coverage ratio (annualized) for senior debt | NPV loan life coverage ratio | Senior debt maturity in years | IRR per annum (real rate in %) |
|---|---|---|---|---|---|---|
| | Minimum | Average | Minimum | | | |
| **Base case** | 1.50× | 1.99× | 2.57× | 2.45× | 13.0 | 9.24% |
| **30% traffic downside** | 1.15 | 1.44 | 1.43 | 2.08 | 15.0 | 6.60 |
| **Macro-economic sensitivities** | | | | | | |
| No growth in traffic volume (%) | 1.14 | 1.78 | 2.39 | 2.45 | 14.5 | 5.24 |
| Toll rates grow at 0% | 1.09 | 1.48 | 2.32 | 2.36 | 14.5 | 5.83 |
| Slower than expected traffic ramp-up | 1.15 | 2.59 | 1.48 | 2.43 | 13.5 | 9.06 |
| Polish inflation at 5% rather than 2% | 1.50 | 1.75 | 2.56 | 2.45 | 13.0 | 9.26 |
| Higher LT interest rates (50 bps) | 1.50 | 1.73 | 2.39 | 2.41 | 13.0 | 9.26 |
| Higher interest rate throughout concession | 1.50 | 2.29 | 1.74 | 2.44 | 14.0 | 9.24 |
| Higher interest and inflation rate | 1.50 | 1.62 | 2.10 | 2.20 | 12.0 | 9.58 |
| Exchange rate (10% of Zloty against the Euro) | 1.50 | 1.67 | 2.30 | 2.53 | 13.5 | 9.22 |
| Higher corporate income tax rate (34% not 22%) | 1.50 | 1.97 | 2.56 | 2.45 | 13.0 | 9.24 |
| **Break-even analysis** | | | | | | |
| Traffic downside of 35% | 1.00 | 1.06 | 1.24 | 0.56 | 15.0 | 6.09 |
| Toll rates grow at 0.4% | 1.00 | 1.36 | 2.29 | 1.89 | 14.5 | 5.15 |
| Traffic growth at a negative 0.55% | 1.00 | 1.43 | 2.34 | 2.10 | 14.5 | 4.22 |
| **Cost overrun sensitivities** | | | | | | |
| Renewal cost plus 100% | 1.50 | 1.61 | 2.35 | 2.39 | 13.0 | 9.08 |
| Fist heavy maintenance plus 100% | 1.50 | 1.82 | 2.57 | 2.44 | 13.0 | 9.08 |

Shortly before the deadline for the financing of the deal, the lead arrangers, after reviewing the traffic data and financial projections, were worried about the financial stability of the project, in particular, whether certain downside scenarios would emerge. An equity gap of €60–90 million would emerge. Despite all the issues that re-opening negotiation with a wide range of parties (18 shareholders and a wide set of lenders) would bring, including the expiration of the concession offer after six weeks, they wondered if they should focus on altering the risk allocation across the timeline of the project, or focus on reshuffling the financing mix and taking the heat out through a different mix of equity, senior debt, mezzanine debt and the guarantees provided by the Polish government. There was quite a lot of pressure mounting, as this trajectory was a critical part of the €30 billion TEN (Trans-European Network) linking European countries together, including its large trading partner, Russia. The concession awarded to the consortium was a 30-year BOT facility and came at a cost of €10 million. The government had the right to terminate the concession for 'cause,' or for defined forms of non-performance such as failure to commence or complete work by certain deadlines, or failure to make required payments to the government. If the government should terminate the concession for cause, it would assume ownership and operation of the concession. The government could also terminate for reasons of public interest. In that case, it would have to compensate the consortium for the cost of fully retiring the consortium, for their debt obligations and for the NPV of the payments made or distributed to the project finance lenders and investors, and those that would have been made if the concession had not been terminated.[13]

In terms of risk identification and sensitivities, the following stages in the process can be identified. We ignore here the impact that the FX crossing between Zloty and Euro might have (at the beginning of the project the Zloty was pegged to a basket of Euro and USD on a 55/45% basis[14]) although at a certain point the Zloty was pegged to the Euro (100%) with a view towards EU accession.

1. **Construction** – In this case, the Euro-denominated contracts were turnkey projects, which means that the consortium had a guarantee that it could commence operations at a certain point in time. The land would be acquired by the government and then provided to AWSA under a long-term lease arrangement. AWSA (through its contractors) would then take care of all the local permits etc. required to build.
2. **Operations** – The data (on traffic etc.) provided above are based on surveys (this was the first toll road in Poland). A capture rate of 50% was used, which was below the actual results as illustrated by other similar projects in the CEE region (which had a realization rate of 70–80%)[15]. The input on the model is based on educated decisions, and the sensitivities to the model were provided above as well. Besides the impact of economic activity and growth (GDP), there is the less quantifiable and often culturally determined time-value trade-off, deciding if a driver would pay to arrive early, or take their time and cruise the toll-free but (much) slower secondary roads. That answer might be different for Polish drivers and international drivers, and undoubtedly would be different for cargo versus passenger

---

[13] See ibid. note 11, p. 32.

[14] Source: IMF country website.

[15] But in line with experiences across the toll-road sector. Forsgren, K. *et al.*, 'The Toll Road Sector: Smooth Conditions Overall But Watch For Caution Flags', Standard & Poor's Infrastructure Finance, October 1999, pp. 148–149.

traffic. In short, there was a certain (albeit low) amount of traffic risk in the model. Recent examples at that time in other CEE countries demonstrated that estimations could be way off and derail the whole project to the point of breaking debt covenants and even insolvency of the project company. Both the construction and operational costs were less relevant in the model, as they were contractually fixed. There was a declining (per completed phase) all-risk insurance scheme in place.

### 6.4.1 Other financial peculiarities

The critical elements in the financial model were the traffic and revenue forecasts (although the project company was entitled to the revenues (other income) from the concessions of gas stations and restaurants etc. they were close to irrelevant and immaterial in this case).

Other key assumptions were:

- Constant purchasing power.
- Decreasing levels of Polish inflation (from 6% to 2%).
- Decreasing corporate taxes in Poland (from 34% to 22%).
- Maximum senior debt would be used up to 1.5 × DSCR in the base-case scenario (see dataset).

Sources of funding (in line with the dataset) were:

- €242 million senior secured from a syndication of banks jointly arranged by Crédit Lyonnais and Commerzbank:
  - Drawdown: 5.5 years.
  - Grace period: 6 months.
  - Semi-annual payments of principal plus interest.
  - Rate: spread (180–235 bps) over 6-month Libor (interest rate swap was forced upon consortium by lenders).
- Three tranches of zero-coupon bonds for €266 million (face value: €800 million), maturity in 2014.
- €235 million in subdebt and equity from lenders and shareholders.
- There was no hedge in place between Zloty revenues and Euro-denominated debt due to:
  - Unavailability of instruments beyond one year (or at a major cost).
  - Difficulty synchronizing hedge with volatile earnings.
  - The consortium had no funding to post collateral to match counterparty risk.
- Principal repayments had a maturity of 13–15 years and were based on a 1.5 × DSCR under a base scenario (assuming traffic 30% below estimation).
- A cash sweep facility was put in place for senior debt to accelerate repayment where possible.
- For the mezzanine debt the interest rate (accrued) would be between 7–9% depending on market conditions at effective start as well as maturity and currency choice. Note that there was hardly any Polish market for senior debt with this maturity and no market for Zloty-denominated mezzanine debt.
- The mezzanine debt portion had backing by the government via a guarantee of €800 million (absolute maximum for the Polish government). The guarantee was valid for the duration

of the concession and therefore also valid if the mezzanine debt needed to be refinanced (which would have been the case if the base scenario had emerged).

- The subordinated debt provided by shareholders did not carry interest until all other senior and mezzanine debt was repaid or monetized, which left them far out in terms of repayment (2026). The rate was 9% over ST-Euribor.
- €43 million had to be accumulated (from operational cash flows) in an account controlled by lenders for capex, maintenance and upgrading.
- Build-up of a sinking fund account.

The concession agreement spelled out a forced cash flow waterfall in terms of repayment order:

- Current operating expenses including land lease fee to government.
- Capex and maintenance reserve account.
- Current interest and principal payments on senior loans.
- Senior debt service reserve account.
- Remaining cash to zero-coupon bond reserve account.
- The government would receive 20% of the distributable cash flows once shareholders in the project received a cumulated real return of 10% on their invested capital, and 50% of the distributable cash flows once the shareholders received a 15% return (or more).

### 6.4.2 Case guidance

The question that ultimately arises is whether the current relation in equity/senior debt and mezzanine debt can be sustained, or whether the relative proportion needs to be altered. That could include changing the instruments' maturities as well as making the choice to use the mezzanine debt products. Implicitly, you need to make up your mind about the stability of the financial forecasts and inputs to the model.

## 6.5  CASE STUDY 2: BUILDING AND OPERATING A WIND PARK

It has become clear that project finance has a number of particularities which also have an impact on the function and positioning of mezzanine debt. One of the key things is the fact that in project finance the project company has no balance sheet strength other than the strength given by its sponsors (or external equity owners) and the syndicate of lenders. A direct consequence is that the ability to repay its debt is a direct function of the cash flow generating capacity (and timing) of the assets being financed. As there is no broader balance sheet or guarantees (although that is changing – see further in this chapter), an adequate understanding of the cash flow aspects of the project is critical (which starts with understanding how the industry in which the project will be active works), as well as understanding the fact that the relations between all parties involved are contractual in nature. Those contracts always, therefore, include details of how those cash flows will be used to pay expenses and repay investors, by defining the type, nature and maturity of the instruments selected and in what mix.

Lenders typically provide about 70–80% of the financing for these projects, and therefore assume a high project-specific risk (hence the syndication) which goes much further than the typical creditworthiness test for senior secured lenders. The sponsors, therefore, are often subject to a share retention agreement which is required by the lenders (which prohibits the sponsors from selling their stake in the project company (of which they often own 100%), at least for a certain period of time or until a certain phase in the project. They are, on top of this, subject to a subordination agreement in cases where the sponsors also provide shareholder loans to the project company. Because of all that, they truly are 'the last ones standing' in terms of being repaid in the project.

Another direct consequence of the lenders taking enhanced risks is their demand to have access to a wider set of guarantees (often in second lien), or a broader balance sheet than that of the project company only. It has therefore become commonplace for the sponsors to provide a secondary guarantee by using a certain part of their balance sheet to secure the loans granted to the project company.

In project finance, the pecking order in which the parties involved are repaid is dictated by the contract between the parties involved. That way a sort of cash flow waterfall is created, where each party creates visibility regarding when and how much they are expected to receive in the case that a certain set of assumptions materializes.

A cash flow waterfall clause will look somewhat similar to the one below, obviously adjusted as necessary to reflect the facts of the specific case:

All project revenues shall be applied in the following order of priority (as will be further detailed in the loan documentation):

- Operating and Maintenance Expenses (incl. payments under the Warrant Maintenance and Service Agreement (WMSA)).
- Taxes incurred, unless contemplated under Operating and Maintenance Expenses.
- Insurance premiums with respect to any insurance required pursuant to the transaction documents, unless contemplated under Operating and Maintenance Expenses.
- Cost, fees and expenses of the administrative parties.
- Interest and fees on Senior Loans.
- Default interest under the Senior Loans.
- Principal on Senior Loans (other than voluntary prepayments).
- Any mandatory prepayment due and payable under Senior Loans.
- Interest and fees on Mezzanine Loan.
- Default interest under the Mezzanine Loan.
- Principal on Mezzanine Loan.
- Any mandatory prepayment due and payable under Mezzanine Loan.
- Funding of Annual & Major Maintenance Accounts, if no WMSA or Replacement WMSA is in place.
- Funding of Debt Service Reserve Account.
- All remaining funds shall be deposited in the Distribution Account.

The bigger picture is clear. First, all operational expenses which relate to the project in the wider sense are paid, followed by the senior lenders (both interest and principal), followed by the mezzanine lenders, the shareholder loan etc. and ultimately the residual cash flow holders – the equity owners of the project company. Often, residual cash flows are held in escrow (often separated for senior and subordinated lenders) as long as certain lenders are not (fully) repaid, to avoid, in essence, subordinated parties (mezzanine lenders or shareholders) benefiting prior to a full repayment of the lenders, which can become a problem if the project, for whatever reason, turns sour after those payments are made to the subordinated parties, without any form of legal claw-back (except for litigation). This clause also protects the lenders against premature dividend payments which the project company (the sponsors) might decide to pay. Any deviation from that clause needs to be matched with cash injections and/ or letters of credit from a financial institution (or other trade finance instrument). Often, there will be a separate 'distribution clause' included in the documents which will read somewhat like the following one:

> The Borrower may not transfer funds from the Distributions Account or declare or pay any dividend, make any other cash distribution on its equity or make a payment under any subordinated debt (including the Affiliate Loans and any other shareholder loans) unless:
>
> 1. Financial Completion has been achieved.
> 2. In the case of dividends, such payment would be made in accordance with applicable law.
> 3. In the case of payments other than dividends (like cash distribution on its equity or making a payment under any of its subordinated debt to its shareholders), such payments would be made only when consistent with the Subordination and Share Retention Agreement (SSRA).
> 4. Each of the Historical Debt Service Coverage Ratio and the Projected Debt Service Coverage Ratio is not less than 1.25:1.0 as of the testing date immediately prior to the relevant Interest Payment Date.
> 5. Only if the Borrower has no Senior Financial Debt as of the relevant Interest Payment Date, each of the Historical Total Financial Debt Service Coverage Ratio and the Projected Total Financial Debt Service Coverage Ratio is not less than 1.20 :1.0 as of the testing date immediately prior to such Interest Payment Date.
> 6. Such payment is made within 30 days after an Interest Payment Date.
> 7. Immediately before and after giving effect to such payment:
>    - No Default occurs or is continuing.
>    - The Debt Service Reserve Account (DSRA) (of US$ XX million) is fully funded and the Borrower has a Minimum Cash balance of at least US$XXX,000.
>    - The Financial Debt to Net Worth Ratio is not more than 70:30; and
>    - There are no arrears on the Senior and Mezzanine Loans; and
> 8. The Borrower shall have certified each of the foregoing.'

Ultimately, the senior lenders are the ones who have a first lien on the assets, the mezzanine lenders (often but not always) have a second lien claim on the assets. This will read somewhat like the following clause:

> **The Senior Loans will be secured by a first-ranking security interest and the Mezzanine Loan will be secured by a second-ranking security interest over the following (collectively, the 'Security'):**
>
> - All assets of the Borrower.
> - The Borrower's rights under all Project Documents, concessions, permits, WMSA, etc. associated with the Project.
> - All shares of the Shareholders in the Borrower, including all rights related thereto.
> - All the accounts of the Borrower (incl. DSRA).
> - The Borrower's rights under all insurance policies.
> - The Borrower's rights under any subordinated loans from the Sponsors or any other Shareholders under the SSRA or any other permitted shareholder loans from the Sponsors or any other Shareholders, including Affiliate Loans; and

- Other forms of security permitted by applicable country laws and appropriate for the Project, including the Borrower's rights under any Hedge Agreement, under all Sponsor/Shareholder Loans made to the Borrower.

Additionally, in most projects, the senior debt comes in tranches with a different maturity and/or different creditworthiness. As previously mentioned, they have a first lien on all the project company's assets. The mezzanine lenders (including the second lien lenders) tend to have a maturity beyond the senior lenders' part. That makes sense; if the maturity of the mezzanine lenders were to occur earlier than that of the senior lenders, it would provide (implicit) priority to the mezzanine lenders as their earlier maturity would drain the cash flow from the project's cash flow waterfall even before the senior lenders were fully repaid, which is somewhat conflicting with the overall philosophy and the relationship between senior and mezzanine lenders.

A product which has become commonplace in project finance, and more common in general, is the unitranche lending product. Rather than being part of the mezzanine product group, it is considered a separate product, and therefore useful if you want a competitor to the mezzanine product group.

The unitranche product is characterized by the fact that the same lender (or syndicate of lenders) provides financing for the secured part as well as for the non-secured (subordinated) part of the financing needs in one product, with one interest rate attached to it. That interest rate will undoubtedly sit somewhere between the rate which would have been charged by senior lenders and that which would have been charged by mezzanine lenders for the project. Consequently, part of the loan will be secured and part will have an open exposure, meaning it has no direct collateral attached. That is at least how it looks from the surface. From the inside, the collateral provided is there to serve the whole loan. The collateral, however, did not have a market value or net asset value to cover the whole loan amount, at least not at the start of the project when the loans were provided. A simple example: if one provides a unitranche loan to a project for buying a property plus some working capital etc. The loan is €200,000, of which the cost of the property is €100,000. There is €100,000 in open exposure. Now, let's say that the loan matures in seven years and that by year five the (execution) value of the property bought has risen to €180,000. The €180,000 will serve as collateral for the whole loan (i.e., the €100,000 which was initially covered by the collateral at the start as well as the remaining €80,000 which will act as collateral for part of the subdebt). Put differently, the excess value is there to secure the whole loan, although its execution value will most likely never do so in full. That position will often then be complemented with a formal second lien on the collateral, but that is not a mainstream position for unitranche products. We will get back to the outlook for this product as a competitor for the mezzanine product group later on in the outlook and way forward for the mezzanine product group chapter (Chapter 11).

Let's return to the project finance theme and look at a specific project that aims to build a windfarm.

The deal includes a 21 MW wind project (delivered by 10 wind turbines). Besides the sustainability argument, these projects are characterized by high capital cost but low operational costs. Although the technology is proven, the pay-back periods are sometimes very long, which might pose problems in some emerging or growth markets where funding with LT-tenors is not (abundantly) available.

The following financing schedule has been put in place.

**Financial estimations (in USD)**

| Investments | In USD (millions) | Financing | In USD (millions) |
|---|---|---|---|
| EPC cost | 50 | Sponsor's equity | 10 |
| Other costs | 9 | Sponsors' shareholders loans | 6 |
| DSRA (Debt service reserve account-opening position) | 1 | Mezzanine loans | 3 |
| Other costs | 2 | Total equity | 19 (30.64%) |
| | | Other liabilities | 0.5 |
| | | Senior loans | 42.5 |
| | | Total liabilities | 43 |
| **Total** | **62** | **Total** | **62** |

The largest costs in this project are the EPC costs (engineering, procurement and construction) which also often cover the warranty and maintenance costs which come with the project. In the windfarm business, firms such as Siemens, GE, Vestas or Suzlon either provide those project services themselves or work with external project and engineering firms to make this happen. A big chunk of the cost therefore comes very early on in the process, and will be earned back over an extended period of time. It is not uncommon for firms such as Vestas and Suzlon to provide vendor finance for these deals.

The other investment position is the DSRA which is a key element in every project. The purpose of the DSRA is to provide a cash buffer during periods where the cash flow available for debt service (often referred to as CFADS) is less than the scheduled payments. The buffer allows for some room to deal with issues of an operational nature or otherwise. Initially, the repayment schedule is in line with the cash flow available at any given point in time in the project based on the projections agreed upon by the parties. In extremis, the debt position needs to be restructured to avoid default by the borrower (i.e., the project company).

The €1 million investment is the opening position. The target balance of the DSRA is somewhere between three and 12 months of scheduled repayments (interest and principal) – this is both for senior and mezzanine debt.

In practice, the funding of the account is agreed upon in the term sheet and can be one of the following:

- The account is funded in full on the last day of construction.
- The account is partially funded on the last day of construction and then further complemented with cash flows from the project.
- The account is completely built up from the cash flows from the project (which has its obvious intrinsic risks).

The clauses above already indicated the funding's position in the cash flow waterfall. It is funded pretty much after the operational costs of the project have been met (and potentially any sort of land lease or concession payments to be made to a public authority, which in essence is also an operational cost). The build-up of the account occurs before any payments are made to the sponsors, which includes both their equity position and the shareholder loans' positions.

Consequently, the buffers operate as follows:

| Position | Indicator (or any other agreed target) | Action |
|---|---|---|
| Going concern | DSCR < 1x | Operational cash flows are either added or released from the account to maintain a certain target |
| Distressed | DSCR > 1x | The necessary funding is released from the DSRA to cover the project's cash flow shortfall in order to avoid the borrower defaulting on the debt somewhere over the next 3–12 months |

The DSRA is a current asset and will, as such, appear on the project company's balance sheet. There are some modeling issues which particularly relate to the position of the DSRA under the different models (in particular the bad case scenario), as well as its consistent relation to the cash flow available to top up the account based on the cash flow forecasts in the model, which in its turn is linked to the cash flows available for shareholders.

The following consistencies should be monitored:

- The cash flow available to top up the account should not exceed the cash flows available to fund the account.
- The balance of the account should never be negative or materially too low.
- The sum of all the cash movements during the project (including the initial funding) should ultimately amount to zero.
- The balance of the account always reflects the repayment schedule for the next 3–12 months and should therefore gradually decline as the project matures and the loans mature.
- A release from the account to top up operational cash flow shortfalls should be no more than to guarantee that the DSCR = 1x.

Something of a side note in this respect is the fact that most of these contracts are bound by reduction of carbon emission targets and carbon credits (often referred to as VER/CER conditions, which deal with the conditions and the certification of the project) and as such they often form a constituting element for approval of the financing.

We now need to look a little more deeply into the inputs to the financial model, and the critical factors which will allow for some sort of scenario modeling on a project (we assume quality, solvent and experienced sponsors):

- Although the contractual affairs are outside the scope of this book, having an adequate PPA (power purchase agreement, or off-take agreement) in place is critical for covering the total earn-back period (i.e., lenders will prefer the PPA to cover the tenor of the loan or a little longer as an implicit, albeit imperfect hedge). The same is true for access to the national or local grid and its physical proximity, as well as adequate O&M (operation & maintenance) and warranties, often all wrapped up in a WMSA contract.
- The pricing at which end product(s) will be sold and how that can change (indexing or otherwise) over time (and who decides the pricing range (cap) – government?).
- Based on the installed capacity (here that was 21 MW) and an estimated wind speed (miles/hour) a certain NCF (net capacity factor) can be determined, which then allows for comparison.

- Local expected demand (for energy in this case) versus actual and expected supply.
- Sustainability and stability of the technology used as well as its longevity and scalability.
- With respect to the EPC phase, the project company disburses payments based on completion milestones and final completion. These intermediate steps will often be (in the case of a windfarm): (1) foundation works, (2) completion of mechanical works, (3) completion of electrical works, (4) intermediate review milestone also known as facility commissioning completion date (FCCD), (5) connecting to the grid and (6) final completion including fine-tuning and final tests.
- Most senior loans come with a grace period of about two years or more.

The construction phase is often characterized by (semi)-turnkey projects with a fixed price, and only operational delays and legal issues (and additional work needed) can disfigure the financial projections.

The moment the project goes live, the revenue stream will be a function of capacity and pricing per GWh. The capacity (the aforementioned NCF) is a function of the technology's performance (which is known) combined preferably with some local expertise (other wind projects) in terms of average wind speed, volatility across the year etc.

Based on those, your estimated GWh per year can be calculated and, given a certain (adjustable) pricing volatility (USD per KWh), the revenues can be estimated. There used to be a time when the revenues from carbon credits were included. In 2012, given the low value of the credits (per ton), this seems to no longer be recommendable.

A sensitivity analysis can then be created by increasing/decreasing the probability factor (which is part of the NCF). That reflects possible higher or lower average wind speeds, the variable in the model. This way, base-case scenarios etc. can be developed and their impact on covenants and the DSCR can be predicted.

## 6.5.1 Security

The securities provided to lenders in project finance include not only all assets of the project company, but also the future profitability of the firm (through its PPA – quality and variety of the off-takers is therefore a necessity), licenses, other accounts and the WSMA. Disbursement of funding is often done based on completion milestones. Once the project is completed, (most of) the actual cost overrun risk goes away. However, that doesn't make the project financially risk-free. Having said that, most sponsors, (beyond the equity and subordination of the shareholder loans) support from additional guarantees or recourse etc. falls away upon the completion of the construction phase, i.e., sponsor support until financial completion (full repayment of all lenders involved) is normally not on the agenda.

# 7

# Real Estate Projects and Mezzanine Finance

In reality, a big chunk of what has been discussed in the context of project finance and mezzanine products is valid in the context of real estate finance as well. At least as long as it is directly linked to the particularities which are the consequence of a project's creditworthiness and its exclusive dependence on the cash flows of the project company. The equity owners are the sponsors of the project, potentially complemented with eternal equity investors.

We will therefore build on the principles previously discussed and focus more on the real estate-specific features of a deal. However, the systemic approach will definitely feel familiar after having reviewed the project finance chapter.

Let's start with an example:

> You are trying to model the distribution of cash flows from a real estate investment. It is essentially a series of cash flows after payment of debt service from month 0 (closing) to month 36. The real estate project has two investors, the Institutional Investor and the Developer. In this case, the Institutional Investor contributes 90% of the required project equity and the Developer contributes the remaining 10%. The cash flow is distributed according to a set of parameters specifying cash flow percentage allocations and IRR targets, known as the cash flow waterfall. As with all for-sale development deals, the early cash flows are negative and then turn positive as unit sales occur. In more recent times, lenders have tended to step in only if there is 50% pre-sold. The order of distribution of the cash flow remaining after debt service is paid is as follows (the waterfall):
>
> Both investors receive the return of their invested capital from cash flow distributions.
>
> 1. Hurdle 1 (after the return of equity to both investors), the Institutional Investor receives 90% of the monthly cash flows and the Developer 10%, proportional to their respective overall equity contributions, until both investors achieve a 12% IRR (all IRRs to be calculated from deal inception/first dollar invested).
> 2. Hurdle 2, (after Hurdle 1 is satisfied), the Institutional Investor receives 60% of the monthly cash flows until the Institutional Investor achieves an 18% IRR.
> 3. The Final Split (after satisfying Hurdle 2) allocates monthly cash flow 50% to each investor.
>
> On an overall project basis, the Developer should realize a disproportionate share of the cash flow after the second hurdle is hit. This is what is known as the 'promote.'

The cash flow waterfall ensures that each cash flow item occurs at the correct seniority to other items (as is the case in project finance). If the underlying assets are mortgages or loans, there are usually two separate waterfalls, because the principal and interest receipts can be easily allocated and matched. However, if the assets are income-based transactions such as rental deals, it is not possible to differentiate so easily between how much of the revenue is income and how much principal repayment. In this case, all the income is used to pay the cash flows due on the bonds as those cash flows become due.

In securitization, securities can be credit enhanced, meaning their credit quality is increased above that of the originator's unsecured debt or underlying asset pool. Individual securities are often split into tranches, or categorized into varying degrees of subordination. Each tranche has a different level of credit protection or risk exposure to the others: there is generally a senior (A) class of securities and one or more junior subordinated (B, C etc.) classes which function as protective layers for the A class.

The senior classes have a first claim on the cash received by the SPV, and the more junior classes only start receiving repayment after the more senior classes have been repaid. Because of the cascading effect between classes, this arrangement is often referred to as a cash flow waterfall. In the event that the underlying asset pool becomes insufficient to make payments on the securities (e.g., when loans default within a portfolio of loan claims), the loss is absorbed first by the subordinated tranches, and the upper-level tranches remain unaffected until the losses exceed the entire amount of the subordinated tranches. The senior securities are typically AAA rated, signifying a lower risk, while the lower-credit quality subordinated classes receive a lower credit rating, signifying a higher risk.

# 7.1 WIDER APPLICATION

Tranches are categorized as senior, mezzanine and subordinated/equity, according to their degree of credit risk. If there are defaults or the CDOs' collateral otherwise underperforms/migrates/amortizes early, scheduled payments to senior tranches take precedence over those for mezzanine tranches, and scheduled payments to mezzanine tranches take precedence over those to subordinated/equity tranches.

Senior and mezzanine tranches are typically rated by one or more of the rating agencies, with the former receiving ratings equivalent to A to AAA and the latter receiving ratings of B to BBB. The ratings reflect the expected credit quality of the underlying pool of collateral, as well as how much protection a given tranche is afforded by tranches which are subordinate to it.

The credit crunch has also left its marks in the real estate sector. Nevertheless, that industry was part of the problem which led to the world's current problems. Not only in terms of the amount of debt used to complete the projects, but more in a general way, there is a problematic relationship between real estate and FIs. When FIs have to decide where to allocate their loan book, they naturally tend to do so with a tilt towards real estate (as that is/was perceived as less risky – equally so these days with respect to sovereign bonds). Ultimately the collateral of a house, warehouse or hotel building is (much) stronger than that of a personal, student or general business loan where the collateral tends to be systematically weaker. However, since water always flows to its lowest point, it will find a way there, causing natural floods which we know in economics as bubbles. Banks actively contribute to this by systematically allocating more capital to the real estate sector. This ensures that prices go beyond their natural D/S price, and bank balance sheets grow naturally faster the more real estate is on their books as collateral, which, in its turn, will push more money into the real estate sector. A vicious cycle, if you want.[1]

As previously mentioned, the crisis had its impact on the way these projects were financed, although the differences are not as significant as you would expect (see Figure 7.1) given the depth of the crisis we went through.

---

[1] See further: L. Nijs, 'Shaping tomorrow's marketplace: investment philosophies for emerging markets and a semi-globalized world,' *Euromoney*, 2011.

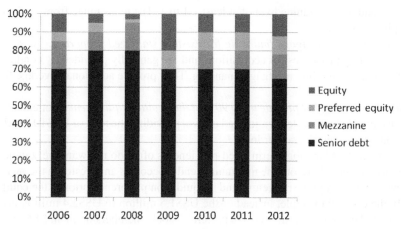

**Figure 7.1**   Construction loan to total development costs
*Source:* Lipper

Although traditionally investors stepped into real estate as either senior lenders or equity providers, mezzanine financing has been on the table for a few decades now as a tool for developers to execute their business plan. Traditionally, situations have looked pretty similar to the example below:

---

### EXAMPLE

Assume that a project has an existing cash flow of US$1 million and a projected cash flow of US$1.35 million. The acquisition price is US$10 million. Additional capital will be required for redevelopment costs including lease up and tenant leasehold improvement of US$1 million (redevelopment costs). A number of lenders are willing to provide US$7.5 million of financing at, for example, 6–7% interest. The mezzanine loan would be for US$1.5 million, which would advance between 75 and 90% of the acquisition costs and 90% of the redevelopment costs. The owner-operator is required to fund 10% of the acquisition cost and 10% of the redevelopment cost. The senior lender will fund 75% of the capital (US$7.5 million), the mezzanine lender will fund between 75% and 90% of the capital (US$1.5 million), and up to 90% of the redevelopment costs (US$900,000).[2]

---

The spectrum of mezzanine applications is, however, wider than the value-added development model. The following five categories can be distinguished.

1. *Traditional mezzanine in a value-added transaction.* This is the most common form of mezzanine financing and is illustrated by the earlier example. It is generally a loan in which property will have debt service coverage after meeting the requirements of the first

---

[2] Warshaw, Burstein, Cohen, Schlesinger & Kuh LLP, 'Mezzanine and equity financing for real estate deals,' 2003.

mortgage and the mezzanine loan of at least 1.1 to 1. The loans range from 75% to 90% of the capital structure.

2. *Traditional second mortgage financing for existing stabilized properties.* These are loans made to existing properties for acquisitions and are generally provided by conduit lenders in order to secure the first mortgage financing. They provide additional leverage for acquisitions.

3. *Interim senior loans that provide up to 90% of the capital requirements.* For example, if the original example had one lender, instead of two, providing the total of US$10.9 million, the loan would be an interim senior loan.

4. *Preferred equity.* Many long-term fixed-rate lenders often do not want mezzanine finance in the form of debt, therefore the mezzanine lender becomes an investor in the owner or the borrower, and has a preferred return and a liquidation preference prior to the equity investors. In the original example, instead of the US$1.5 million to US$2.4 million investment being debt, the investor would receive preferred stock, membership in an LLC, or partnership interests which would provide for a preferred return to the investor. In the event of sale, refinance etc., the investor would be paid its principal before the equity holder.

5. *Equity structured as debt.* Frequently, an equity investor wants the investment structured as debt. This will give it better protection in the event of bankruptcy and, if there is environmental risk, a debt structure provides the investor with better protection. An example of this would be an equity investor investing in a project where the investor is providing up to 97% to 98% of the capital structure and the project is thinking about an environmental clean-up. The equity investor will make their investment as a loan. However, the loan must have normal lender controls as opposed to equity controls, and it should not have more than 50% of the residual economics or it will be deemed equity even if it is structured as debt.

The returns sought by investors are very much subject to criteria such as:

- Type of project
- Location
- Level of subordination
- Value-added criteria
- D/E ratio on project level
- Regulatory aspects
- (Geo)political and country risks
- Market interest rates.

## 7.2 OTHER APPLICATIONS AND RETURN ISSUES

Other mezzanine applications can be summarized as follows:

1. Loans for acquisition of stabilized returns. These loans are made by conduit lenders generally up to 90% of the capital structure with debt service coverage of at least 1.1 to 1.0. These loans generally cost 4% to 7% over the London Inter-Bank Offer Rate (LIBOR), or fixed 10–12% plus points.

2. Interim loans that are made by lenders who are making first mortgage loans up to 90% of the capital structure. These loans (1) require returns that blend the senior component and the mezzanine component, (2) generally have existing debt coverage of at least 1.1 to 1, and (3) are less than 90% of the capital structure. Typically such loans require a 1% origination fee, a 1%

to 2% exit fee, and 200 to 325 over LIBOR depending on the perceived risk and the type of investment. Apartments and retail get the lowest spreads, whereas suburban offices and hotels require the highest spreads.

3. Traditional mezzanine loans for value-added projects. If the loan is up to 90% of the capital requirements, the loan requires interest rates in the 11% to 16% range. If the loan goes to 90% of the capital structure and debt service coverage exceeds 1.1 to 1.0, depending on the perceived risk, the returns will be higher. If debt service coverage is less than 1.1 to 1.0, the returns will go up.

If the investor is exceeding 90% of the capital structure and going up to 95%, the returns generally are in excess of 20%. If it is equity structured as debt, the returns to capital should have minimum returns of 10–12% with a participation in cash flow with returns exceeding 25%. If the investment is structured as preferred equity the returns to the investor will be similar to the debt structure with a slight premium due to the perceived increased legal risk.

Any attempt to indicate potential (expected) returns is therefore somewhat flawed, especially in a day and age with very low interest rates and many markets still suffering from oversupply in many areas of the real estate market. The latter will probably continue, as many projects that were halted during the crisis are now completed as that yields the lowest loss relative to halting the project permanently, given the reimbursement obligation the developer often has vis-à-vis investors in case the project is not completed. Therefore, in some markets, high single-digit returns can be expected in a mezzanine position.

Mezzanine loans were originally only second mortgages, but the needs of the senior lenders have changed that, resulting in additional complexities.

1. Second mortgage that is forecloseable. This is the most traditional structure to the investor and generally requires a lower return to the investor. However, many first mortgages restrict this type of investing. Primarily used when there is construction risk so that the lender: (1) will have a priority over intervening liens of mechanics; (2) can appoint a receiver in the event of default, which gives the lender more control of the property after default; and (3) has a better position in a bankruptcy proceeding.

2. Second mortgage that is nonforecloseable. This is a very common structure where the lender gets a mortgage, which it cannot foreclose and gets additional security such as an assignment of the ownership interests. In the event of default, the investor cannot foreclose the mortgage, but does foreclose on the ownership interest and takes over the ownership of the borrower, subject to the liens and whatever problems exist. The security is not as good, the perceived risk increases, and the rate of return required increases. Many investors prefer the nonforecloseable second mortgage to loan structures such as assignment of ownership interests without a mortgage, because the investors are deemed secured creditors in the event of bankruptcy and they have better protection in the event of hazardous waste issues.

3. Assignment of ownership interests without a mortgage. This form is the same as 'second mortgage that is non forecloseable' except there is no mortgage. An understanding of the legal structure of the assignment is important. The investor generally gets an assignment of the owner's interest in the borrower. The structure is that the borrower is owned by another parent entity and the lender takes as security the ownership interests in the parent entity.

4. Preferred ownership of interest. This structure is not a loan; therefore there can be no foreclosure. Under the ownership agreement (e.g., stockholder agreement, operating agreement, partnership agreement), the investor makes its investment and receives a preferred return as opposed to interest. In the event of non-payment or breach or some other affirmative or negative covenant (e.g., performance or default in mortgages), the preferred owner dilutes the equity, takes over management control, or buys out the equity pursuant to a buy–sell agreement. This

structure has the least protection but can grant the investor more control in the event of default and it will effectively block any bankruptcy because the investor gets a seat on the board of directors or managers and has the right to veto bankruptcy. From a lender's perspective, it is potentially more difficult to get control because the investor will make contract claim and the resolution of that could substantially delay the process.

The arguments for preferring mezzanine over equity (or the other way around) can be summarized as follows:

## ADVANTAGES TO EQUITY:

1. Developer usually needs less cash.
2. In the event of default or actual receipt of returns less than projected or less than the mezzanine lender requires, there is no loss of equity through foreclosure and you don't have a debt forgiveness tax liability.
3. Mezzanine is additional leverage with all its risks.
4. No need for inter-creditor and subordination agreement with senior lender.
5. More equity might result in better senior loan terms.
6. Some senior lenders simply don't like mezzanine loans behind them, or won't allow an assignment of the partnership interests.
7. No personal guaranties (as there might be with mezzanine).

## ADVANTAGES TO MEZZANINE

1. When the returns are bigger, it's generally better to put up more capital and keep a larger portion of the profits.
2. Mezzanine doesn't share in the profits, and their return is capped.
3. Mezzanine has much less control of the day-to-day operation; they are a lender with lender controls similar to a first mortgagee (albeit somewhat tighter).
4. The mezzanine investor's return requirements are usually less than the equity investor's requirements, (preferred equity returns are slightly higher but similar to mezzanine, generally without participation in cash flow or the return is capped).

## SUMMARY OF GENERAL REASONS TO CHOOSE EITHER MEZZANINE OR EQUITY:

1. One or the other may be a requirement of the senior lender (won't allow mezzanine behind them; can't work out an inter-creditor; etc.), or might influence the cost of the senior.
2. Developer wants to keep as much upside as possible, in which case mezzanine (or preferred equity) is preferable.
3. Developer just doesn't want an equity partner, nor is willing to cede control.
4. Developer just doesn't like more debt, or is unwilling to guarantee anything.

Before we can take this further, we first need to enhance our understanding of the potential risk–return dynamics in the real estate sector and its individual subsectors. There are many different ways to do this, but I was charmed by the most structural approach provided a few years ago by Muldavin[3], to which the previously quoted pieces of text are owed as the article provides a comprehensive read on the topic of mezzanine finance and real estate (albeit geared towards the US market).

It is indicated that the different types of mezzanine investing are assessed by the level of risk undertaken, and commonly measured by loan-to-value and loan-to-cost ratios. For example, investing in the 70–80% loan-to-value or loan-to-cost slice is lower in risk than a mezzanine investment which provides capital up to a 95% loan-to-value and loan-to-cost ratio. Given the wide range of risk and return available in mezzanine investments, this investment category calls for further definition.

Muldavin separates mezzanine real estate investing into four distinct types, incorporating both risks and investment purposes in a single definition. As presented in Table 7.1, the four types of mezzanine investment are:

- **Stabilized:** Existing property with acceptable current cash flow coverage to the mezzanine investment.
- **Value added:** Existing asset with moderate to substantial lease-up and/or releasing risk. Generally requires some cosmetic rehabilitation.
- **Development:** To-be-built property with substantial development, construction and lease-up risk.
- **Securitized mortgage pool:** Typically associated with the purchase of the unrated class of CMBS, these investments are similar to stabilized mezzanine but on a pool basis.

These definitions provide an immediate link to the type of property and nature of the risks involved in each type of mezzanine investing. Loan-to-value and loan-to-cost ratios by themselves inadequately describe the risks in a mezzanine investment. As shown in the table, loan-to-value ratios overlap significantly among the four types of mezzanine real estate investments. More importantly, the new definitions can also be directly linked to specific return expectations.

As mentioned before, mezzanine investing risks are similar to those found in other real estate investments, but they incorporate both debt and equity risk characteristics depending on the particular type and structure of the investment. Key risk issues therefore include:

- Value changes
- Magnitude and timing of cash flow
- Financial risk
- Quality of underwriting
- Management control
- Exit timing
- Management quality
- Development risk, and
- Construction risk.

Clearly, the most important risk (beyond those which occur in the operational stage) comes from a severe market downturn that would affect the magnitude and timing of cash flows, as

---

[3] Tim Ballard and Scott Muldavin, 'Does mezzanine investing in real estate make sense today?' (2000) *Real Estate Finance* 1–9.

**Table 7.1**   Risk and rewards investing in the real estate sector (adjusted from Muldavin's research)

| Mezzanine investment type | Property characteristics | Typical deal structures | Total return expectations (*) | Key risk issues |
| --- | --- | --- | --- | --- |
| Stabilized | • Existing cash flow<br>• Limited lease-up risk<br>• Minor rehabilitation or repositioning | • 70% to 85% LTV piece<br>• No participation in cash flow or residual value 3 to 7-year term<br>• Exit through refi. or mortgage amortization<br>• Cash flow sweep/lockbox | 14–18% IRR | • Severe value decline<br>• Magnitude and timing of cash flow interest rate risk<br>• Quality of underwriting<br>• Management control |
| Value-added | • Some existing cash flow<br>• Moderate rehabilitation, repositioning<br>• Moderate to substantial lease-up, releasing required<br>• Completed property will represent 75% to 80% loan-to-value based upon the total capital structure | • 70% to 95% LTC piece 10% to 15% interest rate, with participation in cash flow and/or residual value 18-month to 3-year term<br>• Exit through refi. or sale<br>• Value creation should allow return of 100% of capital through refi. | 18–25% IRR | • Severe value decline<br>• Magnitude and timing of cash flow<br>• Interest rate risk<br>• Quality of underwriting<br>• Exit timing<br>• Management control |
| Development | • No existing cash flow<br>• To-be-built property<br>• Completed property will represent 75%–80% loan-to-value based upon the total capital structure | • 70% to 95% LTC piece<br>• Participation in cash flow and residual value 3-year term<br>• Exit through refi., sale, or 'presale'<br>• Value creation should allow return of 100% of capital through refi. | 20–30% IRR | • Significant value decline<br>• Magnitude and timing of cash flows<br>• Financial risk<br>• Quality of underwriting<br>• Exit timing Development risk<br>• Construction risk<br>• Management control |
| Securitized | • Mortgages securitized by a pool of properties<br>• Existing cash flow<br>• Stabilized underlying assets | • 70% to 75% LTV tranche of CMBS 10-year term | 20–25% IRR | • Severe value decline<br>• Financial risk<br>• Quality of underwriting<br>• Management quality<br>• Cross-defaulted first loss<br>• Management control |

(*)Returns presume leverage at the property level but not at the fund or investor level. Returns are net of 1% asset management fee and 20% of profits typically paid to sponsor. It can be added that the returns are merely indicative, and have come down significantly since publication of the article. As indicated before, the wider range of high single to mid double-digit returns are more adequate in the current environment anno 2012. In some emerging market regions, that range can be pushed up a few hundred bps. But ultimately, all depends on the location and specifics of the project.

well as the value of the asset. Given the risk position between the first mortgage and straight equity investment, investors must carefully look at the current conditions of the market cycle and expected market swings to determine appropriate return premiums for investing at the mezzanine level.

The quality and methodology of underwriting is also a critical risk in mezzanine real estate investing. How detailed is the underwriting on each asset? Are property values and cash flows based on optimistic projections of market change, or are they realistic and appropriate? Most importantly, mezzanine real estate investments need to be underwritten from an equity perspective, with specialized understanding of management and control issues as well as specific focus on a timely exit.

Lastly, for mezzanine investments with a strong debt component, financial risks resulting from increasing interest rates must also be taken into consideration. Appropriate controls need to be in place to deal with potential problems in this area.

The typology in the chart feeds through in the structuring of individual mezzanine deals. As Muldavin argues:

> Mezzanine real estate investments have customized deal structures based on the strengths of the borrower and property, the level and timing of capital required, and other project-specific issues. However, as shown in the chart, each mezzanine investment type we have identified has certain deal structure commonalities.

> For example, stabilized mezzanine investments do not typically receive participation in cash flow or residual value and provide a longer loan term, reflective of traditional debt investment. Value added and development mezzanine investments often cover up to 90% or 95% of a property's initial capital and typically incorporate participation in cash flow and residual value. Loan terms are typically eighteen to thirty-six months, with refinancing or sale used as an exit strategy. Last, securitized mezzanine investments are commercial mortgage-backed securities, with the complex pool-based structuring requirements typical of these deals. It is important to understand that most mezzanine real estate investments appear to borrowers as a single higher-interest-rate mortgage. For example, in the first quarter of 2000, a borrower could typically obtain a mortgage at approximately 8.5% for 75% of the value of a property. However, given the need for additional capital, the borrower may be interested in a loan to value (LTV) of 90% and is willing to pay interest rates of 10% or more for such a loan. When the 90% LTV loan is originated, the higher-return mezzanine-level investment for the 75%–90% slice of the loan can be bifurcated from the first mortgage to create a separate 'mezzanine' investment. Accordingly, many mezzanine real estate investments are created from bifurcated portions of larger first mortgages, which are sold to traditional lenders or securitized by a CMBS sponsor. Mezzanine investments can be made on top of existing first mortgages in some circumstances, but in most cases, including most 'conduit' loans headed for the commercial-mortgage-backed securities markets, intercreditor agreements and other first mortgage restrictions limit this practice.

Return expectations vary significantly based upon the structure of a particular mezzanine investment. Required returns will increase as the level of lease-up and/or construction risk increases. Returns will also increase as the loan-to-value level increases. Accordingly, a 95% loan-to-cost mezzanine investment for a new construction project would have the highest return expectations, and a 70% to 80% mezzanine loan-to-value on a stabilized asset would have the lowest return expectations. Return expectations will also vary within each type of mezzanine real estate investment, based on the size of the investment, the financial strength of the property and borrower, and the certainty of the exit strategy and loan payoff of the mezzanine investment. For example, return expectations will be higher if investors assume more risk in the exit strategy.

A final factor influencing investor returns is leverage at the fund level. Returns which are already leveraged at the property level can be further enhanced by leveraging the pool of capital used to invest in mezzanine opportunities.

The risk–return matrix is ultimately, and as indicated in Chapter 6, orchestrated around market and financial risk on the one hand, and deal structure risk on the other. Mezzanine investors need to structure deals with controls that guarantee them input into major decisions should certain events or agreed-upon performance hurdles not occur. Muldavin comments on the appropriate positioning of mezzanine products in real estate financing when arguing: 'Mezzanine real estate investment, while often characterized as "mezzanine debt," is really a specialty investment with more equity than debt-like features. Accordingly, an investment in a mezzanine real estate financing could be allocated as "opportunistic" real estate equity, an alternative high-yield investment, or some other specialty real estate investment.'

What follows is a case study to illustrate, by bringing a variety of issues together, the impact of what has been discussed above.


## 7.3  CASE STUDY: FINANCING A REAL ESTATE COMPANY IN THE CEE REGION

In this case study, the intended investment is at the level of the (real estate and development) company, not at the level of a specific project. The company can, however, be assessed as a portfolio of projects, diversifying some of the more accentuated project-specific risks.

The company is active (investing, managing and developing) in a wide range of CEE and CIS countries, and provides a natural diversification in terms of country-specific risks related to the real estate market. They are active in both the residential and commercial part of the market. The existing shareholders are divided on a 50/50 basis, on the one hand the founder and CEO with two of his disciples and on the other a set of three CEE focused investment firms who have been with them ever since their inception in 2000. The founder c.s. however, holds the majority voting rights (55%) and therefore qualifies as an activist shareholder with a highly visible and quality reputation in the markets they are active in. The team is highly qualified for the job and holds very deep sector expertise in the country in which it is active.

Prospects are looking good across the countries involved, and credit seems available after the dust settled due to the region being hit heavily in the early stages of the 2008 financial crisis. As it stands in 2012, they have been impacted, but more by the Eurozone crisis than by region or country-specific issues. The banking sector has recovered and is open for business but on a more selective basis than before the crisis, which is probably not such a bad thing overall. The firm has 30 projects in nine countries.

The pipeline for the next couple of years tells us that the asset base will grow by about €200 million, which will be financed through additional equity coming from shareholders (€65 million), mezzanine debt (€60 million), straight senior debt at project level (€60 million) and €20 million from retained earnings. The additional financing will make their solvency drop from 69% to 60% over the next three years and the target IRR for shareholders is set at around 20–25%, coming down from > 30% in the period before 2008.

The firm is, as previously indicated, looking for €60 million in mezzanine debt. It would prefer plain subordinated debt in two tranches of €30 million each with a two-year grace period. Disbursement of the first tranche would be at close, and the second part after three years. Tenor would be seven years. The front-end, appraisal and commitment fees are set at 1, 0.5 and 0.5%. Interest would be set at Euribor + 650 bps. The second tranche would only be disbursed based on certain milestones, which predominantly include the satisfying progress of the projects and the strict monitoring of the covenants.

The firm approached us, ABC investors, to consider this investment. During the discussions internally at ABC regarding this case, it frequently came up that overall, the compensation on the instrument seemed low relative to the expected IRR for shareholders and the level of subordination this instrument would be subject to. Therefore, it was decided to counter offer, replacing the plain subdebt with either step-up rates or a convertible loan. It was expected that the firm would not accept step-up rates, given its already steep use of senior debt and the impact on the cash flow waterfall it would have. The convertible loan option would give ABC part of the equity upside, which it would be able to monetize in the process of a later IPO or strategic sale, something the founder already indicated is on the cards towards the end of the seven-year period (give or take three years) of the loan. This would require ABC to put in some sort of tag-along rights.

The conversion of the full loan would lead to a 6% stake for ABC given the projections, and the (total) IRR would be somewhere between 15–20% dependent on the time of conversion. After discussions with the real estate firm, they indicated they were willing to OK the convertible products, but could offer only a 20% discount on the fair value of the stocks (at conversion) and where the conversion of the full principal amount would lead to a 7% stake in the firm.

Other covenants which could be agreed upon were:

- Solvency            > 28%
- DSCR               > 1.25%
- Current ratio       > 1.15
- Net debt/EBITDA     < 4.5
- ABC exposure        < 10% of total assets.

The loan will be provided to a Lux. Holding, which holds each of the OpCos in the nine CEE/CIS countries, which, in their turn, hold the project companies.

Quality of management, shareholders and corporate governance structures pose no problem. Their books are audited by Deloitte and no issues were identified in any of the years since inception.

The market outlook is where the big problem rests in this case. Or, to put it differently, the performance of their existing projects (no new ones were brought on board ever since the beginning of the crisis in 2008) is unlikely to mirror future projects (hence the reduction in expected shareholder IRR to 20–25%). Current results are therefore an imperfect guide in understanding future performance, and market risk is the big unknown in the equation. In 2008, markets literally fell off a cliff and valuations came down. In 2009, markets were pretty much paralyzed and only in 2010 were existing projects finalized (as liquidating projects was often more expensive for the developers relative to dumping new projects on a market still absorbing existing inventory). That depressed the prices in 2010 to early

2011 even further. Since early 2012, prices have stabilized and even reported small gains. Depending on the region, prices were even going up a bit as they had quoted below fair value during the most graphic parts of the crisis. Also, rental prices seemed to have gained momentum since early 2012.

The firm can fall back on some distinct advantages: (1) it takes on smaller projects which the markets are able to absorb relatively easily and so there is sufficient liquidity in its market segment and (2) it is active in both Ukraine and Poland, two countries which will be/are benefiting from the 2012 European soccer championship, and so the firm had no dead weight on its books coming from past projects.

Given its solvency, with no inventory and currently no projects under development, it seems to be in pretty good shape. Audited details are given below. One of the good things that came with the crisis was significantly lower construction costs (20–25% lower), which obviously will benefit the firm. The crisis also created a serious shake-out amongst developers, so overall competition is lower and valuations more attractive than before the crisis started. The choice to only build real estate in a modular fashion also allowed the company to cut costs where needed, make its headcount more flexible and manage opex in line with levels of economic activity in the market.

Local currency instability and political instability are, in 2012, the larger causes for concern. Political instability comes from different sources, one of the largest being societies voting against governments imposing tough austerity packages on countries and country-specific features, like the Tymoshenko issues in Ukraine which isolated Ukraine on a diplomatic and wider level from its natural allies.

The firm is also confident that banks are willing to come through with first lien senior debt for the individual projects. The firm's strategy to build modularly, or only when at least 50% is either pre-let or pre-sold, has contributed to the banks being confident to push through on their projects. The smaller size of their projects relative to the market makes them more easily digestible for the market, which adds to that positive momentum. Overall stabilizing of real estate prices, supply being adjusted to real demand and the overall lack of good quality real estate in some regions makes the market attractive for a niche player. However, real estate markets will always stay cyclical, and that fact needs to be factored into the equation.

The financials of the firm are provided in the tables below:

| Euro in 000's | 2008 | 2009 | 2010 | 2011 |
|---|---|---|---|---|
| Revenue | 2,932 | 1,443 | 1,845 | 2,454 |
| EBITDA | 1,412 | 1,234 | 1,345 | 1,456 |
| Net earnings | −1,543 | −350 | 450 | 1,243 |
| BS total | 105,089 | 130,087 | 140,084 | 120,072 |
| Solvency (%) | 49 | 23 | 35 | 51 |
| Debt/EBITDA | 6.5 | −2.1 | 1.21 | 1.34 |
| Current ratio | 1.3 | 0.8 | 1.1 | 1.4 |
| DSCR | 2.4 | 1.4 | 2.0 | 2.2 |
| CF from operat. | −2,474 | −3,384 | −3,123 | −4,382 |
| CF from investing | −4,234 | 432 | −120 | −1,430 |
| CF from financing | 5,467 | 4,343 | 5,500 | 6,500 |
| CF at year-end | −1,241 | 1,391 | 2,257 | 688 |

## 7.3.1 Projections

| Euro in 000's | 2012 | 2013 | 2014 | 2015 | 2016 | 2017 |
|---|---|---|---|---|---|---|
| Revenues | 2,709 | 3,100 | 3,450 | 4,908 | 5,250 | 6,000 |
| EBITDA | 1,540 | 1,870 | 2,100 | 3,130 | 3,400 | 3,900 |
| Net earnings | 1,430 | 1,604 | 1,705 | 2,300 | 2,800 | 2,950 |
| EBITDA margin (%) | 57 | 60 | 61 | 64 | 65 | 65 |
| Net margin (%) | 53 | 52 | 49 | 47 | 53 | 49 |
| CF including investments | 45,000 | 55,000 | 65,000 | 87,000 | 110,000 | 125,000 |
| BS total | 140,373 | 190,797 | 299,989 | 430,736 | 505,999 | 550,848 |
| Equity | 71,000 | 105,000 | 160,000 | 270,000 | 309,000 | 340,000 |
| Solvency (%) | 50 | 54 | 56 | 65 | 62 | 67 |
| Current ratio | 1.9 | 2.2 | 1.8 | 1.7 | 1.9 | 2.0 |
| Asset turnover (%) | 19 | 25 | 34 | 45 | 41 | 40 |
| Loan-to-value (%) | 50 | 55 | 54 | 51 | 49 | 55 |
| RoAE (%) | 12 | 21 | 25 | 24 | 28 | 21 |
| RoAA (%) | 9 | 11 | 14 | 19 | 13 | 11 |
| DSCR | 1.24 | 1.45 | 2.1 | 2.7 | 2.1 | 1.8 |

The main drivers of revenue and earnings growth in the coming years can be brought back to a number of items:

- Pre-sold homes and apartments.
- Rental income from retail and commercial market.
- Sale of retail and office projects (particularly after 2014).

The mortgage market in many CEE markets is young but developed and is continuously being refined.

## 7.3.2 Points for consideration

It will not be possible to conduct a full cash flow analysis, given the lack of the full balance sheet and income statements. That was not the purpose here, as we looked at those principles in Chapter 6 when discussing project finance. Please ignore any potential FX issues or exposures which might come with the fact pattern provided. However, it is possible to reflect on a number of the structural questions underlying this deal:

1. Is it fair to argue that plain subdebt would provide too little upside for the risk that is in this deal, relative to the level of subordination of this new chunk of mezzanine debt coming in?
2. If the answer to Q1 is yes, the next question is whether the convertibility added to the loan is the right mechanism/instrument (that is including the convertibility mechanism as described). Were there better mechanisms including the step-up rates as initially preferred by ABC?
3. Are there ways to protect yourself against structural market risks as given in the case?

4. The demand–supply relation is very un-transparent in this case. Would that require some exceptional dealing? What could that be? Would a pledge on the shares of the holding company be an option? A pledge on the shareholders' loans and/or intercompany loans?

5. Is the discount offered on the shares upon conversion sufficient to provide a meaningful equity kicker?

6. What other features would need to be built into the deal structure to mitigate potential risks:
   a. Share retention? Common in many mezzanine debt products.
   b. Allocation of capital to certain projects and countries?
   c. Convertibility option (obviously), exercise valuation and exercise period?
   d. Tag-along rights to facilitate exit after conversion?
   e. Right of first refusal providing the ability to block the transfer of shares to third parties or non-qualified parties in the deal?
   f. Prepayment or cancellation of the instrument in case of change of control?
   g. Positive, negative and financial covenants (including most likely a negative pledge)?
   h. Conditions which constitute a default?

7. Would it have been better for ABC to provide a unitranche facility to the real estate company, or at least a facility with a second lien on all the individual projects covered by the loan? What would the potential issues in this case be? Does a second lien facility help in these kinds of deals (i.e., where valuations could drop)?

8. Since cash flows are earned at the OpCo level (country-by-country) a clause will have to be included which allows for sufficient dividends to be up-streamed to the Lux. Holding to facilitate payments (due on a quarter-by-quarter basis).

9. The firm is a developer and uses subcontractors to effectively build the properties – that poses execution risk to which the firm and its borrowers are similarly exposed. Additionally, the real estate sector is regulated by heavy compliance and permits, which feeds corruption in some of the countries in which the firm is active. Although there are OECD guidelines re: corporate governance and direct or indirect government payments, these operational risks can result in significant exposures for the firm due to civil and/or criminal charges. For sure, guidelines for management need to be written into the contract as a positive covenant, although it is clear that some might be partly out of control of the firm's management. Are there other ways possible to protect against such risks? Hiring forensic auditors and/or consultants?

10. Two other material elements of risk are the way individual projects are leveraged (limit it contractually to, for example, 30/70 equity/debt? Or in line with market practice?) and how the different parts of the real estate market behave under different macro-economic conditions.

11. Another element of risk besides the cyclicality of the real estate business is the potential risk if the financial crisis were to have a second leg; it would evaporate the availability of senior credit in the markets in which the firm is active.

# 8
# Mezzanine and the Private Equity Space

It has been around four decades now since the first LBOs (leveraged buy-outs) emerged. A novel concept in the 70s, whereby investment firms took ownership of a company (often 100%, but definitely a majority stake) and funded the acquisition with only a sliver of their own equity and the rest with a syndication of all sorts of debt instruments. The idea was that the acquisition debt would be paid off (to a large degree) by the time that the firm was resold or brought back to the public market.

A definition of an LBO could therefore be:

> A transaction in which an investor group acquires a company by taking on an extraordinary amount of debt with plans to repay the debt with funds generated from the company or with revenues earned from selling off the newly acquired company's assets. It seeks to force realization of the firm's potential by taking control of the firm. The leveraging up of the purchase is a temporary state pending the realization of that excess value. It allows for a democratic means of ownership and control, i.e. a management team can take a firm to the next level or spin-off and follow its own independent course.

The target market for this kind of transaction was:

- Private businesses where the owner wanted to exit the business.
- Private or public businesses where the management wanted to take control of the firm and take the firm to the next step – later known as MBO (management buy-out) or where new management came in (MBI – management buy-in) who were looking for ownership but lacked the equity funding to acquire full ownership that way.
- Public businesses which, for whatever reason, had fallen from grace in the public market. At a later stage that was complemented with businesses which had to go through some sort of restructuring or totally re-invent themselves, and where the public markets didn't show any compassion so there was a need for the firm to go through that phase in the quietness of private ownership (P2P – public to private transactions). Most of these firms ultimately ended up being relisted again after the conversion was completed, and the firm could follow its own course.
- Generally, companies with low levels of existing debt on their books.
- Companies with quite a lot of fixed assets which could be used as collateral.
- Sizeable scope for creating efficiencies, cost reductions or creating value by reorganizing the firm.
- Strong, predictable operating cash flows with which the leveraged company could service and pay down acquisition debt.
- Mature, steady (non-cyclical), and perhaps even boring companies.
- Well-established business and products and leading industry position.
- Moderate capex and product development (R&D) requirements so that cash flows were not diverted from the principal goal of debt repayment.
- Limited working capital requirements.
- Strong tangible asset coverage.

- Undervalued or out-of-favor.
- Seller was motivated to cash out of their investment, or to divest non-core subsidiaries, perhaps under pressure to maximize shareholder value.
- Strong management team.
- Viable exit strategy.

For comparative purposes only, in the box below, the acquisition criteria of the saga of Omaha are described in the annual report of Berkshire Hathaway, 2009.[1]

---

# BERKSHIRE HATHAWAY INC.
# ACQUISITION CRITERIA

We are eager to hear *from principals or their representatives* about businesses that meet all of the following criteria:

(1) Large purchases (at least $75 million of pre-tax earnings unless the business will fit into one of our existing units).
(2) Demonstrated consistent earning power (future projections are of *no* interest to us, nor are 'turnaround' situations).
(3) Businesses earning good returns on equity while employing little or no debt.
(4) Management in place (we can't supply it).
(5) Simple businesses (if there's lots of technology, we won't understand it).
(6) An offering price (we don't want to waste our time or that of the seller by talking, even preliminarily, about a transaction when price is unknown).

The larger the company, the greater will be our interest: We would like to make an acquisition in the $5–20 billion range. *We are not interested, however, in receiving suggestions about purchases we might make in the general stock market.*

We will not engage in unfriendly takeovers. We can promise complete confidentiality and a very fast answer — customarily within five minutes — as to whether we're interested. We prefer to buy for cash, but will consider issuing stock when we receive as much in intrinsic business value as we give. *We don't participate in auctions.*

Charlie and I frequently get approached about acquisitions that don't come close to meeting our tests: We've found that if you advertize an interest in buying collies, a lot of people will call hoping to sell you their cocker spaniels. A line from a country song expresses our feeling about new ventures, turnarounds, or auction-like sales: 'When the phone don't ring, you'll know it's me.'

---

A number of elements are essential in understanding the LBO model. Typical LBO targets are firms which are relatively mature, with stable cash flows and often a significant branding or other IP firepower (often supporting these stable cash flows). The consumer sector, with its distinct brands or businesses with significant fixed assets, is likely to be a source of prime targets. Additionally, low valuations help, or as one prime PE manager once mentioned during a very early breakfast meeting: 'the alpha is in the purchase price, the rest is nonsense' – I

---

[1] Annual report, Berkshire Hathaway 2009, p. 21. Reproduced with permission of the author.

rephrased the last part to make it sound nicer, but the message is clear. On the other hand, firms with continuous high needs for capex or high-growth firms, which are in situations where they absorb the full free cash flow (FCF) to grow the business, show intrinsic weaknesses which mean the model will not work in an optimal way. Everything has to do with the availability of free cash flow to absorb the interest expense which comes with elevated levels of acquisition debt. It is ultimately those FCFs that enable the acquisition to be financed that way.

The world has changed significantly in the last 30 years, although the model has stayed relatively similar over time. The buy-out industry has known more booms and busts in that period than any other industry, partly due to the direct link to and need for cheap acquisition finance. If there is something that contracts during a financially induced crisis, it is the availability of (cheap) credit. The other aspect is that in the last 30 years, corporations have started to use more and more leverage to fund activities themselves, which overall leaves less room for additional acquisition debt.

As it stands in 2012, fundraising for LBOs is not anywhere close to the 2008 levels (see Figure 8.1), and the trend has become to spread capital over more funds and to allocate based more on specialism, rather than using capital for more general larger buy-out funds.[2] This is part of a more general trend in the asset management industry to spread across managers and strategies in order to work towards achieving better levels of diversification.[3] There is, however, no (in)direct evidence that this conduct pays off. Geographical coverage in general in the PE industry is gradually moving towards emerging markets, although in most cases the EM coverage is growth and development capital with only a minority proportion of deals qualifying as traditional LBOs.

The typical modeling steps and application issues are as follows (though not necessarily followed in this order by every LBO firm):

- Develop operating assumptions and projections for the standalone company to arrive at EBITDA and cash flow available for debt repayment over the investment horizon (typically three to seven years).
- Estimate the multiple at which the sponsor is expected to exit the investment (should generally be similar to the entry multiple).
- Determine the maximum purchase price which can be paid for a business, based on certain leverage (debt) levels and equity return parameters.
- Develop a view of the leverage and equity characteristics of a leveraged transaction at a given price.
- Determine key leverage levels and capital structure (senior and subordinated debt, mezzanine financing, etc.) which result in realistic financial coverage and credit statistics.
- Calculate the minimum valuation for a company since, in the absence of strategic buyers, an LBO firm should be a willing buyer at a price that delivers an expected equity return which meets the firm's hurdle rate.
- Calculate equity returns (IRRs) to the financial sponsor and sensitize the results to a range of leverage and exit multiples, as well as investment horizons.
- Solve for the price which can be paid to meet the above parameters (alternatively, if the price is fixed, solve for achievable returns).

---

[2] Dan McCrum, 'Private equity fundraising by top 50 drops,' *Financial Times*, April 29, 2012.
[3] Ruth Sullivan, 'Most fund managers "inefficient,"' *FTfm*, May 7, 2012.

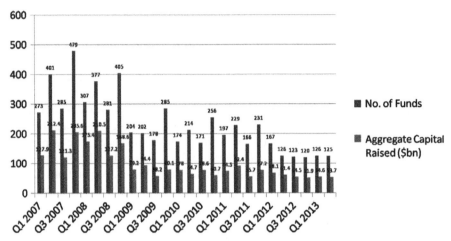

**Figure 8.1**  Global private equity fundraising, Q1 2007–Q4 2012
*Source:* Preqin, Author's own

Repeatedly, the question is raised about the value creation in a model like this. The answer deserves a separate book. Two short features I might add here: In 2011, the British Venture Capital Association (BVCA) released a report where, covering the year 2010, it analyzed the question of value creation and its origins. Its conclusions were that roughly 80% of the returns come from leverage and only 20% from value creation. I guess that makes sense. PE firms are, in general, relatively small firms and can only spend so much time on a particular portfolio company. On top of that, it is very likely that the managers of that firm are pretty good at what they do, otherwise the PE firm wouldn't have bought the firm to begin with, as it is that management team which needs to turn the company around (or take it to the next level, and putting in place a new management team after being PE acquired is often a risk factor). For completeness purposes it must be added that other studies have allocated more of the total return to value-creating activities conducted or initiated by the PE firm.[4] Although, in general, management teams seem happy with the PE ownership, there are distinct exceptions to that. A second recent example is the experience of Jimmy Choo's owner, Tamara Mellon, of what she called the PE hamster wheel after being owned by PE firms for 10 years, during a significant growth phase for the firm.[5]

## 8.1  DRIVERS OF RETURN

Basically, there are two drivers of return in LBOs: leverage and value creation (which can be of a strategic, operational and/or financial nature and will result in margin expansion, cost

---

[4] See, for example, O. Gottschalg, E. Talmor and F. Vasvari, 'Private equity fund level return attribution: Evidence from UK based buy-out funds,' LBS/HEC Working Paper, June 2010.
[5] Vanessa Friedman, 'Private equity versus private ownership, or the lessons of Jimmy Choo,' *Financial Times*, November 14, 2011 and Dan McCrum and Vanessa Friedman, 'Tamara Mellon puts the boot in to buyouts,' *Financial Times*, April 6, 2012.

cutting and efficiency improvements), which translate into earnings growth and a higher multiple valuation (although part of the latter can always be allocated to prevailing market conditions). Let's put that in an example:

A company with earnings of €20 million is bought for €160 million, thus on an earnings multiple of eight. It is held for three years and then sold for €240 million, by which time its earnings have increased to €25 million, and so the exit earnings multiple is 9.6. The original purchase price is funded with €40 million in equity and €120 million in debt.

| | | | | |
|---|---|---|---|---|
| Earnings at start | 20 M | | Earnings at exit | 25 M |
| Multiple at start | 8× | | Multiple at exit | 9.6× |
| Enterprise value | 160 M | | Enterprise value | 240 M |
| **Capital structure** | | | | |
| Equity | 40 | | Equity | 120 |
| Debt | 120 | | Debt | 120 |
| Enterprise value | 160 | | Enterprise value | 240 |
| Gains: 120M − 40M = 80M | | | | |
| Money multiple: 120M / 40M = 4× | | | | |

Contribution by:

- Earnings increase: (25M × 8) − (20M × 8) = 200M − 160M = 40M
- Multiple increase: (25M × 9.6) − (25M × 8) = 240 − 200 = 40M
- Total contribution 80M

Percentage contribution:

- Earnings increase: (40M/80M) × 100 = 50%
- Multiple increase: (40M /80M) × 100 = 50%

The dynamics here are clear – the more leverage, the more it magnifies the equity returns for investors. The downside has become clear as well: leverage creates fixed costs and the more cyclical the business, the more of a problem it might become when the economy turns south or when new growth doesn't show up at the time it is expected. The interim question is obviously whether it is better to allocate most of the free resources to acquisition debt repayment rather than spending it on capex, innovation, real growth or dividends. This is a question which has many answers, and the good news is that we don't have to answer this one in the context of this book.

Although there is a cascade of steps in a traditional LBO/MBI/MBO process, our focus here is on the debt capacity analysis and the sources of funding. Acquisition funding is allocated to the acquisition holding rather than the operational company. That poses all sorts of issues which relate to the fact that the holding doesn't earn any cash flows itself, and therefore needs structures in place with upstream cash flows to fund the repayment of the acquisition debt. We will not cover those, as it would take us too far away from the funding and mezzanine topic.

The starting point for our analysis is the firm and its financials and projections at entry point. Understanding the firm and its industry is key, despite the fact that the LBO process is a purely financial-model-driven exercise.

Our ultimate question is how many free cash flows are available to fund acquisition debt after the firm has paid its opex, interest on its debt and taxes. Our cash flow statement starts from net income and adds back all relevant items such as non-cash charges etc. to arrive at the cash flows for the year. However, these cash flows are not entirely freely available to pay off debt. We need to account for expenses and investments we will make in the coming year(s). To grow the business, our working capital will likely rise, and potentially new capex will have to be incurred as well as keeping the firm's dividend policy alive (to some degree). These items are regularly ignored in practice when using projected EBITDA (as a proxy for free cash flow). However, EBITDA doesn't look at forward projects' expenses and investments, but only at this year's (and then still ignores some of the expenses). Looking at EBITDA will basically show that there will be no further investments or incremental expenses needed to grow the business in line with the plan. Or, put more directly, you cut or reduce those line items to (almost) zero. That will maximize your debt capacity to fund the acquisition with debt (and magnify your equity returns).

In a structured way that becomes:

### EBITDA = Earnings Before Interest Taxes Depreciation and Amortization

> EBITDA = Operating Income + Depreciation + Amortization
> = EBIT + Depreciation + Amortization
> = Net Income + Income Tax Expense + Interest Expense + Depreciation + Amortization

### Cash Flow from Operations (CFO/OCF)

> CF from Operations
> = Net Income + Depreciation + Amortization − Chg in Non-Cash Current Assets (Inventory, A/R) + Chg in Non-Debt Current Liabilities (A/P, Deferred Revs) + Non-Cash Items
> = Net Income + Depreciation + Amortization − Chg Non-Cash Working Capital + Non-Cash Charges

The key operational distinction between EBITDA and CFO/OCF is the Change in Net Working Capital. CFO/OCF is also burdened by taxes and interest expense.

### Free Cash Flow (FCF)

> Unlevered FCF = Free Cash Flow to Firm (FCFF) = EBIT(1 − T) + D&A − Change in Non-Cash WC − Capex

The FCFF represents the cash flows available to *all* investors after mandatory cash outflows for business needs have been taken out (including taxes).

The reason we need FCF instead of EBITDA and OCF is the capex adjustment. See Table 8.1.

**Table 8.1**   Financial dynamics underlying an LBO

| Cash flow for leverage | Credit statistics for LBO(*) | |
|---|---|---|
| Revenue | Total Debt/EBITDA | 4.5x – 5.5x |
|   – Expenses | Senior Bank | 3.0x |
|   – D&A | Debt/EBITDA | |
| = EBIT | EBITDA/Interest | > 2.0x |
| = FCF available to pay interest | Coverage | |
|   – Cash tax | (EBITDA – | > 1.6x |
|   + D&A | Capex)/Interest | |
|   – Non-discretionary capex | Coverage | |
|   – Change in WC | | |
| = FCF available to pay interest and principal | (*)These parameters will change with market conditions. Also, the financing limit will depend on the circumstances specific to the transaction and the growth potential of the target | |

| Definitions of cash flow measures[6] | Most common debt capacity ratios |
|---|---|
| **Revenues** | |
|   – Operating Expenditure | • Equity incl. subdebt/T. Assets |
|   + Depreciation and Amortization | • Equity excl. subdebt/T. Assets |
|   + Long-Term Rentals | • Current ratio |
| **= Operating EBITDA** | |
|   – Cash Interest Paid, Net of Interest Received | • Senior debt/EBITDA |
|   – Cash Tax Paid | • All debt/EBITDA |
|   + Associate Dividends | • DSCR excl. Investments |
|   – Long-Term Rentals | • DSCR incl. Investments |
|   +/– Other Changes Before FFO | |
| **= Funds Flow from Operations (FFO)** | |
|   +/– Working Capital | |
| **= Cash Flow from Operations (CFO)** | |
|   +/– Non-operational Cash Flow | |
|   – Capital Expenditure | |
|   – Dividends Paid | |
| **= Free Cash Flow (FCF)** | |
|   + Receipts from Asset Disposals | |
|   – Business Acquisitions | |
|   + Business Divestments | |
|   +/– Exceptional and Other Cash Flow Items | |
| **= Net Cash In/Outflow** | |
|   +/– Equity Issuance/(Buy-back) | |
|   +/– Foreign Exchange Movement | |
|   +/– Other Items Affecting Cash Flow | |
| **= Change in Net Debt** | |
|   Opening Net Debt | |
|   +/– Change in Net Debt | |
| **Closing Net Debt** | |

---

[6] Source: fitchratings.com.

## 8.2 LBO STRUCTURE

A typical LBO structure is reflected in Figure 8.2:

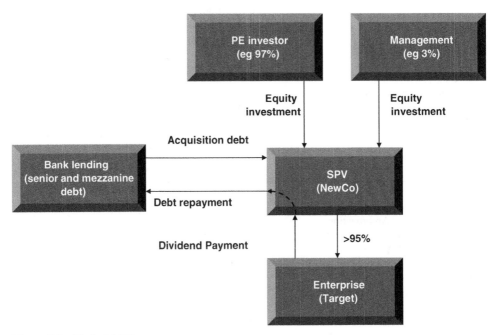

**Figure 8.2** Typical LBO structure

Depending on the situation, there will be a management team holding a certain amount of equity in the deal, either due to the nature of the deal (MBO/MBI), or as an incentive put in place by the PE firm to encourage the management team to deliver on the business plan underlying the assumptions used to build the LBO model and acquisition finance facilities.

The leverage provided by banks and other institutional investors (often in syndication) knows limitations as determined by debt capacity, which was discussed earlier in this chapter. The indirect limitations of the use of leverage are:

1. Solvency requirements (e.g., certain criteria) put up by debt providers to stay in business as a credible party to do business with.
2. Future financial flexibility, including the need to free up cash in case interesting projects or acquisition targets show up. Heavy indebtedness triggers situations where the firm loses a certain level of flexibility on how to finance its future operations, as certain channels of (cheap) funding might close down due to the incremental levels of debt the firm is carrying on its books. Can also impact situations where future capex needs are (partially) ignored in the above debt capacity analysis, and now need to be financed externally, most likely at a higher cost.
3. Financial risk related to IRR/ROI. As indicated before, the higher levels of fixed-cost debt increased to absolute levels of operational leverage (fixed cost to total cost) at the firm. It

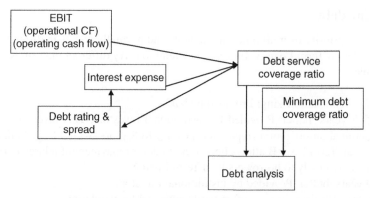

**Figure 8.3**   Leverage and debt capacity in an LBO

will make the firm naturally more prone to cyclical aspects of the industry or the market as a whole, and make them qualify as more risky from an investor point of view (as the volatility of the return increases as well as the return on equity) – see Figure 8.3.

The logical steps in the process are:

- Find operating cash flow and interest expense.
- Find minimum debt service capacity ratio.
- Use these to estimate debt capacity.

The financial structure of an LBO in terms of its product mix tends to look as reflected in Table 8.2. Existing senior debt at the level of the target company is often refinanced at the moment the LBO transaction is put in place:

**Table 8.2**   Default debt finance model for an LBO

| | | |
|---|---|---|
| 45–55% of total funding | Senior debt | Bank debt (A, B, C) up to 4.25–4.75x EBITDA (although lower currently); 5–7 years payback; 2x interest coverage |
| | Second lien | Senior debt + second lien up to 5.25–5.75x EBITDA (although currently lower); 7–10 years payback |
| 20–25% of total funding | Mezzanine/High-yield | Cash interest debt up to 6.5–7x EBITDA |
| | PIK notes | Non-cash interest debt |
| 25–30% of total funding (*) | Equity | Provided by PE fund; 4–7 years exit |

(*) Prior to the financial crisis of 2008, this part often constituted only as little as 10–15% of the total funding volume, the rest being made up by the other categories. The crisis rebalanced that somewhat and it is currently common for banks to want to see more skin in the game from PE firms.

## 8.2.1 Senior debt

This portion has priority over all other instruments and normally comes in different tranches, hence the indication Term Loan A, B or C. They tend to carry different maturities.

For example:

- Term A, 5–7 years, amortizing: Provided by banks.
- Term B, 5–8 years, bullet: Provided by institutional investors. This layer of debt usually involves nominal amortization (repayment) over 5 to 8 years, with a large bullet payment in the last year. Term Loan B allows borrowers to defer repayment of a large portion of the loan, but is more costly to borrowers than Term Loan A.
- Term C, 9 years, bullet: Provided by institutional investors.
- Floating rate (LIBOR + spread), often partly swapped for fixed rate.

These instruments carry the lowest risk, as they come with tight covenant conditions and have priority in terms of repayment (also in cases of default or liquidation). They tend to have either fixed or marginally floating interest charges – usually the latter (but always with spreads significantly over LIBOR) – attached and normally have a grace period (of up to 2–3 years). Depending on the credit terms, bank debt may or may not be repaid early without penalty. Part of this tranche is typically a revolver facility which can be used by the firms on a need-to-have basis across the cycle of the intended investment (see Chapter 10). How much of the total deal can be financed with senior debt depends on the level of existing debt in the firm, the value of the collateral, how much FCF is available and/or expected, as discussed earlier, and where that puts the firm on a peer review basis in the industry.

Part of this chunk of the total financing package (which is all bank debt) qualifies as:

- Bridge finance (see further for different meanings of the same concept): Short-term bank loans, typically to be refinanced in 1–6 months, which are put in place to get the deal done and cover expenses and which may be characterized by step-up spreads and other incentives to pay down early.
- Revolver: Bank facility the company can 'draw down' for working capital (functions like a credit card), certain capital investments or unforeseen costs. They come with ongoing fees, borrowing limits, covenants and conservative repayment terms. A company will draw down the revolver up to the credit limit when it needs cash, and repay the revolver when excess cash is available (there is no repayment penalty). The revolver offers companies flexibility with respect to their capital needs, allowing them access to cash without having to seek additional debt or equity financing.

  There are two costs associated with revolving lines of credit: The interest rate charged on the revolver's drawn balance, and an undrawn commitment fee. The interest rate charged on the revolver balance is usually LIBOR plus a premium which depends on the credit characteristics of the borrowing company. The undrawn commitment fee compensates the bank for committing to lend up to the revolver's limit, and is usually calculated as a fixed rate multiplied by the difference between the revolver's limit and any drawn amount.

  Subordinated bridge facilities and PIK bridge facilities are normally refinanced before maturity, often through the target's holding issuing debt instruments.

## 8.2.2  Second lien

Often used in conjunction with mezzanine debt, in a mix that is usually driven by what the market will tolerate. Providers are often alpha-seeking higher risk tolerant institutional investors like hedge funds. They are considered secured (as senior debt) though obviously with a weaker link, and at a cost often closer to senior debt than traditional mezzanine instruments. More and more, banks offer the unitranche model as a package for both senior and slightly beyond senior debt at rates which keep the total cost of funding at acceptable levels.

The maturity of these instruments is, in principle, longer than the longest term loan (Term Loan C), as an earlier maturity would implicitly break the seniority schedule. A second lien or mezzanine loan which would mature before all senior loans is still more junior to the senior loans, but would drain cash flow from the cash flow waterfall which is earmarked for repayment of the senior debt (interest and principal), and would make the senior debt more risky and less secured than intended. The senior and mezzanine loans are often structured with a bullet payment at the end (at least for the principal part). The second lien product group is senior to the unsecured mezzanine group but junior to the senior tranches. It is therefore not subordinated in right of payment to first lien lenders.

---

### DIFFERENCE BETWEEN DEBT SUBORDINATION AND LIEN SUBORDINATION:

1. **Basics.** In traditional contractual subordination, the debt claim itself is subordinated. If a subordinated debt holder obtains anything of value in a bankruptcy from any source, it agrees to turn it over to the holders of senior debt until the senior debt is paid in full. In lien subordination, the liens are subordinated; the underlying debt claim is not. What this means is that the holder of second lien debt only agrees to turn over proceeds from sales of shared collateral to the holders of first lien debt. The holder of a second lien secured claim does not have to turn over funds to the holders of first lien debt distributed to it from other sources.
2. **Priority vis-à-vis the trade.** In its simplest terms, debt subordination places the subordinated debt behind the senior debt, but does not place it ahead of any other of the borrower's debt (unless holders of that other debt agree, in turn, to subordinate their debt to the subordinated debt). By contrast, although lien subordination does place second lien debt behind first lien debt to the extent of the value of the first lien creditor's interest in the collateral, it also places the second lien debt ahead of the trade and other unsecured creditors, to the extent of the value of its interest in the collateral. This is the key benefit for second lien creditors.
3. **Anti-layering covenant issues.** A typical 'anti-layering' covenant will prohibit an issuer from incurring new debt which is subordinated 'in right of payment,' unless that new debt is also subordinated to (or *pari passu* with) the debt containing the anti-layering provision. However, a typical anti-layering covenant does not restrict the incurrence of second lien debt because it isn't subordinated 'in right of payment.'
4. **Payment blockage issues.** Unlike traditional subordinated debt, second lien debt is not typically subject to payment blockage provisions of any kind.

**5. Remedy standstill provisions.** The remedy bars in second lien deals typically only apply to remedies associated with the collateral. Most second lien deals specifically preserve all, or almost all, of the remedies which would be available to an unsecured creditor, with a few exceptions (as we will discuss below). In the case of bond deals issued in public offerings (or in private placements with registration rights), certain legislation like the US Trust Indenture Act (or similar Acts) prohibits any bar on actions to collect payments due and owing to bond holders, but it does allow limits on enforcement actions against collateral.

## 8.2.3 Mezzanine/HY loans

This is where most of the structuring takes place. Both product groups are contractually subordinated (see further in this chapter). The more senior mezzanine products (which have no roll-up of interest) enjoy upstream guarantees into the holding the more they are structurally subordinated. The junior mezzanine products (roll-up of interest payments) and PIK notes don't enjoy upstream guarantees, and are ranked after trade creditors. In effect, they are equity owners and deeply subordinated. In contrast to most mezzanine loans, the HY yield group, which pays a fixed interest (in contrast to most mezzanine loans), is – often also structurally – subordinated, but with light covenants.

### What is a covenant-light loan?

A covenant-light loan is a loan without maintenance-style financial covenants (such as maximum leverage, minimum interest coverage and cash flow cover) which are required to be tested (and passed) each quarter or half-year.

Maintenance coverage is typically set at a 20–30% headroom against the financial base case used to structure the deal. The purpose of such maintenance covenants is to allow creditors to monitor the issuer's actual performance against the anticipated performance, and since the covenants typically assume improving metrics over the life of the loan, they cement the 'de-risking' profile of the borrower over time.

Should there be a breach in any of these tests, creditors have either the option to amend the covenants, normally with a fee, via a loan amendment (if the causes of the breach are considered temporary) or to waive the breach subject to the borrower taking action to address the underlying causes. The last option is to declare an event of default, accelerate the loan and enforce their security rights.

### Leveraged (often syndicated) loans

Loans, often provided in syndication by lenders (to spread risk) to leveraged borrowers – those whose credit ratings are speculative grade (traditionally double-B plus and lower), and who are paying spreads (premiums above LIBOR or another base rate) sufficient to attract the interest of non-bank term loan investors (that spread typically will be LIBOR+200 or higher, though this threshold rises and falls, depending on market conditions). Banks which initially didn't lend to leveraged borrowers started doing so in the 80s/90s, as it was an easy way to put quite a bit of money to work with little effort and at little cost to the firm. There are three main types of leveraged loan syndications:[7]

- An underwritten deal
- A best-efforts syndication
- A club deal.

*Underwritten deal*   In an underwritten deal, the arrangers guarantee the entire amount committed, and then syndicate the loan.

If the arrangers cannot get investors to fully subscribe the loan, they are forced to absorb the difference, which they may later try to sell. This is easy, of course, if market conditions – or the credit's fundamentals – improve. If not, the arranger may be forced to sell at a discount and, potentially, even take a loss on the paper. Or the arranger may just be left above their desired hold level over the credit.

So, why do arrangers underwrite loans? There are two main reasons:

1. Offering an underwritten loan can be a competitive tool to win mandates.
2. Underwritten loans usually require more lucrative fees because the agent is on the hook if potential lenders balk.

Of course, with flex-language now common, underwriting a deal does not carry the same risk it once did, when the pricing was set in stone prior to syndication.

*Best-efforts*   In a 'best-efforts' syndication, the arranger group commits to underwrite less than the entire amount of the loan, leaving the rest of the credit to the vicissitudes of the market. If the loan is undersubscribed, the credit may not close, or may need major surgery – such as an increase in pricing or additional equity from a private equity sponsor – to clear the market.

Traditionally, best-efforts syndications were used for riskier borrowers or for complex transactions. Since the late 1990s, however, the rapid acceptance of market-flex language has made best-efforts loans the rule, even for investment-grade transactions.

*Club deal*   A 'club deal' is a smaller loan (usually US$25 million to US$100 million, but as high as US$150 million) which is pre-marketed to a group of relationship lenders.

The arranger is generally a first among equals, and each lender gets a full cut, or nearly a full cut, of the fees.

Syndicated leverage loans have a credit rating and an active secondary market. Typically, they are callable at par without penalty. They can be secured or unsecured but are always senior debt. Leveraged syndicated loans are typically senior to all other debt in the borrower's capital structure, while syndicated loans of investment grade firms are often at the same level of seniority as senior bonds.

Leveraged loans need to be distinguished from leveraged secured credit, which is an asset-based loan secured by a company's A/R, inventory, equipment etc. whereby the lender

---

[7] Further information can be found at: www.leveragedloan.com.

takes a first lien on the assets being financed. They can be attractive, as they are profiled for lenders with different characteristics than traditional lenders. They tend to come with fewer covenants and might free up more funding than would be justified if judged on a pure cash flow basis. You can even take it a step further and securitize certain assets like franchise receivables or future contractual cash flow streams in order to lower funding costs and enhance flexibility.

### High-yield loans/bonds[8] aka junk bonds:[9]

Bonds which are non-investment grade (directly or after fall-back). Originally, speculative grade bonds were bonds which had been investment grade at time of issue, but where the credit rating of the issuer had slipped and the possibility of default increased significantly. These bonds are called 'fallen angels.' Over time, more and more of these facilities were provided to LBO operators, but also to other corporations for operational purposes, often if firms were constrained by bank credit availability. These loans were then often repackaged into CLOs (Collateralized Loan Obligations) or CDOs (Collateralized Debt Obligations) with a view to providing a higher rating to the senior tranches above the rating of the original debt. The senior tranches of high-yield CDOs could meet the minimum credit rating requirements of pension funds and other institutional investors, despite the significant risk in the original high-yield debt. The rest of the story is history. HY loans come with tight covenants which are mainly centered around:

- The inability to incur further indebtedness.
- Performing restricted payments (dividends or other distributions to shareholders, intra-group loan repayments or investments as well as asset transfers (sale, sale-and-leaseback etc.)).
- Granting liens over its property or assets.
- Entering into non-arm's length dealing with other groups and/or related companies.
- Events of default include any failure to pay interest and/or principal, any breach of covenants and the instigation of insolvency or other related proceedings against the issuer or the group.
- Most often, there is a 'cross-holding default,' which implies that a default on one of the loans or bonds triggers an acceleration of all other instruments.
- It typically also includes a grace period and a non-redemption period.

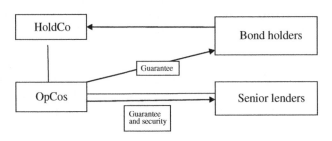

---

[8] For valuation-related issues of HY bonds: Thomas S. Y. Ho and Sang Bin Lee,' Valuing High Yield Bonds: a Business Modeling Approach', Working Paper, 2003.

[9] For a market perspective, see: Ed Altman, 'The Anatomy of the High Yield Bond Market,' Working Paper, 1998.

The above diagram reflects the US position. In Europe, however, HY bond holders typically suffer(ed) from:

- Structural subordination: due to the fact that the bond holders or HY issuer don't have a guarantee, but can only rely on an intercompany loan from the holding to the OpCo's.
- Payment blockage.
- Standstill provisions.

Consequently, they have started to ask for stronger upstream guarantees and protection from the operational companies as well as security interests over the OpCo's assets. Given their deep level of subordination, they are actually equity risk wrapped in a fixed-income product, but do, however, correlate to equities[10] because of their underlying fundamentals. This is especially true now since, in the aftermath of the financial crisis, the senior lenders have become more vocal in insisting on strict and deep subordination for the HY/mezzanine lenders. They in their turn are looking for better pricing of their equity-like products.

---

## Lien, structural and contractual (or debt) subordination[11]

Subordination is an arrangement where one creditor or group of creditors (the junior creditor(s)) agrees not to be paid by a borrower or other common debtor until another creditor or group of creditors (the senior creditor(s)) have been paid.

There are essentially three types of subordination: structural, contractual and lien subordination.

In the case of a **contractual subordination**, loans are made to the same company but the senior creditor and junior creditor agree priority of payment by contract. Partial debt subordination would usually permit a subordinated lender to receive some or all of its scheduled payments in the absence of an event of default under the senior credit facility. Complete debt subordination means that the subordinated lender would not receive any payment on its loans until the senior lender received payment in full on its senior loans. Second lien loans generally contained limited debt subordination provisions which were only triggered by collection actions. In contrast, current transactions involving mezzanine and other institutionally subordinated debt typically provide the senior lender with the ability to implement a payment blockage against the subordinated lender for a specified period of time (generally set in the range of 90 to 180 days), for an event of default which does not involve the failure to make a payment on senior debt, and a permanent payment blockage for a default due to failure to pay all, or any portion, of the senior debt.

---

[10] 'High-Yield Bonds and Their Correlation to Equities,' in *The Educated Investor*, December 2008.
[11] For more on the topic, see: Ron Carleton and Tim Delaney, 'Using Subordination to Define Intercreditor Priority' (2009) *RMA Journal* **16**.

**Structural subordination** arises when the senior creditor lends to a company (usually one of the operating subsidiaries in which assets are held) which is lower in the group structure than the company (most often a holding company) into which the junior creditor lends.

Structural subordination means that the priority of payment of an obligation as a practical matter is determined by the structure of the financing transaction and the recipient of the loan, rather than by any express contractual agreement by a lender to subordinate its priority.

Junior creditors as creditors of a holding company effectively rank behind creditors of the operating subsidiaries lower down in the group structure. This is because, where a holding company and its subsidiaries become insolvent, the operating subsidiaries' creditors will be paid out before any distribution is made to the holding company as shareholder in the subsidiary. The holding company will only be able to meet the claims of its creditors from the proceeds realized from the subsidiaries if it receives a distribution from the liquidator of a subsidiary.

**Lien subordination**[12] means that one lender agrees that the priority of its liens on property which serve as common collateral will be subordinate to the liens of another lender. Subordinated secured lenders possess certain rights because of their status as lien holders which, in the absence of an agreement to the contrary, would interfere with the rights of senior lenders in workouts or bankruptcies. A typical lien subordination enables the senior lender to collect on the proceeds of its collateral before the subordinated lender, and the subordinated lender will agree to some short period of time before taking any foreclosure action against shared collateral. This is called a 'remedy standstill' provision. The senior lender expects to be in the driver's seat for a period of time (a range of 90 to 180 days) when it comes to dealing with, and exercising remedies against, the shared collateral. The generally accepted principle is that the subordinated lender should be permitted to exercise remedies in the event that the senior lender fails to commence an exercise of its remedies after this standstill period. Acquirers may want to move forward with documentation based on their lenders' mutual agreement that the second lien will be a 'silent second', or that it will be 'deeply' subordinated, but they do so at their peril. The meaning of both of those terms will vary from one deal to the next, based upon numerous factors, including the composition of the senior and subordinated lender groups, the difficulty of syndicating those loans, the nature and value of the collateral for those loans, and the relative size of those loans. A deal can be delayed or sidetracked because of the lenders' failure to agree on what each side meant by the use of those terms.

Remedy standstill provisions will normally be accompanied by terms which require the subordinated lender to turn over any amounts that it may recover in a liquidation or bankruptcy to the senior lender. This type of 'turnover clause' is intended to prevent a subordinated lender from receiving more than it would have been entitled to receive under the inter-creditor agreement. Turnover provisions involve drafting nuances which may fundamentally modify their effect. For example, if the inter-creditor agreement

---

[12] Based on and see for more: 'Defining Intercreditor and Subordination Terms in Deal Negotiations' by Gary B. Rosenbaum, Partner, McDermott Will & Emery LLP.

were to permit the subordinated lender to foreclose at the end of the remedy standstill period, then the drafting of the turnover provision might permit a subordinated lender to argue that it should not be obligated to turn over any funds that it received following the end of the standstill period to the senior lender.

A more in-depth analysis will be provided in the later chapter on legal and term sheet issues (Chapter 10).

Leveraged loans, however, often came with very light covenants compared to their senior debt peers, which gave them the name covenant-light loans. Covenant-light loans are loans which have bond-like financial incurrence covenants, rather than the traditional maintenance covenants which are normally part and parcel of a loan agreement. What's the difference?

Incurrence covenants generally require that if an issuer takes an action (paying a dividend, making an acquisition, issuing more debt), it would need to still be in compliance. So, for instance, an issuer which has an incurrence test that limits its debt to 5x cash flow would only be able to take on more debt if, on a pro forma basis, it was still within this constraint. If not, it would have breached the covenant and be in technical default on the loan. If, on the other hand, an issuer found itself above this 5x threshold simply because its earnings had deteriorated, it would not violate the covenant.

Maintenance covenants are far more restrictive. This is because they require an issuer to meet certain financial tests every quarter, whether or not it takes an action. So, in the case above, had the 5x leverage maximum been a maintenance rather than incurrence test, the issuer would need to pass it each quarter, and would be in violation if either its earnings eroded or its debt level increased.

For lenders, clearly, maintenance tests are preferable because they allow them to take action earlier if an issuer experiences financial distress. What's more, the lenders may be able to wrest some concessions from an issuer that is in violation of covenants (a fee, incremental spread, or additional collateral) in exchange for a waiver.

Conversely, issuers prefer incurrence covenants precisely because they are less stringent. Covenant-light loans, therefore, thrive when the supply/demand equation is tilted persuasively in favor of issuers.

Pricing of both products is still built, in a traditional sense, around default and 'loss-given default' risk. Loans usually offer borrowers different interest-rate options. Several of these options allow borrowers to lock in a given rate for one month to one year. Pricing on many loans is tied to performance grids, which adjust pricing by one or more financial criteria. Pricing is typically tied to ratings in investment-grade loans, and to financial ratios in leveraged loans.

Syndication pricing options include Prime, LIBOR, CD and other fixed-rate options:

- Prime is a floating-rate option. Borrowed funds are priced at a spread over the reference bank's prime lending rate. The rate is reset daily, and borrowings may be repaid at any time without penalty. This is typically an overnight option, because the prime option is more costly to the borrower than LIBOR or CDs.
- The LIBOR (or Eurodollar) option is so called because the interest on borrowings is set at a spread over LIBOR for a period of one month to one year. The corresponding LIBOR rate is used to set pricing. Borrowings cannot be prepaid without penalty.

- The CD option works precisely like the LIBOR option, except that the base rate is certificates of deposit, sold by a bank to institutional investors.
- Other fixed-rate options are less common but work like the LIBOR and CD options. These include federal funds (the overnight rate charged by the Federal Reserve to member banks) and cost of funds (the bank's own funding rate).

As the name implies, LIBOR floors put a floor under the base rate for loans. For instance, if a loan has a 3% LIBOR floor and three-month LIBOR falls below this level, the base rate for any resets defaults to 3%. For obvious reasons, LIBOR floors are generally seen during periods when market conditions are difficult and rates are falling, as an incentive for lenders. The debt rating model banks use to price the leveraged loan is based on a regression analysis, and the pricing grid (seven levels) is based on the company's financial data for the last 2–3 years. It tells them how much to lend and at what spread, but also the amount of economic capital that needs to be allocated to the loan exposure. Indirectly, the pricing level is a function of the analyzed credit risk, but also the covenants that come with the product (negotiated). Four steps can be distinguished:

**Main differences between syndicated loans and the HY bonds product groups[13]**
Although both product groups look pretty similar on the surface, there are some distinct differences. Leveraged syndicated loans primarily bear interest at a variable rate, usually based on a margin above LIBOR (London interbank offer rate) or another base rate, with changes in the interest rate at intervals selected by the borrower, varying from one to six months. Because they are variable-rate products, syndicated loans are almost always pre-payable without premium. Bonds, in contrast, are fixed-rate instruments and do not freely allow prepayment. Bonds may include a call provision giving the issuer a onetime right after a set period of time (often five years) to prepay and retire the bonds, usually at a premium above par. Leveraged syndicated loans typically have a short term to maturity of one to five years. High-yield bonds are usually medium-term instruments with maturities of five to ten years. Interest on syndicated loans is typically paid monthly or quarterly. Interest on high-yield bonds is often paid semiannually or annually. Bonds are term obligations which are fully funded at the issuance of the bonds. Leveraged syndicated loans typically include revolving credit facilities as well as term loan facilities.

The most obvious difference between the two forms of debt is that high-yield bonds are typically unsecured subordinated debt while leveraged syndicated loans are senior secured debt. Leveraged syndicated loans are typically secured by a lien on all of the borrowing entity's assets and a lien on all of the borrower's subsidiaries' assets. The borrower in a leveraged syndicated transaction is commonly either the parent corporation or a holding

---

[13] Derived from and see further on this topic: Gary D. Chamblee and Jolie Amie Tenholder, 'Converging Markets: Leveraged Syndicated Loans and High-Yield Bonds' (November–December 2005) *Commercial Lending Review* 7–16.

company owned by the parent corporation. In either case, each of the borrower's subsidiaries, both direct first-tier subsidiaries and lower-tier subsidiaries, guarantees the loan to the borrower by so-called upstream guarantees which are then secured by the assets of each of the guarantor subsidiaries.

Despite these differences, high-yield bonds (or what were once called 'junk bonds') are often described as the closest asset class to leveraged syndicated loans, and the similarities between the two types of debt have increased at an accelerating rate over the last decade. What are the common characteristics that have led these two forms of debt to increasingly compete in the marketplace for the attention of both borrowers and investors?

### What is the difference between leveraged and junk bonds?

High-yield bonds and leveraged syndicated loans share the characteristic of being classified as below investment grade. The dividing line between investment-grade debt and below-investment-grade debt depends on who is doing the rating. Irrespective of the credit rating firms you go to, credit ratings are generally divided into two categories: investment grade and speculative. Because speculative-grade bonds are considered to have a higher default risk and a lower credit quality than those issued by higher-rated investment-grade issuers, the issuers must typically offer a higher rate of return to attract investors, and are therefore classified as high-yield bonds in addition to being below investment grade. The highest quality investment-grade bonds are rated as 'Aaa' by Moody's and as 'AAA' by Standard & Poor's. Any bond rated below 'Baa' by Moody's is classified as speculative or below investment grade, and any bond rated below 'BBB' by Standard & Poor's is classified as speculative.

The world of syndicated loans is similarly divided into two broad categories: investment grade (or non-leveraged loans) and leveraged loans. Leveraged loans involve a higher ratio of debt to equity and are considered to be less creditworthy than investment-grade syndicated loans. Different banks, rating agencies and investors use different methods to distinguish between the two. Some rating agencies use the company default spread to determine whether it is investment grade (non-leveraged) or not. For example, everything over LIBOR + 125 bps is considered leveraged. Others use the loan's credit rating to determine what is leveraged or not. The qualification is then reserved for those loans with ratings at the lowest end of the spectrum (for example below BB or B). The bank loan ratings process (in contrast to corporate ratings) focuses on a specific loan, and includes an analysis of the overall quality and scope of collateral (that is, a first lien on all assets compared to a lien on selected assets), loan-to-value ratios and strength of loan covenants. If the collateral and loan covenant package is sufficiently strong, the bank loan rating may be 'notched up,' meaning that the loan has been given a higher rating than the overall corporate credit rating for the issuer.

Although both product groups have been created within the emergence of the LBO sphere, their use over time has become more popular, and has expanded to include corporate funding beyond the M&A area.

Although covered extensively in Chapter 10, a few words here on the covenants for both product groups will prove useful.

The structure and content of covenants in leveraged syndicated loan transactions are similar in many ways to the covenants in high-yield bond transactions. Some typical covenants which the two forms of debt share in common include the following: limits on indebtedness; liens; transactions with affiliates; restricted payments; the sale of assets, mergers and consolidations; and changes in ownership. In addition, most of these covenants in both types of transactions are applicable to the borrower/issuer and to the significant or 'restricted' subsidiaries of the borrower/issuer. Often, in leveraged syndicated loans, the covenants may extend to all subsidiaries of the borrower/issuer. The main concern in setting these covenants for both the lenders in a syndicated loan and the investment bankers in a bond transaction is to ensure that the borrower/issuer has sufficient funds to pay the debt, whether that comes from the borrower/issuer's business or the business operations of its subsidiaries through dividends or otherwise, and that concern is the main impetus for the covenants and how they are negotiated. This emphasis on the borrower/issuer's ability to repay its debt is important both for investors' ability to be paid in due course and to keep the value of the asset as it is traded in the secondary markets.

Covenants in both leveraged syndicated loans and high-yield bonds include a covenant limiting the incurrence of indebtedness. In both cases, there are many carve-outs and exceptions, which are called permitted debt. Permitted debt usually includes existing indebtedness and new indebtedness which refinances existing indebtedness, indebtedness related to the transaction documents (including guarantees) and a variety of other types of indebtedness central to the borrower/issuer's business and to the underlying loan or bond documents. Indebtedness covenants in both types of transactions usually include a category of permitted debt in the form of a specific sum (in dollars) as a catchall or 'basket' for any other indebtedness which does not fall into one of the other permitted categories. In leveraged syndicated loans, any indebtedness other than permitted debt is typically not allowed, but often in high-yield bond transactions indebtedness outside of the permitted debt may be allowed if the issuer meets certain financial ratios, usually a debt-to-earnings ratio (leverage ratio) or an earnings-to-fixed-charges ratio (fixed-charge coverage ratio).

Documentation for both leveraged syndicated loans and high-yield bonds usually includes a covenant restricting liens on the borrower/issuer's assets. Both types of transactions will include carve-outs or 'permitted liens' for existing liens at the time of the transaction, purchase money liens, liens for taxes and assessments and liens for the refinancing of other permitted liens. An unsecured high-yield bond transaction may commonly include more permitted liens than a secured, leveraged syndicated loan transaction.

Both leveraged syndicated loans and high-yield bonds will also include covenants restricting dividend payments. Generally, all such payments are restricted unless no default would be caused by the making of dividend payments, and such payments are either by one of the borrower/issuer's subsidiaries, or are, in an aggregate amount, less than some particular financial trigger. The financial trigger is often tied to the borrower/issuer's consolidated net income. However, in some instances, leveraged syndicated loans may be more restrictive than high-yield bond offerings by including an overall cap on the dividends which may be made during the existence of the credit facility.

Covenants which provide limitations on transactions with affiliates and on the sale of assets by the borrower/issuer and its subsidiaries, or certain significant subsidiaries, are included in both leveraged syndicated loan and high-yield bond documentation. Both leveraged syndicated loans and high-yield bonds will require that transactions with an affiliate be on an arm's-length basis for fair market value. High-yield bond deals often go further in requiring that if there are transactions with affiliates, depending upon the size of such transactions, the parties must provide evidence of board approval and fairness opinions. Covenants restricting asset sales also require that such sales be for fair market value. Covenants in a high-yield transaction addressing sales of assets often permit such sales if their proceeds are primarily given in cash and are used to purchase new assets or to repay specified outstanding debt. On the other hand, covenants in leveraged syndicated loan transactions are often more stringent in that the bulk of permitted asset sales are limited to sales in the ordinary course of business, and to sales of equipment or real estate where the proceeds are used to buy replacement equipment or real estate.

Financial covenants are generally found in leveraged syndicated loan transactions but not in high-yield bond deals. Whereas bond deals may weave in financial aspects such as limiting dividends or allowing indebtedness based on financial triggers, such financial aspects are implicated when some additional action has been taken by the issuer (for example, the issuer has paid dividends). Leveraged syndicated loans have explicit requirements that net worth, earnings, leverage ratios, fixed-charge coverage ratios and/or other similar financial requirements and ratios must be maintained. If the financial requirements set out in the covenants are not met, there may be a default on the leveraged syndicated loan.

In addition, financial covenants often play a part in pricing for leveraged syndicated loans. While high-yield bond deals have fixed rates, leveraged syndicated loans have a floating rate which is commonly adjusted for a fiscal period if certain financial covenant calculation results change (alternately, the pricing may be adjusted based on the debt rating of the borrower). It is particularly common for the applicable interest rate in a leveraged syndicated loan to change based on the leverage ratio of the borrower.

As discussed earlier, the covenants in leveraged syndicated loan and high-yield bond transactions are often very similar. Though they differ to a reasonable extent, such differences may often be caused by the fact that the lenders under the loan transaction have a secured interest, and therefore have an expectation of being paid first in the case of a default, while the unsecured investors in a bond transaction have concerns as to which debt may be paid prior to their interests and wish to ensure that there are not too many liens by third parties with priority over their unsecured interests. Covenants in both loan and bond deals may be amended, but because of the structure of a loan, and particularly if the lenders still have obligations to fund a revolving loan, it is often easier to amend a covenant in a loan than in a bond transaction where it may be more difficult to obtain the necessary number of investors' approval for an amendment. In addition, the term of a syndicated loan is typically shorter than the term of a bond. Thus, if a covenant is exceptionally restrictive, at the end of the loan term, a different covenant may be negotiated in a new loan, whereas the bond covenants may continue through the life of multiple loans and multiple sets of loan covenants. Credit agreements for syndicated loans now fully anticipate that interests in the loans will be traded in the secondary market.

These markets are always in action. Recent developments can be monitored through the AFME European or US High Yield and Leveraged Loan reports (Sifma). Issuance in 2012 is on the rise and constitutes a fourfold increase in issuance volume compared to 2011 so far, at least for the leveraged loan market. A small drop has been experienced in the high-yield market in 2012 so far compared to last year.

A last category in this tranche is **seller's notes:** A portion of the purchase price in a (typically smaller) LBO may be financed by a seller's note. In this case, the buyer issues a promissory note to the seller saying that it agrees to repay (amortize) over a fixed period of time. The seller's note is attractive to the financial buyer because it is generally cheaper than other forms of junior debt, and easier to negotiate terms with the seller than a bank or other investors. Also, the acceptance of a seller's note by the seller signals their faith and confidence in the business being sold. However, seller financing may be unattractive to the seller because they retain the risks associated with the business without having any control over it. Additionally, the seller's receipt of proceeds from the sale is delayed. It is often called 'hope-we-get-paid someday finance' as it is frequently a last resort measure and can indicate that the buyer has little wiggle room in getting the deal financed, so the seller will offer seller finance in line with current market conditions at that time. Arrangement can be PIK or structurally subordinated, and is mostly deeply subordinated. Pricing is often attractive relative to the subordination level. The arrangement can be, but is not necessarily, combined with earn-out provisions, which allows the seller to generate additional future income based on the (future) performance of the sold business. Goals are often sales or earnings-based.

### 8.2.4 PIK notes

The big difference between PIK notes and the other products in the mezzanine group is the fact that both the principal and the interest component accrues until maturity. That not only makes the product deeply subordinated and prone to pretty much every shock in business or overall economic conditions, but also is built on the assumption that by this step in the tiering of the financial package for the acquisition, there is no actual FCF (according to projections) at the firm matching potential interest due (the cash flow waterfall has dried up). Therefore the liability is pushed forward towards maturity on the understanding that incremental cash flows will be available to account for the payments. PIK notes tend to receive ratings at the lower end of the junk spectrum, as they are structurally subordinated with no guarantees or security pledges. The product group is also known as toggle notes. Partial PIK notes are possible when there is room available for some additional interest payments prior to maturity. PIK notes are often provided at HoldCo level (with no guarantee or pledge), hence the terminology HoldCo PIK notes.

### 8.2.5 Equity

It is what it says it is. The equity provided by a PE firm which normally has a specific target return in mind, which impacts valuation assumptions and exit targets. Target annualized IRR is (at least) 20% looking at the global marketplace. Economic reality tells us that actual performance hovers around that number in quite a wide bandwidth across time and vintage years.

In most cases, PE players tend to use convertible preferred shares (CPS) where possible, given their distinct benefits. However, in many emerging countries, this security type is not available and therefore firms need to turn to common equity or security characterized with overall less flexibility than the CPS. That lack of flexibility makes it more difficult to orchestrate exits, as one often needs to turn to IPOs and trade sales to provide the necessary liquidity. Consequently, more and more firms are using securities with natural expiration (e.g., redeemable preferred shares etc.) or with the ability to create synthetic exits.[14]

---

[14] Sev Vettivetpillai, 'Private equity must no longer rely on IPOs,' *Financial Times*, March 11, 2012.

The cascade given below translates into a parallel cascade of subordination levels:

| Operational Company/Holding Company | Senior debt | Closest to the operational cash flows |
|---|---|---|
| **Dividends** | Second lien | Subordinated debt in HoldCo which receives dividends from OpCo after servicing the term loans |
| Holding Company | Mezzanine/High yield | |
| | PIK notes | |
| | Equity (Sponsor and management) | Residual cash flow owners |

There is an inherent conflict of interest between PE firms and their lenders, which can be summarized as follows:

| Equity investor's aims | Lenders' objectives |
|---|---|
| Achieve maximum leverage | Get maximum investor commitment |
| Freedom of action | Tight ratios |
| Loose or light covenants | Tight covenants |
| Minimum events of default | EoD enables to negotiate |
| Optimize WACC | Adequate return for risk |

In the case of a secondary buy-out, where an LBO operator buys a portfolio company from another LBO operator, the process repeats itself in pretty much an identical fashion.

## 8.3 TAX IMPLICATIONS

In order to finance the amounts due on acquisition finance, an acquisition holding will charge (often through an intercompany loan) the amounts due on the acquisition debt. That interest charge can be offset against the remaining operational profits in the OpCo. Through the process of consolidation for corporate tax purposes, that will not lead to an additional tax charge at the level of the HoldCo, where it will be used to offset the amounts due (interest and/or principal) on the acquisition debt. It is, however, common practice for the OpCo to also tolerate the charge of the tax shields which result from the inter-company loan. That benefit is also passed on as a buffer to the HoldCo which enhances its debt repayment capacity. That buffer will either be consumed in later years when the OpCo is not able to generate sufficient FCF to absorb the intercompany loan charge for that period and/or be used to accelerate repayment of the acquisition debt still outstanding. In the case of an earlier than expected sale, the remaining amounts due on the acquisition debt will be paid off using part of the purchase price, and will never be passed on to the next owner of the business.

## 8.4 ALTERNATIVE TRANSACTIONS USING SIMILAR FINANCING STRUCTURES

There are quite a number of transactions which use similar techniques to the LBO model – we mentioned similar approaches for MBO/MBI transactions (which are essentially factually different in nature, but similar in their objectives relative to an LBO), but also beyond those there are a number of transactions applying similar techniques. A number of the most common are:

- **Leveraged recapitalization:** A strategy where a company takes on significant additional debt with the purpose of either paying a large dividend or repurchasing shares. The result is a far more financially leveraged company (significant change of the capital structure), usually in excess of the 'optimal' debt capacity. After the large dividend has been paid, the market value of the shares will drop. A share is referred to as a 'stub' when a financial recap results in its price declining to 25% or less of its previous market value. In a successful recap, the value of the dividend plus the value of the stub exceeds the pre-recap share price. Leveraged recapitalizations are used by closely held companies as a means of refinancing, generally to provide cash to the shareholders while not requiring a total sale of the company. There are downsides, however. This form of recapitalization can lead a company to focus on short-term projects which generate cash (to pay off the debt and interest payments), which in turn leads the company to lose its strategic focus.[15] Leveraged recapitalization can also occur in cases where LBO operators hold their portfolio company longer than expected, and the existing set of acquisition debt is starting to mature. To replace the existing acquisition debt and to capitalize on the additional equity value created during the holding period, a complete new set of acquisition debt is brought on board to bridge the period until exit. Those situations, however, need to be distinguished from situations where the PE firm provides a bridge loan or bridge facility to the portfolio company while bridging the period to an IPO or exit, where the exit is more tangible, visible and/or predictable.
- **Dividend recapitalization:** As indicated, a form of leveraged recapitalization. The goal of raising leveraged finance is to pay a dividend to shareholders (which, under normal conditions, would be paid out of retained earnings or the year's earnings). Although the dividend recap is not a transaction exclusively for the buy-out field, it is common practice among PE firms to use it as such, particularly in cases where the repayment of the original acquisition debt is up to speed. The buffer it yields allows the PE firm to take new leveraged debt on board during the holding period of the portfolio company, in order to pay the shareholders a dividend providing interim liquidity to the PE. Although it sounds somewhat counter-intuitive to pay yourself a dividend as a shareholder with debt you raised (or at the least it sounds un-careful), there are possible situations where it technically could make sense. That is particularly the case if leveraged debt is relatively cheap compared to the rest of your balance sheet and the returns you can make as a firm given the business you're in. Then, rather than consume earnings from the firm which it can re-invest in good projects which will earn an interest return, dividends are paid at a cost (much) lower than the return on those projects. The differential is the firm's 'saving' relative to paying the dividend out of earnings. That is, unless you consider that one shouldn't pay a dividend if the business can grow at decent levels while maintaining good returns. Ultimately, it piles up debt and fixed commitments which might turn against the firm when recession kicks in or the

[15] U.C. Peyer and A. Shivdasani, 'Leverage and Internal Capital Markets: Evidence from Leveraged Recapitalizations' (March 2001) *Journal of Financial Economics* **59**(3):477–515.

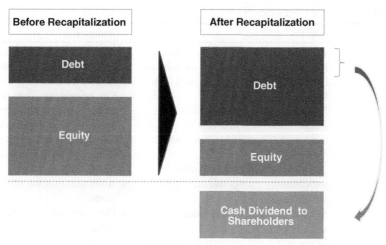

**Figure 8.4**   Dividend recapitalization

business tanks otherwise.[16] Dividend recapitalizations by PE firms have become more frequent in recent years, as the exit of their portfolio companies (holding periods) has become longer than anticipated, which, under these circumstances, allows the firms to capture some of the equity value without disposing of their equity stake (see Figure 8.4).

• Some of the indicated techniques are also used as **shark repellants** (i.e., to avoid or fight off a (hostile) takeover bid). This is done by adding debt whilst eliminating idle cash and debt capacity. Prospective bidders would face the daunting task of returning the firm to leverage ratios closer to historical industry levels. The recap may also give management a higher percentage of share ownership and control. Although such recaps are designed as a takeover defense, a high percentage of firms which adopt them are subsequently acquired. The technique can also be employed proactively, as a means of placing free cash flows into shareholders' hands and employing debt's disciplinary effect to improve performance, thus increasing shareholder value.

## 8.5  SUMMARY OF DIFFERENT COMPARTMENTS IN THE LBO STRUCTURE[17]

In Table 8.3 the main categories of the LBO structure are summarized based on the discussion above.

---

[16] Julie Creswell, 'Profits for Buyout Firms as Company Debt Soared,' *New York Times*, October 4, 2009 and Julie Creswell and Peter Lattman, 'Private Equity Thrives Again, but Dark Shadows Loom,' *New York Times*, September 29, 2010.
[17] Source: www.macabacus.com.

**Table 8.3** Tranches in the LBO structure

| Sources of funds | Key terms | Comments |
| --- | --- | --- |
| Bank Debt | • Typically 30–50% of capital structure<br>• Based on asset value as well as cash flow<br>• LIBOR-based (i.e., floating rate) term loan<br>• 5–8-year maturity, with annual amortization often in excess of that which is required (average life 4–5 years)<br>• 2.0x–3.0x LTM EBITDA (varies with industry, ratings and economic conditions)<br>• Secured by all assets and pledge of stock<br>• Maintenance and incurrence covenants | • Bank debt will also include an unfunded revolving credit facility to fund working capital needs<br>• Can be split into Term A (shorter term, higher amortization) and Term B (longer term, nominal amortization, bullet payment)<br>• Generally, no minimum size requirement<br>• Amortizes over the life of the loans<br>• Generally, no prepayment penalties |
| High-yield and Subordinated Debt | • Typically 20–30% of capital structure<br>• Generally unsecured<br>• Fixed coupon<br>• May be classified as senior, senior subordinated or junior subordinated<br>• Longer maturity than bank debt (7–10 years, with no amortization and a bullet payment)<br>• Incurrence covenants | • Public and 144A high-yield offerings are generally US$150m or larger; for offerings below this size, assume mezzanine debt. In some cases, it may be appropriate to include warrants such that the expected IRR is 17–19% to the bond holder<br>• Senior and senior subordinated offerings are generally cash-pay; junior subordinated offerings (which would generally be issued in combination with senior subordinated offerings) may be zero coupon and issued at a holding company<br>• Bullet payment (non-amortizing) |
| Mezzanine Debt | • Can be preferred stock or debt<br>• Convertible into equity<br>• IRRs in the high teens to low twenties on 3–5-year holding period | • Occasionally used in place of high-yield debt<br>• Generally a combination of cash pay and PIK; can be both, or change over time<br>• Often includes warrants to enhance IRR to desired level above coupon rate |
| Total Debt | • Typically 3.0x–6.0x LTM EBITDA<br>• Interest coverage at least 2.0x LTM EBITDA/first year interest | • Total debt varies by sector, market conditions and other factors |
| Common Equity | • Typically 20–35% of capital structure<br>• 20–30% IRR on about a 5-year holding period<br>• Exit multiple = entry multiple<br>• Management options of 5–10% | • Required IRR may be lower for larger or less risky transactions |

## 8.6 SUMMARY OF TYPES OF SECURITIES IN THE LEVERAGE STRUCTURE OF AN LBO

Table 8.4 provides an overview of the individual securities in the leverage structure and their characteristics and use in such structures.

**Table 8.4**  Comparison of security classes

| Security class | Leveraged loans | High-yield | Mezzanine | Equity |
|---|---|---|---|---|
| Security | First lien | Unsecured | Unsecured | None |
| Ranking | Senior | Contractual subordinated | Structural/contractual subordinated | Junior |
| Covenants | Generally comprehensive | Incurrence-based | Less restrictive, mostly financial and maintenance-based | None |
| Term | 5 years | 10 years | 8 years | Open ended |
| Coupon | Cash paid – floating | Cash paid – fixed | Cash paid – fixed/PIK | Dividends |
| All-in rate(*) | L+ 550 bps | T+600 bps | 10–18% | Variable |
| Warrants | None | Generally not | Almost always | Not applicable |
| Pre-payment penalties | Minimal | Heavy penalties/call premiums attached | Moderate | Not applicable |
| Capital providers | Banks, non-banks | Public offering | Private capital | Public/private |
| Recovery (%) (*) | 80 | 40 | 20 | 0 |
| Liquidity | Medium | Medium/High | None | High |
| Rating requirements | Required | Required | None | None |
| Buyers of paper | CLOs/buyers of institutional paper | Institutional investors, CBOs/ HNWI | Insurance firms, mezz. funds, PE funds | General public, institutional investors |

PIK: Pay in kind, L: LIBOR, T: 10-year US Treasury, CLO: Collateralized Loan Obligation, CBO: Collateralized Bond Obligation
(*) In both cases, it is undeniably the case that the numbers or spreads will evolve over time and subject to geographical and macro-economic variables. They can be seen as an average position in the market anno 2012–2013.

## 8.7 CASE STUDY: BUYING ORANGINA – A TYPICAL LBO WITH SOME INTERESTING QUESTIONS AHEAD!

By November 2005 Europe had developed a pretty decent buy-out market. Slightly in contrast to the US, the European buy-out market was predominantly orchestrated through auctioning with the bulge bracket FIs as an intermediary.

The main players in this case were Lion Capital and The Blackstone Group. Lion Capital was a young buy-out player in Europe with focus on the consumer market, mainly operating out of London (by 2012 it had become a household name in the PE field, with investments (and exits) across the wider European spectrum. One of its first high-profile deals was Jimmy Choo shoes.) It was operating its first fund (€820 million), and was in the process of building a track record. The poster child was Javier Ferrán, who had been CEO at Bacardi Limited amongst other positions during his long tenure at the Bacardi Group, and who had joined the firm some time before this deal emerged in 2005.

The other player needs less of an introduction. The Blackstone Group, a diversified financial conglomerate (anno 2012) mainly known for its buy-out funds (although they only constitute a modest part of the total organization). Founded in 1985 as an advisory boutique, it had propelled itself, by 2005, into the top ranks of what came to be known as the buy-out industry. It already had a significant number of funds and assets under management (of which the size had grown exponentially going from one fund to the next). In November 2005, it had close to US$15 billion under management in its four buy-out funds, and was raising its fifth fund, which closed in 2007 at US$21.7 billion.

Being at the top of the market in 2005, credit was abundantly available and the buy-out market was on fire. Blackstone, although it was a market leader, had been very slow moving into Europe, partly due to the different way buy-out firms were perceived in that market. So the firm had money to spend but not so much of a reputation in the European market yet.

In November 2005, Lion Capital (Lion) and the Blackstone Group (BG) were engaged in an auction to buy Cadbury Schweppes European beverages (further referred to as 'Orangina'). Cadbury Schweppes' European beverages business contained, besides Orangina which came with its very brand-specific bottles, a number of other confectionery and beverage businesses. Those included brands such as Apollinaris water, Schweppes tonic and soda water, and a portfolio of regional brands. In November 2007, the consortium had already gone through two rounds of bidding.

With about seven parties left,[18] they tried to avoid going into a third round of bidding as they considered they were already at the upper range of the valuation scale, especially given the fact that sales at the auctioned business had already been falling for five years, and Cadbury Schweppes had been eager to sell the business for a few years, as it was considered to have become non-strategic. Nevertheless, they were both very eager to get this deal fished in, as it would give Lion the necessary credibility and visibility, and the Blackstone Group more weight in the European market, allowing them to hit the ground running in continental Europe. More rounds of bidding typically not only mean higher valuations, but also clustering of competitors into club deals to increase financial firepower, in particular given the restrictions PE managers have on how much of each fund they can spend on any particular deal.

Valuations have always been an issue, partly due to the auctioning process, triggering the winner's curse, but also due to the effect of abundant credit availability which, at that time, had pushed leverage for the larger buy-out deals in Europe up to almost 6x EBITDA (higher than in the US). Buy-out funds committed up to 30% of the deal price via their own equity, the rest being financed by FIs as well as the wider market, including hedge funds through the process of syndication and the CLO process (Collateralized Loan Obligations).

It was clear that whatever the price this deal was going to close on, Lyon Capital had to go back to its LPs (Limited Partners) for further funding or co-investment, given the 30% per deal limitation it had on its fund. That was even with the help of the BG, which could commit more

---

[18] See Saigol, Schmith and Boschat, 'Goldman opens bidding for Schweppes', Financial news online, September 2, 2005.

than US$1 billion per deal given the size of its most recent fund at that time, a competitive advantage which made the group attractive as a partner in a club-deal, but not sufficient to get the deal done at current valuations.

The two PE firms were no strangers to each other, as they had been looking at another deal together (the acquisition of Allied Domecq), a deal which ultimately didn't go through.

At the time of the deal, the European soft-drinks market was valued at about €140 billion.[19] The consumer market has always been on top of the buy-out list due to its stable cash flows across cycles, and often strong branding dynamics which made them ideal buy-out targets which could sustain a decent portion of acquisition debt.

Weather and tourism were major drivers behind the market's dynamics, which were pretty favorable for the market during 2005. Many classifications existed, e.g., carbonated, still drinks, nectars, sport drinks. Also, the 'low calorie' segment had been growing consistently over the last five years. Increasing wealth in the region and efforts to have consumer taste shifted away from alcohol did the rest of the work. Compounded growth the last 10 years had been around 3% for the market as a whole, with the carbonated drinks market at the lower end of that with only 1.6% and still drinks and sport drinks at almost 9%.[20]

Coca-Cola and Pepsi Cola topped the ranks with Orangina as a relevant third. The heart of its brands included Orangina, a carbonated orange fruit drink containing orange pulp, as well as Schweppes containing tonic water and fruit-flavored soda. They were all leading brands in Europe (or parts of Europe). Also included, but of minor importance, were Oasis and TriNa, still fruit-flavored soft drinks. Schweppes Tonic was the top tonic water across Europe; Orangina the number one orange carbonated soft drink in France (it still is in 2013), and Oasis and TriNa the top still soft drinks in France and Spain. Yet at the point of this deal in 2005, the division's same-store sales were down by approximately 1% and profit down by about 6%.

The Orangina business was a bit of an odd one. It was actually left over from an earlier deal (in 1999) when Cadbury Schweppes sold its non-US soft drinks business to Coca-Cola. However, anti-trust concerns prohibited the full asset base from being transferred. It left Cadbury Schweppes with an assortment of brands including Schweppes Tonic, Oasis, TriNa, Canada Dry, Champomy, Vida, Gini and Pampryl, with coverage across Europe and beyond.

They were forced to rebuild some economies of scale back into the business, which they did by acquiring Orangina and La Casera, a Spanish carbonated lemonade, in 2001, followed in 2002 by taking over Apollinaris bottled water. The company became vertically integrated in a number of countries including France, Spain, Germany, Belgium and Portugal. In other countries third-party bottlers handled the market.

The hodgepodge of failed divestments and seemingly random acquisitions had led to under-investment in this part of the business, and a complete lack of management focus, to a large degree explaining its poor performance during 2005.

### 8.7.1 Getting the deal done!

This deal received significant interest in the market from financial as well as strategic buyers.[21] It was expected to be priced at about 9x EBITDA. The market buzz was that the business

---

[19] Based on industry reporting Deloitte (2005).

[20] Ibid. note 19.

[21] It was all over the financial press for months, putting additional pressure on all parties involved in the deal.

would come with a price tag of about €2–2.2 billion. It raised the question of whether that was a fair value price for a business which was performing so poorly at the time. Due to the significant interest, an auction was unavoidable. The process was handled by Goldman Sachs with its notorious marketing machine behind it, so if there was one certain thing, it was that the deal wouldn't come cheap. The teams realized that there was often significant alpha in the purchase price in deals of this nature.

One of the problems here was the fact that, due to the myriad of transactions leading to the business as it was in 2005, they weren't really buying a firm with a solid structure and management and marketing machine built around it, but rather a set of brands, splashed out over a set of legal entities located all over Europe. It had some sort of team, which was helped by the larger corporate support of the Cadbury Schweppes Group. The latter would obviously disappear after the sale of the business. Marketing had been poor, and the question emerged as to whether the existing team would be able to pull off any meaningful business plan which would lead to value creation and an exit value in line with targeted returns.

After convincing yourself that this would be an operable business on a stand-alone basis, the next bump in the road would be how much funding was needed to turn this into a top-class business again, and how, in the next few years, it would impact the bottom line. Ultimately, as mentioned above, stable cash flows of a mature business are somewhat of a condition for a well performing buy-out.

On a consolidated level there were four distinct issues:

1. Consistency of running the business at the time, and how it would impact the business once it was no longer a corporate division. The recent acquisitions were hardly integrated and the business lacked a real spine, including asymmetry in management functions between the Orangina management and firm management, as well as some key departures in recent years.
2. These were poster child brands and therefore triggered some level of price inelasticity as long as they were supported by consistent and significant marketing efforts. Those efforts had been lacking for some time, which would force the PE firms to look carefully at how it would affect free cash flow in the coming few years when they would be rebuilding the brands. The firm hadn't invested much in innovation either, which was felt particularly in the diet drinks sphere, which had grown significantly in recent years in market terms, but Orangina only managed to get about 2% of that market. Nevertheless, it had products which were complementary vis-à-vis its direct competitors (Coca-Cola and Pepsi Cola) as well as the fact that its products had features (e.g., pulp) that competitors' products didn't have.
3. One of the issues behind the curtain was the fact that there was a variety of distribution networks for these products, each with its distinct characteristics. Going through a hypermarket (where brands are important and consequently there is price elasticity) is a different ballgame compared to wining and dining environments, where brands are less important or at least where brands compete on more of a level playing field. In terms of sales, Orangina was sold through different channels depending on the country analyzed, with different perspectives as a consequence.
4. The last issue goes back to the point of country specificity. The consumer market is known for its heavy regulation (mainly related to food pricing), an issue which had to be looked at on a per-country basis. For example, in France, where sales had been falling for years, there was a law in place during 2005 (which was going to be repealed in 2006) which caused a pricing issue, whereby manufacturers' payments to retailers for promotion or shelf placement could not be passed on to the consumer by reducing the price of the product below its invoiced cost. Repealing this rule would affect food pricing in the country, but

how it would affect individual brands was uncertain. There was also EU legislation upcoming which would bring down price protection for sugar, which would help bring down the cost structure of the product. (Note: if this case had happened in early 2012, the same question would have emerged since the EU approved, from January 1, 2012, the use of Stevia, a surrogate for sugar, which had been available for some time in the US market.)

## 8.7.2 Valuation, pricing and deal mechanics

Although this particular transaction is full of issues which could make it worth looking at, the focus going forward will be on the financial part of the deal, and in particular the valuation, pricing and financing issues.

The consortium ultimately made an offer of €1.848 billion with 7.3x EBITDA leverage. It decided to put in 30% using its equity (about €600 million). Banks were willing to step in, lured by strong cash flows. They also felt comfortable due to the company's set of A-brands holding strategic positions in key markets across a range of segments. The fact also remained that, despite everything that had happened in the last couple of years, the business was still resilient and produced cash flows. In that sense, breaking apart the asset structure to manage those brands independently could create tremendous value at the end of the road. Nevertheless, there were also risks involved, as indicated earlier. On top of this, and given its 30% exposure limit, Lion Capital would have to go back and syndicate its LPs to come up with the difference. The firm needed about €300 million, which was above 30% of €820 million (the size of its only fund at the time), and that needed to happen under the time pressure which often comes with auction processes.

Hereafter some further case-related datasets are included, which give the data on the financing, structuring issues and debt capacity analysis for the deal, including the mezzanine-related products used.

## 8.7.3 Case guidance

There are two relevant questions to focus on going forward. Firstly, is the deal fully priced at the offering price of €1.85 billion? The second revolves around the choices of (mezzanine) debt financing proposed, and the impact these would have on the debt capacity analysis given the sensitivity around the financial projections, and the unknowns surrounding the costs of ramping up marketing, operational excellence etc.

Based on the projections (see below), the offering price equals about 10x EBITDA. Another element which can be thrown into the mix is the fact that its peers, Coca-Cola and Pepsi Cola, were trading in the market at respectively 13.85 and 15.88x EBITDA (at that time), which would give Orangina a valuation of around €2.15 to 2.47 billion, closer to the initial pricing Cadbury Schweppes had in mind before going into the process.

With such an amount of uncertainty surrounding the business's performance, the expected increase in costs and pay-off period combined with a 2/1 leverage Debt to Equity, this deal could be considered as what the French would call a true 'tour de force.' The other thing is that this was likely a low-growth deal, where volume was expected to be flat between 2005 and 2010. Marketing expenditures etc. would lead to growth in net sales, but would it have been realistic to expect that the firm would grow beyond the market as a whole, given the shape it was in? It would have needed to grab quite some market share to do so, and it wasn't particularly well positioned in the higher growth segments of the soft-drinks market.

## 8.7.4  Datasets

---

### DATASET 1: BLACKSTONE FUNDS[22]

Blackstone, as indicated, had a number of funds up and running at the time of the deal in 2005, which it has since added to. They include (vintage year):

- Blackstone Capital Partners I – (1987) Committed Capital US$800 million.
- Blackstone Capital Partners II – (1994) Committed Capital US$1,270 million.
- Blackstone Capital Partners III – (1997) Committed Capital US$3,780 million.
- Blackstone Capital Partners IV – (2000) Committed Capital US$2,019 million.
- Blackstone Capital Partners V – (2006) Committed Capital €21,700 million (in process of raising at time of deal).
- Blackstone Capital Partners VI – (2010) Committed Capital US$13,500 million (closed after exit and sale to Suntory).

---

### DATASET 2: ORANGINA FINANCIALS (ACTUAL AND PROJECTIONS)[23]

| In mn of € | Actual | | | Estimated | Projected | | | | |
|---|---|---|---|---|---|---|---|---|---|
|  | 2002 | 2003 | 2004 | 2005 | 2006 | 2007 | 2008 | 2009 | 2010 |
| P&L |  |  |  |  |  |  |  |  |  |
| Net sales | 977.9 | 1,003.9 | 955.1 | 952.9 | 960.0 | 997.9 | 1,036.0 | 1,074.9 | 1,115.0 |
| Cost of goods | 362.3 | 346.5 | 378.5 | 373.1 | 376.4 | 387.2 | 398.4 | 413.6 | 425.9 |
| Gross profit before marketing | 615.6 | 657.4 | 576.6 | 579.8 | 583.6 | 610.7 | 637.6 | 661.3 | 689.1 |
| Marketing expenses | 106.5 | 112.6 | 105.9 | 107.3 | 112.5 | 131.6 | 134.2 | 133.4 | 137.9 |
| Marketing exp. as % of net sales | 10.9% | 11.2% | 11.1% | 11.3% | 11.7% | 13.2% | 12.9% | 12.4% | 12.4% |
| Gross profit after mark. exp. | 509.1 | 544.8 | 470.7 | 472.5 | 471.1 | 479.1 | 503.4 | 527.9 | 551.2 |
| EBITDA | 182.9 | 199.6 | 188.4 | 184.5 | 193.5 | 201.4 | 212.3 | 220.5 | 239.6 |
| Change in working capital | <12.3> | 26.9 | <14.4> | <27.4> |  |  |  |  |  |
| Restructuring payments | <29> | <6.4> | <39.5> | <35.7> | <3.4> |  |  |  |  |
| Net capex | <14> | <45.9> | <42.9> | <24.3> | <33.6> | <28.8> | <25.2> | <29.1> | <25.9> |
| Pre-tax operating cash flow | 112.76 | 174.2 | 91.6 | 97.1 | 156.5 | 172.6 | 187.1 | 191.4 | 213.7 |

---

[22] Derived from the company website: www. blackstone.com
[23] Author estimations based on consolidated Cadbury Schweppes financials, public information and firm and deal dynamics.

## DATASET 3: BREAK-DOWN OF ACQUISITION DEBT[24]

| Debt | | Millions of € | Maturity | xFY2005 EBITDA | % of total | Interest compensation (%) |
|---|---|---|---|---|---|---|
| | Senior debt Tranche A | 250 | 7 | 1.36 | 12.9 | 5.5 |
| | Senior debt Tranche B | 260 | 8 | 1.41 | 13.44 | 6.1 |
| | Senior debt Tranche C | 260 | 9 | 1.41 | 13.44 | 6.6 |
| | Bridge facility Apollonaris etc. (sell-off businesses) | 150 | 2.5 (*) | 0.813 | 7.73 | 5.4 |
| | First lien facilities | 920 | | 5.0 | 47.42 | |
| | Second lien | 120 | 9.5 | 0.65 | 6.18 | 8.95 |
| | **Senior debt + second lien** | **1,040** | | **5.64** | **534.6** | |
| | Mezz. bridge facility | 300 | 10 | 1.62 | 154.46 | 8.2 +PIK margin of 6.5% |
| | | | | 7.3 | | |
| | **Total debt facility** | **1,340** | | **7.26** | **69.07** | |
| **Equity** | | 600 | | 3.25 | 30.92 | |
| | **Lion Capital** | **300** | | | | |
| | **Blackstone** | **300** | | | | |
| | **Total sources** | **1,940** | | 10.51 | 100 | |

(*) Will be paid off immediately after brands are sold after acquisition, hence the significantly shorter maturity.

---

[24] Ibid. note 24. A logical pattern was followed in building the acquisition debt schedule, i.e. ranking, volume and pricing, based on a standardized LBO debt package design. Actual numbers in the case might have differed from the standardized model although total acquisition debt will be in line due to known equity investments by PE firms, as those were publicly communicated. Maturity of debt instruments was estimated based on normal PE investment duration and banking (syndication) practices. Pricing of the instruments was based on market conditions in 2005 and took into account the ultimate price paid for the business – 'pricing levels' might have deviated in the actual case. An additional restructuring and revolving credit facility is normally granted using a similar duration as the deal. This is not reflected in the debt package as it is often undrawn at the moment of the close of the deal and is a more operational feature.

## DATASET 4: ESTIMATED DEBT REPAYMENT SCHEDULE[25]

| € Millions | 2006 | 2007 | 2008 | 2009 | 2010 | 2011 | 2012 | 2013 |
|---|---|---|---|---|---|---|---|---|
| Total net cash position | <81.5> | <79.6> | <76.7> | <71.9> | <64.8> | <56.5> | <48.5> | <38.9> |
| Net total debt | 921.0 | 871.3 | 789.4 | 674.7 | 554.2 | 415.3 | 253.5 | 83.6 |
| Net senior debt | 739.2 | 697.4 | 623.7 | 500.1 | 384.4 | 241.4 | 88.4 | 0.0 |

The last stage of our analysis is whether the total debt facility put in place is sustainable vis-à-vis the projected cash flows. To do that effectively, we retake our debt schedule and add an additional row where we calculate the effective interest paid on each instrument (consider the notes which were provided with the chart initially):

**Actual cost of leverage in the Orangina deal**

| | | Millions of € | Maturity | xFY2005 EBITDA | % of total | Interest compensation (%) | Interest in millions of € |
|---|---|---|---|---|---|---|---|
| Debt | | | | | | | |
| | Senior debt: Tranche A | 250 | 7 | 1.36 | 12.9 | 5.5 | |
| | Senior debt: Tranche B | 260 | 8 | 1.41 | 13.444 | 6.1 | |
| | Senior debt: Tranche C | 260 | 9 | 1.41 | 13.444 | 6.6 | |
| | Bridge facility for sell-off business | 150 | 2.5 | 0.813 | 7.73 | 5.4 | |
| | First lien facilities | 920 | | 5.0 | 47.4 | | |
| | Second lien | 120 | 9.5 | 0.65 | 6.18 | 8.95 | |
| | Senior debt + second lien | 1,040 | | 5.64 | 53.6 | | |
| | Mezz. bridge facility | 300 | 10 | 1.62 | 154.46 | 8.2 +PIK margin (6.5%) | |
| | Total debt facility | 1,340 | | 7.26 | 69.07 | | |
| Equity | | 600 | | 3.25 | 30.92 | | |
| | Lion Capital | 300 | | | | | |
| | Blackstone | 300 | | | | | |
| | Total sources | 1,939 | | 10.51 | 100 | | |

---

[25] Ibid. note 24.

Once we have that, we can go back to our debt repayment schedule and combine it with the EBITDA from the projections chart. What is left to calculate is the total debt repayment per annum (which you can, as you know what the interest per instrument is and when the principal amount becomes due). Offsetting your projected annual EBITDA against the repayments due (for that year) provides the coverage ratio, which will tell you how sensitive the model is, how stretched the debt portion in the financing mix as well as in what years the risk of a breach of covenants is most likely to occur. Ultimately, the debt capacity of a firm in the case of an LBO comes down to the idea of how much room there is left in terms of free cash flows (EBITDA is used here as an indicator for that), i.e., after the usual items such as WC, capex, dividends etc., or what is effectively available in terms of funding to repay the additional acquisition debt. The corporate debt which was attached to the business that was bought is already paid, and reflected in the net earnings, the basis for calculating the CF from operations. Unfortunately, all too often, the WC and new capex are squeezed to maximize the FCF, as it allows the business to use more leverage to finance the deal, thereby enhancing returns on the equity invested by the LBO operators. It shows years later when the firm is sold on or IPO'd through below-par performance relative to peers in the market. This has made investors suspicious of buying into PE-led IPOs (or at least at elevated prices). In effect, the assets are exhausted and need revitalization after years of being ignored. That takes time and money.

In terms of debt capacity analysis, you need the free capacity left after opex and WC/capex/dividends are accounted for. Around that sensitivity pattern you can then build a set of mezzanine products which take into account those sensitivities, maturities of the mezzanine products vis-à-vis the estimated exit period and possible early repayment options if the business is sold earlier than expected, taking into account the expected rate of return of the LBO project.

**Debt capacity analysis**

| € Millions | 2006 | 2007 | 2008 | 2009 | 2010 | 2011 | 2012 | 2013 |
|---|---|---|---|---|---|---|---|---|
| Total net cash position | <81.5> | <79.6> | <76.7> | <71.9> | <64.8> | <56.5> | <48.5> | <38.9> |
| Net total debt | 921.0 | 871.3 | 789.4 | 674.7 | 554.2 | 415.3 | 253.5 | 83.6 |
| Net senior debt | 739.2 | 697.4 | 623.7 | 500.1 | 384.4 | 241.4 | 88.4 | 0.0 |
| Payments to retire acquisition debt | | | | | | | | |
| EBITDA | 193.5 | 201.4 | 212.3 | 220.5 | 239.6 | | | |
| Coverage | | | | | | | | |

## 8.7.5 How did it all end?

The deal was ultimately accepted in November 2005 and the deal closed early 2006. They ultimately used €450 million of their own equity and threw €1.4 billion debt at the deal, using favorable market conditions to their advantage.

In the course of 2009 (to be precise towards the end of 2009), the Japanese drinks distributor Suntory made an offer on the Orangina business. Its offer was €2.6 billion (converted from USD using FX at time of deal). The consortium consequently got 2x its money back in the space of three years, which one could consider 'fizzy' returns given the shape the market was in globally at the moment of the deal (Note: consider how different the returns would have been if no or little leverage had been used to finance the deal). The consortium sold the business and therefore kept it for a much shorter time than initially anticipated, especially given the financial crisis the world was still in at the end of 2009. Suntory, a well-established name in Japan and Asia, had been looking to enter the European market (as demand in Asia and in particular Japan was declining, and its market share seemed saturated) for some time, and saw the well-developed brand portfolio of Orangina as a proper way to penetrate the European market. Suntory went public in the course of 2013.

During the consortium's holding period, it sold the water business Apollinaris to Coca-Cola in the course of 2006, only months after closing the deal in early 2006 – as intended. The exit demonstrated that, despite market conditions, there is a market for high quality consumer brands as they can be sold to strategic or trade buyers in contrast to other businesses which need an IPO to monetize the business, a window that, during 2009 was globally shut (or almost).

# 9

# Mezzanine Products and the World of the Rating Agencies and Accountancy Boards

## 9.1 RATING AGENCIES AND THE DEBT–EQUITY CONTINUUM

The world of the rating agencies and their output has undeniably been subject to much scrutiny around the globe ever since the start of the financial crisis in 2008. From the looks of it, everything has been said about the good, the bad and the ugly in this context, and that is a good thing because it means I can skip that part and focus on the particularities of the rating agencies' approach and methodologies towards mezzanine products and hybrid capital in general.

A credit rating evaluates the creditworthiness of an issuer of specific types of debt, specifically debt issued by a business enterprise such as a corporation or a government. It is an evaluation of the debt issuer's likelihood of default[1] made by a credit rating agency.

It took a while for the credit agencies to come up to speed on hybrid capital, as their initial methodologies were not naturally tuned in to this phenomenon. Other factors which have contributed to the rise of hybrid capital and the need for rating agencies to come up with some sort of comprehensive model to evaluate these products were:

- Improved structuring and rating criteria clarification.
- Liquid market and low interest rates – 'yield hungry investors'.
- Equity accounting treatment possible under IFRS.
- Increasingly supportive legal and tax systems.
- Multiple issuer objectives.

Also, the drivers which were already known from an issuer point of view contributed to the rise of mezzanine products. Amongst the arguments are:

- Reduce average cost of capital.
- Coupon payments tax deductible (in contrast to dividends).
- Diversify funding.
- Non-dilutive equity substitute (attractive for government-owned and family-owned companies).
- Funding of acquisitions, pensions, share repurchases, refinancing of debt.
- Bolster credit ratings and enhance financial flexibility.

---

[1] Christian Kronwald, *Credit Rating and the Impact on Capital Structure*, Norderstedt, Germany: Druck und Bindung, 2009, p. 3.

Since rating agencies are concerned with the creditworthiness of the firm, and its relationship with its debt and equity holders, the two dominant questions with respect to hybrid capital for any rating agency are:

1. How is the relationship between mezzanine investors and the senior debt holders? What impact do the mezzanine products have on the overall credit quality of the firm? The ultimate question here is about the equity content of the products, i.e., its ability to absorb losses.
2. How much risk does the hybrid instrument carry for the investor? This will be mainly determined through the analysis of the product's subordination and notching in the cash flow waterfall.

In terms of a mezzanine product's features, when answering the above two questions, the rating agencies look at the following items:

| | |
|---|---|
| • Term | • Alternative payment mechanisms and requirements |
| • Call/redemption provisions | • Dividend look-backs |
| • Step-ups | • Subordination |
| • Replacement provisions | • Management intentions |
| • Put provisions | • Market expectations |
| • Conversion provisions | • Regulatory classification and intent |
| • Optional deferral (limitations; cumulative versus non-cumulative) | • Legal form/nomenclature |
| • Mandatory deferral | • Tax treatment |
| • Regulatory deferral | • Accounting treatment. |

The next step we have to take is to go through the two questions and flesh them out a little further.

The first question basically comes down to the issue of how much *equity strength* there is in a particular mezzanine product. The equity strength is a proxy for the product's loss absorption capacity, and therefore will determine its relation and place in the capital structure of any organization.

Critical concepts which will be tested are:

1. Equity requires no ongoing payments which could lead to default.

    The deferral of the coupon (optional, mandatory, ASCM, regulatory) will be the key item.
2. Has no maturity or repayment requirement.

    Features analyzed will be the term of the hybrid instrument and any call/redemption requirements.
3. Provides a cushion for creditors in case of bankruptcy.

    The analysis will come down to the level of effective subordination and notching of the product in the cash flow waterfall.
4. Expected to remain a permanent feature of the capital structure.

The following criteria will be lead indicators in this respect:

- Step-ups and incentive to repay
- Replacement provisions
- Management intentions
- Tax and accounting treatment.

Even when analyzing those features, arriving at a meaningful conclusion, or at least some sort of methodology whereby the user will understand the pecking order of the criteria, requires a more holistic view of any mezzanine product.

It is fair to assume that a qualitative hybrid, from a rating point of view, will most likely score strongly on all dimensions and not just on one or two; for example, an instrument that can be deferred but will mature in 10 years' time. An extra layer of subordination doesn't advance the credit status of the product, as it doesn't offset difficult deferability criteria.

Having said that, the ultimate dominant driver will be the deferability and permanence criteria (of the terms of the instrument). This makes sense as the ratings focus on default risk. The level of subordination of a product in itself does not, therefore, form a critical element in the analysis. It becomes problematic if the product is part of a wider debt package (for example, a PIK loan in an LBO).

Typical assumptions which are built into the mezzanine product are:

- Non-payment doesn't (automatically) equal legal default or trigger of cross-holding default.
- Unfettered, unconditional and deferability of more than five years.
- No step-up in compensation. Possibility of call option built in after five years without incentive to use call option.
- Tax deductibility of the instrument's proceeds by the issuer.

With respect to the aforementioned 'permanence' criteria, it can be pointed out that the economic and not the legal or stated maturity prevails, by assessing the rationale, timing and likelihood of any possible redemptions or repurchases. Any step-up incentive incentivizes redemption and therefore impacts the permanence criteria negatively. The relationship between step-ups and incentive to redeem is difficult and intent-based. The replacement of the product after redemption is intent-based, and not legally binding or enforceable, whereas to receive a high level of equity content for the product would require legally binding replacement covenants.

Another relevant feature of the analysis is the impact the hybrids have on the organization's balance sheet. Although the criteria evolve over time, the hybrid should not account for more than 15% of the balance sheet capacity (total book capacity, i.e., adjusted equity + debt + hybrids) of an organization to be considered an engineered balance sheet. The numerator of the formula accounts for all hybrids at full principal value, regardless of their equity credit score (also not weighted by equity content).

Over time, the equity content of a mezzanine product can be negatively impacted by:

- The passage of time, as residual life of the product reduces.
- The actual experience with the product: repeated tax-law changes which impact the status of its proceeds, weak replacements of stepping-up instruments.
- The analysis over time of the legal feasibility of covenanted replacement language in the contract.

By analyzing each product based on its features and using the methodology indicated, one would naturally end up with a long list of positions where products would be located between very strong equity-like characteristics on the one hand, and very weak debt-like characteristics of a product on the other. The latter will demonstrate very limited or no loss absorbing capacity and the former perfect, or near perfect, equity-like loss absorbing capacity.

In order to make the list user-friendly, most rating agencies have created different classifications on the spectrum, demonstrating higher or lower equity content for the products.

Conclusively, the following equity content categories can be identified:[2]

| High | Includes features which support current rating. Typically involves mandatory component – either regarding deferral of ongoing payments or near-term conversion into common | Treated entirely as equity |
| --- | --- | --- |
| Intermediate | Encompasses most preferred stock instruments, from 30-year trust preferred with five-year cumulative deferral rights to perpetual, with non-cumulative deferral rights | Now to be treated 50/50, debt/equity. Alternatively, as before: ratios calculated based on 100% equity, 100% debt |
| Minimal | Includes instruments with little or questionable permanence; terms or nomenclature which restrict or discourage discretion over payments; costs or conversion terms which may become unattractive to issuer | Treated entirely as debt |

It needs to be mentioned here that, for the purpose of analyzing hybrid capital within the context of a financial services firm or bank, conceptual differences will apply for reasons such as:

- Different leverage characteristics of financial services entities versus corporates.
- Greater funding appetite of financial services entities versus corporates; hence, greater concern with preserving capital market access.
- Role of regulation in financial services.

In an industry as determined by regulation as the financial services industry, the regulator can:

- Determine what is capital.
- Define and enforce minimum capital standards.
- Determine if a bank is solvent.
- Set the terms for qualifying hybrid capital (maturity, triggers for payment deferral, calls and replacement).
- Have power to intervene and stop payments on hybrid securities.

Any possible rating methodology for hybrid capital needs, ultimately, to be aligned with the drivers of regulatory policy.

---

[2] Andreas Zsiga, S&P's approach to hybrid capital, 2006, presentation.

The classification of hybrid securities for financial services companies has known the following categories in the S&P methodology (see Table 9.1) – see FI section further on in this chapter for actual updated table:

**Table 9.1**   S&P hybrid securities' categorization for financial industries

| Category | Inclusion in capital measures (*) | Examples |
| --- | --- | --- |
| **Cat.1 High Equity content** | Up to 35% of ATE or up to 25% of TAC | • Short-dated mandatory convertible securities (< 3 years)<br>• High quality hybrids with participating coupons |
| **Cat.2 Intermediate Equity content**<br><br>**Cat.2 Strong** | Up to 25% of ATE or up to 15–25% of TAC | • Perpetual preferred shares<br>• Most bank and insurer undated deferrable Tier 1 instruments<br>• Insurance long-dated deferrable instruments with residual maturity of > 20 years |
| **Cat.2 Adequate** | Up to 10% of ATE or up to 15–25% of TAC | • Most, but not all, bank Upper Tier 2 instruments<br>• Limited life preferred shares (e.g., US trust preferred)<br>• Insurance deferrable instruments with residual maturity < 20 years |
| **Cat.3 Minimal Equity content** | Not included in ATE or TAC | • Dated hybrid instruments with a residual maturity < 5 years<br>• Auction-preferred securities<br>• Non-deferrable subordinated debt<br>• Instruments with put options |

(*) TAC= Total Adjusted Capital, ATE = Adjusted Total Equity.

From a comprehensive rating perspective, hybrid capital is one of the many things which determine a rating for a company, and different attributes of hybrid capital are relevant for different parts of the analytical framework.

Aspects across the relevance spectrum and related to different technical aspects of the framework are:

• Aspect of ongoing payments is considered in fixed-charge coverage and cash flow adequacy.
• Equity cushion in leverage and asset protection.
• Need to refinance upon maturity in liquidity.
• Potential for conversion in financial policy.
• Cost of paying for funds is also a component of both earnings and cash flow analysis.

At this stage, we need to tackle an essential aspect of the rating entourage which deserves to be mentioned earlier on in this chapter, and that is the different positioning of different rating profiles. The following categories can be identified:

1. **Issuer credit rating (ICR)** – Current opinion of issuer's ability and willingness to meet its financial commitments on timely basis.
2. **Issue ratings** – Addresses timeliness; also addresses potential for recovery of principal in event of bankruptcy or liquidation of issuer – that is, ranking of issue.

The assignment of issue ratings reflects the incremental risk of hybrid products compared to the ICR and traditional senior debt. Preferred equity and certain other hybrid instruments afford enhanced equity benefits to issuers mainly through:

1. **Deferability** – ongoing payment requirements are more flexible than conventional debt interest.
2. **Subordination** – contractual lower ranking to conventional debt.

These characteristics make mezzanine instruments more risky for investors than plain vanilla senior debt.

Regarding the **deferability item:** the deferability issue is directly linked with payment risk on the side of the issuer (creditworthiness).

The following features in hybrid contracts can enhance payment risk from the issuer:

- Optional deferral
  - Management entitled to suspend/cancel distributions without triggering a legal default.
  - We assume reluctance to exercise given reputation risk.
  - Risk for financial distress increases the likelihood.
  - 'Pressure point' may differ for different types of issuers.
- Mandatory deferral
  - Requirement to suspend payments at breach of pre-determined triggers.
  - Typically linked to financial parameters.
  - Dividend pusher can reduce the risk (but also equity content).
  - Payment risk linked to risk of breaching trigger.
- Regulatory deferral
  - Regulator authority to direct companies to defer hybrid's payments.
  - Payment risk assessment requires consideration of sector and country-specific factors.
  - Identification of financial measures to which the regulator is particularly sensitive is key.
  - Regulatory triggers – whether or not clearly defined – amount to de facto mandatory deferral.

The ultimate question is how payment risk can be blended in a ranking schedule in an objective way, and what the criteria and concerns would be. A key consideration in this respect is what the combined significance is of different sources of deferral risk.

In practice, where risk is relatively remote, but still material, one-notch differential versus subordinated rating (i.e., two notches versus ICR) is applied. This is typical notching for issues with optional deferral only. When there are heightened concerns that the issuer may defer, the gap between ICR and issue rating is increased. The combinations of different forms of deferral may or may not increase deferral risk, i.e., a mandatory trigger with significant erosion, or before optional deferral is likely, increases payment risk and will lead to additional notching. A mandatory trigger remote with optional deferral likely before breach does not increase payment risk and will not lead to additional notching.

The payment risk for financial institutions and the question of how to blend it into issue ratings leads to the following observations:

- For regulated financial institutions, explicit mandatory deferral triggers do not add to risk stemming from regulation if triggers just replicate capital standards that the regulator applies in determining whether to order deferral.

- With banks, it is particularly unlikely that optional deferral would be unilaterally exercised.
- Presumption that bank regulators would act preemptively to force banks to raise capital to prevent regulatory capital guidelines from being breached.
- In most instances, one notch is taken away only for deferral risk in rating issues of investment grade banks, even where there is a combination of optional and regulatory deferral.

Regarding the **subordination item**, the following guidelines can be observed:

- It adversely affects ultimate recovery prospects of subordinated obligation holders in bankruptcy, since claims of priority creditors must be satisfied first.
- For investment grade issuers, one notch is taken away from ICR for issues which are subordinated (but not deferrable).
- No distinction in notching between gradations of subordination.
- Ultimate recoveries for different classes of subordinated instruments tend to be similar, and poor.

As a conclusive and general statement regarding the criteria for rating hybrid products, it needs to be mentioned that the evolution in the market, the regulatory changes across the world, financial innovation, design of techniques applied and covenants designed to meet regulatory hurdles all lead to the fact that the methodology is under constant review, refinement and further clarification of criteria to align with the unlimited levels of innovations the product group can tolerate. This includes a further refinement of hybrids applied in other spheres and applications.[3]

In recent years, up till the start of the financial crisis, some of the aspects which were evolving in a significant fashion were the treatment and impact of:

- Mandatory deferrals.
- Tight replacement clauses.
- ACSMs (Alternative Coupon Satisfaction Mechanisms): if a trigger event occurs and continues for more than one year (for example), the capital securities contain an alternative coupon satisfaction mechanism which requires the company to issue common stock.
- Change of control clauses.
- Conversion calls.
- Rating-agency/equity-content calls.
- Legally binding replacement covenant.
- Immediate stock settlement.

The overall conclusion can be that equity credit crashes in unmitigated step-up and call situations, and an overreliance on hybrids could raise issues about the health of the financial policy and over-accentuates disincentives to defer. ACSMs have the potential to disincentivize a deferral.

---

[3] See, for example, the recently issued report by Fitch: 'Criteria for Rating U.S. Equity REITs and REOCs,' February 2012 as well as a newly published criteria report which replaces both 'Treatment of Hybrids in Corporate and REIT Credit Analysis,' dated July 11, 2011 and (along with the criteria

footnote (*continued*)

report titled 'Rating Bank Regulatory Capital and Similar Securities,' also published on that day) 'Rating Hybrid Securities' dated July 28, 2011. Both previously published criteria reports have been withdrawn. The updated Non-Financial Corporate and REIT criteria were substantially the same as the previous criteria, so it did not automatically trigger any immediate rating changes in these sectors.

Key aspects of the new criteria include:

- Simplified Categories for Debt and Equity Allocation: The categories are reduced from the former five to three going forward: 100% equity; 50% equity and 50% debt; or 100% debt.
- Focus on Preserving Ongoing Viability: To attain equity credit, hybrids must support the ongoing viability of an organization; the terms of the instrument should avoid mandatory payments, the ability to incur covenant defaults, or events of default that could trigger a general corporate default or liquidity need. Structural features that constrain a company's ability to activate the equity-like features of a hybrid make an instrument more debt-like and eliminate equity treatment. While this was also the case under the prior guidelines, it is more strictly applied in the new criteria.
- No Explicit Limit on Amount of Equity from Hybrids: The amount of adjusted equity that can be derived from hybrid instruments is not subject to a cap, a change from the prior criteria. Under the prior criteria an explicit limit of 30% of total equity and equity from hybrids applied, but the amount of hybrids of individual corporate issuers never approached that proportion.
- Interest Expense and Dividends of Hybrids Are Not Adjusted: While the amount of debt and equity are adjusted to allocate the hybrid's principal, Fitch analysts use the full amount of hybrid interest or dividends to calculate fixed-charge coverage ratios, despite provisions allowing the deferral or omission of payments. This is consistent with the former criteria.
- New Guidelines Follow the Earlier Exposure Draft: The Corporate and REIT criteria generally correspond to the indications provided in 'Exposure Draft: Proposed Revisions to Hybrid Equity Credit Criteria' of February 10, 2011. A difference relative to the Exposure Draft is that cumulative corporate preferred and preference shares will be allocated 50% to debt and 50% to equity, while only those with a non-cumulative deferral option will be eligible for the 100% equity category. The Exposure Draft had indicated that both cumulative and non-cumulative preferred instruments would receive 100% equity treatment. In the REIT sector, no distinction is made between cumulative and non-cumulative preferred capital; both are assigned to the 50% debt/50% equity category to calculate Risk Adjusted Capital Ratios, and to the 100% equity category to calculate Financial Leverage Ratios.

Hybrids are therefore evaluated, in determining equity credit, as to the extent they contribute to financial flexibility and support the ongoing viability of an organization. To achieve any equity allocation, an instrument should avoid mandatory payments, covenant defaults or events of default (EODs) which could trigger a general corporate default or liquidity need. Structural features which constrain a company's ability to activate the equity-like features of a hybrid make an instrument more debt-like.

Hybrid instruments with going-concern loss absorption are typically deeply subordinated instruments with very low recovery prospects in liquidation or bankruptcy. Such an instrument will therefore be treated as highly loss absorbing and rated at least two notches below the Issuer Default Rating (IDR) for most corporate issuers. Hybrids in certain sectors which typically exhibit higher recovery values, such as utilities and REITs in select EMEA jurisdictions, are typically rated a net one notch below the IDR.

Going-concern loss-absorption hybrid securities issued by financial institutions are expected to be rated in accordance with the principles outlined in the agency's criteria titled 'Rating Bank Regulatory Capital and Similar Securities.'

Other recent hybrid-instruments-related Fitch publications are:

- 'Corporate Rating Methodology' (August 12, 2011)
- 'Rating Bank Regulatory Capital and Similar Securities' (December 15, 2011)
- 'Treatment of Hybrids in Bank Capital Analysis' (July 11, 2011).

Bringing the two critical elements together leads to the summary shown in Table 9.2:

**Table 9.2**   Implications of deferability and its consequences

| Deferability | |
|---|---|
| Optional | Mandatory |

Key question: When, how much and for how long is cash preserved for the benefit of senior debt holders?

**When?**

| | |
|---|---|
| 1. Any hindrance reduces equity content, as do 'pushers' (e.g., cannot defer directly after a shareholder distribution; if net income exceeds coupons; if a given credit ratio is too strong) | • Present in about half the contracts<br>• Trigger definitions influence equity content<br>• Trigger criteria: |
| 2. Long 'lookback periods' are problematic: > 12 months (6 for HYs) disqualifies for 'intermediate' | – Cash flow / interest < 2.5×/3.0× or 15% cash flow/adjusted debt |
| 3. 'Dividend stopper(*)' typically does not reduce equity content | – cash flow from operations/revenues < 5%/7%<br>– Ill-structured mandatory referrals trigger extra notching without necessarily enhancing equity content |
| 4. ACSM may disincentivize deferral | |

**How much and for how long?**

| | |
|---|---|
| If cumulative, forced settlement before five years is inconsistent with 'intermediate' equity content. Aim: preserve cash as soon and as long as stress requires. Optional deferral's value to the particular credit soon and as long as stress requires. | • If not properly addressed step-ups can significantly reduce equity content in an instrument<br>• Different appreciation of step-ups for a high-yield versus an investment-grade issuer<br>• Step-up = in-built, instrument-specific incentive to call (destroys permanence):<br>  – Absent step-up, typical five-year call does not reduce equity content.<br>  – Insignificant step-up is ok |

| | |
|---|---|
| Deeply subordinated products and equity-like products tend to contribute to cash preservation at first sight, however: | Different remedies to step-up (result in different equity content results): |
| 1. To assess unfettered optional deferability, ACSMs need to be monitored for optionally deferred amounts which were restricted to common shares, or where stock dilution was not tightly capped or with a hard settlement deadline earlier than five years<br>  • Heavy common-stock dilution (at a potentially low price) makes repurchasing unwieldy, i.e., it disincentivizes deferring in the first place. | 1. **Intent-based replacement covenants**<br>  • 'As equity-like as': ambiguous and controversial<br>  • Only moral dynamic<br>  • Remedies step-ups that are 10 years out or more (seven for high-yields)<br>  • Must unambiguously require identical key features of replacing versus replaced instruments<br>  • Remains non-legally binding and untested. Absence of step-up still significantly better. |
| 2. For corporates with maximum five-year deferability, an optional deferral with the following settlement alternatives is consistent with 'intermediate' equity content:<br>  • PIK (the least problematic)<br>  • 25% cap on hybrid settlement | 2. **Legally binding enforceable covenants**<br>  • In investment grade, enables calls to be before year ten but step-up not to exceed 100bp<br>  • Assumes supportive local law<br>  • Necessary for 'High Equity Content' |

*(continued)*

## Deferability

| Optional | Mandatory |
|---|---|
| • 2% cap on common share issuance (refers to the whole cumulative deferral, not per year of settlement nor per year of coupon deferred; to the underlying shares in case of settlement by warrants)<br>• More structuring flexibility if the first hard deadline is after five years. | • Even for 'intermediate,' we would question why such a tool would not be used if available in the specific jurisdiction.<br>• Covenants enhance structuring flexibility. |

**A call option is not a call option:**
- 'Change-of-control' clauses typically don't require replacement language
  - Wording should not endanger financial standing pre-change of control
  - Are senior bonds at least as well protected?
- 'Conversion calls' typically don't require replacement language
  - Issuer can call the portion of the hybrid whose equity content equates to the amount of equity stemming from the conversion of a convertible bond
  - Acceptable because not given specific equity credit to plain vanilla convertibles
  - Does not require replacement clause, 'Rating-agency/equity-content calls' do require replacement language
  - Issuer can call entire instrument if any agency has lowered its equity-content denomination
  - Initial equity content needs to be put back in place.

- Different types of call options imply different replacement requirements

Instrument characteristics used most often in practice:

- With mandatory deferral, step-up and lookback
- Only optionally-deferrable with step-up but no lookback
- Only optionally-deferrable with lookback but non-cumulative and with no step-up.

(*) Dividend stopper: A 'dividend stopper' is a term which states that the issuer will not, within a specified period of time (usually known as the 'stopper period'), pay a coupon on another security or class of securities if it does not pay a dividend on the security in question. A dividend stopper is generally included in the terms of instruments which provide for 'discretionary' returns, for example, a preference share that requires a directors' declaration. The effect of the dividend stopper is that it effectively counteracts the discretion and places pressure on the entity to pay the required return on the discretionary instrument. A 'dividend pusher' is a term (found in the prospectus) whereby the coupon is mandatory if remuneration is given to another specified security or class of securities within a specified period of time (usually known as the 'pusher period'). Within the context of financial services companies, an important comment needs to be made based on the new Basel III criteria and the interpretation given re. dividend stoppers. See glossary for further details and variations on this concept.

As discussed in Chapter 5, which looked at the financial services industry, the 7th criterion under the new Basel rules for inclusion of an instrument as an additional Tier 1 instrument reads as follows:

> 7. Distributions are paid only after all legal and contractual obligations have been met and payments on more senior capital instruments have been made. This means that there are no preferential distributions, including in respect of other elements classified as the highest quality issued capital.

In the December 2011 frequently asked questions document, the following question (and feedback) was included regarding dividend stoppers in the light of this criterion:[4]

> **Criterion 7 sets out the requirements for dividend/coupon discretion for Additional Tier 1 Capital. Are dividend stopper arrangements acceptable (e.g. features that stop the bank making a dividend payment on its common shares if a dividend/coupon is not paid on its Additional Tier 1 instruments)? Are dividend stopper arrangements acceptable if they stop dividend/ coupon payments on other Tier 1 instruments in addition to dividends on common shares?**

> Dividend stopper arrangements that stop dividend payments on common shares are not prohibited by the Basel III rules text. Furthermore, dividend stopper arrangements that stop dividend payments on other Additional Tier 1 instruments are not prohibited. However, stoppers must not impede the full discretion that the bank must have at all times to cancel distributions/payments on the Additional Tier 1 instrument, nor must they act in a way that could hinder the recapitalisation of the bank (see criterion 13). For example, it would not be permitted for a stopper on an Additional Tier 1 instrument to:

> - Attempt to stop payment on another instrument where the payments on this other instrument were not also fully discretionary.
> - Prevent distributions to shareholders for a period that extends beyond the point in time that dividends/coupons on the Additional Tier 1 instrument are resumed.
> - Impede the normal operation of the bank or any restructuring activity (including acquisitions/ disposals).

> A stopper may act to prohibit actions that are equivalent to the payment of a dividend, such as the bank undertaking discretionary share buybacks.

## 9.1.1 Permanence and deferral characteristics

In summary, Table 9.3 provides an overview of the main permanence and deferral characteristics:

**Table 9.3**   Implications of permanence and deferral clauses included in hybrid securities

| Permanence | Deferral (optional) | Deferral (mandatory) |
|---|---|---|
| Coupon step-up rate (year/amount in bps) | For how long? | Deferral trigger type |
| Conversion, rating agency call | Shareholder distribution stopper | Deferral trigger level |
| Existence of tax and/or accounting calls | Pusher (shareholder distribution lookback period) | Recently experienced level of trigger ratio |
| Replacement instrument issuance timing (months prior to redemption) | Cumulatively/settlement mode | Cumulatively/settlement mode |

---

[4] Basel III definition of capital – Frequently asked questions – December 2011 update which can be found at http://www.bis.org/publ/bcbs211.pdf.

## 9.1.2 Simplified continuum for banks' (FIs') and insurers' hybrid capital security

Applied to the FI sector, the following 'equity strength' continuum can be developed – see Table 9.4:

**Table 9.4**    Hybrid capital spectrum for FIs based on their equity strength

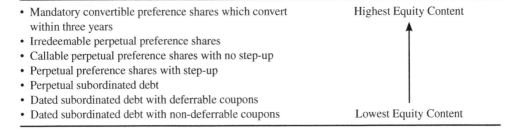

- Mandatory convertible preference shares which convert within three years       Highest Equity Content
- Irredeemable perpetual preference shares
- Callable perpetual preference shares with no step-up
- Perpetual preference shares with step-up
- Perpetual subordinated debt
- Dated subordinated debt with deferrable coupons
- Dated subordinated debt with non-deferrable coupons       Lowest Equity Content

## 9.2 CASE STUDY: FITCH'S APPROACH TO RATING HYBRID FOR CORPORATES[5]

As is obvious by now, any hybrid instrument is distinguished from a straight debt instrument by its ability to absorb losses in a going concern (i.e., without triggering a general corporate default and without having an effect on senior obligations). This going concern loss absorption may take various forms, including some which contribute to the financial flexibility of the organization (e.g., coupon deferral) and others which absorb loss more directly pre-bankruptcy (e.g., the write-down of principal or conversion to a more deeply subordinated instrument). Taken together, the most commonly encountered forms of going concern loss absorption are cumulative coupon deferral, non-cumulative coupon omission, principal write-down (either with or without the potential to be written back up) and contingent conversion into a more equity-like instrument (typically common equity or potentially some form of preference share).

There are other types of hybrid securities which do not include going concern loss absorption features. An example is a convertible debt security or similar synthetic unit based on an ordinary senior or subordinated debt obligation, coupled with an exchange or conversion (into common or preferred shares) which is not triggered by the issuer's distress. Where rated, the rating of such instruments principally reflects the characteristics of the host (i.e., pre-conversion) instrument, and the mandatory exchange or conversion into a more junior instrument would not be viewed as non-performance. These hybrids are accorded equity credit by Fitch Ratings if they have an assured conversion to a form of equity, but are not designed to provide going concern loss absorption correlated with the timing of their issuer's distress.

---

[5] The content described in the next few paragraphs is based on Fitch's framework for assessing hybrids and, as a consequence, cannot be used as an independent theoretical framework without backtesting it against other methodologies (which will, however, be very similar). Part of the exercise is to demonstrate the slight variations in approach to the same problem. The content of these paragraphs is based on Fitch's research paper: 'Rating hybrid securities,' December 2009 and 'Equity credits for hybrids and other capital securities,' December 2009.

Under most circumstances, Fitch regards going concern loss absorption by a rated instrument to be non-performance from a rating perspective. There are two notable exceptions to this approach: (i) a short-lived cumulative deferral; and (ii) payment-in-kind (PIK) notes.

As mentioned earlier in this chapter, the approach used in practice is essentially one of notching a particular security from an anchor or reference rating, typically the Issuer Default Rating (IDR). The notches represent incremental risk relative to that reference rating. They do not represent absolute amounts of incremental risk. That incremental risk is typically a function of increased loss severity after default, but, in the case of hybrid instruments, there is also an element which represents the heightened risk of non-performance in a going concern which has not defaulted on any other obligations. Given both the significant variety of features within the hybrid asset class and the relatively limited granularity of the long-term rating scale, Fitch believes that it is neither possible nor desirable to subtract notches for every conceivable feature, as this would potentially result in too wide a rating spread for any given issuer. It should also be noted that Fitch does not rate duration risk, and therefore does not rate the extension risk that is often present in hybrid securities, such as the risk that a security will not be called at its call date, or that an issuer will take advantage of an option included in the documents to extend maturity.

With respect to the rating of hybrid capital within the framework of regulated industries, and in particular the banking and insurance sector, they indicate:

> When hybrid instruments are deployed in regulated industries as a cost-efficient means of meeting regulatory capital requirements, they are more subject to changes in regulatory practice than other asset classes. This is particularly the case in the banking industry – by far the largest user of hybrid capital – where the role and definition of capital, including hybrid capital, in the financial crisis from mid-2007 has come under close scrutiny. The process of change resulting from this scrutiny is far from complete and the future evolutionary path is far from clear. As a result, guidelines on this matter are likely to be subject to more exceptions and more frequent changes than is normally the case with rating criteria.

We are already aware that loss-absorption capacity is the prime aspect for rating equity content. Fitch breaks the assessment up by looking at the different stages of the product's life-cycle.

## 9.2.1 At initiation and thereafter when fundamentals are acceptable; coupon payments are occurring as expected

To characterize them, hybrid instruments with going concern loss absorption are typically deeply subordinated instruments with very low recovery prospects in liquidation or bankruptcy. The instrument will therefore be treated as being highly loss-absorbing and rated at least two notches below the IDR.

Where the instrument has features which materially increase the likelihood of the loss absorption mechanism's activation, Fitch will lower the instrument rating by at least one additional notch. The most typically encountered of such features is a mandatory loss absorption trigger which is easily activated. An example would be an annual profits test.

There are two forms of loss absorption which Fitch regards as particularly aggressive and, therefore, meriting further notching. The first is permanent write-down of principal (i.e., the payment schedule does not return to the levels anticipated pre-loss absorption once an issuer returns to financial health). Within this category, Fitch includes instruments which are dated and where any principal write-down (including one which could be reversed) is crystallized at maturity – i.e., the investor is only entitled to the written-down amount. The second particularly aggressive form of loss absorption is the contingent conversion of a debt instrument into common equity (or another very equity-like instrument).

Consequently, Fitch will generally rate instruments with permanent principal write-down or contingent convertible securities (so-called CoCos as discussed earlier in Chapter 5) at least three notches lower than the issuer's IDR. As with other hybrids, wider notching is likely to be deployed if the conversion trigger is viewed as being easily activated. Similarly, in rare cases, narrower notching may be used if the trigger for the write-down or conversion is considered to be exceptionally remote. A trigger may be considered exceptionally remote if, for example, the write-down of principal only occurs after the loss of all equity and substantially all hybrid capital for a strong bank of systemic importance. The notching scheme illustrated in Table 9.5 is indicative of the treatment of all obligations in the corporate hierarchy, including the typical forms of hybrid instruments with going concern loss absorption which are most likely to be notched either two or three notches below the IDR. It is possible that hybrid securities will be devised with special features which require a modification of this notching approach, such as the notching being reduced, or more likely increased. Equally, if loss absorption triggers are constructed where Fitch does not have the required visibility or ability to adequately assess the risk of loss absorption being initiated, Fitch may not be able to rate the hybrid instrument. For example, the agency would be very unlikely to rate a hybrid security which has a loss absorption trigger related to a commodity price or equity valuation.

There are a number of exceptions to the notching table as provided:[6]

1. Low Speculative Grade Issuers

    When an issuer has an IDR of B+ or lower, Fitch undertakes a bespoke analysis of the recovery prospects of its various classes of debt and assigns them Recovery Ratings. This bespoke approach is more specific, and therefore overrides the generic notching set out in Table 9.5.

2. Unusually Strong or Weak Baseline Recoveries

    For types of issuers or industries where Fitch expects unusually strong or weak recoveries in the event of default, the notching approach set out in the table may be modified. These relatively rare cases generally coincide with senior unsecured debt which is rated above or below the IDR, rather than at the same level, as is most common across Fitch. In such cases, the agency will typically reflect the unusually strong or weak recoveries through either additional or reduced notching for the hybrids from the IDR. Examples of organizations which are assumed to have unusually weak or strong recoveries include utility companies (senior debt is rated above the IDR) and non-operating insurance holding companies (senior debt is rated below the IDR).

3. Bank Hybrids and State Support[7]

    In the case of banks, there is an assumption that state support cannot be relied upon to extend to instruments which have been given regulatory capital treatment and have going concern loss absorption features. In the case of banks, therefore, notching of hybrid ratings is based on a notional unsupported IDR. This may well be multiple notches lower than the bank's published support-driven IDR.

---

[6] See further on notching Moody's: 'Updated summary guidance for notching bonds, preferred stocks and hybrid securities of corporate issuers,' February 2007.

[7] See also below for a more detailed analysis.

**Table 9.5**   Typical notching relative to IDR

| Recovery prospects | Investment grade and high speculative grade |
|---|---|
| Outstanding | +2 |
| Superior | +1 |
| Good | +1 |
| Average | 0 |
| Below average | −1 |
| Poor (including all instruments with going concern loss absorption) | −2 or −3 |
| Hybrid instruments with easily activated going concern loss absorption | −3 or more |
| Hybrid instruments with aggressive loss-absorption including contingent convertible securities | −3 or more |

### 9.2.2  As fundamentals decline and the probability of some form of loss absorption increases

If Fitch considers that the probability of the loss absorbing features being activated has materially increased, a rating committee will consider the likely rating of the hybrid if the loss
absorption features are activated as in Section 9.2.3. They will then lower the instrument
rating below the band indicated in the previous table, to a rating which is intermediate to, or
approaches, the expected rating in the event of loss absorption being activated.

### 9.2.3  When loss absorption features are activated

Fitch takes into consideration the form and expected duration of loss absorption. Factors considered include:

- The issuer's fundamental financial condition.
- Cumulative deferral or non-cumulative payment suspension; probability of resuming payments; any mitigants (such as alternative coupon satisfaction mechanisms (ACSM, known
  in some markets as alternative settlement mechanisms or ASM)).
- Forced loss absorption through conversion to an equity instrument or write-down of principal, if applicable; whether, after write-down, the instrument is subject to writing value
  back up.
- Other forms of loss absorption, if relevant:
  - (a) If the loss absorption is in the form of a cumulative deferral which is expected to be
    short-lived in nature, or that deferral is effectively mitigated for the investor by an
    ACSM or other mechanism, Fitch will typically lower the rating during the payment
    suspension to a rating no higher than the BB category (high speculative grade or, in very
    limited cases, to the BBB category, low investment grade). The actual rating determined
    will generally be based, in part, on the net present value evaluation of the likely impair-
    ment of cash flows, if any, over the instrument's lifetime, as well as the issuer's credit
    outlook. Under these circumstances, the rating is likely to be accompanied by a Rating
    Watch, the direction of which will depend on the particular circumstances of the case.

**Table 9.6**  Ratings of non-performing hybrid securities

| Obligation rating | Non-performing obligation |
|---|---|
| B | Loss absorption has been triggered, but the rated obligation is expected to return to performing status with only very low economic losses being sustained. |
| CCC | Loss absorption has been triggered, but the rated obligation is expected to return to performing status with only moderate economic losses being sustained. |
| CC | Loss absorption has been triggered, and the rated obligation is only expected to return to performing status with high economic losses being sustained. |
| C | Loss absorption has been triggered, and the rated obligation is only expected to return to performing status with severe economic losses being sustained. |

(b) Where the loss absorption takes the form of a cumulative deferral which is expected to be other than short-lived, is on a non-cumulative basis or involves principal write-down, then the hybrid is deemed to be impaired and the rating table applicable to non-performing instruments is applied. The actual rating determined will be based, in part, on the net present value evaluation of the likely impairment of cash flows, if any, over the instrument's lifetime. In cases where a contingent conversion into common equity is activated, Fitch will lower the rating to C, and simultaneously withdraw the rating.

(c) If the activation of loss absorption is viewed by Fitch as a precursor to a liquidation, bankruptcy, restructuring or, in the case of a regulated industry such as banking, a statutory supervisory intervention, hybrid instrument ratings will be evaluated on a case-by-case basis, but are likely to be very low given their typically very deep subordination. Ratings may be revised up or down during a deferral or non-payment period to reflect changes in fundamental prospects and outlook for loss absorption or resumption of performance (see Table 9.6).

## 9.2.4  When normal payments are resumed (and the instrument resumes debt-like performance)

As a hybrid instrument returns to normal performance and the risk of loss absorption features being reactivated recedes, its rating will return to being assessed on the basis of the stage one methodology outlined earlier in this chapter. If the risk of reactivation is deemed material, this return to stage one notching may be gradual. There is no prejudice to the instrument for the prior interruption of payments.

### Effect of ACSM on hybrid ratings and notching

Some hybrid securities, especially those with mandatory deferral mechanisms, incorporate ACSMs. The operation of the ACSM allows, or in some cases requires, the issuer to use the proceeds of a new issue of common stock or a junior hybrid security to pay coupons, which would otherwise have been avoided or deferred because of the mandatory deferral provision. The operation of the ACSM can protect securities' holders from the risk of a random event which triggers a mandatory deferral when the issuer is not in a distressed situation and still has the financial flexibility to issue capital securities. However, investors cannot count on the success of the ACSM to avoid a deferral if the issuer is really in a distressed state, and cannot access the capital markets to issue new capital securities. Based on the inability to rely upon the successful application of the ACSM mechanism in all circumstances, Fitch gives no recognition to the ACSM as a factor influencing the notching or rating of a hybrid security in Stage 1 (at initiation of ratings or when fundamentals remain acceptable). However, as the issuer moves into Stages 2 and 3, when a possible deferral of coupons is foreseen or comes close to occurring, Fitch's rating committee will take into consideration its view of the issuer's likelihood to make use of the ACSM, and the probability that a capital market issue will be achieved to avoid deferral. If Fitch's rating committee has a high degree of confidence that effective operation of the ACSM will maintain payments without delay, or with only a brief delay, then the instrument may be spared the rating transition from Stage 2 into Stage 3.

On a comparative note,[8] Moody's had already published its 'Moody's Tool Kit: A framework for assessing hybrid securities' in December 1999, which has been updated on a number of occasions, for example with the report issued in November 2003 called 'Hybrid Securities Analysis, New Criteria for Adjustment of Financial Ratios to Reflect the Issuance of Hybrid Securities Product of the New Instruments Committee'. Moody's most recent update to the framework for assessing hybrids took place in July 2010. S&P's most recent report on rating hybrid instruments dates from March 2011 and is called 'Credit FAQ: Providing A Perspective

---

[8] Intellectual honesty requires a benchmark, which can be provided by at least summarizing the Moody's and S&P frameworks. They try to do the same, but with different accents, and often different mechanics. Whether they lead to a different outcome or structural approach, and whether it is significant, is a matter of taste. It is my understanding that the ultimate impact on the outcome is modest. The review is based on Larsen and Magnussen, 'Corporate hybrid capital: exploring the debt/equity continuum,' Danske Research, August 2010. The authors point out that despite the €20 billion issuance by corporates in Europe in the period 2003–2010, corporate hybrid capital is an established asset class, albeit fairly heterogeneous with many variations on the debt/equity continuum.

**Motives behind issuance of hybrid capital**

While Fitch revised its hybrid rating methodology in January 2010, Moody's published its long-awaited revised methodology in July 2010. As a result, transparency for issuers and investors regarding the assignment of equity credit and issue ratings has increased. Together with intact rationale for issuance and our expectation of demand from yield-seeking investors to move down the capital structure on solid names, we expect this to result in more issuance over the coming quarters. From the issuer's perspective, the combination of equity and debt-like characteristics offers a highly flexible alternative in the Treasurer's tool-box when deciding on the capital structure and funding strategies. Broadly, hybrids provide debt-like cost of capital while containing senior rating-supportive equity characteristics. Through hybrid capital, issuers can access funding that will count partly as debt and partly as equity for credit rating purposes. In addition to rating considerations, IFRS and tax authority treatment are also important determinants of the final structure. Ideally, the hybrid will be regarded by tax authorities as sufficiently debt-like to qualify for tax deductibility of interest payments, but enough like equity to be considered as equity under IFRS accounting rules. Besides obtaining 'cheap equity' as just described, the main reasons for issuing hybrids are senior rating defense, increased financial flexibility and access to equity-like funding for non-listed companies. Senior rating defense refers to a range of situations including the financing of acquisitions, capital expenditure, pension deficits and shareholder rewards.

Broadly they assess the equity content of a hybrid against the key defining characteristics of plain vanilla equity, i.e., (i) no maturity; (ii) no ongoing payments the absence of which might trigger default; and (iii) loss absorption. The more rating agencies believe that the hybrid will cushion investors in senior unsecured notes by acting like common equity during periods of stress, the greater the equity content that is assigned, and vice versa. The objective of the summary is to demonstrate how S&P and Moody's

footnote (*continued*)

view corporate hybrids and to highlight selected key structuring considerations to achieve a desired equity credit or issue rating. The structuring considerations below apply to issuers with an investment grade issuer rating.

### Assigning equity credit to hybrid capital

S&P places different hybrid structures on the debt/equity continuum into one of three categories: High (100% equity credit), Intermediate (50%) and Minimal (0%). Hybrids with less than 20 years to maturity or limitations on the deferability of coupon payments are typically classified as Minimal, whereas hybrids mandatorily convertible into common equity are candidates for the High category. We have not found a single structure outside the Intermediate category in the universe of European corporate hybrids rated by S&P. While a hybrid issued with a Minimal equity credit is unlikely to fulfill its purpose from an issuer's perspective, the crowded 50% equity credit category also reflects a grandfathering when S&P strengthened its view on built-in call incentives in 2007 (see below).

Moody's classifies hybrids into five baskets labeled A to E, where basket A is the most debt-like (0% equity credit) and E the most similar to equity (100%). Intermediate baskets are categorized as B, C and D, representing equity credits of 25%, 50% and 75%, respectively. The majority of hybrids rated by Moody's are placed in basket C or D.

Moody's revised the criteria to receive a given equity credit in July 2010, and it will not grandfather the existing basket treatment for outstanding hybrids.

Overall, Moody's has increased its focus on loss absorption characteristics in advance of default. Thus, it views the timing of coupon deferral as an issuer weakens financially (rather than when close to default), and whether or not deferred coupons are cumulative, as largely determinant of the loss absorption capability. To be eligible for basket D, non-cumulative mandatory deferral at strong triggers is generally necessary. Both S&P and Moody's treat the hybrid as partly debt and partly equity, with weightings depending on equity credit when calculating adjusted credit metrics. It is primarily through this operation that rating agencies acknowledge the hybrid in the issuer's capital structure.

### Notching of hybrid issue ratings

Obviously, the special characteristics of hybrid capital, resulting in the assignment of equity credit, impose incremental risks on hybrid investors compared with investors in senior unsecured notes. Relative to the senior issuer rating, S&P typically lowers the hybrid security issue rating by one notch for subordination (without distinguishing between gradations of subordination), one notch for optional deferral and an additional notch for mandatory deferral (i.e., a maximum three-notch differential). Until Moody's revised its methodology in July 2010, it was less restrictive than S&P in terms of issue notching, and it operated with a general rule of a maximum of two notches when the senior issuer rating was investment grade. When no preferred stock is outstanding and a deeply subordinated hybrid is senior only to common equity, which is typical for European corporate hybrid issuers, Moody's previously notched down twice, irrespective of coupon deferral features. Now, Moody's has added an extra notch (i.e., a maximum three-notch differential, like S&P) for non-cumulative hybrids with strong mandatory coupon deferral triggers. As a result, the assignment of equity credit and notching is now better aligned, which was one of the purposes behind Moody's revised methodology. Around 45% of the rated universe is currently notched down twice by S&P from the senior issuer rating, and 55% is notched down three times. 50% of the rated universe is currently notched down twice by Moody's, while the proportion of hybrids notched down three times has increased to 30% following the recent downgrades.

### Key structuring considerations

Both S&P and Moody's ultimately take a holistic approach to instrument characteristics and consider the overall effect of hybrid capital on the issuer's credit profile when assigning equity credit. However, an absence or presence of certain equity features plays an important role and can disqualify the hybrid from a given equity credit assignment.

footnote (*continued*)

Below the key hybrid structuring considerations are highlighted to achieve a desired equity credit, as well as differences and similarities between Moody's revised methodology and S&P.

**Ongoing payments**

Most hybrids have a stated coupon, where the payment may be deferred at the discretion of management (optional deferral) or where it must be deferred on breach of a financial trigger (mandatory deferral). Deferrals can be non-cumulative or cumulative (i.e., the issuer must honor deferred payments), with settlement in cash or through an alternative coupon settlement mechanism (ACSM), closely resembling payment in kind.

In case of optional deferral, both S&P and Moody's are generally indifferent between cumulative and non-cumulative coupons, but allocate less equity content to instruments with constraints on deferability. Such a constraint could be a maximum deferral period, which S&P regards as inconsistent with Intermediate equity content if below five years. A dividend pusher forcing hybrid coupon payments if dividends are paid on common stock in a look-back period exceeding one year also disqualifies Intermediate equity content from S&P. Moody's lowers equity content, all else being equal, if the look-back period exceeds six months. S&P generally has a neutral view on a dividend stopper, where coupon deferral prohibits divided payments on common stock.

Moody's overall views non-cumulative hybrids senior only to common equity that tend to absorb losses for a 'going' concern (i.e., well ahead of default) as eligible for basket D, whereas cumulative hybrids senior only to common equity that tend to absorb losses for a 'gone' concern (i.e., where default is imminent) are eligible for basket C at best.

However as corporate issuers are not assumed to defer optionally until default is imminent, a hybrid with optional deferral is only seen as absorbing losses for a 'gone' concern, and is eligible for basket C irrespective of whether coupons accumulate or not. To be classified as effectively non-cumulative and eligible for basket D, mandatory deferral at strong triggers is necessary. Under S&P's methodology, mandatory deferral triggers set at a level close to the issuer's current rating (i.e., within two to three notches of the current rating) qualify for High equity content. Weaker but meaningful triggers qualify for Intermediate.

S&P views a requirement of ACSM settlement of optionally-deferred coupons within five years as inconsistent with Intermediate equity content, as the prospect of having to sell common equity or additional hybrids at a time when pricing could be depressed is likely to postpone deferral in the first place. ACSM settlement of mandatorily deferred coupons is generally eligible for Intermediate equity content. In July 2010, Moody's strengthened its view on ACSM settlement, leading to less equity content. The agency no longer views ACSM settlement as tantamount to a non-cumulative hybrid, but only as absorbing losses for a 'gone' concern eligible for basket C. However, basket D may still be assigned to mandatory deferral with strong triggers if non-cumulative coupons can be ACSM settled at the issuer's option.

**Permanence**

Rating agencies require hybrid capital to be sufficiently permanent to justify equity content, and most hybrids come with long or even perpetual maturity. S&P requires a time to maturity of at least 20 years to warrant Intermediate or High equity content, implying that equity content is eliminated when the remaining time to maturity falls below this threshold. Following the July 2010 revision, Moody's views 60 years as tantamount to perpetuity, and hybrids must have at least an initial 30-year maturity at issuance for the assignment of equity credit. Equity credit will be eliminated when the remaining time to maturity is 10 years. It is common for hybrids to be callable, either starting on a certain date and continuing for a defined period, or on discrete days. Simple callability does not necessarily limit equity credit, but it can be constrained by built-in call incentives (such as a coupon step-up), depending on the type of replacement language. In May 2007, S&P strengthened its view on built-in call incentives and replacement language, but grandfathered the existing treatment of outstanding hybrids as it reflected

footnote (*continued*)

best practice at the time. This grandfathering is rather unusual, in our view, but likely reflects that most of the outstanding hybrids issued during the last wave in 2005 to 2006 would no longer qualify for any equity content if structured under the revised criteria by S&P. If a hybrid has a step-up exceeding 25bp or a discrete call date followed by five or more years during which it is not callable, S&P assumes that the issue will be called when the step-up occurs or on the discrete call date. Hence, after its 2007 revision, S&P requires a legally binding replacement capital covenant (RCC) rather than a mere expression of intent, to qualify for Intermediate equity content. In S&P's view, an RCC restricting management in the future is necessary to restore sufficient assurance of permanence, by stipulating that replacement is effected by an issue of similar or greater equity content.

However S&P views step-ups of more than 100bp (for investment-grade issuers) as defining the effective maturity date of the hybrid, even if the security has an RCC. Also, irrespective of an RCC, an initial call date less than five years from the date of issuance generally disqualifies an Intermediate equity credit from S&P.

All corporate hybrids rated by S&P since May 2007 with moderate built-in call incentives have been structured with an RCC to preserve Intermediate equity content. Some are structured in a special way, to effectively circumvent the RCC but still receive Intermediate equity content from S&P. The perpetual hybrid is callable in year seven without a step-up, and in year twelve where the coupon steps up by 100bp. However, the RCC only becomes effective one day after the first call date. This allows the issuer to call the hybrid in year seven without triggering the RCC.

While Moody's increased its focus on loss absorption characteristics in advance of default in its July 2010 revision, unlike S&P it no longer views replacement language as a key consideration. Furthermore, rather than factoring the time to the first call date or the replacement security into a basket, both are factored into the overall senior issuer rating.

However, built-in call incentives still hurt equity content. A hybrid with a coupon step-up above 100bp will be assigned equity content reflecting effective maturity on this date. Equity content is also reduced if a call date with a 100bp step-up occurs earlier than 10 years after issuance.

In terms of priority in event of default, S&P generally considers the distinction between subordination and deep subordination as a secondary factor in the assignment of equity credit compared with other key defining characteristics of equity. Moody's assignment of equity content as detailed above is eligible for deeply subordinated securities senior only to common equity that cannot default or cross-default other than at maturity, and that have limited influence on the outcome of a bankruptcy proceeding. If these conditions are not satisfied, equity credit is capped at basket B. In our view, these criteria are mainly relevant for financial institutions that have a more tiered capital structure.

**Capacity limit for hybrids in the capital structure**
Hybrid capital is only beneficial up to a certain point, as both Moody's and S&P have capacity limits regarding the proportion of hybrids in the capital structure and associated equity credit. While hybrid capital cushions the position of senior note holders at times of stress, the rating agencies aim to prevent over-engineered balance sheets.

| S&P equity credit cap | Moody's credit cap |
| --- | --- |
| Hybrid capital can comprise 15% of total book capitalization (i.e., the sum of equity, debt and hybrids) making normal S&P adjustments. Above this level, the hybrid counts as pure debt. | The hybrid capital notional multiplied by the equity credit ratio can account for 25% of equity (making the usual Moody's adjustments) plus hybrid notional multiplied by the equity credit ratio. Above this level, the hybrid counts as pure debt. |

Source: S&P & Moody's

footnote (*continued*)

Both rating agencies stress that while hybrid capital counts as pure debt above a certain threshold when calculating adjusted credit metrics, the exact threshold may vary between sectors and issuers. Moody's introduced a 25% equity credit cap in March 2008, with the object of limiting the equity credit contribution of hybrids relative to straight common equity. The limit on equity credit reflects the view that common equity may be more predictable as a source of credit support in stressful conditions, and should be the dominant component of a company's capital structure. S&P's 15% equity credit cap is calculated using the hybrid capital principal value (without adjusting for equity content) and includes debt in the total capitalization.

Key structuring considerations for corporates: rating agency guidelines when senior issuer rating is investment grade

|  | S&P | Moody's |
|---|---|---|
| Share of hybrid allowed in the capital structure | Hybrid principal/(hybrid principal +equity excl. goodwill + debt)<=15% | Hybrid equity credit/(equity + hybrid equity credit) <= 25% |
| Equity credit | Minimal (0%), Intermediate (50%) and High (100%). | Baskets A to E covering equity credit of 0%, 25%, 50%, 75% and 100%, respectively. |
| Coupon deferral | **Optional deferral:** Indifferent between cumulative and non-cumulative. Not eligible for Intermediate if maximum deferral period below five years. **Mandatory deferral:** Triggers close to current rating (i.e., within two to three notches) qualify for High. Weaker but meaningful triggers qualify for Intermediate. | **Optional deferral:** Indifferent between cumulative and non-cumulative, eligible for basket C. In general, restricted options to defer qualify for basket C at best. **Mandatory deferral:** Strong triggers qualify for basket D if non-cumulative. |
| ACSM to settle cumulative dividends | **Optional deferral:** Not eligible for Intermediate if ACSM settlement within five years of initial deferral. **Mandatory deferral:** ACSM settlement eligible for Intermediate but not High. | **Optional and/or mandatory deferral:** ACSM settlement is eligible for basket C. However, basket D may still be assigned to mandatory deferral with strong triggers if non-cumulative coupons can be ACSM settled at the issuer's option. |
| Dividend pusher and dividend stopper | Not eligible for Intermediate if dividend pusher look-back period exceeds one year. Neutral view on dividend stopper. | Dividend pusher: Moody's lowers equity content, all else equal, if look-back period exceeds 6 months. |
| Time to maturity | Time to maturity of at least 20 years to warrant Intermediate or High. Equity credit is eliminated when the remaining time to maturity falls below this threshold. | Moody's views 60 years as tantamount to perpetuity and hybrids must have at least an initial 30-year maturity at issuance for the assignment of equity credit. Equity credit will be eliminated when the remaining time to maturity is 10 years. |

(*continued*)

On The Criteria For Hybrid Instruments Issued By Corporate Entities', which is an FAQ following the five core documents on hybrid capital ratings, being:

- 'Unregulated Issuers' Hybrid Instruments: Rating Methodology and Assessment of Equity Content,' issued March 17, 2011.
- 'Hybrid Capital Handbook: September 2008 Edition,' issued September 15, 2008.
- 'Criteria Assumptions Regarding Coupon Step-Ups in Equity Hybrids Issued by Banks and Insurers,' published September 16, 2009.
- 'Methodology for Rating Bank Non-deferrable Subordinated Debt (Lower Tier 2 Regulatory Capital),' published August 4, 2009.
- 'Assumptions: Implications of the December 2009 Basel III Proposals for Our Bank Hybrid Criteria,' published February 9, 2010.
- 'Criteria Clarification On Hybrid Capital Step-Ups, Call Options, And Replacement Provisions,' published October 22, 2012.

Late 2012 S&P published an advance notice of proposed criteria change on equity content in corporate hybrid capital instruments, indicating that it is reviewing the assumptions and

footnote (*continued*)

|  | S&P | Moody's |
|---|---|---|
| Built-in call incentives and replacement language | If (1) <u>step-up</u> is in the range 26–100bp or (2) a *discrete call date* is followed by five or more years of non-call, a legally binding RCC is necessary to qualify for Intermediate. Initial call date (even without step-up) less than five years from issuance disqualifies Intermediate even if RCC. Step-up above 100bp defines effective maturity date even if RCC and hence does not qualify for Intermediate if call date within 20 years. | Replacement language is not a key consideration and rather than factor time to the first call date or the replacement security into a basket, both are factored into the overall <u>senior issuer rating</u>. However, built-in call incentives still hurt **equity content** (1) 100bp step-up within 10 years from issuance results in lower equity content (2) step-up above 100bp defines effective maturity date and equity content is assigned accordingly (see Time to maturity). |
| Subordination | Distinction between subordination and deep subordination <u>a secondary factor</u> to other characteristics | The abovementioned equity content is eligible for deeply subordinated securities senior only to common equity that cannot default or cross-default other than at maturity and that have limited influence on the outcome of a bankruptcy proceeding. If these conditions are not satisfied, equity credit is capped at basket B (<u>mainly relevant for financial institutions</u> that have a more tiered capital structure). |
| Notching | One notch for subordination, one notch for optional deferral, one notch for mandatory deferral | Two notches if deeply subordinated and senior only to common equity. An additional notch if non-cumulative with strong mandatory trigger |

methodologies it uses to determine the equity content of certain corporate hybrid capital instruments, i.e., the degree to which these instruments are included in our measures of capital for issuers, especially those classified as having 'high' equity content.[9] Fitch's latest review occurred in January 2010 for corporations and in late 2012 for financial institutions.[10]

---

## EXAMPLE: COMPARATIVE PRODUCT ANALYSIS AND CALCULATION (FITCH-BASED METHODOLOGY) – SEE TABLES 9.7 AND 9.8

Hypothetical case: €200 million issuance of hybrid security.

**Hybrid A:** Mandatory convertible securities, three years to conversion, interest deferrable, fixed exchange rate;

**Hybrid B:** Deferrable trust preferred securities, 15 years remaining to maturity, three years cumulative deferral;

**Hybrid C:** Senior convertible note with no deferral of interest, redeemable with common stock at the issuer's option.

**Table 9.7**   Calculating risk-adjusted credit ratios

| Background information (in millions of Euro) | Issuer's rating BBB |
|---|---|
| Other debt | 300 |
| Shareholder's equity | 500 |
| Total capital before hybrid issue | 800 |
| EBITDA | 200 |
| Operating cash flow before interest expense | 150 |
| Pre-tax net income | 140 |

**Table 9.8**   Hybrid report interpretation

|  | Hybrid A | Hybrid B | Hybrid C |
|---|---|---|---|
| Amount of hybrid issued | 200 | 200 | 200 |
| Implied equity allocation (%) | 95 | 65 | 0 |
| **Adjusted leverage measures** | | | |
| Other debt | 300 | 300 | 300 |
| Debt attributed to hybrid | 10 | 70 | 200 |
| Total risk-adjusted debt | 310 | 370 | 500 |

*(continued)*

---

[9] The review will apply to hybrid capital instruments issued globally by corporate entities and by North American insurance holding companies, except for leveraged buy-out companies (LBOs). The review will not affect the criteria for assessing equity content for hybrid capital instruments issued by banks or by insurance companies that are subject to prudential regulation. In November 2012 it issued a request for comments on the topic, seeking market feedback.

[10] See Fitch (2012) 'Assessing and rating bank subordinated and hybrid securities.' Sector specific rating criteria (this document replaces two of its previous documents on the topic, i.e., (1) Rating bank regulatory capital and similar securities of December 2011 and (2) Treatment of hybrids in bank capital analysis (July 2012).

**Table 9.8**   (*continued*)

|  | Hybrid A | Hybrid B | Hybrid C |
|---|---|---|---|
| **Adjusted leverage measures** (*cont'd*) |  |  |  |
| Shareholder's equity | 500 | 500 | 500 |
| Equity attributed to hybrid | 190 | 130 | 0 |
| Total risk-adjusted equity | 690 | 630 | 500 |
| Total capital | 1,000 | 1,000 | 1,000 |
| Risk-adjusted Debt/Capital (%) | 31 | 37 | 50 |
| Risk-adjusted Debt/EBITDA (×) | 1.6 | 1.9 | 2.5 |
| Risk-adjusted Debt/OCF (×) | 2.1 | 2.5 | 3.3 |
| **Adjusted coverage measures** |  |  |  |
| Interest of other debt | 22.5 | 22.5 | 22.5 |
| Interest of dividend on hybrid: |  |  |  |
| Non-deferrable | 0 | 0 | 14.5 |
| Deferrable | 14.0 | 14.0 | 0 |
| Total interest | 36.5 | 36.5 | 36.5 |
| Total non-deferrable interest | 22.5 | 22.5 | 36.5 |
| Coverage (×) |  |  |  |
| EBITDA/Total interest | 5.5 | 5.5 | 5.5 |
| Pre-tax interest/Total income | 3.8 | 3.8 | 3.8 |
| Alternate stress case coverage (×) |  |  |  |
| EBITDA/Non-deferrable interest | 8.9 | 8.9 | 5.5 |
| Pre-tax income/Non-deferrable interest | 6.2 | 6.2 | 3.8 |

## 9.3  MEZZANINE DEBT, RATING AGENCIES, THE REGULATOR AND FINANCIAL INSTITUTIONS AFTER 2008[11]

It was mentioned earlier in this chapter that heavily regulated industries pose additional complications with respect to the positioning and rating of hybrid capital for corporations active in those industries. In Chapter 5, we elaborated extensively on the implications of Basel III on the regulated balance sheet of FIs. Before the financial crisis kicked in, hybrid capital was a popular way to pick up attractive spreads when investing in banks which were considered very creditworthy. Hybrid capital gave issuing banks access to the best of both worlds: better capital ratios without dilution plus tax efficiency. Bank returns on equity benefited as a result. In the period up till the crisis, the rating on hybrid capital was often only two notches lower than that for senior notes.

During the Basel I and II regulatory regime, there were a few major types of hybrids including trust preferreds (TRUPS) and more recently issued forms of hybrid capital such as income trust securities and REIT preferreds. These have been complemented later on with more exotic variances of those products as well as look-alikes.

---

[11] The preliminary comments in this part will show natural similarities with the earlier general part which mainly focused on corporates.

## 9.3.1 The impact of Basel III[12]

Due to the adoption of Basel III, most forms of previously issued hybrid capital no longer count toward Tier 1 capital requirements. In general, bonds which were issued before September 2010 will lose 10% Tier 1 credit per year until called or the credit runs out (see Figure 9.1). There are a couple of exceptions to this rule, one being bonds with step-up coupons; these will lose all equity credit once their call or step-up dates are reached. In the US, due to Dodd–Frank legislation, TRUPS received Tier 1 credit only until January 2013 but will be phased out completely by January 2016 (see Figure 9.2). It is assumed this will be done on a straight-line basis, although it seems that the pace is at the regulator's discretion.

Bank regulators have placed greater emphasis on the Tier 1 common/core Tier 1 ratio since the introduction of Basel III as a means of measuring capital sufficiency. As hybrids are effectively excluded from Tier 1 common, their future role as regulatory capital instruments has waned. Some of these hybrid securities will become eligible for Tier 2 credit as subordinated debt. For securities such as income trust securities, which convert to preferred stock, they can become Tier 1 non-common instruments. In any event, from a bank's perspective, the wonderful combination of tax deductibility and Tier 1 regulatory capital credit will not exist in the future – see Table 9.9.

Current and future issuance in US bank hybrid capital will be largely restricted to perpetual non-cumulative preferred stock. Recently, we have seen a number of high-quality regional banks issue preferred stock to boost their non-common Tier 1 ratio – US Bancorp 6.5% perpetuals callable in 2022 and PNC 6.75% perpetuals callable in 2021 were both issued in the last six months.

Some European banks have, as previously discussed, issued a newer form of hybrid instrument known as contingent convertible securities (CoCos) which would allow Tier 2 credit initially, but could convert to equity to boost core Tier 1 during periods of stress. These have not taken off to the extent expected. This may have been due to overall investor risk aversion during the aftermath of the financial crisis, but it is also likely because US regulators have yet to provide clear guidelines on whether CoCos would receive regulatory approval in the US.

**Figure 9.1** Basel III timeline – Tier 1 hybrid phase out

**Figure 9.2** Dodd–Frank timeline – TRUPS Tier 1 phase out

---

[12] Spencer Phua, 'Hybrid Capital: Going the way of the dinosaur?,' *ING Investment Perspectives*, February 2012.

**Table 9.9**  Basel III is changing the definition of regulated capital

|  | Current | Basel III |
| --- | --- | --- |
| Tier 1 Common | Common and preferred stock | Common stock |
| Tier 1 Non-Common | Trust preferred and hybrids | Preferred stock (non-cumulative and non-redeemable) |
| Tier 2(*) | Subdebt and reserves | Subdebt and reserves |
| SIFI Buffer |  | Common stock |

(*) Often Tier 2 is subdivided into higher and lower Tier 2, which indicates seniority of lower Tier 2 instruments over higher Tier 2 instruments (which are more senior than Tier 1 products).

## 9.3.2  Phasing out of hybrid capital due to regulatory changes

We are aware by now of the rating approach to hybrids in general. Broadly, they assess the equity content of a hybrid against the key defining characteristics of plain vanilla equity, i.e., (i) no maturity; (ii) no mandatory ongoing payments and (iii) loss absorption. The more rating agencies believe that the hybrid will cushion investors in senior unsecured notes by acting like common equity during periods of stress, the greater the equity content that is assigned, and vice versa.

There are noteworthy differences in approach, however, and features of the framework are in constant evolution.[13]

S&P places different hybrid structures on the debt/equity continuum into one of three categories: High (100% equity credit), Intermediate (50%) and Minimal (0%). Hybrids with less than 20 years to maturity, or limitations on the deferability of coupon payments, are typically classified as Minimal, whereas hybrids mandatorily convertible into common equity are candidates for the High category.

Moody's classifies hybrids into five baskets labeled A to E, where basket A is the most debt-like (0% equity credit) and E the most similar to equity (100%). Intermediate baskets are categorized as B, C and D, representing equity credits of 25%, 50% and 75%, respectively.

Moody's revised the criteria to receive a given equity credit in July 2010, and it will not grandfather the existing basket treatment for outstanding hybrids. The agency ended the process of assigning new baskets without significant rating changes on the back of this.

Overall, Moody's has increased its focus on loss absorption characteristics in advance of default. Thus, it views the timing of coupon deferral as an issuer weakens financially (rather than when close to default), and whether or not deferred coupons are cumulative, as largely determinant of the loss absorption capability. To be eligible for basket D, non-cumulative mandatory deferral at strong triggers is generally necessary. Both S&P and Moody's treat the hybrid group as partly debt and partly equity, with weightings depending on equity credit when calculating adjusted credit metrics. It is primarily through this operation that rating agencies acknowledge hybrid products in the issuer's capital structure – see Table 9.10.

---

[13] See further: Arnt and Hovard, 'Hybrid bank capital: Features and treatment by regulators and rating agencies,' August 2010.

**Table 9.10**   Examples of triggers which cause deferral of coupon

| Examples of triggers which cause deferral of coupon[14] | | |
| --- | --- | --- |
| Trigger type | Industry | Trigger strength |
| Net loss | Bank & Insurance | Strong |
| Minimum regulatory capital | Bank & Insurance | Weak |
| Solvency | Bank & Insurance | Very weak |

## 9.3.3 Notching down and structuring[15]

Obviously, the special characteristics of hybrid capital, resulting in the assignment of equity credit, impose incremental risks on hybrid investors compared with investors in senior unsecured notes. Relative to the senior issuer rating, S&P typically lowers the hybrid security issue rating by one notch for subordination (without distinguishing between gradations of subordination), one notch for optional deferral and an additional notch for mandatory deferral (i.e., a maximum three-notch differential).

Until Moody's revised its methodology in July 2010, it was less restrictive than S&P in terms of issue notching, and it operated with a general rule of a maximum of two notches when the senior issuer rating was investment grade. Now, Moody's has added an extra notch (i.e., a maximum three-notch differential, like S&P) for non-cumulative hybrids with strong mandatory coupon deferral triggers. As a result, the assignment of equity credit and notching is now better aligned, which was one of the purposes behind Moody's revised methodology.

---

[14] Source: Moody's

[15] As the 'structuring' features are more or less the same as an item discussed earlier (although comparisons will be made between Moody's and S&P's approach which were not highlighted before, I took the liberty of moving that review to the note section – Source: ibid note 8).

Both S&P and Moody's ultimately take a holistic approach to instrument characteristics and consider the overall effect of hybrid capital on the issuer's credit profile when assigning equity credit. However, an absence or presence of certain equity features plays an important role, and can disqualify hybrid capital from a given equity credit assignment. Below, we highlight key hybrid structuring considerations to achieve a desired equity credit, as well as differences and similarities between Moody's revised methodology and S&P.

**Ongoing payments (deferral possibilities)**

Most hybrids have a stated coupon, where the payment may be deferred at the discretion of management (optional deferral) or where it must be deferred on breach of a pre-defined financial trigger (mandatory deferral). Deferrals can be non-cumulative or cumulative (i.e. the issuer must honor deferred payments), with settlement in cash or through an alternative coupon settlement mechanism (ACSM), closely resembling payment-in-kind.

In case of optional deferral, both S&P and Moody's are generally indifferent between cumulative and non-cumulative coupons, but allocate less equity content to instruments with constraints on deferability. Such a constraint could be a maximum deferral period, which S&P regards as inconsistent with Intermediate equity content if below five years. A dividend pusher forcing hybrid coupon payments if dividends are paid on common stock in a look-back period exceeding one year also disqualifies a product from Intermediate equity content for S&P. Moody's lowers equity content, all else being the same, if the look-back period exceeds six months. S&P generally has a neutral view on a dividend stopper, where coupon deferral prohibits divided payments on common stock.

Moody's overall views non-cumulative hybrids which are senior only to common equity which tends to absorb losses for a 'going' concern (i.e. well ahead of default) as eligible for basket D, whereas

footnote (*continued*)

cumulative hybrids which are senior only to common equity, which tend to absorb losses for a 'gone' concern (i.e. where default is imminent) are eligible for basket C at best.

A key distinction between corporate hybrids and hybrids from financial institutions is that the latter are defined as being regulated industries. In practice, this implies that where corporate issuers are assumed not to defer optionally until default is imminent, this is not the case for financial institutions where the regulator is assumed to press the case for coupon deferral at an earlier stage. In practice this means that loss absorption is more probable for financial institutions than it is for corporates. To be classified as effectively non-cumulative and eligible for basket D at Moody's, mandatory deferral at strong triggers is necessary. Under S&P's methodology, mandatory deferral triggers set at a level close to the issuer's current rating (i.e. within two to three notches of the current rating) qualify for High equity content. Weaker triggers may qualify for Intermediate equity content.

S&P views a requirement of ACSM settlement of optionally-deferred coupons within five years as inconsistent with Intermediate equity content, as the prospect of having to sell common equity or additional hybrids at a time when pricing could be depressed is likely to postpone deferral in the first place. ACSM settlement of mandatorily deferred coupons is generally eligible for Intermediate equity content. In July 2010, Moody's strengthened its view on ACSM settlement, leading to less equity content. The agency no longer views ACSM settlement as synonymous with a non-cumulative hybrid.

### Permanence
Rating agencies require hybrid capital to be sufficiently permanent to justify equity content, and most hybrids come with long or even perpetual maturity. S&P requires an effective time to maturity of at least 20 years to warrant Intermediate or High equity content, implying that equity content is eliminated when the remaining time to maturity falls below this threshold. Following the July 2010 revision, Moody's views 60 years as tantamount to perpetuity, and hybrids must have at least an initial 30-year maturity at issuance for the assignment of equity credit. Equity credit will be eliminated when the remaining time to maturity is 10 years.

### Call possibilities and step-ups
It is common for hybrids to be callable, either starting on a certain date and continuing for a defined period, or on discrete days. Simple callability does not necessarily limit equity credit, but it can be constrained by built-in call incentives (such as a coupon step-up). S&P views step-ups of more than 100bp or half the initial spread as defining the effective maturity date of the hybrid. Also, an initial call date less than five years from the date of issuance generally disqualifies a product from equity credit for S&P. Moody's increased its focus on loss absorption characteristics in advance of default in its July 2010 revision. Rather than factoring the time to the first call date into an equity basket, it is merely factored into the overall senior issuer rating. However, built-in call incentives still hurt equity content. Like S&P, Moody's considers a step-up in excess of 100bp to be the effective maturity date. Equity content is also reduced if a call date with a 100bp step-up occurs earlier than 10 years after issuance.

Another key difference between financial institutions and corporates relates to the replacement capital covenant (RCC). For the latter, S&P requires a legally binding RCC rather than a mere expression of intent, to qualify for Intermediate equity content. For financial institutions it is assumed that the regulator will prevent a call if it deems that the company has insufficient capital – i.e. a legally binding RCC is not necessary.

### Subordination
In terms of priority in the event of default, S&P generally considers the distinction between subordination and deep subordination as a secondary factor in the assignment of equity credit compared with other key defining characteristics. Moody's assignment of equity content is eligible for deeply subordinated securities (senior only to common equity and called 'preferred' securities in Moody's terminology) which cannot default or cross-default other than at maturity. Furthermore, they must have limited influence on the outcome of a bankruptcy proceeding. If these conditions are not satisfied, equity credit is capped at basket B.

### 9.3.4 Capacity limits in the balance sheets of financial institutions and insurers

For both rating agency and regulatory purposes, hybrid capital is only beneficial up to a certain point. At S&P, banks can count in hybrids with High equity content up to 50% of adjusted common equity (ACE). Hybrids with Intermediate equity content can account for up to 33% of ACE. For insurance companies, High equity content hybrids may account for up to 35% of total adjusted capital (TAC) whereas Intermediate equity content hybrids may only account for up to 25% (in Europe). S&P's equity credit cap is calculated using the hybrid capital principal value.

Moody's introduced a 25% equity credit cap in 2008, with the objective of limiting the equity credit contribution of hybrids relative to straight common equity. The limit on equity credit reflects the view that common equity may be more predictable as a source of credit support in stressful conditions, and should be the dominant component of a company's capital structure.

### 9.3.5 Basel III and Solvency II

The implications of Basel III have been discussed both in this chapter and in Chapter 5. Bear in mind that one of their key objectives was to arrive at a consistent definition and structuring of capital for FIs. The goal is to ensure that the future tiering of bank capital will be limited: Tier 1 must absorb losses on a going concern basis and Tier 2 must absorb losses on a gone concern basis. Sub-categories of Tier 2 capital will therefore be removed, i.e., there will be a harmonization of LT2 and UT2 instruments.

According to the Basel Committee, Tier 1 instruments must be comprised of instruments which are subordinated, have fully discretionary non-cumulative dividends or coupons and have neither a maturity date nor an incentive to redeem (i.e., no step-up). Payments (coupons) on Tier 1 bonds will be considered a distribution of earnings (dividends). Innovative hybrid capital instruments with an incentive to redeem through features like step-up clauses, currently limited to 15% of the Tier 1 capital base, will be phased out. The current limitation on Tier 2 capital (that it cannot exceed Tier 1 capital) will be removed and replaced by minimum Tier 1 and total capital requirements. The future role of Tier 2 capital is likely to be determined by the difference between the total capital requirement and the Tier 1 requirement. If the difference is large, Tier 2 capital is likely to continue to play a role, as it would provide a cheaper way to address regulatory limits. Outstanding hybrids will be subject to grandfathering, but nothing has been communicated as to its reach so far. Our assumption is that it will run until first call date at least, as this would ensure that banks do not receive adverse capital treatment compared to what was expected at the time of issuance.

The philosophy of Solvency II for the insurance industry is somewhat the same as under Basel III.

The table below shows the new regulatory limits. As can be seen, qualifying hybrid instruments cannot constitute more than 20% of Tier 1 capital. Furthermore, the minimum amount of non-hybrid to cover the minimum capital requirement (MCR) is 64% (80% − (0.2*80%)) while the minimum amount of non-hybrid to cover the solvency capital requirement (SCR) is 40% (50% − (0.2*50%)). Under the current solvency rules, hybrid debt may constitute up to 50% of the minimum requirement. Finally, Tier 1 bonds must meet the specific criteria listed.[16]

| Capital limits under Solvency II[17] | | | |
|---|---|---|---|
| | Tier 1 | Tier 2 | Tier 3 |
| MCR cover | >80% | <20% | Not allowed |
| SCR cover | >50% | <50% | <15% |
| Amount of qualifying debt allowed | <20% | <100% | <100% |

S&P's latest intervention in its rating framework for hybrids, 'Clarification Of The Equity Content Categories Used For Bank And Insurance Hybrid Instruments With Restricted Ability To Defer Payments,' published February 9, 2010 and 'Unregulated Issuers' Hybrid Instruments: Rating Methodology And Assessment Of Equity Content,' issued March 17, 2011 impacted the following topics more specifically:

- Revising the equity content categories by converting 'Intermediate: Strong' and 'Intermediate: Adequate' into a single 'Intermediate' category.
- Revising the approach to bank 'step-up' hybrids.

---

[16] Since the implementation date and content is still somewhat in progress at the moment of the drafting of the manuscript the critical features of Tier 1 bonds are listed here (source: ibid. note ix):
Under Solvency II, Tier 1 bonds must – as a minimum – possess the following features:

- Principal loss absorbency mechanisms for which the trigger event is a breach of 75% of the SCR or a breach of the SCR which is not resolved within two months.
- Be undated or have an original maturity of at least 10 years. The maturity date is deemed to be the first opportunity to repay or redeem unless there is a contractual obligation to replace with an item of the same or higher quality capital (RCC).
- Not callable or repayable without supervisory permission, and if the SCR is breached, although the supervisor may waive this if the item is replaced with equal or higher quality and MCR is complied with.
- No step-up.
- Should have both an optional coupon skip and a mandatory coupon skip linked to a breach of the SCR.
- A fixed coupon is allowed, but skipped coupons are canceled unless there is an immediate equity settled ACSM.

For Tier 2 the following criteria must be fulfilled:

- Be undated or have an original maturity of at least five years. The maturity date is deemed to be the first opportunity to repay or redeem unless there is a contractual obligation to replace with an item of the same or higher quality capital.
- Not callable or repayable without supervisory permission, and if the SCR is breached although supervisor may waive this if the item is replaced with another Tier 1 or Tier 2 item and MCR is complied with.
- May have a moderate incentive to redeem; step-ups must not exceed either 100bp or 50% of initial credit spread.
- Cumulative deferral of coupon on a breach of the SCR.
- Almost all of the current outstanding Tier 1 instruments will not be eligible for inclusion under these requirements and will be classified as Tier 2 instead. However, grandfathering is expected although details are still lagging as to the length of the period.

[17] Source: QIS 5 specifications & Danske Markets.

- Clarifying the link with regulatory classifications of hybrids, and the approach to hybrids which are subject to regulatory grandfathering.
- Revising the approach to 'High' equity content hybrids for banks, with reference to contingent capital structures and hybrids with write-down features.
- Clarifying the treatment of government-owned hybrids issued as part of a bank rescue or support package.
- How they intend to treat 'Bail-In' hybrids within our equity content framework.

What follows are the relevant changes which were put in place (see Tables 9.11 to 9.13) to the criteria for assessing hybrids in the FI sector.

**Table 9.11**  Standard & Poor's maximum equity content for hybrid instrument categories – financial institutions (updated table 2011)

| Category (equity content designation) | Maximum included in Standard & Poor's Total Adjusted Capital (TAC) | Qualifying instruments |
|---|---|---|
| **High equity content** | Amount equivalent to up to 50% of Adjusted Common Equity (ACE) | Short-dated mandatory convertible securities (which convert in less than three years for issuers with an SACP(*) above BBB-, within two years for issuers with an SACP in the BB category, and within one year for issuers with an SACP in the B category) |
| | | Certain government-owned hybrids (these are included in TAC with no limit) |
| **Intermediate equity content** | Amount equivalent to up to 33% of ACE | Subordinated instruments, preferred stock, or trust preferred instruments which meet the following conditions:<br><br>• Ability to stop paying coupons, or write down principal, or convert into equity, without triggering a default or wind-up of the issuer;<br>• No material restriction on the ability to defer or otherwise absorb losses;<br>• Perpetual or with a residual life of at least 20 years;<br>• Do not contain a step-up clause within the next 20 years;<br>• Coupons can be cumulative or non-cumulative. |
| **Minimal equity content** | Not included in TAC | • Issues which otherwise qualify for 'Intermediate,' but have remaining lives of less than 20 years, or where there is a step-up feature associated with a call option within 20 years;<br>• Hybrid instruments which have a material restriction on the ability to defer;<br>• Instruments which do not have the ability to stop paying coupons, or otherwise absorb losses, without triggering a default or wind-up of the issuer. |

(*) The SACP is the 'stand-alone credit profile' which is used as the standard for assessing bank hybrids. S&P uses a stand-alone approach rather than its issuer credit rating (ICR), except in those cases where we expect the hybrid to receive group support.

**Table 9.12**    Provisions in hybrid instruments viewed as the equivalent of maturity(*)

Hybrid equity content treatment in our ratios ends when less than 20 years remain until the 'effective maturity.' At that point it is treated as debt for ratio purposes, with the benefits incorporated qualitatively in our analysis. This table summarizes which maturity-like provisions are viewed as an 'effective maturity.'

|  | Call with moderate step-up or equivalent (For investment-grade issuers 26 bps–100 bps is viewed as moderate. 'Moderate' can vary depending on local interest rates.) |
| --- | --- |
| S&P's approach | For regulated banks and for finance companies: This is viewed as an effective maturity even when there is a replacement capital covenant (RCC). |
| Rationale | Regulated banks and finance companies frequently access wholesale debt markets to refinance maturing liabilities and fund growth. In our opinion, failure by the bank to redeem a hybrid with step-up at the call date would damage the bank's access to these wholesale markets. |

**How the company is likely to react under varying circumstances**

| Doing well | Will redeem. |
| --- | --- |
| Under moderate stress | Likely to redeem even if more expensive to replace. |
| Under heavy stress | Still a risk of retiring the instrument even if it is more expensive to replace. |

(*)'Step-up equivalents' are features which, similar to an increase in the coupon, motivate the issuer to call the issue.

**Table 9.13**    Rating bank hybrids

| Assigning issue ratings to bank hybrids (*) | Approach |
| --- | --- |
| The minimum notching for a bank hybrid(**) | SACP of BBB- or higher: 2 notches below SACP; SACP of BB+ or lower: 3 notches below SACP |
| Instrument contains a clause stating that the bank must pass an earnings test to pay the hybrid coupon | Deduct at least one more notch |
| Instrument contains a 'contingent' clause leading to equity conversion and/or principal write-down | Deduct one more notch |
| When bank is not paying a common dividend | Deduct one more notch |
| Instrument contains a 'contingent' clause leading to equity conversion and/or principal write-down but the 'contingent' trigger is either based on rating transitions, or we consider the trigger to be exceptionally sensitive and vulnerable. | Assign a CCC issue rating |
| The entity announces that interest payments will be stopped on the hybrid or its principal will not be repaid when due | Assign a CC issue rating |
| The entity announced a distressed exchange offer on the instrument | Assign a CC issue rating |
| The hybrid has suspended its coupon, written down principal or there has been a distressed exchange | Assign an issue rating of C |

(*)In some cases, we will not use all notches if that would lead to a rating of C or D being assigned to a hybrid that is being fully serviced. In those cases, we assign an issue rating of CC, which is the lowest rating for a hybrid that is still being serviced.
(**) We deduct more notches than this minimum to reflect specific features as described in the following rows. The additional notching is cumulative. We deduct the notches from the SACP except for some circumstances where we start from an ICR.

Under the proposed criteria, the minimum notching for a bank hybrid is:

- Two notches below the SACP when the SACP is BBB- or higher.
- Three notches below the SACP when the SACP is BB+ or lower.
- When notching down from an ICR which incorporates support, a minimum of two notches if the ICR is BBB- or higher.
- When notching down from an ICR which incorporates support, a minimum of three notches if the ICR is BB+ or lower.

## 9.4 APPENDIX 1:[18] EQUITY–CONTENT MAXIMIZATION AND STRUCTURING CRITERIA AT MOODY'S

**Table 9.14**  Equity-content maximization and structuring criteria at Moody's

| | | 1 | 2 | 3 | 4 | 5 | 6 | 7 | 8 | 9 | 10 | 11 | 12 | 13 | 14 |
|---|---|---|---|---|---|---|---|---|---|---|---|---|---|---|---|
| Coupon skip | Mandatory weak (1) | X | | | | | | | | | | | | | |
| | Restricted optional (2) | | | x | | | | | | | x | | | | |
| | Mandatory moderate (3) | | | | | | | | | | | x | | | |
| | Optional | X | | | x | x | | x | x | | | x | | | |
| | Optional & mandatory strong (4) | | | | | | x | | | x | | | | X (5) | x |
| Settlement | Cumulative | X | X | x | x | x | x | | | x | | | | | |
| | Non-cumulative | | | | | | | | x | | x | x | X | x | X |
| Ranking | Subordinated | X | X | x | x | x | X | | | | | | | | |
| | Preferred | | | | | | | x | x | x | x | x | X | X | |
| | Equity | | | | | | | | | | | | | | x |
| Maturity | < 30 years | X | | | | | | | | | | | | | |
| | 30–59 years | | | x | | | | | x | | | | | | |
| | >= 60 years | | X | | x | x | x | x | | x | x | x | x | X | |
| | Irredeemable | | | | | | | | | | | | | | x |
| Bank basket | | A | B | B | B | B | B | C | C | C | C | C | D | D | E |
| Non-bank basket | | A | B | B | B | B | B | C | C | C | C | C | D | D | E |

(1) Mandatory weak triggers include minimum regulatory capital ratios set at low levels;
(2) Restricted optional is when the issuer either has to breach certain triggers or stop payments on parity or junior securities for more than six months before being able to skip hybrid coupons;
(3) Mandatory moderate triggers include a balance sheet loss trigger for banks;
(4) Optional and mandatory strong triggers includes both optional skip mechanisms and strong or 'meaningful' triggers such as net loss triggers for banks;
(5) The mandatory coupon suspension is non-cumulative; the optional coupon suspension can either be cumulative or non-cumulative.

---

[18] Source: Appendices 1 and 2, ibid. note 8.

## 9.5 APPENDIX 2: S&P'S AND MOODY'S KEY STRUCTURING CONSIDERATIONS[19]

**Table 9.15** Key structuring considerations: rating agency guidelines when senior issuer rating is investment grade

|  | S&P | Moody's |
| --- | --- | --- |
| Share of hybrid allowed in the capital structure | **Banks:** High equity content up to 50% of adjusted common equity (ACE). Intermediate equity content up to 33% of ACE. **Insurance:** High equity content up to 35% of total adjusted capital (TAC). Intermediate equity content up to 25%. | Hybrid equity credit/(equity + hybrid equity credit) <= 25% |
| Equity credit | Minimal (0%), Intermediate (50%) and High (100%) | Baskets A to E covering equity credit of 0%, 25%, 50%, 75% and 100%, respectively. |
| Coupon deferral | **Optional deferral:** Indifferent between cumulative and non-cumulative. Not eligible for Intermediate if maximum deferral period below five years. **Mandatory deferral:** Triggers close to current rating requirement qualify for High. Weaker but meaningful triggers qualify for Intermediate. | **Optional deferral:** Indifferent between cumulative and non-cumulative, eligible for basket C. In general, restricted options to defer qualify for basket C at best. **Mandatory deferral:** Strong triggers qualify for basket D if non-cumulative. |
| ACSM to settle cumulative dividends | **Optional deferral:** Not eligible for Intermediate if ACSM settlement within five years of initial deferral. **Mandatory deferral:** ACSM settlement eligible for Intermediate but not High. | **Optional and/or mandatory deferral:** ACSM settlement is eligible for basket C. However, basket D may still be assigned to mandatory deferral with strong triggers if non-cumulative coupons can be ACSM settled at the issuer's option. |
| Dividend pusher and dividend stopper | Not eligible for Intermediate if *dividend pusher* look-back period exceeds one year. Neutral view on *dividend stopper*. | *Dividend pusher:* Moody's lowers equity content, all else equal, if look-back period exceeds six months. |
| Time to maturity | Time to maturity of at least *20 years* to warrant Intermediate or High. Equity credit is eliminated when the remaining time to maturity falls below this threshold. | Moody's views *60 years* as tantamount to perpetuity and hybrids must have at least an initial *30 year* maturity at issuance for the assignment of equity credit. Equity credit will be eliminated when the remaining time to maturity is *10 years.* |

---

[19] Source: S&P, Moody's and Danske Markets. Note 1. Both S&P and Moody's ultimately take a holistic approach to instrument characteristics and consider the overall effect of hybrid capital on the issuer's credit profile when assigning equity credit. However, an absence or presence of certain equity features plays an important role and can disqualify the hybrid from a given equity credit assignment.

|  | S&P | Moody's |
|---|---|---|
| Built-in call incentives and replacement language | *Step-up* of more than 100bp or half the initial spread, the call date will be treated as the effective maturity date. Initial call date (even without step-up) less than five years from issuance disqualifies Intermediate even if RCC. | RCC is not a key consideration. Built-in call incentives hurt *equity content* (1) 100bp step-up within 10 years from issuance results in lower equity content (2) step-up above 100bp defines effective maturity date |
| Subordination | Distinction between subordination and deep subordination a *secondary factor* to other characteristics | Equity content is eligible for deeply subordinated securities senior only to common equity which cannot default or cross-default other than at maturity and that have limited influence on the outcome of a bankruptcy proceeding. If these conditions are not satisfied, equity credit is capped at basket B |
| Notching | One notch for subordination, one notch for optional deferral, one notch for mandatory deferral | Two notches if deeply subordinated and senior only to common equity. An additional notch if non-cumulative with strong mandatory trigger |

## 9.6 THE INTRICACIES OF THE ACCOUNTING WORLD

Accounting philosophies aren't very easy, especially not since they are principle-based. The consequence is that, just like legislation, they are perpetually behind the curve and have trouble catching up with and adjusting to reality.

It therefore comes as no surprise that the qualification, recognition, measurement and reporting of hybrid securities has been not only very troublesome and volatile over time, with a set of rules which is in constant movement, but also that we are still left with the question of whether the rules as they currently stand reflect the 'true and fair view' that the accounting rules want to offer to investors. In reviewing this interesting but somewhat troubled part of the overall mezzanine spectrum, I will focus on the IFRS rules only. Since the recent evolution of the accounting standards has been based on a joint project between the IASB and the FASB, somewhat similar positions are taken by both with respect to hybrid products. The two governing accounting bodies (IASB and FASB) are working on a convergence project to arrive at some sort of single global set of accounting rules. As of mid-2012 it seems that they are working towards initial finalization of that project around mid-2013. It should also be noted that I tried to be as complete as possible within the space the topic justifies in a book like this.[20] There are, however, many more details, nuances and twists to many of the issues described. My focus will be on the accounting classification of the instrument, and less on the accounting treatment of the instrument's proceeds unless a holistic approach is needed, in which case they will be included.

Historically, the positioning of debt and equity did not pose particular problems, since the legal classification was used and followed consequently, although the economic consequences

---

[20] Since the topic deserves a book of its own.

of many products in terms of debt or equity are far less clear-cut than the legal classification would make one believe. The problem is not just the classification of often complex hybrid instruments, but also the fact that a classification as liability combined with the notion of reporting at 'fair value' and principles such as 'mark-to-market' can imply significant volatility in reported results.

The four most relevant pieces of information in this respect are:

- IAS 32, which deals with the presentation from the perspective of the issuer (which has been modified a number of times during the last 15 years).
- IAS 39, which deals with measurement and recognition of financial assets and financial liabilities.
- IFRS 7, which deals with the disclosure rules.
- IFRS 9, financial instruments (replacing IAS 39).

IFRS is part of a project started by the IASB (International Accounting Standards Board) in November 2009 as a comprehensive project to replace IAS 39.[21] The objective of this project is to improve the usefulness of financial statements for users by simplifying the classification and measurement requirements for financial instruments.[22]

The review breaks down into three phases.

## 9.6.1 Classification and measurement

The IFRS 9 *Financial Instruments* was published in November 2009, and contained requirements for financial assets. Requirements for financial liabilities were then later added in October 2010. Most of the requirements for financial liabilities were carried forward unchanged from IAS 39. However, some changes were made to the fair value option for financial liabilities, to address the issue of own credit risk (see below). All the way into 2010 and 2011 the IASB was tweaking content through smaller adjustments to IFRS 9, and I wouldn't be surprised to see further modifications suggested by the IASB after the close of the manuscript, as it continues to be on the IASB meeting schedule during the remainder of 2012 and into 2013. Effective mandatory implementation now seems to be set for January 1, 2015 (coming from January 1, 2013).

IFRS 9 specifies how an entity should classify and measure financial assets, including some hybrid contracts. It requires all financial assets to be:

(a) Classified on the basis of the entity's business model for managing the financial assets and their contractual cash flow characteristics.
(b) Initially measured at fair value plus particular transaction costs (in the case of a financial asset not at fair value through profit or loss).
(c) Subsequently measured at amortized cost or fair value.

---

[21] See also Chiara del Prete, 'EFRAG study on accounting for hybrid financial instruments,' Working Paper, January 2012.
[22] The project is run in cooperation with the FASB. For the FASB status on the same issue, see: 'Financial instruments – a new classification and measurement model on the horizon,' E&Y Technical Line, July 2011.

Remember, IFRS's objective is 'To establish principles for the financial reporting of financial assets that will present relevant and useful information to users of financial statements for their assessment of the amounts, timing and uncertainty of the entity's future cash flows'.[23]

These requirements improve and simplify the approach for classification and measurement of financial assets compared with the requirements of IAS 39.

### 9.6.2 Impairment methodology

The supplementary document *Financial Instruments: Impairment* was published in January 2011. It has been redrafted and re-issued many times since 2011 and expanded to include credit losses on impairment (December 2012). That resulted in a new exposure draft issued in March 2013 which is currently up for debate. This part of the total overhaul of IAS 39 is still ongoing.

### 9.6.3 Hedge accounting

The exposure draft *Hedge Accounting* was published in December 2010. This part of the process is still ongoing and has been going through different reviews, with a newly issued draft in September 2012. Since submission of the manuscript of this book in May 2013 the IAS Board has been finalizing its deliberations regarding this project. It is therefore expected that the final version will be issued some time in Fall/Winter 2013 through a new version of IFRS 9.

That more or less completes (for now) the picture of the debt–equity continuum from an interdisciplinary perspective. Table 9.16 is a framework overview, and therefore requires many nuances regarding its individual inputs, which either have been discussed (in this or previous chapters) or will be discussed in this chapter.

IAS 32 helps us to put things in perspective terminology-wise:

A **financial asset** is any asset which is:

> Cash.
> Another entity's equity instrument.
> A contractual right: to receive cash or another financial asset from another entity, or to exchange financial assets or financial liabilities with another entity under conditions that are potentially favorable to the entity.

**Table 9.16**  Cross-discipline treatment of securities

| Discipline | Accounting (IFRS) | Legal | Rating | Taxation |
|---|---|---|---|---|
| Equity | Equity | Equity | 100% | Dividend payment: not tax-deductible |
| Hybrid instruments | Equity(*) | Subordinated: senior to ordinary shares only | 50/50% equity and debt | Interest payment: tax-deductible |
| Senior debt | Debt | Senior debt: no subordination | 100% debt | Interest payment: tax deductible |

(*) Many nuances need to be put in place here, and often the qualification of a debt product will end up being a liability rather than equity.

---

[23] IFRS 9, *Financial Instruments*, IASB 2009.

A contract which will or may be settled in the entity's own equity instruments and is: a non-derivative for which the entity is, or may be, obliged to receive a variable number of the entity's own equity instruments, or a derivative which will, or may be, settled other than by the exchange of a fixed amount of cash or another financial asset for a fixed number of the entity's own equity instruments.

A **financial liability** is any liability which is:

A contractual obligation: to deliver cash or another financial asset to another entity, or to exchange financial assets or financial liabilities with another entity under conditions that are potentially unfavorable to the entity.

A contract which will or may be settled in the entity's own equity instruments and is: a non-derivative for which the entity is, or may be, obliged to deliver a variable number of the entity's own equity instruments, or a derivative that will or may be settled other than by the exchange of a fixed amount of cash or another financial asset for a fixed number of the entity's own equity instruments.

An **equity instrument** is any contract which evidences a residual interest in the assets of an entity after deducting all of its liabilities.

**Fair value** is the amount for which an asset could be exchanged, or a liability settled, between knowledgeable, willing parties in an arm's length transaction.

A **puttable instrument** is a financial instrument which gives the holder the right to put the instrument back to the issuer for cash or another financial asset, or is automatically put back to the issuer on the occurrence of an uncertain future event or the death or retirement of the instrument holder.

It will prove paramount to review the legal form and economic substance of any financial instrument. The economic substance will thereby dictate the accounting position.

A financial instrument is defined as a contract between two parties, whereby the instrument can qualify as an asset to one party while being, at the same time, a financial liability or equity instrument to the other party. An equity instrument is, therefore, a contract which represents a residual interest in the net asset of the company. A financial liability is a contractual obligation to deliver cash (or another financial asset), or to exchange financial assets or financial liabilities under conditions which are potentially unfavorable.

Whatever shape or form, financial instruments should be classified as debt or equity according to their economic substance, even if they contain both debt and equity components (referred to as compound instruments).

An equity instrument is characterized as having the following characteristics:

- The instrument contains no contractual obligation.
- The instrument may be settled in a fixed number of the issuer's own equity instruments.

A critical feature (with a few exceptions) in differentiating a financial liability from an equity instrument is the existence of a contractual obligation of one party to the financial instrument, to either deliver cash or another financial asset to the other party, or an obligation to exchange financial assets or financial liabilities with the holder under conditions which are potentially unfavorable to the issuer.

Basically, the holder of an equity instrument cannot compel an issuer to make such distributions, because the issuer has no contractual obligation to deliver cash or another financial asset to the equity holder. Note that dividends do not make an equity instrument a financial liability, since dividends are not obligatory, notwithstanding that some preferred shares carry a cumulative provision.

Conversely, if an entity does not have an unconditional right to avoid delivering cash or another financial asset to settle a contractual obligation, the obligation meets the definition of a financial liability, except for those instruments classified as equity instruments (puttable instruments).

Finally, the substance of a financial instrument, rather than its legal form, governs its classification on an entity's balance sheet. Substance and legal form are usually consistent, but not necessarily. For example, some financial instruments take the legal form of equity but are liabilities in substance (term preferred shares), while others may combine features associated with both equity instruments and financial liabilities (convertible debt). Therefore, the issuer of a non-derivative financial instrument must evaluate the terms of the financial instrument to determine whether it contains both a liability and an equity component. Note that classification of the liability and equity components of a convertible instrument is not revised as a result of a change in the likelihood that a conversion option will be exercised, even when exercise of the option may appear to have become economically (dis)advantageous to some holders.

As noted above, puttable instruments are treated differently from other financial instruments. A puttable instrument is one which gives the holder the right to force the entity to accept the instrument back, i.e., 'put' the instrument back to the issuer. For example, a puttable bond would be considered a puttable financial instrument, since the holder has the right to redeem the unit for cash at any time or at certain points in time.

Puttable financial instruments are classified as equity only if all of the following conditions apply:

- The holder must be entitled to a pro-rata share of the entity's net assets on liquidation.
- The instrument is in a class of instruments which is the most subordinate, and all instruments in that class have identical features.
- Apart from obligations to deliver cash or another financial asset on redemption, the instrument has no other characteristics that would meet the definition of a financial liability.
- The total expected cash flows attributable to the instrument over its life are based substantially on the profit or loss, the change in the recognized net assets, or the change in the fair value of the entity's recognized and unrecognized net assets. Also, the issuer has no other instrument on issue, or contract, which has: (1) total cash flows based substantially on the profit or loss, change in recognized net assets or change in fair values of recognized and unrecognized net assets; and (2) the effect of substantially restricting or fixing the residual return to the puttable instrument holders.

### 9.6.4 Substance over form

A contract is not an equity instrument just because it can result in the receipt or delivery of the entity's own equity instruments. An entity may have a contractual right or obligation to receive or deliver a number of its own shares or other equity instruments which varies, so that the fair value of the entity's own equity instruments, which they will receive or deliver, is equal to the amount of the contractual right or obligation. For example, an entity may be required to deliver as many of its own equity instruments as are equal in value to €10,000. Such a contract is a financial liability, even though the entity must or can settle it by delivering its own equity instruments. It is not an equity instrument because the entity uses a variable number of its own equity instruments as a means to settle the contract. Perhaps most telling, it is not an equity instrument as the contract does not evidence a residual interest in the entity's assets after deducting all of its liabilities.

- Direct versus indirect

    A financial instrument may indirectly establish a contractual obligation to deliver cash or another financial asset through its terms and conditions, even though it does not explicitly establish an obligation. For example, an instrument may stipulate that on settlement, the entity will deliver either cash or another financial asset, or its own shares, whose value will be determined to exceed substantially the value of the cash, or other financial asset. In this example, the entity does not have an explicit contractual obligation to deliver cash or another financial asset. Nevertheless, the value of the share settlement alternative is such that the entity will choose to settle in cash rather than in shares. In any event, the holder has, in substance, been guaranteed an amount which is at least equal to the cash settlement option. This type of financial instrument constitutes a financial liability.

- Contingent settlement provisions

    A financial instrument may require the entity to deliver cash or another financial asset, or otherwise to settle it in such a way that it would be a financial liability, in the event of uncertain future events which are beyond the control of both the issuer and the holder of the instrument occurring or not occurring (or on the outcome of uncertain circumstances). For example, the settlement of the instrument may be dependent on things such as a change in a stock market index, consumer price index, interest rate or taxation requirements, or the issuer's future revenues, net income or debt-to-equity ratio. The issuer of such an instrument does not have the unconditional right to avoid delivering cash or another financial asset (or otherwise settle it in such a way that it would be a financial liability). Therefore, it is a financial liability for the issuer.

    Notwithstanding the preceding, a financial instrument would not be a financial liability if the part of the contingent settlement provision which could require settlement in cash or another financial asset (or otherwise in such a way that it would be a financial liability) is not genuine, or if the obligation is only payable in the event of liquidation. Essentially, if the contingency is such that settlement in cash or another financial instrument (or otherwise in such a way that it would be a financial liability) is unlikely, it would not be a financial liability.

- Settlement options

    When a derivative financial instrument gives one party a choice over how it is settled – either the issuer or the holder can choose settlement net in cash or by exchanging shares for cash – it is a financial asset or a financial liability, unless all of the settlement alternatives would result in it being an equity instrument. An example of such a derivative financial instrument would be a share option which stipulates that it can be settled (i.e., exchanged), at the issuer's option for cash, or by issuing their own shares for cash. In this case, the share option would be a financial liability, as not all settlement options result in an equity instrument being issued.

## 9.6.5  Examples of equity instruments

According to our understanding so far, equity instruments will be:

- Non-puttable ordinary shares.
- Some types of preferred shares (see further on in this chapter).
- Warrants or written call options which allow the holder to subscribe to or purchase a fixed number of non-puttable ordinary shares in the issuing entity, in exchange for a fixed amount of cash or another financial asset, or the fixed-stated principal of a bond.

To qualify as an equity instrument it is therefore not only necessary to imply that the reporting firm needs to issue/receive its own shares, but also that the consideration needs to be fixed.
  Conversely, an instrument would be a liability if it gives the holder the right to obtain:

- A variable number of non-puttable ordinary shares in the issuing entity in exchange for a fixed amount of cash or another financial asset; or
- A fixed number of non-puttable ordinary shares in the issuing entity in exchange for a variable amount of cash of another financial asset.

The following (provisional) table[24] (Table 9.17) provides some initial indications based on the characteristics of some mezzanine products. Where an instrument contains both liabilities and equity, the liability would generally be measured at the future cash flows' present value, with the remaining consideration exchanged for the instrument being booked as equity (see also further on in this chapter).

**Table 9.17**  Provisional overview of accounting classification for some hybrid instruments

| Instrument | Classification |
| --- | --- |
| Mandatorily redeemable preferred shares | Even though these are equity in legal terms, the substance is that the instrument contains a liability due to the contractual obligation to repay (redemption is mandatory) |
| Shares where the holder has the right to sell them back to the company for a fixed amount (puttable) | Even though these are equity in terms of legal form, the substance is that the instrument contains a liability due to the contractual obligation to repay if the holder presents the shares. Therefore, a liability exists unless certain restrictive criteria are met (discussed further later in this chapter) |
| Liability which may be repaid in cash or a variable number of shares, which will approximate the face value of the amount owing | Even though the amount can be repaid with shares, the number of shares varies depending on the amount owed and the share value. The entity is therefore locked into repaying a certain value and this is a liability |
| Financial instruments which may require the entity to repay if a certain event occurs (such as a decline in the entity's shares below a pre-determined benchmark) | Due to the fact that there is uncertainty which is beyond the control of the company, these are treated as liabilities |

---

[24] Source: Wiecek & Young, 'IFRS Primer: International GAAP basics,' 2010, p. 170.

Equity treatment depends on the lack of an obligation to deliver cash or financial assets, with the following features attached:

- No maturity.
- Option to settle in cash does not create a liability.
- Interest payment optional only (dividend pusher possible).

Let's look first at the classification and measurement requirements of IAS 39/IFRS 9 and following that we can start to position hybrid instruments on the spectrum. We will focus on those parts which directly relate to mezzanine products, and not on the issues which are naturally linked to other applications of derivatives. Therefore, issues which come with the new hedge accounting statements are not covered.

A. Classification and measurement[25]

IFRS 9 requires that financial assets are classified at either fair value or amortized cost, and this classification determines their ongoing measurement in financial statements. However, IFRS 9 requires two tests to be satisfied if a financial asset is to be measured at amortized cost:

(a) **The 'business model' test:** The objective of an entity's business model has to be to hold financial assets in order to collect contractual cash flows.
(b) **The 'characteristics of the instrument' test:** The contractual terms of the financial asset give rise on specified dates to cash flows which are only payments of principal and interest on the principal outstanding. Cash flow (i.e., interest) is consideration for the time value of money, and for the credit risk associated with the principal amount outstanding during a particular period of time.

Where either of these tests is not satisfied, financial assets are to be measured at fair value.

---

[25] Appendix 2 of the IFRS guidelines provides some non-exhaustive examples:

| Instrument | Analysis |
| --- | --- |
| **A. Instrument A** is a bond with a stated maturity date. Payments of principal and interest on the principal amount outstanding are linked to an inflation index of the currency in which the instrument is issued. The inflation link is not leveraged and the principal is protected. | The contractual cash flows are solely payments of principal and interest on the principal amount outstanding. Linking payments of principal and interest on the principal amount outstanding to an unleveraged inflation index resets the time value of money to a current level. In other words, the interest rate on the instrument reflects 'real' interest. Thus, the interest amounts are consideration for the time value of money on the principal amount outstanding. However, if the interest payments were indexed to another variable such as the debtor's performance (e.g., the debtor's net income) or an equity index, the contractual cash flows would not be payments of principal and interest on the principal amount outstanding. That is because the interest payments are not consideration for the time value of money and for credit risk associated with the principal amount outstanding. There is variability in the contractual interest payments that is inconsistent with market interest rates. |

footnote (*continued*)

| Instrument | Analysis |
| --- | --- |
| **B.** **Instrument B** is a variable interest rate instrument with a stated maturity date that permits the borrower to choose the market interest rate on an ongoing basis. For example, at each interest rate reset date, the borrower can choose to pay three-month LIBOR for a three-month term or one-month LIBOR for a one-month term. | The contractual cash flows are solely payments of principal and interest on the principal amount outstanding as long as the interest paid over the life of the instrument reflects consideration for the time value of money and for the credit risk associated with the instrument. The fact that the LIBOR interest rate is reset during the life of the instrument does not in itself disqualify the instrument. However, if the borrower is able to choose to receive one-month LIBOR for three months and that one-month LIBOR is not reset each month, the contractual cash flows are not payments of principal and interest. The same analysis would apply if the borrower were able to choose between the lender's published one-month variable interest rate and the lender's published three-month variable interest rate. However, if the instrument has a contractual interest rate which is based on a term that exceeds the instrument's remaining life, its contractual cash flows are not payments of principal and interest on the principal amount outstanding. For example, a constant maturity bond with a five-year term that pays a variable rate which is reset periodically but always reflects a five-year maturity does not result in contractual cash flows which are payments of principal and interest on the principal amount outstanding. That is because the interest payable in each period is disconnected from the term of the instrument (except at origination). |
| **C.** **Instrument C** is a bond with a stated maturity date and pays a variable market interest rate. That variable interest rate is capped. | The contractual cash flows of both: (a) an instrument that has a fixed interest rate and (b) an instrument that has a variable interest rate are payments of principal and interest on the principal amount outstanding as long as the interest reflects consideration for the time value of money and for the credit risk associated with the instrument during the term of the instrument. Therefore, an instrument which is a combination of (a) and (b) (e.g., a bond with an interest rate cap) can have cash flows that are solely payments of principal and interest on the principal amount outstanding. Such a feature may reduce cash flow variability by setting a limit on a variable interest rate (e.g., an interest rate cap or floor) or increase the cash flow variability because a fixed rate becomes variable. |
| **D.** **Instrument D** is a full recourse loan and is secured by collateral. | The fact that a full recourse loan is collateralized does not in itself affect the analysis of whether the contractual cash flows are solely payments of principal and interest on the principal amount outstanding. |
| **E.** **Instrument E** is a bond which is convertible into equity instruments of the issuer. | The holder would analyze the convertible bond in its entirety. The contractual cash flows are not payments of principal and interest on the principal amount outstanding because the interest rate does not reflect only consideration for the time value of money and the credit risk. The return is also linked to the value of the issuer's equity. |

B. The business model test[26]

The business model test distinguishes the objective of holding financial assets to collect contractual cash flows from the objective of realizing fair value changes. However, it accepts that some asset sales may occur without compromising the objective of holding financial assets to collect contractual cash flows. For example, it would be acceptable to sell some financial assets to meet investment policy criteria (e.g., due to credit downgrades) or to fund capital expenditures.

The business model test is applied at a higher level than an individual financial asset, although not necessarily at the level of the reporting entity as a whole. For example, an entity may apply the business model to a portfolio of financial assets.

C. The instrument test

The instrument test requires that, to be eligible for measurement at amortized cost, the contractual cash flows arising on a financial asset must be only payments of interest and principal in the currency in which the financial asset is denominated. Interest paid must

footnote (*continued*)

| Instrument | Analysis |
|---|---|
| **F. Instrument F** is a loan which pays an inverse floating interest rate (i.e., the interest rate has an inverse relationship to market interest rates). | The contractual cash flows are not solely payments of principal and interest on the principal amount outstanding. The interest amounts are not consideration for the time value of money on the principal amount outstanding. |
| **G. Instrument G** is a perpetual instrument, but the issuer may call the instrument at any point and pay the holder the par amount plus accrued interest due. Instrument G pays a market interest rate, but payment of interest cannot be made unless the issuer is able to remain solvent immediately afterwards. Deferred interest does not accrue additional interest. | The contractual cash flows are not payments of principal and interest on the principal amount outstanding. That is because the issuer may be required to defer interest payments and additional interest does not accrue on those deferred interest amounts. As a result, interest amounts are not consideration for the time value of money on the principal amount outstanding. If interest accrued on the deferred amounts, the contractual cash flows could be payments of principal and interest on the principal amount outstanding. The fact that Instrument G is perpetual does not in itself mean that the contractual cash flows are not payments of principal and interest on the principal amount outstanding. In effect, a perpetual instrument has continuous (multiple) extension options. Such options may result in contractual cash flows which are payments of principal and interest on the principal amount outstanding if interest payments are mandatory and must be paid in perpetuity. Also, the fact that Instrument G is callable does not mean that the contractual cash flows are not payments of principal and interest on the principal amount outstanding unless it is callable at an amount which does not substantially reflect payment of outstanding principal and interest on that principal. Even if the callable amount includes an amount which compensates the holder for the early termination of the instrument, the contractual cash flows could be payments of principal and interest on the principal amount outstanding. |

[26] Further analysis of both tests can be found in Appendix B of IFRS 9.

only reflect consideration for the time value of money and the credit risk associated with the instrument over its lifetime.

Stand-alone derivatives are leveraged, and therefore are not eligible for amortized cost. Hybrid contracts which provide for contractual cash flows other than payments of interest and principal on the principal outstanding are not eligible for measurement at amortized cost either. However, certain contractual terms affecting the cash flows arising on debt instruments such as prepayment options, extension options, interest rate caps and floors and reset options are, in some cases, considered payments of principal and interest. Such contracts are eligible for the amortized cost category if the entity's objective for holding such financial assets is to collect contractual cash flows.

Equity instruments are not eligible for the amortized cost category because their cash flows do not have the characteristics of payments of interest and principal.

D. Fair value option

IFRS 9 permits (i.e., it is an option) an entity to designate an instrument, which would otherwise have been classified in the amortized cost category, to be at fair value through profit or loss if that designation eliminates or significantly reduces a measurement or recognition inconsistency (sometimes referred to as an 'accounting mismatch').

E. Embedded derivatives

An embedded derivative is a component of a hybrid contract which also includes a non-derivative host, with the effect that some of the combined instrument's cash flows vary in a way similar to a stand-alone derivative (as is the case in a convertible bond or convertible preference shares). An embedded derivative causes some or all of the cash flows (which otherwise would be required by the contract) to be modified according to a specified interest rate, financial instrument price, commodity price, foreign exchange rate, index of prices or rates, credit rating or credit index, or other variable, provided, in the case of a non-financial variable, that the variable is not specific to a party to the contract. A derivative which is attached to a financial instrument but is contractually transferable independently of that instrument, or has a different counterparty, is not an embedded derivative, but a separate financial instrument.

IFRS 9 (introduced in 2009) has removed the requirement in IAS 39 to split out and separately account (bifurcate) derivatives embedded in (non-derivative) host financial assets.[27] The standard requires a reporting entity to assess the hybrid financial asset (i.e.,

---

[27] To be precise: the IFRS 9 states that:

If a hybrid contract contains a host which is within the scope of this IFRS, an entity shall apply the requirements just mentioned to the entire hybrid contract (so do not bifurcate).

If a hybrid contract contains a host which is not within the scope of this IFRS, an entity shall apply the requirements of IAS 39 to determine whether it must separate the embedded derivative from the host. If the embedded derivative must be separated from the host, the entity shall:

(a) Classify the derivative in accordance with IFRS 9 for derivative assets or of IAS 39 for all other derivatives.

(b) Account for the host in accordance with other IFRSs.

The latter situation is outside the scope of mezzanine products and therefore not further examined.

the combined financial asset host and embedded derivative) in its entirety, to determine whether the instrument's cash flows are principal and interest on the outstanding principal (see further on in this chapter).

The existing IAS 39 requirements for measurement of financial liabilities were kept in place insofar as:

(a) Financial liabilities which are held for trading and derivatives are measured at fair value through profit or loss.
(b) Hybrid instruments (i.e., host contracts with embedded derivatives) which are not measured at fair value should be:
  (i) Accounted for at amortized cost if the embedded derivatives are closely related.
  (ii) Bifurcated into a host contract and a derivative component if the derivative component is not closely related; the host contract should be measured at amortized cost, and the derivative should be measured at fair value through profit or loss.
(c) All other financial liabilities should be measured at amortized cost.

F. Non-recourse financial assets

The fact that a financial asset is non-recourse does not in itself preclude the financial asset from satisfying the characteristics of the instrument test. The creditor is, however, required to assess (look through to) the particular underlying assets or cash flows, to determine whether the contractual cash flows of the financial asset being classified are payments of principal and interest on the principal amount outstanding. If the terms of a financial asset give rise to any other cash flows, or limit the cash flows in a manner inconsistent with payments representing principal and interest, the financial asset does not satisfy the characteristics of the instrument test. Whether the underlying assets are financial assets or non-financial assets does not in itself affect this assessment.

G. Initial and subsequent measurement and gains/losses on the instrument

- At initial recognition, the firm shall measure a financial asset at its fair asset value plus the transaction costs (under certain conditions) that are directly attributable to the acquisition of the financial asset.
- After initial recognition: measurement of the financial asset at fair value or amortized cost.
- A gain or loss on a financial asset which is measured at fair value and is not part of a hedging relationship shall be recognized in profit or loss, unless the financial asset is an investment in an equity instrument and the entity has elected to present gains and losses on that investment in other comprehensive income.
- A gain or loss on a financial asset which is measured at amortized cost and is not part of a hedging relationship shall be recognized in profit or loss when the financial asset is derecognized, impaired or reclassified, and through the amortization process.

H. Hybrid's positioning

IAS 39 dealt with the requirements in relation to hybrid instruments.

IAS 39 required embedded derivatives which are not closely related to the host instrument to be separated when:

(a) They are embedded in instruments which are not carried at fair value through profit or loss.
(b) A separate instrument with the same terms as the embedded derivative would meet the definition of the derivative.
(c) Embedded derivatives can be separated reliably.

The premise for bifurcation requirements in IAS 39 was that:

(a) Fair value is the only relevant measure for derivatives.
(b) Entities should not circumvent the principle of measuring derivatives at fair value by embedding them into another contract which is not carried at fair value through profit or loss.

The bifurcation requirements relied on the definition of a derivative and the distinction established through examples between closely and non-closely related embedded derivatives. Only non-closely related embedded derivatives needed to be separated. Closely related embedded derivatives cannot be separated.

As a result, entities were required to consider whether bifurcation requirements applied if they classified their financial instruments into one of the following categories:

(a) Held-to-maturity, which enables entities to carry, at amortized cost, a financial asset that:
   (i) Is not a derivative.
   (ii) Has fixed or determinable payments and fixed maturity.
   (iii) An entity has the positive intention and ability to hold to maturity.
(b) Loans and receivables, which enables entities to carry, at amortized cost, a financial asset that:
   (i) Is not a derivative.
   (ii) Has fixed or determinable payments.
   (iii) Is not quoted in an active market.
   (iv) Is not held for trading purposes.
   (v) Is not one for which the holder may not recover substantially all of its initial investment, other than because of credit deterioration.
(c) Available-for-sale, which enables entities to measure, at fair value, through other comprehensive income a financial asset that:

   Is not held for trading and:
   • Either it does not meet the requirements of the held-to-maturity and loans and receivables categories, or
   • The entity designates the instrument into the available for sale category by choice.
(d) Liabilities not held for trading, which encompasses all financial liabilities that:

   (i) Are not derivatives.
   (ii) The entity does not intend to trade for short-term gains.

## 9.6.6 IFRS 9 requirements in relation to hybrid instruments

IFRS 9, which was introduced in 2009, was long-awaited, much discussed and was put in place to end the controversial and obscure practice surrounding the reporting of financial products, and (embedded) derivatives in particular.

As mentioned above, IFRS 9 requires that financial assets which meet the business model and characteristics of the instrument tests should be carried at amortized cost. Other financial assets are measured at fair value.

The effect of the IFRS 9 requirements for financial assets is that simple instruments which are held for their contractual cash flows would be reported at amortized cost in the primary financial statements and fair value would be disclosed in the notes. On the other hand, leveraged instruments and those instruments which entities acquire for purposes other than merely realizing their contractual cash flows, would be re-measured at fair value in each reporting period.

The basis for conclusions to IFRS 9 explains that the IASB considered the following three approaches for accounting for instruments which have features that are not just payments of principal and interest on the principal outstanding:

(a) To maintain the requirements in IAS 39.
(b) To use the 'closely/non-closely related' notion to determine the classification for the contract in its entirety.
(c) To use the same classification approach for all financial assets, irrespective of whether they are hybrid contracts or not.

The IASB noted the following disadvantages of the first two approaches:

(a) They rely on the assessment of whether an embedded derivative is 'closely related' to the host. The 'closely related' assessment in IAS 39 is based on a list of examples which are inconsistent and unclear. That assessment is also a significant source of complexity.
(b) These approaches would result in hybrid contracts being classified using conditions different from those that would be applied to all non-hybrid financial instruments. Consequently, some hybrid contracts whose contractual cash flows do not solely represent payments of principal and interest on the principal amount outstanding might be measured at amortized cost. Similarly, some hybrid contracts whose contractual cash flows do meet the conditions for measurement at amortized cost might be measured at fair value.
(c) These approaches would not make it easier for users of financial statements to understand the information that financial statements present about financial instruments.

The IASB agreed on the third approach (a single classification for all financial assets) and pointed to the following advantages:

(a) Using a single classification approach improves comparability by ensuring consistency in classification, and hence makes it easier for users to understand the information that financial statements present about financial instruments.
(b) The current underlying rationale for separate accounting for embedded derivatives is not to reflect risk management activities, but to avoid entities circumventing the recognition and measurement requirements for derivatives. Therefore, it is an exception to the definition of the unit-of-account (the contract) motivated by a wish to avoid abuse. Eliminating an anti-abuse exception would reduce complexity.
(c) The embedded derivative feature affects the cash flows ultimately arising from the hybrid contract. Thus, applying the classification approach to the hybrid contract in its entirety would depict more faithfully the amount, timing and uncertainty of future cash flows.

## 9.6.7 Hybrid financial liabilities

As mentioned above, the IASB decided to keep the existing IAS 39 requirements for financial liabilities, though it took a new approach – when the fair value option is applied – to the recognition of the changes in a financial liability's fair value due to changes in the entity's own credit risk. Therefore, the IASB decided to go with the following model: fair value measurement with separate presentation in OCI of fair value changes arising from changes in own credit risk.

The IASB decided to keep the embedded derivatives requirements in IAS 39 for the classification and measurement of financial liabilities, noting that:

(a) The benefits of changing practice at this point do not outweigh the costs of the disruption that such a change would cause.

(b) The issue of credit risk is addressed for most liabilities, because they would continue to be subsequently measured at amortized cost, or would be bifurcated into a host which would be measured at amortized cost, and an embedded derivative which would be measured at fair value.

(c) Liabilities which are held for trading (including all derivative liabilities) would continue to be subsequently measured at fair value through profit or loss, which is consistent with the widespread view that all fair value changes for those liabilities should affect profit or loss.

### 9.6.8 Preferred shares

The issuer must consider whether it has a contractual obligation to transfer cash or other financial assets to the holder of the share. For example, if, under its terms of issue, a preference share is mandatorily redeemable on a certain date, the issuing company has such a contractual obligation. The preference share will therefore be a financial liability, not an equity instrument. If the preference share is non-redeemable, but the company has a contractual obligation to pay a dividend, it will again be a financial liability. If, however, payment of a dividend is solely at the discretion of the directors (whether or not unpaid dividends accumulate), there is no contractual obligation to make a payment and the preference share will be classified as an equity instrument. Where a preference share is classified as a financial liability, the preference dividend paid will be shown as 'interest' in the company's income statement. This does not, however, affect the tax treatment (non-deductibility) of such dividends.

## 9.7  DEMARCATION LINES AND PRODUCT MODELING

### 9.7.1  Contractual obligation to deliver cash or other financial assets

From the discussion above, it is clear that a liability is characterized by the contractual obligation to deliver cash or another financial asset, or to exchange financial assets or liabilities with the holder, under conditions that are potentially unfavorable to the issuer.

The absence of an obligation to deliver cash or a financial asset is a key criterion, and needs to be interpreted as showing that the issuer has an unconditional right to avoid doing so in all future circumstances, other than an unforeseen liquidation. The consequence is that the instruments covered are those which include the situation where the issuer's ability to discharge its obligation is restricted, or where the holder needs to perform a certain action to oblige the issuer to commit to the contractual obligation.

IAS provides further guidance, and does so by using preferred shares as a framework for discussion. It should be noted that the theoretical analysis applies to instruments with the same or similar characteristics.

To identify whether a preferred share is a liability or equity, IAS provides the following distinction:

- Instruments mandatorily redeemable, or redeemable at the holder's option.
- Those redeemable only at the issuer's option or not redeemable.

From there on, and as a kind of (attempted) summary for the topic, the mezzanine product group can be further analyzed. In the following table, I have tried to bring together the many positions, opinions, contractual clauses and instruments that are out there, and which are all part of the mezzanine product group and their classification under IFRS rules. As indicated earlier, some of the positions taken are open for discussion within the context of the original criteria provided in IAS 32 (see above). With one notable exception, the classification is based on the instruments' characteristics and term, rather than their position on the balance sheet, or their level of subordination – see Table 9.18.

**Table 9.18**    Accounting classification of hybrid instruments

| (characteristic of) Instrument | Classification |
| --- | --- |
| Step-up loans/bonds (plain vanilla) | Liability |
| PIK loans/bonds (plain vanilla) | Liability |
| HY loans/bonds (plain vanilla) | Liability |
| PP loans/bonds (plain vanilla) | Liability |
| Convertible loans (plain vanilla) | • Before conversion: liability<br>• After conversion: equity |
| Preferred shares | • Mandatorily redeemable or redeemable by holder: liability<br>• Non-mandatorily redeemable or redeemable by issuer or not redeemable: liability in cases of mandatory dividend; otherwise equity<br>• Non-mandatorily redeemable or redeemable by issuer or not redeemable: equity when dividend payment is solely up to the BoD<br>• Cumulative dividend clause or not is irrelevant |
| Warrants | Equity after exercise |
| Perpetual debt repayable only at the issuer's option and option to defer coupon payments | Equity[28] (other perpetual debt: liability) |
| (Silent) partnership stake | Liability in cases where the partner can withdraw the balance standing to their capital account (it is irrelevant that it is only the residual stake in the partnership's assets which can be withdrawn). However, in practice often registered as equity on the partnership's balance sheet |

---

[28] As far as I'm concerned this qualification is up for debate between the issuer and their auditors. Definitely a liability if the coupon payments can't be deferred by the issuer.

| (characteristic of) Instrument | Classification |
| --- | --- |
| Instruments with dividend blocker clause | Equity |
| Perpetual instrument with a step-up clause | Irrelevant. If dividend is mandatory = liability; if dividend is discretionary = equity |
| Instruments characterized by relative subordination | Irrelevant, main conditions apply |
| Linked instruments | *Accessorium sequitur principale* |
| Instruments which include 'change of control,' 'taxation change' or 'regulatory change' clauses | Liability |
| Puttable instruments | Liability unless(**): <br><br> • Narrowly-defined category of puttable instruments **and** <br> • Instrument is most subordinated by reporting entity(*) **or** <br> • Instruments repayable on a pre-determined liquidation |
| Contingent settlement provisions | Liability unless payable **only** upon liquidation, change of control, settlement provision is not genuine (i.e., highly unlikely) |

(*) This is a significant departure from the IAS's standard approach, where the classification of an instrument should be determined only by reference to the contractual terms of that instrument, other than those instruments in issue, i.e., subordination normally does not matter. This departure implies that two firms can classify an identical product differently, if it is one entity's most subordinated instrument, but not the other's. It therefore gives the impression that the IAS standard is looking more for a desired accounting outcome, rather than a clear principle.
(**) IAS 32 classifies a puttable instrument as an equity instrument if it has all of the following features:

• It entitles the holder to a pro-rata share of the entity's net assets in the event of the entity's liquidation. The entity's net assets are those assets which remain after deducting all other claims on its assets. A pro-rata share is determined by:
  – Dividing the entity's net assets on liquidation into units of equal amount.
  – Multiplying that amount by the number of units held by the financial instrument holder.
• The instrument is subordinate to all other classes of instruments. To be in such a class the instrument:
  – Has no priority over other claims to the assets of the entity on liquidation.
  – Does not need to be converted into another instrument before it is in the class of instruments which is subordinate to all other classes.
• All instruments in the subordinated class need to have identical features (all puttable with their repurchase or redemption price calculated in the same way). Subordination is measured at the time of the instrument's classification and is done by calculating the instrument's claim on a liquidation.
• Implicitly, the conditions include that the issuer has no obligation to deliver cash or another financial asset, or to exchange financial assets or liabilities with another entity that are potentially unfavorable to the entity.
• The issuing entity may also not have instruments in place which substantially fix or restrict the residual return to the instrument's holder. That can be instruments:
  – Where total cash flows substantially are based on specific assets of the issuer.
  – Instruments with total cash flows based on a % of revenues (PP loans?).
  – Contracts designed to reward individual employees for services rendered to the entity.
  – Contracts requiring the payment of an insignificant % of profits for services rendered or goods provided.

# 10
# Term Sheets, Inter-creditor Agreements and Debt Restructuring

This chapter, before we're ready to conclude on the topic, will take us into the somewhat more legal side of mezzanine finance. Also known as contractual finance, the pricing of any mezzanine instrument is a function not only of creditworthiness and equity risk which the instrument is exposed to (i.e., subordination), but also how the instruments are legally structured. In that sense, the product group is made up of boilerplate (or master) instruments, which can be further tailored by using a certain set of covenants, thereby reducing or expanding the effective riskiness of the instrument in a particular deal.

An individual review of all products and their term sheets would be extremely academic and would front-load the discussion with facts rather than a perspective on the product group. However, I have opted to include a model contract for each product, which can be reviewed on the individual merits of each of the products, in Appendix 1 of this book.

In this chapter, I will focus more on the contractualized framework of the position of mezzanine instruments, the role of inter-creditor agreements and the position of mezzanine investors in cases of (un)voluntary debt restructuring. By doing so, I will still (try to) review a significant (and most relevant) part of the covenant spectrum, but framed more towards application in certain factual situations, and focused towards the implications of certain choices.

## 10.1 GROUPS OF COVENANTS

Covenants are traditionally categorized into three types, each of which directs the parties into engaging or refraining from a certain action:

- Positive (or affirmative) covenants: these are covenants which require the issuer to take certain actions or guarantee certain outcomes. For example, maintaining certain levels of liquidity, ensuring that insurance is in place or reporting certain financial data every quarter.
- Negative (or restrictive) covenants: these are covenants which restrict the issuer from engaging in certain transactions and/or avoiding the firm ending up in certain (financial) positions. For example, not selling certain strategic assets, engaging in an acquisition or taking on board additional debt above certain thresholds.
- Financial covenants can be positive or negative in nature. Financial covenants are standards for the financial strength and performance of the borrower which serve as protection for both the bank and the borrower.

Covenants can be temporarily or permanently waived by the holder based on either discretionary grounds or objectively pre-determined standards.

The option to restructure the debt portfolio of a company before declaring an official 'breach of covenants' can also be included.

Given the position mezzanine providers are in, the covenants often include a cross-default clause. Cross-defaults are provisions in which, if a borrower with multiple debt obligations defaults on one of their debts, this triggers an automatic default on all other debts held by the same lender (or often all lenders). It is important to note that a cross-default action will also apply to loans which are obtained through subsidiaries, in the event that the parent company defaults on a loan issued by a common lender. At the same time, a default on a debt obligation by the subsidiary can also make any loans issued to the parent company move into default, at the discretion of the lender.

Also, in a cross-default clause it is possible for the lender to exercise discretion and to work something out with the borrower, as the lender often well understands that executing the clause will most likely provide limited effective recourse on the assets (especially from the position of a mezzanine lender). Additionally, the expenses (and potential real economic damage done to the firm) which come with an execution might further hinder any economically sound business activity going forward.

It is useful at this stage to accentuate the difference between 'cross-acceleration' and 'cross-default' provisions. A cross-acceleration clause operates by defaulting a borrower under Agreement A when it defaults under Agreement B and the lender under Agreement B accelerates repayment. A cross-acceleration provision effectively gives the lender under Agreement A the benefit of the default provisions in Agreement B. In contrast to a cross-acceleration, a cross-default clause in Agreement A causes an automatic event of default under that agreement when the borrower defaults under Agreement B, even if the lender under Agreement B does not accelerate repayment.

From a general point of view one could argue that the spectrum of covenants (regardless of whether they are positive or negative in nature) is focused around four anchor concepts:[1]

1. Payout Covenants

    This group is comprised of covenants limiting the borrower's ability to initiate distributions to its shareholders by formally announced dividends, spin-offs, stock repurchases, stock redemptions or otherwise. Payout covenants may limit distributions by the issuer alone, or may limit business group payouts, namely by subsidiaries and affiliates of the issuer.

2. Capital Structure Covenants

    Capital structure covenants restrict the debtor's freedom to finance its business through relatively risky capital structures. This group includes covenants which limit the total debt a debtor may incur, either in a total amount, through assets to liabilities or current assets to current liabilities ratio, and covenants which limit the aggregation of debt through its controlled subsidiaries. In addition, negative pledge clauses are covenants which often curtail the debtor's practical ability to finance itself with additional debt. Negative pledge clauses protect the holders of unsecured debt, while secured debt is complemented by covenants restricting junior liens. By imposing the aforementioned limitations, these covenants effectively design the firm's capital structure.

3. Asset Substitution Covenants

    These covenants limit the firm from engaging in various transactions which may result in substitution of high risk and volatile assets for solid and low risk assets. Such transactions may include asset sales and investments by the borrower firm alone, or through its subsidiaries.

---

[1] See further: David Hahn, 'The roles of acceleration,' Bar Ilan University, Faculty of Law, Working Paper (accessible through www.ssrn.com).

4. Event Risk Covenants

This group includes covenants which make substantial alterations of the firm's risk profile, initiated by the firm or a third party, events of default. Alterations of the firm's risk profile include the acquisition of a certain percentage of the debtor's shares by a third party, a merger or consolidation, a change in the composition of the board of directors, or a repurchase by the borrower of a certain percentage of its own shares. Change of control exacerbates the risk to other creditors when it involves a leveraged acquisition. Event risk covenants may be accompanied by a clause which entitles the creditors to contractual remedies only when they trigger a credit rating decline.

These kinds of covenants (or most of them) can be found (in a slimmed-down version) in traditional loans and senior debt instruments as well. What follows is an analysis of those covenant groups which are specific for unsecured, subordinated debt instruments given the specific position these holders are in.

One of the specific needs for mezzanine holders is to get a better grip on where exactly they will end up, and to stay on the maturity schedule and cash flow waterfall. Covenants can act as risk reducers without being a holy grail for the overall problem of mezzanine lenders being impacted by actions taken by borrowers after signing up for the mezzanine instruments.

Covenants can protect a bond holder from detrimental action by equity owners and preserve the priority of a bond or loan, as well as accelerate a restructuring to preserve or distribute value to creditors. Covenants provide meaningful control over a company's strategy or operations, or act as a safeguard against declining enterprise value. Ultimately, it is the mezzanine provider that is most vulnerable to changes in a firm's risk profile after they signed up to provide mezzanine finance.

Covenants can therefore stabilize and/or improve the risk/reward characteristics of an individual investment. Four structural elements can play a role here:

1. Seniority

The seniority of a bond will determine how a class of creditors will fare (i.e., their priority in receiving any recovery) in the event of a default. A bond's priority can be altered by a number of factors, including:

- Senior versus subordinated status – the contractual priority is listed in an indenture.
- 'OpCo' versus 'HoldCo' issuance level – bonds issued at the operating company (OpCo) are closer to the assets and typically receive recoveries first.
- Security/liens – much like a home mortgage, bond holders receive the benefit of the value of assets specifically supporting a bond issue.
- Subsidiary guarantees – a bond which has guarantees from the issuer's operating subsidiaries receives credit support from the subsidiaries as well as the parent.

Bonds with more senior claims (as defined by one of the factors above) historically have experienced higher recovery rates in the event of default. Certain covenants, including the limitation on indebtedness and liens tests described below, further define one's place in the capital structure and protect it going forward.

2. Maintenance versus incurrence tests

Maintenance and incurrence tests are two categories of covenants which require a borrower to adhere to certain financial metric limits. Maintenance tests, which are typically found in leveraged loans, require that a company maintain compliance with financial metrics in order to avoid defaulting on its debt. A common example of a maintenance test would be a 6.0x maximum debt-to-EBITDA leverage ratio, which if the company exceeded for any reason, would result in a technical default. This contrasts with incurrence tests (which need to be met at specific points or periods in time), which are used in high-yield bond indentures and kick in only when a company incurs additional debt or makes restricted payments to the detriment of bond holders. A company with a 6.0x debt/EBITDA leverage debt incurrence test would violate the covenant if the company actively added debt which caused it to exceed 6.0x leverage, but not if its EBITDA declined and caused its leverage to increase.

3. Definition and fine print

Many basic covenants, such as a leverage limit in the limitation on indebtedness test, contain written exceptions (also known as carve-outs) which can dilute their value to bond holders. An example of this would be a credit facilities carve-out that allows a company to make additional borrowings on its bank line, even when it would be in violation of its headline leverage or coverage-based limitation on indebtedness test. Furthermore, the definitions section in an indenture can allow a company more flexibility (at the bond holders' expense) than an initial reading of a covenant would have suggested. The paragraph-long limitation on liens section in a bond indenture often has pages of permitted liens listed in the definitions section, which vastly increase the risk of structural subordination for bond holders.

4. Early redemptions

Early redemption features can have a material impact on the total return of a bond, depending on a bond's call features. Mezzanine products typically have a non-call period during which a company's option to retire the issue is limited but not impossible. For example, most bonds contain a 'make whole' call feature which allows the company to call bonds during the non-call period at a premium of US Treasuries or otherwise plus 50 bps. Investors are typically very satisfied when a 'make whole' call is made on a bond in their portfolios, because the 'make whole' price is typically well in excess of market prices. An equity clawback call is another matter. Equity clawbacks allow the issuer to refinance a certain amount of the outstanding bonds with proceeds from an equity offering, whether initial or follow-on offerings. A typical clawback would be for up to 35% of the outstanding bond issue at a price equal to par, plus the annual coupon. Investors are less enthusiastic about equity clawback calls, which tend to be at prices below where the market values the security. A recent and rather unfavorable development of issue structures has been the addition of a 10% annual call in some new issues.


## 10.2  REVIEW OF KEY COVENANTS FOR MEZZANINE PRODUCTS[2]

1. Limitation on Indebtedness

The Limitation on Indebtedness covenant, which is also known as a debt incurrence or debt test, is one of the most common high-yield covenants. There is no standardized financial metric for the Limitation on Indebtedness test, but the two most frequently used ratios are leverage (debt/EBITDA) and interest coverage (EBITDA/interest expense).

---

[2] Based on, and see further: Western Asset, 'Introduction to HY Bond Covenants,' June 2011.

A Limitation on Indebtedness covenant restricts an issuer from incremental borrowing beyond a prescribed level. This covenant also typically includes carve-outs which permit additional debt above and beyond the base calculation, including credit facilities, the refinancing of existing debt and miscellaneous needs. This covenant may also contain subtests which limit secured debt, helping preserve a bond's place in the capital structure. Particular focus is normally given to lease commitments, which have an underlying lending contract, but where the future liabilities (partly caused by the IFRS treatment) of repayment are normally not included in the debt ratio analysis or debt/equity assessment.

2. Limitations on Restricted Payments

   The Limitation on Restricted Payments (RP) covenant limits cash outflows, dividends, acquisitions and investments by the company. This covenant helps protect asset coverage for bond holders and limits the power of equity holders. An RP 'basket', from which the company is able to make restricted payments, is typically calculated using either: (a) 50% of net income, or (b) 100% of EBITDA less 1.4x interest expense. Investments in restricted subsidiaries are typically not subject to RPs, allowing the company to invest in its core business without violating covenants. A properly written RP covenant starts with limited restricted-payment capacity at the date of a new bond issue, with capacity increasing over time as the company generates earnings. A tight RP test is frequently a catalyst for bonds to be tendered in acquisition/LBO situations.

3. Limitations on Liens

   The Limitation on Liens covenant restricts a company's ability to secure future debt with company assets. This covenant protects a bond's place in the capital structure and can support recoveries in the event of default. A typical liens test permits a company's existing bank credit facility to be secured, and may also include additional permitted liens capacity that could subordinate a new bond issue. The Limitation on Liens covenant is also typically the one meaningful covenant in investment-grade bonds. In investment-grade indentures, the liens covenant is typically referred to as a negative pledge, which requires that an unsecured bond issue is given security when new secured debt is placed on the balance sheet. Both a careful analysis and understanding of the definitions and carve-outs for the liens test are important, given the potential for unexpected, additional secured debt.

4. Limitations on Asset Sales

   The Limitation on Asset Sales covenant prevents a company from selling assets out from under a bond holder without using the proceeds to either: (a) reinvest in the business or (b) offer to pay back bond holders at par (a 'Net Proceeds Offer'). Asset sales are usually defined as a transaction of material size to the company; proceeds need to represent fair market value of the assets being sold and must be at least 75% cash. Companies typically have 365 days to reinvest the proceeds of an asset sale – making a Net Proceeds Offer a lengthy process for bond holders. This covenant can sometimes be diluted when specific assets are exempted in the indenture from treatment under the Limitation on Asset Sales covenant.

5. Change of Control

   A Change of Control (CoC) covenant allows investors to put (sell) their bonds back to the company at 101% of par value when a specified event has changed the ownership/control of the company. The importance of this covenant typically depends on the trading prices of bonds, as well as the intentions of the new owners (such as pursuing an LBO versus an acquisition by an investment-grade company). Bond issuers have increasingly complicated this historically simple covenant by adding conditions, including carve-outs for 'permitted holders' (current owners or logical acquirers). Some CoC covenants are triggered only by a rating decline, while others are not triggered if a public company acquires the high-yield firm. As a result, a close reading of an indenture's definition of CoC can be important.

6. Reports

The Reports covenant ensures the bond holder's access to financial information from the company. The Reports covenant is particularly important for holders of '144A' bonds which will not be registered by the SEC or required to file financials on the EDGAR system (or similar systems of registration in other parts of the world). For 144A issuers, the Reports covenant will often require the filing of SEC-like financial reports. The Reports covenant also specifies the amount of time a company has to file its financial reports, typically set at 45 days after the end of a quarterly period, and 90 days after the end of an annual period.

7. Mergers

The Mergers covenant prevents a company from merging with another company unless: (a) the company is the surviving corporation out of the merger and continues to observe the indenture, or (b) the acquirer delivers a supplemental indenture to the trustee expressly assuming the old bonds and terms of the old indenture. In addition, the combined company must not be in default and must be able to incur US$1 of additional debt under the debt incurrence test. These requirements effectively prevent a company from avoiding its obligations to bond holders by selling out to another company.

8. Events of Default

The Events of Default covenant lists the conditions under which the company is in violation of the terms of its requirements. Events of default can include bankruptcy of the company or its material subsidiaries, not paying principal or interest as scheduled, not filing financial statements on time, or a legal judgment against the company in excess of a certain amount. Events of default typically have grace periods which allow the company an amount of time to cure the event of default, after which an actual default occurs and the bonds are immediately due. The typical grace period for missed timely payments of principal and interest is 30 days, and 60–90 days for other covenants. Trustees are responsible for policing bond covenants and declaring events of default; however, a group representing more than 25% of bond holders can typically declare a default as well.

## 10.3  OTHER COVENANTS

In addition to the key high-yield covenants described above, there are many more which are used less frequently and may or may not be critical when considering an investment. These other covenants include:

- Covenant Suspension/Fall-Away – companies with aspirations of investment-grade ratings may include this covenant, which suspends or removes most financial covenants when the company is rated investment-grade;
- Amendment/Consent Solicitation – most indentures specify that an affirmative vote of greater than 50% of bond holders by value is sufficient to amend the indenture or waive an event of default;
- Inter-creditor Agreement – for secured bonds from a corporation which has another class of secured debt outstanding (e.g., first lien bank loan and first lien bond), the Inter-creditor

Agreement section discusses the priority of payments in a default scenario. Note that secured bonds are typically at a disadvantage to bank loans in terms of collateral control and even priority of payment;

- Anti-layering – second lien secured bonds often have explicit or implicit (via incurrence/liens tests) anti-layering language which limits the ability of the company to place new debt in between the bonds and a standard first lien bank facility or bond;
- Limitation on Dividends of Restricted Subsidiaries – this covenant prevents restricted subsidiaries from encumbering their assets and/or cash flows outside of the ways envisioned in the indenture, in order to preserve value for the parent/issuer;
- Designation of Unrestricted Subsidiaries – companies can 'un-restrict' their subsidiaries by treating the transfer of the subsidiary's value as a restricted payment, subject to the size of the basket;
- Future Subsidiary Guarantees – this covenant ensures that subsidiary guarantors are managed in the spirit of the original indenture, with new subsidiaries adding their guarantees to the indenture and sold/unrestricted subsidiaries dropping their guarantees;
- Transactions With Affiliates – this covenant prevents a company from transferring value into affiliated companies above a certain size unless the transaction is 'arm's length' or is counted as a restricted payment/permitted investment.

## 10.4  CASE STUDIES: THE GOOD, THE BAD AND THE UGLY[3]

The following three case studies illustrate the potential benefits and risks which covenants can represent for mezzanine investors.

### 10.4.1  Good covenants

In November 2010, a high-yield document management services company brought an inaugural high-yield bond issue with a 10.5% coupon and a 2016 maturity.

**Key Covenants:**
- A conservative 4.5x maximum leverage Limitation on Indebtedness covenant that will limit the company's ability to issue much more additional debt, given its current leverage ratio of nearly 4.0x.
- Carve-outs to the Limitation on Indebtedness covenant were limited to approximately US$105 million, with the credit facility carve-out reduced to only US$50 million if leverage exceeds 4.5x.
- Permitted liens in the Limitation on Liens covenant were restricted to only credit facility borrowings and a US$5 million miscellaneous carve-out, preventing the company from securing excessive amounts of future debt ahead of the unsecured notes.
- Restricted-payment capacity in the Limitation on Restricted Payments covenant shrinks by US$15 million when leverage exceeds 3.0x.

---

[3] Ibid. note 2.

This robust covenant package will protect bond holders in a downside scenario from a combination of excessive leverage, subordination from new secured debt and depletion of asset coverage via restricted payments.

## 10.4.2  Bad covenants

In March 2011, a high-yield auto supplier which had recently emerged from bankruptcy came to market with a US$500 million senior note issue which had a 6.75% coupon and a 2019 maturity. In addition to the cyclical nature of the auto industry and the company's historical financial problems, the new deal included a number of covenant features which were unattractive.

**Key Covenants:**
- Subsidiary guarantees on only approximately 20% of the company's assets, making the new bonds effectively subordinate to any debt at subsidiaries representing the bulk of the company's value (see this chapter's earlier section on seniority).
- Over US$2 billion of additional secured debt is permitted under the Limitation on Liens covenant, which (if issued) could deeply subordinate the new unsecured bonds.
- The Limitation on Restricted Payments covenant would allow nearly US$2 billion of dividends to shareholders under a permissive leverage-based limit and a US$400 million miscellaneous carve-out.
- The bonds came with a bond holder-unfriendly eight-year maturity, with a three-year call structure and an unusual 10% annual call at 103% of par.

Especially in the context of the company's 2009–2010 bankruptcy, this weak covenant package represented an excessive amount of risk for new bond holders and was not compensated for by the anemic 6.75% coupon (40 bps less than the high-yield market at the time).

## 10.4.3  Ugly covenants

An investment-grade newspaper company was taken private in a leveraged buy-out (LBO) in 2007. Its bond indenture contained a 'negative pledge' (see this chapter's earlier section on Limitation on Liens) which would typically prevent its formerly investment-grade notes from being subordinated behind secured debt. However, the indenture did not provide subsidiary guarantees, which then allowed the new owners of the newspaper company to add structurally senior bank debt at the subsidiary level, effectively deeply subordinating the formerly investment-grade bonds. Contrast the bond holder experience in this case with that of bond holders of an investment-grade Spanish-language television network that also LBO'd in 2007. Its bond indenture also contained a negative pledge clause. However, the television network bond indenture also contained subsidiary guarantees. As a result of this difference, the newspaper company's formerly investment-grade bonds traded as low as two cents on the dollar in 2009, while the Spanish-language television network's formerly investment-grade bonds were retired at 100 cents on the dollar.

A similar situation occurred for legacy investment-grade bonds of a large electric utility when the company was taken private in 2007. A negative pledge in the investment-grade bonds' indenture was written to include only 'capital stock' (but not assets) of subsidiaries, which allowed the company to secure huge amounts of new debt at its subsidiaries. Furthermore, a lack of subsidiary guarantees in the investment-grade indenture allowed the company to place structurally senior guaranteed debt at the parent level as well. The poorly written fine print in the electric utility's legacy investment-grade bonds ultimately cost bond holders dearly, with some bonds trading as low as 50 cents on the dollar today.

## 10.5 A COMPARISON OF DEBT ASSET CLASSES[4]

Bond covenants become more relevant the more a company is levered, and therefore prone to externalities and macro-economic or other business shocks. Therefore, intensity and priority of covenants will differ depending on the product. See Table 10.1 for a review of a number of mezzanine products in this respect, relative to investment-grade products.

Covenants are a key component of a bond's risk profile. A company's fundamentals, credit position and valuation will paint the overall picture, but covenants can alter a bond's risk profile significantly in a good or bad way, and could make the investment either attractive or completely un-investible, despite the issuers' fundamentals referring to the economic and financial fundamentals of the issuer. It points at the fact that a good deal for both parties involved will most likely lead to a negotiated deal, rather than a boilerplate model. Ultimately, when setting a required rate of return for investors, covenant quality will be taken into account. On the other hand, good covenants alone aren't enough to justify buying a high-yield bond deal.

### 10.5.1 Covenants which relate specifically to liquidity events in private market transactions

One of the issues with the mezzanine product group is that some of its products will make you end up with effective equity, either directly or after conversion. That will be the case for:

- Convertible loans
- Convertible preferred shares
- Warrants.

That in itself is not a problem, unless you end up with equity in a private company and low liquidity in the market for those shares. Quite often, an extra complication is that after conversion, the effective shareholding is often below the minority protection levels included in corporate laws. It is an unholy position to be in, and one can easily be subject to a smoke-out by the majority owners, often at unattractive valuations.

Therefore, protective covenants are often put in place to exit the arrangement one way or the other. The effective design of these covenants is subject to negotiations. Hereafter follows an overview of some of the techniques used:

- **Put/call options:** put and call options allow the buyer and the seller to buy or sell their share back, either at market conditions at the moment the transaction effectively takes place, or at pre-determined conditions or valuations (IRR-driven). The call normally front-runs the put time-wise. Other criteria for consideration are the time or period for the options to become

---

[4] Ibid. note 2.

**Table 10.1**  Comparison of bond/loan covenants

|  | Investment grade | Leveraged loan | High-yield loan |
| --- | --- | --- | --- |
| **Security** | Unsecured | First lien | Typically unsecured |
| **Subsidiary guarantee** | Typically no | Yes | Usually |
| **Typical maturities** | 5–30 years | 7 years | 5–10 years |
| **Callable** | Non-callable | Callable at par | Callable at par + ½ coupon |
| **Financial covenants** | None | Maintenance | Incurrence |
| **Other covenants** | Negative pledge | RP, liens, asset sales, mergers etc. | RP, liens, asset sales, mergers etc. |
| **Public filings** | Yes | No | Only if 'registered securities' |

effective. Can also be used for situations where the lender receives the shares after conversion (warrants, convertible loans).

- **Step-up dividends:** if a preferred stock instrument has no maturity or is not redeemable, the question becomes: what will happen if the company cannot or does not want to facilitate a buy back? Often it is agreed that the company can buy back or the lender can sell back the securities. However, what about cases where the company cannot buy back (no capital available, also not by the underlying shareholders at a private level), or doesn't want to facilitate buy back because it considers the initially agreed valuations/or buy-back conditions now unattractive? In that case, a step-up dividend can be considered for preferred shares after a certain period beyond the initially intended investment period. The step-up dividend will increase, and thereby achieve levels on par or above the intended or actual return on equity of the existing shareholders who cannot or don't want to buy-out under certain conditions. That might sound somewhat like bullying, but sometimes a little endorsement will work miracles to unlock an illiquid situation. There is no shareholder group which will allow a permanent erosion of equity returns by preference shareholders. That will definitely be the case if the instrument is cumulative.

- **Equity-to-debt swap:** the increased step-up dividend solution is not possible when owning 'normal' common stock. Therefore, a somewhat more dramatic solution is needed. An automatic equity-to-debt swap can be considered at a fixed point in time after the initially intended investment period. It will automatically convert the equity positions into a debt position. The conversion will happen at either prevailing market conditions at the mentioned swap date, or pre-determined conditions. Which debt instrument the equity will be converted into, its maturity, its interest rate etc. need to be orchestrated. The existing intercreditor agreement will indicate if approval from existing (senior) lenders for the swap is needed, and what will happen if certain covenants are breached because of the transaction.

- **Ring-fencing assets for liquidation:** although this is not preferred, indicating up-front the pool of lien-free assets (at the firm or other assets the shareholders control) which can be liquidated to finance the buy back of the shares can be considered.

- **Drag-along rights:** drag-along rights are not a solution in themselves, but allow the minority shareholder to find a solution and drag the majority shareholder in an exit organized by the (in this case) investor/minority shareholder under the terms and conditions agreed with the minority shareholder. It is somewhat of a nuclear option, and should be executed as a last resort technique.

## 10.5.2  Mezzanine providers and inter-creditor agreements

Each time an organization uses multiple providers of debt financing or the same providers at different points in time to finance its activities, the question arises of how potential conflicts of interest between those providers, or tranches of finance from the same providers, will be dealt with. An inter-creditor agreement is put in place to do exactly that. Obviously, the content is geared towards moments of distress and/or (voluntary or mandatory) reorganization of the firm's debt structure.

The agreement spells out aspects of their relationship to each other and to the borrower so that, in the event a problem emerges, there will be ground rules in place to handle the situation. The specifics of an inter-creditor agreement vary depending on the borrower, the type of debt, and other factors, such as the presence of cosigners.

Inter-creditor agreements provide information about lien positions and security interests. They also discuss the liabilities and rights of the parties involved. For example, a bank might indicate that it has a security interest in a vehicle, which means that another creditor cannot confiscate and sell the vehicle to satisfy a debt, because the bank has the first right to do so. Likewise, an inter-creditor agreement might provide information about liens on other property, such as real estate.

Creditors are not all created equal. An inter-creditor agreement spells out the differences between different creditors and their rights in the event of a bankruptcy or default. The agreement may also include a buy-out clause, which gives one creditor the option of buying out another creditor's debt, usually in response to a trigger event such as a bankruptcy filing.

Creditors can make arrangements of this nature without the consent of the borrower, just as they are free to sell debt without asking the borrower. Borrowers may be notified after the fact about sales of debt and other agreements which are made in regards to their debt. It is advisable to read notices sent from creditors with care in case they contain important information, such as changes in repayment terms or notifications about changes to the lending agreement. Debtors do have the right to contest changes made to their lending agreements, although if they do, the creditor may refuse to extend additional credit, or may demand payment in full.

Common inter-creditor provisions are shown in Table 10.2:

**Table 10.2**   Key inter-creditor provisions

| Primary provision | Comments |
| --- | --- |
| Mutual acknowledgment of, and agreement not to challenge, liens and relative lien priorities | • Relative priority among parties effective even if senior lien or claim is effectively challenged by debtor or third parties<br>• Turnover provisions for non-complying recoveries by second lien creditors |
| Second lien creditors are subject to a remedies standstill notwithstanding second lien defaults | • Standstill may be limited to a specified time period |
| Second lien creditors are subject to payment blockage if there are first lien defaults | • Default, event of default and/or acceleration of first lien debt may be a trigger for payment blockage<br>• Payment blockage may be limited to a specified time period |

(*continued*)

**Table 10.2** (*continued*)

| Primary provision | Comments |
| --- | --- |
| Second lien creditors consent to possible future changes in first lien documents | • Amount of covered first lien debt may be capped<br>• Pricing and maturity changes may be subject to restrictions<br>• Second lien creditors agree not to change the second lien documents |
| Other consents and waivers by second lien creditors in favor of first lien creditors | • Consent to asset sales approved by first lien creditors, and release of second liens on collateral released by first lien creditors<br>• Waive marshaling rights, claims relating to exercise of remedies and subrogation rights (until first lien claims have been paid in full) |
| Option in favor of second lien creditors to buy first lien debt at par | • Triggered by remedies standstill/payment blockage<br>• Deadlines to exercise and close option |
| Post-bankruptcy provisions | • Pre-bankruptcy provisions remain applicable<br>• Second lien creditors consent to DIP financing and priming lien by first lien creditors (or to which first lien creditors have consented)<br>• Second lien creditors consent to use of cash collateral to which first lien creditors have consented<br>• Second lien creditors consent to all adequate protection afforded to first lien creditors<br>• Second lien creditors waive adequate protection rights, except rights to adequate protection liens junior to first lien creditors' adequate protection liens<br>• Second lien creditors consent to exercise of remedies by first lien creditors, and agree not to exercise their own remedies<br>• First lien is reinstated with respect to any claim arising from an avoidance recovery<br>• Second lien creditors agree that first lien creditors control plan votes on second lien claims |

It is fair to state, in general terms, that the position of the mezzanine provider within the context of an inter-creditor agreement is often grim, partly due to the nature of being subordinated and unsecured, partly because senior lenders, especially ever since the 2008 crisis, have been insisting on clear subordination of mezzanine providers, to secure their positioning in the cash flow waterfall.

Another reason is that, since inter-creditor agreements are mostly used in cases of distress or more formalized in cases of bankruptcy/liquidation proceedings, the very nature of being unsecured and subordinated translates into being unlimitedly pushed back in the cash flow waterfall in favor of advisory and bankruptcy proceedings-related fees, senior and junior lenders stepping in with super-priority to refinance the firm in a 'survivable' way etc. The case study at the end of this chapter provides further food for thought in this respect. That is why mezzanine lenders often step in during bankruptcy proceedings with additional 'rescue' finance, i.e., to secure (or even improve) their CF waterfall position relative to the situation without them stepping in, or even better than that, prior to going into bankruptcy proceedings.

1. **Bankruptcy proceedings:** it should be clear that, within the context of an inter-creditor agreement, senior lenders will try to demand all control in the case of the debtor's bankruptcy, thereby compromising the mezzanine lenders' position. Mezzanine lenders should therefore aim to at least negotiate provisions of the inter-creditor agreement which address the right to seek adequate protection without the senior lender's consent, the right to object to the senior lender's cash collateral arrangement on grounds other than adequate protection, the right to object to a senior lender's request for relief from an automatic stay, and rights (including the right to object) with respect to a sale of the collateral and to vote on a plan.

2. **Foreclosures:** the same line of reasoning is pretty much valid with respect to foreclosures. Senior lenders will limit the ability of mezzanine lenders to interfere in the process, although bankruptcy and foreclosure proceedings are two separate and distinct proceedings. Negotiations here should aim to preserve the mezzanine lender's right to challenge the commercial reasonableness of a sale of collateral, allow it to submit a credit bid on a sale of collateral, and clarify its ability to keep informed of the foreclosure process.

3. **Payment blockage:** although payment blockages are commonly requested by senior lenders, mezzanine providers should negotiate appropriate limits on the scope of such payment blockages. Common restrictions include imposing time limits (90 to 180 days is common), limiting payment blockages to material defaults, requiring notice of the triggering event, limiting the number of payment blockages that may be imposed in a specific period, and allowing the mezzanine lender to recover catch-up payments upon the expiration of the blockage period.

4. **Standstill period:** inter-creditor agreements commonly require the mezzanine lender to forbear from exercising its rights and remedies for a certain period of time following the occurrence and continuance of a default. Because the senior lender has more protection from the collateral, it can often afford the debtor more time to right the ship, even if collateral value is deteriorating. Mezzanine lenders, on the other hand, typically have limited or no cushion on the collateral value, and may otherwise choose to foreclose and assert other rights and remedies immediately upon a default. For this reason, mezzanine lenders should ensure there are limits on the standstill period clearly set forth in the inter-creditor agreement.

5. **Ability of lenders to amend loan documents:** mezzanine lenders should negotiate limits on the ability of the senior lender to amend the terms of the senior loan documents. Common limits include placing a cap on the total amount of senior debt subject to the senior lien or, alternatively, caps on each component of the senior credit facility, as well as limits on the senior lender's ability to extend the maturity date of the senior loans, increase the interest rate or make the covenants more onerous.

6. **Clawback clauses:** inter-creditor agreements generally require the mezzanine lender to turn over to the senior lender any payments made to it during a blockage period. However, a court may require that the original payment by the borrower to the mezzanine lender (i.e., the one turned over to the senior lender) be disgorged for preference or fraudulent conveyance reasons. In that circumstance, it is important to provide, in the inter-creditor agreement, that the senior lender must reimburse the mezzanine lender for the disgorged payment which was turned over to the senior lender.

7. **Subrogation rights:** senior lenders' proposed inter-creditor agreements frequently contain a waiver of the mezzanine lender's subrogation rights. Subrogation rights allow a mezzanine lender to step into the shoes of the senior lender after the senior lender has been paid

off. Changes to federal bankruptcy law have made it clear that a mezzanine lender's right of subrogation has no impact on the senior lender. Accordingly, a senior lender has no valid reason to demand that the mezzanine lender waive its subrogation rights.

8. **Right to buy out senior lenders:** one of the ways a mezzanine lender can protect itself is to ensure that it has the right to buy out the senior debt at par under certain circumstances. Without a provision in the inter-creditor agreement, a mezzanine lender has no inherent right to do this, and there may be situations, such as a declining pool of collateral, which would make it advantageous for a mezzanine lender to step into the shoes of a senior lender and control a liquidation process.

### 10.5.3 Lien subordination and inter-creditor agreements[5]

Second lien financing instruments have become attractive financing tools over the last decade. Second lien financing offers borrowers an additional source of capital that generally has lower interest rates, and therefore substantially reduced cash outflows for debt service, than with the payment subordinated and unsecured alternatives. The lower coupon on second lien financings, as compared to unsecured mezzanine financing generally, reflects the parties' assumption that the second lien creditors would obtain some value from their liens based on valuation of the collateral base at closing. Second lien lenders also assume that they would not be in the same position as unsecured, payment subordinated mezzanine debt, though the inter-creditor agreements initially prevalent in the market have not always supported that assumption. First lien lenders want to ensure that they have, for at least some defined period of time, exclusive rights to manage the common collateral and any foreclosure sale, and the use and disposition of common collateral, as well as the exercise of certain other material secured creditor rights during a bankruptcy proceeding. Second lien lenders have often sought backstop protection, such as a purchase option to acquire the first lien debt at par, though many purchase options in inter-creditor agreements do not work from a practical standpoint. Strangely, very few inter-creditor agreements provide the second lien lenders with the right to disclaim the lien entirely, terminate the inter-creditor agreement, or eliminate the waivers of rights contained in the inter-creditor agreement.

### 10.5.4 A quick reminder of the distinction between lien and payment subordination

Lien subordination involves two senior creditors with security interests in the same collateral, one of which has lien priority over the other. To the extent of any value derived from the collateral (e.g., its liquidation proceeds upon a sale), the senior lien lender is repaid first from collateral proceeds, and the junior lien lender collects only from any remaining collateral value. If the collateral proceeds are insufficient to repay the senior lender in full, then both the senior lien and junior lien lenders, and all other unsecured senior creditors, rank equally in their right to repayment of their remaining debt from the borrower's other assets or resources.

By contrast, in payment subordination, the senior lender enjoys the right to be paid first from all assets of the borrower or any applicable guarantor, whether or not they constitute

---

[5] See further: Robert L. Cunningham and Yair Y. Galil, 'Lien Subordination and Intercreditor Agreements' (May 2009) *The Review of Banking and Financial Services* **25**(5).

collateral security for the senior or subordinated lenders. Because payment subordination depends only on the amount owed, and not on the value of any particular collateral, it is a more fundamental form of subordination and is generally more advantageous to a senior lender.

In a second lien financing, the lien subordination is effected contractually by means of an inter-creditor agreement between the first lien and the second lien creditors or their representatives. Although the first lien creditors will often also insist on timing the filing of perfection documents, so as to ensure that they are first to perfect and thus enjoy statutory first-in-time priority, this serves merely as a backstop; the inter-creditor agreement establishes the lien priority by agreement of the parties, and generally explicitly overrides the statutory result notwithstanding the timing of perfection of the two sets of creditors' liens. In addition, the inter-creditor agreement establishes multiple rights and obligations, and waivers of rights, among the creditors beyond those that would result from a simple statutory priority, and will often fundamentally and adversely affect rights which the second lien lenders would have as unsecured creditors in a bankruptcy proceeding. These provisions are generally intended to prevent the second lien creditors from interfering with the first lien creditors' pursuit of remedies against the common collateral, and from exercising certain rights in a borrower's bankruptcy proceeding which could adversely affect the lien priority of, or the value of the collateral to, the first lien lender. Thus, the second lien is said to be 'silent' to a greater or lesser degree.

The drafting of inter-creditor agreements governing lien subordination was initially based upon the inter-creditor and subordination agreements used in a payment subordination context. Often, these agreements carried over several payment subordination concepts which may not be appropriate to pure lien subordination, resulting in a substantial erosion of what many experts would consider to be appropriate rights of second lien lenders.

More recently, the ABA Model Intercreditor Agreement Task Force has been developing a model first lien/second lien inter-creditor agreement[6] which brings into focus a number of issues between first and second lien lenders that have often been ignored in the past.

According to Cunningham and Yalil there are four critical themes to the application of an inter-creditor agreement in cases of lien subordination: (1) 'absolute' priority of security interests; (2) composition of first lien obligations; (3) cap on first lien obligations; and (4) relative enforcement rights in the collateral.

1. 'Absolute' priority of security interests:

   The typical first lien/second lien inter-creditor agreement is intended to effect a 'pure' lien subordination, in which the second lien lender does not subordinate its debt claim, but only its lien on certain specified assets in which both the first and second lien lenders have a security interest (Common Collateral). Both parties are intended to have valid, perfected liens on the Common Collateral, the priority of the first lien lenders' liens is intended to be absolute, regardless of the timing or manner of perfection, and once the value of the Common Collateral is exhausted upon liquidation, assuming a deficiency in recovery by the first lien lenders, both the first lien and the second lien lenders typically become senior unsecured creditors, ranking equally in rights to payment from the debtor's remaining assets, together with all other senior unsecured creditors.

   Often, the question arises as to whether the definition of Common Collateral, as is often the case with definitions of core terms, raises a conceptual question: does Common Collateral include all assets in which the security documents of the first lien lender purport to

---

[6] Which can be found in Appendix 2.

create a lien, whether or not perfected or valid? Alternatively, is it limited to the assets in which the first lien lender and the second lien lender each have a valid, perfected lien at the time of determination? It comes down to an absolute versus relative approach.[7] Let's look at an example for both methods:[8]

## EXAMPLE 1

Assume that a borrower has US$110 million of asset value upon liquidation, all of which assets are intended to constitute Common Collateral, and that the borrower has US$50 million of first lien debt, US$50 million of second lien debt and US$50 million of additional unsecured creditors.

*Full perfection of all liens.* In this example, consistent with the expectations of the parties, the first lien lenders and the second lien lenders would each recover 100% of their secured claims, leaving US$10 million to satisfy the claims of unsecured creditors.

*Perfection of second liens; non-perfection of first liens.* In this example, under the first lien relative priority approach, the first lien lenders' liens would be avoided and the second lien lenders, as a matter of law, would have the only secured claims and would ordinarily be entitled to a full recovery, leaving the unsecured first lien creditors to share recovery of 60% of their claims with the other unsecured creditors. However, under the first lien absolute priority approach, the second lien lenders would receive a recovery of US$50 million and would be required, under the terms of the inter-creditor agreement, to turn over that entire recovery to the unsecured first lien lenders. This would mean they would receive by subrogation an unsecured claim in bankruptcy entitling them to a recovery of only 60% of their claim in subrogation, in lieu of the 100% recovery they would have had if the first lien creditors had maintained perfection of their liens. The second lien lenders, as effective insurers of the first lien's validity, are victims of the first lien lenders' negligence. It is important to note that in this example, had the second lien lenders been unsecured lenders not subject to an inter-creditor agreement, they would have recovered 73.33% of their unsecured claim, a far better recovery than they receive as secured creditors under the first lien absolute priority approach.

## EXAMPLE 2

Assume that a borrower has only US$75 million of asset value upon liquidation, all of which assets are intended to constitute Common Collateral, and that the borrower has US$50 million of first lien debt, US$50 million of second lien debt, and US$50 million of additional unsecured creditors.

*Full perfection of all liens.* In this example, consistent with the expectations of the parties, the first lien lenders would recover 100% of their secured claims and the second lien lenders would recover 50% of their secured claims, leaving no assets to satisfy the unsecured claims of the second lien lenders and the other unsecured creditors.

---

[7] For further analysis, see article mentioned in note 5.

[8] Ibid. note 5.

*Perfection of second liens; non-perfection of first liens.* In this example, under the first lien relative priority approach, the first lien lenders' liens would be avoided and the second lien lenders, as a matter of law, would have the only secured claims and would ordinarily be entitled to a full recovery, leaving the unsecured first lien creditors to share recovery of 25% of their claims with the other unsecured creditors. However, under the first lien absolute priority approach, the second lien lenders would receive a recovery of US$50 million and would be required, under the terms of the inter-creditor agreement, to turn over that entire recovery to the unsecured first lien lenders. This would mean they would receive by subrogation an unsecured claim in bankruptcy entitling them to a recovery of only 25% of their claim in subrogation, in lieu of the 50% recovery they would have had if the first lien creditors had maintained perfection of their liens. The second lien lenders, as effective insurers of the first lien validity, are again victims of the first lien lenders' negligence. Again, it is important to note that in this example, had the second lien lenders been unsecured lenders not subject to an inter-creditor agreement, they would have recovered 50% of their unsecured claim.

A reasonable argument can be made that the first lien relative priority approach results in a windfall to the second lien lenders in Example 2 above, in that they would recover more than they would have if the first lien lenders had perfected their liens as anticipated.

Limiting the Common Collateral to assets in which the first lien creditors and second lien creditors both have valid, perfected, unavoidable liens, or alternatively restricting the relative priorities provision to the first lien creditors' valid, perfected, and unavoidable liens, raises a further question: What courses of action are available to the second lien creditors if the first lien creditors' liens are not valid, perfected, and unavoidable? Most inter-creditor agreements provide that the parties will not challenge each other's liens and priority. However, first lien creditors will react negatively to an agreement which permits the second lien creditors to attack the first priority liens without limit. On the other hand, the first lien relative priority approach inherently requires some methodology for a legal determination of whether assets are or are not included in the Common Collateral pool (to which the lien subordination applies), and therefore whether the first lien creditors' lien on the assets in question is invalid or unperfected.

One possible resolution to this conundrum allows the second lien creditors to challenge lien priorities as a shield but not as a sword, i.e., as a defense against a breach of contract claim brought by the first lien creditor.

2. Composition of first lien obligations:

Given their lien subordinated position, second lien creditors' recovery prospects may decrease materially if there is any increase in the amount of first lien obligations secured by the Common Collateral. Accordingly, second lien creditors typically insist on defining explicitly the types of first lien obligations that may have the benefit of the inter-creditor agreement's lien subordination provisions – and the types that will not.[9] Often, inter-creditor agreements distinguish between a bankruptcy situation and non-distress situations.

---

[9] For an overview of assets typically in-/excluded in inter-creditor agreements, see the article mentioned in note 5.

3. Cap on first lien obligations:

Second lien creditors – after negotiating the composition of the first lien obligations which will enjoy the benefits of the inter-creditor agreement's subordination provisions – typically negotiate a cap on the overall principal amount thereof. For a variety of reasons, beyond the scope of this book, the setting of this cap is relatively complicated.

The tension can be described as follows: first lien creditors will typically insist that various accumulations of interest, fees, costs, indemnities and other miscellaneous amounts payable under the terms of the first lien facility, as well as items such as hedging and cash management obligations, not be subject to the cap. The second lien lenders will insist on limiting the interest, fees, expenses and other amounts included in the first lien obligations cap to those items which relate to principal amounts included in the first lien obligations, and on an overall cap on interest rate and fee increases under the first lien documents. They will often also allow unlimited cash management obligations.

Once the treatment of these issues is agreed, the creditors need to determine the size of the cap. It is generally in the interests of the second lien creditors to agree to some additional debt capacity under the cap, since the first lien creditors will often be the best (cheapest and quickest) source of additional liquidity in times of need. A typical inter-creditor agreement will provide for a 'cushion' of 10–15% of the initial principal amount in a non-bankruptcy context, perhaps with an additional cushion of 10–15% to provide priming DIP financing if insolvency proceedings have commenced.[10]

Once the composition and amount of the cap are agreed, the parties still need to determine how to treat any amounts in excess of the cap. The goal of the second lien lenders should be to subordinate this to the lien securing the second lien obligations, the lien securing any principal amount of first lien obligations in excess of the cap, together with interest and other amounts ancillary thereto, by assigning third lien priority to all first lien obligations in excess of the cap. This approach most closely aligns with the parties' expectations and assigns a specific waterfall of priorities.

The first lien creditors will generally want to impose an analogous cap on the second lien obligations, so that the debt to which their third priority 'tail' is lien subordinated is capped at a known amount.

4. Relative enforcement rights in the collateral:

- ***Non-interference with enforcement by first lien creditors***. In line with the basic understanding that, subject to minimal limitations, the first lien creditors have exclusive rights to control the maintenance and disposition of the Common Collateral, the second lien

---

[10] Often the setting of the cap is reflected in a formula which reads as follows: '"First Lien Cap" means [(A)% of [(B) – (C) – (D)]] plus (E), where (A) is ___%, (B) is $[_____], (C) is the amount of all repayments and prepayments of principal applied to any term loans constituting First Lien Obligations, (D) is the amount of all repayments and prepayments of any revolving loans or reimbursement of drawings under letters of credit constituting First Lien Obligations, to the extent accompanied by a corresponding permanent reduction of commitments under the applicable revolving facility or letter of credit commitment amount (excluding reductions in sub-facility commitments not accompanied by a corresponding permanent reduction in the revolving facility or letter of credit commitment amount and reductions under (A) and (B) as a result of a Refinancing), [and (E) is an amount equal to all Second Lien adequate protection payments if and to the extent paid from any DIP Financing or Proceeds of Collateral.] [In the event of an Insolvency Proceeding, the First Lien Cap shall be increased by $_____.]'

creditors normally agree not to enjoin or otherwise interfere with the first lien creditors' exercise of their remedies against the Common Collateral.

- **Standstill on second lien enforcement.** In addition to agreeing not to challenge Common Collateral maintenance and enforcement actions by the first lien creditors, the second lien creditors are usually barred for some period of time (standstill period) from taking enforcement action of their own against the Common Collateral in response to a default under the second lien credit facility.
- While the second lien creditors normally are subject to an enforcement standstill with regard to their remedies against the Common Collateral, they will usually seek to retain as many of their unsecured creditors' remedies against the borrower and any guarantors as possible. The typical argument made by second lien creditors in this regard is that they should not, by extending credit as a second lien lender, be placed in a worse position than an unsecured lender.

Among the unsecured creditors' remedies which the second lien creditors insist on retaining are the right to accelerate their loan on default; the right to demand payment from the borrower or any guarantor; the right to commence litigation and obtain a judgment against the borrower or any guarantor; and the right to commence an involuntary bankruptcy proceeding against the borrower or any guarantor. Nevertheless, if the second lien creditors are awarded a judgment lien against any of the Common Collateral in response to their exercise of unsecured creditors' remedies, that judgment lien normally will be subject to the enforcement standstill relating to the Common Collateral.

In a bankruptcy context, the second lien creditors' desire to retain and exercise their unsecured creditors' remedies usually results in intense negotiations, as the first lien creditors will not want to leave the second lien creditors with rights and remedies which could encumber the first lien creditors' control over the Common Collateral. The issues which arise between the first lien and second lien lenders in bankruptcy proceedings against the borrower are numerous and complex, and a full discussion of those issues is beyond the scope of this book.

There are a number of particularities with respect to mezzanine loan and inter-creditor agreements. The ABA model inter-creditor agreement as can be found in Appendix 2[11] to this book therefore needs to be treated as a starting point rather than anything else. It is necessary to tweak the provisions, and often engaging in hefty negotiations between senior and mezzanine lenders is the only solution to model the agreement in line with the deal's particular risks, positioning the mezzanine group or individual provider in such a way that the risk/reward trade is geared positively, and the downside risk is minimized given the specific risk mezzanine lenders incur in a specific deal. The following box provides some specific pointers with respect to some of the Achilles' heels of mezzanine lenders and inter-creditor agreements within the context of real estate deals. Although most of them are geared towards the specifics of a real estate deal, some elements have relevance beyond the real estate sector.

---

[11] The first lien/second lien ICA was drafted by the American Bar Association and published in 2010. Further reporting can be found in: Committee on Commercial Finance, ABA Section of Business Law 'Report of the Model First Lien/Second Lien Intercreditor Agreement Task Force' (May 2010) *The Business Lawyer* **65**:809 and further.

## REAL ESTATE, MEZZANINE LOANS AND
## INTER-CREDITOR AGREEMENTS[12]

In general terms, mezzanine lenders may feel that they do not have leverage to improve the terms of their inter-creditor agreements with senior lenders. Because senior lenders customarily make loans only up to a certain percentage of the property's total value, known as the loan-to-value ratio, mezzanine loans offer an additional source of financing for acquiring, developing or redeveloping various projects. Over the years, the portion of a project's total value which senior lenders are willing to lend has risen at the top of the market to often 80–85%, before dropping back to 70% and often less. Also due to the fact that the loan-to-value ratio has more and more been replaced by a loan-to-cost formula, the portion of senior debt has fallen back even more. Mezzanine providers therefore typically account for about 10–20% of total funding. Additionally, senior lenders generally look for a debt service coverage ratio (i.e., the ratio of net operating income of the property to the debt service payable on the loan for a period) of at least 1.15:1. Mezzanine lenders may accommodate a debt service coverage ratio of as low as even 1.05:1 (taking total senior and mezzanine debt into account).

While senior loans are secured by a mortgage covering the property itself, mezzanine loans are usually secured not by a collateral interest in the property, i.e., a mortgage or a deed of trust, but only by a pledge of equity interests in the property-owning entity, typically a limited liability company. Accordingly, if the property is worth less than or equal to the amount of the senior loan, then the mezzanine loan collateral would be worthless.

The mezzanine loan has additional risk as the mezzanine lender is generally entitled to be paid the principal of the mezzanine loan only after the senior lender is fully repaid. Furthermore, in many mezzanine loans, only a portion of interest may be currently payable, with the balance accrued and payable at the maturity of the loan, often expressed as an 'IRR catch-up' which gives the mezzanine lender a specified internal rate of return over the life of the loan.

Beyond the general complications in an inter-creditor agreement, the following issues deserve enhanced attention within the context of real estate deals:

1. Collateral for the mezzanine loan
    Mezzanine loans typically are not secured by the real property, but by a pledge of the ownership interests in the property-owning entity, which is the borrower under the senior loan. Whether it is formed as a limited liability company or a limited partnership, 100% of the equity interests in the entity which owns the real property is pledged as security for the mezzanine loan's repayment. In the event of a default under the mezzanine loan, the mezzanine lender may foreclose upon the pledged equity interests and take over ownership and control of the property owner.

---

[12] Based on: Mark Fawer and Michael Waters, 'Mezzanine Loans and the Intercreditor Agreement: Not etched in stone,' *Real Estate Finance Journal*, Spring 2007 and Jeffery A. Lenobel, 'Mezzanine Lenders and Intercreditor Agreements,' *Distressed Asset Investor*, July 2010.

However, a real estate foreclosure action is typically conducted in court, and may take upwards of one and a half years, in contrast to how swift normal foreclosure proceedings are.

The value of this pledged collateral is dependent on mezzanine lenders ensuring that there are not multiple pledges of interests in the property-owning entity, and that only one person or entity owns all of the membership or other interests in the property owner (hence an SPV is used, which holds the real estate). While the pledge of membership interests in the property-owning entity is usually the main security, there are other options for mezzanine lenders. In some cases, mezzanine lenders may be permitted to obtain a second priority mortgage on the property as additional security, which affords the mezzanine lender a higher level of security than a pledge alone. Those projects may include new construction of condominiums or townhouses, or sale of lots for condominiums or townhouses, where the collateral diminishes over time as sales are made and as the senior mortgage is released from the units that are sold. Such cases provide mezzanine lenders with greater justification for a second mortgage so that it may monitor sales and make sure that it is paid whatever it is entitled to upon the sale of units or lots, after the first mortgage is paid off.

2. Guarantees as additional collateral

Along with the pledge of equity interests as collateral, mezzanine lenders typically seek guarantees from a creditworthy entity or individual(s) which serve as credit enhancement. Because the borrower has more opportunity to impair the collateral's value in a mezzanine loan, these guarantees are usually greater in scope than the limited guarantees for the senior loan. For instance, full recourse may be triggered not only by a voluntary or collusive involuntary bankruptcy filing, but also by bad faith interference with the mezzanine lender's exercise of its remedies, unauthorized transfers of interests in the property or pledged equity interests, or a refinancing or unauthorized modification of the senior loan.

One of the items typically covered by the inter-creditor agreement, then, is the extent to which a mezzanine lender is permitted to accept payments from a guarantor. Senior lenders will be concerned that payments made to the mezzanine lender by a guarantor may deplete the guarantor's resources, and hinder their ability to make payments under the guarantee for the senior loan, should that become necessary. That leaves mezzanine lenders with a range of options for negotiating these terms with the senior lender. In the strictest case, the terms may include an absolute restriction against accepting payments from the guarantor until after the senior loan is repaid. Mezzanine lenders, however, should seek a more flexible agreement which would permit them to accept payments so long as there have been no demands made under the guarantees under the senior loan, or to accept payments so long as they do not reduce the net worth of the guarantor below a certain threshold. Besides addressing the issue of accepting payments from the guarantor, an even bigger question is whether the mezzanine lender may accept payments from the borrower.

3. Payments from the borrower

In the most conservative inter-creditor agreements, other than regular installments of interest (which are typically made from an interest reserve), the mezzanine lenders may not accept any other payments from the borrower to pay down the mezzanine loan, until the senior loan is paid off in full. Less restrictive inter-creditor agreements may allow the mezzanine lender to accept prepayments or repayments of the mezzanine loan, so long as those payments come from an external source and not from the property itself.

4. Control over construction and condominium conversion

In new construction projects, or projects where there are otherwise substantial construction and upgrade costs, the senior loan documents will spell out provisions governing the use of the proceeds of the senior loan and the mezzanine loan, as well as the borrower's required equity in the project, procedures for approving 'change orders,' the funding of cost overruns, required retainage, approval of construction plans, the project schedule, the contractors and design professionals, and other details of the construction, as well as timing of advances of the senior loan for repayment of 'hard' and 'soft' construction costs. The mezzanine lender should attempt to maintain some control over the construction and costs, as cost overruns may need to be paid by the borrower, adversely impacting the borrower's ability to repay the mezzanine loan. Additionally, the mezzanine lender may insist on having the right to review and approve the condominium offering plan, the declaration of condominium, the obligations of the sponsor to perform work, including common area renovations and upgrades to the condominium units, and the minimum sale prices. Reductions in sales prices or increases in sponsor costs and obligations may jeopardize the borrower's ability to repay the mezzanine loan.

5. The right to modify loan documentation

Senior lenders will typically seek to retain the right to modify their documents. Mezzanine lenders, however, should be aware that if the senior lender seeks to make certain categories of modifications to the senior loan documents, these modifications may enhance the senior lender's position while diminishing the value of the collateral under the mezzanine loan, or otherwise adversely affecting the mezzanine loan and the borrower's ability to repay the mezzanine loan. Therefore, the mezzanine lender should seek to ensure that such changes cannot be made to the senior loan documents without its consent. Usually, inter-creditor agreements include reciprocal clauses that govern the loan document modifications which the parties may not make without the other's consent.[13]

---

[13] Generally, a senior lender will agree in the inter-creditor agreement not to take the following actions without the mezzanine lender's consent:
- Increase the principal amount of the senior loan. There are, however, exceptions in which the senior lender or the mezzanine lender may increase the size of its respective loan without seeking the other's consent. One exception is for 'protective advances' made by the senior lender to preserve the property, such as for emergency repairs which the borrower fails to make. Another exception is for the accrual of interest, in which unpaid interest is added to the principal amount.
- Increase the interest rate or change hedging or interest rate cap agreements.
- Accelerate the maturity date (except in case of default).
- Increase the rate of amortization.

6. Default under the mezzanine loan

In the event of a default under the mezzanine loan, senior lenders will generally try to prevent the mezzanine lender from foreclosing, because the senior lender may wish to keep the original borrower. Under the worst terms, the mezzanine lender cannot take any action unless the senior lenders are fully paid off. Mezzanine lenders, however, should negotiate for, at the very least, the right to proceed with a foreclosure on the pledge of interests in the property owner, especially if, after a limited time period, the senior lender fails to cure the mezzanine loan default on behalf of the borrower. The mezzanine lender should also negotiate the right to seek payments from the mezzanine loan's guarantors, provided that any such enforcement would not cause a violation of any of such guarantors' liquidity or net worth covenants under the senior loan.

7. Default under the senior loan

Every inter-creditor agreement will require the senior lender, at a minimum, to give notice of the default to a mezzanine lender and accept a cure of that default from

---

footnote (*continued*)

- Modifications to the casualty and condemnation clauses that would require the borrower to use the proceeds of insurance from a casualty or any award from a condemnation to repay the senior loan before being applied to the restoration of the property. Because the borrower may not be able to secure outside sources of financing for restoration after the senior loan is repaid, the property may be in a state where it is neither producing income nor readily marketable because of the unrepaired damage, adversely affecting the ability of the borrower to repay the mezzanine loan.
- Modifications to the cash management arrangement. Senior lenders generally require all the borrower's revenues to be paid into a blocked account that follows a strict waterfall of how that money may be used. Typically, the cash would first be used to pay the senior lender's costs and expenses, then to the payment of interest and scheduled amortization of the loan principal, then to fund reserves for insurance, taxes and required repairs, and finally to the borrower. The mezzanine lender should require that any funds that would otherwise be released to the borrower under this waterfall would, so long as the mezzanine loan is outstanding, instead be paid to the mezzanine lender, and that there is no deviation from this waterfall.
- The addition of a 'kicker' or contingent interest, which would reduce the value of the collateral left for the mezzanine lender.
- In projects involving new construction or substantial construction and upgrade costs, modifications to the provisions of the senior loan documents regarding changes to the construction plans, the project schedule, the project budget, the borrower's required equity in the project, procedures for approving 'change orders,' the funding of cost overruns, required retainage, the approved contractors and design professionals and the timing of advances of the senior loan for construction costs.

  In a condominium conversion or offering, modifications to the provisions of the senior loan documents regarding changes to minimum 'release prices,' the condominium offering plan, the declaration of condominium and the sponsor's obligations.
- Expansion of the events of default. Additional events of default increase the likelihood that the borrower will default and cause an acceleration of the senior loan, which would require the mezzanine lender to pay off the senior loan in full or eventually have its collateral interest extinguished or reduced in foreclosure.

the mezzanine lender. Where it becomes more controversial is in negotiating the permissible actions in the following three categories of default:

- Those that are monetary.
- Those that are curable and non-monetary.
- Those that are incurable and non-monetary.

In any case, if a senior loan default is not cured by the mezzanine lender, the senior lender may commence a mortgage foreclosure action.

8. Right to pay off or purchase the senior loan at par

   In the event of a default under the senior loan, a foreclosure on the property could wipe out the borrower's interest in the property and, therefore, absent the mezzanine lender holding a subordinate mortgage, the security for the mezzanine loan. The mezzanine lender's options in that case are to not only cure the default, but also to pay off the senior loan at par and without payment of any onerous pre-payment or yield maintenance penalties, late charges or interest at a default rate. However, even in cases where the mezzanine provider has the funding to pay off or purchase the senior loan(s), they should be aware that the collateral comes as is, i.e., whatever the borrowers have done to the real estate – placed additional sub-debt, subject to tax liens and other existing claims of tenants, judgment creditors and mechanic lienors – all of which have priority over the interest of the mezzanine lender.

9. Rights to sell the loans

   The senior lender will generally try to restrict the right of the mezzanine lender to sell or assign the mezzanine loan, or, in the most severe cases, prohibit a sale entirely. The mezzanine lender, however, should seek to preserve its flexibility to sell the mezzanine loan or participation interests therein, and its ability to pledge the mez-zanine loan. The compromise position typically involves restricting such transactions to those involving a 'qualified transferee' (or the rating agencies otherwise provide a no-downgrade letter with respect to the transfer), which may include insurance companies, banks, savings and loan associations, colleges, universities, nationally recognized commercial credit corporations, investment banks having an investment-grade senior debt rating, real estate investment trusts, real estate mortgage investment conduits, pension funds, mutual funds and governmental entities, and which may be required to meet minimum capital requirements and possess expertise in similar real estate transactions. Mezzanine lenders should also have the unqualified right to assign the mezzanine loan to any of their affiliates or any successor by merger or acquisition.

### Documentation issues

When compiling documentation for real estate deals, the following content requires inclusion when lending subordinated debt:

(1) What is the collateral?
   (a) Subordinated mortgage
   (b) Security interest in equity.

(2) Control over the source of revenue
   (a) Consent rights for major property events (e.g., zoning change, management, hotel flagging, new construction)
   (b) Consent rights over operating budgets
   (c) Notice rights for problems (e.g., environmental hazards, casualty).
(3) Flow of funds
   (a) Compelling distribution of revenue if borrower of subordinated debt is not the income-generator
   (b) Lockboxes and separate accounts.
(4) Documentation structure
   (a) Separate mezzanine loan agreement
   (b) 'B note'
   (c) Participation interest in the whole loan.
(5) Inter-creditor/Risk Control
   (a) Cure/notice rights for senior loan defaults
   (b) Right to foreclose on equity collateral and keep senior loan in place
   (c) Recourse guaranty/bankruptcy protection
   (d) Right to accept cures and pursue recourse guaranty even if common guarantor
   (e) Purchase rights for senior loan.

In addition to the normal controls over the borrower and the property, consideration should be made for the following additional risks and concerns of a senior lender when there is subordinated debt:

(1) What security do the junior loans have, and what happens if they foreclose?
   (a) Second mortgage – foreclosure means new property owner
   (b) Security in equity – foreclosure means new 'parent' of property owner.
(2) What rights should the junior lenders have to foreclose, and what should the remedies of the senior lender be?
   (a) Cure rights by senior lenders
   (b) 'Standstill arrangements'
   (c) Covenants from junior lenders regarding permitted activities after foreclosure
   (d) Prohibitions on putting the borrower or its affiliates into bankruptcy
   (e) Structural solutions to avoid bankruptcy (sometimes referred to as the 'springing member' structure).
(3) What controls (e.g., consent rights) has the junior lender tried to assert against the borrower or its parent?
   (a) Will those consent rights interfere with the property owner's ability to manage the property? (e.g., if the property owner needs to get multiple consents to change a line in the annual budget/sign a lease, is there unworkable interference in the ability to conduct business?)
   (b) If the senior lender consents, does the junior lender have the ability to unreasonably withhold its consent?
(4) Cure rights, consent and/or notice rights in general for problems/major changes under all junior debt.

## TYPICAL COVENANTS IN REAL ESTATE DEALS[14]

| Affirmative covenants | Negative covenants |
|---|---|
| (1) Existence; compliance with legal requirements | (1) Liens |
| (2) Payment of taxes and other charges | (2) Dissolution |
| (3) Notice of litigation | (3) Change in business |
| (4) Access to the property for lender | (4) Debt cancellation |
| (5) Notice of defaults | (5) Zoning |
| (6) Cooperation in legal proceedings | (6) No joint assessment |
| (7) Award and insurance benefits | (7) Name, identity, structure or principal place of business |
| (8) Further assurances | (8) ERISA |
| (9) Payment of recording and intangible taxes | (9) Affiliate transactions |
| (10) Financial reporting | (10) Transfers |
| (11) Business and operations | (11) Limitations on securities issuances |
| (12) Costs of enforcement | (12) Distributions |
| (13) Estoppel statements | (13) Refinancing or prepayment of mortgage loan |
| (14) Use of loan proceeds | (14) Acquisition of the mortgage loan |
| (15) Performance of obligations by borrower | |
| (16) Confirmation of representations (upon securitization) | |
| (17) Leasing matters | |
| (18) Management agreement | |
| (19) Environmental matters | |
| (20) Alterations | |
| (21) Compliance with Office of Foreign Assets Control | |
| (22) O&M program (regarding abatement of hazardous materials) | |
| (23) Appraisal | |
| (24) Mortgage reserve funds | |
| (25) Notices | |
| (26) Special distributions | |
| (27) Mortgage borrower covenants (cause property owner to comply) | |
| (28) Mortgage loan estoppels | |
| (29) Replacement documents | |

---

[14] The ABA inter-creditor model (see note 11) is to be complemented with the CRE financial council inter-creditor model specifically designed for the real estate sector. A full copy of the text can be found at: http://www.crefc.org/Industry_Standards/Standard_Loan_Documents/Standard_Loan_Documents/.

## TYPICAL EVENTS OF DEFAULT

(1)  Non-payment of debt
(2)  Non-payment of taxes and other charges
(3)  Lapse of insurance policies or non-delivery of copies
(4)  Transfer or encumbrance of collateral in violation of documents (including critical indirect interests)
(5)  Falsity or misleading nature of representations or warranties
(6)  Assignments for benefit of creditor by borrower, property owner, guarantor, critical direct or indirect parent, or other bankruptcy or insolvency event
(7)  Assignment of rights under loan documents
(8)  Breach of negative covenants
(9)  Breach of leasing covenants
(10)  Default under a property management agreement which permits the property manager to cancel the agreement
(11)  Violation of single-purpose entity requirements
(12)  Permitting liens on real property or other collateral
(13)  Violation of covenants relating to ERISA
(14)  Failure to deliver estoppel certificates when required
(15)  Defaults under guaranties and indemnities
(16)  Defaults under any pledge or security agreement for any portion of the collateral, whether superior or inferior
(17)  Termination or downgrading of interest rate cap agreements
(18)  Untruth of the assumptions in any non-consolidation opinion (whether untrue at closing or in the future)
(19)  Failure of first lien priority against relevant collateral (if applicable)
(20)  Default under the property loan
(21)  Any other default of terms, covenants or conditions of the loan.

## 10.6  CASE STUDY: LYONDELLBASELL AND LYONDELL CHEMICAL COMPANY[15]

**Are you, as a mezzanine investor, always drawing the shortest straw in a restructuring process?**

In February 2009, during the midst of the financial crisis, LyondellBasell Industries S.C.A. (LyondellBasell) was on shaky ground. It was headquartered in The Netherlands, in Rotterdam to be specific, which is not surprising as Rotterdam is among the largest ports in Europe and, indeed, the world. LyondellBasell was a global leading diversified chemicals company and it had been in a tough spot for a while. Rising wages and commodity

---

[15] Regarding the case described, I have been living through the eyes of one of my clients: a supplier to LyondellBasell, which ultimately had to take a significant haircut on its outstanding A/R vis-à-vis Lyondell Chemical Company. I have tried to not let that position color the story (without a 100% guarantee). However, I have stuck to the facts of the case using the materials and data that were made publicly available or have become available during the Chapter 11 debates and court proceedings.

prices combined with weakening global demand as a starter, with (very) high debt levels coming a close second, making the firm somewhat 'on a tear'. It had been experiencing deteriorating financial performance for a couple of quarters, and consequently went into bankruptcy in January 2009 under Chapter 11 of the bankruptcy code in the USA (the parent company and its 79 subsidiaries). That happened after the management team had already gone through an extensive set of meetings with the company's creditors with a view to putting together some sort of 'debtor-in-possession' (DIP) loan facility which it was hoped would put them back on track towards a financially sustainable future, but one adjusted to the new economic reality. The DIP facility is open to parties operating within the Chapter 11 procedure. Now, given the fact that we were in the middle of a severe crisis, the DIP negotiations were extremely difficult, with the global credit markets in a twist, most lenders not willing to lend and credit spreads consequently at unseen levels. LyondellBasell, from its side, was looking for US$8 billion in DIP facilities.

The fact that there was an extremely complex (one could say opaque) holding system in place on an international level didn't really help. The full LyondellBasell Group operated under the protective Chapter 11 terms, although it didn't file for any similar protective (bankruptcy or insolvency) procedures in other countries (where its subsidiaries were located). The parent company had guaranteed the debt of most subsidiaries, and operations were highly intertwined between those subsidiaries that were within the bankruptcy proceedings and those that were not.

By February 2009, it had gone through a set of sessions at the NY Bankruptcy Court to hammer out the DIP facility. Parties to the discussion were obviously the secured and unsecured creditors. Their position was that the terms of the DIP were not adequate and/or unfair. Nevertheless, it seemed to be the only way out for LyondellBasell and other options seemed unrealistic at that point.

**A few things you need to know about the firm, its owners and history, and what got them in trouble to begin with**

LyondellBasell, as previously mentioned, was a holding company located in The Netherlands, and by far its largest owner was Access Industries, which owned 97% of the shares (a private US holding company owned by the Russian businessman Len Blavatnik). The firm, in its current status, was the result of a merger in 2007 between US-based Lyondell and Holland-based chemical company Basell. It was one of the largest (independent) chemical companies in the world with about US$45 billion in revenues, and about 15,000 employees worldwide. Access Industries bought Basell in 2005 for US$5.2 billion, through an LBO. Access Industries was a holding which focused on natural resources, chemicals, TMT and media through long-term strategic investment.

In terms of activities[16], it produced and sold a wide array of its own products, and its operations were vertically and globally integrated. Essentially, it was amongst the largest producers of chemicals, polymers and derivative products. On top of this, it refined crude oil and produced of gasoline blending components. It was also active in the development and licensing of technologies for the production of polymers.

Given its wide product group, it had always been able to smooth the very cyclical prices (and demand) for chemical products, and so was relatively stable in sales and margin terms across the business cycles. Dataset 1 provides some further details on Lyondell. Depending on

---

[16] Source: company website.

the type of product, LyondellBasell had a market share of between 5 and 8%, positioning it in the top five producers in the world across the product group.

The merger between Lyondell and Basell in 2007 happened under a US$48 price tag (in cash) per outstanding share in Lyondell, or a 6.2x multiple based on 2007 earnings and a 20% premium over its closing stock price. The price tag of US$12.37 billion (and about US$1 billion in transaction-related expenses) was financed through a series of secured senior debt. In the process, Lyondell's existing debt of US$7.5 billion was refinanced as well.[17]

The combination of the two firms was expected to deliver significant synergies including cost savings related to employees and manufacturing plants, operational improvements in the area of manufacturing and technology, and margin enhancement by being able to produce at lower cost and innovate and develop new products at a lower R&D cost. Synergies in 2010 were valued at US$420 million EBITDA.[18]

The corporate structure was complicated before, and even more so after, the transaction. The operational companies were not directly held by Access Industries, but through two sub-holdings, being LyondellBasell Finance Corporation, which held the US assets, and Dutch-based holding LyondellBasell Industries Holdings B.V., which held the European business.

After the previously highlighted buy-out, the firm's performance deteriorated significantly. In 2008, it suffered from higher input prices, in particular for crude oil and other raw materials. A little further down the road in late 2008, the implications of the global economic crisis kicked in (on top of a few accidents and Acts of God which hit the firm). Even more importantly, the profit margins on a number of key products had already been declining for a few years, and were expected to decline further, along with global demand which visibly deteriorated at the end of 2008. After all, the chemicals business is a high-volume, commoditized and very cyclical business to be in.

As a direct consequence of the oil price dropping considerably in late 2008, prepayments of over a billion US$ were triggered on some of its senior secured debt.

The post-merger results were far off in terms of cash flows. Management did the usual trick, cutting back on capex and working capital while looking for additional funding for an amount of US$750 million senior unsecured revolver, which it sourced from a different subsidiary of the Access Industries family.

A lot of it was too little too late, and performance and cash flows continued to deteriorate.

By the end of 2008, with everything put together, it had to seek an extension on payment due on an US$8 billion facility, and as a consequence some of the new revolver facilities which had been negotiated closed down due to the 'event of default by missing payments on the facility'.

Dataset 2 provides an estimated and (significantly) simplified overview of the pre-petition debt and the historical financial statements.

Early 2009, the firm filed for creditor protection under Chapter 11 facilities. All US business except for the parent company and all non-US businesses except for a German subsidiary were included in the filing.[19]

The bankruptcy court allowed some immediately needed payments to suppliers, and the ability to enter into an emergency facility loan of US$100 million, as well as an additional draw down of over US$2 billion of the US$8 billion DIP facility mentioned earlier.

---

[17] Source: SEC filings.
[18] Sources: Credit Suisse analyst coverage.
[19] Source: company website press release January 8, 2009.

**A few things you need to know about the Chapter 11 facility**

Under the Chapter 11 facility, lenders who are willing to lend to the bankrupt firm after it is filed (so post-petition) are entitled to superior priority in terms of repayment under its restructuring plan, obviously relative to those unsecured lenders that have debt facilities outstanding pre-petition (as well as most post-petition claims).[20] That makes sense as, without that protection, a firm in trouble might not be able to find emergency funding at all for the firm to finance future operations. Disruption in operations, caused by a lack of emergency funding, might cause even more financial damage to the firm and its debtholders.

Further, existing pre-petition secured lenders cannot seize collateral or otherwise due to a mechanism called the 'automatic stay'. The bankruptcy judge can 'lift the stay', and can allow payments or otherwise if they were convinced that it would contribute to the preservation of the firm. For example, critical suppliers can be paid if that results in their willingness to continue supplying and keep the firm in business. During that period, no interest is paid on pre-petition debt, and interests do not accrue on unsecured pre-petition debt, though they can accrue for secured pre-petition debt but only if the collateral's market value was higher than the existing face value of the remaining debt outstanding (and limited to that differential).[21] The DIP facility is essentially there to ensure that the firm can continue operating and investing, and to execute the turnaround program and become profitable again.

DIP financing was introduced in 1978 as part of a larger reform of the US bankruptcy laws. It has become common practice for bankrupt firms to look for DIP financing prior to filing for Chapter 11. With a deal already in place with DIP financiers, they could enter the procedure and get the DIP deal signed off at an early stage, and ensure (hopefully) the continuity of operations. Banks have been developing specialist teams to engage in such lending practices as, under the right conditions and structured the right way, it can become an attractive investment for the bank.

DIP financiers were normally larger commercial banks and specialized financing companies, and more recently hedge funds and institutionalized lenders joined that list. In 2008, that became a problem as the economic crisis went hand in hand with a financial crisis, so the typical DIP lenders were often experiencing liquidity problems of their own[22] and therefore many firms were experiencing significant problems raising funding of whatever nature from a market which was experiencing contracting credit markets.

Within the DIP financing scheme the following options were possible, depending on the priority given to the DIP lenders:[23]

- The debtor borrowed 'in the ordinary course of business' (for example, for buying inventory from vendors). The debt would then be treated as an unsecured first priority administrative claim. Administrative claims rank just behind pre-petition secured debt in priority of payment. Part of that is obviously the fees paid to financial and legal professionals involved in the

---

[20] See section 364 of the US Bankruptcy Code.

[21] Ibid. note 6.

[22] Banks had their fair share of problems, as well as hedge funds, whilst experiencing redemptions.

[23] See further: J. Friedland, M. Bernstein, G. Kuney and J. Ayer, *Obtaining DIP Financing and Using Cash Collateral*, Informational Brief Issue 8.11, January 2009.

procedures, or who advised the debtor, and committees appointed by the bankruptcy judge. The full Chapter 11 claim ranking can be found in Dataset 3.

- The debtor borrowed 'outside the ordinary course of business'. (e.g., for general financing purposes). Three situations were possible:

1. The debt would be treated as an unsecured first-priority administrative claim, similar to post-petition trade debt.
2. If no lender could be found willing to lend under these conditions, the bankruptcy judge could provide DIP lenders a super-priority administrative claim (ranking ahead of all other administrative claims), or could provide those DIP lenders with a security interest in an unencumbered or uncollateralized property (i.e., assets which were not already pledged as collateral for some other debt or liability). A judge can, at all times, combine the super-priority administrative claim with a security interest in an uncollateralized asset or pool of assets.
3. If there were still no DIP lenders available under the conditions mentioned under 2., the judge could approve giving a DIP lender a security interest in a property which already served as a collateral for existing outstanding pre-petition debt. This new security could be junior, *pari passu* or senior to the existing pre-petition debt. If it were senior to the pre-petition security interest, the pre-petition secured lender would have been what is called 'primed' by the DIP lender. There is no higher priority to be given to restructuring lenders under Chapter 11. Before that could happen, as it was quite an aggressive position, it would be necessary for the court to be shown that the pre-petition lender's security interest was 'adequately protected', and that they would not suffer any economic loss due to the priming taking place (that was to be evidenced by the fact that the pre-petition lender's collateral was sufficient to cover both its own claim and that of the new DIP lender, or because it was granted a replacement lien on some other property). It is no surprise that, in reality, pre-petition lenders almost always object to having their loans primed.

During the procedures before the court, and before the court would provide the DIP lenders with a particular level of priority, the debtor would have to demonstrate that it was impossible to provide financing by offering a lower level of priority. Studies demonstrate that an increasing number of bankruptcy courts in recent years have granted DIP lenders with secured positions, including those situations where the new DIP lender was allowed to prime pre-petition secured creditors.

If all those options did not result in new lending facilities becoming available, the alternative option would be to look for (additional) financing from pre-petition creditors, who were already owed money by the firm. To sweeten the deal, the existing pre-petition lenders, who obviously considered this as throwing good money after bad, were often given a higher priority or more senior secured interest than the DIP lenders' pre-petition claim, which would, in turn, be partially or wholly paid down using a portion of the DIP loan proceeds. DIP roll-ups were commonplace in 2007–2009 when credit markets contracted globally and re-financing was extremely challenging. Most roll-ups involved secured revolving credits, and where judges were more inclined to OK deals of this nature if it could be shown that the resulting benefits to the debtor outweighed any harm to creditors whose claims were not rolled up.

Lenders were often attracted to the DIP financing market due to:

- The fact that they received a super-priority claim and/or a security interest in the debtor's assets.
- DIP lenders were normally paid at the conclusion of the bankruptcy which, according to research, lasted for about 20 months, and so the loan maturity on the DIP facilities was relatively short (15–24 months).
- The DIP loan was repaid by cash available or refinanced with new debt (exit debt) which normally was issued at the moment that the company emerged from the Chapter 11 procedure. That exit debt was then raised through the normal banking facility.
- Although DIP financing seems very risky, historical default rates for DIP loans are extremely low, often lower than normal senior secured loans.

## 10.6.1 Specifics of the Lyondell DIP facility

No doubt, the Lyondell DIP facility is one of the largest DIP facilities ever arranged. Of the US$8 billion DIP loans the firms arranged before filing for Chapter 11, the judge provided immediate access to over US$2 billion, pending finalization of the details between the firm and the lenders.

Also here, the typical institutions involved were commercial banks, investment banks, hedge funds and private equity funds including names such as Goldman Sachs, Cerberus Capital Management. Citigroup, ABN-AMRO, UBS, Oaktree Capital Management and others.[24]

All the DIP lenders had pre-petition debt in place with the firm. Most of the secured pre-petition debt (provided by commercial and investment banks) arranged by lenders was related to the acquisition of Lyondell in 2007. That included a whole list of specific facilities such as the 'senior secured credit facility', 'asset-backed inventory facility', 'accounts receivable securitization facility' and the 'interim loan facility'. Dataset 4 provides an overview. The pre-petition claims held by hedge funds and PE firms were often bought from the banks in the secondary market, after the acquisition and often at a discount.

The proposed DIP facilities consisted of three (separate) facilities:

1. A US$1.51 billion revolving credit facility (RC facility).
2. A US$3.250 billion general purpose term loan facility (GP facility).
3. A US$3.250 billion term loan facility (roll-up facility) which would finance a partial roll-up of the pre-petition senior secured credit facility.

The amounts under the RC and GP facilities would be used for general corporate purposes and to fund ongoing working capital needs.

A summary of other DIP characteristics:

- In order to participate in the roll-up facility, a pre-petition creditor had to participate in the GP facility, obviously to avoid free-riding at no cost or additional risk. The deal was that for every dollar invested under the GP facility, it would be entitled to roll-up US$4 of its

---

[24]J. Blakeley, DIP Dimensions: Lyondell Chemical Company, *The Deal Pipeline*, February 12, 2009.

pre-petition claims into the roll-up facility, which implies an effective conversion of its pre-petition claim into a secured super-priority administrative claim.

- All three tranches of financing would mature on, and be payable in cash on, either December 15, 2009 or the effective date of the firm's reorganization plan. Any extension of the maturity would require the consent of all the financiers involved in the DIP facility. The loans would accelerate, and become fully due and payable, if the borrowers defaulted on any of the loan terms.
- All three loan tranches would be treated as super-priority administrative claims, although the roll-up facility would be junior to the RC facility and the GP facility (which were *pari passu* to each other).
- All three loan tranches would also be secured by first- and second-priority liens on various assets of the firm. A second priority lien (or second lien) would have a claim, in the case of liquidation, on any liquidation proceeds which remained after the claims of creditors (those who held first liens on that asset and had been paid in full). If the proceeds were not sufficient to repay the first lien holder, the second lien holder would go home empty-handed.
- The portion of the pre-petition senior secured credit facility that was not refinanced by the DIP roll-up facility would continue to have a first lien over LyondellBasell's European operations, although if liens on US assets granted to the roll-up lenders were not sufficient to make those lenders whole, they would be entitled to a pro-rata share of the European collateral.
- The liens which would be granted to the DIP lenders were 'priming liens', representing a more senior security interest in the collateral that currently secured the debtors' pre-petition secured debt. They ensured that the pre-petition debt holders would be 'adequately protected'. The firm proposed to grant those creditors a subordinate lien on the assets that would secure the DIP facilities, a super-priority administrative expenses claim for any diminution in the value of their pre-petition security interest, and a number of smaller measures.
- The DIP borrowings would be guaranteed by LyondellBasell subsidiaries located in the US and Europe. Each borrower under the DIP facilities would also agree to guarantee the obligations of all the other borrowers.

Finally, the court would issue a temporary injunction to avoid 'acceleration of payment' on the publicly-traded bonds of the parent company LyondellBasell. Some bondholders argue that the parent guaranteed some trade and mezzanine debt of some of the subsidiaries now under Chapter 11 and that that in itself would constitute 'an event of default'.

## 10.6.2  Resistance against the proposed DIP facility

Quite a number of objections were raised against the proposed DIP facility. They opposed an amendment to the pre-petition 2007 secured revolving credit facility, under which lenders who participated in the roll-up facility would be treated 'as separate tranche DIP lenders,' and 'given full voting rights on most issues under the term DIP credit agreement.' They argued that the 'treatment of the rolled up loans as refinanced loans with full voting rights under the term DIP credit agreement was never contemplated and gives the holders of roll-up DIP loans extraordinary control over the DIP financing and unnecessarily poses risks to the roll-up DIP lenders' liens in non-US collateral'. Their position was that 'the roll-up DIP loans should continue to constitute loans outstanding under the pre-petition 2007 secured revolving credit facility'.

Some of them threatened to withdraw their commitment under the GP facility. However, the other DIP lenders indicated that they would be willing to cover the withdrawal when needed.

Further objections were formulated against the proposed DIP facility by the unsecured creditors. The following arguments were put on the table:[25]

- The financial covenants were, in general, too onerous.
- The maturity date of December 15, 2009 and related milestones in the Chapter 11 process were 'not justified on any reasoned economic, credit, risk or other basis, were precipitously early and devoid of any realistic mechanism to seek and effect any necessary extension'.
- The DIP lenders were granted excessive control over the debtor's operations, through mechanisms that would allow the lenders to 'install captive management and wrest operational control away from the debtors'.
- The pricing of the DIP facility was 'nothing short of confiscatory: with an all-in cost including upfront and exit fees of approximately 20%'.
- The continued payment of interest on the US$3.25 billion of pre-petition debt which would be 'rolled up' under the DIP facility made no economic sense, and would result in 'negative arbitrage', because to pay for the interest the debtor would have to borrow under the DIP facility at an all-in annual cost of 20%.
- The DIP loan inappropriately limited the liability of the DIP lenders for their pre-petition conduct with respect to Lyondell, specifically in connection with Access Industries' 2007 leveraged acquisition of Lyondell Chemical, under which US$12.3 billion of borrowed funds were 'siphoned off Lyondell's former shareholders, leaving the debtors with insufficient capital and liquidity to service their resulting debt burden . . .'.

### 10.6.3 The outcome

The DIP facility was necessary to restructure the business and ensure that the debtors emerged from Chapter 11 with viable operations. If the judge ruled in favor of the dissatisfied creditors, the whole DIP facility, and even the entire reorganization, would be put at risk. Finding replacement financing would prove to be impossible, which could lead to full bankruptcy and liquidation of the entire firm. The deal ultimately, luckily enough, went ahead.[26] Dataset 5 displays some of the financial data provided by the firm, which support a 'going concern' scenario after the firm exited the Chapter 11 proceedings on a sustainable and viable basis.

---

[25] Those objections were formulated by the Official Committee of Unsecured Creditors.

[26] T. Kary, *Lyondell Chemical Wins Approval for 8 USD Billion Bankruptcy Loan*, www.Bloomberg.com (February 28, 2009).

## 10.6.4 Datasets

---

### DATASET 1: FINANCIAL PERFORMANCE OF BASELL AND LYONDELL PRIOR TO THE LBO (IN US$ BILLIONS).[27]

|  | 2003 | 2004 | 2005 | 2006 |
|---|---|---|---|---|
| **Revenues** | | | | |
| Basell | 6.5 | 8.4 | 10.7 | 13.3 |
| Lyondell | 10.0 | 14.0 | 20.0 | 24.0 |
| **Adjusted EBITDA** | | | | |
| Basell | 0.4 | 0.8 | 1.0 | 1.3 |
| Lyondell | 0.6 | 1.3 | 2.2 | 2.8 |
| | **Basell** | **Lyondell** | | |
| Total asset | 11.0 | 16.5 | | |
| Total debt | 4.4 | 6.6 | | |
| Total equity | 2.3 | 3.5 | | |

---

### DATASET 2: LYONDELLBASELL INDUSTRIES AF SCA – OUTSTANDING PRE-PETITION DEBT[28]

| Debt | Face value ($US in millions) |
|---|---|
| **A. Debt owed by entities which are included in the Chapter 11 filing** | |
| **First lien debt** | |
| **Senior secured credit facility** | |
| Revolver | 991 |
| Term loan A | 1,865 |
| Term loan B | 9,350 |
| Lyondell notes maturity 2010 | 102 |
| Lyondell notes maturity 2020 | 228 |
| Equistar notes maturity 2026 | 144 |
| **Total** | **12,680** |
| **Second and third lien debt** | |
| Fixed-rate second lien loan | 3,400 |
| Floating-rate second lien loan | 1,300 |
| Floating rate third lien loan | 3,000 |
| **Total** | **7,700** |

*(continued)*

---

[27] Source: Senior secured credit facility presentation, Investor presentation, April 2008 (retrieved: company website: www.Lyondellbasell.com)

[28] Author's assessment based on available information. Reality might have been somewhat different and excluding intercompany financing and relation between the individual components to each other through various inter-creditor agreements whose impact is not reflected here.

| Debt | Face value ($US in millions) |
|---|---|
| **Unsecured notes** | |
| Basell senior notes maturity 2015 (US denominated) | 635 |
| Basell senior notes maturity 2015 (Euro denominated) | 715 |
| Millennium notes maturity 2026 | 265 |
| **Total** | **1,615** |
| **B. Other debt not included in the Chapter 11 filing** | |
| Senior notes | 300 |
| **Senior secured credit facility** | **600** |
| **Total consolidated debt** | **22,895** |

# HISTORICAL FINANCIAL STATEMENTS ($ MILLIONS)[29]

## A. LyondellBasell Industries AF SCA

| Balance Sheet | Dec. 31, 2007 | Sept. 30, 2008 |
|---|---|---|
| Cash & cash equivalents | 560 | 623 |
| Restricted cash | 1,471 | 1,432 |
| Short-term investments | 0 | 169 |
| Accounts receivable | 4,165 | 4,291 |
| Inventories | 5,178 | 5,935 |
| Prepayments and other assets | 620 | 560 |
| **Total current assets** | **11,994** | **13,010** |
| Property plant and equipment | 17,146 | 16,746 |
| Investments | 2,382 | 2,406 |
| Goodwill and other intangibles | 7,731 | 7,399 |
| Other assets | 475 | 508 |
| **Total assets** | **39,728** | **40,069** |
| Current maturities of LT debt | 459 | 1,478 |
| Short-term debt | 2,415 | 2,465 |
| Accounts payable and accrued liabilities | 6,392 | 5,713 |
| Deferred income taxes | 432 | 576 |
| **Total current liabilities** | **9,698** | **10,232** |
| Long-term debt | 21,541 | 22,203 |
| Other liabilities | 1,881 | 1,977 |
| Deferred income taxes | 4,543 | 3,839 |
| Minority interest | 144 | 133 |
| Total stockholder equity | 1,921 | 1,685 |
| **Total liabilities and equity** | **39,728** | **40,069** |

[29] Derived from consolidated financials on company website.

| Income Statement (*) | Dec. 31, 2006 | Dec. 31, 2007 | Sept. 30, 2008 |
|---|---|---|---|
| Revenue | 35,743 | 44,320 | 54,602 |
| Operating expenses | (33,737) | (42,257) | (53,416) |
| Operating income (loss) | 2,006 | 2,063 | 1,186 |
| Interest expense | (2,236) | (2,232) | (2,204) |
| Interest income | 117 | 103 | 120 |
| Other income, net | 38 | 134 | 83 |
| Income from associations and JVs | 223 | 164 | 143 |
| Income (loss) from continuing operations | 148 | 232 | (672) |
| (Provision for) benefit from income tax | (85) | (25) | 234 |
| Net income from continuing operations | 63 | 207 | (438) |
| Income from discontinued operations | 0 | 0 | (15) |
| Net income (loss) | 63 | 207 | (423) |
| Depreciation & amortization | 1,627 | 1,772 | 1,870 |
| EBITDA | 4,528 | 5,071 | 3,917 |

(*) 12 months ending at

## B. Lyondell Chemical Company[30]

| Balance Sheet | Dec. 31, 2007 | Sept. 30, 2008 |
|---|---|---|
| Cash & cash equivalents | 370 | 406 |
| Deposits with related parties | 135 | 1,091 |
| Short-term investments | 0 | 169 |
| Accounts receivable | 1,377 | 953 |
| Inventories | 3,354 | 3,267 |
| Prepayments and other assets | 232 | 178 |
| Note receivable from related parties | 2 | 0 |
| **Total current assets** | **5,470** | **6,064** |
| Property plant and equipment | 12,504 | 12,289 |
| Investments in JVs | 564 | 543 |
| Note receivable from related parties | 835 | 835 |
| Goodwill and other intangibles | 7,645 | 6,971 |
| Other assets | 187 | 181 |
| **Total assets** | **27,392** | **27,117** |
| Current maturities of LT debt | 435 | 1,359 |
| Related party borrowing | 717 | 751 |
| Accounts payable and accrued liabilities | 3,145 | 2,251 |
| Deferred income taxes | 431 | 557 |
| **Total current liabilities** | **4,728** | **4,918** |
| Banks and other unrelated parties | 9,454 | 10,087 |
| Related parties | 8,000 | 8,000 |
| Other liabilities | 827 | 823 |
| Deferred income taxes | 3,884 | 3,402 |
| Minority interest | 126 | 115 |
| Total stockholder equity | 373 | (228) |
| **Total liabilities and equity** | **27,392** | **27,117** |

(*continued*)

---

[30] Duff & Phelps, Valuation Analysis of LyondellBasell Industries AF S.C.A. and Certain Subsidiaries

| Income Statement (*) | Dec. 31, 2006 | Dec. 31, 2007 | Sept. 30, 2008 |
|---|---|---|---|
| Trade revenue | 19,183 | 27,387 | 31,588 |
| Related party revenue | 1,334 | 787 | 551 |
| Operating expenses | (18,725) | (27,371) | (32,389) |
| Operating income (loss) | 1,792 | 803 | (250) |
| Interest expense | (648) | (670) | (1,426) |
| Interest income | 39 | 37 | 88 |
| Other income, net | (28) | 91,550 | (162) |
| Income (loss) from continuing operations | 1,155 | 15 | (1,175) |
| (Provision for) benefit from income tax | (413) | 68 | 498 |
| Net income from continuing operations | 742 | (53) | (1,252) |
| Income from discontinued operations | (556) | (94) | 51 |
| Net income (loss) | 186 | (147) | (1,201) |

(*) 12 months ending at

## DATASET 3: HIERARCHY OF CLAIMS IN CHAPTER 11[31]

1. Secured claims
2. Super-priority claims (e.g., DIP financing)
3. Priority claims:
   3.1  Administrative expenses (legal and professional fees related to the filing and case overall)
   3.2  Wages, salaries and commissions
   3.3  Employee benefit claims
   3.4  Claims against facilities (that store grain or fish products)
   3.5  Consumer deposits
   3.6  Alimony and child support
   3.7  Tax claims
   3.8  Unsecured claims based on commitments to a federal depository institutions regulatory agency
   3.9  General unsecured claims
   3.10 Preferred stock
   3.11 Common stock.

---

[31] Stuart C. Gilson, *Creating Value through Corporate Restructuring: Case Studies in Bankruptcies, Buy-outs and Break-ups*, NY, John Wiley & Sons, Inc., 2001, p. 228.

## DATASET 4: LYONDELL DEBTORS: LENDER COMMITMENT UNDER DIP FINANCING (IN US$ IN MILLIONS)[32]

| RC Facility | |
| --- | --- |
| Goldman Sachs | 326 |
| Merrill Lynch | 326 |
| ABN AMRO | 326 |
| Citigroup | 301 |
| UBS | 236 |
| | **1,540** |
| **GP Facility** | |
| UBS | 770 |
| Apollo Management | 710 |
| Cerberus Capital Management | 237.5 |
| ABN AMRO | 230 |
| Angelo Gordon Co. | 200 |
| Silver Point Capital | 200 |
| Appaloosa Management | 200 |
| Merrill Lynch | 150 |
| Oak Hill Capital Partners | 122.5 |
| Citigroup | 110 |
| Goldman Sachs | 110 |
| Farallon Capital Management | 75 |
| Oaktree Capital Management | 75 |
| Strategic Value Partners | 60 |
| | 3,250 |

## DATASET 5: LYONDELLBASELL AF SCA – HISTORICAL AND PROJECTED EBITDA ($ MILLIONS) [33]

| Year | EBITDA |
| --- | --- |
| 2006 | **4,528** |
| 2007 | **5,071** |
| 2008 | **3,047** |
| 2009 | **2,109** |
| 2010 | **2,356** |
| 2011 | **3,711** |
| 2012 | **4,253** |
| 2013 | **4,603** |

---

[32] R. Kellerhals, *Creditors and Banks Spar Over DIP*, High yield report 2009 (Factiva); *Lyondell Loan Exemplifies New Bankruptcy Landscape*, Bloomberg News, February 4, 2009.
[33] Ibid. note 30.

## LYONDELLBASELL AF SCA (CORE BUSINESS – FINANCIAL FORECASTS ($ MILLIONS)

| | 2009 | 2010 | 2011 | 2012 | 2013 | 2014 | 2015 | 2016 | 2017 | 2018 |
|---|---|---|---|---|---|---|---|---|---|---|
| **NOPAT** | 263 | 471 | 1,369 | 1,733 | 1,980 | 2,372 | 2,444 | 2,517 | 2,580 | 2,644 |
| **D&A** | 1,705 | 1,631 | 1,604 | 1,586 | 1,557 | 1,137 | 1,171 | 1,206 | 1,236 | 1,267 |
| **Net WC** | 34 | 11 | (104) | (260) | (915) | (7) | (5) | (5) | (5) | (5) |
| **CAPEX** | (775) | (1,010) | (1,030) | (1,090) | (1,000) | (1,197) | (1,233) | (1,270) | (1,301) | (1,334) |
| **FCF** | 1,226 | 1,103 | 1,840 | 2,203 | 2,522 | 2,305 | 2,377 | 2,448 | 2,510 | 2,573 |

## 10.6.5 Case guidance

Although the case deals specifically with the peculiarities of the DIP financing scheme under a Chapter 11 program, it can be mentioned here that most of the legal restructuring programs follow very similar dynamics, although details, procedures and consequences of choices are often different. This is logical, and most likely not very important within the context of the impact of mezzanine finance and the implications of a bankruptcy or even outright liquidation. When reviewing the case, the following questions can guide the analysis from a mezzanine point of view:

1. How deeply subordinated were the mezzanine lenders when going into the Chapter 11 filing? Was this primarily due to the LBO in 2007 and could the debt package have been better constructed than was the case?
2. Were there economic indicators that the market was gradually suffering from eroding margins that could question further capex investments in the field?
3. How much would the mezzanine investors have to write off going into the Chapter 11 proceedings? How much if the new proposed package were to be agreed? Or, put differently: would their risk profile change significantly given the significantly deeper levels of subordination they would experience? Build a cash flow waterfall to support your position.
4. Are there potential techniques to protect your position as a mezzanine lender in these discussions? Would the complex legal structure and guarantee structure require a different approach to subordination and the implicit risk that the mezzanine products carry?
5. Would you put up (additional) conditions as a mezzanine lender for accepting the DIP deal as it stood at the time?
6. Would you conclude that mezzanine lenders (or unsecured lenders in general) are 'out there on a limb' in bankruptcy and restructuring cases? Do you think that is due to the specifics of the case or would that be true in general? If the latter, would you consider that an (un)intended consequence of the DIP financing and Chapter 11 rules in this respect? Are you of the opinion that there is an asymmetry between the position of the senior versus the mezzanine lenders after the close of the Chapter 11 filing?
7. If you consider there is a structural problem with these bankruptcy hierarchies, what would you consider changing in the rules, and what would be the objective?

# 11

## Outlook

### 11.1 INTRODUCTION

The outlook for mezzanine reads a bit like the good, the bad and the ugly of the financial markets and everything that has happened since 2008.

It is fair to say that, in general terms, the outlook for mezzanine is pretty good anno 2013 and going forward. A few elements have contributed to that, including the fact that since 2008, and especially now that it is clear how the final format of Basel III will look, financial institutions are repositioning their loan portfolios, thereby often overweighting sovereign bonds over operational loans.[1] For risky loans, a higher level of capital will have to be held at the bank, and therefore cannot be deployed in its effort to maximize its own ROE and shareholder value. Its retraction from the market has left a void which can only be filled with either equity or mezzanine capital, the former of which is often unavailable for (smaller) SMEs. As cash flows have become more volatile given the protracted period of volatility in the market, cash flow visibility has significantly reduced, something credit analysts are still learning to cope with.

Secondly, the financial repression, arranged by central banks in the aftermath of the first part of the financial crisis, which investors have experienced globally not only led to extremely low yield levels on T-bonds and other acclaimed risk-less assets, but also pushed savvy investors in relatively risk-elevated fixed-income products (as well as higher yielding sukuks (i.e., bond look-alike Islamic products) like leveraged and high-yield loans and bonds as a direct alternative to equity allocations.

Also, the lower interest rate levels have pushed up demand for refinancing activities by corporate and sovereigns alike.

Thirdly, many investors have shifted gearing after being confronted with a significant J-curve in the aftermath of the crisis on their PE investments, and rather than waiting for returns, they re-allocated future allocations to mezzanine, often providing similar returns compared to PE (at least judging by the industry's average PE performance).

Finally, the emerging equity gap (partly driven by the absolute reluctance by retail investors to invest in the stock market any longer, and the fact that there is very little of an equity culture in emerging markets to fund pension plans) in the world has led and will lead to mezzanine products being used as a direct alternative to replace equity products and senior debt alike.

---

[1] The fact that FIs are allowed under the final liquidity rules (part of Basel III, as has been communicated in January 2013) not to hold any risk capital against sovereign bonds is striking in contrast with experience in recent years. The final liquidity coverage ratios can be found here: http://www.bis.org/press/p130106b.pdf. Further guidance and implementation issues are extensively discussed and can be found here: http://www.bis.org/publ/bcbs238.pdf.

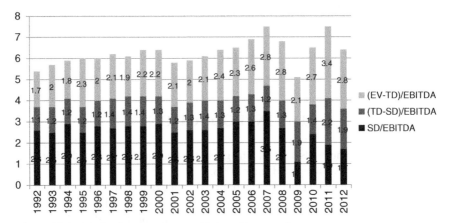

**Figure 11.1**   Median leverage loan multiples: all transactions

In numerical terms, those trends are confirmed by the most recent report by CEPRES, who, in their 2012 report, highlight the following dynamics (see Figure 11.1):[2]

- Senior debt volume in transactions is down 45% from the 2007 peak, whilst mezzanine is up 85% and equity financing up 20%, showing the increasing importance of private debt.
- Strong price stability was maintained by mezzanine deals in Europe during the latest financial crisis.
- Bargaining power for mezzanine terms improved in some market segments.
- The PIK return component on invested capital showed a 40% increase.
- The pricing for mezzanine debt (both interest spread and PIK) is running at a 20-year high water mark level.
- Europe shows increasing use of mixed equity kickers whilst North America tends to bifurcate equity flavor on the majority of deals.

## 11.2  THE NOT-TOO-DISTANT PAST

The mezzanine product group is here to stay, as it not only provides the flexibility needed for companies to weather downturns, but also provides the opportunity for private equity players to drive enhanced value from their portfolio companies, as it allows deals with protracted periods of underperformance. In mid-market transactions, for example, senior debt has often been limited to 3–3.5x EBITDA, which is generally not sufficient when sponsors are contemplating entry multiples of 7x and above.

Intellectual honesty does force us, however, amidst this tsunami of optimism, to point out the fact that often, mezzanine lenders have taken a serious beating during the years since 2008. In fact, in some restructuring cases, the mezzanine position has been completely wiped out together with the equity position. In such cases, where valuation of the company is key, and where during periods of significant stress, the visibility of valuations is extremely reduced,

---

[2] CEPRES, 'Mezzanine market report 2012,' April 2012 (www.cepres.com).

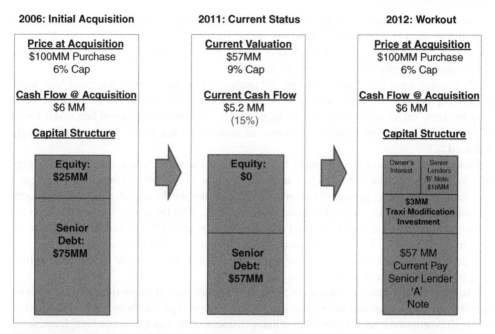

**Figure 11.2**  The opportunity: restructuring and workouts as an investment opportunity in the current cycle

there is the constant risk that senior lenders will walk away with the firm at what would be considered absurd valuations under normal conditions. Often negotiated behind closed doors, we got a glimpse of that when some of these cases spilled over into court,[3] finding a court which was willing to think about the dynamics of valuation principles under stress.

Indeed, documentation permitting, some senior lenders don't even feel the need to talk to junior lenders. However, it should be stressed here that flexibility allows mezzanine lenders to be a key element in the restructuring process, by providing new or enhanced liquidity on the balance sheet of the restructured entity or group, an argument not to be ignored in a debt market as we know it today, characterized by many black holes. Disputes between lenders tend never to come at the benefit of the restructured firm. Ultimately, senior lenders are called senior for a reason and mezzanine providers are in the game for a different reason. Their different risk/return profile has the risk of loss priced in. Having said that, mezzanine lenders can play a critical role in all sorts of restructuring or recapitalization projects (see Figure 11.2).

## 11.3  NEW KIDS ON THE BLOCK

Financial innovation and the contractual flexibility of the mezzanine finance groups trigger a continuous stream of new products mirroring needs as they occur in the market. With senior lenders having vacated a part of the credit market, mezzanine providers had the opportunity

---

[3] For example, in the UK the British car-cleaning company IMO Car Wash.

to expand into what was formerly a purely senior lender space. The consequence was that a one-stop product covering both senior and junior lending needs was well favored. Although the unitranche product existed for a longer period of time, it clearly experienced a serious renaissance in the aftermath of the recent financial crisis.

That is also not the first time. For over 30 years it's been a consistent source of long-term, patient capital which continues to provide an attractive risk-adjusted return to lenders and their backers. Yet, in each of the past financial cycles, stretch senior, second lien, older forms of unitranche, junk bonds and opportunists in search of attractive yields have supposedly replaced it.

Unitranche seems to be consistently the most dominant of the 'alternative' product group. The logic is simple: streamlined when arranging, simple when documenting, easy when communicating. One lender instead of two or even three means one document, one set of covenants etc. and one party to talk to during good times and bad. With the ability to combine both the senior and junior portions of the capital structure into a single debt instrument, the unitranche structure provides similar leverage to a traditional senior cash flow/mezzanine structure, with the same weighted average cost of capital, yet often with more favorable terms for amortization, prepayment penalties and covenant packages.[4]

The product is, however, not always as straightforward as you might think. While a senior stretch loan can be qualified as a hybrid loan taking the center ground between an asset-backed and cash flow-based loan, a unitranche colludes characteristics together in one legal framework.

## 11.4  THE UNITRANCHE PRODUCT

The unitranche product is a hybrid product mainly used in the mid-market, i.e., for companies with an EBITDA of less than €30 million or sales below €300 million with an average ticket of about €70–100 million.

Further, it has the following characteristics:

- Unitranche loans are documented in a single loan agreement, often with a single lender. If a borrower has a more traditional capital structure with a senior secured loan facility and a separate second lien or mezzanine loan, these are documented separately and often have different covenant packages, so that the borrower must be aware of and comply with the different restrictions and limitations in each agreement.
- Unitranche loans are often term loans, especially if they are used to finance acquisitions where the total amount of the loan proceeds must be funded on the acquisition closing date. In some transactions, the borrower also has a separate lending facility which is often provided by an affiliate of the unitranche lender. If the borrower has a revolving loan, it typically ranks with the unitranche term loan (or just behind it), so both loans can be documented under the same credit agreement.
- Unitranche loans have a single interest rate based on the separate rates applicable to the senior and junior components of the loan. This blended interest rate is determined by the lender, based on the weighted average interest rates of the first and second lien components

---

[4] Ronald Kahn, 'Mezzanine gets another chance to shine,' PEhub.com, October 2011.

of the loan. The borrower is usually unaware of how the loan is split into its respective components, or how the interest payments are allocated between them.

- In many cases, unitranche loans do not include call protection (also known as a prepayment premium). This means the borrower can repay all or any portion of the loan at any time it chooses without restriction or penalty. However, in a unitranche loan that does include call protection, because the loan is a single facility, the borrower cannot avoid making a prepayment premium if it wishes to reduce its overall leverage by paying down some of its debt. This may contrast with a financing arrangement where the borrower has separate facilities, such as first and second lien credit agreements. If the borrower has separate facilities, it may be able to negotiate one facility without a prepayment premium and therefore be able to prepay some of its debt without paying a prepayment penalty.
- Because unitranche loans combine first and second lien facilities, the amount of debt under a unitranche loan exceeds that which would be available to the borrower under a first lien facility alone. Unitranche loans, like traditional bank loans, often contain financial covenants which the borrower must meet during the life of the loan. Many financial covenants measure various aspects of a borrower's financial performance or condition in relation to its outstanding debt. In a unitranche loan, the ratios in the financial covenants are set at levels which permit a total amount of debt as if the borrower had separate first lien and second lien facilities.
- In a unitranche facility, the borrower is not involved in, and is typically not aware of, the inter-creditor arrangements governing the respective components of its loan. Because unitranche loans are typically provided by a single lender and are not generally traded, the inter-creditor terms may be largely academic because the originating lender generally keeps the entire loan until maturity. If some portion of the loan is sold, or different lenders provide the portions of the loan, then the inter-creditor terms become more significant. Although less common, if this occurs it has the potential to make life difficult for the borrower if it needs additional financing or a covenant waiver. The borrower may not have a breakdown of ownership of its loan or be aware of the consent rights of the respective lenders, so the borrower may not know to whom it should make its case and how to concentrate its efforts to get the necessary lender approvals.

The origin in 2005 (GE started experimenting with the product at that time) was clear and straightforward, but over time the unitranche product has developed many faces. These days, it has evolved into a variety of structures.[5] Most unitranche loans now find themselves behind a revolver and are often referred to as split collateral financings. These structures, which were designed to decrease the overall cost of capital, often use an asset-based lender to provide the borrower with a revolver secured by the company's accounts receivable and inventory, with the term loan (or unitranche loan) getting a first lien on all the remaining assets and a second lien on the accounts receivable and inventory.

Because this term loan encompasses both what a senior lender and junior lender would lend, it results in more capital than either type of provider would lend individually, and is considered a unitranche loan. However, not everything is always rosy when it comes to putting a unitranche facility in place. The inter-creditor agreement in split collateral financing is normally more difficult to negotiate than a traditional senior cash flow/mezzanine inter-creditor agreement because, not only does the unitranche lender require no payment blockage and a

---

[5] See further: Ronald Kahn, 'The many faces of unitranche,' PEhub.com, March 2012.

very limited, if any, remedy standstill, but disputes over many other issues including the right to liquidate collateral and the ability to provide DIP financing might occur.

Increasingly, either because borrowers lobby for a lower interest rate, or because the unitranche lender decides that the stated interest rate on their loan isn't high enough, the unitranche lender enlists the asset-based lender to help them out by suggesting that, in addition to providing the revolver, the ABL also provides a first-out tranche to the unitranche/term loan. This ability to 'tranche the unitranche loan' not only results in a lower interest rate for the borrower (compared to what the unitranche lender would otherwise have to charge to meet its desired returns) and a higher rate to the last-out provider (compared to the stated interest rate of the unitranche loan), but it also results in complex legal documentation and, potentially, a different outcome down the road for a borrower.

As previously mentioned, the mezzanine product market is in constant evolution, and this is partly driven by the changing nature of the providers of junior finance. Credit hedge funds, Collateralized Loan Obligations (CLO), Business Development Companies (BDC) and small business investment companies (SBIC) are all (relatively) new players to the game.

Pricing: historically, and floating across cycles, the unitranche instrument has traditionally yielded around 11–12% (the mezzanine average globally is 14%). In 2011–2012, that has come down to 8.5–10%, often now yielding a return below the hurdle rate of the provider. Therefore, more and more unitranche providers are now suggesting that they need to lay off a first-out piece of their unitranche debt so that their remaining last-out piece has a yield which is acceptable to their own investors. In essence, the unitranche is internally divided into a first-out tranche and a last-out tranche (creating more junior and more senior tranches of loans).

The interest rate for the facility is allocated among the lenders disproportionately, to provide the first-out tranche with a lower effective interest rate than the last-out tranche. Under the first-out and last-out arrangements, interest payments are made to an administrative agent who is responsible for distributing to the first-out and last-out lenders their portion of the interest payment based on the agreed allocation.

Mandatory and optional principal payments are usually paid ratably to the first-out and last-out lenders until the occurrence of certain 'waterfall trigger events.' Upon the occurrence of these waterfall trigger events, the first-out lenders will receive priority payment on both their interest and principal until any payment is distributed to the last-out lenders. Waterfall trigger events usually include: (1) a payment default under the credit agreement; (2) failure of the borrower to comply with all or certain financial covenants, usually within a percentage range; (3) bankruptcy and insolvency events; and (4) failure of the borrower to conduct all or a material portion of its business, usually following a certain cure period. The payment waterfall typically only applies with respect to payments and proceeds received by the agent from the collateral, meaning that any other proceeds received by the agent would be distributed ratably to the lenders.[6]

This tranching of the unitranche, while enabling hedge funds to obtain the returns they need to continue providing unitranche facilities, can create other issues for borrowers. This exercise may not be totally transparent to the borrower. Unlike a capital structure where the relationship between traditional senior debt and mezzanine debt is governed by an inter-creditor agreement that's disclosed to the borrower, unitranche tranching is often governed by an 'agreement among lenders' which may not be disclosed to the borrower.[7] More often than not, it seems

---

[6] RK&O, 'The latest innovation in middle market lending: the unitranche facility,' March 2012.
[7] Ronald Kahn, 'Is unitranche still a unitranche?' PEhub.com, June 2011.

that the terms of this type of arrangement are kept confidential by the lenders. As a result, issues like standstill provisions and voting rights may now be unknown to the borrower.

## 11.5  REORGANIZATION OF INSOLVENCY LAWS IN EUROPE

One could argue that Europe has a partially coordinated (not harmonized) bankruptcy law system. Or, put differently, it has a system in place to ensure that the parties (the bankrupt firm as debtor, and its creditors) have no incentive to transfer their assets or court proceedings from one Member State to another to obtain more favorable treatment.

The Regulation applies to insolvency proceedings which comprise the following elements:

- Insolvency proceedings are collective – all the creditors' rights are considered at the same time and individual proceedings are suspended.
- The debtor is insolvent – it has been established that they cannot meet their financial obligations.
- The debtor is disqualified from acting – their powers to manage their assets and dispose of them are limited and under the administrator's control.
- Methods are laid down for the appointment of an administrator.

The courts with jurisdiction to open insolvency proceedings are those for the Member State in which the 'center of a debtor's main interests' is situated. Where a company is concerned, this will generally mean its registered head office.

However, secondary proceedings can be opened later to liquidate assets in another Member State. The law of the Member State in which such insolvency proceedings are opened determines their effects.

The Regulation provides that proceedings opened in several Member States are to be coordinated between them, notably via active cooperation between administrators.

All decisions taken by a court in a Member State which has jurisdiction in the main proceedings is basically recognized automatically in the other Member States without further review.

In March 2012, the European Commission put out a consultation in its 2012 working program, as a first step in the revision of the existing bankruptcy laws in place, 10 years after the Regulation (EC) No 1346/2000 on insolvency proceedings (the 'Insolvency Regulation') which has applied since May 31 2002 came into force.[8] That consultation followed a report by the European Parliament in October 2011 with recommendations to the Commission on insolvency proceedings in the context of EU company law.

The Insolvency Regulation has been in force since May 31 2002, and applies whenever a debtor has assets or creditors in more than one Member State. It sets out provisions in relation to jurisdiction, recognition, applicable law and the coordination of insolvency proceedings opened in several Member States.

That consultancy phase resulted, in December 2012, in a draft proposal[9] for a redrafting of the insolvency proceedings published by the Commission. This is a first step towards an

---

[8] See further: Bob Wessels, 'Revision of the EU Insolvency Regulation: What type of facelift?' 2011.
[9] Proposal for a Regulation of the European Parliament and of the Council amending Council Regulation (EC) No 1346/2000 on insolvency proceedings – 2012/0360(COD).

EU 'rescue and recovery' culture to help companies (and individuals) in financial difficulties. Overall, the focus is more on restructuring and going concerns rather than a prelude to liquidation. In that sense, the European policymakers are moving more towards a Chapter 7/ Chapter 11 distinction as is the case under US insolvency law. It will also increase legal certainty, by providing clear rules to determine jurisdiction, and ensuring that when a debtor is faced with insolvency proceedings in several Member States, the courts handling the different proceedings work closely with one another. Information to creditors will be improved by obliging Member States to publish key decisions – about the opening of insolvency proceedings, for example. All in all, these changes will improve the efficiency and effectiveness of cross-border insolvency proceedings within the EU.

The proposal is, at the close of writing this book, up for a second reading by the European Parliament. It can be envisaged that more transparency regarding treatment of cross-border insolvency cases in the EU could create a wider window for mezzanine lending in Europe, which has, in recent years, moved across borders already, but only with baby steps.

# 11.6  ISLAMIC FINANCE: SUKUKS AND NON-RISK-FREE BOND LOOK-ALIKES

Islamic finance has been marching along in the financial universe ever since the 1980s, but definitely since the 2008 financial crisis. Based on fundamentals completely different than the conventional finance sphere, it has demonstrated significant resilience in the downturn.

A key difference is the absence of interest payments (or interest on interest payments) known as Riba, or in more general terms, any increase in capital without any services provided and risk taking. Riba is not Sharia compliant. It therefore qualifies as a bond look-alike in the Islamic finance world, but it is not really as it lacks the basic criteria of a conventional bond.[10] Unfortunately, it has become commonplace for financial institutions in the ME as well as in SEA and London to issue instruments as being so-called Sharia compliant but which in essence are not, in order to attract interest from larger investors than would be the case if the product were effectively Sharia compliant. There is no direct implication of that non-compliance, but it does hurt the transparency and uniformity the industry so badly needs, as well as its future progress and (product) development.

The closest one can come is to compare a sukuk to an instrument represented by certificates, which represents the entitlement of the certificate holder to the economic value produced by the underlying assets financed with the sukuk, or other assets earmarked in the contract. It therefore provides an open window (and partial ownership) to the profit-generating capacity of the underlying assets within the context of the business model applied. It is therefore dependent on the real profit-making of those assets to generate a return for its investors, which cannot be extracted from other asset owners in the business (which is the case in conventional finance) unless those assets which are financed produced value themselves. They come in

---

[10] See further my previous writings in: L. Nijs: 'Shaping tomorrow's marketplace: investment philosophies for emerging markets and a semi-globalized world,' *Euromoney*, 2011.

many different types depending on the transaction and assets being financed (Sukuk Murabaha, S. Musharaka, S. Istisna'a, S. Al Ijara and S. Al Isthithmar).

In order to be Sharia compliant, the instrument cannot be traded and therefore needs to be held until maturity. The certificates also need to be bought before the financing of the assets occurs. The direct consequence is that a certificate holder can receive no compensation for a long time, and potentially not at all. In fact, it is even possible to lose the principal value of the instrument. Nevertheless, many FIs have developed products where SPVs issuing the certificates (and financing the firm or assets directly) model the cash flows of the sukuk as if it were a conventional bond. In line with what has been mentioned above, there is a lively practice of issuing so-called Islamic finance compliant products which violate the Sharia principles. It qualifies as market-making but might harm the future growth of the industry. It is good to note that since 2010, the AAOIFI (Accounting & Auditing Organization for Islamic Financial Institutions) has been working on a set of (minimum) conditions per product, which would act as a code of conduct (for those institutions that sign up) but which, however, would have only moral authority. Progress is being made but slowly, as many opinions (of different scholars coming from different schools) need to be brought together.

A further complication is the result of the absence of transparent (cross-border) insolvency laws in the Middle East and South East Asian region. The consequence is that open-ended questions related to what happens if the underlying assets become non-performing or the company becomes insolvent are still on the table. Would the implication be that the sukuk holders are entitled (up to the amount invested) to the proceeds of the liquidation of the assets financed (or all assets engaged in the firm or business model)? How would the interaction be with other (conventional) creditors, given the absence of an inter-creditor agreement? Also the treatment of the sukuk's proceeds and qualification of the instrument under international taxation treaties still remains obscure, and therefore hinders the development of the product group's full potential, and industry as a whole.

## 11.7 ORIGINATION SOURCES FOR MEZZANINE

Traditionally, the origination channels for mezzanine products have been the PE sphere and on the sponsorless side of things, interested borrowers could mainly be found in the SME sphere and particularly the smaller end of the SME sphere. They have always been in a tough spot when it comes to raising senior debt and equity alike, and therefore have been engaged borrowers of mezzanine products with preference for plain vanilla subordinated debt.

Part of that story also includes the unwillingness of family-owned or closely-held businesses to dilute control of their assets over time. This does not always yield situations which would make one jealous. Often, having started the firm on a shoestring of capital loaded with senior debt, further growth needs to be (at least partially) financed with additional debt as operational cash flows do not grow fast enough and at large enough volumes to justify meeting the interest and principal amortization hurdle(s) on the initial debt. Also, the need for further financing is less likely to cover fixed assets, which restricts or often fully excludes the availability of pure asset-based senior debt. Under current market conditions, cash flow-based lending is very tight through the traditional banking system, especially when the organization was relatively front-loaded with senior debt.

Over time, the mezzanine sphere, partly driven by the aforementioned PE activity, has been diversifying in terms of its origination sources and channels to now include:

- M&A.
- Refinancing.
- Divestitures by private and/or public companies.
- Secondary/tertiary buy-outs.
- New buy-outs but likely on a very selective basis.
- Refinancing companies with limited access to mainstream capital markets.
- Filling the gap left by CLOs ending their reinvestment periods.
- Replacing existing mezzanine or a new mezzanine tranche.

That also has triggered a new set of additional questions which need to be answered including:

- Pricing and structuring conditions in secondary/tertiary buy-outs.
- Examining where mezzanine fits into capital structures of already levered companies.
- Adequate structuring of growth capital.
- Should certain sectors be avoided when allocating mezzanine capital?

It is also fair to say that in those newer transactions, there is a need to have a mature and liquid HY and/or leveraged loan market available. It can be mentioned that those, at this point in time, are only available in the US and Europe, and only very embryonic in Asia. Indeed, one can even wonder how deep the liquidity is in the European market. I guess that part of the answer will be provided during the upcoming refinancing wall in 2014–2016, where the levels of liquidity and depth of that market will be tested.

## 11.8  THE ROLE OF GOVERNMENTAL ORGANIZATIONS

Receiving too little attention on average, development banks and organizations have become significant providers of mezzanine and private equity products globally, but given their nature, predominantly in emerging markets. They, so to speak, prepare the markets for the arrival of commercial capital which has less or no development objectives, and on average less of a risk appetite for what, on average, are illiquid investments in often even more illiquid markets, where IPO exits are impossible or not preferable and where no secondary markets exist for many debt products.

Nevertheless, they finance (often as a syndication of development banks) firms which often are or become the bedrock of the local economies in their countries, and therefore contribute to the creation and strength of the economic fabric in those countries which then fosters education and social mobility.

Although, in my experience, development banks have become more commercial during the last decade in their approach and way of structuring deals, where returns on deals have become equally important vis-à-vis the development objectives they carry, they continue to be a strong catalyst for growth in many industries and parts of the EM world. Credit should go to them for doing so, including their willingness to structure mezzanine products into frontier markets (known often by a limited legal infrastructure), thereby offering products which, in terms of sophistication, are far ahead of the curve relative to the financial debt products the local banking scene is producing and offering (often restricted by regulation).

Back-to-back with that phenomenon, they are also the largest equity provider, in many EM and frontier countries, of equity capital for private businesses either as direct investments or through emerging PE managers in those countries, accounting for often 50% or more of the committed capital in many PE funds, who allocate a few tens of billions of USD each year to businesses in EM countries. The financial media therefore got stuck in their typical glamorous nihilism when limiting reporting on EM (emerging markets) PE funding and investing to the initiatives undertaken by Bob Geldof and the Africa-earmarked fund of the Carlyle Group and look-alikes in other EMs.

## 11.9  THE REFINANCING WALL: OPPORTUNITIES AND CHALLENGES

In the introductory chapter I mentioned the refinancing wall which is upcoming in the period 2014–2016. Beyond the question of whether the market is going to be ready to provide sufficient liquidity to refinance those instruments, where it can be mentioned that given the state the capital markets were in during mid to late 2012, significant issues (read defaults) might be on the horizon, especially in the PIK, HY and LBO debt market.[11] Relevant questions will then be:

- How will banks participate and at what levels?
- What is the likelihood of a wholesale amend and extend approach to manage the maturity of so many loans?
- What are the main drivers for sponsors choosing mezzanine and what are the main alternatives to mezzanine, e.g., unitranche?
- What will the relationships be between new lenders and sponsors and how will they be managed?
- What will the economic effect on underlying portfolio companies be, given the increase in margin due to senior/mezzanine refinancing?
- How will existing leverage multiples be managed at the time of restructuring?
- Who will the main players in the new order be; will structured credit vehicles return?

## 11.10  PERFORMANCE OF MEZZANINE PRODUCTS

Although sponsored mezzanine will always play a significant role in the market, it is undeniably the case that the sponsorless market for mezzanine has been growing across the cycles, and has become an independent source of capital for organizations, often kicked off in emerging markets by development banks and organizations providing sponsorless mezzanine capital to emerging SMEs.

---

[11] See recently: Robin Wigglesworth, 'Moody's warns on LBO debt default,' *Financial Times*, May 29, 2012 pointing at the finite lifespan of CLOs and vacating banks are the prime drivers behind this process.

In terms of mezzanine products' performance, there is no real answer when judging that question globally. As mentioned earlier, the performance of mezzanine products (although having been close to PE investments) is a function of a couple of things which will also determine the way forward for the product group.

The first element is the cost of funding for the provider. Given the financial repression we have been experiencing ever since the start of the financial crisis, the cost of funding has lowered, but that benefit has often been captured at the level of the provider (banks or funds) rather than put forward to the borrowers, although pricing at that level has come down as well but not as significantly as at the wholesale level.

The second element is the fact that the risk/reward dynamics are co-determined for mezzanine products by the way the deal is structured, the existing senior and junior debt load already in place, the covenants that could be agreed upon, the positioning in the cash flow waterfall and the conditions agreed upon in the inter-creditor agreement. The consequence is that the flexibility feeds through in the pricing model, which implies that a good deal can become non-financeable and that a troubled deal can become realistic through any of the mechanisms listed.

On top of that, there are market differences in terms of structuring techniques and pricing differentials. For example, and judged on an aggregate basis, European mezzanine products rely much more on the equity kicker and less on the interest component for their returns, whereas in the US it is, once again on average, the opposite. A summary of the most dominant differences is given in Table 11.1 below.[12]

**Table 11.1**    Geographical diversification in the use and conditions of mezzanine products

| Characteristic | US mezzanine | Australian mezzanine | European mezzanine |
|---|---|---|---|
| **Capital structure** | Junior unsecured, Contractually subordinated | Junior secured Benefits from the same collateral as senior loans but on a second ranking and/or subordinated basis | Junior (un)secured Some products benefit from the same collateral as senior loans but on a second and/or subordinated basis |
| **Fixed/ floating** | Primarily fixed with PIK component | Both fixed and floating with PIK component | Fixed/floating with PIK component |
| **Pricing** | 1,600–1,800 bps return (middle market) 1,100–1,500 bps return (large cap) | 1,600–1,900 bps (all in) | Senior mezzanine: Euribor + 1,300–1,400 bps Junior mezzanine: Euribor + 1,600–1,700 bps |
| **Equity kicker** | Both warranted and warrant-less deals in the market | Both warranted and warrant-less deals in the market | Both warranted and warrant-less deals in the market |
| **Term** | 6–8 years | 5–7 years | 7–10 years |
| **Prepayment penalties** | Declining premium Some no-call protection | No-call protection typical | No-call protection typical |

---

[12] Source: Adjusted from Babson Capital.

**Table 11.1** *Continued*

| Characteristic | US mezzanine | Australian mezzanine | European mezzanine |
|---|---|---|---|
| **Typical deal size** | Mid cap often no larger than US$50 million<br>Large cap US$50–200 million | AUD 5–150 million | €100–500 million |
| **Public/ private** | Financial sponsor-backed LBO of private companies, growth financing for capital investment or acquisitions by unsponsored private companies | Financial sponsor-backed LBO of private companies, public-to-private, or divestitures by private or public companies | Financial sponsor-backed LBO of private company |
| **Security package/ covenants** | Some covenants as banks, but looser, maintenance-based | Second ranking security with financial and non-financial covenants based on senior terms | Similar covenant package to senior loans with maintenance financial covenants<br>Second or third ranking |

In one of my previous books[13] I discussed the mezzanine product group's performance per region of the world, of which you can find hereafter an updated overview (see Figure 11.3).

During 2012, the market and the mezzanine product group has been demonstrating the dynamics of a bright future, although the regulator isn't making the life of (mezzanine) fund managers very easy, with a myriad of complicated, unnecessary and behind-the-curve pieces

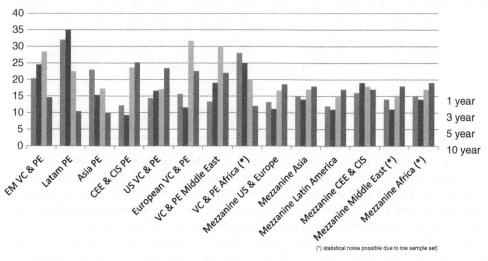

(*) statistical noise possible due to low sample set)

**Figure 11.3** Private equity/mezzanine performance at the end of 2012 – pooled end-to-end returns, net of fees, expenses and carried interest

---

[13] See further: L. Nijs, 'Shaping tomorrow's marketplace: Investment philosophies for emerging markets and a globalized world,' *Euromoney*, 2011.

of legislation including the EU AIFM (Alternative Investment Fund Manager Directive), the US Dodd–Franck Act, the US FATCA (Foreign Account Tax Compliance Act) and Basel III.

Beyond that hurdle, the key word will be flexibility, a characteristic intrinsic to the product group and its structuring capabilities. That needs to be aligned with the need for a certain level of returns providers of capital are looking for, a balancing act in itself.

Ultimately, there is no better deal for borrowers than to be able to tap into synthetic debt (per instrument but also on an aggregate level) which takes into account the sensitivities of the business model and the market(s) and industries it operates in. Ultimately, there is a difference between financial and economic default, and one doesn't want to wreck an otherwise perfectly fine and well-functioning business.

A debt instrument which can maintain its tax-deductibility advantage while preserving the flexibility of an equity product will show some of the characteristics shown in Table 11.2:

**Table 11.2**     Essential dynamics warranting the flexibility of mezzanine products

| Cash flow dynamics of firm/project | Debt characteristic |
| --- | --- |
| Duration | Duration/maturity of instrument(s) |
| Currency | Currency mix (currency swaps) |
| Effect of inflation/uncertainty re: future | Fixed versus floating rate (debt for equity/equity for debt swaps) |
| Growth pattern | Straight versus convertible (based on expected growth dynamics and CF evolution over time) |
| Cyclicality and other effects | Special features (call, put options, commodity linked bonds, weather bonds, catastrophe bonds, PP dependent bonds ...) |

It has been observed that, within the mezzanine product group, certain products are more used in the private and others more in the public capital markets, caused by the nature and liquidity of those respective markets and the (non)-availability of a secondary market for those products.

| Mezzanine financing instruments | Private mezzanine instruments | Subordinated loans (Profit) participating loans 'Silent' participations |
| --- | --- | --- |
| | Public mezzanine instruments | Profit participating rights Convertible bonds Bonds with warrants |

As a final comment on the product group and its outlook: financial Darwinism calls upon the ability to provide flexible solutions in an ever-changing economic landscape. Mezzanine products and their DNA are designed to do just that: provide solutions for situations where the traditional lending group cannot provide answers. This can often happen at a cost lower than equity, and with the benefit of no, or only temporary, dilution of the existing shareholders' equity position. The dynamics of the products, their pricing and total return will ultimately float on the risk-adjusted waves of the pricing ocean, while trying to avoid hazards put in place by regulators and rating agencies. Beyond all that, mezzanine products are here to stay. The market has a need and it is, and will be, served by the mezzanine product group one way or the other. It is the eloquent structurer and negotiator that will allow both the provider and the borrower to benefit from the dynamics this product group offers.

# Appendix 1

# Overview of Term Sheets and/or Model Contracts for the Mezzanine Product Group

## Contents

## APPENDIX 1.A TERM SHEET FOR A SENIOR SECURED LOAN

Based upon the preliminary information provided to XYZ regarding the proposed Facility, the following Summary of Terms outlines (for discussion) the key terms and conditions of a potential transaction. This Summary of Terms is not intended to be a comprehensive list of all relevant terms and conditions of the transactions contemplated herein. Further, these terms are subject to completion of due diligence, legal and other internal review and receipt of related approvals satisfactory to XYZ and any other approval procedures customary for a transaction of this nature. Final terms will be included in definitive documentation based on this Summary of Terms and executed by the applicable parties. This Summary of Terms is intended for the sole benefit of the Company identified in Appendix A and certain of its affiliates and shall not be relied upon by any other person.

**Facility:** A term loan that is full recourse to Borrower(s) (except as provided in Appendix A), secured by a first or junior lien, as applicable, on all of Borrower(s)' assets, and is subject to the terms and conditions contained herein and in the definitive Facility documentation.

**Borrower(s):** As set forth in Appendix A.

**Lender:** XYZ, on a committed basis.

**Guarantor(s):** As set forth in Appendix A. The Borrower(s) and the Guarantor(s) shall hereinafter each be referred to as a 'Loan Party,' and collectively, as 'Loan Parties.'

**Closing Date:** As set forth in Appendix A.

**Loan:** Lender will make available to Borrower(s) a loan in an aggregate amount up to the amount set forth in Appendix A (the 'Loan Amount') in pre-determined draw amounts, as further specified in Appendix A.

**Availability:** On the dates specified in Appendix A, Borrower(s) may request that the Lender fund a draw up to an amount set forth in Appendix A for such date (each such funding, an 'Advance'). At the time of each funding of an Advance by the Lender (each, an 'Advance Date'), Borrower(s) shall be in compliance with all of the covenants, representations and warranties of this Facility.

Unless otherwise agreed by XYZ, Borrower(s) must provide XYZ with its request at least two (2) business days prior to the date on which an Advance will be funded by the Lender. For the avoidance of doubt, notice received by XYZ after 5:00 pm Washington, DC time on any business day shall be deemed to be received on the following business day.

**Use of Funds:** The Borrower(s) shall utilize the proceeds from the Advances as set forth in Appendix A.

**Currencies:** All Advances, prepayments and payments of fees and indemnities and any other payments under the Facility shall be made in United States Dollars.

**Collateral:** As set forth in Appendix A. As security for Borrower(s)' performance of all of their obligations under the Facility and Guarantor(s)' performance of their obligations under the Guaranties, the applicable Loan Parties will grant to the Lender a security interest in and to the Collateral (with the applicable lien priority specified with respect thereto in Appendix A).

**Maturity Date:** The Facility will terminate and the aggregate outstanding Advances, together with interest thereon at the applicable Interest Rate and all fees, expenses, indemnities and other amounts owing to the Lender, will be due and fully payable on the earliest of (i) the Expiration Date (as set forth in Appendix A), (ii) the occurrence of a Termination Event, or (iii) the occurrence of an Event of Default, at the option of the Lender.

**Interest Rate:** Each Advance shall accrue interest at a rate per annum equal to (i) the sum of (x) the greater of (A) three-month LIBOR and (B) the LIBOR Floor, plus (y) the Spread Amount, multiplied by (ii) the outstanding principal balance of such Advance. The Interest Rate shall be determined on the Closing Date and reset on each Interest Payment Date and shall be calculated on a 360-day year basis for the actual number of days elapsed (including the first day but excluding the last day) occurring in the related Interest Period. Interest on the Advances shall be payable in arrears on each Interest Payment Date in respect of the previous Interest Period, and together with all outstanding principal and other amounts owing, on the Maturity Date.

**Interest Period:** For each Advance, (i) initially, the period commencing on the related Advance Date and ending on the calendar day prior to the next succeeding Interest Payment Date, and (ii) thereafter, each period commencing on an Interest Payment Date and ending on the calendar day prior to the next succeeding Interest Payment Date. Notwithstanding the foregoing, no Interest Period may end after the Maturity Date.

**Interest Payment Date:** Set forth in Appendix A.

**LIBOR Floor:** Set forth in Appendix A.

**Spread Amount:** Set forth in Appendix A.

**Mandatory Prepayments:** Subject to any mandatory prepayments from the following amounts required under existing secured credit agreements, Borrower(s) shall apply 100% of the net cash proceeds of any of the following transactions to prepay, on a pro rata basis, the aggregate outstanding Advances: (i) sales, liquidations or other transfers of any Collateral other than sales in the ordinary course of business, (ii) the incurrence by any Borrower of any debt (other than permitted indebtedness including the refinancing of prior indebtedness) or any equity or other capital raises (other than contributions of indemnity payments received by the Company and required to be applied to satisfy obligations of its subsidiaries), either public or private, whether in connection with a primary securities offering, a business combination of any kind, or otherwise, (iii) to the extent unencumbered, non-ordinary course asset sales (including aircraft divestments); provided that, with respect to clause (ii), in no event will any of the Collateral or Lender's security interest therein be released to the applicable Loan Party until the aggregate outstanding Advances, together with interest thereon at the applicable Interest Rate and all fees, expenses, indemnities and other amounts owing to the Lender shall have been paid in full. Notwithstanding anything to the contrary contained herein, any amounts advanced and repaid cannot be re-borrowed.

**Optional Prepayments:** Upon written notice to the Lender at least two business days in advance, Borrower(s) may prepay all or a portion of the outstanding Advances, without penalty; provided that in no event will any of the Collateral be released to the applicable Loan Party until the aggregate outstanding Advances, together with interest thereon at the applicable Interest Rate and all fees, expenses, indemnities and other amounts owing to the Lender shall have been paid in full. Notwithstanding anything to the contrary contained herein, any amounts advanced and repaid cannot be re-borrowed.

**Executive Privileges and Compensation:** Until such time as the Facility is repaid in full and XYZ ceases to own any equity securities of the Company acquired pursuant to this Facility (including any Warrants and underlying Equity Interests acquired by XYZ upon exercise thereof) (the 'Relevant Period'), the following restrictions on executive privileges and compensation shall apply to the 'Relevant Companies,' as defined in Appendix A:

1. The Relevant Companies shall be subject to the executive compensation and corporate governance requirements of Section 111(b) of the EESA and XYZ's guidelines that carry out the provisions of such subsection for systemically significant failing institutions as set forth in Notice 2008-PSSFI.
2. The Relevant Companies and their respective SEOs (as defined below) shall modify or terminate all benefit plans, arrangements and agreements (including golden parachute agreements) to the extent necessary to be in compliance with Section 111(b) of the EESA and the guidelines set forth in Notice 2008-AAAAA.
3. The Relevant Companies shall comply in all respects with the limits on annual executive compensation deductibles imposed by Section 162(m)(5) of the Internal Revenue Code of 1986, as amended, as applicable.
4. None of the Relevant Companies shall pay or accrue any bonus or incentive compensation to the 25 most highly compensated employees (including the SEOs) (collectively, the 'Senior Employees') except as approved by the President's Designee.
5. None of the Relevant Companies shall adopt or maintain any compensation plan that would encourage manipulation of their reported earnings to enhance the compensation of any of its employees; and
6. The Relevant Companies shall maintain all suspensions and other restrictions of contributions to Benefit Plans that are in place or initiated as of the Closing Date. At any time during the Relevant Period, the Lender shall have the right to require any Relevant Company to

claw back any bonuses or other compensation, including golden parachutes, paid to any Senior Employees in violation of any of the foregoing.

Within 120 days of the Closing Date, the principal executive officer (or person acting in a similar capacity) of each Relevant Company shall certify in writing, under penalty of perjury, to the Lender's Chief Compliance Officer that such Relevant Company's compensation committee has reviewed the compensation arrangements of the SEOs with its senior risk officers and determined that the compensation arrangements do not encourage the SEOs to take unnecessary and excessive risks that threaten the value of such Relevant Company. Each Relevant Company shall preserve appropriate documentation and records to substantiate such certification in an easily accessible place for a period not less than three (3) years following the Maturity Date.

'President's Designee' means one or more officers from the Executive Branch designated by the President. 'SEOs' means the Loan Parties' 'senior executive officers' as defined in subsection 111(b)(3) of the EESA and regulations issued thereunder, including the rules set forth in 31 C.F.R. Part 30, or as otherwise may be defined by XYZ. 'Benefit Plan' means, collectively, any compensation, bonus, incentive and other benefit plans (including supplemental executive retirement plans), arrangements and agreements (including golden parachute, severance and employment agreements).

**Asset Divestment:** With respect to any private passenger aircraft or interest in such aircraft that is owned or held by any Loan Party or any subsidiary immediately prior to the Closing Date, such party shall demonstrate to the satisfaction of the President's Designee that it is taking all reasonable steps to divest itself of such aircraft or interest. Further, no Loan Party shall acquire or lease any such aircraft or interest in such aircraft.

**Material Transactions:** The Loan Parties shall provide prompt notice to the President's Designee of any asset sale, investment, contract, commitment, or other transaction not in the ordinary course of business proposed to be entered into with a value in excess of $100 million (a 'Material Transaction'). The President's Designee shall have the right to review and prohibit any such Material Transaction if the President's Designee determines that it would be inconsistent with or detrimental to the long-term viability of such Loan Party.

**Restrictions on Expenses:** During the Relevant Period, the Company shall maintain and implement its comprehensive written policy on corporate expenses ('Expense Policy') and distribute the Expense Policy to all employees of the Company and its subsidiaries covered under the policy. Any material amendments to the Expense Policy shall require the prior written consent of the President's Designee, and any material deviations from the Expense Policy, whether in contravention thereof or pursuant to waivers provided for thereunder, shall promptly be reported to the President's Designee.

The Expense Policy shall, at a minimum: (i) require compliance with all applicable law, (ii) apply to the Company and all of its subsidiaries, (iii) govern (a) the hosting, sponsorship or other payment for conferences and events, (b) travel accommodations and expenditures, (c) consulting arrangements with outside service providers, (d) any new lease or acquisition of real estate, (e) expenses relating to office or facility renovations or relocations, and (f) expenses relating to entertainment or holiday parties; and (iv) provide for (a) internal reporting and oversight, and (b) mechanisms for addressing non-compliance with the policy.

**Restructuring Plan:** By no later than <date>, the Company shall submit to the President's Designee a plan to achieve and sustain the long-term viability, international competitiveness and energy efficiency of the Company and its subsidiaries (the 'Restructuring Plan'), which Restructuring Plan shall include specific actions intended to result in the following:

1. Repayment of the Loan Amount and any other financing extended by the Government under all applicable terms and conditions.
2. Ability of the Company and its subsidiaries to (x) comply with applicable Federal fuel efficiency and emissions requirements, and (y) commence domestic manufacturing of advanced technology vehicles, as described in section xx of the Energy Independence and Security Act of 2007.
3. Achievement by the Company and its subsidiaries of a positive net present value, using reasonable assumptions and taking into account all existing and projected future costs, including repayment of the Loan Amount and any other financing extended by the Government.
4. Rationalization of costs, capitalization and capacity with respect to the manufacturing workforce, suppliers and dealerships of the Company and its subsidiaries; and
5. A product mix and cost structure that is competitive in the United States marketplace.

The Restructuring Plan shall extend through 2010 monthly and annually through 2014 and shall include detailed historical and projected financial statements with supporting schedules and additional information as may be requested by the President's Designee.

**Restructuring Targets:** In addition to the Restructuring Plan, the Company and its subsidiaries shall use their best efforts to achieve the following targets:

1. Reduction of their outstanding unsecured public indebtedness (other than with respect to pension and employee benefits obligations) by not less than two-thirds through conversion of existing public debt into equity or debt (a 'Bond Exchange') and other appropriate means.
2. Reduction of the total amount of compensation, including wages and benefits, paid to their U.S. employees so that, by no later than <date> the average of such total amount, per hour and per person, is an amount that is competitive with the average total amount of such compensation, as certified by the Secretary of Labor, paid per hour and per person to employees of <reference companies> whose site of employment is in the United States (the 'Compensation Reductions').
3. Elimination of the payment of any compensation or benefits to U.S. employees of the Company or any subsidiary who have been fired, laid-off, furloughed, or idled, other than customary severance pay (the 'Severance Rationalization').
4. Application of the work rules to their U.S. employees, beginning not later than <date> in a manner that is competitive with <reference companies> whose site of employment is in the United States (the 'Work Rule Modifications' and, together with the Compensation Reductions and Severance Rationalization, the 'Labor Modifications'); and
5. Provision that not less than one-half of the value of each future payment or contribution made by them to the account of the voluntary employees beneficiary association (or similar account) ('VEBA') of a labor organization representing the employees of the Company and its subsidiaries shall be made in the form of the stock of the Company or one of its subsidiaries (the 'VEBA Modifications'), and the total value of any such payment or

contribution shall not exceed the amount of any such payment or contribution that was required for such time period under the collective bargaining agreement that applied as of the day before the Closing Date.

**Term Sheet Requirements:** By no later than <date>, the Company shall submit to the President's Designee:

1. A term sheet signed on behalf of the Company and the leadership of each major U.S. labor organization that represents the employees of the Company and its subsidiaries (collectively, the 'Unions') providing for the Labor Modifications; and
2. A term sheet signed on behalf of the Company and representatives of the VEBA providing for the VEBA Modifications; and
3. A term sheet signed on behalf of the Company and representatives of holders of the Company's public debt providing for the Bond Exchange.

**Restructuring Plan Report:** On or before <date> the Company shall submit to the President's Designee a written certification and report detailing the progress made by the Company and its subsidiaries in implementing the Restructuring Plan. The report shall identify any deviations from the Restructuring Targets and explain the rationale for these deviations, including an explanation of why such deviations do not jeopardize the Borrower's long-term viability. The report shall also include evidence satisfactory to the President's Designee that the following events have occurred:

1. Approval of the Labor Modifications by the members of the Unions.
2. Receipt of all necessary approvals of the VEBA Modifications other than regulatory and judicial approvals, provided that the Company must have filed and be diligently prosecuting applications for any necessary regulatory and judicial approvals; and
3. The commencement of an exchange offer to implement the Bond Exchange.

**President's Designee Review/Certification:** The President's Designee will review the Restructuring Plan Report and other materials submitted by the Company to determine whether the Company and its subsidiaries have taken all steps necessary to achieve and sustain the long-term viability, international competitiveness and energy efficiency of the Company and its subsidiaries in accordance with its Restructuring Plan. If the President's Designee determines that these standards have been met, he will so certify (the 'Plan Completion Certification').

**Termination Event:** If the President's Designee has not issued the Plan Completion Certification by <date> or such later date (not to exceed 30 days after <date>) as the President's Designee may specify (the 'Certification Deadline'), the maturity of the Loan shall be automatically accelerated and any portion of the Loan Amount not invested in or loaned to the Borrower's principal financial subsidiaries shall become due and payable on the 30th day after the Certification Deadline, without any further action on the part of the Lender.

**Reporting Requirements:** In addition to the foregoing, the Loan Parties shall deliver to the Lender the following periodic reports and certifications:

1. Weekly status report, commencing with the week of <date> detailing the 13-week rolling cash forecast for the Company and its subsidiaries (on a consolidated and consolidating basis).

2. Bi-weekly liquidity status report, commencing with the second week following the Closing Date, detailing, with respect to the Company and its subsidiaries (on a consolidated and consolidating basis): (i) the current liquidity profile; (ii) expected liquidity needs; (iii) any material changes in their business since the date of the last status report; (iv) any transfer, sale, pledge or other disposition of any material asset since the date of the last status report; and (v) any changes to their capital structure.
3. Monthly certification that (i) the Expense Policy conforms to the requirements set forth herein; (ii) the Company and its subsidiaries are in compliance with the Expense Policy; and (iii) there have been no material amendments thereto or deviations therefrom other than those that have been disclosed to and approved by the Lender.
4. Monthly certification that all Benefit Plans with respect to Senior Executive Officers are in compliance with Section 111(b) of the EESA; and
5. Certified copies of all publicly filed financial reports and auditors' opinions.

**Access to Information and Right to Audit:** At all times while the Facility is in effect, the Borrower(s) and each of their direct and indirect subsidiaries shall permit the Lender and its agents, consultants, contractors and advisors, and the Special Inspector General of the Troubled Assets Relief Program, access to personnel and any books, papers, records or other data that may be relevant to the financial assistance, including compliance with the financing terms and conditions.

**Representations and Warranties:** As of each day the Facility is in place, the Loan Parties shall be deemed to make customary corporate and asset-level representations and warranties to the Lender. In addition, with respect to Warrants currently issued to the UST and to be issued to the UST under the Facility as provided below, the Borrower(s) will represent and warrant to the UST that, as of the date of this Indicative Summary of Terms and each date any Warrants are delivered, (i) the Warrants have been duly authorized and constitute a valid and legally binding obligation of the Company enforceable against it in accordance with its terms; (ii) the shares of common stock issuable upon exercise of the Warrants (the 'Warrant Shares') have been duly authorized and reserved for issuance upon exercise of the Warrants, and when so issued in accordance with the terms of the Warrants will be validly issued, fully paid and non-assessable; (iii) Loan Parties have the corporate power to enter into this Facility, to execute and deliver the related Facility documentation and the Warrants and to carry out its obligations hereunder and thereunder (which includes the issuance of the Warrants and Warrant Shares); (iv) the execution, delivery and performance by Loan Parties of the Facility documents and the Warrants, and the consummation of the transactions contemplated hereby and thereby, have been duly authorized by all necessary corporate action on their respective parts, and no further approval or authorization is required on their respective parts; (v) each Facility document, when executed and delivered by the applicable Loan Parties and Lender, is a valid, binding and enforceable obligation of each such Loan Party.

**Conditions Precedent to Closing:** Closing of the Facility and the funding of the first Advance will be subject to the satisfaction of customary conditions precedent, including but not limited to:

1. Execution of mutually satisfactory Facility documentation and completion of all conditions to funding contained therein.

2. Receipt of customary legal opinions from in-house, domestic and local foreign counsel to the Loan Parties acceptable to the Lender including, but not limited to, security interest perfection, PTO filings and analogous foreign law opinions, general corporate matters and enforceability, and an Investment Company Act opinion.

3. Receipt of officer's certificates and standard closing documents and certificates with respect to each Loan Party, each in a form acceptable to the Lender.

4. The Lender's interests in the Collateral shall be perfected in accordance with applicable law (except to the extent that the interests will be perfected on a post-closing basis, as may be agreed to by the Lender) and all necessary waivers, amendments, approvals and consents to the pledge of such Collateral shall have been obtained.

5. With respect to Collateral on which the Lender will have a first priority lien, evidence that all then-existing liens thereon have been released or will be released simultaneously with the funding of the first Advance.

6. With respect to Collateral on which the Lender will have a lien of junior priority, an intercreditor agreement duly executed by the other lienholders, in form and substance acceptable to the Lender in its sole discretion.

7. With respect to any equity investments that constitute Collateral, receipt of approvals duly executed by the Loan Parties' applicable creditors consenting to the pledge of such equity investments, to the extent required.

8. With respect to any real property that constitutes Collateral, receipt of an environmental indemnity from the applicable Loan Party.

9. Receipt of approvals duly executed by the Guarantor(s)' applicable creditors consenting to the guaranty, to the extent required.

10. A waiver shall have been duly executed by the Loan Parties and each SEO and delivered to the UST releasing the UST from any claims that the Loan Parties and/or the SEOs may otherwise have as a result of any modification of the terms of any benefit plans, arrangements and agreements to eliminate any provisions that would not be in compliance with the executive compensation and corporate governance requirements of Section 111 of the EESA and the guidelines set forth in Notice 2008-AAAAA.

11. A waiver shall have been duly executed by each SEO and delivered to the Loan Parties (with a copy to XYZ) releasing the Loan Parties from any claims the SEOs may otherwise have as a result of any modification of the terms of any benefit plans, arrangements and agreements to eliminate any provisions that would not be in compliance with the executive compensation and corporate governance requirements of Section 111 of the EESA and the guidelines set forth in Notice 2008-AAAAA.

12. A waiver shall have been duly executed by the Loan Parties and each Senior Employee and delivered to the UST releasing the UST from any claims that the Loan Parties and such Senior Employees may otherwise have as a result of the Loan Parties' failure to pay or accrue any bonus or incentive compensation as a result of the foregoing.

13. A waiver shall have been duly executed by each Senior Employee and delivered to the Loan Parties (with a copy to XYZ) releasing the Loan Parties from any claims that the SEOs may otherwise have as a result of the Loan Parties' failure to pay or accrue any bonus or incentive compensation as a result of the foregoing.

14. No material pending or threatened litigation not otherwise disclosed to and approved by the Lender.

15. Payment of all fees and expenses due at the Closing Date.

16. Satisfaction of the additional conditions precedent set forth in Appendix A; and

17. Delivery or performance (to the satisfaction of the Lender) of all other conditions to closing and due diligence items that may be requested by the Lender.

**Conditions Precedent to Each Advance:** The obligation of the Lender to make each Advance (including the initial Advance) will be subject to the satisfaction of the following conditions precedent:

1. No unmatured Event of Default or Event of Default shall have occurred and be continuing; and
2. Other customary conditions precedent.

**Covenants:** Unless waived by the Lender, the Loan Parties shall be subject to customary covenants for this type of transaction (with certain exceptions to be mutually agreed), including, but not limited to, the following negative covenants: (i) prohibition on redemption or buy back of any capital stock of the Company (other than pursuant to contracts existing as of <date>), (ii) restriction on transfer of assets, (iii) restriction on issuance of stock that would dilute the Warrants, (iv) negative pledge, (v) no fundamental change, (vi) limitation on transactions with affiliates, (vii) prohibitions on any dividends and distributions (or the economic equivalent) other than what is owed to unaffiliated entities pursuant to contract or law as of <date>, (viii) prompt notice of material adverse change with respect to any Loan Party, (ix) prohibition on creation of any new U.S. pension obligations until all U.S. pension plans maintained by the Company or any of its subsidiaries have been fully funded, and (x) such other covenants as may be deemed appropriate by the Lender.

**Financial Covenants:** At all times, the Company must satisfy each of the financial covenants set forth in Appendix A.

**Events of Default:** Will include, but not be limited to, each of the following events (as the same relates to each Loan Party):

1. Breach of representations, warranties or covenants or other terms and conditions of the Facility.
2. Default on any payment obligation under the Facility.
3. Bankruptcy/insolvency of any Borrower.
4. Going concern qualification with respect to any Borrower or any Guarantor in any correspondence from its accountants.
5. Change in control of any Borrower or any Guarantor.
6. Any Borrower's or any Guarantor's default under any other debt or prepayment obligations, the outstanding principal balance of which equals or exceeds $10 million.
7. Lender ceases to have a perfected first or junior (as applicable) security interest or ownership interest in any material portion of the Collateral.
8. Cross-default to any other facility or arrangement between any Borrower or any Guarantor or any of their affiliates and the Lender.

Upon the occurrence of any of the foregoing, the Lender shall have the option to declare that an Event of Default has occurred, at which time the Facility will terminate and all amounts owing with respect to the Facility will be immediately due and payable without presentment, demand, protest or notice of any kind, all of which shall be waived by the Loan Parties; provided, however, it is understood and agreed that a bankruptcy or insolvency of any Loan Party shall be immediately deemed an automatic Event of Default without the need for the Lender to declare it as such. The Lender shall be entitled to any and all remedies pursuant to the Facility documents and applicable law, each of which shall be cumulative and in addition to every other remedy available to the Lender.

**DIP Loan Conversion:** Upon the filing of a voluntary or involuntary bankruptcy petition by or in respect of any Loan Party, the Lender shall have the exclusive right, exercisable at its option, to convert this Facility into a debtor-in-possession facility in form and substance acceptable to the Lender.

**Joint and Several Liability:** In the event of multiple Borrowers or Guarantors, such parties will be jointly and severally liable to the Lender for all representations, warranties, covenants, obligations and liabilities of each of the Borrowers or Guarantors, as applicable, under the Facility. An unmatured Event of Default or an Event of Default of one party will be considered an unmatured Event of Default or an Event of Default by each party, and the Lender shall have no obligation to proceed against one party before proceeding against the other party. Such parties shall waive any defense to their obligations under the Facility based upon or arising out of the disability or other defense or cessation of liability of one party versus the other. A party's subrogation claim arising from payments to the Lender shall constitute a capital investment in another party subordinated to any claims of the Lender, and equal to a ratable share of the equity interests in such party.

**Summary of Warrant Terms Warrant:** Under the terms of the commitment, the UST will receive Warrants to purchase common shares of the Company.

**Exercise Price Per Share:** The 15-day trailing average price determined as of <date>. The Exercise Price Per Share shall be subject to anti-dilution adjustments.

**Amount:** The total number of Warrants will be equal to 20% of the Maximum Loan Amount divided by the Exercise Price Per Share, provided that the number of Warrants will be capped at 20% of the issued and outstanding common equity interests of the Company, before giving effect to the exercise of the Warrants ('the Warrant Limit').

**Additional Notes:** In the event that the Warrant Limit reduces the number of Warrants issuable to the UST, the UST will receive Additional Notes in an amount equal to 6.67% of the Maximum Loan Amount less a sum equal to one-third of the number of Warrants actually granted to the UST times the Exercise Price Per Share.

**Term:** Perpetual

**Exercisability:** Immediately exercisable, in whole or in part, at 100% of its issue price plus all accrued and unpaid dividends.

**Transferability:** The Warrants will not be subject to any contractual restrictions on transfer. The Company will file a shelf registration statement covering the Warrants and the Equity Interests underlying the Warrants as promptly as practicable after the date of the investment and, if necessary, shall take all action required to cause such shelf registration statement to be declared effective as soon as possible; provided, however, that if the Company is not subject to the periodic reporting requirements of Section 13 or 15(d) of the Exchange Act, it need not file a shelf registration statement unless and until it becomes subject to such requirements.

The Company will also grant to XYZ piggyback registration rights for the Warrants and the Warrant Shares and will take such other steps as may be reasonably requested to facilitate the transfer of the Warrants and the Warrant Shares. The Company will apply for the listing of the Warrant Shares on the national exchange, if applicable, on which its Equity Interests are traded and will take such other steps as may be reasonably requested to facilitate the transfer of the Warrants or the Warrant Shares.

**Voting:** Prior to the occurrence of a Termination Event or an Event of Default, the UST will agree not to exercise voting power with respect to any shares of Equity Interests of the Company issued to it upon exercise of the Warrants.

**Consent:** In the event that the Company does not have sufficient available authorized shares of Equity Interests to reserve for issuance upon exercise of the Warrants and/or equity holder approval is required for such issuance under applicable stock exchange rules, the Company will call a meeting of its equity holders as soon as practicable after the date of this investment to increase the number of authorized shares of Equity Interests and/or comply with such exchange rules, and to take any other measures deemed by XYZ to be necessary to allow the exercise of Warrants into Equity Interests.

**Substitution:** In the event that the Company is not listed or traded at any time on a national securities exchange or securities association, or the consent of the Company's stockholders described above has not been received within six months after the issuance date of the Warrants, the Warrants will be exchangeable, at the option of XYZ, for senior term debt or another economic instrument or security of the Company such that XYZ is appropriately compensated for the value of the Warrants, as determined by XYZ.

**Optional Warrant Redemption:** At any time after the aggregate outstanding Advances, with interest thereon at the applicable Interest Rate, fees, expenses, indemnities and other amounts due to the Lender shall have been paid in full, the Company shall have the right to repurchase any equity security of the Company held by the UST at fair market value or, if no recognized market for such securities exists at the time of prepayment, at the value attributed to such securities by an independent third party appraiser reasonably acceptable to the Lender.

**Private Companies:** If the Company is privately held, in lieu of Warrants, XYZ will receive additional notes ('Additional Notes') with the same priority and general terms as the Facility, in an amount equal to 6.67% of the Maximum Loan Amount.

**Other Terms Fees and Expenses:** The Loan Parties shall be responsible for any and all legal fees, due diligence and other out-of-pocket expenses incurred by or on behalf of the Lender in connection with this Facility, whether or not the Facility closes or funds.

**Governing Law:** Applicable Federal law (including conflicts of law rules), and in the absence of applicable Federal law, the law of the State of New York, without regard to conflict of laws doctrine applied in such state (other than Section 5-1401 of the New York General Obligations Law).

**Not a Commitment:** This term sheet is a summary of indicative terms and conditions purely for discussion purposes, does not constitute a commitment on the part of the Lender and is not binding on the Lender. All terms described herein are subject to due diligence satisfactory to the Lender, receipt of all appropriate credit and other required internal and external approvals, final documentation satisfactory in form and substance to the Lender and its legal counsel.

# APPENDIX A TO SECURED TERM LOAN FACILITY

## Additional Terms

**Company/Borrower:** ABC Inc.

**Guarantor(s):** All material domestic subsidiaries of the Borrower and any successor entity thereto, on a joint and several basis.

**Closing Date:** <date>

**Loan Amount:** Up to $13.40 billion, to be made available to the Borrower, upon request, as follows (subject to the Loan Parties' satisfaction of the other terms and conditions of the Facility):

**Closing Date:** $4.0 billion.
    <date> : $5.4 billion.
    <date> : $4.0 billion, contingent on Congressional action.

**Use of Funds:** The funds advanced may be used by the Borrower for general business purposes.

**Expiration Date:** <date> 5:00 pm Washington, DC time.

**Payment Date:** The last business day of each calendar quarter, commencing with the first calendar quarter in <year>.

**LIBOR Floor:** 2.00%

**Spread Amount:** 300 basis points; provided that upon the occurrence and during the continuance of an Event of Default, the Spread Amount shall be equal to 800 basis points.

**Financial Covenants:** TBD

**Additional Conditions Precedent:** The Common Holders of the Class A Membership Interests of ABC Inc and holders of the Class C Membership Interests of ABC Inc shall have consented in writing to the pledge to the Lender of the Class B Membership Interests and the Preferred Membership Interests under this Facility.

**Collateral:** To the extent legally and contractually permissible, the applicable Loan Parties shall grant to the Lender first-priority liens on all unencumbered assets, and junior liens on all encumbered assets. Notwithstanding anything herein to the contrary, the Loan Parties shall use their best efforts to obtain all necessary waivers, amendments, approvals or consents, as the case may be, to enable the Loan Parties to grant any such lien to the Lender as security for their respective obligations under the Facility.

**Relevant Companies:** <list>

## APPENDIX 1.B TERM SHEET FOR A SUBORDINATED LOAN/BOND

# TERM SHEET

**Company:** XYZ
Subordinated Bond Issue ABC/010101
(the 'Bond Issue/Bonds/Loan')

Issuer/Borrower: XYZ

**Bond Issue Amount:** NOKm 400

**Currency:** NOK

**Coupon Rate:** 3 month NIBOR + 700 bps p.a. during the first 24 months after Settlement

**Date:**

**Step-up:** The coupon rate shall increase to 3 month NIBOR + 1,000 bps p.a. from and including the Interest Payment Date (as defined below) on <date> (24 months after Settlement Date).

**Settlement Date:** Expected to be <date>. Notice is expected to be given a minimum of two banking days prior to the Settlement Date.

**Maturity Date:** Expected to be <date> (5 years after Settlement Date). The Bonds mature at par value (100%) plus accrued unpaid interest.

**First Interest Payment Date:** Expected to be <date> (3 months after Settlement Date)

**Last Interest Payment Date:** Expected to be <date> (5 years after Settlement Date)

**Interest Payments (Payment-in-Kind):** Interest on the Loan will start to accrue on the Settlement Date and shall be payable quarterly in arrears on the interest payment date in February, May, August and November each year, or if not a Norwegian banking day on the first subsequent banking day (each an 'Interest Payment Date'). The day count fraction for the coupon is act/360, modified following.

**Payment-in-Kind Clause:** The Issuer shall (each time) pay interests as additional Bonds at a nominal value of NOK 1.00, rounded down to the nearest NOK. Payment of interest as additional Bonds (based on the NOK 1.00 face value of the Bonds) shall be calculated based on the total number of Bonds held at each Interest Payment Date. The additional Bonds issued upon payment of interest give the same rights as the other issued Bonds as of the registration of the increased outstanding amount of Bonds in VPS. All interest payments as payment-in-kind shall be based upon the total outstanding bonds from time to time, i.e. including previous issued bonds in connection with payment of interest as additional Bonds.

The Issuer may, subject to prior written consent from the Issuer's banks, make interest payments to the bondholders in cash on an Interest Payment Date.

**Issue Price:** 100.00% of par value

**Nominal Value:** The Bonds will have a nominal value of NOK 1.00. Minimum subscription and allotment is NOK 500,000.

**Status of the Bond Issue:** The Bond Issue and accrued interest shall be subordinated to all other debt of the Borrower, with the provision that the Bond Issue and accrued interest shall rank *pari passu* with any other subordinated debt of the Borrower, and shall rank ahead of all amounts payable in respect of the share capital of the Borrower.

**Purpose:** The net proceeds of the Bond Issue shall be employed for refinancing of existing bank debt.

**Change of Control:** In the event of a change of control of the Issuer, the bondholders will, for the following period of 30 banking days from the closing of a transaction being a Change of

Control Event, have the right to have the Bonds redeemed by the Issuer ('put option') at 101% of their principal amount together with accrued interest.

'Change of Control Event' means if any person or group (as defined in the Norwegian Securities Trading Act § 2-5), becomes the owner, directly or indirectly, of shares which represent 50% or more of the votes in the Issuer.

**Issuer's Call Option:** The Issuer may redeem parts of the Loan or the entire Loan as follows any time at price 106% of par value (plus accrued unpaid interest on redeemed amount) during the first month after the Settlement Date, thereafter any time during each month at a price that declines with 25 bps each month (i.e. price 105.75% of par value during the second month, 105.50% during the third month and so on). When the call price has declined to 100.00% of par on the Interest Payment Date in May 2010 (24 months after the Settlement Date), the call price shall remain at price 100.00% of par at any time during the remaining term of the Loan.

This clause, the Issuer's Call Option, shall be removed and shall accordingly not apply from and including 16 banking days after the occurrence of a Change of Control Event. This means that if the Issuer decides to redeem the Loan after a Change of Control Event, the Issuer must inform the Trustee about such decision no later than 15 banking days after the Change of Control Event has occurred.

**Subordination Agreement:** A subordination agreement in form and substance based on the existing subordination agreement dated <date> between the Company, the existing lenders and <company name> as loan trustee, the bondholders in the NOK 200 million 4.50 per cent Subordinated Convertible Bond Issue 200X/20XX dated <date> adjusted and amended to reflect the terms and conditions of this term sheet, and otherwise in form and substance acceptable to all parties. Pursuant to the subordination agreement, the Bonds shall be subordinated to all other debt of the Issuer, with the provision that the Bond Issue and accrued interest shall rank *pari passu* with any other subordinated debt of the Borrower, and shall rank ahead of all amounts payable in respect of the share capital of the Issuer. To such end, the subordination agreement shall provide, *inter alia*, that until the date when all senior debt is paid, no principal amounts owing by the Issuer to the bondholders may be repaid and no redemption may be made in respect of the Bonds without the prior written consent of the facility agent for the senior debt. However, the Issuer may pay ordinary interest, fees and expenses in respect of the Bonds. In the event of a default or potential default with respect to the senior debt, the facility agent may issue a written stop notice, pursuant to which no payments whatsoever and no redemptions may be made in respect of the Bonds without the prior written consent of the facility agent.

**Cross-Default:** The Loan may be declared to be in default if, for each member of the Group, the aggregate amount of financial indebtedness or commitment for financial indebtedness falling within paragraphs (i) to (iv) below exceeds a total of NOK 10 million – or the equivalent thereof in other currencies; (i) any financial indebtedness of, or guaranteed by, the Issuer is not paid when due nor within any originally applicable grace period, (ii) any financial indebtedness is declared to be or otherwise becomes due and payable prior to its specified maturity as a result of an event of default, (iii) any commitment for any financial indebtedness is canceled or suspended by a creditor as a result of an event of default, or (iv) any creditor becomes entitled to declare any financial indebtedness due to and payable prior to specified maturity as a result of an event of default.

**Financial Indebtedness Restriction Clause:** In the event that the financial covenant structure of the Issuer's bank loan agreements (the 'Existing Financial Covenant Structure') is altered to a materially more flexible structure, the Loan Agreement shall be amended to include a limitation on total financial indebtedness for the Group broadly similar to the limitations in the Existing Financial Covenant Structure.

**Issuer's Ownership of Bonds:** The Issuer has the right to acquire and own the Bonds. Such Bonds may, at the Issuer's discretion, be retained by the Issuer, sold or discharged against the Bond Issue.

**Manager:** ABC Securities, Oslo, Norway and DEF Securities Oslo, Norway

**No Dividend:** The Issuer shall not, during the term of the Loan, make any dividend payment, repurchase of shares, share capital distribution or make any other distributions or loans to its shareholders.

**Special Issues:** The Issuer shall not, without the prior written approval of the Trustee, permit any member of the Group to engage in, directly or indirectly, any transaction with any party, except in the ordinary course of such member of the Issuer Group's business and upon fair and reasonable terms that are no less favorable to the member of the Issuer Group than those which might be obtained in an arm's length transaction at the time. The Group shall not, without the approval of the Trustee, or, where necessary, bondholders' meeting: (a) cease to carry on its business, (b) sell or dispose of all or a substantial part of its assets or operations or change the nature of its business or merge with another company in a manner which might jeopardize the Issuer's fulfillment of its obligations under the Loan Agreement. For the avoidance of doubt, the Issuer should generally be allowed to sell assets or businesses conditional on the net proceeds from such sales being used for the repayment of financial debt including this Loan, (c) de-merge, merge or in any other way restructure its business, in a manner which might jeopardize the Issuer's fulfillment of its obligations under the Loan Agreement, (d) make any acquisitions (paid for with cash or shares) unless all shareholder elected representatives of the Issuer's board of directors have unanimously approved such acquisition.

**Group:** The Issuer and all its current and future subsidiaries

**Trustee:** EFG Company, Oslo, Norway

**Registration:** The Norwegian Central Securities Depository (VPS). Principal and interest accrued will be credited to the bondholders through VPS.

**Issuer's Org. Number:** XXX XXX XXX

**Loan Agreement:** The Loan Agreement will be entered into, on standard terms and conditions for such bond issues, by the Issuer and the Trustee acting as the bondholders' representative. The Loan Agreement regulates the bondholders' rights and obligations with respect to the Bond Issue. If any discrepancy should occur between this Term Sheet and the Loan Agreement, then the Loan Agreement shall prevail. The Subscriber is deemed to have granted authority to the Trustee to negotiate and finalize the Loan Agreement and the Subordination Agreement. Minor adjustments to the structure described in this Term Sheet may occur.

The Subscription Agreements will specifically authorize the Trustee to negotiate, execute and deliver the Loan Agreement and the Subordination Agreement on behalf of the prospective bondholders, who will execute and deliver such Subscription Agreements prior to receiving Bond allotments.

On this basis, the Issuer and the Trustee will execute and deliver the Loan Agreement and the latter's execution and delivery is on behalf of all of the subscribers, such that they thereby will become parties to the Loan Agreement on the Subordination Agreement. The Loan Agreement shall specify that all bond transfers shall be subject to the terms thereof, and the Trustee and all bond transferees shall, in taking transfer of Bonds, be deemed to have accepted the terms of the Loan Agreement and subordination agreement, which specifies that all such transferees shall automatically become parties to the Loan Agreement upon completed transfer having been registered with the VPS, without any further action required to be taken or formalities to be complied with. The Loan Agreement shall specify that it shall be made available to the general public for inspection purposes and may, until redemption in full of the Bond Issue, be obtained on request to the Trustee or the Issuer, and such availability shall be recorded in the VPS particulars relating to the Bond Issue.

**Stock Exchange Listing:** An application will initially not be made for the Bonds to be listed on Oslo Børs or any other regulated marketplace. An application may be made during the term of the Bond Issue at the discretion of the Issuer.

**Market Making:** No market-maker agreement has been made for this Bond Issue.

**Eligible Purchasers:** The Bonds are not being offered to and may not be purchased by investors located in the United States except for 'Qualified Institutional Buyers' (QIBs) within the meaning of Rule 144A under the U.S. Securities Act of 1933, as amended ('Securities Act'). In addition to the Subscription Agreement that each investor will be required to execute, each U.S. investor that wishes to purchase Bonds will be required to execute and deliver to the Issuer a certification in a form to be provided by the Issuer stating, among other things, that the investor is a QIB. The Bonds may not purchased by, or for the benefit of, persons resident in Canada.

**Transfer Restrictions:** Bondholders located in the United States will not be permitted to transfer the Bonds except (a) subject to an effective registration statement under the Securities Act, (b) to a person that the bondholder reasonably believes is a QIB within the meaning of Rule 144A that is purchasing for its own account, or the account of another QIB, to whom notice is given that the resale, pledge or other transfer may be made in reliance on Rule 144A, (c) outside the United States in accordance with Regulation S under the Securities Act in a transaction on the Oslo Børs, and (d) pursuant to an exemption from registration under the Securities Act provided by Rule 144 thereunder (if available). The Bonds may not, subject to applicable Canadian laws, be traded in Canada for a period of four months and a day from the date the bonds were originally issued.

**Subject To:** The issue of Bonds shall be subject to: (i) All necessary corporate resolutions for the issuance of the Bonds (ii) Approval from the current lending banks (DnB NOR and Fokus Bank) (iii) Appropriate legal opinion and finalized Loan Agreement and Subordination Agreement and approval of such agreement by the Trustee.

Oslo, <date>
<Companies>

## APPENDIX 1.C TERM SHEET FOR MEZZANINE DEBT

**TERM SHEET[1]**

## Mezzanine Debt

This Term Sheet does not constitute an offer and is solely for discussion purposes. This Term Sheet shall not be construed as creating any obligations on any party whatsoever, and shall

---

not be binding on any party unless the conditions contained herein are satisfied and the terms of the proposed investment are contained within definitive documents which are negotiated, executed and delivered in connection with the closing of such investment.

**Borrower/Issuer:** [_____] and its controlled affiliates and subsidiaries ('Issuer' or the 'Company').

**Equity Sponsors:** [_____], and other person acceptable to Purchaser (including any affiliates thereof).

**Subordinated Notes/[Principal Amount]:** Subordinated Notes in a principal amount up to $[_____] (the 'Notes').

**Purchaser:** [ ] ('Purchaser').

**Credit Facilities:** [_____].

**Agent, Arranger, Underwriter:** [_____].

**Expiration:** This Term Sheet expires on [_____]. An extension may be granted by the Purchaser at the formal request of the Borrower and/or Equity Sponsor.

**Targeted Closing Date:** [_____].

**Purchase Price:** [_____]% of the Face Amount ('Par'). If market conditions change, the Purchaser has the right to review the pricing structure.

**Amortization:** Bullet payment at Maturity.

**Maturity:** [_____] years from closing.

**Purpose:** To provide financing for the [acquisition of _____].

**Security:** Secured obligations by second lien on all assets.

**Guarantee:** The [Borrower's parent and its] subsidiaries shall provide guarantees of the Notes in a form satisfactory to the Purchaser.

**Interest Rate:** The Notes will bear interest at a fixed annual interest rate equal to [_____] percent ([_____]%), payable each calendar quarter in arrears, [of which [_____] percent ([_____]%) will be paid in cash and [_____] percent ([_____]%) will be paid in-kind.] Interest will be calculated on the basis of a 360-day year of twelve 30-day months.

**Up Front Fee:** The Purchaser will receive a fee equal to [_____] percent ([_____]%) of the total amount of the Notes purchased by the Purchaser at closing.

**Default Rate:** [_____]% in excess of the applicable rate.

**Optional Prepayment:** The Notes may be prepaid in accordance with the schedule below at the following redemption prices (expressed in percentages of principal amount to be repaid), plus accrued interest to the date of prepayment:

Loan Year Redemption Price
1 [_____]%
2 [_____]%
3 [_____]%
4 [_____]%

5 [_____]%
thereafter [_____]%

**Mandatory Repayment:** The Company may be required by the Purchaser to repay the Notes upon a Liquidity Event (defined as a liquidation, winding up, change of control, merger, sale of all or substantially all of the assets of the Company or an Initial Public Offering). Repayments under this clause will be at the prices set forth above under the Optional Prepayment clause.

**Subordination:** The Notes will be subordinate in payment to the senior debt of the Borrower or terms acceptable to the Purchaser. Other customary terms and conditions, as well as provisions will be applied. The Notes will be senior to all existing and future subordinated debt and seller debt.

**Warrants [or Equivalent Shares]:** [At the closing of the transaction, the Purchaser will receive detachable and freely transferable warrants or other securities which provide an equivalent equity value in the Company (the 'Warrants') to acquire [_____]% of the fully diluted stock or value in the Company at closing. The Warrants will have a nominal exercise price and will include a cashless exercise feature as well as put provisions. In addition, the Purchaser will receive demand, and unlimited piggyback registration rights; tag along/co-sale, pre-emptive and anti-dilution provisions satisfactory to the Purchaser.] or

[The Subordinated Notes will be sold with detachable and transferable warrants for the purchase of shares at a nominal price (including a cashless exercise feature) representing [_____]% of the fully diluted stock. This warrant position assumes that all of the equity contributed by the Equity Sponsors will be in the form of common stock, and should the contribution be made in a form of security which provides for any form of dividend in cash or payment-in-kind, then the warrant amount shall be adjusted on or before the closing of the Acquisition to maintain a return to the investors as if the equity had been contributed as common equity. The warrants will expire [_____] years from closing, be immediately exercisable, and will have one demand registration and unlimited 'piggy-back' registration rights (in each case, at the Borrower's expense) with respect to stock issued upon exercise, customary anti-dilution provisions that will include dilution protection in the event of issuances below the common stock price (or common stock equivalent) paid by the Equity Sponsors and issuances to management and will contain put and call provisions, preemptive rights and other terms and conditions, in each case acceptable to the Purchaser.

In the event of a sale of all or substantially all of the stock or assets of the Borrower, the stock issuable upon the exercise of the warrants will be subject to 'drag-along' and have the benefit of 'tag-along' provisions.]

**Registration Rights:** After an Initial Public Offering, the warrant holders will have a single demand registration right on Form S-1 and unlimited demand registration rights on Form S-3, all at the Borrower's expense. The warrant holders will also have a pro rata participation right in the event of any private disposition of a controlling interest in the Borrower. The Borrower will have the right to require the warrant holders to participate on a pro rata basis in any such liquidity event.

**Board of Directors/[Observer Rights]:** The Purchaser will have the right to elect [_____] members to the Company's Board of Directors, or alternatively, the Purchaser will be allowed to send [_____] observers to all regular and special meetings of the Board of Directors of the Company.

**Financial and Other Covenants:** The Note and Warrant Purchase Agreement will contain customary covenants (the terms of which will be defined in the Note and Warrant Purchase Agreement) including, but not limited to:

- Limitations on indebtedness, material changes, change of control, liens, restricted payments and investments, asset sales, capital expenditures, changes in nature of business, mergers, acquisitions, dividends, etc.;
- Maintenance of existence;
- Maintenance of eligibility in SBIC program;
- Minimum Fixed Charge Coverage [and Interest Coverage] Ratio[s];
- Minimum EBITDA;
- Leverage Ratio;
- Limitation of Capital Expenditures; and
- [Maintenance of Minimum Tangible Net Worth].

**Documentation:** Documentation will contain such terms, conditions, representations, warranties, reporting requirements, covenants, including financial covenants customary for investments of this type, and subordination terms as the Purchaser or its affiliates may require.

**Reporting Requirements:** The Borrower will furnish the following reports, including, but not limited to:

- Audited financial statements on a [annual][quarterly] basis and unaudited financial statements on a [monthly] basis.
- Any other reports that the Purchaser may reasonably request and as necessary for the Purchaser to comply with the regulations of the Small Business Investment Company Act as required by law.

**Conditions to Closing/[Funding]:** Conditions to closing will include, without limitation, the following:

- The terms, conditions and structure of the [acquisition] (and all documents related thereto) shall be in form and substance satisfactory to the Purchaser and its counsel and all transactions contemplated thereunder shall have been consummated as set forth therein and no conditions or material provisions contained therein shall have been waived or amended unless agreed to by the Purchaser.
- The negotiation, execution and delivery of definitive documentation, including the Note and Warrant Purchase Agreement, the Notes and the Warrants (in form and substance satisfactory to the Purchaser and its counsel).
- The Purchaser shall have received independent legal, tax, insurance, fairness and accounting opinions satisfactory to the Purchaser and its counsel.
- Receipt of (i) SBA Form 480, Size Status Declaration, (ii) SBA Form 652, Assurance for Compliance for Non-discrimination by the Borrower and (iii) use of proceeds certification.
- The absence of any material adverse change or disruption in the financial or capital markets.
- The absence of any change, which the Purchaser deems to be materially adverse, in respect of the business, results of operation, condition (financial or otherwise), value, prospects, liabilities or assets of the Company.
- The management incentive and employment agreements of the Company shall be acceptable to the Purchaser and its counsel.

- [A minimum Adjusted EBITDA on a pro-forma, run-rate basis [ _____ ] of at least $[ _____ ] million on a basis satisfactory to the Purchaser.
- Satisfactory liquidity in the amount of $[ _____ ].
- Satisfactory insurance.
- Satisfactory legal, accounting and financial due diligence.
- Accuracy of representations and warrants under the Note and Warrant Purchase Agreement.
- Approvals of all requisite parties to the Transaction have been received by closing.
- No violation of any securities laws or other applicable laws or regulations.
- No default in any material contracts and absence of any material litigations as of the date of closing and after giving effect to the [acquisition].
- The Purchaser shall have received all fees and expenses (including fees and expenses of counsel) on or before the date of the closing of the [Transaction].
- Absence of any defaults or event of default under the Note and Warrant Purchase Agreement, the Notes or any other related documents.
- Receipt by the Company of all third party consents and governmental approvals.
- Satisfaction that there are no material environmental issues.
- No default in any material contracts and absence of any material litigation as of the date of closing and after giving effect to the acquisition.
- The Equity Sponsors shall have made a cash equity investment in the Company of at least $[ _____ ] million (which shall have been made on terms and conditions acceptable to the Purchaser); and
- Senior financing in the amount of $[ _____ ] will be available to be drawn at closing. Governing Law: State of [ _____ ].

**Events of Default:** Customary Events of Default will include but are not limited to: (i) failure to pay interest or principal when due and payable; (ii) failure to comply with the covenants in the Securities Purchase Agreement; (iii) defaults under other agreements; (iv) breaches of representations and warranties; (v) failure to discharge material judgments; and (vi) bankruptcy or insolvency.

**Assignment/Transfer of Notes:** The Purchaser may syndicate, assign or sell a portion or all of the Notes.

**Transaction Expenses:** The Borrower shall reimburse the Purchaser for all expenses related to the Transaction (whether or not the Transaction closes), including, but not limited to, legal fees and disbursements, consulting fees (which consultants shall be agreed upon with the Equity Sponsors prior to their engagement), and out-of-pocket expenses (including travel and incidental expenses, etc.).

**[Syndication:]** [The Purchaser intends to syndicate a portion of the Notes to other financial institutions. The Borrower and the Equity Sponsors agree to assist and facilitate the Agent's syndication process.]

**Market Conditions:** The Borrower acknowledges and agrees that the financing commitment is subject to the absence of a material adverse change in the condition (whether financial or otherwise) or results of operations of the Borrower and/or its affiliated entities since the period ended _____, _____.

[Furthermore, the financing commitment is subject to the absence of any material disruption of, or material adverse change in, current financial, banking or capital market conditions that, in the Purchaser's judgment, could materially impair the satisfactory syndication of the Notes.]

**Good Faith Deposit:** The Issuer shall pay to the Purchaser a good faith deposit in the amount of $[_____], which, upon closing of the Transaction, will be credited toward the Up Front Fee. Should the Equity Sponsors decline to proceed with the financings as described herein for any reason, the Purchaser shall retain the deposit as compensation for its time and effort in connection with the requested financing.

**Opportunity Cost Fee:** If the Transaction proposed herein is closed within one year from the end of the Exclusivity Period, without Purchaser financing, and the Purchaser is prepared to consummate the proposed financing on substantially the same terms set forth herein, then an Opportunity Cost Fee will be paid to the Purchaser equal to [_____]% of the proposed principal amount of the Notes that the Purchaser was prepared to purchase.

**Termination Fee:** Additionally, if a termination fee is paid to the Equity Sponsors or their affiliates pursuant to any agreement, then a fee equal to [_____]% of the amount remaining after the out-of pocket expenses of the Equity Sponsors are deducted from the termination fee received by the Equity Sponsors shall be payable in cash to the Purchaser within ten business days of the Equity Sponsors receiving such payment. This fee will be in addition to any other fees previously paid to the Purchaser.

**No Shop Clause:** Upon acceptance of this commitment, the Equity Sponsors and the Company agree that until the earlier of (i) closing of the Transaction and (ii) [_____], the Equity Sponsors and the Company will not, and will not permit any of their affiliates to, syndicate or issue, attempt to syndicate or issue, announce or authorize the announcement of the syndication or issuance of, or engage in discussions concerning the syndication or issuance of, any debt facility other than the Notes financing contemplated hereby or solicit any proposal or commitment or engage in any discussions or negotiations concerning the financing of the Transaction by any person other than the Purchaser as contemplated hereunder.

**Pricing Terms:** The Purchaser shall be entitled, after consultation with the Equity Sponsors and the Borrower, to change the pricing, terms and structure of the Notes if the Syndication has not been completed and if the Purchaser determines that such changes are advisable to insure a successful syndication of the Notes.

**Indemnification:** The Equity Sponsors and the Borrower (each an 'indemnifying person'), jointly and severally, agree to indemnify and hold harmless the Purchaser and any and all other financial institutions or banks that become a lender or purchaser under the Notes, each affiliate thereof and each director, officer, employee, agent or representative thereof (each an 'indemnified person') in connection with any losses, claims, damages, liabilities or other expenses to which such indemnified persons may become subject, insofar as such losses, claims, damages, liabilities (or actions or other proceedings commenced or threatened in respect thereof) or other expenses arise out of or in any way relate to or result from the [Acquisition] or this letter or the issuance of the Notes contemplated by this letter, or in any way arise from any use or intended use of this letter or the proceeds of the Subordinated Notes, and the Equity Sponsors and the Borrower, jointly and severally, agree to reimburse each indemnified person for any reasonable legal or other expenses incurred in connection with investigating, defending or participating in any such loss, claim, damage, liability or action or other proceeding (whether or not such indemnified person is a party to any action or proceeding out of which indemnified expenses arise).

**Required Documents/Due Diligence Issues:** Prior to closing, the Borrower will provide the following due diligence documents, and any other information deemed necessary by the Purchaser to complete its credit review process, the form and substance of which must be acceptable to the Purchaser:

- Legal, tax and accounting opinions provided by firms acceptable to the Purchaser.
- Consolidated audited financial statements of the Borrower for the past three years.
- A comprehensive business plan, including financial projections of the operations of the Borrower for the next seven years.
- Visit with management.
- Visit of Company's facilities.
- Interviews with customers, suppliers, etc.
- Data Room visit.
- All available relevant consultant reports will be submitted to the Purchaser.
- Available industry reports will be made accessible; and
- Customary background checks will be initiated.

## APPENDIX 1.D WARRANT PURCHASE AGREEMENT

# TERM SHEET[2]

## Warrant Purchase

This Term Sheet summarizes the principal terms with respect to a potential transaction between _____ (the 'Company') and _____ (the 'strategic Partner').

This Term Sheet is a statement of the present material intentions of the parties, and except that the Company agrees to negotiate in good faith towards conclusion of the transactions referred to below and except as set forth under the headings 'Confidentiality,' 'No Other Agreements,' and 'Due Diligence' below as to which the parties intend to be legally bound, no legally binding agreement or obligation of any party are covered by this Term Sheet. A binding commitment with respect to the transactions (other than as set forth under the headings 'Confidentiality,' 'No Other Agreements,' and 'Due Diligence' below) will result only upon the execution of definitive agreements, if any. No oral modifications to this principle shall be valid.

The Company and Strategic Partner are discussing a transaction on the following terms:

**Warrant:** The Company will issue a Warrant containing the following terms to the Strategic Partner:

(a) Warrant to purchase shares of Series ___ Preferred Stock.
(b) Exercisable in whole or in part at any time and from time to time for [_____] years.
(c) The Warrants, if fully exercised, will represent a number of shares equal to ___% of the Company's outstanding capitalization (on a fully diluted basis) post exercise.
(d) The exercise price will be equal to $ (the last round price of the Company's Series Preferred Stock).

---

[2] © 2007 Arch Capital Advisors. All Rights Reserved.

(e)  The Strategic Partner will also be entitled, at its discretion, to purchase up to $_____ of the Company's fully registered freely tradable common stock at the IPO price when the Company goes public, less the underwriter's discount.

(f)  Method of exercise includes net issuance rights

(g)  Customary adjustments of the Warrant price and number of shares subject to the warrant for stock splits, stock dividends, recapitalizations and the like.

(h)  Warrants may be transferred by the Strategic Partner in conformity with applicable securities laws.

(i)  Registration rights comparable to those applicable to the existing Preferred will apply to the common stock obtained upon conversion of the Preferred Stock issuable upon exercise of the Warrant.

(j)  The parties will not treat the Warrant or the shares as being granted or issued as property transferred in connection with the performance of services or otherwise as compensation for services rendered.

**The Warrant Purchase Agreement:** The issuance of the Warrant will be made pursuant to a Warrant Purchase Agreement that will contain, among other things, at least the types of representations and warranties of the Company and covenants of the Company that are comparable to those that were contained in the Stock Purchase Agreement entered into by the Company in connection with the sale of its recent round of financing, with such changes as are negotiated between the parties.

**Registration Rights:** The Strategic Partner will have piggyback rights for any shares acquired plus be able to participate in demand registrations with other investors.

**Right of First Refusal:** In the event that the Company offers equity securities (other than Reserved Employee Shares, or upon conversion of outstanding Preferred, or upon exercise of outstanding options or warrants, or in connection with an acquisition or in a public offering), the Strategic Partner shall have a right of first refusal to purchase the same percentage of such offering as such holder is entitled to via the Warrant. This right will terminate upon the Company's Initial Public Offering.

**Conditions of Closing:** The closing will be conditioned upon:

(1)  Completion of due diligence to the satisfaction of the Strategic Partner and approval of its Board of Directors.

(2)  Execution by the Company of a Warrant Purchase Agreement and related agreements satisfactory to the Strategic Partner.

(3)  Compliance by the Company with applicable securities laws.

(4)  Opinion of counsel to the Company rendered to the Strategic Partner in form and substance satisfactory to the Strategic Partner.

(5)  Execution of strategic alliance, license agreement or marketing agreement in form satisfactory to the Strategic Partner.

(6)  Such other conditions as are customary for transactions of this type.

**Expenses:** The Company will pay a fixed amount of the Strategic Partner's legal fees equal to $_____, together with out-of-pocket expenses incurred by counsel to _____, payable by wire transfer at the closing.

**Closing:** The closing of the transaction, if all conditions are met, is expected to occur on or before [_____].

## APPENDIX 1.E CONVERTIBLE BOND TERM SHEET

# CONVERTIBLE BOND TERM SHEET

This term sheet (Term Sheet) contains a summary of the principal terms of the New Bonds referred to in the Summons for a meeting of the Bondholders, dated June xx 20xx.

## Security

Series A Senior Secured Bonds convertible into common shares in the share capital of XYZ ('New Bonds'), non-callable

## Issuer

ABC Group Inc.

## Investment Amount

US$8 million (EIGHT MILLION DOLLARS) ('Total Amount'):

1. Tranche A: 30 per cent of Total Amount being US$2,400,000 (TWO MILLION, FOUR HUNDRED THOUSAND DOLLARS) ('Tranche A')
2. Tranche B: 70 per cent of the Total Amount being US$5,600,000 (FIVE MILLION, SIX HUNDRED THOUSAND DOLLARS) ('Tranche B')

　　Subscriptions shall be sought for the Total Amount in accordance with the Pre-Emption Rights timetable below. However, Tranche A shall be allotted on a pro rata basis in accordance with the subscriptions received for the Total Amount. The balance of the Total Amount shall be due and payable by subscribers in the event that Tranche B is called on August 15 20xx.

## Minimum Denomination

100,000 USD

## Coupon

15 per cent per annum pay-in-kind

## Maturity

12 months from Closing Date

## Conversion Right and Price

Convertible into the ordinary shares of AGI at 0.0375 NOK ('Conversion Price') at any time after subscription of the relevant tranche of New Bonds prior to maturity on 10 banking days' prior written notice

## Anti-dilution

Terms not less favorable than those in the loan agreements for the Bonds (defined below)

## Security Interests

A proposed pledge (under the laws of Jersey) over 100 per cent of the shares held by AGI in the Jersey company, ABC Holdings (Jersey) Limited, and an assignment/charge under English law over the receivable related to the payment due from a joint venture partner (l) in respect of the JV memoranda of understandings ('MOU') dated March 20 and April 20 20xx relating to the farm-out by htd. of its xyz On-shore and Off-shore working interests ('JV Farm-Out').

Additional collateral interests granted to the New Bonds may also comprise, without limitation, some or all of: (1) security agreement over all the assets of XYZ; (2) cross guarantees; (3) an assignment or charge over the receivables of any intercompany loan agreements; and (4) such other security interests deemed appropriate in relation to the New Bonds.

## Guarantors & Guarantees

The New Bonds will be guaranteed by eligible entities ('Guarantors') within the XYZ group of companies. The obligations of each Guarantor of the New Bonds will constitute senior, unsubordinated, direct, unconditional, and unsecured obligations of such Guarantor and at all times will rank at least equally with all other present and future unsecured and unsubordinated obligations of the Guarantor.

## Put Options at 105%

Each holder of the Tranche A New Bonds ('Tranche A Bondholders') shall have the option to put some or all of the New Bonds to the Issuer at 105 per cent of the Investment Amount plus accrued interest (the '105 Put Option') within 30 days of the earlier of:

(a) receipt from AGI of a notice of receipt of the sale proceeds ('Sale Notice') from any material transaction entered into by the Company with minimum net proceeds to the Company of US$40 million ('Material Transaction'); or

(b) August 3 20xx. XYZ will be obligated to issue the Sale Notice to the Tranche A Bondholders immediately upon receipt of funds from any Material Transaction.

Upon the expiry of the 105 Put Option each holder of the New Bonds, which, for the avoidance of doubt may include both Tranche A and Tranche B Bondholders, shall have the option to put some or all of the New Bonds to the Issuer at 135 per cent of the Investment Amount plus accrued interest upon 10 banking days' written notice to the Company ('135 Put Option') provided that such notice shall be given no later than November 30 20xx, at which time the 135 Put Option shall expire.

## Pre-emption Rights

Holders ('Bondholders') of:

1. $10 million 10.5 per cent callable convertible bond issue II 2006/2009.
2. $35 million 10 per cent callable bond issue III 2006/2010.
3. $70 million 6 per cent Senior Unsecured convertible bond issue 2007/2012, (together, the 'Bonds') will be entitled to participate in the issuance of New Bonds subject to the Minimum Denomination. Those Bondholders that elect to subscribe for New Bonds by 13:00 hours (Oslo Time) on June 18 20xx ('Subscribing Bondholders') will be given the opportunity to subscribe for any remaining New Bonds not taken up by the Bondholders. To

the extent the New Bonds are oversubscribed the allocations will be scaled back on a pro rata basis. To the extent New Bonds remain unsubscribed as at 13:00 hours (Oslo Time) on June 23 20xx, certain substantial pre-conversion shareholders shall be given the right to subscribe for the remaining New Bonds.

## Use of Proceeds

General corporate and working capital of the XYZ Group. However, any proposal to use the proceeds of the New Bonds to fund the Company's interests in <country> shall be subject to the prior approval of the XYZ Board.

## Ranking

The New Bonds will constitute direct, unconditional and unsubordinated obligations of the Issuer, secured by first ranking Security, and will rank *pari passu* and rateably, without any preference, among themselves.

## Closing Dates

Tranche A: June 25, 20xx (payment to be made within three (3) banking days of Tranche A Closing Date)

Tranche B: In the event that on or before August 3 20xx a Material Transaction occurs as defined in the 105 Put Option para (a) the Tranche B New Bonds shall be issued to the Subscribing Bondholders and the balance of the Total Amount shall be paid to the Company on August 15 20xx (payment to be made within three (3) banking days of Tranche B Closing Date).

In the event that a Material Transaction does not occur on or before August 3 20xx the Subscribing Bondholders shall each be entitled to elect to take up the Tranche B New Bonds and any other Tranche B New Bonds that are unsubscribed. The Subscribing Bondholders have until August 15 to notify the Company in writing that they wish to elect to take up:

(a) Their entitlement to Tranche B New Bonds; and
(b) Further Tranche B New Bonds that are unsubscribed as at close of business on August 15 20xx. . .

## Form of the New Bonds

Registered in a securities depository according to the Norwegian Securities Depository Act

## Pre-emption Rights of New Bondholders

The holders of the New Bonds ('New Bondholders') will have a pre-emption right on the basis of each New Bondholder's pro rata holding of the New Bonds ('Pre-Emption Right') in respect of the subscription to any further series of convertible bonds ('Additional New Bonds') that XYZ may issue. If the New Bondholders elect not to exercise the Pre-Emption Right, subscription to the Additional New Bonds will be offered first to the Bondholders, and if the Bondholders elect not to subscribe to all of the Additional New Bonds, then the Additional New Bonds shall be offered exclusively to the Existing Shareholders.

## Bond Trustee, Principal Paying, Transfer and Conversion Agent

ASA, subject to terms of engagement

## Security Trustee

To be determined

## Withholding Taxes and Tax Redemption

All payments on the New Bonds will be free and clear of, and without withholding or deduction for, any taxes, duties, assessments or governmental charges. If withholding tax is applicable the Issuer will pay the coupons and all amounts on a grossed-up basis.

## Representation and Warranties

Customary representations and warranties for senior secured loans, including without limitation, incorporation, power and capacity, authorization, no conflict, obligations binding, consents and compliance with laws, no defaults, litigation, environment, ownership of assets, original accounts, transaction documents, material adverse change, status of parent, no winding up, security interests and financial indebtedness, no deductions, taxation, subsidiaries, annual and management accounts and group structure.

## Information Undertakings

Customary undertakings including without limitation (1) annual audited consolidated financial statements within 120 days of the end of each financial year; unaudited consolidated financial statements for each monthly management accounting period within 45 days of the end of each such period; an updated 13-week rolling cash flow forecast for each principal entity within the group on a weekly basis; weekly cash balances/cash flows by entity; (2) immediate notice of all budgets and cash calls as and when made available by joint venture and joint operating agreement counterparties; and (3) immediate notification of default, litigation or government action.

## Financial Covenant

Such covenants as may be deemed appropriate.

## General Undertakings

Customary general undertakings, including without limitation, authorizations, compliance with laws, acquisitions, disposals and mergers, change of business, status of parent, senior ranking, disposals, negative pledge, sale and leaseback transactions, factoring receivables, joint ventures, borrowings, guarantees, loans, treasury transactions, principal agreements, banking business, guarantors, insurance, material intellectual property, taxes, pension schemes, arm's length terms, compliance with environmental laws, regulatory clearance, share issues, redemptions and acquisitions of own shares, payment of dividends and other distributions, shareholder payments, payments to members and other persons, defaults, books of account and auditors, conditions subsequent, including granting additional security interests as may be required by the Majority New Bondholders.

## Permitted Transactions

(1) The JV Farm-Out, subject to: (a) Documentation: no waiver, variation or amendment to the terms of, or exercise of a discretion or giving a consent under, the MOU without the Majority

New Bondholders' consent; (b) Price: no change to the MOU consideration without the Majority New Bondholders' consent; (c) Information: to provide the Facility Agent with such information (including material breaches, material notices or material claims) regarding the MOU as the Facility Agent may reasonably require; (d) Claims: take all reasonable action to enforce any material claim that any Group Company may have under the MOU, (e) Clearance: undertaking to comply with all obligations in (1) the MOU in respect of obtaining governmental and regulatory clearances required in connection with the MOU; (2) the Bank of ABC loan for $7 million; (3) the TRO / AAA Energy Project asset swap; and (4) any other transaction which is approved by two-thirds (by value) of the New Bondholders and/or XYZ shareholders (as relevant), in attendance at the requisite meetings.

## Events of Default

Customary events of default and acceleration terms for senior secured loans, including without limitation, non-payment without a cure period, financial covenants, other obligations, material adverse change, misrepresentation, cross-default under any material contract, insolvency, insolvency proceedings, unlawfulness and invalidity, cessation of business, winding up, suspension of payment, regulatory proceedings, change of ownership, audit qualification, expropriation, litigation, material adverse change, failure to deliver or satisfy in a timely manner any condition subsequent.

## Conditions Precedent

(1) Amendments to the Bonds and conversion; (2) requisite board approvals and related corporate actions in respect of the New Bonds; (3) satisfactory completion and execution of all loan documentation relating to the New Bonds; (4) certified copies of relevant constitutional documents and corporate authorities and customary legal opinions; (5) execution of applicable security documents to be delivered on the Closing Date; (6) payment and funding of all costs, fees, expenses payable, and the reserve account, as provided under the Trustee Fee Letter; (7) implementation of a cash management system to the satisfaction of the Majority holders of the New Bonds; (8) delivery of a detailed schedule of all anticipated payments to be made out of proceeds of the New Bonds.

## Conditions Subsequent

XYZ will grant and perfect all security interests requested by the Majority New Bondholders to secure the New Bonds, which may include, without limitation: (1) cross-guarantees governed by English law by all or some of the XYZ Group companies in compliance with the laws of the Guarantor's jurisdiction of incorporation, (2) an assignment/charge under English law over the receivables of relevant XYZ Group companies in respect of current and future intercompany loan agreements, and (3) an assignment/charge under English law over the receivable related to the payment due from the counterparty in respect of the JV MOUs and/or the JV Farm-Out.

## Majority New Bondholders

New Bondholders representing 66 2/3 per cent or more of the outstanding New Bonds.

## Bondholders' Meeting

Provisions similar to those for the Bonds, except for: (1) the quorum for convening a new Bondholders' meeting will be 10 per cent of the New Bonds; (2) the notice period for convening a New Bondholders' meeting will be five (5) banking days; (3) except as provided in (4) below, in a validly convened New Bondholders' meeting, resolutions may be adopted by a simple majority of the New Bonds represented at the New Bondholders' meeting; (4) resolutions that require Majority New Bondholders' consent will include without limitation (a) extension of maturity date, (b) extension to the date for payment of any amount under the New Bonds, (c) any change to the Security under the Security Documents that adversely affects the position of the New Bondholders, (d) any change of the Issuer, the Guarantors, the Bond Trustee and the Security Trustee, (e) any other material change to any of the transaction documents that adversely affects the position of the New Bondholders (including covenants, provisions regarding early redemption, the Pre-Emption Right and the Put Option); and (5) a second New Bondholders' meeting will have no quorum requirement and may be convened provided at least three banking days' notice is given to the New Bondholders.

## Fees and Expenses

All costs and expenses (including legal fees) reasonably incurred by the Bond Trustee, the Security Agent, and each of the New Bondholders in connection with the negotiation, preparation, printing, execution, and perfection of the Bond Agreement, any document referred to in the New Bond loan document, the security and any other transaction documents will be paid by the Issuer promptly on demand whether or not the loan agreement for the New Bonds (the 'Loan Agreement') is duly executed by the relevant parties. For the avoidance of doubt, it is the intention of the relevant parties to execute the Loan Agreement as soon as practicable.

## Eligible Purchasers and Transfer Restrictions

As provided for in the Loan Agreements for the Bonds but, for the avoidance of doubt, Subscribers for the New Bonds must qualify as Accredited Investors under applicable securities laws. The New Bonds may only be transferred on prior written notice to the Bond Trustee and the Company, where such notice shall include the identity of the transferee and the number and face value of New Bonds to be transferred.

## Change of Trustee

As provided for in the Loan Agreements for the Bonds.

## Governing Law

<Country> law, except for applicable security documents.

## Jurisdiction

Courts of <country>.

## Confidentiality

The Term Sheet and its content are intended for the exclusive use of the Issuer and shall not be disclosed by the Issuer to any person other than the Issuer's legal and financial advisors for the purposes of the proposed transaction unless the prior written consent of the steering committee representing the Bondholders is obtained.

Accepted and acknowledged this _ day of June, 2009
ABC Group Inc.
By: _____ _
Name:
Title:


## APPENDIX 1.F CONVERTIBLE PREFERRED SHARES

### TERM SHEET FOR POTENTIAL INVESTMENT
### IN
### NEWCO EMERGING GROWTH, INC.

This Term Sheet summarizes the principal terms with respect to a potential private placement of equity securities of Newco Emerging Growth, Inc., an Idaho corporation (the 'Company') by a group of investors ('Investors') led by xx.[3] This Term Sheet is intended solely as a basis for further discussion and is not intended to be and does not constitute a legally binding obligation except as provided under 'Confidentiality,' 'Exclusivity', and 'Expenses' below. No other legally binding obligation will be created, implied or inferred until a document in final form entitled 'Stock Purchase Agreement' is executed and delivered by all parties. Without limiting the generality of the foregoing, it is the parties intent that, until that event, no agreement shall exist among them and there shall be no obligations whatsoever based on such things as parol evidence, extended negotiations, 'handshakes,' oral understandings, courses of conduct (including reliance and changes of position), except as provided under 'Confidentiality,' 'Exclusivity', and 'Expenses' below.[4]

| | |
|---|---|
| Amount of Investment: | $ _____ [5] |
| Valuation of the Company: | $ _____ [6] Pre-Money on a fully-diluted basis. |
| | $ _____ Post-Money on a fully-diluted basis. |
| Type of Security: | Shares of the Company's Series A Convertible Preferred Stock ('Preferred'), convertible into shares of the Company's Common Stock ('Common'), representing % of the outstanding capital stock of the Company on a fully-diluted basis. |

---

[3] Generally, in venture financings, a single Investor such as a venture capital fund takes the lead in investigating the proposed investment, including performing due diligence and negotiating the terms of the stock acquisition.

[4] The concern addressed by the last two sentences is whether an agreement in principle or term sheet could be construed to be a contract binding on the Investor group. From the Investors' perspective, they will not want to be bound in any way until all conditions precedent have been met, such as completion of due diligence and execution of a definitive purchase agreement.

[5] Sometimes this amount is structured as a range, e.g., 'A minimum of $3 million and a maximum of $6 million.' Also, the investment is sometimes structured as a staged pay-in, with subsequent installments to be invested if the Company has met certain milestones or performance objectives. See 'Milestones.'

[6] This is the agreed upon valuation of the Company prior to the Investors contributing money to the Company. Valuation per share will often take into account outstanding stock options together with authorized but unissued options.

Price Per Share:                $ _____ ('Original Purchase Price').

Milestones:                     It is contemplated that the Investors will purchase the Pre-
                                ferred in [two] tranches, the first $ ___ _ upon [completion of
                                the first milestone, e.g., the successful field trial of a product
                                (the "Product') or the signing of a letter of intent to join in
                                a business partnership to market the Product]. The second
                                $ ___ _, comprising the balance of the investment, will be ad-
                                vanced upon [completion of the second milestone, e.g., pur-
                                chase orders for a specified amount of Product, the achieve-
                                ment of a specified amount of revenue, or the execution of a
                                formal strategic alliance with a major manufacturer].

Company Capitalization:         The current capitalization of the Company is set forth in
                                Exhibit 1, and the capitalization of the Company after this
                                proposed financing is set forth in Exhibit 2.[7]

Terms of Preferred Stock:       (1) Dividend Provisions: [Starting on January 1, 2000 the
                                holders of the Preferred will be entitled to receive dividends
                                [at the rate of __ % of the Original Purchase Price] when-
                                ever funds are legally available and when and as declared by
                                the Board. No dividend shall be paid on the Common at a
                                rate greater than the rate at which dividends are paid on the
                                Preferred (based on the number of shares of Common into
                                which the Preferred is convertible on the date the dividend
                                is declared). Dividends on Preferred will be in preference
                                to dividends paid on the Common. Dividends on the Pre-
                                ferred will be [cumulative] [noncumulative]. No dividends
                                will be paid on the Common until such time as the holders
                                of Preferred have received aggregate dividends equal to the
                                Original Purchase Price of the shares of Preferred purchased
                                in the offering.[8]
                                (2) Liquidation Preference: In the event of any liquidation,
                                dissolution or winding up of the Company, the holders of
                                Preferred will be entitled to receive in preference to the hold-
                                ers of Common an amount ('Liquidation Preference') equal
                                to the Original Purchase Price plus any dividends declared

---

[7] Exhibit 1 should show outstanding warrants, stock options, employee reserved stock and options, and outstanding Common, Preferred, and convertible securities. It may be useful for Exhibit 2 to show the capitalization of the Company taking into account the effect of anti-dilution provisions of any prior Preferred Stock issuances.

[8] Because most emerging growth companies will not typically be in a position to pay dividends to the holders of the Preferred Stock, some dividend provisions are drafted as to not mandate or cumulate dividends. However, in most financings, the Investors will require that dividends accrue and cumulate whether or not declared by the Board. Where dividends are cumulative, companies will want all previously accrued but unpaid dividends to be waived upon the automatic conversion of the Preferred Stock; Investors will want the unpaid dividends to be paid or to be converted into Common Stock. If dividends are required, the Company will want the dividends not to commence immediately and to have the option to pay such dividends in cash or stock. In the latter case, dividends are often structured as 'pik preferred' dividends, e.g., 'payment in kind' dividends for additional shares of Preferred Stock.

[cumulated] on the Preferred but not paid [and then to share with the holders of the Common[9] in the remaining assets on an as-if converted basis[10]]. At the option of the holders of the Preferred, the effectuation by the Company or third-party acquirers of a transaction or series of transactions in which more than [50%] [80%] of the voting power of the Company is disposed of to a single person or group of affiliated persons or the consolidation or merger of the Company with or into any other corporation or corporations or the sale of all or substantially all of its assets shall be deemed to be a liquidation, dissolution or winding up for purposes of the Liquidation Preference.

(3) Conversion: A holder of Preferred will have the right to convert Preferred, at the option of the holder, at any time, into shares of Common. The total number of shares of Common into which Preferred may be converted initially will be determined by dividing the Original Purchase Price by the conversion price. The initial conversion price ('Conversion Price') will be the Original Purchase Price. The Conversion Price will be the subject of adjustment to reflect stock dividends, stock splits and similar events as provided in paragraph (5) below.

(4) Automatic Conversion:[11] The Preferred will be automatically converted into Common, at the then applicable Conversion Price, upon the closing of a sale of the Company's shares of Common Stock pursuant to a firm commitment underwritten public offering by the Company at a public offering price per share (prior to underwriter commissions and

---

[9] If the Company has other series or classes of Preferred Stock, this provision will need to address the liquidation preferences of those past issuances vis-à-vis the new Preferred issuance. For example, is a Series B round to be equal or superior to the liquidation of the Series A round?

[10] The bracketed language provides for a 'participating preferred,' where on liquidation of the Company the Preferred first receives an amount equal to the original purchase price and unpaid dividends, or a multiple of the original purchase price, with the remainder of the Company's assets divided on a pro-rata basis with the Common as if the Preferred were converted. The Company will typically strongly resist this participating feature or attempt to mitigate its effect (e.g., the participating feature will not apply if the Investors have made at least a 25% annual compounded return on their investment, or a higher multiple such as 4–6 times the original purchase price). This participating provision results in the payment of the Liquidation Preference on each share of Preferred from the proceeds of a merger or sale of the Company. After such payment, all holders of Preferred and Common typically share the balance on an 'as converted' basis. Entrepreneurs who hold Common are often disappointed when they realize that the payment of the Liquidation Preference results in sharply lower per share prices for their Common. A participating preferred provision can also result in situations where Investors may favor a sale of the Company that the founders would oppose.

[11] The purpose of this automatic conversion provision is to clean up and simplify the Company's capitalization structure at the Initial Public Offering stage. The underwriters in an IPO will want the capitalization structure simplified as much as possible without unusual rights outstanding to minority shareholders.

discounts) that is not less than $ xx[12] in an offering greater than [$xx million] (a 'Qualified IPO').[13]

(5) Anti-dilution Provisions: The conversion price of the Preferred will be subject to adjustment (a) for stock dividends, stock splits, or similar events, and (b) to prevent dilution in the event that the Company issues additional shares at a purchase price less[14] than the applicable Conversion Price. No adjustment to the Conversion Price will occur for any issuance of additional shares at a purchase price in excess of the current Conversion Price.[15] Conversion Prices will not be adjusted because of (a) conversion of Preferred Stock, (b) the issuance and sale of, or grant of options to purchase, .... shares[16] of Common Stock pursuant to the Company's employee stock purchase or option plans (the 'Reserved Employee Shares'), or (c) options or stock issued to equipment lessors and bank lenders [or stock issued in connection with mergers and acquisitions by the Company].

(6) Voting Rights: Except with respect to election of Directors, a holder of Preferred will have the right to that number of votes equal to the number of shares of Common issuable upon conversion of its Preferred at the time the shares

---

[12] This number will vary depending on the state of the Company's progress at the time of this financing. The Investors will not want to be forced to convert to Common Stock unless they have received a sufficient return on their investment.

[13] This number is typically $10 million to $15 million. Automatic conversion of the Preferred is also sometimes required (i) when less than 25% of the Preferred shares issued in the financing remain outstanding or (ii) upon the affirmative vote of more than 50% (or 66-2/3%) of the outstanding Preferred.

[14] Adjustment mechanisms can take several forms. The most favorable to the Investor is the so-called 'full ratchet provision' which provides that upon a dilutive financing, the conversion price of the diluted shares is adjusted downward to the issuance price of the dilutive financing. A less onerous mechanism is the so-called 'weighted average.' The trend is for the former because of the perception that there is a greater risk of down rounds in the current economic times. An additional provision, the so-called 'pay to play provision,' which can be burdensome from the Investor's standpoint, provides that the Investors must participate pro rata in the dilutive financing (or perhaps even in all future financings) in order to retain anti-dilution protection for their shares. Lead Investors sometimes require a pay to play provision to prevent 'free riding' by minor Investors. The 'pay to play' provision could also provide that any Investor that does not participate pro rata in future financings (or dilutive future financings) would be converted to Common Stock.

[15] Occasionally, the Company is able to request and obtain a provision that requires the anti-dilution provisions to take into account future Company issuances of stock at a price *greater* than the Conversion Price, to ameliorate the effect to stock issued at lower than the Conversion Price. However, the Investors will usually not allow the Conversion Price to ever be higher than the initial Conversion Price due to such a provision.

[16] This number is typically 10%–20% of the Company's capital stock. This provision can be alternatively worded to exclude any stock options or stock to employees approved by the Board. See 'Reserved Employee Shares.'

are voted.[17] Election of Directors will be as described under 'Board Representation' below.

(7) Protective Provisions: [So long as there are at least ------ shares of Preferred outstanding[18]] consent of the holders of at least [a majority] [two-thirds] of the outstanding Preferred will be required for any action which would: (a) amend or repeal any provision of, or add any provision to, the Company's Articles of Incorporation or Bylaws to change the rights of the Preferred, or increase or decrease the number of authorized shares of the Preferred; (b) create any new series or class of shares having a preference or priority as to dividends or assets superior to or on a parity with that of the Preferred; (c) create any bonds, notes or other obligations convertible into, exchangeable for or having option rights to purchase shares of stock with any preference or priority as to dividends or assets superior to or on a parity with that of the Preferred; (d) reclassify any class or series of Common into shares with a preference or priority as to dividends or assets superior to or on a parity with that of the Preferred; (e) apply any of its assets to the redemption or acquisition of any shares of Common, except from employees, advisors, officers, directors, consultants and service providers of the Company on terms approved by the Board; or (f) agree to a merger, sale or consolidation of the Company with another entity or the effectuation of any transaction or series of related transactions in which more than [50%] of the voting power of the Company is disposed [other than pursuant to a Qualified IPO].[19]

Redemption:[20]

The Company shall redeem the Preferred in [three] equal annual installments commencing [six] years from the date of purchase by paying in cash an amount equal to the Original Purchase Price plus any declared but unpaid dividends [plus ___ % for each year the Preferred Stock is outstanding]. To the extent that the Company may not, at any such date, legally

---

[17] In addition, the Preferred, voting as a class, must approve a sale or merger of the Company, or other event in which the Liquidation Preference comes into play.

[18] The Company may request the bracketed language, so that the protective provisions would no longer apply if the number of outstanding shares of the Preferred were reduced to a designated percentage (e.g., 25%).

[19] The Common holders may request that the Preferred holders must vote in favor of a merger or sale so long as the Preferred have received a designated return on their investment.

[20] The Company will typically resist a redemption feature, on the theory that the expected liquidity will be achieved when the Company goes public or is acquired. The venture Investors may insist on the redemption feature to force the Company to cash them out at some point (assuming funds are available), if the other liquidity options have not materialized, especially if the fund is nearing the end of its life and must have liquidity to make distributions to its partners.

Information and Registration
Rights:[22]

redeem such Preferred, such redemption will take place as soon as legally permitted.[21]

(1) Registration Rights Agreement: The information and registration rights between the Company and any past purchasers of the Company's stock shall be merged with the registration rights of the Investors in this transaction to be set forth in an Investor Rights Agreement (the 'Rights Agreement'). (2) Information Rights: So long as an Investor holds Preferred (or Common issued upon conversion of Preferred), the Company will deliver to such Investor annual [audited/unaudited] and quarterly [unaudited] financial statements. So long as the Investor holds at least [5%] [10%] of the Preferred (or Common issued upon conversion of the Preferred), and the Company has not gone public, the Company will timely furnish such Investor with budgets and monthly financial statements.

(3) Demand Rights: If, at any time after the earlier of the Company's Initial Public Offering and the date [three] years from the [first] [last] purchase of the Preferred (but not within 180 days of the effective date of a registration), Investors holding at least [25–50%] of the Preferred (or Common issued upon conversion of the Preferred) request that the Company file a registration statement for at least [25–50%] of the Common issued or issuable upon conversion of the Preferred (or any lesser percentage if the aggregate offering price to the public would exceed $[2,000,000]), the Company will use its [reasonably diligent] [best] efforts to cause such shares to be registered. The Company will not be obligated to effect more than [two] registrations (other than on Form S-3) under these demand registration rights provisions.[23]

(4) Registrations on Form S-3: Holders of at least [25–50%] of the Preferred (or Common issuable upon conversion of the Preferred) will have the right to require the Company to file up to [four] registration statements of its Common on Form S-3 (or any equivalent successor form) if the anticipated aggregate offering price to the public would exceed [$500,000–$1,000,000].

---

[21] Investors may require that if a redemption is not made on schedule, the Conversion Price of the shares not redeemed shall be reduced by some percentage. In some cases, the unredeemed shares' Conversion Price continues to be adjusted downward until the shares are redeemed.

[22] A short form provision that would replace sections (1) through (9) under this 'Information and Registration Rights' section is as follows: 'The Investors shall have demand, piggyback and S-3 registration rights and related rights, as well as information rights and related rights, in the manner customary for transactions of this nature, all as to be detailed in the definitive documents.'

[23] The Company may request that it will not be obligated under the demand registration rights provisions if SEC Rule 144, 144A, or a comparable rule is available to the Investors for the proposed sale.

(5) Piggyback Registrations: The Investors will be entitled to 'piggyback' registration rights on registrations of the Company or on any demand registrations, subject to the right of the Company and its underwriters, in view of market conditions, to reduce or eliminate the number of shares of the Investors proposed to be registered.[24]

(6) Registration Expenses: All registration expenses (exclusive of underwriting discounts and commissions [and the fees of one special counsel for the selling shareholders]) shall be borne by the Company.

(7) Transfer of Registration Rights: The registration rights may be transferred to a transferee (other than a competitor of the Company) who acquires at least [25%] of the shares held by a holder of Preferred (or Common issued upon conversion of Preferred). Transfer of registration rights to a limited or general partner or any Investor will be without restriction as to minimum shareholding.[25]

(8) Future Purchasers of Company Securities:[26] Subsequent purchasers of the Company's securities may be granted information and registration rights upon consent of the holders of at least 51% of the holders of registration rights.[27]

(9) Other Registration Provisions: Other provisions will be contained in the Stock Purchase Agreement with respect to registration rights as are customary, including cross-indemnification, the Company's ability to delay the filing of a demand registration for a period of not more than 180 days, the agreement by the purchasers of Preferred if requested by the underwriter in a public offering not to sell any Company securities they hold for a period of up to [180 days] following the effective date of the registration statement of such offering, underwriting arrangements and the like. The registration rights will apply only to Common issued upon conversion of Preferred and the Company shall have no obligation to register an offering of Preferred.

Board Representation:     The authorized number of directors of the Company will not be less than nor more than __ to be initially fixed at __. So long as [25%] or more of the Preferred issued in this

---

[24] The Company may request that the piggyback rights not be exercisable if the Investors are able to use the benefits of SEC Rule 144, 144A, or a comparable rule. The Investors may request that any underwriter cutbacks from piggyback rights be effectuated first from the founders and other shareholders before any cut back of Investors' shares.

[25] This is intended to allow distribution of securities from a venture fund to its partners.

[26] The Company must address the issue of what registration rights can be given to future investors, and what consents from this round of Investors will be necessary.

[27] The Company will prefer that it be allowed to grant *pari passu* registration rights to future investors without the consent of any of the holders of registration rights granted in this financing.

|  | financing remains outstanding, the holders of Preferred (voting as a class) will elect ___ director(s), the Common (voting as a class) will elect ___ director(s), and the holders of Preferred and Common voting together as one class will elect ___ director(s). If at any time, less than [25%] of the Preferred remains outstanding, all of the directors will be entitled to vote as if all of the Preferred were converted into Common. The Company's Board of Directors will meet at least quarterly. The Company's Bylaws will provide that any two directors or holders of at least [25%] of the Preferred may call a meeting of the Board. |
|---|---|
| Use of Proceeds: | The proceeds from the sale of the Preferred will be used for general working capital purposes.[28] |
| Employment Relationships: | The Company has, or will have, prior to the closing, employment agreements with the following persons: ___. The Company will hire persons acceptable to the Investors to the following positions:[29] |
| Stock Restriction and Vesting Agreement: | The founders of the Company and [all] [certain] other holders of Common of the Company who are [key] employees of, or consultants to, the Company will execute a Stock Restriction and Vesting Agreement with the Company pursuant to which the Company will have a repurchase option to buy back at cost a portion of the shares of Common held by such person in the event that such shareholder's employment with, or consulting to, the Company is terminated prior to the expiration of [48] months from the date of the [first] [last] purchase of the Preferred or date of first employment or consulting, whichever is later (the 'Starting Date').[30] A portion of the shares will be released from the repurchase option based upon continued employment with the Company as follows: [1/48th] will be released from the repurchase option at the end of each month from the Starting Date. In addition, the Company will have a right of first refusal with respect to any employee's or consultant's shares proposed to be resold. The price at which the Company may exercise its right of first refusal will be equal to the lower of (i) the price offered by |

---

[28] If the proceeds are to be used for a specific purpose, this provision will need to be amended accordingly.

[29] In early stage companies, venture Investors often insist that a new chief executive officer, acceptable to the Investors, be employed.

[30] This vesting provision can be heavily negotiated, with the primary issues revolving around: (1) which founders and employees are subject to this vesting provision; (2) whether all of the shares will be subject to vesting; (3) how long the vesting period is to last; and (4) whether monthly or other time period vesting should occur. Founders are often deemed to be vested in at least a portion of their stock, reflecting service to the Company prior to the Preferred investment. Founders also sometimes request that accelerated vesting occur in the event major milestones are met or the Company is sold.

|                              | the proposed third party purchaser or (ii) the price most recently set by the Board of Directors as the fair market value of the Company's Common Stock. The right of first refusal will terminate upon completion of a public offering by the Company. |
| Market Standoff Provisions:  | The Company, prior to closing, will cause all present holders of the Company's Common and all present holders of options to purchase, or rights to convert into, the Company's Common to execute a Market Standoff Agreement with the Company pursuant to which such holders will agree, if so requested by the Company or any underwriter's representative in connection with the first public offering of the Company's Common, not to sell or otherwise transfer any securities of the Company during a period of up to [180 days] following the effective date of the registration statement. The Company will require all future purchasers of stock prior to the Company's Initial Public Offering to execute such a Market Standoff Agreement.[31] |
| Reserved Employee Shares:    | The Company may reserve up to [10–20%] share of Common (the 'Reserved Employee Shares'), [inclusive] [exclusive] of shares presently reserved for issuance upon the exercise of outstanding options, for issuance to employees, officers and consultants. The Reserved Employee Shares will be issued from time to time under such arrangements, contracts or plans as are recommended by management and approved by the [Compensation Committee of the] Board of Directors. Issuance of shares or options to employees in excess of the Reserved Employee Shares [will be dilutive events requiring adjustment of the Conversion Price as described above and] will be subject to the Investors' right of first refusal described below. Holders of Reserved Employee Shares will be required to execute Stock Restriction and Vesting Agreements and Market Standoff Agreements as described above. |
| Right of First Refusal:      | In the event that the Company offers equity securities (other than Reserved Employee Shares, or upon conversion of outstanding Preferred, or upon exercise of outstanding options, warrants, or in connection with an acquisition of technology or a business or in a public offering), each Investor [who holds at least % of the Preferred issued in this financing] |

---

[31] The length of the Market Standoff will vary depending on the quality and size of the underwriter involved in the Company's Initial Public Offering. Many 'small cap' underwriters, who specialize in smaller issues and IPOs of 'penny stocks' will require that the Market Standoff extend as long as two years following the Initial Public Offering. The purpose of these provisions is to enable the underwriter to stabilize the market following the IPO and to prevent the founders and other major stockholders from immediately dumping their shares into the public market.

shall have a right of first refusal to purchase a pro rata percentage of shares in the new offering, based on the holder's percentage ownership interest in the Company. This right will terminate upon the Company's Initial Public Offering.

Co-Sale Agreement:    The founders of the Company shall execute a Co-Sale Agreement in which, if any founder proposes to sell shares of the Company, each Investor will be entitled to participate in such sale by selling the same percentage of its stock as such founder is selling of such founder's Common.[32] This right will terminate upon the Company's Initial Public Offering.

Sale of the Company:    If an affiliated third party makes a bona fide offer for all of the stock or substantially all the assets of the Company (or to lease its product line on an exclusive basis) and the holders of [a majority] [two-thirds] of the Preferred elect to sell, the founders shall have [30–60] days to match the offer and, failing their ability to do so (with financing in place), they shall sell their shares or vote to sell assets or lease product to the third party on the terms set forth in the offer.

Confidential Information and Inventions Assignment Agreement:    Each officer, director and key employee of the Company will enter into a Confidential Information and Inventions Assignment Agreement in a form reasonably acceptable to the Company and the Investors.

Stock Purchase Agreement:    The purchase of the Preferred, if consummated, will be made pursuant to a Stock Purchase Agreement (with exhibits) drafted by counsel to the Investors and acceptable to the Company and the Investors.

The Stock Purchase Agreement will contain, among other things, appropriate representations and warranties of the Company,[33] covenants of the Company,[34] and conditions to the obligations of the Investors.

Conditions of Closing:    The closing for the purchase of the Preferred will be conditioned upon:

(1) Completion of due diligence to the satisfaction of the Investors in their sole discretion.

(2) Execution by the Company of a Stock Purchase Agreement and related agreements satisfactory to the Investors in their sole discretion.

(3) Compliance by the Company with applicable federal and state securities laws.

---

[32] Founders will sometimes request exclusions from this restriction, e.g., that the founders are allowed to sell up to $100,000 of their stock without the co-sale rights coming into effect.

[33] The venture Investors may also want representations and warranties from the founders, such as with respect to technology and inventions developed by the founders.

[34] Covenants will often include requirements by the Company to provide Investors (or Investors who hold a designated minimum number of shares) with monthly, quarterly and annual financial and other information.

(4) Opinion of counsel to the Company rendered to the Investors in form and substance satisfactory to the Investors.

(5) Key man life insurance having been obtained for the benefit of the Company on [key employee(s)] for $ [provided that the Company can obtain such insurance at normally prevailing rates for persons in good health].

[(6) Other material conditions.]

(7) Such other conditions as are customary for transactions of this type.

**Expenses:** The Company and the Investors will each bear their own legal and other expenses with respect to the transaction, except that, [assuming a successful completion of the offering], the Company will pay the reasonable legal fees and expenses incurred by a single counsel to all Investors, [subject to a cap of $], payable at closing or payable immediately if the Company elects not to proceed with this transaction.

**Finders:** The Company and the investors each will indemnify the other for any finders' fees for which that party is responsible.

**Closing:** The closing of the transaction, if all conditions are met, is expected to occur on or before _____ _ 20XX.

**Confidentiality:** The Investors agree that (except as may be required by law) they will not disclose or use and they will cause their Representatives (as defined below) not to disclose or use, any Confidential Information (as hereinafter defined) with respect to the Company furnished, or to be furnished, by the Company to the Investors in connection herewith at any time or in any manner and will not use such information other than in connection with their evaluation of the Company and the Preferred. For purposes of this paragraph, 'Confidential Information' means any information identified as such in writing to the Investors by the Company. If the purchase of the Preferred is not consummated, the Investors will promptly return all documents, contracts, records and properties to the Company. The provisions of this paragraph shall survive the termination of this Term Sheet.

**Exclusivity:** The Company agrees that until, 20XX (the 'Termination Date'), or if a definitive Stock Purchase Agreement shall have been executed prior to such date, thereafter pursuant to the terms of such Agreement, the Company will, and the Company will cause its Representatives (as defined below) to, (i) immediately terminate all existing discussions with any corporation, partnership, person or other entity or group (other than the Investors and their Representatives) concerning any merger, purchase or sale of material assets or shares of capital stock, consolidation, reorganization, recapitalization, business combination or similar transaction (collectively, a 'Transaction') involving the Company; and (ii) shall not, nor shall it direct or authorize any of its Representatives to, directly or indirectly, solicit, initiate or participate in any way in discussion or negotiations with, or provide any information to, any corporation, partnership, person or other entity or group (other than the Investors and their Representatives) concerning any Transaction involving the Company which would prevent the Investors' acquisition of the Preferred substantially in accordance with the terms set forth herein. The Company represents that neither it nor any of its affiliates is party to or bound by any agreement with respect to any such transaction other than as contemplated by this Term Sheet. For purposes of this Term Sheet, 'Representatives' shall mean a party's directors, officers, employees, agents, advisors, consultants, attorneys, financing sources, accountants and affiliates.

| | |
|---|---|
| Counsel to the Investor: | Phone: _____ |
| | Fax: _____ |
| | Attn: _____ |
| Counsel to the Investor: | Phone: _____ |
| | Fax: _____ |
| | Attn: _____ |
| Distribution List: | The parties list for distribution of documents is set forth as Exhibit 3. |

Exhibit 1: Current capitalization of the company
Exhibit 2: Capitalization of the company after the proposed financing
Exhibit 3: Distribution list for documents

## APPENDIX 1.G TERM SHEET FOR SENIOR SECURED FINANCING

## SUMMARY OF TERMS OF SENIOR SECURED FINANCING

| | |
|---|---|
| Issuer: | ABC Inc. together with all related operating subsidiaries (the 'Company'). |
| | Transaction Overview........................ MMM shall purchase BBB, Inc. in a transaction (the 'Transaction') valued at no more than $xx million resulting in pro forma combined Company EBITDA of no less than $xx million. The Company shall issue no less than $xx million of common stock on the Closing Date and shall further agree to issue an additional $xx million of equity (the 'Additional Equity') within six months of the Closing Date, with the Additional Equity to be provided by an acceptable institutional investor. |
| Issue: | Senior Secured Notes (the 'Notes'). |
| Amount: | $x,000,000 funded at close (the 'Term Loan') plus an additional $x,000,000 acquisition line (the 'Acquisition Line'). |

| | |
|---|---|
| Investors: | XXX or one or more of its affiliates and other investors mutually acceptable to XXX and the Company. |
| Use of Proceeds: | The Term Loan shall be used to (i) refinance existing indebtedness and capital leases, (ii) fund the acquisition of BBB, and (iii) pay fees and expenses in connection with the Transaction. Total funded indebtedness on the Closing Date shall not exceed 3.35x, including seller debt, capital lease obligations and any other indebtedness. The Acquisition Line will be available to fund the purchase of related Bears following the issuance of the Additional Equity. The Acquisition Line will be available until the later to occur of (1) the 12-month anniversary of the issuance of the Additional Equity or (2) the 18-month anniversary of the Closing Date. |
| Interest Rate: | LIBOR plus 5.75% per annum payable in cash on all funded amounts outstanding. Interest shall be payable monthly in arrears. |
| Closing Fee: | 1.0% of the Amount committed. |
| Unused Acquisition Line Fee: | A commitment fee shall be payable on a monthly basis on the unused portion of the Acquisition Line at the rate of: (x) 0.50% per annum during the first 12 months following the Closing Date and (y) 0.75% per annum following the 12-month anniversary of the Closing Date until the termination of the availability of the Acquisition Line. |
| Closing Date: | Anticipated to be on or before April 15, 2OOX. |
| Maturity: | 5 years from the Closing Date. |
| Mandatory Amortization: | $5.0 million upon the issuance of the Additional Equity. |
| Cash Flow Sweep: | 50% of cash flow after maintenance capital expenditures and acquisitions shall be applied to repay the principal loan balance. |
| Maximum Leverage: | Future acquisitions will be subject to a maximum funded debt to pro forma EBITDA ratio of 3.0x. |
| Optional Redemption: | The Company may redeem some or **all** of the Notes at any time prior to maturity at the following redemption prices, plus accrued and unpaid interest: |
| Year Redemption Price: | Year 1     104% |
| | Year 2     103% |
| | Year 3     102% |
| | Year 4     101% |
| | Year 5     Par |
| Security Interest: | The Notes will be secured by a first lien on and security interest in substantially all of the assets and properties owned by the Company, including a pledge of **all** of the capital stock of the Company and its subsidiaries, subject only in priority to a prior ranking lien on accounts receivables securing the credit facility. |

Ranking:

The Notes will be a senior secured obligation and will rank senior to **all** of the Company's existing and future subordinated indebtedness.

Covenants:

The Notes will contain covenants, including, but not limited to, covenants with respect to: (i) limitations on the incurrence of additional indebtedness and the issuance of disqualified capital stock; (ii) minimum EBITDA; (iii) maximum leverage ratio, minimum interest coverage and minimum fixed charge coverage ratios; (iv) limitations on investments and restricted payments; (v) limitations on the sale of assets; (vi) limitations on lines of business; (vii) limitations on transactions with affiliates; (viii) limitations on liens; (ix) restrictions on mergers, consolidations and the transfer of all or substantially all of the assets of the Company to another person; (x) limitations on capital expenditures and lease liabilities; and (xi) certain additional financial covenants.

Due Diligence:

The Lender shall complete a due diligence review, which shall include, but not be limited to: (i) meetings with the Company's management team, (ii) visits to the Company's and BBB's diagnostic imaging facilities, (iii) participation in the financial and accounting due diligence engagement to evaluate BBB's financial position, and (iv) an accounting review of BBB's existing operations.

Representations and Warranties:

The definitive documentation for the Notes will contain the usual representations and warranties.

Events of Default:

The definitive documentation for the Notes will contain usual events of default.

Expenses:

The Company shall reimburse the Lender for all reasonable out-of-pocket expenses incurred in connection with the transaction, including, without limitation, related due diligence and preparation, negotiation, execution, delivery, administration and enforcement of the definitive documentation.

Governing Law:

All documentation in connection with the Notes shall be governed by the laws of the State XX applicable to agreements made and performed in such state.

Appendix:

Senior Secured Second Lien Term Loan

Borrower:

('The Borrower'), assumed to be the same as the Obligors under the credit agreement governing the new Senior Secured First Lien Credit Facility ('First Lien Credit Facility').

Credit Facility:

Senior Secured Second Lien Term Loan (the 'Second Lien Credit Facility').

Principal Amount:

$XX,000,000.

Purchaser:

XXX a fund managed by XXX, or any of its affiliated funds (the 'Purchaser').

| | |
|---|---|
| Use of Proceeds: | The proceeds will be used to (i) finance the purchase of the Borrower's Convertible Preferred Stock by an employee stock ownership trust (the 'ESOT') in connection with the ESOP Transaction (the 'ESOP Transaction') and (ii) pay fees and expenses related to this transaction. |
| Targeted Closing Date: | To be determined, but expected to be on or before March 31, 20xx. |
| Purchase Price: | 100% of the Face Amount ('Par'). |
| Upfront Fee: | One percent (1.00%) of the Principal Amount of the Second Lien Credit Facility, payable at closing. |
| Interest Rate: | LIBOR plus seven percent (7.00%), payable in cash each calendar quarter in arrears. The Interest Rate will step down to LIBOR plus six and one half percent (6.50%) when (i) the First Lien Term Loan and the Revolving Credit Facility are both in pro forma compliance with the Borrowing Base, (ii) after the Senior Secured Second Lien Term Loan has been reduced to $10,000,000 outstanding, (iii) if, and only if, the Borrower is in pro forma compliance with all Covenants set forth in the Senior Credit Facility and the Second Lien Credit Facility, and (iv) when pro forma Total Debt/EBITDA is less than 1.5x. |
| Tenor: | Four and one-half (4.5) years (assumed to be 6 months after the maturity of the First Lien Credit Facility). |
| Amortization: | Bullet payment at maturity. |
| Optional Prepayment: | The Second Lien Credit Facility may be prepaid at the Borrower's option at any time after the date of issuance in accordance with the schedule below and at the following redemption prices (expressed in percentages of principal amount to be prepaid) with minimum prepayment amount of $x,000,000, plus accrued interest to the date of the prepayment: |

| Year | Redemption price |
|---|---|
| 1 | 104% |
| 2 | 103% |
| 3 | 102% |
| 4 | 101% |
| Thereafter | 100% |

During the 1st anniversary of the Closing Date, the Borrower will pay the redemption price set forth in the schedule above for any prepayments, whether optional or mandatory (defined below), made to the Second Lien Credit Facility. At any time after the lSI anniversary of the Closing Date, the Borrower will pay the redemption prices set forth in the schedule above for all optional prepayments and all mandatory prepayments (defined below) made to the Second Lien Credit Facility with the exception of mandatory prepayments made with 75% of Excess Free Cash Flow (to be defined).

Mandatory Prepayment:      The Second Lien Credit Facility shall be prepaid with (a) 75% of Excess Free Cash Flow (to be defined), with a reduction to be agreed based upon achievement and maintenance of a leverage ratio to be agreed, (b) 100% of the net cash proceeds of all asset sales or other dispositions of property by the Borrower (subject to exceptions and reinvestment provisions to be agreed upon), (c) 100% of the net cash proceeds of issuances of debt obligations of the Borrower (subject to exceptions to be agreed upon) and (d) 50% of the net cash proceeds of issuances of equity securities of the Borrower, with a reduction to be agreed based upon achievement and maintenance of a leverage ratio to be agreed.

Guarantors:      Mandatory prepayments described above shall be applied first to the First Lien Credit Facility up to the point that the First Lien Term Loan and the Revolving Credit Facility are both in pro forma compliance with the Borrowing Base and thereafter to the principal of Second Lien Credit Facility until paid in full.

Note:      Prepayments to the Seller Subordinated Notes will be allowed (i) after the First Lien Term Loan and the Revolving Credit Facility are both in pro forma compliance with the Borrowing Base, (ii) after the Senior Secured Second Lien Term Loan has been reduced to $xx,000,000 outstanding, (iii) if, and only if, the Borrower is in pro forma compliance with all Covenants set forth in the Senior Credit Facility and the Second Lien Credit Facility, and (iv) when Total Debt/EBITDA is less than 1.5x. At such time, prepayments may be made from 50% of Excess Free Cash Flow, so long as the Senior Secured Second Lien Term Loan also receives 50% of Excess Free Cash Flow as defined under the loan documents.

Guarantors:      The Second Lien Credit Facility will be guaranteed on a senior secured second lien basis by any present or future direct and indirect domestic subsidiaries of the Borrower, assumed to be the same Guarantors as under the credit agreement governing the First Lien Credit Facility.

Security:      The Second Lien Credit Facility will be secured by a perfected second priority security interest and lien upon all tangible and intangible assets of the Borrower, assumed to be identical to the assets securing the First Lien Credit Facility.

Inter-creditor Terms:      The Second Lien Credit Facility will be senior to all existing and future subordinated debt as will be reflected in documentation acceptable to the· Purchaser. General intercreditor terms for the Second Lien Credit Facility shall include, but not be limited to:

- Second Lien Credit Facility is lien subordinated and not payment subordinated to the First Lien Credit Facility.

- Application of proceeds from collateral (including, but not limited to, those outlined in the Mandatory Prepayment provision) not applied to the First Lien Credit Facility shall be applied to the Second Lien Credit Facility in accordance with Mandatory Prepayment provision.

Management Access and Reporting Right:
XXX will have the right to receive all information, reports, and access provided to the senior lenders under the Reporting Requirements set forth in the Senior Credit Agreement. In addition, the Senior Secured Second Lien Lenders will meet quarterly with management to receive a formal update on the performance of the business and its prospects. Failure by the company to comply with such a meeting request will be an event of default under the Senior Secured Second Lien Loan Agreement.

Documentation:
Documentation will contain such terms, conditions, representations, warranties, reporting requirements, covenants, including financial maintenance and incurrence covenants, as is customary for investments of this type.

Financial and Other Covenants:
Financial covenants are expected to be consistent with the financial covenants set forth in the credit agreement governing the First Lien Credit Facility and are expected to include but not be limited to:

(i)   Minimum Debt Service Coverage.
(ii)  Maximum Senior Funded Debt to EBITDA.
(iii) Maximum Total Funded Debt to EBITDA.
(iv)  Maximum Capital Expenditures; and
(v)   Limitations on Officers' Salaries.

Events of Default:
Customary Events of Default will include, but not be limited to: (i) failure to pay interest or principal when due and payable; (ii) failure to comply with the covenants and other terms contained in related transaction documents; (iii) failure to discharge material judgments; (iv) cross-default and cross-acceleration with other indebtedness; and (v) bankruptcy or insolvency.

Fees, Costs and Expenses:
All reasonable costs, fees and expenses (including, without limitation, all legal, accounting and consulting fees and disbursements) incurred or to be incurred by XXX, subject to the Closing Expense Cap, in connection with the examination, review, documentation, and/or closing of this transaction whether or not this transaction ultimately closes.

Conditions to Closing:       XXX's satisfactory completion of its due diligence including, but not limited to:

- Due diligence with respect to the operations of the Borrower including, but not limited to, review of financial condition and historical financial statements, review of management forecasts, review of management agreements, review of all material contracts, evidence of meeting material laws and regulations, customer calls.
- Receipt and satisfaction with financial and third-party accounting due diligence.
- Review and satisfaction with all collateral and systems audits conducted by XX.
- Satisfaction with all borrowing base and liquidity calculations under the First Lien Credit Facility.
- Receipt and satisfaction with legal diligence conducted by Company's legal counsel and XXX's legal counsel, including, but not limited to tax and ERISA due diligence.
- Satisfaction with the capital structure at closing including the equity ownership of the Company and all financings related to the transaction.
- Satisfactory review of all opinions, regulatory, tax or other matters related to the ESOP Transaction; and
- Satisfactory completion of all documents, agreements and approvals necessary to execute this transaction.

# Appendix 2

# First Lien/Second Lien
# Inter-creditor Agreement

*[First Lien Agent]*

*[Second Lien Agent]*

*[Control Agent]*

*[Borrower]*

*[Holdings]*

*[Guarantor Subsidiaries]*

*[date]*

Updates of the ABA model agreement can be found at: http://apps.americanbar.org/dch/
committee.cfm?com=CL190029

# Table of Contents

# PREAMBLE

## Parties

- _____, as collateral agent for the holders of the First Lien Obligations defined below (in such capacity, **_First Lien Agent_**)[1]
- _____, as collateral agent for the holders of the Second Lien Obligations defined below (in such capacity, **_Second Lien Agent_**)
- _____, as control agent for First Lien Agent and Second Lien Agent (in such capacity, the **_Control Agent_**)
- _____, (**_Borrower_**)
- _____, (**_Holdings_**)
- The Guarantor Subsidiaries (as defined below).

## Background

The Borrower, the Borrower's parent company, Holdings, certain lenders and agents, and the First Lien Agent have entered into a **_First Lien Credit Agreement_** dated the date hereof providing for a revolving credit facility and term loan.

The Borrower, Holdings, certain lenders and agents, and the Second Lien Agent have entered into a **_Second Lien Credit Agreement_** dated the date hereof providing for a term loan.

Holdings has guaranteed, and Holdings and the Borrower have agreed to cause certain current and future Subsidiaries of the Borrower [and Holdings] (the **_Guarantor Subsidiaries_**) to guarantee the Borrower's Obligations under the First Lien Credit Agreement and the Second Lien Credit Agreement.

Each of the Borrower, Holdings, each Guarantor Subsidiary, and each other Person that executes and delivers a First Lien Collateral Document or a Second Lien Collateral Document as a 'grantor' or 'pledgor' (or the equivalent) is a **_Grantor_**.

A Grantor may enter into Hedge Agreements and Cash Management Agreements with one or more lenders under the First Lien Credit Agreement or their affiliates as counterparties, which may be included in the First Lien Obligations defined below.[2]

The First Lien Obligations and the Second Lien Obligations are secured by Liens on substantially all the assets of the Borrower, Holdings and the Guarantor Subsidiaries.

The Parties desire to set forth in this First Lien/Second Lien Inter-creditor Agreement (this **_Agreement_**) their rights and remedies with respect to the Collateral securing the First Lien Obligations and the Second Lien Obligations.

# AGREEMENT

---

[1] The first and second lien agents are parties to the inter-creditor agreement, but the first and second lien lenders are not. Therefore, the first and second lien credit agreements should each (i) bind each lender to the terms of the inter-creditor agreement, (ii) authorize the agent to enter into the inter-creditor agreement on behalf of the lenders and to exercise all the agent's rights and comply with all its obligations under the inter-creditor agreement, and (iii) specify what lender direction or authorization is required for the agent to agree to consents, waivers or amendments, or to take or refrain from other actions under the inter-creditor agreement.

[2] The parties may wish to provide for hedge agreements provided by a second lien lender or affiliate.

# 1 LIEN PRIORITIES[3]

## 1.1 Seniority of Liens securing First Lien Obligations

(a) A Lien on Collateral securing any First Lien Obligation that is included in the Capped Obligations up to but not in excess of the First Lien Cap will, at all times, be senior and prior in all respects to a Lien on such Collateral securing any Second Lien Obligation, and a Lien on Collateral securing any Second Lien Obligation will, at all times, be junior and subordinate in all respects to a Lien on such Collateral securing any First Lien Obligation that is included in the Capped Obligations up to but not in excess of the First Lien Cap.

(b) A Lien on Collateral securing any First Lien Obligation that is not included in the Capped Obligations will, at all times, be senior and prior in all respects to a Lien on such Collateral securing any Second Lien Obligation, and a Lien on Collateral securing any Second Lien Obligation will, at all times, be junior and subordinate in all respects to a Lien on such Collateral securing any First Lien Obligation that is not included in the Capped Obligations.

(c) The Lien on Collateral securing any First Lien Obligation that is included in the Capped Obligations in excess of the First Lien Cap will have the priority set forth in Section 1.11, 'Subordination of Liens securing Excess First Lien Obligations.'

(d) Except as otherwise expressly provided herein, the priority of the Liens securing First Lien Obligations and the rights and obligations of the Parties will remain in full force and effect irrespective of

   (1) how a Lien was acquired (whether by grant, possession, statute, operation of law, subrogation, or otherwise),

   (2) the time, manner, or order of the grant, attachment, or perfection of a Lien,

   (3) any conflicting provision of the U.C.C. or other applicable law,

   (4) any defect in, or non-perfection, setting aside, or avoidance of, a Lien or a First Lien Loan Document or a Second Lien Loan Document,

   (5) the modification of a First Lien Obligation or a Second Lien Obligation,

   (6) the modification of a First Lien Loan Document or a Second Lien Loan Document,

   (7) the subordination of a Lien on Collateral securing a First Lien Obligation to a Lien securing another obligation of a Grantor or other Person that is permitted under the

---

[3] The heart of the inter-creditor agreement is the lien subordination provision pursuant to which the second lien lenders agree that their lien on the common assets will be junior and second in priority to the lien of the first lien lenders, including typically both liens on personal property and liens on real estate. Even at this preliminary stage of the inter-creditor agreement, the first lien lenders and the second lien lenders are likely to have different points of view as to how broadly the lien subordination provision should be worded. The first lien lenders are likely to insist that their lien on the common assets should remain superior (at least up to the amount of the first lien cap) even if the first lien lenders fail to perfect their lien properly or allow their lien to lapse or their lien is avoided in bankruptcy or otherwise. Second lien lenders will often take the position that only collateral in which both first and second lien lenders have a valid and perfected security interest not subject to avoidance as a preferential transfer or otherwise by the debtor or a trustee in bankruptcy should be subject to the lien priority provisions. See alternative Section 1.1 and notes to that section and alternative Section 1.7. In practice, the view of the first lien lenders has typically prevailed on this issue although there is increasing recognition of the unintended 'payment subordination' by the second lien lenders that may result if the first lien lapses or is avoided in bankruptcy, and the second lien lenders are forced by their agreement to an 'absolute' priority provision to be subordinate to the now unsecured first lien lenders.

First Lien Loan Documents as in effect on the date hereof or secures a DIP Financing deemed consented to by the Second Lien Claimholders pursuant to Section 6.1, '*Use of cash collateral and DIP financing*,'

(8) the exchange of a security interest in any Collateral for a security interest in other Collateral,

(9) the commencement of an Insolvency Proceeding, or

(10) any other circumstance whatsoever, including a circumstance that might be a defense available to, or a discharge of, a Grantor in respect of a First Lien Obligation or a Second Lien Obligation or holder of such Obligation.

**[Alternative Section Favorable to Second Lien Lenders][4]**

## [1.1 Seniority of Liens securing First Lien Obligations

(e) A Lien on Collateral securing any First Lien Obligation that is included in the Capped Obligations up to but not in excess of the First Lien Cap will, at all times, be senior and

---

[4] First and second lien lenders typically agree not to challenge the priority, perfection or validity of their respective liens. However, a first lien agent may fail to perfect, or maintain perfection, of its lien, or may be determined by a court to have participated in a fraudulent transfer or other transaction that results in their claims being disallowed or equitably subordinated. This has occurred in several recent high-profile cases. In such situations, second lien lenders will often argue, particularly in negotiated middle-market transactions, that an agreement to continue to treat an unperfected or equitably subordinated first lien lender as being perfected and senior to the second lien lender converts lien subordination into payment subordination to unsecured or equitably subordinated indebtedness that is not reflected in the coupon on or underwriting assumptions for the second lien obligations. This could place the second lien lenders in a far worse position than if they were unsecured creditors. Therefore, second lien lenders often take the position that only collateral in which both first and second lien lenders have a valid and perfected security interest not subject to avoidance as a preferential transfer or otherwise by the debtor or a trustee in bankruptcy should be subject to the lien priority provisions of the inter-creditor agreement. Payment subordination as described in this note can occur if (i) the lien securing first lien obligations maintains priority, and a turn-over right, under the inter-creditor agreement even if invalid, unperfected, equitably subordinated or avoidable, or (ii) first lien obligations include amounts 'whether or not allowable in an insolvency proceeding' and the amounts are not allowed. This can result in payment subordination of the claims of second lien lenders to the extent of first lien claims not allowed in an insolvency proceeding, which also leaves the second lien lenders with no enforceable subrogation rights in respect of such claims, and in a position that may be worse than that of an unsecured creditor. On the other hand, application of proceeds to second lien claimholders from unperfected first lien collateral may result in a greater recovery than had the first lien collateral been perfected, and some inter-creditor agreements attempt to address this issue. As an example, consider a debtor with $100 million of assets, $50 million of first lien debt, $50 million of second lien debt and $50 million of unsecured obligations. If the first lien lenders' claims are unsecured for failure to maintain perfection, the second lien lenders will recover in full ($50 million) on their lien, but pay the entire recovery over to the first lien lenders, and have only an unsecured subrogation claim from the first lien lenders, which will result in a recovery of only $25 million, all due to the failure of the first lien lenders to perfect. If the first lien lenders' claims are equitably subordinated or disallowed because of bad acts of the first lien lenders, the result for the second lien lenders will be catastrophic. In the example above, they would turn over their $50 million recovery to the first lien lenders, who would be paid in full notwithstanding their bad acts, and the innocent second lien lenders would have no recovery at all. For a detailed discussion of this issue, please see, among other articles, Robert L. Cunningham and Yair Y. Galil, Lien Subordination and Inter-creditor Agreements, *Review of Banking and Financial Services* **25**:49 (2009).

prior in all respects to a Lien on such Collateral securing any Second Lien Obligation, and a Lien on Collateral securing any Second Lien Obligation will, at all times, be junior and subordinate in all respects to a Lien on such Collateral securing any First Lien Obligation that is included in the Capped Obligations up to but not in excess of the First Lien Cap so long as the Lien securing the First Lien Obligations is valid, perfected, [and unavoidable] [and is not avoided in an Insolvency Proceeding].

(f) A Lien on Collateral securing any First Lien Obligation that is not included in the Capped Obligations will, at all times, be senior and prior in all respects to a Lien on such Collateral securing any Second Lien Obligation, and a Lien on Collateral securing any Second Lien Obligation will, at all times, be junior and subordinate in all respects to a Lien on such Collateral securing any First Lien Obligation that is not included in the Capped Obligations so long as the Lien securing the First Lien Obligations is valid, perfected, [and unavoidable] [and is not avoided in an Insolvency Proceeding].

(g) The Lien on Collateral securing any First Lien Obligation that is included in the Capped Obligations in excess of the First Lien Cap will have the priority set forth in Section 1.11, *'Subordination of Liens securing Excess First Lien Obligations.'*

(h) Except as otherwise expressly provided herein, the priority of the Liens securing First Lien Obligations and the rights and obligations of the Parties will remain in full force and effect irrespective of

    (1) how a Lien was acquired (whether by grant, possession, statute, operation of law, subrogation or otherwise),

    (2) the time, manner or order of the grant, attachment or perfection of a Lien,

    (3) any conflicting provision of the U.C.C. or other applicable law,

    (4) the modification of a First Lien Obligation or a Second Lien Obligation,

    (5) the modification of a First Lien Loan Document or a Second Lien Loan Document,

    (6) the subordination of a Lien on Collateral securing a First Lien Obligation to a Lien securing another obligation of a Grantor or other Person that is permitted under the First Lien Loan Documents as in effect on the date hereof or secures a DIP Financing deemed consented to by the Second Lien Claimholders pursuant to Section 6.1, *'Use of cash collateral and DIP financing,'*

    (7) the exchange of a security interest in any Collateral for a security interest in other Collateral, or

    (8) the commencement of an Insolvency Proceeding.]

**[End of Alternative Section]**

## 1.2 No payment subordination[5]

The subordination of Liens securing Second Lien Obligations to Liens securing First Lien Obligations set forth in the preceding section affects only the relative priority of those Liens, and does not subordinate the Second Lien Obligations in right of payment to the First Lien Obligations. Nothing in this Agreement will affect the entitlement of any Second Lien Claimholder to receive and retain required payments of interest, principal and other amounts in respect of a Second Lien Obligation unless the receipt is expressly prohibited by, or results from the Second Lien Claimholder's breach of, this Agreement.

---

[5] The typical second lien financing inter-creditor agreement does not require payment subordination.

## 1.3  First Lien Obligations and Second Lien Obligations

(a) *First Lien Obligations* means all Obligations of the Grantors under
   (1) the First Lien Credit Agreement and the other First Lien Loan Documents,
   (2) the guaranties by Holdings and the Guarantor Subsidiaries of the Borrower's Obligations under the First Lien Loan Documents,
   (3) any Hedge Agreement entered into with an agent or a lender (or an Affiliate thereof) under the First Lien Credit Agreement (even if the counterparty or an Affiliate of the counterparty ceases to be an agent or a lender under the First Lien Credit Agreement),
   (4) any Cash Management Agreement, or
   (5) any other agreement or instrument granting or providing for the perfection of a Lien securing any of the foregoing.

Notwithstanding any other provision hereof, the term '*First Lien Obligations*' will include accrued interest, fees, costs and other charges incurred under the First Lien Credit Agreement and the other First Lien Loan Documents, whether incurred before or after commencement of an Insolvency Proceeding, and whether or not allowable in an Insolvency Proceeding. To the extent that any payment with respect to the First Lien Obligations (whether by or on behalf of any Grantor, as proceeds of security, enforcement of any right of set-off or otherwise) is declared to be fraudulent or preferential in any respect, set aside or required to be paid to a debtor in possession, trustee, receiver or similar Person, then the obligation or part thereof originally intended to be satisfied will be deemed to be reinstated and outstanding as if such payment had not occurred.

**[Alternative Definition More Favorable to Second Lien Lenders]**

[(a) *First Lien Obligations* means all Obligations of the Grantors under
   (1) the First Lien Credit Agreement and the First Lien Loan Documents,
   (2) the guaranties by Holdings and the Guarantor Subsidiaries of the Borrower's Obligations under the First Lien Loan Documents,
   (3) any Hedge Agreement entered into with an agent or a lender (or an Affiliate thereof) under the First Lien Credit Agreement (even if the counterparty or an Affiliate of the counterparty ceases to be an agent or a lender under the First Lien Credit Agreement),
   (4) any Cash Management Agreement, or
   (5) any other agreement or instrument granting or providing for the perfection of a Lien securing any of the foregoing, except that such Obligations will only be considered First Lien Obligations to the extent
      (i) they are secured by a valid, perfected and unavoidable Lien on the Collateral in favor of the First Lien Agent,[6] and
      (ii) a claim for such Obligations would be allowed or allowable in an Insolvency Proceeding applicable to the relevant Grantor.]

**[End of Alternative Definition]**

(b) *Second Lien Obligations* means all Obligations of the Grantors under
   (1) the Second Lien Credit Agreement and the other Second Lien Loan Documents,
   (2) the guaranties by Holdings and the Guarantor Subsidiaries of the Borrower's Obligations under the Second Lien Loan Documents,

---

[6] These changes in the definition of 'First Lien Obligations' would typically be used in connection with the alternative definition of 'First Lien Cap' and the alternative lien priority provisions in Section 1.1 noted as being more favorable to second lien lenders.

(3) any Hedge Agreement entered into with an agent or a lender (or an Affiliate thereof) under the Second Lien Credit Agreement if such agent or lender is not an agent or lender under the First Lien Credit Agreement (even if the counterparty or an Affiliate of the counterparty ceases to be an agent or a lender under the Second Lien Credit Agreement),

(4) any agreement or instrument granting or providing for the perfection of a Lien securing any of the foregoing, [except that the aggregate principal amount of the Second Lien Obligations (other than Obligations under Hedge Agreements or Cash Management Agreements) in excess of the Second Lien Cap (as defined below) will not be Second Lien Obligations].[7]

Notwithstanding any other provision hereof, the term '*Second Lien Obligations*' will include accrued interest, fees, costs and other charges incurred under the Second Lien Credit Agreement and the other Second Lien Loan Documents, whether incurred before or after commencement of an Insolvency Proceeding, [and whether or not allowable in an Insolvency Proceeding].

(c) The inclusion of Obligations under Hedge Agreements in the First Lien Obligations will not create in favor of the applicable counterparty any rights in connection with the management or release of any Collateral or of the Obligations of any Grantor under any First Lien Collateral Document, and the inclusion of Obligations under Hedge Agreements in the Second Lien Obligations will not create in favor of the applicable counterparty any rights in connection with the management or release of any Collateral or of the Obligations of any Grantor under any Second Lien Collateral Document.

(d) The First Lien Agent and the holders of First Lien Obligations are, together, the *First Lien Claimholders*. The Second Lien Agent and the holders of Second Lien Obligations are, together, the *Second Lien Claimholders*.

## 1.4 First Lien Cap[8]

*Capped Obligations* means First Lien Obligations for the payment of principal of Loans and reimbursement obligations in respect of Letters of Credit [Obligations under Interest Rate Protection Agreements] and interest, premium, if any, and fees accruing or payable in respect thereof or in respect of commitments therefor.

---

[7] Second lien caps are less common than first lien caps. If there is a second lien cap, the following definition should be added:

> **Second Lien Cap** means $_____ minus the aggregate amount of principal payments on the term loan under the Second Lien Credit Agreement (other than payments in connection with a Refinancing).

[8] The Model Agreement includes a fairly broad definition of 'First Lien Obligations' that encompasses principal, interest, fees, indemnity obligations, the cost of unwinding hedging obligations and cash management obligations. However, it also provides for a 'first lien cap' in an agreed-upon maximum principal amount. The standard definition of 'first lien cap' is limited to a cap on principal and a related cap on interest, premiums and fees on the capped principal amount. The alternative definition more favorable to second lien lenders includes optional limits on other first lien obligations, including separate caps on interest payments and on obligations under hedge agreements. Many inter-creditor agreements provide for a first lien cap but fail to address the consequences of the first lien lenders exceeding the cap. The Model Agreement specifically provides in Section 1.1 ('*Seniority of Liens securing First Lien Obligations*') that the lien on collateral securing first lien obligations will have priority over the second lien obligations up to but not in excess of the first lien cap. The Model Agreement also deals with the question of how the first lien lenders' lien securing first lien obligations in excess of the cap should

***First Lien Cap*** means the sum of

(a) the excess of

    (1) the aggregate principal amount of First Lien Obligations (including the undrawn amount of all letters of credit constituting First Lien Obligations (***Letters of Credit***) and the aggregate original principal amount of any term loan that is a First Lien Obligation but excluding First Lien Obligations under Hedge Agreements) up to, but not in excess of, $_____,[9] over

    (2) the sum of (A) principal payments applied to term loans that are First Lien Obligations, (B) permanent reductions of revolving credit loans (and accompanying commitments) under the revolving credit facility provided for in the First Lien Credit Agreement, and (C) reimbursements of drawings under Letters of Credit constituting First Lien Obligations to the extent that any such reimbursement results in a permanent reduction of the Letter of Credit commitment amount under the First Lien Loan Documents, excluding reductions resulting from a Refinancing, plus

---

footnote (*continued*)

be handled. See Section 1.11, '*Subordination of Liens securing Excess First Lien Obligations*,' which provides, among other things, that the second lien lenders will be subordinate only to the extent that the principal amount of the first lien loan does not exceed the first lien cap. Similarly, the buy-out provisions of the Model Agreement that permit the second lien lenders to purchase the first lien loan at par following the occurrence of an event of default only apply to the portion of the first lien loan that does not exceed the agreed-upon cap and the uncapped portion of the loan. While a first lien cap is designed to protect the second lien lenders from unanticipated increases in the first lien debt, the first lien lenders will want to make sure that they have a sufficient 'cushion' under the first lien cap to increase the first lien loan by a reasonable amount to deal with additional cash needs by the borrower as part of a loan workout or otherwise. The first lien lenders also should consider including an additional 'cushion' for debtor-in-possession ('DIP') financing to be provided by the first lien lenders in the event of bankruptcy. The definition of first lien cap in the Model Agreement includes optional provisions for including DIP financing under the first lien cap. The Task Force has intentionally omitted any provision stating that a breach of the agreement occurs if the first lien lenders exceed the cap. Instead, the agreement provides that exceeding the cap will result in a subordination of the excess amount to the lien of the second lien lenders as provided in Section 1.11. The parties may wish to consider including an express agreement by the first lien lenders not to exceed the first lien cap but, in most cases, the Task Force believes that the subordination of the excess will provide a sufficient and appropriate remedy for the second lien lenders. Section 1.11(e) expressly provides that the second lien lenders reserve any rights against the borrower under the second lien loan documents for any event of default resulting from the incurrence of obligations exceeding the first lien cap.

[9] In the absence of unusual provisions in the first lien credit agreement (e.g., delayed draw term loans or accordion features), a typical first lien cap for a negotiated transaction would be in the range of 110–115% of the aggregate commitment under the first lien loan documents, with 110% being the most common percentage. If the modification section restricts extending scheduled amortization, consider whether the borrower should be prohibited from reallocating its term facility to revolving exposure. This form of agreement assumes that the parties have negotiated a reducing cap as opposed to, for instance, a leverage-based incurrence option or a flat, non-reducing cap. If the parties have agreed to a form of non-reducing cap, then appropriate changes will need to be made to the definition of 'First Lien Cap.' This definition of first lien cap applies only to principal. Second lien lenders may argue that the cap should be expanded to include other first lien obligations, including interest, costs, expenses, indemnities and obligations under hedge agreements and cash management agreements. See the alternative definition of first lien cap more favorable to second lien lenders.

(b) amounts in respect of accrued, unpaid interest, fees and premium (if any), in each case above accruing in respect of or attributable to, but only in respect of or attributable to, the aggregate principal amount of First Lien Obligations (including the undrawn amount of all Letters of Credit constituting First Lien Obligations and the aggregate original principal amount of any term loan that is a First Lien Obligation) at any one time not to exceed the amount referred to in clause (a) above,[10] *provided* that the First Lien Cap shall not apply to any First Lien Obligations other than Capped Obligations, [and plus

(c) Obligations owing by Grantors to First Lien Claimholders under non-speculative Hedge Agreements] [Obligations owing by Grantors to First Lien Claimholders under Interest Rate Protection Agreements designed to protect a Grantor against fluctuations in interest rates on an aggregate principal amount of First Lien Obligations (including the undrawn amount of all Letters of Credit constituting First Lien Obligations and the aggregate original principal amount of any term loan that is a First Lien Obligation) at any one time not to exceed the amount referred to in clause (a) above, plus amounts in respect of accrued, unpaid interest on such Obligations,] [plus

(d) the aggregate amount of all Second Lien Adequate Protection Payments to the extent paid from a DIP financing or Proceeds of Collateral[11], [and

(e) if there is an Insolvency Proceeding, $_____].[12]

**[Alternative Definition of First Lien Cap for First Lien Loans Involving a Borrowing Base]**

[*First Lien Cap*[13] means the excess of

(f) the sum of (1) the aggregate principal amount of First Lien Obligations (including the undrawn amount of all letters of credit constituting First Lien Obligations (*Letters of Credit*)

---

[10] It is common to see first lien caps that apply only to principal and do not directly address whether or not interest, fees and premium (if any) on the 'excess principal' above the first lien cap should be entitled to the same priority as interest and fees on outstanding principal up to the cap. That approach may leave open the question of how the 'excess' fees, interest and premium (if any) should be treated for priority purposes. The alternative followed in the Model Agreement is to provide in this section that interest, fees and premium (if any) on principal up to the first lien cap will have the same priority as such principal, while interest, fees and premium (if any) on principal in excess of the first lien cap will be treated as 'excess first lien obligations' under Section 1.11(c). Second lien lenders may logically object to the ability of the first lien lenders to capitalize all interest and add that capitalized interest as an additional priority principal obligation in excess of the stated dollar cap amount. First lien lenders may logically object to not having the ability to capitalize interest to help a debtor though difficult periods without eroding any principal cushion they may have available within the capped amount. The parties should attempt to balance these concerns by negotiation, perhaps by specifying when capitalized interest will not utilize the principal cap.

[11] Include if Section 6.4 permits second lien adequate protection payments.

[12] The parties also need to decide whether a separate basket for potential DIP financing and carve-outs should be included. *See also* Section 6.1 and notes to that section.

[13] If this alternative definition of 'First Lien Cap' is used, then the following definition should be added to Section 8.1:

> *Availability* means, at any time, the aggregate amount of the revolving loans, letter of credit accommodations, and other credit accommodations available to the Borrower from the First Lien Lenders based on the Borrowing Base (as such term, and the definitions used in such term, are defined in the First Lien Loan Documents as in effect on the date hereof) (determined without regard to any revolving loans, letter of credit accommodations, or other credit accommodations then outstanding).

but excluding for purposes of this section (a) only the principal amount of any term loan that is a First Lien Obligation and any First Lien Obligations under Hedge Agreements) up to, but not in excess of, the lesser of (A) $_____, and (B) [110%] of Availability as determined by the First Lien Agent at the time each principal amount is made, issued or otherwise incurred, plus (2) the aggregate original principal amount of any term loan that is a First Lien Obligation, over

(g)  the sum of (1) the aggregate amount of all payments of the principal of any term loan included in the First Lien Obligations, and (2) the amount of all payments of revolving loans or reimbursements of drawings under Letters of Credit that permanently reduce the accompanying revolving credit commitment or letter of credit commitment amount under the First Lien Credit Agreement (excluding reductions in sub-facility commitments not accompanied by a corresponding permanent reduction in the revolving facility or letters of credit commitment amount, excluding reductions under (A) and (B) as a result of a Refinancing, and *provided* that the First Lien Cap shall not apply to any First Lien Obligations other than Capped Obligations), [plus

(h)  [Obligations owing by Grantors to First Lien Claimholders under non-speculative Hedge Agreements] [Obligations owing by Grantors to First Lien Claimholders under Interest Rate Protection Agreements designed to protect a Grantor against fluctuations in interest rates on an aggregate principal amount of First Lien Obligations (including the undrawn amount of all Letters of Credit constituting First Lien Obligations and the aggregate original principal amount of any term loan that is a First Lien Obligation) at any one time not to exceed the amount referred to in clause (a) above, plus amounts in respect of accrued, unpaid interest on such Obligations], [plus

(i)  all Second Lien Adequate Protection Payments to the extent paid from any DIP Financing or Proceeds of Collateral][14]], [plus

(j)  if there is an Insolvency Proceeding, $_____]].]

**[End of Alternative Definition]**

**[Alternative Definition More Favorable to Second Lien Lenders][15]**

*Capped Obligations* means First Lien Obligations for the payment of principal of Loans and reimbursement obligations in respect of Letters of Credit, and interest, premium, if any, and fees accruing or payable in respect thereof or in respect of commitments therefor, [plus obligations under Interest Rate Protection Agreements in respect of interest on First Lien Principal Obligations not in excess of the First Lien Cap].

---

[14] Include if Section 6.4 permits second lien adequate protection payments.

[15] If this alternative definition of 'First Lien Cap' is used, then the following definitions should also be included in Section 8.1:

*Excess Second Lien Principal Obligations* means Second Lien Principal Obligations in excess of the Second Lien Cap.

*First Lien Principal Obligations* means, at any time of determination, the aggregate unpaid principal of the loans outstanding under the First Lien Loan Documents together with the undrawn amount of all outstanding Letters of Credit under the First Lien Loan Documents.

*Second Lien Principal Obligations* means, at any time of determination, the aggregate unpaid principal of the loans outstanding under the Second Lien Loan Documents [together with the undrawn amount of all outstanding Letters of Credit under the Second Lien Loan Documents].

[*First Lien Cap* means the sum of

(k) the excess of (1) the outstanding amount of First Lien Principal Obligations not to exceed in the aggregate [the sum of (x)] $_____ of term Indebtedness [plus (y) the lesser of (A) [110]% of [Availability] as determined by the First Lien Agent at the time each principal amount is made, issued or otherwise incurred, and (B) $_____ of revolving credit Indebtedness included in the First Lien Obligations [(including the outstanding undrawn amount of, and reimbursement obligations in respect of, letters of credit constituting First Lien Obligations (*Letters of Credit*))] [(calculated, in the case of any First Lien Principal Obligations issued at a discount, at the aggregate amount due at maturity thereof)]], over (2) the aggregate amount of all repayments of term Indebtedness, and all repayments or reductions of revolving credit Indebtedness, included in the First Lien Principal Obligations, [and of reimbursement obligations under Letters of Credit] (to the extent effected with a corresponding permanent commitment reduction under the First Lien Credit Agreement but excluding reductions as a result of a Refinancing) (First Lien Principal Obligations in excess of the First Lien Cap being the *Excess First Lien Principal Obligations*), plus

(l) accrued but unpaid interest, commitment, facility, utilization and other analogous fees and, if applicable, prepayment premiums on the First Lien Principal Obligations referred to in clause (a) above [(at [rates] [interest rate margins] not in excess of __ basis points [or __%] above the [rates] [interest rate margins] provided for under the First Lien Credit Agreement as in effect on the date hereof)], plus

(m) all fees, expenses, premium (if any), reimbursement obligations and other amounts of a type not referred to in clause (a) or (b) above payable in respect of the amounts referred to in clauses (a) and (b) above, [plus

(n) Obligations under Hedge Agreements in respect of interest on First Lien Principal Obligations referred to in clause (a) above not to exceed $_____ in the aggregate] in each case payable pursuant to the First Lien Loan Documents *provided* that the First Lien Cap shall not apply to any First Lien Obligations other than Capped Obligations.

For purposes of this definition, all payments of First Lien Principal Obligations will be deemed to be applied first to reduce the First Lien Principal Obligations referred to in clause (a)(1) above and thereafter to reduce any Excess First Lien Principal Obligations.]

**[End of Alternative Definition]**

Any net increase in the aggregate principal amount of a loan or Letter of Credit (on a U.S. Dollar equivalent basis) after the loan is incurred or the Letter of Credit issued that is caused by a fluctuation in the exchange rate of the currency in which the loan or Letter of Credit is denominated will be ignored in determining whether the First Lien Cap has been exceeded, [except with respect to the principal amount of First Lien Obligations made, issued or advanced after the calculation of such fluctuation in exchange rate].[16]

## 1.5 First and Second Lien Collateral to be identical

(a) The Parties intend that the First Lien Collateral and the Second Lien Collateral be identical, except [specify any exceptions]. Accordingly, subject to the other provisions of this Agreement, the Parties will cooperate

---

[16] In asset-based transactions with foreign currencies, changes in exchange rates are taken into account in calculation of availability from time to time. The language above should not reverse that requirement to the detriment of the second lien lenders.

(1) to determine the specific items included in the First Lien Collateral and the Second Lien Collateral, the steps taken to perfect the Liens thereon, and the identity of the Persons having First Lien Obligations or Second Lien Obligations, and

(2) to make the forms, documents and agreements creating or evidencing the First Lien Collateral and Second Lien Collateral and the guaranties of the First Lien Obligations and the Second Lien Obligations materially the same, other than with respect to the first and second lien nature of the Liens.

(b) Until the Discharge of First Lien Obligations, and whether or not an Insolvency Proceeding has commenced, the Borrower and Holdings will not grant, and will use their best efforts to prevent any other Person from granting, a Lien on any property

(1) in favor of a First Lien Claimholder to secure the First Lien Obligations unless the Borrower, Holdings or such other Person grants (or offers to grant with a reasonable opportunity for the Lien to be accepted) the Second Lien Agent a junior Lien on such property to secure the Second Lien Obligations (however, the refusal of the Second Lien Agent to accept such Lien will not prevent the First Lien Claimholder from taking the Lien), and

(2) in favor of a Second Lien Claimholder to secure the Second Lien Obligations unless the Borrower, Holdings or such other Person grants (or offers to grant with a reasonable opportunity for the Lien to be accepted) the First Lien Agent a senior Lien on such property to secure the First Lien Obligations (however, the refusal of the First Lien Agent to accept such Lien will not prevent the Second Lien Claimholder from taking the Lien).

(c) Subject to Section 1.1, '*Seniority of Liens securing First Lien Obligations,*' if a Second Lien Claimholder hereafter acquires a Lien on property to secure a Second Lien Obligation where the property is not also subject to a Lien securing the First Lien Obligations, then such Second Lien Claimholder will give the First Lien Agent written notice of such Lien no later than five Business Days after acquiring such Lien. If the First Lien Agent also obtains a Lien on such property or if such Second Lien Claimholder fails to provide such timely notice to the First Lien Agent, then such property will be deemed to be Collateral for all purposes hereunder.

## 1.6  Pledged Collateral

(a) If the First Lien Agent has any Collateral in its possession or control (such Collateral being the *Pledged Collateral*), then, subject to Section 1.1, '*Seniority of Liens securing First Lien Obligations,*' and this Section 1.6, the First Lien Agent will possess or control the Pledged Collateral as gratuitous bailee and/or gratuitous agent for perfection for the benefit of the Second Lien Agent as secured party, so as to satisfy the requirements of Sections 8-106(d)(3), 8-301(a)(2) and 9-313(c) of the U.C.C. In this Section 1.6, 'control' has the meaning given that term in Sections 8-106 and 9-3 14 of the U.C.C.

(b) The First Lien Agent will have no obligation to any First Lien Claimholder or Second Lien Claimholder to ensure that any Pledged Collateral is genuine or owned by any of the Grantors or to preserve rights or benefits of any Person except as expressly set forth in this Section 1.6. The duties or responsibilities of the First Lien Agent under this Section 1.6 will be limited solely to possessing or controlling the Pledged Collateral as bailee and/or agent for perfection in accordance with this Section 1.6 and delivering the Pledged Collateral upon a Discharge of First Lien Obligations as provided in subsection (d) below.

(c) The Second Lien Agent hereby waives and releases the First Lien Agent from all claims and liabilities arising out of the First Lien Agent's role under this Section 1.6 as bailee and/or agent with respect to the Pledged Collateral [except for claims arising by reason of the First Lien Agent's gross negligence or willful misconduct].

(d) Upon the Discharge of First Lien Obligations, the First Lien Agent will deliver or transfer control of any Pledged Collateral in its possession or control, together with any necessary endorsements (which endorsements will be without recourse and without any representation or warranty),

(1) *first*, to the Second Lien Agent if any Second Lien Obligations remain outstanding, and

(2) *second*, to the Borrower,

and will take any other action reasonably requested by the Second Lien Agent (at the expense of the Borrower or, upon default by the Borrower in payment or reimbursement thereof, the Second Lien Agent) in connection with the Second Lien Agent obtaining a first-priority interest in the Pledged Collateral.

(e) If the Second Lien Agent has any Pledged Collateral in its possession or control, then, subject to Section 1.1, '*Seniority of Liens securing First Lien Obligations*,' and this Section 1.6, the Second Lien Agent will possess or control the Pledged Collateral as gratuitous bailee and/or gratuitous agent for perfection for the benefit of the First Lien Agent as secured party, so as to satisfy the requirements of Sections 8-106(d)(3), 8-301(a)(2) and 9-313(c) of the U.C.C.

(f) The Second Lien Agent will have no obligation to any First Lien Claimholder or Second Lien Claimholder to ensure that any Pledged Collateral is genuine or owned by any of the Grantors or to preserve rights or benefits of any Person except as expressly set forth in this Section 1.6. The duties or responsibilities of the Second Lien Agent under this Section 1.6 will be limited solely to possessing or controlling the Pledged Collateral as bailee and/or agent for perfection in accordance with this Section 1.6 and delivering the Pledged Collateral upon a Discharge of Second Lien Obligations [up to any Second Lien Cap] as provided in subsection (h) below.

(g) The First Lien Agent hereby waives and releases the Second Lien Agent from all claims and liabilities arising out of the Second Lien Agent's role under this Section 1.6 as bailee and/or agent for perfection with respect to the Pledged Collateral [except for claims arising by reason of the Second Lien Agent's gross negligence or willful misconduct].

(h) Upon the Discharge of Second Lien Obligations up to any Second Lien Cap, the Second Lien Agent will deliver or transfer control of any Pledged Collateral in its possession or control, together with any necessary endorsements (which endorsements will be without recourse and without any representation or warranty),

(1) *first*, to the First Lien Agent if any First Lien Obligations remain outstanding, and

(2) *second*, to the Borrower,

and will take any other action reasonably requested by the First Lien Agent (at the expense of the Borrower or, upon default by the Borrower in payment or reimbursement thereof, the First Lien Agent) in connection with the First Lien Agent obtaining a first-priority interest in the Pledged Collateral.

## 1.7 Limitations on duties and obligations

(a) (1) The First Lien Agent will be solely responsible for perfecting and maintaining the perfection of its Liens on the First Lien Collateral, and (2) except for the First Lien Agent's obligations under Section 1.6, '*Pledged Collateral*,' the Second Lien Agent will be solely responsible for perfecting and maintaining the perfection of its Liens on the Second Lien Collateral.

(b) This Agreement is intended solely to govern the respective Lien priorities as between First Lien Claimholders and Second Lien Claimholders and does not impose on the First Lien

Agent or the Second Lien Agent any obligations in respect of the disposition of Proceeds of foreclosure on any Collateral that would conflict with a prior perfected claim in favor of another Person, an order or decree of a court or other Governmental Authority, or applicable law.

(c) Notwithstanding any other provision of this Agreement, the First Lien Agent will only be required to verify the payment of, or other satisfactory arrangements with respect to, First Lien Obligations arising under Cash Management Agreements or Hedge Agreements if the First Lien Agent receives notice of such Obligations, together with any supporting documentation the First Lien Agent requests, from the applicable Person.

(d) Except for obligations expressly provided for herein, the Control Agent and First Lien Claimholders will have no liability to any Second Lien Claimholder for any action by a First Lien Claimholder with respect to any First Lien Obligations or Collateral, including

  (1) the maintenance, preservation or collection of First Lien Obligations or any Collateral, and

  (2) the foreclosure upon, or the sale, liquidation, maintenance, preservation or other disposition of, any Collateral.

(e) The First Lien Agent will not have by reason of this Agreement or any other document a fiduciary relationship with any First Lien Claimholder or Second Lien Claimholder. The parties recognize that the interests of the First Lien Agent and the Second Lien Agent may differ, and the First Lien Agent may act in its own interest without taking into account the interests of any Second Lien Claimholder.

## 1.8 Prohibition on contesting Liens; no marshaling

(a) The First Lien Agent will not contest in any proceeding (including an Insolvency Proceeding) the validity, enforceability, perfection or priority of any Lien securing a Second Lien Obligation, but nothing in this Section 1.8 will impair the rights of any First Lien Claimholder to enforce this Agreement, including the priority of the Liens securing the First Lien Obligations or the provisions for exercise of remedies.

(b) The Second Lien Agent will not contest in any proceeding (including an Insolvency Proceeding) the validity, enforceability, perfection or priority of any Lien securing a First Lien Obligation up to the First Lien Cap with respect to the Capped Obligations and in their entirety with respect to First Lien Obligations that are not Capped Obligations, but nothing in this Section 1.8 will impair the rights of any Second Lien Claimholder to enforce this Agreement, including the priority of the Liens securing the Second Lien Obligations or the provisions for exercise of remedies.[17]

---

[17] In light of the recent *ION Media* decision, if the second lien claimholders wish to preserve an express right to challenge priority on the grounds that certain property does not constitute 'first lien collateral,' they may wish to consider arguing for adding language to the effect that: 'Nothing in this Section 1.8(b) shall prevent the Second Lien Agent or any Second Lien Claimholder from asserting that any property does not constitute First Lien Collateral under the First Lien Collateral Documents.' In the memorandum decision by the Bankruptcy Court in *In re ION Media Networks, Inc.*, 419 B.R. 585 (Bankr. S.D.N.Y. 2009), the inter-creditor agreement included an express acknowledgment by the parties 'to the relative priorities as to the Collateral . . . as provided in the Security Agreement' and an agreement by the parties that such priority would not be affected or impaired by 'any nonperfection of any lien purportedly securing any of the Secured Obligations.' *Id.* at 594 (emphasis omitted). The purchaser of the second lien

(c) Until the Discharge of First Lien Obligations, the Second Lien Agent will not assert any marshaling, appraisal, valuation or other similar right that may otherwise be available to a junior secured creditor.[18]

**[Additional Sections More Favorable to Second Lien Lenders]**

[(d) The assertion in any proceeding (including an Insolvency Proceeding) or otherwise by one Party (Party A) of the invalidity or nonperfection of the other Party's (Party B's) security interest as a defense to a claim or assertion by Party B against Party A for or alleging breach of this Agreement arising out of Party A's exercise or assertion of claims or other rights or enforcement of remedies under this Agreement or any First Lien Loan Documents or Second Lien Loan Documents, as applicable, will not be a 'contest' for purposes of this Section 1.8.

(e) A Second Lien Claimholder who intends to assert a claim or exercise a right or remedy that would violate this Agreement but for the invalidity or nonperfection of the Lien purporting to secure First Lien Obligations will give the First Lien Agent at least five Business

---

footnote (*continued*)

obligations argued in a motion objecting to confirmation of the debtor's plan of reorganization that certain FCC licenses owned by a special purpose vehicle within the debtor's capital structure were immune from being encumbered due to their special character and that the licenses therefore did not constitute 'collateral' for purposes of the inter-creditor agreement. *Id.* at 589. While the first lien lender had a security interest in the proceeds of the FCC licenses, there were no proceeds to which the lien could attach. *Id.* The court found that the use of the term 'purportedly securing' in the inter-creditor agreement to describe the liens granted in the security agreement 'evidenced the intent of the secured parties to establish their relative legal rights [with respect to the FCC licenses themselves] *vis à vis* each other, 'regardless not only of the ultimate validity of any lien therein granted by the debtors, but also regardless of whether a lien was even intended to be granted in the FCC licenses.' *Id.* at 594. The court's attempt to determine and enforce the intent of the parties based on the negotiated terms of the agreement is a positive step for the enforcement of inter-creditor agreements based on the agreement of the parties rather than bankruptcy policy grounds. However, the court, in attempting to determine the parties' intent, arguably ignored the clear language of the security agreement, which expressly excluded the FCC licenses from the collateral, and the fact that a lien on the FCC licenses (as opposed to proceeds thereof) would be prohibited by law. Notwithstanding the foregoing, the court concluded that 'at bottom, the language of the Intercreditor Agreement demonstrates that the Second Lien Lenders agreed to be 'silent' as to any dispute regarding the validity of liens granted by the Debtors in favor of the First Lien Lenders and conclusively accepted their relative priorities regardless of whether a lien ever was properly granted, [or intended to be granted] in the FCC Licenses.' *Id.* First lien lenders can accomplish the result implicit in the court's decision in a manner that does not ignore the law and the express language of the security agreement by (i) contractually prohibiting the second lien lenders from asserting claims such as those asserted by the second lien lender in *ION Media*, (ii) ensuring that the language of the granting clause in the security agreement picks up all general intangibles relating to the FCC licenses, including all enterprise value relating to the ownership thereof, as well as all proceeds of the disposition thereof, (iii) insulating the FCC licenses in a bankruptcy remote license subsidiary, and prohibiting any debt (other than the debt of the second lien lenders) in that subsidiary, (iv) subordinating the guarantee or other claims of the second lien lenders against the FCC license subsidiary, and (v) taking a first priority lien on the equity in that subsidiary.

[18] Note that the marshaling waiver is not limited to collateral upon which both the first lien and second lien lenders have a lien. Many transactions may involve some collateral, such as foreign collateral, where there is no shared lien, and careful consideration should be given to the marshaling waiver in those circumstances.

Days' prior notice of the contemplated action, stating the basis for the claimant's belief that the invalidity or nonperfection exists.

(f) No First Lien Claimholder or Second Lien Claimholder will assert a claim that challenges the perfection or validity of a Lien or Indebtedness of another Claimholder that is based on allegations

   (1) of fraudulent conveyance, unlawful payment of distributions to equity holders or other like allegations, or

   (2) that could be asserted with comparable merit against Liens, interests or rights of the Person asserting the claim.]

**[End of Additional Sections]**

## 1.9 Confirmation of subordination in Second Lien Collateral Documents

The Borrower will cause each Second Lien Collateral Document to include the following language (or language to similar effect approved by the First Lien Agent) and any other language the First Lien Agent reasonably requests to reflect the subordination of the Lien:

> Notwithstanding anything herein to the contrary, the Lien and security interest granted to the Second Lien Agent pursuant to this Agreement and the exercise of any right or remedy by the Second Lien Agent hereunder are subject to the provisions of the Inter-creditor Agreement, dated _____ (as amended, restated, supplemented or otherwise modified from time to time, the 'Inter-creditor Agreement'), among _____, as First Lien Agent, _____, as Second Lien Agent, _____, as Control Agent, and the Grantors (as defined therein) from time to time party thereto and other persons party or that may become party thereto from time to time. If there is a conflict between the terms of the Inter-creditor Agreement and this Agreement, the terms of the Inter-creditor Agreement will control.

## 1.10 Release of Liens [or guaranties]

(a) If the First Lien Agent releases a Lien on Collateral, [or releases a Grantor from its Obligations under its guaranty of the First Lien Obligations which guaranty is secured by a Lien on Collateral,[19]] in connection with:

   (1) an Enforcement Action, or

   (2) a Disposition of any Collateral under the First Lien Loan Documents other than pursuant to an Enforcement Action (whether or not there is an event of default under the First Lien Loan Documents), then any Lien of the Second Lien Agent on such Collateral, [and the Obligations of the Grantor under such guaranty of the Second Lien Obligations] will be, except as otherwise provided below, automatically and simultaneously released to the same extent, and the Second Lien Agent will promptly execute and deliver to the First Lien Agent [or the Grantor] such termination statements, releases and other documents as the First Lien Agent [or the Grantor] requests to effectively confirm the release, *provided* that such release will not occur without the consent of the Second Lien Agent

---

[19] The bracketed language is an alternative favorable to first lien claimholders. Rights to release a grantor should be considered carefully and may be limited to subsidiaries, as this provision has the effect of subordinating the claims of second lien claimholders to unsecured creditors of the grantor.

(i)   for an Enforcement Action, as to any Collateral the net Proceeds of the disposition of which will not be applied to repay (and, to the extent applicable, to reduce permanently commitments with respect to) the First Lien Obligations, or

(ii)  for a Disposition, if the Disposition is prohibited by a provision of the Second Lien Credit Agreement [other than solely as the result of the existence of a default or event of default under the Second Lien Loan Documents].[20]

(b)  The Second Lien Agent hereby appoints the First Lien Agent and any officer or agent of the First Lien Agent, with full power of substitution, as its true and lawful attorney-in-fact with full power and authority in the place and stead of the Second Lien Agent or in the First Lien Agent's own name, in the First Lien Agent's discretion to take any action and to execute any and all documents and instruments that may be reasonable and appropriate for the limited purpose of carrying out the terms of this Section 1.10, including any endorsements or other instruments of transfer or release. This appointment is coupled with an interest and is irrevocable until the Discharge of First Lien Obligations or such time as this Agreement is terminated in accordance with its terms.

(c)  Until the Discharge of First Lien Obligations, to the extent that the First Lien Agent

(1)  releases a Lien on Collateral or a Grantor from its Obligations under its guaranty, which Lien or guaranty is reinstated, or

(2)  obtains a new Lien or additional guaranty from a Grantor, then the Second Lien Agent will be granted a Lien on such Collateral and an additional guaranty, as the case may be, subject to Section 1.1, *'Seniority of Liens securing First Lien Obligations.'*

## 1.11 Subordination of Liens securing Excess First Lien Obligations[21]

(a)  If this Agreement provides for a Second Lien Cap, then all Liens securing Second Lien Obligations up to but not exceeding the Second Lien Cap will be senior in all respects and prior to any Lien on the Collateral securing any Excess First Lien Obligations, as defined

---

[20] Bracketed language is a first lien favorable alternative.

[21] Many inter-creditor agreements simply state that amounts in excess of the first lien cap are not first lien obligations. These agreements do not address the matter further. This leaves a lot of room for speculation. What is the result of the first lien creditors exceeding the cap? The second lien lenders may argue that exceeding the cap is a breach of the inter-creditor agreement by the first lien creditors and should allow the second lien creditors to assume first lien priority. That would be a result outside of the intent of the parties to the inter-creditor agreement. Even though obligations in excess of the first lien cap are not intended by the parties to be treated as 'first lien obligations,' the liens securing the first lien obligations (including U.C.C. Financing Statements and mortgages or deeds of trust) are usually filed before the second lien U.C.C. Financing Statements and mortgages or deeds of trust and would therefore remain first priority liens under the 'first to file' rule. There is no guidance with respect to treatment of the excess in such a case. A common alternative in inter-creditor agreements in which the parties and their counsel have actually considered this issue is to assign third lien priority to all first lien obligations in excess of the first lien cap. This most closely aligns with the parties' expectations and assigns a specific 'waterfall' of priorities. Section 1.11 takes that approach and goes further to deal with other priority issues relating to any second lien cap included in the inter-creditor agreement. See also Section 4.1, which establishes a 'waterfall' for the application of proceeds received in connection with an enforcement action by either the first lien lenders or the second lien lenders. Although much less common than first lien caps, second lien caps do appear in some inter-creditor agreements, particularly more negotiated middle-market transactions.

below (but only with respect to such excess amounts), and all Liens securing any Excess First Lien Obligations will be junior and subordinate in all respects to any Lien securing a Second Lien Obligation up to but not exceeding the Second Lien Cap. All Liens securing Excess First Lien Obligations will be senior in all respects and prior to any Lien on the Collateral securing any Excess Second Lien Obligations and all Liens securing any Excess Second Lien Obligations will be junior and subordinate in all respects and prior to any Lien securing Excess First Lien Obligations.

*Example[22]: Suppose First Lien Obligations are $150 million, with a First Lien Cap of $100 million; Second Lien Obligations are $50 million, with a Second Lien Cap of $20 million; and the total Collateral has a fair market value of $175 million. Then First Lien Claimholders will have a first priority Lien on the first $100 million of Collateral (including Proceeds), Second Lien Claimholders will have a second priority Lien in the next $20 million of Collateral, First Lien Claimholders will have a third priority Lien in the remaining $55 million of Collateral up to the $50 million of Excess First Lien Obligations, and Second Lien Claimholders will have a fourth priority Lien in the remaining $5 million of Collateral. If all of the Collateral is sold at its fair market value, then the $175 million in sales proceeds will be sufficient to pay the First Lien Obligations of $150 million in full and $25 million of the Second Lien Obligations. See also Section 4.1, 'Application of proceeds.'*

(b) If this Agreement provides for a First Lien Cap but does not provide for a maximum limitation of the amount of the Second Lien Obligations (i.e., a Second Lien Cap), then all Liens securing Second Lien Obligations will be senior in all respects and prior to any Lien on the Collateral securing any Excess First Lien Obligations, as defined below (but only with respect to such excess amounts), and all Liens securing any Excess First Lien Obligations will be junior and subordinate in all respects to any Lien securing a Second Lien Obligation.

*Example: Suppose First Lien Obligations are $150 million, with a First Lien Cap of $100 million; Second Lien Obligations are $50 million with no Second Lien Cap; and the total Collateral has a fair market value of $175 million. Then First Lien Claimholders will have a first priority Lien on the first $100 million of Collateral (including Proceeds), Second Lien Claimholders will have a second priority Lien in the next $50 million of Collateral, and First Lien Claimholders will have a third priority Lien on the remaining $25 million in Collateral. If all of the Collateral is sold at its fair market value, then the $175 million in sales proceeds will be sufficient to pay $125 million of the First Lien Obligations of $150 million and the Second Lien Obligations totaling $50 million in full. See also Section 4.1, 'Application of proceeds.'*

(c) **Excess First Lien Obligations** means any First Lien Obligations that are included in the Capped Obligations and that are in excess of the First Lien Cap.

(d) With respect to the Excess First Lien Obligations and Collateral (including Proceeds),

(1) First Lien Claimholders will have rights and obligations (other than the obligations in respect to the Standstill Period) analogous to the rights and obligations Second Lien Claimholders have under this Agreement with respect to the Second Lien Obligations [not in excess of any Second Lien Cap] and the Collateral (including Proceeds), and

(2) Second Lien Claimholders will have rights and obligations analogous to the rights and obligations First Lien Claimholders have under this Agreement with respect to the First Lien Obligations that are included in the Capped Obligations and that are not in excess of the First Lien Cap, and the Collateral (including Proceeds).

---

[22] This and the following example are part of the agreement itself, rather than being comments to the agreement.

(e) Nothing in this Section 1.11 will waive any default or event of default under the Second Lien Loan Documents resulting from
  (1) the incurrence of Obligations under the First Lien Loan Documents in excess of the First Lien Cap with respect to the Capped Obligations, or
  (2) the grant of Liens under the First Lien Collateral Documents securing any such excess amounts, or the right of Second Lien Claimholders to exercise any rights and remedies under the Second Lien Loan Documents as a result thereof.

# 2 MODIFICATION OF OBLIGATIONS[23]

## 2.1 Permitted modifications[24]

Except as otherwise expressly provided in this Section 2,
(a) the First Lien Obligations may be modified in accordance with their terms, and their aggregate amount increased or Refinanced, without notice to or consent by any Second Lien

---

[23] The modification provisions are intended to balance the desire of each class of creditor to administer freely its loan documents and refinance the debt thereunder against the interest of the other class of creditor in protecting against any modification or refinancing that alters any fundamental assumption about the borrower's capital structure relied on in underwriting the transaction. Fundamental issues usually addressed in the modification provisions include prohibitions on:

  i) increasing the maximum permitted advances of first lien/second lien obligations above negotiated caps;
  ii) extension of the maturity of the first lien obligations beyond the maturity date of the second lien obligations;
  iii) accelerating the amortization/maturity of the second lien obligations or increasing any mandatory prepayment obligations; and
  iv) increasing interest rates above specified levels.

Additional restrictions may or may not appear in the inter-creditor agreement or in the first lien loan documents or second lien loan documents.

The scope of restrictions on amendments is highly negotiated and varies depending on the market in question. While first lien and second lien claimholders will usually object to the borrower or its counsel becoming deeply involved in negotiating the terms of the inter-creditor agreement, the borrower will be highly motivated to scrutinize the modification restrictions and the debt cap definitions. The borrower's interests will be aligned with those of the first lien claimholders, as these provisions greatly impact the future flexibility of the borrower to incur additional debt, refinance existing debt on market terms and obtain covenant relief.
[24] The Model Agreement starts with the baseline concept that the first lien claimholders and second lien claimholders are generally free to amend their respective loan documents and refinance the obligations thereunder subject to meeting a limited set of parameters. This concept respects the status of the second lien obligations as debt that is senior in priority of payment and may be contrasted with the approach generally taken with respect to mezzanine or other payment subordinated obligations. Payment subordinated obligations are most often subject to broad restrictions on amendments and other modifications and will almost always prohibit any prepayment or refinancing of the subordinated obligations until the senior obligations are paid in full. While the Model Agreement focuses primarily on the economic terms of the obligations and does not prohibit the first and second lien claimholders from tightening or adding covenants or events of default, such amendments are usually prohibited by covenants in the first lien credit agreement in order to preserve any negotiated covenant cushion existing at the outset of the transaction. Likewise, cross-default provisions in the second lien loan documents should be reviewed and qualified as necessary to preserve any such negotiated covenant cushion.

Claimholder, *provided* that the holders of any Refinancing Indebtedness (or their agent) bind themselves in writing addressed to Second Lien Claimholders to the terms of this Agreement, and

(b) the Second Lien Obligations may be modified in accordance with their terms, and their aggregate amount increased or Refinanced, without notice to or consent by any First Lien Claimholder, *provided* that the holders of any Refinancing Indebtedness (or their agent) bind themselves in writing addressed to First Lien Claimholders to the terms of this Agreement.

However, no such modification may alter or otherwise affect Sections 1.1, '*Seniority of Liens securing First Lien Obligations*,' or 1.8, '*Prohibition on contesting Liens; no marshaling*.'

## 2.2 Modifications requiring consent[25]

Notwithstanding the preceding Section 2.1, [and except as otherwise permitted as DIP Financing provided by the First Lien Lenders and deemed consented to by the Second Lien Lenders pursuant to Section 6.1, '*Use of cash collateral and DIP financing*'] the Second Lien Agent must consent to any modification to or Refinancing of the First Lien Obligations, and the First Lien Agent must consent to any modification to or Refinancing of the Second Lien Obligations, that:

(a) increases the aggregate principal amount of loans, letters of credit, bankers' acceptances, bonds, debentures, notes or similar instruments or other similar extensions of credit [(but excluding obligations under Hedge Agreements or Cash Management Agreements) [and, for Second Lien Obligations, any increase resulting from payment of interest in kind

---

[25] The 'laundry list' approach set forth in the Model Agreement is frequently encountered in middle-market transactions. Larger syndicated loan transactions and bond second lien deals often have fewer restrictions on the modification or refinancing of the first lien obligations. The restrictions in this section may also be largely addressed in the applicable loan documents rather than in the inter-creditor agreement. As discussed above, restrictions on any modification or refinancing must be carefully considered relative to the definitions used to formulate any debt caps. See also note 12 above concerning potential restrictions on amendments that reallocate portions of term facility exposure to revolving exposure in cases where the second lien claimholders are seeking to require a minimum amount of amortization. While it is a case involving payment subordinated obligations, a worst-case scenario for a second lien claimholder (or a best-case scenario for a first lien claimholder) concerning flexibility to modify a class of debt with senior lien priority is illustrated by *In Re Musicland Holding Corp.*, 374 B.R. 113 (Bankr. S.D.N.Y. 2007). In that case, a senior revolving credit facility was successfully modified pursuant to the terms of a broadly drafted inter-creditor agreement to incorporate an additional term loan facility that 'leapfrogged' the subordinated creditors in the priority of distribution of the debtor's Chapter 11 estate. *Id.* at 118–19.

The amount of any permitted percentage increase in the interest rate is among the items subject to negotiation between the parties. A maximum 2% per annum increase has been a common agreed upon amount; however, this negotiated amount is being revisited by many in the aftermath of the recent market disruption and widespread re-pricing of transaction exposure. The alternative text with respect to asset-based lending transactions is often strongly resisted. To the extent that such alternative text is included, the first lien claimholders should consider whether sufficient flexibility to make protective advances or over-advances generally is included in the first lien loan documents or needs to be expressly addressed in the inter-creditor agreement.

permitted under the Second Lien Credit Agreement as in effect on the date hereof]] or commitments therefor beyond

(1) for the First Lien Obligations, the amount permitted by the First Lien Cap, or[26]

(2) for the Second Lien Obligations, the [amount theretofore permitted under the First Lien Credit Agreement] [the amount permitted by the Second Lien Cap];

(b) increases

(1) the interest rate or yield, including by increasing the 'applicable margin' or similar component of the interest rate or by modifying the method of computing interest, or

(2) a letter of credit, commitment, facility, utilization, or similar fee so that the combined interest rate and fees are increased by more than [_____]% per annum[27] in the aggregate [at any level of pricing], but excluding increases resulting from

(A) increases in an underlying reference rate not caused by a modification or Refinancing of such Obligations,

(B) accrual of interest at the 'default rate' defined in the loan documents at the date hereof or, for a Refinancing, a rate that corresponds to the default rate, or

(C) application of a pricing grid set forth in the loan documents at the date hereof;

(c) for the First Lien Obligations, extends a scheduled amortization payment or the scheduled final maturity date of the First Lien Credit Agreement or a Refinancing beyond the scheduled final maturity date of the Second Lien Credit Agreement or Refinancing;

(d) for the First Lien Obligations, modifies a mandatory prepayment provision in a manner [prohibited by the Second Lien Credit Agreement] [that allows amounts that would otherwise be required to be used to prepay First Lien Obligations to be retained by the Grantors to an amount greater than permitted under the Second Lien Credit Agreement];

(e) for the First Lien Obligations, increases the amount of Proceeds of dispositions of Collateral that are not required to be used to prepay First Lien Obligations and that may be retained by the Grantors to an amount greater than permitted under the Second Lien Credit Agreement;

(f) for the First Lien Obligations, modifies a covenant or event of default that directly restricts one or more Grantors from making payments under the Second Lien Loan Documents that would otherwise be permitted under the First Lien Loan Documents as in effect on the date hereof;

(g) for the Second Lien Obligations, modifies covenants, defaults or events of default to make them materially more restrictive as to any Grantor, except for modifications to match changes made to the First Lien Obligations so as to preserve, on substantially similar economic terms, any differential that exists on the date hereof between the covenants, defaults or events of default in the First Lien Loan Documents and the covenants, defaults or events of default in the Second Lien Loan Documents;

(h) for the Second Lien Obligations, accelerates any date upon which a scheduled payment of principal or interest is due, or otherwise decreases the weighted average life to maturity;

(i) for the Second Lien Obligations, changes a prepayment, redemption or defeasance provision so as to require a new payment or accelerate an existing payment Obligation; or

---

[26] Consider whether subordination of excess first lien obligations is a sufficient remedy, or whether the agreement should also include an outright prohibition on extensions of credit in excess of the cap.

[27] The amount of any permitted percentage increase in the interest rate is subject to negotiation between the parties. A maximum 2% per annum increase is a typical agreed-upon amount.

(j)  for the Second Lien Obligations,
  (1)  changes a term that would result in a default under the First Lien Credit Agreement,
  (2)  increases the Obligations of a Grantor, or
  (3)  confers additional rights on a Second Lien Claimholder in a manner materially adverse to a First Lien Claimholder.

**[Additional Section for Asset-Based Lending Transaction]**

[(*) for the First Lien Obligations, increases the Advance Rate applicable to the Borrowing Base to a rate higher than the Advance Rate on the date hereof, or modifies the definitions of 'Borrowing Base,' 'Eligible Account,' 'Eligible Inventory' or 'Reserves' in the First Lien Credit Agreement on the date hereof so as to increase the amount of credit available to the Borrower, *provided* that the First Lien Agent's discretion to establish additional reserves, to release reserves and to determine eligibility will not be affected or limited in any manner.]

**[End of Additional Section]**

## 2.3  Parallel modifications to Second Lien Obligations[28]

Subject to Section 2.2, *'Modifications requiring consent,'* if a First Lien Claimholder and a Grantor modify a First Lien Collateral Document, the modification will apply automatically to any comparable provision of a Second Lien Collateral Document in which the Grantor grants a

---

[28] Consistent with the expectation of the first lien claimholders to control issues related to common collateral, the Model Agreement provides that when the first lien claimholders amend the provisions of the first lien collateral documents, such revisions will automatically apply with respect to corresponding provisions of the second lien collateral documents. This 'drag-along' concept is intended to cover only provisions that relate to the collateral and, accordingly, applies only to the collateral documents. It does not apply to covenants in the first lien credit agreement or second lien credit agreement that may relate directly or indirectly to the collateral, such as disposition or insurance covenants or tangible net worth requirements. To that end, the counsel to the first lien claimholders will closely review any such restrictions in the second lien credit agreement for appropriate cushion, where applicable, to allow some flexibility in dealing with the borrower on such issues without the need to obtain an amendment or waiver from the second lien claimholders. The drag-along provision obviates the need to negotiate cushion on potentially highly focused covenants and threshold amounts in the second lien collateral documents, which are generally duplicated from the corresponding first lien collateral documents. That said, the automatic amendment provisions will not apply to amendments that require the release of collateral, except to the extent that such releases are required by other sections of the Model Agreement. Releases of collateral in the context of an enforcement action or dispositions are addressed in Section 1.10, *'Release of Liens or guaranties,'* and releases in the context of an insolvency proceeding are addressed in Section 6.2, *'Sale of Collateral.'* The automatic amendment provisions are, likewise, qualified to protect the second lien agent from being required to assume additional responsibilities, to protect the second lien claimholders from amendments that permit additional liens that could undermine their collateral position, and, in the case of the optional language, to protect from an amendment that could prejudice a second lien claimholder to a larger degree than a first lien claimholder. Such optional language may be objectionable to first lien claimholders based on the language being somewhat vague in nature and open to interpretation. Second lien claimholders may object to this section – especially in financings where specialized covenants are essential to preserve the expected value of the collateral or the validity of the liens. One such area that comes to mind would be customary geographic restrictions, maintenance and insurance requirements applicable in vessel financings. Provisions pertaining to the application of casualty and condemnation proceeds also merit careful consideration.

Lien on the same Collateral, without the consent of any Second Lien Claimholder and without any action by the Second Lien Agent or any Grantor, *provided* that no such modification will

(a) remove or release Second Lien Collateral, except to the extent that (1) the release is permitted or required by Section 6.1, '*Use of cash collateral and DIP financing*,' and (2) there is a corresponding release of First Lien Collateral,

(b) impose duties on the Second Lien Agent without its consent, [or]

(c) permit other Liens on the Collateral not permitted under the terms of the Second Lien Loan Documents or Section 6, '*Insolvency Proceedings*,' of this Agreement, [or

(d) be prejudicial to the interest of Second Lien Claimholders to a greater extent than First Lien Claimholders (other than by virtue of their relative priorities and rights and obligations hereunder)].

## 2.4 Notice of modifications[29]

The First Lien Agent will notify the Second Lien Agent, and the Second Lien Agent will notify the First Lien Agent, of each modification to the First Lien Obligations or Second Lien Obligations, respectively, within ten Business Days after the modification's effective date and, if requested by the notified Agent, promptly provide copies of any documents executed and delivered in connection with the modification.

Notice and copies will not be required to the extent the Borrower or a Grantor has provided the same to the Agent to be notified.

## 3 ENFORCEMENT[30]

### 3.1 Who may exercise remedies

(a) Subject to subsections (b) and (c) below, until the Discharge of First Lien Obligations up to the First Lien Cap with respect to the Capped Obligations and in their entirety with

---

[29] In order to allow the first lien claimholders and second lien claimholders to track compliance of the other party with the provisions in Section 2 of the Model Agreement, we have provided a mutual notice provision. This notice requirement applies after the effectiveness of the modification in question and, while a claim for damages is theoretically possible, the failure to give such notice is not intended to impair the effectiveness of the agreement. Often, parties may prefer to put the burden of providing notices on the borrower; however, this provision is consistent with the general theme in the Model Agreement of attempting to foster reasonable cooperation between the creditors on administrative issues. As the notice provision is also acknowledged by the borrower, it also may provide a waiver by the borrower of confidentiality provisions that might otherwise restrict communication between the creditors on issues covered by the inter-creditor agreement.

[30] In addition to enjoying relative lien priority over second lien claimholders, first lien claimholders are afforded enforcement priority over the second lien claimholders with respect to the collateral. This lien enforcement priority is not unlimited, however. First lien claimholders are permitted a finite period in which to exercise their exclusive right to bring enforcement actions with respect to the collateral. This exclusive enforcement period afforded the first lien claimholders (which is referred to in the Model Agreement and in practice as a 'Standstill Period' – i.e., a period during which second lien claimholders agree to refrain from exercising their subordinate security interests) frequently is a matter of intense negotiation. The length of the standstill period typically ranges from 120 to 180 days, depending upon

respect to First Lien Obligations that are not Capped Obligations, First Lien Claimholders will have the exclusive right to

(1) commence and maintain an Enforcement Action (including the rights to set off or credit bid their debt),

(2) subject to Section 1.10, *'Release of Liens or guaranties,'* make determinations regarding the release or disposition of, or restrictions with respect to, the Collateral, and

(3) otherwise enforce the rights and remedies of a secured creditor under the U.C.C. and the Bankruptcy Laws of any applicable jurisdiction, so long as any Proceeds received by the First Lien Agent and other First Lien Claimholders in the aggregate in excess of those necessary to achieve Discharge of First Lien Obligations up to the First Lien Cap with respect to First Lien Obligations that are Capped Obligations and in their entirety with respect to First Lien Obligations that are not Capped Obligations are distributed in accordance with Section 4.1, *'Application of proceeds,'* except as otherwise required pursuant to the U.C.C. and applicable law,[31] subject to the relative priorities described in Section 1.1, *'Seniority of Liens securing First Lien Obligations.'*

---

footnote (*continued*)

factors such as the relative bargaining strength of the parties, the nature of the borrower's business and the collateral, and other factors that may reduce or lengthen the amount of time necessary for first lien claimholders to evaluate whether or not to commence an enforcement action. Accordingly, the Model Agreement provides a range of days for the standstill period, rather than suggesting a single, specific period. Along with their exclusive right during the standstill period to commence an enforcement action with respect to the collateral, first lien claimholders have the exclusive right during the standstill period to exercise certain other rights and remedies. First lien claimholders may exercise all the rights and remedies of a secured creditor under the Uniform Commercial Code. Additionally, first lien claimholders may agree to release or dispose of the collateral (or to place or eliminate restrictions with respect to the collateral), so long as the consent of second lien claimholders is obtained if the proceeds received by first lien claimholders in connection with any such events are not applied to reduce the first lien obligations or if any such action is prohibited under the second lien loan documents. Following the expiration of the standstill period, second lien claimholders may commence an enforcement action against the collateral under certain conditions. These conditions include the requirement that first lien claimholders have not commenced an enforcement action with respect to all or a material portion of the collateral prior to the end of the standstill period and are not then continuing the diligent pursuit of such enforcement action (or diligently attempting to vacate any stay or prohibition against such enforcement action) and the requirement that second lien claimholders have not rescinded any acceleration of the second lien obligations. Even during the standstill period, second lien claimholders may take certain actions to preserve their position as provided in the Model Agreement. For example, second lien claimholders are granted the rights to file a proof of claim, to vote on a plan of reorganization and to make other filings, arguments and motions with respect to the second lien obligations and the collateral in any insolvency proceeding involving the borrower. A question of much current interest is whether or not the second lien claimholders should be allowed to join in an involuntary bankruptcy petition against the borrower in the exercise of their reserved rights as unsecured creditors or whether any right to join in an involuntary petition should be expressly excluded on the grounds that it effectively undermines the rights of the first lien claimholders to bring an enforcement action under the standstill provisions. *See* Section 3.1(d) below, including optional language prohibiting the second lien claimholder from initiating or joining in an involuntary bankruptcy petition.

[31] Under Section 9-617(a) of the U.C.C., the lien securing the second lien obligations will not automatically attach to the proceeds of collateral received following a foreclosure of the first lien, as the second lien will be discharged. U.C.C. § 9-617(a) (2008).

(b) Notwithstanding the preceding Section 3.1(a), Second Lien Claimholders may commence an Enforcement Action or exercise rights with respect to a Lien securing a Second Lien Obligation if

   (1) [120–180] days have elapsed since the Second Lien Agent notified the First Lien Agent that the Second Lien Obligations were due in full as a result of acceleration or otherwise (the *Standstill Period*),[32]

   (2) First Lien Claimholders are not then diligently pursuing an Enforcement Action with respect to all or a material portion of the Collateral or diligently attempting to vacate any stay or prohibition against such exercise, [and]

   (3) any acceleration of the Second Lien Obligations has not been rescinded, [and

   (4) [no] [the applicable] Grantor is [not] then a debtor in an Insolvency Proceeding].[33]

(c) Notwithstanding Section 3.1(a), [but subject to Section 1.5, '*First and Second Lien Collateral to be identical*'] a Second Lien Claimholder may

   (1) file a proof of claim or statement of interest, vote on a plan of reorganization (including a vote to accept or reject a plan of partial or complete liquidation, reorganization, arrangement, composition or extension), and make other filings, arguments and motions, with respect to the Second Lien Obligations and the Collateral in any Insolvency Proceeding commenced by or against any Grantor, in each case in accordance with this Agreement,

   (2) take action to create, perfect, preserve or protect its Lien on the Collateral, so long as such actions are not adverse to the priority status in accordance with this Agreement of Liens on the Collateral securing the First Lien Obligations or First Lien Claimholders' rights to exercise remedies,

   (3) file necessary pleadings in opposition to a claim objecting to or otherwise seeking the disallowance of a Second Lien Obligation or a Lien securing the Second Lien Obligation,

   (4) join (but not exercise any control over) a judicial foreclosure or Lien enforcement proceeding with respect to the Collateral initiated by the First Lien Agent, to the extent that such action could not reasonably be expected to interfere materially with the Enforcement Action, but no Second Lien Claimholder may receive any Proceeds thereof unless expressly permitted herein, and

   (5) bid for or purchase Collateral at any public, private or judicial foreclosure upon such Collateral initiated by any First Lien Claimholder, or any sale of Collateral during an Insolvency Proceeding; *provided* that such bid may not include a 'credit bid' in respect of any Second Lien Obligations unless the proceeds of such bid are otherwise sufficient to cause the Discharge of First Lien Obligations up to the First Lien Cap with respect to the Capped Obligations and in their entirety with respect to First Lien Obligations that are not Capped Obligations.

---

[32] Second lien lenders may seek to have an earlier trigger for the commencement of a standstill such as certain actions by the first lien lenders, and they may also oppose acceleration as a requirement for the commencement of the standstill.

[33] Second lien claimants will likely take the position that the bankruptcy laws should dictate what rights the first and second lien claimholders have if an insolvency proceeding is commenced, and that a blanket prohibition on remedies is not appropriate. However, first lien claimants do not want the second lien claimants to exercise remedies against any loan parties or accompanying collateral that may not be subject to the protection of the bankruptcy court and may prefer to exercise remedies contemporaneously against all the loan parties.

**[Optional Provisions]**

[(6) take or fail to take any Lien securing First Lien Obligations or any other collateral security therefor, or take or fail to take any action necessary or appropriate to ensure that any Lien is enforceable, perfected or entitled to priority as against any other Lien or to ensure that any Proceeds of any property subject to a Lien are applied to the payment of any Obligation secured thereby, or

(7) otherwise release, discharge or permit the lapse of any Lien securing a First Lien Obligation.]

**[End of Optional Provisions]**

(d) [Notwithstanding any provision of this Agreement] [Except as otherwise expressly set forth in this Section 3.1 [and _____]],[34] Second Lien Claimholders may exercise any rights and remedies that could be exercised by an unsecured creditor [other than initiating or joining in an involuntary case or proceeding under the Bankruptcy Code with respect to a Grantor] [prior to the end of the Standstill Period] against a Grantor that has guaranteed or granted Liens to secure the Second Lien Obligations in accordance with the terms of the Second Lien Loan Documents and applicable law, *provided* that any judgment Lien obtained by a Second Lien Claimholder as a result of such exercise of rights will be included in the Second Lien Collateral and be subject to this Agreement for all purposes (including in relation to the First Lien Obligations).

**[Optional Provision]**

[(e) The First Lien Agent will promptly notify the Second Lien Agent of the Discharge of First Lien Obligations.]

**[End of Optional Provision]**

## 3.2  Manner of exercise[35]

(a) A First Lien Claimholder may take any Enforcement Action
   (1) in any manner in its sole discretion in compliance with applicable law,
   (2) without consultation with or the consent of any Second Lien Claimholder,
   (3) regardless of whether an Insolvency Proceeding has been commenced,

---

[34] Consider specifying provisions precluding objections to claims, liens and other agreed provisions that might be more favorable to second lien lenders.

[35] The right of first lien claimholders to take an enforcement action against the collateral is generally unfettered. The only real limitation on such right is that first lien claimholders must comply with applicable law. First lien claimholders otherwise are free to take an enforcement action without consultation with or the consent of second lien claimholders. This is so irrespective of whether an insolvency proceeding has been commenced, whether any second lien loan document provides to the contrary, or whether the enforcement action is adverse to the interest of second lien claimholders. Additionally, first lien claimholders are not impeded in bringing any enforcement action by any action or failure to act of the borrower, any guarantor, any other first lien claimholder or any other party. Nor are first lien claimholders impeded in bringing an enforcement action by the non-compliance by any person other than first lien claimholders with any provision of the inter-creditor agreement, the first lien loan documents or the second lien loan documents, even if the first lien claimholders are aware of such non-compliance. Second lien claimholders specifically agree not to contest, protest or otherwise take any action to interfere with any enforcement action properly conducted by first lien claimholders.

(4) regardless of any provision of any Second Lien Loan Document (other than this Agreement), and

(5) regardless of whether such exercise is adverse to the interest of any Second Lien Claimholder.

(b) The rights of a First Lien Claimholder or the Control Agent to enforce any provision of this Agreement or any First Lien Loan Document will not be prejudiced or impaired by

(1) any act or failure to act of any Grantor, any other First Lien Claimholder or the Control Agent, or

(2) non-compliance by any Person other than such First Lien Claimholder with any provision of this Agreement, any First Lien Loan Document or any Second Lien Loan Document, regardless of any knowledge thereof that any First Lien Claimholder or the Control Agent may have or otherwise be charged with.

(c) No Second Lien Claimholder will contest, protest, object to or take any action to hinder, and each waives any and all claims with respect to any Enforcement Action by a First Lien Claimholder in compliance with this Agreement and applicable law.

## 3.3 Specific performance[36]

The First Lien Agent and the Second Lien Agent may each demand specific performance of this Agreement, and each waives any defense based on the adequacy of a remedy at law and any other defense that might be asserted to bar the remedy of specific performance in any action brought by a Second Lien Claimholder or a First Lien Claimholder, respectively.

## 3.4 Notice of exercise[37]

The First and Second Lien Agents will each provide reasonable prior notice to the other of its initial material Enforcement Action.

# 4 PAYMENTS

## 4.1 Application of proceeds[38]

Until the Discharge of First Lien Obligations and the Discharge of Second Lien Obligations, and regardless of whether an Insolvency Proceeding has been commenced, Collateral or Proceeds received in connection with an Enforcement Action or subject to Section 6.7, '*Reorganization securities*,' received in connection with any Insolvency Proceeding involving a Grantor will be applied

---

[36] The Model Agreement recognizes that the right to bring an enforcement action or prevent an unauthorized enforcement action is an essential right for which the parties have specifically bargained under the Model Agreement. Accordingly, the Model Agreement grants each party the right to demand specific performance under the Agreement, and each party waives the right to assert the adequacy of a remedy at law or any other defense that might be asserted to bar the remedy of specific performance.

[37] First lien claimholders and second lien claimholders have a common interest in the collateral and a common desire to ensure that enforcement actions are conducted in a manner that will yield the maximum possible proceeds for application to the first lien obligations and the second lien obligations. Accordingly, both first lien claimholders and second lien claimholders agree to give each other notice of their commencement of an initial material enforcement action.

[38] As has been detailed earlier, among the primary benefits to the first lien claimholders of the Model Agreement are the priority of their liens over those of the second lien claimholders and the enforcement priority that they enjoy relative to their liens. *See* note 33 to Section 3. The enforcement priority is effectuated by

(a) ***first,*** to the payment in full or cash collateralization of all First Lien Obligations that are not Excess First Lien Obligations,

(b) ***second,*** to the payment in full of the Second Lien Obligations [that are not Excess Second Lien Obligations],

(c) ***third,*** to the payment in full of any Excess First Lien Obligations, [

(d) ***fourth,*** to the payment in full of any Excess Second Lien Obligations],[39] and

(e) ***fifth,*** to the applicable Grantor or as otherwise required by applicable law.

in each case as specified in the First Lien Documents or the Second Lien Documents, or as otherwise determined by the First Lien Claimholders or the Second Lien Claimholders, as applicable.

---

footnote (*continued*)

the standstill period, which provides the first lien claimholders a 'head start' relative to enforcement of their liens. The Model Agreement also continues the exclusivity relative to lien enforcement if, prior to the expiration of the standstill period or prior to the permitted commencement of lien enforcement by the second lien claimholders, as applicable, the first lien claimholders have commenced and thereafter are diligently pursuing the exercise of their rights or remedies with respect to all or any material portion of the collateral. As a corollary to the exclusive enforcement remedies, this section provides for the application of proceeds received in connection with an enforcement action. Commonly referred to as a 'waterfall' provision, the section expressly provides that it is applicable before or after the commencement of an insolvency proceeding. It should be noted, however, that this section does not apply to payments or other distributions made in an insolvency proceeding unless those payments or other distributions are received in connection with an enforcement action. It should also be noted that the section is applicable to collateral or proceeds received in connection with an enforcement action irrespective of whether the action was taken by the first lien claimholders or the second lien claimholders. In the unlikely event that the first lien claimholders have allowed the standstill period to expire and the second lien claimholders exercise their rights to take enforcement actions, this section still requires that the proceeds of such exercise be run through the waterfall. While, as to collateral that is subject to Article 9, this would appear to conflict with Section 9-615(a) of the U.C.C., Section 9-615(a) is not one of the sections of the U.C.C. that Section 9-602 expressly states cannot be waived or varied by the debtor. Presumably, the execution of the Model Agreement by the various grantors would be deemed to be a waiver of the provisions of Section 9-615(a) when the proceeds result from an enforcement action taken by the second lien claimholders. The waterfall provision establishes a priority of application of the proceeds of the collateral, first to the first lien obligations (up to the amount of the first lien cap), second to the second lien obligations (up to the amount of any second lien cap), third to the excess first lien obligations (i.e., the amount of the obligations owing under the first lien loan documents in excess of the first lien cap), and fourth to the excess second lien obligations (i.e., the amount of the obligations owing under the second lien loan documents in excess of a second lien cap). In each case, the application within a particular tier is as specified in the applicable loan documents. Presumably, the loan documents will contain their own order of application of payments, including applying collateral proceeds to the costs and expenses of enforcement, to accrued and unpaid interest, and to the outstanding principal balance of the loans. When combined with the other provisions of the Model Agreement, this section completes a trifecta, i.e., the liens of the first lien claimholders have priority, the enforcement rights of the first lien claimholders have priority, and the first lien claimholders have priority as to the application of the proceeds of any enforcement action. The section does not distinguish between cash proceeds and non-cash proceeds, but should be interpreted to require the application of cash proceeds to the applicable obligations as and when received and to defer the application of the non-cash proceeds to the applicable obligations until such non-cash proceeds have been monetized.

[39] Some inter-creditor agreements do not address the consequences of the first lien lender exceeding the first lien cap or the second lien lender exceeding a second lien cap. In the absence of an agreement between the parties as to the effect of the first lien lender exceeding the first lien cap, the second lien lender might argue

[Notwithstanding the foregoing, until the Discharge of First Lien Obligations up to the First Lien Cap with respect to First Lien Obligations that are capped Obligations and in their entirety with respect to First Lien Obligations that are not Capped Obligations, any non-cash Collateral or non-cash Proceeds will be held by the First Lien Agent as Collateral unless the failure to apply such amounts as set forth above would be commercially unreasonable.[40]]

## 4.2 Insurance[41]

The First Lien Agent and Second Lien Agent will be named as additional insureds and/or loss payees, as applicable, under any insurance policies maintained by any Grantor. Until the Discharge of First Lien Obligations up to the First Lien Cap with respect to the Capped Obligations and in their entirety with respect to First Lien Obligations that are not Capped Obligations, and subject to the rights of the Grantors under the First Lien Loan Documents,

(a) The First Lien Agent will have the exclusive right to adjust settlement for any losses covered by an insurance policy covering the Collateral, and to approve an award granted in a condemnation or similar proceeding (or a deed in lieu of condemnation) affecting the Collateral, and

(b) all Proceeds of such policy, award or deed will be applied in the order provided in Section 4.1, '*Application of proceeds*,' and thereafter, if no Second Lien Obligations are outstanding, to the payment to the owner of the subject property, such other Person as may be entitled thereto, or as a court of competent jurisdiction may otherwise direct.

## 4.3 Payment turnover[42]

Until the Discharge of First Lien Obligations up to the First Lien Cap with respect to the Capped Obligations and in their entirety with respect to First Lien Obligations that are not

---

footnote (*continued*)

that the breach by the first lien lender of the inter-creditor agreement should preclude it from enforcing the agreement. One alternative for addressing this issue is to provide in the inter-creditor agreement that excess first lien obligations (i.e., obligations in excess of the first lien cap) will be given a priority immediately after the second lien obligations. This 'waterfall' may be implemented without formally classifying the excess amount as 'subordinated debt,' as such classification of a portion of the first lien obligations as 'third lien' or 'subordinated' may run afoul of the terms of the first lien lender's credit approval. *See* Section 1.11.

[40] *See* U.C.C. § 9-615(c) (2008).

[41] This section is an ancillary set of provisions in aid of the other priorities set forth elsewhere in the Model Agreement. First, it provides that the first lien agent and the second lien agent are to be named as additional insureds and loss payees, as applicable, of insurance policies maintained by the grantors. Of course, this includes insurance policies beyond those that cover casualty losses to the collateral. Second, the section provides that the first lien agent will have the exclusive right to adjust settlement of any claims under an insurance policy covering the collateral as well as approve any award in a condemnation or similar proceeding affecting the collateral. Last, continuing the priority theme discussed above, the section provides that the proceeds of any policy covering the collateral or proceeds of any award will be applied in a manner consistent with the waterfall provision relative to proceeds received from enforcement actions.

[42] The requirement in this section that a second lien claimholder turn over any amounts it receives in connection with the exercise of enforcement actions (and certain other actions) is essential to the operation of the waterfall provisions of Section 4.1. The section requires that all such amounts be segregated and held in trust for the benefit of the first lien agent and promptly paid over to the first lien agent. Once the second lien claimholders have turned over the proceeds of their enforcement activities, the first lien agent should apply those proceeds in accordance with the waterfall.

Capped Obligations, whether or not an Insolvency Proceeding has commenced, Collateral or Proceeds (including insurance proceeds or property or Proceeds subject to Liens referred to in paragraph (d) of Section 1.5, '*First and Second Lien Collateral to be identical*') received by a Second Lien Claimholder in connection with an Enforcement Action or, subject to Section 6.7, '*Reorganization securities*,' received in connection with any Insolvency Proceeding, will be

(a) segregated and held in trust, and
(b) promptly paid over to the First Lien Agent in the form received, with any necessary endorsements or as a court of competent jurisdiction may otherwise direct. The First Lien Agent is authorized to make such endorsements as agent for the Second Lien Claimholder. This authorization is coupled with an interest and is irrevocable until the Discharge of First Lien Obligations.

## 4.4  Refinancing after discharge of First Lien Obligations[43]

If, after the Discharge of First Lien Obligations, the Borrower issues or incurs Refinancing[44] of the First Lien Obligations that is permitted to be incurred under the Second Lien Loan Documents, then the First Lien Obligations will automatically be deemed not to have been discharged for all purposes of this Agreement (except for actions taken as a result of the initial Discharge of First Lien Obligations). Upon the Second Lien Agent's receipt of a notice stating that the Borrower has entered into a new First Lien Loan Document and identifying the new First Lien Agent (the *New Agent*),

(a) the Obligations under such Refinancing indebtedness will automatically be treated as First Lien Obligations for all purposes of this Agreement, including for purposes of the Lien priorities and rights in respect of Collateral set forth herein,
(b) the New Agent under such new First Lien Loan Documents will be the First Lien Agent for all purposes of this Agreement,
(c) The Second Lien Agent will promptly
 (1) enter into such documents and agreements (including amendments or supplements to this Agreement) as the Borrower or the New Agent reasonably requests to provide to the New Agent the rights contemplated hereby, in each case consistent in all material respects with the terms of this Agreement, and
 (2) deliver to the New Agent any Pledged Collateral held by it together with any necessary endorsements (or otherwise allow the New Agent to obtain control of such Pledged Collateral), and

---

[43] The first lien obligations may be paid off and, subsequently, the borrower may seek to incur new indebtedness on a first lien basis. This section allows for that possibility and provides that the newly incurred indebtedness should be entitled to the benefits of the Model Agreement to the same extent as if the original first lien obligations were not retired. The provisions of the section should not be interpreted to permit the incurrence of indebtedness that is not permitted under the second lien loan documents or to permit indebtedness in excess of the amount of the first lien cap to enjoy a first priority with respect to the collateral. If such refinancing indebtedness is incurred, the second lien agent is required to enter into appropriate documents and agreements to give effect to the substitution, and the new agent is required to agree with the second lien agent that it is bound by the terms of the Model Agreement.

[44] Second lien claimholders may resist the application of this Section 4.4 to situations other than the incurrence of new first lien obligations that are used to refinance then-existing first lien obligations, as opposed to a permanent subordination of second lien obligations to future first lien obligations not to exceed the first lien cap.

(d)  the New Agent will promptly agree in writing addressed to the Second Lien Agent to be bound by the terms of this Agreement.

If any Obligations under the new First Lien Loan Documents are secured by Collateral that does not also secure the Second Lien Obligations, then the Grantors will cause the Second Lien Obligations to be secured at such time by a second priority Lien on such Collateral to the same extent provided in the First Lien Collateral Documents and this Agreement.

## 5  PURCHASE OF FIRST LIEN OBLIGATIONS BY SECOND LIEN CLAIMHOLDERS[45]

### 5.1  Purchase right

(a)  If there is
   (1)  an acceleration of the First Lien Obligations in accordance with the First Lien Credit Agreement,
   (2)  a payment default under the First Lien Credit Agreement that is not cured, or waived by First Lien Claimholders, within sixty days of its occurrence, or
   (3)  the commencement of an Insolvency Proceeding,[46] (each a *Purchase Event*), then Second Lien Claimholders may purchase all, but not less than all, of the First Lien Obligations that are included in the Capped Obligations up to but not in excess of the First Lien Cap plus all, but not less than all, of the First Lien Obligations that are not included in the Capped Obligations (the *Purchase Obligations*). Such purchase will

---

[45] If the collateral agent for the first lien lenders arranges a private sale of the collateral to a third party at a price sufficient to satisfy both the first lien obligations and the second lien obligations, then the second lien lenders will be protected as secured parties second only to the first lien lenders and with a claim superior to all unsecured creditors. However, if the first lien lenders pursue a public sale of the collateral under the U.C.C., the first lien lenders can credit bid and purchase the collateral at the sale. Since the first lien lenders will not bid more than the amount of the first lien debt, the second lien lenders' lien on the collateral will be extinguished unless the second lien lenders elect to outbid the first lien lenders at the public sale. A more orderly alternative to the uncertainties of a private or public sale of the collateral under the U.C.C. is for the second lien lenders to be granted a right in the inter-creditor agreement to purchase the first lien debt following an acceleration of the first lien debt, the filing of bankruptcy proceedings, or for a short period of time (e.g., sixty days) following an uncured payment default. The purchase price is at par. Because first lien credit facilities often include hedge arrangements provided by one of the first lien lenders (usually the agent) or an affiliate of one of the first lien lenders, the Model Agreement includes specific provisions for the unwinding of any hedging obligations. Similarly, provisions are included to deal with undrawn letters of credit and with prepayment premiums. During most of the years that first lien/second lien transactions were closed, first lien debt typically traded on the secondary market at par or close to par. The right of the second lien lenders to purchase all of the first lien position at par was therefore a valuable right. During the financial crisis, first lien debt positions have often traded considerably below par, making it impractical and financially unfeasible for second lien lenders to purchase first lien debt under the inter-creditor agreement at par. Still, even during distressed times, the option to purchase provisions provides a valuable starting point and framework for negotiations between first and second lien lenders for purchase of the first lien position by the second lien lenders following a default.

[46] Second lien claimholders may wish to include additional purchase events such as (i) notice of a disposition or enforcement action that would force a lien release, or (ii) a payment default under the first lien credit agreement not cured or waived by a specified time period.

(A) include all principal of, and all accrued and unpaid interest, fees and expenses in respect of all First Lien Obligations outstanding at the time of purchase that are included in the Capped Obligations up to but not in excess of the First Lien Cap plus all principal of, and all accrued and unpaid interest, fees and expenses in respect of all First Lien Obligations that are not included in the Capped Obligations,

(B) be made pursuant to an *Assignment Agreement* [(as such term is defined in the First Lien Credit Agreement)] [substantially in the form attached hereto as Exhibit A (the bracketed provisions therein to be appropriately modified to reflect the terms of the First Lien Documents and the outstanding First Lien Obligations)] [in form and substance reasonably satisfactory to, and prepared by counsel for, the First Lien Agent (with the cost of such counsel to be paid by the Purchasing Creditors)], whereby Second Lien Claimholders will assume all funding commitments and Obligations of First Lien Claimholders under the First Lien Loan Documents, and

(C) otherwise be subject to the terms and conditions of this Section 5. Each First Lien Claimholder will retain all rights to indemnification provided in the relevant First Lien Loan Documents for all claims and other amounts relating to periods prior to the purchase of the First Lien Obligations pursuant to this Section 5.

(b) First Lien Claimholders will not commence an Enforcement Action while Second Lien Claimholders have a right to purchase the First Lien Obligations under this Section 5.[47]

## 5.2 Purchase Notice

(a) Second Lien Claimholders desiring to purchase all of the Purchase Obligations (the *Purchasing Creditors*) will deliver a *Purchase Notice* to the First Lien Agent that

(1) is signed by the Purchasing Creditors,

(2) states that it is a Purchase Notice under this Section 5,

(3) states that each Purchasing Creditor is irrevocably electing to purchase, in accordance with this Section 5, the percentage of all of the Purchase Obligations[48] stated in the Purchase Notice for that Purchasing Creditor, which percentages must aggregate exactly 100% for all Purchasing Creditors,[49]

(4) represents and warrants that the Purchase Notice is in conformity with the Second Lien Loan Documents and any other binding agreement among Second Lien Claimholders, and

---

[47] This concept may work only for purchase options that have a limited exercise window. First lien claimholders should have an exception if exigent circumstances exist.

[48] First lien claimholders may wish to consider requiring that the purchase notice include all excess first lien obligations.

[49] Second lien claimholders may also negotiate the right to receive (or preferably to have the second lien agent receive on their behalf) notice ten to fifteen days in advance of any acceleration or commencement of an enforcement action, or the taking of any action by the first lien claimholders, and of an estimate of the amount of first lien obligations (not in excess of the first lien cap), within which time, pursuant to specified procedures set forth in the inter-creditor agreement or in the second lien credit agreement, (i) the second lien agent would notify the second lien claimholders of the event underlying the notice, (ii) each second lien claimholder would have a specified number of business days to notify the second lien agent as to whether it wishes to exercise its purchase right, and whether it is willing to purchase more (or less) than its pro rata share of the first lien obligations (and commitments) and irrevocably commit to purchasing its allocable portion of the first lien obligations not in excess of the first lien cap, (iii) non-committing second

(5) designates a ***Purchase Date*** on which the purchase will occur, that is (x) at least five but not more than [fifteen] Business Days after the First Lien Agent's receipt of the Purchase Notice, and (y) not more than sixty days after the Purchase Event.

A Purchase Notice will be ineffective if it is received by the First Lien Agent after the occurrence giving rise to the Purchase Event is waived, cured or otherwise ceases to exist.

**[Alternative Subsection Favorable to Second Lien Lenders]**

[(5) designates a Purchase Date on which the purchase will occur that is at least five but not more than [fifteen] Business Days after the First Lien Agent's receipt of the Purchase Notice.

The Purchase Notice must be received by the First Lien Agent during the period following the occurrence of, and during the continuance of, a Purchase Event.]

**[End Of Alternative Subsection]**

(b) Upon the First Lien Agent's receipt of an effective Purchase Notice conforming to this Section 5.2, the Purchasing Creditors will be irrevocably obligated to purchase, and the First Lien Creditors will be irrevocably obligated to sell, the First Lien Obligations in accordance with and subject to this Section 5.

## 5.3 Purchase Price

The ***Purchase Price*** for the Purchase Obligations will equal the sum of

(a) the principal amount of all loans, advances or similar extensions of credit included in the Purchase Obligations (including unreimbursed amounts drawn on Letters of Credit, but excluding the undrawn amount of outstanding Letters of Credit), and all accrued and unpaid interest thereon through the Purchase Date ([including] [excluding] any acceleration prepayment penalties or premiums[50]),

---

footnote (*continued*)

lien claimholders would lose their purchase right as to the event that is the subject of the notice, (iv) the second lien agent would allocate the total amount of first lien obligations not in excess of the first lien cap pro rata among the second lien claimholders wishing to exercise the purchase right (with any shortfall being allocated equitably to those willing to purchase more than their pro rata share), and (v) the second lien agent would send a binding notice to the first lien agent committing the purchasing second lien claimholders to consummate the purchase by a pre-negotiated deadline. A standstill would exist during the period specified prohibiting the first lien claimholders from taking any of the specified actions with an exception for exigent circumstances. This right allows the second lien claimholders to exercise their purchase right before significant damage (e.g., the loss of trade credit, the triggering of cross-acceleration clauses in other debt, etc.) is done to the enterprise value of the grantors that may result from an acceleration or the commencement of enforcement actions. The Model Agreement sets forth relatively basic purchase option mechanics. For syndicated transactions with a large number of lenders, consideration should be given to setting forth in detail procedures for the allocation and exercise of the purchase right.
[50] Another option for the parties to consider regarding prepayment premiums is to provide that the purchasing creditors will pay to the first lien agent as a deferred portion of the purchase price any prepayment premium that is actually paid to the purchasing creditors within a designated period of time but will not pay any prepayment premium at the closing of the purchase unless the premium was then due and payable.

(b) the net aggregate amount then owing to counterparties under Hedge Agreements that are First Lien Loan Documents, including all amounts owing to the counterparties as a result of the termination (or early termination) thereof to the extent not allocable to Excess First Lien Obligations,

(c) the net aggregate amount then owing to creditors under Cash Management Agreements that are First Lien Loan Documents, including all amounts owing to the creditors as a result of the termination (or early termination) thereof to the extent not allocable to Excess First Lien Obligations, and

(d) all accrued and unpaid fees, expenses, [indemnities] and other amounts owed to the First Lien Creditors under the First Lien Loan Documents on the Purchase Date to the extent not allocable to Excess First Lien Obligations.

## 5.4 Purchase closing

On the Purchase Date,

(a) the Purchasing Creditors and First Lien Agent will execute and deliver the Assignment Agreement,

(b) the Purchasing Creditors will pay the Purchase Price to the First Lien Agent by wire transfer of immediately available funds,

(c) the Purchasing Creditors will deposit with the First Lien Agent or its designee by wire transfer of immediately available funds, [105%] of the aggregate undrawn amount of all then outstanding Letters of Credit and the aggregate facing and similar fees that will accrue thereon through the stated maturity of the Letters of Credit (assuming no drawings thereon before stated maturity), and

(d) The Second Lien Agent will execute and deliver to the First Lien Agent a waiver of all claims arising out of this Agreement and the transactions contemplated hereby as a result of exercising the purchase option contemplated by this Section 5.

## 5.5 Excess First Lien Obligations not purchased

Any Excess First Lien Obligations will, after the closing of the purchase of the First Lien Obligations in accordance with this Section 5, remain Excess First Lien Obligations for all purposes of this Agreement.[51]

## 5.6 Actions after purchase closing

(a) Promptly after the closing of the purchase of all Purchase Obligations, the First Lien Agent will distribute the Purchase Price to First Lien Claimholders in accordance with the terms of the First Lien Loan Documents.

---

[51] Please note Section 1.11(e), which provides in part that, with respect to the excess first lien obligations, first lien claimholders will have rights and obligations (other than the obligations in respect to the standstill period) analogous to the rights and obligations that second lien claimholders have under the Agreement with respect of the second lien obligations. With respect to any excess first lien obligations remaining after the exercise of the purchase option by the second lien lenders, Section 5.5 and Section 1.11(e) would result, for example, in the first lien lenders having the same rights and obligations with respect to the excess first lien obligations that the second lien lenders have under the insolvency provisions in Section 6.

(b) After the closing of the purchase of all Purchase Obligations, the Purchasing Creditors may request that the First Lien Agent immediately resign as administrative agent and, if applicable, collateral agent under the First Lien Loan Documents, and the First Lien Agent will immediately resign if so requested. Upon such resignation, a new administrative agent and, if applicable, a new collateral agent will be elected or appointed in accordance with the First Lien Loan Documents.

(c) The First Lien Agent will apply cash collateral to reimburse Letter of Credit issuers for drawings under Letters of Credit, any customary fees charged by the issuer in connection with such draws, and facing or similar fees. After giving effect to each such payment, any remaining cash collateral that exceeds [105%] of the sum of the aggregate undrawn amount of all then outstanding Letters of Credit and the aggregate facing and similar fees that will accrue thereon through the stated maturity of such Letters of Credit (assuming no drawings thereon before stated maturity) will be returned to the Purchasing Creditors (as their interests appear). When all Letters of Credit have been canceled with the consent of the beneficiary thereof, expired, or been fully drawn, and after all payments from the account described above have been made, any remaining cash collateral will be returned to the Purchasing Creditors, as their interests appear.

(d) If for any reason other than the gross negligence or willful misconduct of the First Lien Agent, the cash collateral is less than the amount owing with respect to a Letter of Credit described in the preceding subsection (c), then the Purchasing Creditors will, in proportion to their interests, promptly reimburse the First Lien Agent (who will then pay the issuing bank) the amount of the deficiency.

## 5.7  No recourse or warranties; defaulting creditors

(a) First Lien Claimholders will be entitled to rely on the statements, representations and warranties in the Purchase Notice without investigation, even if First Lien Claimholders are notified that any such statement, representation or warranty is not or may not be true.

(b) The purchase and sale of the First Lien Obligations under this Section 5 will be without recourse and without representation or warranty of any kind by First Lien Claimholders, except that First Lien Claimholders represent and warrant that on the Purchase Date, immediately before giving effect to the purchase,

  (1) the principal of and accrued and unpaid interest on the First Lien Obligations, and the fees and expenses thereof, are as stated in the Assignment Agreement,

  (2) First Lien Claimholders own the First Lien Obligations free and clear of any Liens (other than participation interests not prohibited by the First Lien Credit Agreement, in which case the Purchase Price will be appropriately adjusted so that the Purchasing Creditors do not pay amounts represented by participation interests), and

  (3) each First Lien Claimholder has the full right and power to assign its First Lien Obligations and such assignment has been duly authorized by all necessary corporate action by such First Lien Claimholder.

**[Alternative Section Favorable to First Lien Lenders]**

[(b) The purchase and sale of the Purchase Obligations under this Section 5 will be without recourse and without any representation or warranty whatsoever by First Lien Claimholders, except that First Lien Claimholders represent and warrant that on the Purchase Date, immediately before giving effect to the purchase, First Lien Claimholders

(4) own the Purchase Obligations free and clear of all Liens (other than participation interests not prohibited by the First Lien Credit Agreement, in which case the Purchase Price will be appropriately adjusted so that the Purchasing Creditors do not pay amounts represented by participation interest), and

(5) have the right to convey whatever claims and interests they may have in respect of the Purchase Obligations.]

**[End of Alternative Section]**

(c) The obligations of First Lien Claimholders to sell their respective Purchase Obligations under this Section 5 are several and not joint and several. If a First Lien Claimholder (a *Defaulting Creditor*) breaches its obligation to sell its Purchase Obligations under this Section 5, no other First Lien Claimholder will be obligated to purchase the Defaulting Creditor's Purchase Obligations for resale to the holders of Second Lien Obligations. A First Lien Claimholder that complies with this Section 5 will not be in default of this Agreement or otherwise be deemed liable for any action or inaction of any Defaulting Creditor, *provided* that nothing in this subsection (c) will require the Purchasing Creditors to purchase less than all of the Purchase Obligations.

(d) The Borrower and Holdings irrevocably consent, and will use their best efforts to obtain any necessary consent of each other Grantor, to any assignment effected to one or more Purchasing Creditors pursuant to this Section 5.

# 6 INSOLVENCY PROCEEDINGS[52]

## 6.1 Use of cash collateral and DIP financing[53]

(a) Until the Discharge of First Lien Obligations up to the First Lien Cap with respect to the Capped Obligations and in their entirety with respect to First Lien Obligations that are not Capped Obligations, if an Insolvency Proceeding has commenced, the Second Lien Agent,

---

[52] Holders of a secured claim in bankruptcy have a variety of statutory rights to protect the creditor's interest in the grantor's property. When lenders hold a collective security interest under one granting clause, they act by majority instruction to the agent or at times by unanimous instruction. When the secured claims are divided into separate granting clauses, two groups (the first lien claimholders and the second lien claimholders) may assert the rights of secured creditors. Absent agreement to the contrary, the second lien claimholders' assertion of these rights may be made in a manner that is in conflict with the interests of the first lien claimholders. Such actions may include consenting or objecting to financing secured by priming liens on the collateral, consenting or objecting to the use of cash collateral to operate during the bankruptcy, or consenting or objecting to sale of collateral free and clear of liens. On the other hand, if the second lien claimholders waive these rights as secured creditors, the grantors and first lien claimholders could agree to the use and disposition of collateral in a manner that could cause the diminution of the value of the interest of the second lien claimholders in the collateral. As such, one of the key functions of an inter-creditor agreement is to set forth the extent to which the rights of second lien claimholders in collateral may be asserted in a manner that does not conflict with the interests of the first lien claimholders during the bankruptcy.

[53] In a Chapter 11 bankruptcy where substantially all of the debtors' assets have been pledged to secure the first and second lien debt, the debtors will have an urgent need to use cash collateral starting with the first days of the case. In addition, in most situations, the debtors will also want to incur DIP financing

as holder of a Lien on the Collateral, will not contest, protest or object to, and each Second Lien Claimholder will be deemed to have consented to,

(1) any use, sale or lease of 'cash collateral' (as defined in Section 363(a) of the Bankruptcy Code), and

(2) The Borrower or any other Grantor obtaining DIP Financing if the First Lien Agent consents[54] in writing to such use, sale or lease, or DIP Financing, *provided* that

    (A) The Second Lien Agent otherwise retains[55] its Lien on the Collateral, [and]

    (B) any Second Lien Claimholder may seek adequate protection as permitted by Section 6.4, '*Adequate protection*,' and, if such adequate protection is not granted, the Second Lien Agent may object under this Section 6.1 solely on such basis[.][,]

    [(C) after taking into account the use of cash collateral and the principal amount of any DIP Financing (after giving effect to any Refinancing of First Lien Obligations) on any date, the sum of the then outstanding principal amount of any First Lien Obligations and any DIP Financing does not exceed the First Lien Cap[56] on such date,[57]

---

footnote (*continued*)

both to provide the debtors with liquidity and also to inspire confidence in customers, vendors and employees. DIP lenders generally insist on super priority claims and priming liens that are senior to both the existing first and second liens. The first lien claimholders generally want to facilitate the debtors' use of cash collateral under a budget that they approve, so as to preserve the value of the first lien claimholders' collateral. They are also the most frequent source for DIP financing, given the reluctance of secured lenders to permit other lenders to prime their liens. In order for the debtors to have the right to use cash collateral of the first and second lien claimholders, or to have priming liens on collateral pledged to secure the first and second lien loans approved, they must either obtain the consent of both first and second lien claimholders, or secure an order of the bankruptcy court finding that adequate protection has been given to such claimholders to protect them from any loss of value from the use or priming. A finding of adequate protection can be difficult or impossible to obtain, and is not a requirement that debtors or first lien claimholders want to have imposed at the outset of the bankruptcy. As such, most inter-creditor agreements include a deemed consent to the use of cash collateral by the second lien claimholders if supported by the first lien claimholders, as well as a deemed consent to permit a priming DIP financing if consented to by the first lien claimholders. The deemed consent typically has certain limitations and conditions. For example, a pre-consent to a DIP financing is typically conditioned on the amount of the DIP financing not exceeding a specified amount. The second lien claimholders will often reserve the right to object to provisions of a proposed DIP financing that would have the effect of dictating the terms of a restructuring, or that would require the company to liquidate its assets on a rapid schedule. While the second lien claimholders' right to object to use of cash collateral or a priming DIP is limited, second lien claimholders typically do have the right to insist on replacement liens in the debtors' post-bankruptcy assets to the extent of any loss of value in the collateral so long as any such replacement liens are junior to the approved DIP financing and any replacement liens granted to first lien claimholders.

[54] *See* note to Section 6.2 below.

[55] First lien claimholders will want no interference with the use of cash collateral, but second lien claimholders will not want to have their other interests 'primed' or have their liens stripped, by reason of the broad concept of 'use' of collateral.

[56] As noted above in connection with the definition of 'First Lien Cap,' it may be desirable to formulate the cap differently in the context of a DIP financing. Common approaches include (i) an incremental cushion for a DIP financing, or (ii) a cap that is the lesser of the first lien cap and some cushion over outstanding first lien obligations at the commencement of the case.

[57] This clause is applicable when the first lien cap is tied to a borrowing base. With respect to principal amounts of new loans that increase the first lien obligations and reduce the amount of collateral available

(D) such DIP Financing and the Liens securing such DIP Financing are *pari passu* with or superior in priority to the then outstanding First Lien Obligations and the Liens securing such First Lien Obligations,[58] and

(E) the interest rate, fees, advance rates, lending limits and sublimits are commercially reasonable under the circumstances.[59]] [Upon written request from the First Lien Agent, the Second Lien Agent, as holder of a Lien on the Collateral, will join any objection by the First Lien Agent to the use, sale or lease of cash collateral for any purpose other than adequate protection payments to Second Lien Claimholders.][60]

[(b) Any customary 'carve-out' or other similar administrative priority expense or claim consented to in writing by the First Lien Agent to be paid prior to the Discharge of First Lien Obligations up to the First Lien Cap with respect to the Capped Obligations and in their entirety with respect to First Lien Obligations that are not Capped Obligations will be deemed for purposes of Section 6.1(a)

(3) to be a use of cash collateral, and

(4) [not to be] a principal amount of DIP Financing at the time of such consent.][61]

[No Second Lien Claimholder may provide DIP Financing to a Borrower or other Grantor secured by Liens equal or senior in priority to the Liens securing any First

---

footnote (*continued*)

for second lien obligations, most agreements limit the amount of diminution that would be suffered. However, most agreements do not limit the amount of diminution that may result from the use of cash collateral or other diminution of the borrowing base. Consideration should be given as to whether cash collateral objections could be asserted by the second lien agent if the amount of collateral diminution, when added to the first lien obligations, would exceed the first lien cap by reason of the erosion of the borrowing base.

[58] First lien claimholders should consider deleting this requirement based upon the protection provided to second lien claimholders from the first lien cap and the fact that the first lien claimholders can condition consent to the DIP financing upon an inter-creditor agreement with the DIP lender that subordinates the lien securing the DIP financing to the lien securing the first lien obligations. In addition, it may be beneficial to the first lien claimholders to have a DIP financing that is 'junior' to the first lien obligations in connection with plan confirmation requirements for the payment in full of all DIP obligations.

[59] First lien claimholders may regard this proviso as creating the potential for delay and uncertainty. The second lien claimholders have the right to assert objections that may be asserted by unsecured creditors that the terms of the DIP financing are not appropriate.

[60] The market has developed to generally give first lien claimholders the power to compel second lien claimholders to consent to the diminution of collateral, in the form of use of cash collateral or permitting additional secured financing even if the first lien obligations are sufficiently oversecured that first lien claimholders are otherwise not motivated to police the excess use of cash collateral or DIP financing. On the other hand, the market has not similarly developed to give first lien claimholders the ability to use second lien claimholders' rights of adequate protection in order to more effectively prevent the diminution of collateral. This draft proposes the first set of rights in favor of first lien claimholders and references the second as an alternative favorable to the first lien claimholders. To the extent that the second lien claimholders are required to join in, or prosecute, such an objection, they should consider requiring that their expenses be paid by the first lien claimholders, which could increase the size of the first lien claim, but will assure that the second lien claimholders will not go out of pocket.

[61] Some inter-creditor agreements attempt to restrict first lien claimholders from consenting to the subordination of the lien securing first lien obligations and, in turn, such agreements often exclude DIP financing from the scope of such restriction. However, the treatment of 'carve-outs' is often omitted or not considered the same as if the first lien agent made advances to fund retainers for professionals. This form treats carve-outs as a use of collateral, but not as though they are the same as if being incurred or used as of the date such 'carve-out' obligations are incurred. An alternative approach would be to treat

Lien Obligations, [*provided* that if no First Lien Claimholder offers to provide DIP Financing to the extent permitted under Section 6.1(a) on or before the date of the hearing to approve DIP Financing, then a Second Lien Claimholder may seek to provide such DIP Financing secured by Liens equal or senior in priority to the Liens securing any First Lien Obligations, and First Lien Claimholders may object thereto].][62]

[(c) nothing in this Section 6.1 limits or impairs the right of the Second Lien Agent to object to any motion regarding DIP Financing (including a DIP Financing proposed by one or more First Lien Claimholders) or cash collateral to the extent that

(5) the objection could be asserted in an Insolvency Proceeding by unsecured creditors generally, [is consistent with the other terms of this Section 6.1, and is not based on the status of any Second Lien Claimholder as holder of a Lien], or

(6) the DIP Financing does not meet the requirements of Section 6.1(a).][63]

## 6.2 Sale of Collateral[64]

The Second Lien Agent, as holder of a Lien on the Collateral and on behalf of the Second Lien Claimholders, will not contest, protest or object, and will be deemed to have consented pursuant to Section 363(f) of the Bankruptcy Code, to a Disposition of Collateral free and clear of its

---

footnote (*continued*)

administrative carve-outs as extensions of credit that need to be capped. If this approach is taken, additional consideration should be given to the first lien cap and the inclusion of additional, incremental amounts in the event of an insolvency proceeding, and to the need to reflect clear dollar limits on administrative carve-outs in the DIP orders. For a discussion of 'carve-outs' generally, see Richard Levin (2002) Almost All You Ever Wanted to Know About Carve Out, *American Bankruptcy Law Journal* 76: 445.

[62] First lien claimholders may want an absolute bar on second lien claimholders attempting to provide 'priming' DIP financing, while second lien claimholders will generally resist any limitation against DIP financing due to the ability of third parties to propose the same. A compromise position is bracketed.

[63] Second lien claimholders may seek to preserve unsecured creditor objections to a DIP financing, while first lien claimholders may expect second lien claimholders not to object in any capacity so long as a DIP financing satisfies the parameters specified in the inter-creditor agreement. The parties may want to consider alternative permitted objections to DIP financing or cash collateral orders such as: (a) provisions that purport to bind parties to a plan, (b) provisions that compel the sale of collateral, and (c) provisions that are otherwise inconsistent with the inter-creditor agreement and priorities of the liens.

[64] Second lien creditors typically agree not to contest or object to a sale, lease, exchange or transfer of collateral under Section 363 of the Bankruptcy Code if the first lien creditors have consented in writing to such disposition, provided that (i) the liens of the second lien creditors attach to the proceeds of such disposition to the extent so ordered by the court, (ii) the net cash proceeds are applied to reduce the first lien obligations permanently, and (iii) the second lien creditors will not be deemed to have waived any right to bid in connection with such disposition (subject to the lien priorities set forth in the inter-creditor agreement). Once again, second lien creditors may attempt to retain the right to assert any objection that may be available to unsecured creditors generally. First lien creditors will most likely object to this inclusion, as it provides the second lien creditors an opportunity to interfere with the first lien creditors' exercise of remedies. Alternatively, the first lien creditors may require that such second lien objections be otherwise consistent with the other terms of the inter-creditor agreement. The first lien creditors may also argue that the second lien creditors have the ability to protect themselves by the exercise of their buy-out right. Some inter-creditor agreements also require that the second lien creditors, solely in their capacity as holders of a lien on the collateral, join the first lien creditors in any objection to a sale of collateral to the extent asserted by the first lien creditors. The second lien creditors would typically resist this. In transactions where each party has priority in certain types of collateral, the parties should consider agreeing on a methodology to allocate value received in a disposition among the various categories of assets.

Liens or other interests under Section 363 of the Bankruptcy Code if the First Lien Agent consents in writing to the Disposition, *provided* that

(a) either (i) pursuant to court order, the Liens of Second Lien Claimholders attach to the net Proceeds of the Disposition with the same priority and validity as the Liens held by Second Lien Claimholders on such Collateral, and the Liens remain subject to the terms of this Agreement, or (ii) the Proceeds of a Disposition of Collateral received by the First Lien Agent in excess of those necessary to achieve the Discharge of First Lien Obligations, up to the First Lien Cap with respect to the Capped Obligations and in their entirety with respect to First Lien Obligations that are not Capped Obligations, are distributed in accordance with the U.C.C. and applicable law[,] [.]

[(b) the net cash Proceeds of the Disposition that are applied to First Lien Obligations permanently reduce the First Lien Obligations pursuant to Section 4.1, '*Application of proceeds*,' or if not so applied, are subject to the rights of the Second Lien Agent to object to any further use notwithstanding Section 6.1(a),[65] and

(c) Second Lien Claimholders [may] [are not deemed to have waived any rights to][66] credit bid on the Collateral in any such Disposition in accordance with Section 363(k) of the Bankruptcy Code.[67]]

Notwithstanding the preceding sentence, Second Lien Claimholders may object to any Disposition of Collateral that could be raised in an Insolvency Proceeding by unsecured creditors generally [so long as not otherwise inconsistent with the terms of this Agreement].[68]

---

[65] Second lien claimholders may seek to preserve rights to object to any proposed sale where liabilities of grantors are assumed (given that this permits trade debt to leapfrog the second lien in terms of priority) or where proceeds are not solely applied to repay first lien obligations or second lien obligations. Provisions of this kind may present impediments to sales, present complexities and require careful negotiation and drafting. For example, cure payments in connection with the assumption and assignment of contracts would need to be carved out, as would payments of DIP financings (if not included in 'First Lien Obligations') and administrative claims entitled to a 'carve-out' under any adequate protection arrangements.
[66] Second lien claimholders may want assurances that they will be permitted to credit bid their claims in any bankruptcy sale. First lien claimholders will want merely to preserve any rights that second lien claimholders may have, not assure that they have such rights.
[67] It may be desirable to include a provision that any credit bid must respect the priorities set forth in the intercreditor agreement, i.e., any credit bid of second lien obligations must contemplate the payment in full in cash of first lien obligations (other than excess first lien obligations) on closing of any resulting disposition.
[68] Second lien lenders will generally expect to be permitted to assert any rights they may have to object to dispositions of collateral that would be available to unsecured creditors in a bankruptcy proceeding. First lien lenders may seek to restrict such rights, or to condition the exercise of such rights on there having been a concession or determination that all or a portion of the second lien obligations are unsecured, arguing that second lien claimholders have the ability to protect themselves through exercise of their buyout rights and that a price for the priority that second lien claimholders enjoy over other creditors is that they must give up any rights to interfere with collateral dispositions that first lien claimholders support. An alternative approach is to rely solely on a provision like Section 3.1(d), which generally preserves unsecured creditor rights. This approach can be favorable to the second lien, depending on how drafted, since it then applies to all aspects of the agreement that are not expressly carved out. The first lien may expect that certain waivers by second lien claimholders will be unqualified, such as waivers of objections to DIP financings supported or provided by the first lien, objections to liens or claims of first lien claimholders, and where commencement of an involuntary bankruptcy is included in the term 'Enforcement Action,' the right to initiate or join in an involuntary bankruptcy.

[Upon the First Lien Agent's request, the Second Lien Agent, solely in its capacity as holder of a Lien on Collateral, will join any objection asserted by the First Lien Agent to any Disposition of Collateral during an Insolvency Proceeding.][69]

## 6.3 Relief from the automatic stay[70]

Until the Discharge of First Lien Obligations up to the First Lien Cap with respect to the Capped Obligations and in their entirety with respect to First Lien Obligations that are not Capped Obligations, no Second Lien Claimholder may, [during any Standstill Period,][71] seek relief from the automatic stay or any other stay in an Insolvency Proceeding in respect of the Collateral without the First Lien Agent's prior written consent [or oppose any request by the First Lien Agent for relief from such stay][72] [, except to the extent that

[a First Lien Claimholder (in such capacity)] [the First Lien Agent] seeks or obtains relief from or modification of such stay[, or a motion for adequate protection permitted under Section 6.4, 'Adequate Protection,' is denied by the Bankruptcy Court]].[73]

## 6.4 Adequate protection[74]

(a) No Second Lien Claimholder will contest, protest or object to
    (1) a request by a First Lien Claimholder for 'adequate protection' under any Bankruptcy Law, or

---

[69] First lien lenders may seek to require the second lien agent to actually support objections that the first lien may have to sales of collateral and other matters in an insolvency proceeding. This is not a usual provision, and many second lien lenders would resist it. To the extent that it is insisted upon, second lien claimholders should consider limiting this undertaking to withholding consent to the applicable disposition of collateral or filing a pleading indicating support for the first lien agent's objections, and also including a requirement that the second lien claimholders be indemnified for any expenses or other losses incurred in complying with this requirement (that any reimbursement by first lien claimholders not add to the amount of priority first lien obligations).

[70] The commencement of a bankruptcy case imposes an automatic stay on actions to foreclose on collateral or otherwise to seek collection of pre-bankruptcy claims. Secured creditors may nonetheless seek a bankruptcy court order lifting the stay and permitting the creditors to take enforcement actions against collateral under appropriate circumstances. First lien claimholders want to control the timing of any effort to pursue remedies against collateral following the bankruptcy filing, and it is thus typical for inter-creditor agreements to prevent or severely limit second lien claimholders from seeking relief from the stay to take action against shared collateral.

[71] Second lien lenders may seek to retain the right to take action following the standstill period (which would then be modified such that it does not extend indefinitely in bankruptcy). First lien lenders and borrowers would generally resist this.

[72] Many agreements only require that second lien claimholders not seek relief themselves. More first lien favorable provisions would go on to preclude second lien claimholders from opposing relief sought by the first lien. This clause would operate in conjunction with Section 6.4(b)(1) and could be provided for there as well.

[73] First lien lenders would prefer the agreement not to seek relief from the stay to be unqualified.

[74] As noted above, in order for the debtors to use cash collateral or grant priming liens on collateral, the debtors must either obtain consent of the secured lenders or must provide adequate protection for any diminution in the value of the secured lenders' interest in the collateral. Adequate protection can take the form of cash payments of fees and/or interest, principal reductions or liens on replacement collateral. If the second lien claimholders retain their right to seek adequate protection in connection with a proposed priming DIP financing or use of cash collateral, this can add a significant and perhaps prohibitive cost to the debtors.

It has become customary for inter-creditor agreements to provide that second lien claimholders may only seek adequate protection in the form of replacement liens on collateral and many agreements

(2) an objection by a First Lien Claimholder to a motion, relief, action or proceeding based on a First Lien Claimholder claiming a lack of adequate protection.

(b) Notwithstanding the preceding Section 6.4(a), in an Insolvency Proceeding:

(1) Except as permitted in this Section 6.4, no Second Lien Claimholders may seek or request adequate protection or relief from the automatic stay imposed by Section 362 of the Bankruptcy Code [or other relief].[75]

(2) [If a First Lien Claimholder is granted adequate protection in the form of additional or replacement Collateral in connection with a motion described in Section 6.1,[76] *'Use of cash collateral and DIP financing,'* then] the Second Lien Agent may seek or request adequate protection in the form of a Lien on [such] additional or replacement Collateral, which Lien will be subordinated to the Liens securing the First Lien Obligations and any DIP Financing (and all related Obligations) on the same basis as the other Liens securing the Second Lien Obligations are subordinated to the Liens securing First Lien Obligations under this Agreement.

(3) Any claim by a Second Lien Claimholder under Section 507(b) of the Bankruptcy Code will be subordinate in right of payment to any claim of First Lien Claimholders under Section 507(b) of the Bankruptcy Code and any payment thereof will be deemed to be Proceeds of Collateral [, *provided* that, subject to Section 6.7, *'Reorganization securities,'* Second Lien Claimholders will be deemed to have agreed pursuant to Section 1 129(a)(9) of the Bankruptcy Code that such Section 507(b) claims may be paid under a plan of reorganization in any form having a value on the effective date of such plan equal to the allowed amount of such claims[77]].

[(4) So long as the First Lien Agent is receiving payment in cash of [all] Post-Petition Claims [consisting of all interest at the applicable rate under the First Lien Loan Documents], the Second Lien Agent may seek and, subject to the terms hereof, retain payments of Post-Petition Claims [consisting of interest at the [non-default] [applicable] rate][78] under

---

footnote (*continued*)

restrict replacement liens unless the first lien claimholders also have been granted replacement liens in the same collateral as adequate protection. Note that the first lien claimholders may well have differing interests from the second lien claimholders in terms of whether replacement collateral is needed as adequate protection, because the first lien claimholders can have a significant cushion when the second lien claimholders do not. As such, the first lien claimholders may not insist upon, or be entitled to receive, replacement liens, while the second lien claimholders may suffer loss of value without them.

[75] A pro-second lien provision would eliminate a general restriction against seeking adequate protection and limit the waivers to cash collateral, DIP financing and asset sales.

[76] While common in the marketplace, second lien claimholders and their counsel may question why this should be a condition to second lien claimholders obtaining junior replacement liens on collateral.

[77] The parties should consider whether the payment of administrative claims arising under Section 507(b) should be paid over to the first lien agent as proceeds of collateral and be applied to reduce the first lien obligations permanently. If first lien claimholders seek confirmation of a plan, the right of second lien claimholders to assert a claim under Section 507(b) may preclude confirmation of the plan. The bracketed text would permit the confirmation of the plan so long as second lien claimholders' Section 507(b) claim would otherwise be satisfied under a 'cram-down'-type test. The parties may wish to consider an alternative treatment for Section 507(b) claims that may include being silent (pro-second) or subordinating the right to assert Section 507(b) claims in their entirety until the discharge of first lien obligations.

[78] Second lien adequate protection payments could include any or all post-petition claims, or other amounts as may be negotiated between the parties.

the Second Lien Loan Documents (*Second Lien Adequate Protection Payments*). If a Second Lien Claimholder receives Second Lien Adequate Protection Payments before the Discharge of First Lien Obligations up to the First Lien Cap with respect to the Capped Obligations and in their entirety with respect to First Lien Obligations that are not Capped Obligations, then upon the effective date of any plan or the conclusion or dismissal of any Insolvency Proceeding, the Second Lien Claimholder will pay over to the First Lien Agent pursuant to Section 4.1, '*Application of proceeds*,' an amount equal to the lesser of (i) the Second Lien Adequate Protection Payments received by the Second Lien Claimholder and (ii) the amount necessary to Discharge the First Lien Obligations. [Notwithstanding anything herein to the contrary, First Lien Claimholders will [not] be deemed to have consented to, and expressly [waive] [retain] their rights to object to, the payment of Second Lien Adequate Protection Payments.[79]]]

## 6.5 First lien objections to second lien actions[80]

Subject to Section 3.1, '*Who may exercise remedies*,' nothing in this Section 6 limits a First Lien Claimholder from objecting in an Insolvency Proceeding or otherwise to any action taken by a Second Lien Claimholder, including the Second Lien Claimholder's seeking adequate protection [or asserting any of its rights and remedies under the Second Lien Loan Documents or otherwise].

**[Alternative Section Favorable to Second Lien Lenders][81]**

## [6.5 First lien objections to second lien actions

Subject to Section 3.1, '*Who may exercise remedies*,' nothing in this Section 6 limits a First Lien Claimholder from objecting in an Insolvency Proceeding or otherwise to any action taken by a Second Lien Claimholder, including the Second Lien Claimholder's seeking adequate protection (other than adequate protection permitted under Section 6.4(b)) or asserting any of its rights and remedies under the Second Lien Loan Documents or otherwise.]

**[End of Alternative Section]**

---

[79] The bracketed language gives the parties the option to negotiate whether adequate protection payments may be contested or not by the first lien claimholders. To the extent the first lien agent asserts a lien on substantially all property of the applicable grantor, the first lien agent likely would assert that any payment constitutes 'proceeds' of collateral and would be subject to turnover and application to payment of the first lien obligations. Second lien claimholders would want to provide expressly that any payments turned over to the first lien agent will be applied to reduce the first lien cap permanently.

[80] The first lien claimholders prefer to have complete freedom to act in the bankruptcy, even where this means that they may choose to contest the claims and liens of the second lien claimholders or to oppose actions by the second lien claimholders that are not inconsistent with the inter-creditor agreement. For example, the first lien claimholders may want to support the position that the second lien is wholly unsecured because this may facilitate the completion of a bankruptcy plan or sale. This provision preserves the right of the first lien claimholders to object generally to actions taken, or relief requested, by second lien claimholders.

[81] The second lien favorable version specifies that the first lien claimholders may not object to the second lien claimholders' seeking of adequate protection consistent with the agreement.

## 6.6  Avoidance; reinstatement of obligations[82]

If a First Lien Claimholder or a Second Lien Claimholder receives payment or property on account of a First Lien Obligation or Second Lien Obligation, and the payment is subsequently invalidated, avoided, declared to be fraudulent or preferential, set aside or otherwise required to be transferred to a trustee, receiver or the estate of the Borrower or other Grantor (a ***Recovery***), then, to the extent of the Recovery, the First Lien Obligations or Second Lien Obligations intended to have been satisfied by the payment will be reinstated as First Lien Obligations or Second Lien Obligations, as applicable, on the date of the Recovery, and no Discharge of First Lien Obligations or Discharge of Second Lien Obligations, as applicable, will be deemed to have occurred for all purposes hereunder. If this Agreement is terminated prior to a Recovery, this Agreement will be reinstated in full force and effect, and such prior termination will not diminish, release, discharge, impair or otherwise affect the obligations of the Parties from the date of reinstatement. [Upon any such reinstatement of First Lien Obligations, each Second Lien Claimholder will deliver to the First Lien Agent any Collateral or Proceeds thereof received between the Discharge of First Lien Obligations and their reinstatement in accordance with Section 4.3, '*Payment turnover.*'][83] [No Second Lien Claimholder may benefit from a Recovery, and any distribution made to a Second Lien Claimholder as a result of a Recovery will be paid over to the First Lien Agent for application to the First Lien Obligations in accordance with Section 4.1, '*Application of proceeds.*'][84]

---

[82] A debtor or bankruptcy trustee may have the ability to 'avoid' or set aside pre-bankruptcy payments or transfers of value as fraudulent or preferential transfers. Fraudulent transfers can be transfers with actual intent to hinder, delay or defraud creditors. More common in large and mid-size cases are allegations of constructive fraud, where a payment or other transfer was made while the debtor was insolvent and for less than reasonably equivalent value. An example is the debtor repaying debt that was incurred as a result of a leveraged buy-out, where the value from incurring the debt flowed to shareholders rather than the borrower. Preferential transfers are those made to creditors within the ninety days prior to a bankruptcy (a year in the case of insider creditors) that result in the creditor receiving more than if the payment had not been made and the debt had been liquidated. Preferences are not a concern where a creditor is, at all points since the offending transfer, oversecured. If a payment is avoided, the creditor will have a claim against the debtor for the value disgorged. Where a first lien loan or a second lien loan has been repaid prior to bankruptcy, the possibility exists that the payment could be subject to avoidance on one of the above theories. The purpose of Section 6.6 is to specify that if that does occur, the inter-creditor agreement continues to govern the relationship between the first and second lien claimholders, with respect to their claims against the debt as a result of the disgorgement. The more controversial language at the end of the section endeavors to compel second lien claimholders to disgorge to the first lien claimholders amounts that they may have received constituting collateral proceeds during the time between the initial payment to the first lien claimholder and the avoidance of that payment. Second lien claimholders often will strenuously resist any contractual undertaking that would require them to disgorge, on the basis that the payment made to them was permitted under the inter-creditor agreement when made and they may well have passed the payment along to their own investors, with no power to obtain a return of such payment. When determining whether and to what extent to resist such provisions, note that the second lien claimholders are likely to be subject to a similar risk of avoidance. As such, though undertaking a contractual obligation to disgorge may be unpalatable, it may not greatly increase the actual risk of disgorgement.

[83] Second lien claimholders will oppose disgorgement of proceeds of collateral received after the first lien obligations are discharged. The parties may negotiate a middle ground where disgorgement is applicable only if demanded within a set time period after payment is received by second lien claimholders.

[84] Second lien claimholders will object to a pro rata disgorgement of avoidance action proceeds on the grounds that general unsecured creditors would have the right to share in such payments, and that the lien subordination should only pertain to the receipt of proceeds of collateral.

## 6.7 Reorganization securities[85]

Nothing in this Agreement prohibits or limits the right of a Second Lien Claimholder to receive and retain any debt or equity securities that are issued by a reorganized debtor pursuant to a plan of reorganization or similar dispositive restructuring plan in connection with an Insolvency Proceeding, [*provided* that any debt securities received by a Second Lien Claimholder on account of a Second Lien Obligation that constitutes a 'secured claim' within the meaning of Section 506(b) of the Bankruptcy Code will be paid over or otherwise transferred to the First Lien Agent for application in accordance with Section 4.1, '*Application of proceeds,*' unless such distribution is made under a plan that is consented to by the affirmative vote of all classes composed of the secured claims of First Lien Claimholders].

If, in an Insolvency Proceeding, debt Obligations of the reorganized debtor secured by Liens upon any property of the reorganized debtor are distributed pursuant to a plan of reorganization or similar dispositive restructuring plan, both on account of First Lien Obligations and on account of Second Lien Obligations, then, to the extent the debt Obligations distributed on account of the First Lien Obligations and on account of the Second Lien Obligations are secured by Liens upon the same property, the provisions of this Agreement will survive the distribution of such debt Obligations pursuant to such plan and will apply with like effect to the Liens securing such debt Obligations.[86]

## 6.8 Post-Petition Claims[87]

(a) No Second Lien Claimholder may oppose or seek to challenge any claim by a First Lien Claimholder for allowance or payment in any Insolvency Proceeding of First Lien Obligations consisting of Post-Petition Claims.[88]

---

[85] In a restructuring, it is common for holders of first and second lien debt to receive debt or equity securities in the reorganized company. One purpose of Section 6.7 is to confirm that this is permissible and that second lien claimholders can receive distributions prior to payment in full of the first lien claimholders. The first lien favorable variation specifies that distributions to the second lien claimholders on account of their secured claims are only permitted if the first lien claimholder classes support the plan. Another purpose of this section is to specify that, if both first and second lien claimholders do receive new secured debt that shares collateral, the inter-creditor provisions will continue to govern the relative priorities and other rights of such secured debt.

[86] There is a hypothetical issue with the fact that this provision covers all debt securities issued with respect to the second lien obligations, in that it is possible that the second lien obligations could be bifurcated into a secured and unsecured component, and that secured debt obligations could be issued with respect to the unsecured component. To the extent that other unsecured creditors also receive the same type of security or the same security, the obligations issued to second lien claimholders could be treated differently because of this provision. Consider whether this potential should be addressed by carving out debt obligations to the extent issued to any unsecured claim held by second lien claimholders and, potentially, to the extent such debt obligations are also issued to other creditors holding unsecured claims.

[87] In this section, the second lien claimholders agree not to oppose the allowance of post-petition claims held by the first lien claimholders and the first lien claimholders agree not to oppose the allowance of post-petition claims held by the second lien claimholders. This waiver applies to valuation of the collateral as a component of determination of the secured claim held by the first and second lien claimholders. In addition, the waiver prevents either the first lien or second lien claimholders from objecting to the allowance of the amount of first and second lien debt held by the other parties.

(b) No First Lien Claimholder may oppose or seek to challenge in an Insolvency Proceeding a claim by a Second Lien Claimholder for allowance [and any payment permitted under Section 6.4, '*Adequate protection*,'] of Second Lien Obligations consisting of Post-Petition Claims.

## 6.9 Waivers[89]

The Second Lien Agent waives

(a) any claim it may hereafter have against any First Lien Claimholder arising out of any cash collateral or financing arrangement or out of any grant of a security interest in connection with the Collateral in an Insolvency Proceeding, so long as such actions are not in express contravention of the terms of this Agreement; [and]

(b) any right to assert or enforce any claim under Section 506(c) or 552 of the Bankruptcy Code as against First Lien Claimholders or any of the Collateral to the extent securing the First Lien Obligations[90] [; and

(c) solely in its capacity as a holder of a Lien on Collateral, any claim or cause of action that any Grantor may have against any First Lien Claimholder, except to the extent arising from a breach by such First Lien Claimholder of the provisions of this Agreement].

---

footnote (*continued*)

Finally, if and to the extent the first lien claimholders have allowed secured claims, the second lien claimholders agree not to oppose the payment of the first lien debt. While this latter waiver is less common in the marketplace, it is consistent with the notion that the second lien claimholders have no right to payment from collateral until after the first lien claimholders have been paid and, therefore, the second lien claimholders should benefit, dollar-for-dollar, from the repayment of the first lien debt. The practical effect of these waivers is that third parties with an incentive to challenge the extent, validity and priority of the first and/or second lien debt will be the ones to challenge the secured claims and there should not be a challenge commenced by either of the first or second lienholders against the other.

[88] Many inter-creditor agreements qualify the agreement not to object to claims based upon the extent of the value of any collateral securing the first lien obligations without regard to the existence of the lien securing the second lien obligations. This language is regarded as inconsistent with the notion that the parties to the inter-creditor agreement should not interfere with each others' claims against the grantors.

[89] In the mezzanine world, where the junior creditor could not receive payment on its unsecured claims until the senior debt was paid in full, an election by the senior lender under Section 1111(b) of the Bankruptcy Code could cause the waiver of the unsecured creditor 'dividend' and make it more difficult for the junior creditor to ever receive payment under a plan. Hence, the subordination agreements in a mezzanine context often contained a 'waiver' of any claims resulting from the senior lender making the Section 1111(b) election. The Model Agreement deletes this waiver as the Task Force believes that the Section 1111(b) election does not affect the rights of the second lien claimholders. The other waivers that relate to cash collateral, financing and granting of security interests are general provisions that are consistent with the DIP financing and cash collateral provisions discussed above. Some second lien claimholders may prefer to be governed by those more specific sections and may object to the more general waiver.

[90] Any payment received by a second lien claimholder as a result of a surcharge against collateral under Section 506(c) of the Bankruptcy Code would result in the receipt of proceeds of collateral that would otherwise be required to be applied to payment of the first lien obligations.

## 6.10  Separate grants of security and separate classification[91]

The grants of Liens pursuant to the First Lien Collateral Documents and the Second Lien Collateral Documents constitute two separate and distinct grants. Because of, among other things, their differing rights in the Collateral, the Second Lien Obligations, to the extent deemed to be 'secured claims' within the meaning of Section 506(b) of the Bankruptcy Code, are fundamentally different from the First Lien Obligations and must be separately classified in any plan of reorganization in an Insolvency Proceeding. Second Lien Claimholders will not seek in an Insolvency Proceeding to be treated as part of the same class of creditors as First Lien Claimholders and will not oppose or contest any pleading by First Lien Claimholders seeking separate classification of their respective secured claims.

## 6.11  Effectiveness in Insolvency Proceedings[92]

The Parties acknowledge that this Agreement is a 'subordination agreement' under Section 510(a) of the Bankruptcy Code, which will be effective before, during and after the commencement of an Insolvency Proceeding. All references in this Agreement to any Grantor will include such Person as a debtor-in-possession and any receiver or trustee for such Person in an Insolvency Proceeding.

# 7  MISCELLANEOUS

## 7.1  Conflicts

If this Agreement conflicts with the First Lien Loan Documents or the Second Lien Loan Documents, this Agreement will control.

## 7.2  No waivers; remedies cumulative; integration

A Party's failure or delay in exercising a right under this Agreement will not waive the right, nor will a Party's single or partial exercise of a right preclude it from any other or further exercise of that or any other right.

---

[91] Many forms in the marketplace have elaborate provisions dealing with the classification of claims. The Model Agreement attempts a more streamlined provision that should be sufficient under most circumstances. We believe that the more lengthy waiver grew out of structures where the second lien claimholders held claims under the same security documents, thereby creating the risk of classification in the same class. Separate granting clauses, at least with respect to the secured claims held by the first lien claimholders and second lien claimholders, should result in separate classification as a matter of law.

[92] Section 510 of the Bankruptcy Code contains a general reference to the enforceability of 'subordination' agreements. There is some difference of opinion as to whether the reference to subordination is to 'debt subordination,' 'lien subordination' or both. From the perspective of waivers and estoppel, the Model Agreement takes the position that the claimholders should not dispute that the reference in Section 510 includes 'lien subordination.' Therefore, no claimholder should be permitted to avoid its contractual obligations set forth in the inter-creditor agreement by arguing that the bankruptcy court lacks jurisdiction to enforce a contract between two non-debtors. Of course, the parties cannot confer jurisdiction on the court where none would otherwise exist, but at least this acknowledgment should be evidence of the parties' intent and should dissuade parties from conduct inconsistent with that intent.

The rights and remedies provided in this Agreement will be cumulative and not exclusive of other rights or remedies provided by law.

This Agreement constitutes the entire agreement between the Parties and supersedes all prior agreements, oral or written, relating to its subject matter.

## 7.3  Effectiveness; severability; termination

This Agreement will become effective when executed and delivered by the Parties.

Each First Lien Claimholder and each Second Lien Claimholder waives any right it may have under applicable law to revoke this Agreement or any provision thereunder or consent by it thereto.

This Agreement will survive, and continue in full force and effect, in any Insolvency Proceeding.

If a provision of this Agreement is prohibited or unenforceable in a jurisdiction, the prohibition or unenforceability will not invalidate the remaining provisions hereof, or invalidate or render unenforceable that provision in any other jurisdiction.

Subject to Sections 1.6(d) and 1.6(g), *'Pledged Collateral,'* 4.1, *'Application of proceeds,'* 4.4, *'Refinancing after discharge of First Lien Obligations,'* 6.5, *'First lien objections to second lien actions,'* and 6.6, *'Avoidance; reinstatement of obligations,'* this Agreement will terminate and be of no further force and effect

(a)  for First Lien Claimholders, upon the Discharge of First Lien Obligations, and

(b)  for Second Lien Claimholders, upon the Discharge of Second Lien Obligations.

## 7.4  Modifications of this Agreement

A modification or waiver of any provision of this Agreement will only be effective if in writing signed on behalf of each Party or its authorized agent, and a waiver will be a waiver only for the specific instance involved and will not impair the rights of the Parties making the waiver or the obligations of the other Parties to such Party in any other respect or at any other time. Notwithstanding the foregoing, neither the Borrower nor Holdings will have a right to consent to or approve a modification of this Agreement except to the extent its rights are directly affected.

## 7.5  Information concerning the financial condition of the Borrower and it's subsidiaries

The Control Agent, First Lien Claimholders and Second Lien Claimholders will each be responsible for keeping themselves informed of

(a)  the financial condition of the Grantors, and

(b)  all other circumstances bearing upon the risk of nonpayment of the First Lien Obligations or the Second Lien Obligations.

Neither the Control Agent nor any First Lien Claimholder will have any duty to advise any Second Lien Claimholder, and no Second Lien Claimholder will have any duty to advise the Control Agent or any first Lien Claimholder, of information known to it regarding any such condition or circumstances or otherwise.

If the Control Agent or a First Lien Claimholder provides any such information to a Second Lien Claimholder, or a Second Lien Claimholder provides any such information to the Control

Agent or any First Lien Claimholder, the Control Agent or the First Lien Claimholder, or Second Lien Claimholder, respectively, will have no obligation to:

(c) make, and it does not make, any express or implied representation or warranty, including as to accuracy, completeness, truthfulness or validity,

(d) provide additional information on that or any subsequent occasion,

(e) undertake any investigation, or

(f) disclose information that, pursuant to applicable law or accepted or reasonable commercial finance practices, it desires or is required to maintain as confidential.

## 7.6  No reliance

(a) The First Lien Agent acknowledges that it and each other First Lien Claimholder has, independently and without reliance on any Second Lien Claimholder, and based on documents and information the First Lien Claimholder deemed appropriate, made its own credit analysis and decision to enter into the First Lien Loan Documents and this Agreement, and will continue to make its own credit decisions in taking or not taking any action under the First Lien Loan Documents or this Agreement.

(b) The Second Lien Agent acknowledges that it and each other Second Lien Claimholder has, independently and without reliance on any First Lien Claimholder, and based on documents and information the Second Lien Claimholder deemed appropriate, made its own credit analysis and decision to enter into the Second Lien Loan Documents and this Agreement, and will continue to make its own credit decisions in taking or not taking any action under the Second Lien Loan Documents or this Agreement.

## 7.7  No warranties; independent action

(a) Except as otherwise expressly provided herein,

   (1) no Second Lien Claimholder has made any express or implied representation or warranty to any First Lien Claimholder, including with respect to the execution, validity, legality, completeness, collectability or enforceability of any Second Lien Loan Document, the ownership of any Collateral or the perfection or priority of any Liens thereon, and

   (2) each Second Lien Claimholder may manage and supervise its loans and extensions of credit under the Second Lien Loan Documents in accordance with applicable law and as it may otherwise, in its sole discretion, deem appropriate.

(b) Except as otherwise expressly provided herein,

   (1) no First Lien Claimholder has made any express or implied representation or warranty to any Second Lien Claimholder, including with respect to the execution, validity, legality, completeness, collectability or enforceability of any First Lien Loan Document, the ownership of any Collateral or the perfection or priority of any Liens thereon, and

   (2) each First Lien Claimholder may manage and supervise its loans and extensions of credit under the First Lien Loan Documents in accordance with law and as it may otherwise, in its sole discretion, deem appropriate.

No Second Lien Claimholder will have any duty to any First Lien Claimholder, and no First Lien Claimholder will have any duty to any Second Lien Claimholder, to act or refrain from acting in a manner that allows, or results in, the occurrence or continuance of an event of default or default under any agreements with the Borrower or any other Grantor (including the First Lien Loan Documents and the Second Lien Loan Documents), regardless of any knowledge thereof that it may have or be charged with.

## 7.8  Subrogation

If a Second Lien Claimholder pays or distributes cash, property or other assets to a First Lien Claimholder under this Agreement, the Second Lien Claimholder will be subrogated to the rights of the First Lien Claimholder with respect to the value of the payment or distribution, *provided* that the Second Lien Claimholder waives such right of subrogation until the Discharge of First Lien Obligations up to the First Lien Cap with respect to the Capped Obligations and in their entirety with respect to First Lien Obligations that are not Capped Obligations. Such payment or distribution will not reduce the Second Lien Obligations.

## 7.9  Applicable law; jurisdiction; service

This Agreement, and any claim or controversy relating to the subject matter hereof, will be governed by the law of the [State of New York].

All judicial proceedings brought against a Party arising out of or relating hereto may be brought in any state or federal court of competent jurisdiction in [the state, county and city of New York]. Each Party irrevocably

(a)  accepts generally and unconditionally the nonexclusive personal jurisdiction and venue of such courts,
(b)  waives any defense of forum non conveniens, and
(c)  agrees that service of process in such proceeding may be made by registered or certified mail, return receipt requested, to the Party at its address provided in accordance with Section 7.11, '*Notices*,' and that such service will confer personal jurisdiction over the Party in such proceeding and otherwise constitutes effective and binding service in every respect.

## 7.10  Waiver of jury trial

Each Party waives its right to jury trial of any claim or cause of action based upon or arising hereunder. The scope of this waiver is intended to encompass any and all disputes that may be filed in any court and that relate to the subject matter hereof, including contract claims, tort claims, breach of duty claims and all other common law and statutory claims. Each Party acknowledges that this waiver is a material inducement to enter into a business relationship, that it has already relied on this waiver in entering into this Agreement, and that it will continue to rely on this waiver in its related future dealings. Each Party further represents and warrants that it knowingly and voluntarily waives its jury trial rights following consultation with legal counsel. This waiver is irrevocable, meaning that it may not be modified either orally or in writing (other than by a mutual written waiver specifically referring to this Section 7.10 and executed by each of the Parties), and will apply to any subsequent modification hereof. In the event of litigation, this Agreement may be filed as a written consent to a trial by the court.

## 7.11 Notices

(a) Any notice to a First Lien Claimholder or a Second Lien Claimholder under this Agreement must also be given to the First Lien Agent and the Second Lien Agent, respectively. Unless otherwise expressly *provided* herein, notices and consents must be in writing and will be deemed to have been given (i) when delivered in person or by courier service and signed for against receipt thereof, (ii) upon receipt of facsimile, and (iii) three Business Days after deposit in the United States mail with first-class postage prepaid and properly addressed. For the purposes hereof, the address of each Party will be as set forth below the Party's name on the signature pages hereto, or at such other address as the Party may designate by notice to the other Parties.

(b) Failure to give a notice or copies as required by Section 2.4, *'Notice of modifications,'* [or] Section 3.4, *'Notice of exercise,'* [or Section 3.1(e) regarding notice of Discharge of First Lien Obligations] will not affect the effectiveness or validity of any modification or of this Agreement, or the effectiveness or validity of the exercise of remedies otherwise permitted hereunder and under applicable law, impose any liability on any First Lien Claimholder or Second Lien Claimholder, or waive any rights of any Party.

## 7.12 Further assurances

The First Lien Agent, the Second Lien Agent and the Borrower will each take such further action and will execute and deliver such additional documents and instruments (in recordable form, if requested) as the First Lien Agent or the Second Lien Agent may reasonably request to effectuate the terms of and the Lien priorities contemplated by this Agreement.

## 7.13 Successors and assigns

This Agreement is binding upon and inures to the benefit of each First Lien Claimholder, each Second Lien Claimholder, the Control Agent and their respective successors and assigns. However, no provision of this Agreement will inure to the benefit of a trustee, debtor-in-possession, creditor trust or other representative of an estate or creditor of the Borrower, or other Grantor, including where such estate or creditor representative is the beneficiary of a Lien securing Collateral by virtue of the avoidance of such Lien in an Insolvency Proceeding.

If either the First Lien Agent or the Second Lien Agent resigns or is replaced pursuant to the First Lien Credit Agreement or Second Lien Credit Agreement, as applicable, its successor will be a party to this Agreement with all the rights, and subject to all the obligations, of this Agreement. Notwithstanding any other provision of this Agreement, this Agreement may not be assigned to any Person except as expressly contemplated herein.

## 7.14 Authorization

By its signature hereto, each Person signing this Agreement on behalf of a Party represents and warrants to the other Parties that it is duly authorized to execute this Agreement.

## 7.15  No third-party beneficiaries

No Person is a third-party beneficiary of this Agreement and no trustee in bankruptcy for, or bankruptcy estate of, or unsecured creditor of, any Grantor will have or acquire or be entitled to exercise any right of a First Lien Claimholder or Second Lien Claimholder under this Agreement, whether upon an avoidance or equitable subordination of a Lien of First Lien Claimholder or Second Lien Claimholder, or otherwise. None of the Borrower, any other Grantor, or any other creditor thereof has any rights hereunder, and neither the Borrower nor any Grantor may rely on the terms hereof. Nothing in this Agreement impairs the Obligations of the Borrower and the other Grantors to pay principal, interest, fees and other amounts as provided in the First Lien Loan Documents and the Second Lien Loan Documents. Except to the extent expressly provided in this Agreement, no Person will have a right to notice of a modification to, or action taken under, this Agreement or any First Lien Collateral Document (including the release or impairment of any Collateral) other than as a lender under the First Lien Credit Agreement, and then only to the extent expressly provided in the First Lien Loan Documents. Except to the extent expressly provided in this Agreement, no Person will have a right to notice of a modification to, or action taken under, this Agreement or any Second Lien Collateral Document (including the release or impairment of any Collateral) other than as a lender under the Second Lien Credit Agreement, and then only to the extent expressly provided in the Second Lien Loan Documents.

## 7.16  No indirect actions

Unless otherwise expressly stated, if a Party may not take an action under this Agreement, then it may not take that action indirectly, or assist or support any other Person in taking that action directly or indirectly. 'Taking an action indirectly' means taking an action that is not expressly prohibited for the Party but is intended to have substantially the same effects as the prohibited action.

## 7.17  Counterparts

This Agreement may be executed in counterparts (and by different parties hereto in different counterparts), each of which will constitute an original, but all of which when taken together will constitute a single contract. Delivery of an executed counterpart of a signature page of this Agreement or any document or instrument delivered in connection herewith by telecopy or electronic facsimile or other electronic means will be effective as delivery of a manually executed counterpart of this Agreement or such other document or instrument, as applicable, and each Party utilizing telecopy, electronic facsimile or other electronic means for delivery will deliver a manually executed original counterpart to each other Party on request.

## 7.18  Original Grantors; additional Grantors

The Borrower and each other Grantor on the date of this Agreement will constitute the original Grantors party hereto. The original Grantors will cause each Subsidiary of the Borrower and of Holdings that becomes a Grantor after the date hereof to contemporaneously become a Party hereto (as a Guarantor Subsidiary) by executing and delivering a joinder agreement (in form and substance satisfactory to the First Lien Agent) to First Lien Agent. The Parties further agree that, notwithstanding any failure to take the actions required by the immediately preceding sentence, each Person that becomes a Grantor at any time (and any security granted by any such Person) will be subject to the provisions hereof as fully as if it constituted a Guarantor Subsidiary Party hereto and had complied with the requirements of the immediately preceding sentence.

# 8  DEFINITIONS[93]

## 8.1  Defined terms

Unless otherwise stated or the context otherwise clearly requires, the following terms have the following meanings:

*Affiliate* means, for a specified Person, another Person that directly, or indirectly through one or more intermediaries, controls or is controlled by or is under common control with the specified Person. For these purposes, 'control' means the possession, directly or indirectly, of the power to direct or cause the direction of the management or policies of a Person, whether through the ownership of voting securities, by contract or otherwise, and 'controlled' has a correlative meaning.

*Agreement* is defined in the Preamble.

*Assignment Agreement* is defined in Section 5.1 (a)(B).

*Bankruptcy Code* means the federal Bankruptcy Code.

*Bankruptcy Law* means the Bankruptcy Code and any similar federal, state or foreign bankruptcy, insolvency, receivership or similar law affecting creditors' rights generally.

*Borrower* is defined in the Preamble.

*Business Day* means a day other than a Saturday, Sunday or other day on which commercial banks in [New York City] are authorized or required by law to close.

*Capped Obligations* is defined in Section 1.4.

*Cash Management Agreement* means an agreement to provide cash management services, including treasury, depository, overdraft, credit or debit card, electronic funds transfer or

---

[93] Much of the detail, and key substantive terms and distinctions, are found in the definitions. A few of the important ones are discussed briefly in footnotes below, but all of them should be scrutinized as the most mundane could be important in a particular transaction. A quick note as to form: Breaking with tradition, at least for many of us, the Model Agreement does not group all of the defined terms into a separate section but rather sprinkles many of them throughout the agreement, providing a definition when a term is first employed. As editor Howard Darmstadter pointed out to the drafters of the Model Agreement, it is easier to read a document from the start if uninterrupted by searches for definitions. More common and obvious terms are found in the definition section at the end. Note also that Section 8.2, '*Usages*,' sets forth various conventions as to certain terms and points of interpretation, including as to the calculation of time periods and the time of day, and that a reference to an agreement includes its amendments. Comments on the following few key definitions appear in notes to each of the applicable definitions: 'Cash Management Agreement,' 'First Lien Obligations,' 'Hedge Agreement,' and 'Obligations.' These terms all relate to the breadth of the Model Agreement – it includes all of the obligations and indebtedness held by the First Lien Lenders, and certain affiliates and potentially others, including obligations relating to bank products and cash management arrangements such as interest rate swaps and automated clearing services. This broad scope is mitigated by the concept of the first lien cap, and care should be taken as to its definition, as more fully discussed in note 11, and as to the definition of first lien obligations, as to which an alternative definition is provided.

other cash management arrangements, to which a Grantor is a party and a lender under the First Lien Credit Agreement or an Affiliate of such lender is the applicable counterparty at the date hereof or at the time it enters into such agreement (even if such counterparty later ceases to be such a lender or Affiliate).

*Collateral* means all of the property of any Grantor, whether real, personal or mixed, that is (or is required to be) both First Lien Collateral and Second Lien Collateral, including any property subject to Liens granted pursuant to Section 6, '*Insolvency Proceedings*,' to secure both First Lien Obligations and Second Lien Obligations.[94]

**[Alternative Definition][95]**

[*Collateral* means, at any time of determination, the First Lien Collateral and all other property of any Grantor in which each of the First Lien Agent and the Second Lien Agent has, pursuant to the First Lien Collateral Documents and the Second Lien Collateral Documents, respectively, a valid and perfected Lien (which Lien has not been avoided, disallowed, set aside, invalidated or subordinated pursuant to Chapter 5 of the Bankruptcy Code or otherwise) securing payment of First Lien Obligations or Second Lien Obligations, respectively, and including any Lien granted pursuant to Section 6, '*Insolvency Proceedings*,' to secure both First Lien Obligations and Second Lien Obligations.]

**[End of Alternative Definition]**

*Control Agent* is defined in the Preamble.

*Defaulting Creditor* is defined in Section 5.7(c).

*DIP Financing* means the obtaining of credit or incurring debt secured by Liens on the Collateral pursuant to Section 364 of the Bankruptcy Code (or similar Bankruptcy Law).

*Discharge of First Lien Obligations*[96] means, except to the extent otherwise expressly provided in Section 5, '*Purchase of First Lien Obligations by Second Lien Claimholders*,'

(a) payment in full in cash of the principal of and interest (including interest accruing on or after the commencement of an Insolvency Proceeding, whether or not such interest would be allowed in the proceeding)[97] on all outstanding Indebtedness included in the First Lien Obligations,

(b) payment in full in cash of all other First Lien Obligations that are due and payable or otherwise accrued and owing at or prior to the time such principal and interest are paid (other

---

[94] Note the alternative definition, available for use with the alternative provisions of Section 1.1. As a general matter, the first lien claimholders and second lien claimholders typically expect to hold liens on the same pool of assets (very often all assets), but exceptions to this often occur and the definition as well as the substantive provisions in Section 1.5 may need to be adjusted.

[95] If the parties use the alternative Section 1.1, then this definition of 'Collateral' can be used.

[96] This term is employed throughout the Model Agreement to indicate when the second lien claimholders are no longer subject to the restrictions of the inter-creditor agreement and therefore is a key definition. See, in particular, note 45. Also, the parties should consider whether certain restrictions against the second lien claimholders contained in the inter-creditor agreement, as well as certain other provisions of the Model Agreement, should apply only until the first lien obligations have been paid to the amount of the first lien cap or whether such restrictions or provisions should continue to apply until all first lien obligations have been paid in full.

[97] If the parties agree as provided in Section 1.3 that the first lien agent should not continue to have priority if its lien is not properly perfected, lapses or is avoided in bankruptcy, then the language in parentheses concerning post-petition claims should be deleted.

than indemnification Obligations for which no claim or demand for payment, whether oral or written, has been made at such time),[98]

(c) termination or expiration of any commitments to extend credit that would be First Lien Obligations [(other than pursuant to Cash Management Agreements or Hedge Agreements, in each case as to which satisfactory arrangements have been made with the applicable lender or Affiliate)], and

(d) termination or cash collateralization (in an amount and manner reasonably satisfactory to the First Lien Agent, but in no event greater than 105% of the aggregate undrawn face amount) of all Letters of Credit.

**[Alternative Clause]**

[(d) [termination or cash collateralization (in an amount reasonably satisfactory to the First Lien Agent) of any Hedge Agreement issued or entered into by any First Lien Claimholder] [termination of any Hedge Agreement and the payment in full by wire transfer of immediately available funds of all Obligations thereunder].

**[End of Alternative Clause]**

*Discharge of Second Lien Obligations* means

(e) payment in full in cash of the principal of and interest (including interest accruing on or after the commencement of an Insolvency Proceeding, whether or not such interest would be allowed in the proceeding) on all outstanding Indebtedness included in the Second Lien Obligations, and

(f) payment in full in cash of all other Second Lien Obligations that are due and payable or otherwise accrued and owing at or prior to the time such principal and interest are paid (other than indemnification Obligations for which no claim or demand for payment, whether oral or written, has been made at such time).

*Disposition* means an 'Asset Sale' (as defined in the First Lien Credit Agreement), or other sale, lease, exchange, transfer or other disposition.

*Enforcement Action*[99] means an action under applicable law to

(g) foreclose, execute, levy, or collect on, take possession or control of, sell or otherwise realize upon (judicially or non-judicially), or lease, license, or otherwise dispose of (whether

---

[98] Clause (b) excludes indemnification obligations for which no claim has been made. Consideration should be given to whether 'Discharge of First Lien Obligations' should also include cash collateralization for contingent exposure on claims that have been made, threatened or, in some cases, may reasonably be expected to be asserted.

[99] This definition is broad in scope, capturing in clauses (a), (c) and (d) not only the foreclosure against collateral and other standard secured party remedies, but also the initial steps of a consensual disposition of collateral as described in clause (b). However, it does not include the filing of an involuntary bankruptcy proceeding or the exercise of other unsecured creditor remedies. The broad scope benefits the first lien claimholders since the first lien claimholders are given the exclusive right to exercise enforcement actions (Section 3.1), and certain events such as the automatic release of liens on collateral securing second lien obligations are triggered by the first lien agent's enforcement action (Section 1.10). On the other hand, Section 5.1(b) bars the first lien claimholders from commencing any enforcement action so long as the second lien claimholders' purchase option right under Section 5 is outstanding, thereby benefiting the second lien claimholders by the broad definition.

publicly or privately), Collateral, or otherwise exercise or enforce remedial rights with respect to Collateral under the First Lien Loan Documents or the Second Lien Loan Documents (including by way of set-off, recoupment notification of a public or private sale or other disposition pursuant to the U.C.C. or other applicable law, notification to account debtors, notification to depositary banks under deposit account control agreements, or exercise of rights under landlord consents, if applicable),

(h) solicit bids from third Persons to conduct the liquidation or disposition of Collateral or to engage or retain sales brokers, marketing agents, investment bankers, accountants, appraisers, auctioneers or other third Persons for the purposes of valuing, marketing, promoting and selling Collateral,

(i) to receive a transfer of Collateral in satisfaction of Indebtedness or any other Obligation secured thereby, [or]

(j) to otherwise enforce a security interest or exercise another right or remedy, as a secured creditor or otherwise, pertaining to the Collateral at law, in equity or pursuant to the First Lien Loan Documents or Second Lien Loan Documents (including the commencement of applicable legal proceedings or other actions with respect to all or any portion of the Collateral to facilitate the actions described in the preceding clauses, and exercising voting rights in respect of equity interests comprising Collateral), [or]

(k) effect the Disposition of Collateral by any Grantor after the occurrence and during the continuation of an event of default under the First Lien Loan Documents or the Second Lien Loan Documents with the consent of the First Lien Agent or the Second Lien Agent, as applicable,][100] *provided* that 'Enforcement Action' will [not] be deemed to include the commencement of, or joinder in filing of a petition for commencement of, an Insolvency Proceeding against the owner of Collateral.[101]

***Equity Interest*** means, for any Person, any and all shares, interests, participations or other equivalents, including membership interests (however designated, whether voting or nonvoting) of equity of the Person, including, if the Person is a partnership, partnership interests (whether general or limited) or any other interest or participation that confers on a holder the right to receive a share of the profits and losses of, or distributions of assets of, the partnership, but not including debt securities convertible or exchangeable into equity unless and until actually converted or exchanged.

***Excess First Lien Obligations*** are defined in Section 1.11(c).
***Excess First Lien Principal Obligations*** are defined in Section 1.4(a).
***First Lien Agent*** is defined in the Preamble.

---

[100] *See* Section 1.10, '*Release of Liens [or guaranties]*.' First lien claimholders may wish to cause a disposition of collateral by an action of the grantor in lieu of a foreclosure sale.

[101] Consider whether the enforcement action concept should, or should not, include commencement of an involuntary bankruptcy proceeding. First lien lenders may consider a right to interrupt their efforts to realize on collateral through filing an insolvency proceeding against a grantor as inconsistent with the proposition that the second lien will defer to the first lien in such efforts. A second lienor may argue that it should not be required to forfeit a right that it would have if it were entirely unsecured. In considering how much to value this right (or to fear it), the parties should note that to commence, or join in commencing, an involuntary bankruptcy petition, a second lienor would likely have to concede that its claims are not fully secured, making this a somewhat unattractive option. A common solution to this issue is to permit second lien claimholders to commence an involuntary insolvency proceeding after the expiration of the standstill period, making the remedy similar to that exercisable by unsecured mezzanine creditors.

*First Lien Cap* is defined in Section 1.4.

*First Lien Claimholders* are defined in Section 1.3(d).

*First Lien Collateral* means the assets of any Grantor, whether real, personal or mixed, as to which a Lien is granted as security for a First Lien Obligation.

## [Alternative Definition][102]

[*First Lien Collateral* means the assets of any Grantor, whether real, personal or mixed, as to which a Lien is granted as security for a First Lien Obligation pursuant to the First Lien Collateral Documents, which Lien is, at any time of determination, a valid and perfected Lien that has not been avoided, disallowed, set aside, invalidated or subordinated pursuant to Chapter 5 of the Bankruptcy Code or otherwise.]

## [End of Alternative Definition]

*First Lien Collateral Documents* means the [security] [Collateral] documents defined in the First Lien Credit Agreement, and any other documents or instruments granting a Lien on real or personal property to secure a First Lien Obligation or granting rights or remedies with respect to such Liens.

*First Lien Credit Agreement* is defined in the Preamble.

*First Lien Lenders* means the 'Lenders' under and as defined in the First Lien Loan Documents.

*First Lien Loan Documents* means

(l)  the First Lien Credit Agreement and the 'Loan Documents' defined in the First Lien Credit Agreement,

(m) each other agreement, document or instrument providing for, evidencing, guaranteeing or securing an Obligation under the First Lien Credit Agreement,

(n)  any other document or instrument executed or delivered at any time in connection with the Borrower's Obligations under the First Lien Credit Agreement, including any guaranty of or grant of Collateral to secure such Obligations, and any inter-creditor or joinder agreement to which holders of First Lien Obligations are parties, and

(o)  each other agreement, document or instrument providing for, evidencing, guaranteeing or securing any DIP Financing provided by or consented to in writing by the First Lien Lenders and deemed consented to by the Second Lien Lenders pursuant to Section 6.1, '*Use of cash collateral and DIP financing*,' to the extent effective at the relevant time, [provided that any such documents or instruments to which any First Lien Claimholder is a party in connection with a DIP financing (other than a DIP financing deemed consented to by Second Lien Lenders pursuant to Section 6.1, '*Use of cash collateral and DIP financing*') will not be deemed First Lien Loan Documents unless so designated in writing by the First Lien Agent].[103]

---

[102] If the parties use the alternative definition of 'Collateral,' then this definition of 'First Lien Collateral' can be used.

[103] Many inter-creditor agreements fail to address whether a non-conforming DIP financing (i.e., one that is not consented to by second lien claimholders) would be subject to the remaining terms and provisions of the inter-creditor agreement insofar as the new DIP financing would likely be, at least in part, a refinancing of the first lien obligations. Second lien claimants may resist this provision as it gives first lien claimholders the benefit of opting into the pro-senior inter-creditor agreement provisions for a non-conforming DIP financing.

***First Lien Obligations*** are defined in Section 1.3(a).

***Governmental Authority*** means any federal, state, municipal, national, or other government, governmental department, commission, board, bureau, court, agency, or instrumentality, or political subdivision thereof, or any entity or officer exercising executive, legislative, judicial, regulatory or administrative functions of or pertaining to any government or any court, in each case whether associated with a state of the United States, the United States, or a foreign entity or government.

***Grantor*** is defined in the Preamble.

***Guarantor Subsidiaries*** are defined in the Preamble.

***Hedge Agreement*** means

(p) an Interest Rate Protection Agreement, or
(q) a foreign exchange contract, currency swap agreement, futures contract, option contract, synthetic cap or other similar agreement or arrangement, each of which is for the purpose of hedging the foreign currency risk associated with the operations of any Grantor,

in either case, to the extent that the incurrence of the obligations in respect thereof was permitted under the First Lien Loan Documents as in effect on the date hereof.

***Holdings*** is defined in the Preamble.

***Indebtedness*** means and includes all Obligations that constitute 'Indebtedness' under the First Lien Credit Agreement or the Second Lien Credit Agreement, as applicable.

***Insolvency Proceeding*** means

(r) a voluntary or involuntary case or proceeding under the Bankruptcy Code with respect to a Grantor,
(s) any other voluntary or involuntary insolvency, reorganization or bankruptcy case or proceeding, or any receivership, liquidation, reorganization or other similar case or proceeding with respect to a Grantor or a material portion of its property,
(t) a liquidation, dissolution, reorganization or winding up of a Grantor, whether voluntary or involuntary and whether or not involving insolvency or bankruptcy, or
(u) an assignment for the benefit of creditors or other marshaling of assets and liabilities of a Grantor.

***Interest Rate Protection Agreement*** means an interest rate swap, cap or collar agreement, or other similar agreement or arrangement designed to protect a Grantor against fluctuations in interest rates.

***Letters of Credit*** are defined in Section 1.4.

***Lien*** means any lien (including, without limitation, judgment liens and liens arising by operation of law, subrogation or otherwise), mortgage or deed of trust, pledge, hypothecation, assignment, security interest, charge or encumbrance of any kind (including any agreement to give any of the foregoing, any conditional sale or other title retention agreement, and any lease in the nature thereof), and any option, call, trust, U.C.C. financing statement or other preferential arrangement having the practical effect of any of the foregoing, including any right of set-off or recoupment.

***Modify***, as applied to any document or obligation, includes

(v) modification by amendment, supplement, termination or replacement of the document or obligation,
(w) any waiver of a provision (including waivers by course of conduct), and
(x) the settlement or release of any claim, whether oral or written, and regardless of whether the modification is in conformity with the provisions of the document or obligation governing modifications.

*New Agent* is defined in Section 4.4.

*Obligations* means all obligations of every nature of a Person owed to any obligee under an agreement, whether for principal, interest or payments for early termination, fees, expenses, indemnification or otherwise, and all guaranties of any of the foregoing, whether absolute or contingent, due or to become due, now existing or hereafter arising, and including interest and fees that accrue after the commencement by or against any Person of any proceeding under any Bankruptcy Law naming such Person as the debtor in such proceeding, regardless of whether such interest and fees are allowed claims in such proceeding.

*Party* means a party to this Agreement.

*Person* means any natural person, corporation, limited liability company, trust, business trust, joint venture, association, company, partnership, Governmental Authority or other entity.

*Pledged Collateral* is defined in Section 1.6(a).

*Post-Petition Claims* means interest, fees, costs, expenses and other charges that pursuant to the First Lien Credit Agreement or the Second Lien Credit Agreement continue to accrue after the commencement of an Insolvency Proceeding, to the extent such interest, fees, expenses and other charges are allowed or allowable under Bankruptcy Law or in the Insolvency Proceeding.

*Proceeds means*

(y)  all 'proceeds,' as defined in Article 9 of the U.C.C., of the Collateral, and

(z)  whatever is recovered when Collateral is sold, exchanged, collected or disposed of, whether voluntarily or involuntarily, including any additional or replacement Collateral provided during any Insolvency Proceeding and any payment or property received in an Insolvency Proceeding on account of any 'secured claim' (within the meaning of Section 506(b) of the Bankruptcy Code or similar Bankruptcy Law).[104]

*Purchase Date* is defined in Section 5.2(a)(5).

*Purchase Event* is defined in Section 5.1(a).

*Purchase Notice* is defined in Section 5.2(a).

*Purchase Obligations* are defined in Section 5.1(a).

*Purchase Price* is defined in Section 5.3.

*Purchasing Creditors* are defined in Section 5.2(a).

*Recovery* is defined in Section 6.6.

*Refinance* means, for any Indebtedness, to refinance, replace, refund or repay, or to issue other Indebtedness in exchange or replacement for such Indebtedness in whole or in part, whether with the same or different lenders, agents or arrangers. 'Refinanced' and 'Refinancing' have correlative meanings.

*Second Lien Adequate Protection Payments* are defined in Section 6.4(b)(4).

*Second Lien Agent* is defined in the Preamble.

*Second Lien Claimholders* are defined in Section 1.3(d).

*Second Lien Collateral* means all of the property of any Grantor, whether real, personal or mixed, as to which a Lien is granted as security for a Second Lien Obligation.

*Second Lien Collateral Documents* means the [security] [Collateral] documents defined in the Second Lien Credit Agreement, and any other documents or instruments granting a Lien on real or personal property to secure a Second Lien Obligation or granting rights or remedies with respect to such Liens.

---

[104] Consider whether this additional clause is necessary or should be used in lieu of negotiated provisions regarding bankruptcy distributions in Section 6.7, '*Reorganization securities*.'

**Second Lien Credit Agreement** is defined in the Preamble.

**Second Lien Lenders** means the 'Lenders' under and as defined in the Second Lien Loan Documents.

**Second Lien Loan Documents** means

(aa) the Second Lien Credit Agreement and the 'Loan Documents' defined in the Second Lien Credit Agreement,

(bb) each other agreement, document, or instrument providing for, evidencing, guaranteeing or securing an Obligation under the Second Lien Credit Agreement, and

(cc) any other document or instrument executed or delivered at any time in connection with the Borrower's Obligations under the Second Lien Credit Agreement, including any guaranty of or grant of Collateral to secure such Obligations, and any inter-creditor or joinder agreement to which holders of Second Lien Obligations are parties, to the extent effective at the relevant time.

**Second Lien Obligations** are defined in Section 1.3(b).

**Standstill Period** is defined in Section 3. 1(b)(1).

**Subsidiary of a Person** means a corporation or other entity a majority of whose voting stock is directly or indirectly owned or controlled by the Person. For these purposes, 'voting stock' of a Person means securities or other ownership interests of the Person having general power under ordinary circumstances to vote in the election of the directors, or other persons performing similar functions, of the Person. References to a percentage or proportion of voting stock refer to the relevant percentage or proportion of the votes entitled to be cast by the voting stock.

**U.C.C**. means the Uniform Commercial Code (or any similar legislation) as in effect in any applicable jurisdiction.

## 8.2  Usages

Unless otherwise stated or the context clearly requires otherwise:

*Agents.* References to the First Lien Agent or the Second Lien Agent will refer to the First Lien Agent or the Second Lien Agent acting on behalf of itself and on behalf of all of the other First Lien Claimholders or Second Lien Claimholders, respectively. Actions taken by the First Lien Agent or the Second Lien Agent pursuant to this Agreement are meant to be taken on behalf of itself and the other First Lien Claimholders or Second Lien Claimholders, respectively.

*Singular and plural.* Definitions of terms apply equally to the singular and plural forms.

*Masculine and feminine.* Pronouns will include the corresponding masculine, feminine and neuter forms.

*Will and shall.* 'Will' and 'shall' have the same meaning.

*Time periods.* In computing periods from a specified date to a later specified date, the words 'from' and 'commencing on' (and the like) mean 'from and including,' and the words 'to,' 'until' and 'ending on' (and the like) mean 'to but excluding.'

*When action may be taken.* Any action permitted under this Agreement may be taken at any time and from time to time.

*Time of day.* All indications of time of day mean [New York City] time.

*Including.* 'Including' means 'including, but not limited to.'

*Or.* 'A or B' means 'A or B or both.'

*Statutes and regulations.* References to a statute refer to the statute and all regulations promulgated under or implementing the statute as in effect at the relevant time. References to a specific provision of a statute or regulation include successor provisions. References to a section of the Bankruptcy Code also refer to any similar provision of Bankruptcy Law.

*Agreements.* References to an agreement (including this Agreement) refer to the agreement as amended at the relevant time.

*Governmental agencies and self-regulatory organizations.* References to a governmental or quasi-governmental agency or authority or a self-regulatory organization include any successor agency, authority or self-regulatory organization.

*Section references.* Section references refer to sections of this Agreement. References to numbered sections refer to all included sections. For example, a reference to Section 6 also refers to Sections 6.1, 6.1(a), etc. References to a section or article in an agreement, statute or regulation include successor and renumbered sections and articles of that or any successor agreement, statute or regulation.

*Successors and assigns.* References to a Person include the Person's permitted successors and assigns.

*Herein, etc.* 'Herein,' 'hereof,' 'hereunder,' and words of similar import refer to this Agreement in its entirety and not to any particular provision.

*Assets and property.* 'Asset' and 'property' have the same meaning and refer to both real and personal, tangible and intangible assets and property, including cash, securities, accounts and general intangibles.

SIGNATURES

First Lien Agent:
[Name of First Lien Agent],
as First Lien Agent by:
Name:
Title:
[Notice Address]
Control Agent:
[Name of Control Agent],
as Control Agent by:
Name:
Title:
[Notice Address]
Second Lien Agent:
[Name of Second Lien Agent],
as Second Lien Agent by:
Name:
Title:
[Notice Address]
Acknowledged and Agreed to by: Borrower:
[Name Of Borrower]
By:
Name: Title:
[Notice of Address]
Holdings:
[Name Of Holdings]
By:

Name: Title:
[Notice Address]
The other Grantors:
[Name of Grantor]
By:
Name: Title:
[Notice Address]
[Name of Grantor]
By:
Name: Title:
[Notice Address]

# Glossary

**Abuse of law** Provision in legislation that intends to capture situations where parts of material are being used to construct (legal) situations that although not conflicting with the literal reading of the law are conflicting with the underlying philosophy and intent of that particular piece of legislation. Often to be found in commercial and tax legislation, but also in civil and criminal codes. The consequence is often that the regulator can look through the designed structure or re-qualify the consequences of the structure.

**Binomial option pricing** One of the methods to value options, based on a generalizable numerical method (based on algorithms that use numerical approximation). It uses a 'discrete-time' (lattice) model of the varying price over time of the underlying financial instruments.

**Black–Scholes formula** Default model to value options based on five critical inputs and a number of assumptions.

**Call option** Financial derivative that allows the holder to buy a certain asset (underlying the option) at a certain price and at a certain time or period in the future.

**Capital protection (soft, hard)** Capital protection is a clause in many fixed-income contracts that points to the fact that the holder is protected against a permanent impairment of the capital invested. Initially that protection was permanent and non-conditional. Over time, variations of soft protection clauses have emerged in contracts whereby the protection is either conditional and/or no longer 100% (but less), hence the term soft protection.

**Cash sweep** Clause in many deeply subordinated mezzanine products. Describes the mandatory use of excess free cash flows to pay down outstanding debt rather than distribute it to shareholders.

**Commercial paper** An unsecured (no collateral), short-term debt instrument issued by a corporation, typically for the financing of accounts receivable, inventories and meeting short-term liabilities. Maturities on commercial paper rarely range any longer than 270 days. In order to issue commercial paper, a firm needs to hold an A-rating, as it is directly issued to investors and not via an investment bank. That implies that there is direct counterparty risk. The instrument is considerably cheaper than issuing normal bonds.

**Contingent convertible bonds** A type of security similar to a normal convertible loan. It also includes an embedded option for convertibility. In this case, however, the convertibility is automatic and the criteria that trigger conversion are pre-defined (e.g., drop in credit rating, stock price falls below a certain level etc.).

**Contingent value rights** A type of right given to shareholders of an acquired company (or a company facing major restructuring) that ensures they receive additional value if a specified event occurs. A contingent value right is similar to an option because it often has an expiration date that relates to the time the contingent event must occur. A firm can, for example, buy another firm where the price is contingent on certain things happening (certain profitability, FDA approval of certain drugs etc.).

**Convertible loan** A subordinated loan that includes the 'option' to convert the instrument into common or preferred stock at a pre-determined conversion rate and conversion time or period. Tends to trigger an interest lower than subordinated loans with a similar risk profile without a convertibility option.

**Covenants** Set of conditions included in a loan/or bond contract indicating that the borrower must fulfill certain conditions (positive covenants) or which forbids the borrower from undertaking certain actions (negative covenants), or which possibly restricts certain activities to circumstances when other conditions are met (maintenance covenance).

**Cross-holding acceleration provision** A contract provision that allows a lender to require a borrower to repay all or part of an outstanding loan if certain requirements are not met (i.e., official default on payment). An acceleration clause outlines the reasons that the lender can demand loan repayment. The cross acceleration points at the fact that the acceleration can cover all loans outstanding (even at the level of subsidiaries), also covering those loans on which the company didn't default.

**Cross-holding default provision** A provision in a bond indenture or loan agreement that puts the borrower in default if the borrower defaults on another obligation.

**Cumulation clause** Clause indicating whether or not interest (loan), dividends (preferred shares) due but not paid will be rolled ('in arrears') over to next year (and whether they will have priority over payments due that next year).

**Debt service coverage ratio** The amount of cash flow available to meet annual interest and principal payments on debt, including sinking fund payments. It is calculated by dividend net operating income/Total net debt. The extensive formula can be framed as: (Annual Net Income + Amortization/Depreciation + Interest Expense + other non-cash and discretionary items (such as non-contractual management bonuses))/(Principal Repayment + Interest payments + Lease payments).

**Deemed dividend** Certain payments made by corporations can be re-qualified by tax authorities if the legal qualification does not match the economic substance underlying the transaction, or where the transaction was constructed with a sole purpose to avoid taxes. Once re-qualified, the payment will be treated and taxed as if it was a dividend, although it isn't a dividend (hence the term deemed dividend).

**Dividend pusher** A 'dividend pusher' is a term (found in the prospectus or loan covenants) whereby the coupon is mandatory if remuneration is given to another specified security or class of securities within a specified period of time (usually known as the 'pusher period').

**Dividend stopper/blocker** A 'dividend stopper' or 'blocker' is a term which states that the issuer will not, within a specified period of time (usually known as the 'stopper period'), pay a coupon on another security or class of securities if it does not pay a dividend on the security in question. A dividend stopper is generally included in the terms of instruments that provide for 'discretionary' returns, for example, a preference share that requires a directors' declaration. The effect of the dividend stopper is that it effectively counteracts the discretion and places pressure on the entity to pay the required return on the discretionary instrument.

**Equity-to-debt swap** Clause in a contract (can also be separate transaction in case of a financial restructuring) that will convert the equity position of a certain shareholder into debt in the company. The clause will determine what type of debt the equity portion will be converted into and how the equity portion will be valued before being converted. Can be put in place to trigger a liquidity moment for investors or as part of a balance sheet restructuring (D/E ratio will change).

**Escrow account** A financial instrument held by a third party on behalf of the other two parties in a transaction. The funds are held by the escrow service until it receives the appropriate written or oral instructions or until obligations have been fulfilled. Securities, funds and other assets can be held in escrow. Often used in a real estate sale, but also in M&A deals and in project finance. Used as a security account when payments or other obligations are not fulfilled by one of the parties involved in the deal. In project finance it is also used to ensure that there is always sufficient liquidity to meet debt holders and other operational expense claims.

**Grace period** Period at the beginning of a loan or bond obligation during which no interest payments are due, or when there are interest payments due during that period, not meeting those payment obligations will not trigger the usual penalties. Very common in mezzanine contracts and can last up to three years.

**High-yield bonds (junk bonds)** A high-paying bond with a lower credit rating than investment-grade corporate bonds, Treasury bonds and municipal bonds. Because of the higher risk of default, these bonds pay a higher yield than investment-grade bonds. Based on the two main credit rating agencies, high-yield bonds carry a rating below 'BBB' from S&P, and below 'Baa' from Moody's. Bonds with ratings at or above these levels are considered investment grade. To compensate for this risk, yields will typically be very high, often equity-like. Also known as 'junk bonds,' although this term is often reserved to only the lower tranches of the non-investment grade spectrum (B+ or lower).

**Incurrence tests** An 'incurrence' covenant is only tested when the issuer takes a voluntary action, for example, when it incurs additional debt or sells an asset. That is in contrast to 'maintenance' covenants which are tested on pre-determined dates (e.g., quarterly or semi-annually). These incurrence tests are often to be found in high-yield bond covenants.

**Inter-creditor agreement** An inter-creditor agreement is an agreement between one or more creditors who have shared interests in a particular borrower. The agreement spells out aspects of their relationship to each other and to the borrower so that, in the event a problem emerges, there will be ground rules in place to handle the situation. The specifics of an inter-creditor agreement vary depending on the borrower, the type of debt and other factors, such as the presence of cosigners.

Inter-creditor agreements provide information about lien positions and security interests. They also discuss the liabilities and rights of the parties involved. For example, a bank might indicate that it has a security interest in a vehicle, which means that another creditor cannot confiscate and sell the vehicle to satisfy a debt, because the bank has the first right to do so. Likewise, an inter-creditor agreement might provide information about liens on other property, such as real estate.

Creditors are not all created equal. An inter-creditor agreement spells out the differences between different creditors and their rights in the event of a bankruptcy or default. The agreement may also include a buy-out clause, which gives one creditor the option of buying out another creditor's debt, usually in response to a trigger event such as a bankruptcy filing.

**Junior debt** Debt that is either unsecured or has a lower priority than another debt claim on the same asset or property. It is a debt that is lower in repayment priority than other debts in the event of the issuer's default. Junior debt is usually an unsecured form of debt, meaning there is no collateral behind the debt.

**Kurtosis** A statistical measure used to describe the distribution of observed data around the mean. A high kurtosis portrays a chart with fat tails and a low, even distribution, whereas a low kurtosis portrays a chart with skinny tails and a distribution concentrated toward the mean.

**Leveraged buy-out** The acquisition of another company using a significant amount of borrowed money (bonds or loans) to meet the cost of acquisition. Often, the assets of the company being acquired are used as collateral for the loans in addition to the assets of the acquiring company. The purpose of leveraged buy-outs is to allow companies to make large acquisitions without having to commit a lot of capital. The financing package includes a variety of senior debt, second lien debt, mezzanine loans and PIK notes as well as a sliver of debt (pre-crisis as low as 10–15%; post-crisis often 20–30%).

**Loan life coverage ratio** A financial ratio used to estimate the ability of the borrowing company to repay an outstanding loan. The Loan Life Coverage Ratio (LLCR) is calculated by dividing the net present value (NPV) of the money available for debt repayment by the amount of senior debt owed by the company or NPV of Cash Flow Available for Debt Service ('CFADS')/Outstanding Debt in the period. The NPV (CFADS) is measured only up until the maturity of the debt tranche. The ratio gives an estimate of the credit quality of the project from a lender's perspective.

**Loan-to-value ratio** A lending risk assessment ratio that financial institutions and other lenders examine before approving a mortgage or real estate finance. Typically, assessments with high LTV ratios are generally seen as higher risk and, therefore, if the mortgage or real estate finance is accepted, the loan will generally cost the borrower more to borrow or he or she will need to purchase mortgage insurance. The LTV ratio is calculated as: Mortgage amount or financing required/Appraised value of property to be bought or built. The ratio can be extended to become the combined loan-to-value ratio which then in the numerator includes all loans raised to finance the purchase or construction of a property.

**Maintenance test** Contractual covenants are either positive (one should do something as a lender) or negative (one should avoid or refrain from something). **Financial covenants** enforce minimum financial performance measures against the borrower, such as: The company must maintain a higher level of current assets than of current liabilities. Broadly speaking, there are two types of financial covenants: maintenance and incurrence.

Under maintenance covenants, issuers must pass agreed-to tests of financial performance such as minimum levels of cash flow coverage and maximum levels of leverage. If an issuer fails to achieve these levels, lenders have the right to accelerate the loan. In most cases, though, lenders will pass on this draconian option and instead grant a waiver in return for some combination of a fee and/or spread increase; a repayment or a structuring concession such as additional collateral or seniority. In the past maintenance tests were associated with leveraged loans and incurrence tests with investment-grade loans and bonds. More recently, the evolution of covenant-light loans has blurred the line. The financial maintenance covenants can be classified as follows:

1. A coverage covenant requires the borrower to maintain a minimum level of cash flow or earnings, relative to specified expenses, most often interest, debt service (interest and repayments) and fixed charges (debt service, capital expenditures and/or rent).
2. A leverage covenant sets a maximum level of debt, relative to either equity or cash flow, with total-debt-to-EBITDA level being the most common. In some cases operating cash flow is used as the divisor. Moreover, some agreements test leverage on the basis of net debt (total less cash and equivalents) or senior debt.
3. A current-ratio covenant requires that the borrower maintain a minimum ratio of current assets (cash, marketable securities, accounts receivable and inventories) to current liabilities (accounts payable, short-term debt of less than one year), but sometimes a 'quick ratio,' in which inventories are excluded from the numerator, is substituted.
4. A tangible-net-worth (TNW) covenant requires that the borrower have a minimum level of TNW (net worth less intangible assets, such as goodwill, intellectual assets, excess value paid for acquired companies), often with a build-up provision, which increases the minimum by a percentage of net income or equity issuance.
5. A maximum-capital-expenditures covenant requires that the borrower limit capital expenditures (purchases of property, plant and equipment) to a certain amount, which may be increased by some percentage of cash flow or equity issuance, but often allowing the borrower to carry forward unused amounts from one year to the next.

**Maturity**  The period of time for which a financial instrument remains outstanding. Maturity refers to a finite time period at the end of which the financial instrument will cease to exist and the principal is repaid with interest. The term is most commonly used in the context of fixed-income investments, such as bonds and deposits.

**Negative amortization**  An increase in the principal balance of a loan caused by making payments that fail to cover the interest due. The remaining amount of interest owed is added to the loan's principal, which ultimately causes the borrower to owe more money. This occurs in PIK loans and in particular in 'pay if you can' and 'Pay when you want' variants.

**Negative pledge**  A negative covenant in an indenture stating that the corporation will not pledge any of its assets if doing so gives the lenders less security. May also be referred to as a 'covenant of equal coverage.' By including a negative pledge clause in a bond indenture, the bondholders of the current bond issue prevent the company from issuing any debt in the future which would jeopardize their current priority claim on the company's assets. Including a negative pledge clause in a bond indenture increases the safety of the bond issue from the investors' perspective, and therefore often allows the bond issuer to borrow funds at a slightly lower interest rate.

**Option**  A derivative product that allows the holder to buy (call) or sell (put) a certain amount of the underlying asset (stock, bonds, can be essentially anything) at a pre-determined price. An option is considered out of the money when the call option has a strike price that is higher than the market price of the underlying asset, or a put option has a strike price that is lower than the market price of the underlying asset. An out-of-the-money option has no intrinsic value, but only possesses extrinsic or time value. As a result, the value of an out-of-the-money option erodes quickly with time as it gets closer to expiry. If it is still out of the money at ex-piry, the option will expire worthless. An option is at the money when an option's strike price is identical to the price of the underlying security. Both call and put options will be simul-taneously 'at the money.' For example, if a stock is trading at 65, then the 65 equity call option is at the money and so is the 65 equity put option for that company. An at-the-money option has no intrinsic value, but may still have time value. Options trading activity tends to be high when options are at the money. An option is 'in the money' when (1) the option's strike price is below the market price of the underlying asset or (2) for a put option, when the strike price is above the market price of the underlying asset. Being in the money does not mean you will profit, it just means the option is worth exercising. This is because the option costs money to buy.

*Pari passu*  (Literally: equal footing) Refers to loans, bonds or classes of shares that have equal rights of payment, or equal seniority. In addition, secondary issues of shares that have equal rights with existing shares rank *pari passu*. Also applicable in situations of bankruptcy or liquidation of company assets.

**PIK notes**  A financial instrument that pays interest or dividends to investors of bonds, notes or preferred stock with additional debt or equity instead of cash. Payment-in-kind securities are attractive to companies which would prefer not to make cash outlays. They are often used in leveraged buy-outs. They tend to pay a relatively high rate of interest but are considered risky. Quite often it is already assumed that the instrument itself at maturity needs to be rolled over, which results in very far out maturities with no interim liquidity. 'Pay if you can' and 'pay if you want' loans as well as 'toggle notes' are variants of the master PIK note instrument.

**Preferred stock**  A security with both equity and debt characteristics. It often has a fixed dividend attached (payment of that dividend is still dependent on the decision of the Board of Directors). It normally carries no voting right and has priority of repayment in case of liqui-dation of the issuing company. Features of the product can be **cumulative or not** (if the divi-dend is not paid in one or multiple years it will go into 'arrears' and will be priority paid the following year or it will be lost (although it was fixed)), **redeemable – or callable** – allowing the issuer to call the instrument (often at a premium to fair value), and **convertible** (indicat-ing the instrument can be converted into a pre-determined amount of common stock (in the issuing company) based on the indicated conversion ratio. The latter feature is often used in private equity cases.

**Profit participating loans**  Loans (often in syndication including multiple lenders) to compa-nies whereby the compensation on the loan is partly or fully dependent ('contingent') on the profitability, solvency or cash-generating ability of the firm. The profit sharing can be based on a % of sales, EBIT, free cash flows, net profit or any other (combination of) criteria. These can be fixed floor negotiated (% or absolute amount based). Loan participations can either be made on a *pari passu* basis with equal risk sharing for all loan participants, or on a senior/subordinated basis, where the senior lender is paid first and the subordinate loan participation paid only if there are sufficient funds left over to make the payments. Such senior/subordinated loan participations can be structured either on a LIFO (Last In First Out) or FIFO (First In First Out) basis. Despite sharing in profits, participating loans do not give rise to an ownership relationship. Participation in losses is contractually excluded. In the event of bankruptcy, providers of participating loans share in the results of the liquidation in the same way as other loan creditors.

**Profit participating rights** Equity investments under company law that entitle the holder to rights over the company's assets (e.g., participation in profits or in the surplus on liquidation, subscription for new stock), but not to the right to be consulted on business decisions. This means that the holder of profit participating rights has no voting or management rights that would permit intervention in the business affairs of the company, but simply a right to a specific monetary claim and no more.

**Put option** Derivative that allows (no obligation) the holder to sell (or exchange) the underlying security at a specific date or time in the future at a pre-determined price (strike price).

**Recapitalization** A recapitalization involves a significant change in the company's balance sheet, removing certain items and replacing them by other securities, in order to make the balance sheet more stable, sustainable and better positioned to deal with the economic situation the firm is in or the market it is active in. There are a number of types of recapitalization: (1) leveraged recapitalization where the company raises bonds with a view towards buying back its own shares (replacing equity by debt). Arguments to conduct a leveraged recapitalization are: (1) desire of current shareholders to partially exit the investment, (2) providing support of falling share price, (3) disciplining a company that has excessive cash, (4) protection from a hostile takeover, (5) rebalancing positions within a holding company or (6) exit of one of the shareholders while the firm remains a 'going concern.' (2) dividend recapitalization: in such a recapitalization the debt that is raised goes to existing shareholders (through paying a dividend) without one shareholder exiting the firm. The debt raised is to fund the dividend so that the shareholder can realize value without exiting. Raising debt to pay dividends may have a minor or major impact on the company's balance sheet depending on the size of the one-off dividend payment made.

**Redeemability** For fixed income instruments, it refers to the act of an (or clause allowing the) issuer repurchasing a bond at or before maturity. Redemption is made at the face value of the bond unless it occurs before maturity, in which case the bond is bought back at a premium to compensate for lost interest. The issuer has the right to redeem the bond at any time, although the earlier the redemption takes place, the higher the premium usually is. This provides an incentive for companies to do this as rarely as possible.

**Redemption blocker clause** Term included in many discretionary securities which states that, following a deferred coupon, the issuer will not redeem (or call) other securities of equal or lower ranking until coupons have been resumed and paid for a certain period of time (usually 12 months) on the security in question.

**Redemption clause** Clause that can be found in bonds or loans dealing with the act of an issuer repurchasing a bond at or before maturity. Redemption is made at the face value of the bond unless it occurs before maturity, in which case the bond is bought back at a premium to compensate for lost interest. The issuer has the right to redeem the bond at any time, although the earlier the redemption take place, the higher the premium usually is. This provides an incentive for companies to do this as rarely as possible.

**Second lien loan** These are essentially senior secured obligations, and therefore differ from typical unsecured and subordinated products in the mezzanine product group. In the event of a bankruptcy or liquidation, the assets used by the company as security would first be provided to the first lien secured lenders as repayment of their borrowings. To the extent that the value of the assets is sufficient to satisfy the company's obligations to the first lien secured lenders, any additional proceeds from the sale of the pledged assets would then be made available to the second lien lenders as repayment of the second lien loan. In contrast to unsecured debt, second lien loans receive a pledge of specific assets of the borrower. Although the second lien loan's security interest is subordinated to the first lien loan's interest in the pledged assets of the company, the ranking of first lien and second lien loans is the same (*'pari passu'*) in the event the pledged assets are not sufficient to satisfy the outstanding borrowings.

**Senior debt** Those instruments that hold (contractual) priority over other non-secured or junior portions of the debt the company holds. In most cases, senior debt is backed by collateral that the holder can turn to in case the issuer defaults on its payments under the senior debt.

**Silent participation** The 'silent' participation is closer in legal form to a stockholding than are subordinated or participating loans. The distinguishing feature of this form of financing is that one or more persons take an equity stake in a company, but without assuming any liability to the company's creditors. The typical 'silent' participation affects only the company's internal affairs and is not apparent to outside observers. The details of participation in profits or losses, involvement in the company's management, supervision and information rights etc. can be structured flexibly. A major feature of this type of financing is that the silent investor participates in losses. However, it is possible to remove this feature partially or completely.

**Skew(ness)** Describes the asymmetry from the normal distribution in a set of statistical data. Skewness can come in the form of 'negative skewness' or 'positive skewness,' depending on whether data points are skewed to the left (negative skew) or to the right (positive skew) of the data average. Skewness is extremely important to finance and investing. Most sets of data, including stock prices and asset returns, have either positive or negative skew rather than following the balanced normal distribution (which has a skewness of zero). By knowing which way data are skewed, one can better estimate whether a given (or future) data point will be more or less than the mean. Essentially, it tells investors how the risk distribution occurs in a particular investment or asset class and consequently how much risk is hidden in the tail risks. That is particularly important as our quantitative models for risk as we know them are not extremely well equipped to measure extremely high or low probability risks.

**Step-up rate loans** A bond that pays an initial coupon rate for the first period, and then a higher coupon rate for the following periods. A step-up bond is one in which subsequent future coupon payments are received at a higher, pre-determined amount than previous or current periods. These bonds are known as step-ups because, quite literally, the coupon 'steps up' from one period to another. For example, a five-year bond may pay a 5% coupon for the first two years of its life and a 7% coupon for the final three years. Such a bond would most likely offer a coupon below current rates at the time of inception, compensating the seller for offering higher coupons in coming periods.

**Subordination** Indicates that the payment due under the instrument is subordinated in right of payment to the issuer senior (bank) financing. The holders of this instrument will only be receiving interest payments or principal repayments if all other senior lenders have been satisfied. Subordination can be contractual, structural or effective. Contractual means it is made explicit in the contract that the instrument is subordinated. Structural means that it has a maturity and position in the debt portfolio of a company that, although not contractually subordinated, will only receive payments after all other senior lenders have been paid (no interest payments and maturity is longer than for senior loans). Effective subordination happens when there is no contractual or structural subordination but where the implications of other features will automatically lead to a de facto effective subordination (e.g. given other guarantees that were provided by the company to other lenders).

**Subrogation** The right for a party (historically mainly an insurer) to pursue a third party that caused an insurance loss to the insured. This is done as a means of recovering the amount of the claim paid to the insured for the loss. In the context of mezzanine it is often used in the inter-creditor agreement where the mezzanine lenders want to ensure that they can step into the shoes ('subrogate') of the senior lenders (once they have been satisfied) and enforce repayment of their claims. If subrogation is not included in the ICA, mezzanine holders can find it hard to enforce their claim when seniors don't lift the standstill period and clawback clause.

**Tenor** The amount of time left for the repayment of a loan or contract or the initial term length of a loan. Tenor can be expressed in years, months or days. Tenor is sometimes used interchangeably with 'maturity,' although tenor is not often used to describe the terms of fixed-income instruments such as government bonds and corporate bonds. Instead, non-standardized contracts like insurance policies and bank loans tend to be described in terms of tenor.

**Thin capitalization** In general terms, it refers to every position whereby a company has used a lot of gearing (i.e., leverage) and consequently has much more debt than equity on its books. But more specifically, it refers to specific parts of the tax code that limit the ability of the issuer to deduct the interest due on loans that exceed a certain (pre-determined) gearing level. The description of those gearing levels differs per country, and absolute levels differ as well and are often a combination of multiple criteria.

**Unitranche loan** A type of debt that combines senior and subordinated debt into one debt instrument; it is usually used to facilitate a leveraged buy-out although in recent years it has been used in stand-alone positions as well. The borrower would pay one interest rate to one lender, and the rate would usually fall between the rate for senior debt and subordinated notes. The unitranche debt instrument was created to simplify debt structure and accelerate the acquisition process. Unitranche lending has its contractual variations, because the loan has often become split in recent years between secured and unsecured instruments (to satisfy different type of investors – i.e., a type of tranching of the unitranche). The interest rate benefit of a secured debt instrument is at least partially obscured by the increased risk attached to the unsecured portion of the instrument. A potential benefit is the fact that the pledges provided for the secured part are further available once a part of the secured portion has been amortized, so the product creates a gliding pledge to also cover the unsecured portion when time advances towards maturity.

**Volatility** A statistical measure of the dispersion of returns for a given security or market index. Volatility can either be measured by using the standard deviation or variance between returns from that same security or market index (for example, the beta for stocks). In other words, volatility refers to the amount of uncertainty or risk about the size of changes in a security's value. A higher volatility means that a security's value can potentially be spread out over a larger range of values. This means that the price of the security can change dramatically over a short time period in either direction. A lower volatility means that a security's value does not fluctuate dramatically, but changes in value at a steady pace over a period of time. It is often claimed that the higher the volatility, the riskier the security. That statement is based on a wrong understanding of the difference between 'volatility' and 'risk.' Risk is a function of time while volatility is constant. **Volatility** is a measure for variation in price of a financial instrument over time. Historic volatility is derived from time series of past market prices. Volatility does not measure the direction of price changes, merely their dispersion. The **implied volatility** of an option contract is the volatility of the price of the underlying security that is implied by the market price of the option based on an option pricing ('BS') model. An investment class's volatility is therefore constant. Risk, however, is not constant. It is a function of time. For stocks, time and risk are inversely related. Price versus value underlies the misconception.

**Warrants** A (derivative) security that gives the holder the right to purchase securities (usually equity) from the issuer at a specific price within a certain time frame. The main difference between warrants and call options is that warrants are issued and guaranteed by the company, whereas options are exchange instruments and are not issued by the company. Also, the lifetime of a warrant is often measured in years, while the lifetime of a typical option is measured in months. The instrument can occur independently or as a subchapter of an (unsecured) loan or bond instrument.

# Case Guidance/Solutions

The case studies included in this book were predominantly included to facilitate understanding of the theory discussed in the respective chapters and to accommodate enhanced understanding of some of the practicalities and technicalities that surround the implementation of mezzanine products in different types of situations and settings. Given that perspective, the analysis of the issues is more important than the answers to the questions posed at the end of the cases. Nevertheless, it might help some readers to have some level of direction provided when navigating through the cases or as an after-read. The following feedback on (most of) the cases will try to do exactly that. I have tried to make the feedback more exploratory and orientation-based rather than prescriptive in nature. That makes sense, as most mezzanine deals are negotiated solutions. Therefore, there are no real answers, and clearly not one correct answer, but merely more optimal and less optimal outcomes given the complexities and technicalities of a certain case. That understanding was observed when drafting the following guidance on the cases.

## KRATOS ACQUISITION FINANCE

The central question in this case relates to the financing of the acquisition by Kratos of the Odin company. However, to understand the intrinsic risk in the acquisition we need to have a closer look at the industry, the expected synergies etc. before looking at the financing question.

The bearings industry is essentially a mature, commoditized and, to a large degree, consolidated industry despite the many refined, diverse and technically ever-improving applications in recent years. However, this hadn't really resulted in top-line growth or much new product development for that matter. That has led to a focus on cost savings which has impacted innovation dynamics in the industry. From that perspective, the proposed transaction makes sense for a company and industry looking for operational efficiencies. There was both the opportunity for economies of scale and cross-selling across the different distribution channels (little product overlap but customer overlap significant) to the market within, forcing Kratos to step away from its LT strategy.

The estimated 80 million in annualized savings equates to about 480 million as expressed as perpetuity. An acquisition of this size does not normally fit in a strategy which includes capital investment reduction and cash preservation but ultimately it comes down to the price paid and the cash flows (and timing of those) the target can produce. Complementary product groups and synergies make Odin more valuable to Kratos than to its current owner, where it has become somewhat of a secondary asset rather than anything else.

Re-taking the financial projections for Odin from the case and adding the margin structure provides the following chart:

| In USD | 2008 | 2009 | 2010 | 2011 | 2012 | 2013E | 2014E | 2015E | 2016E | 2017E |
|---|---|---|---|---|---|---|---|---|---|---|
| **Net sales** | 1,239.5 | 1,239.5 | 1,161 | 1,004.3 | 1,204 | 1,282 | 1,365.3 | 1,454.1 | 1,548.6 | 1,649.2 |
| **Operating income** | 137.2 | 145.7 | 172.6 | 102.1 | 85.2 | 90.7 | 96.6 | 102.9 | 109.5 | 116.7 |
| **Sales growth (%)** | | 0.0 | −6.3 | −13.5 | 19.9 | 6.5 | 6.5 | 6.5 | 6.5 | 6.5 |
| **Operating margin (%)** | 11.1 | 11.8 | 14.9 | 10.2 | 7.1 | 7.1 | 7.1 | 7.1 | 7.1 | 7.1 |
| **Capex** | 36.7 | 30.1 | 25.2 | 23.4 | 23.8 | 25.3 | 26.9 | 28.7 | 30.6 | 32.5 |
| **Depreciation expense** | 28.6 | 25.2 | 21.8 | 19.3 | 21.0 | 21.8 | 23.2 | 25.6 | 28.8 | 32.9 |

The projected margins outlook will change somewhat, where in recent years Odin's margins were much higher than those of Kratos. A more modest estimation of margins is required going forward. When performing a valuation of Odin, I guess a two-step approach is recommended. First, a valuation of Odin on a stand-alone basis and then afterwards a valuation of Odin as integrated in Kratos (recognizing those discussed synergies). During the first step, it is recommended to use the WACC of Odin on a stand-alone basis. For consistency purposes that can also be done in step 2. However, it can be claimed that the long-term cost of funding of Kratos going forward will not be the current cost of funding of Odin. Although that might be true (as it can be perfectly imagined that the acquisition debt will be paid down in an accelerated way, shifting the D/E relation in the long run more towards the optimal capital structure), we are valuing the integrated businesses today with the data we can observe. If the changes are expected to be significant, a valuation model can bring in different costs of funding which differ between the growth and terminal period or even on a per-year basis. Within the context of this case guidance we have not observed any difference within the valuation model.

But, let's not forget about the essentials here. And that is the issue of the impact of financing the transaction and its collateral impact on the balance sheet of Kratos as well as the bond rating of the company. And the starting point pre-transaction was a BBB rating (and that was already borderline) which wasn't all that great to begin with. It is very likely that Kratos will lose its investment-grade status when pushing too much debt into the financing mix. Too much equity, however, will not be appreciated by the existing shareholders, which subsequently will have its impact on the stock price, which was already priced below fair value. In this case too much debt would mean a 100% debt financing arrangement, while a 50% debt/50% equity mix would likely justify Kratos keeping its BBB rating, and thereby preserving financial flexibility going forward.

Re-taking the financial ratio chart of the chart, we can assess the financing implications of this deal.

| | AAA | AA | A | BBB | BB | B | CCC | Kratos (current) | Combined with 100% debt | Combined with 50% |
|---|---|---|---|---|---|---|---|---|---|---|
| **EBIT interest coverage (x)** | 23.4 | 13.3 | 6.3 | 3.9 | 2.2 | 1 | 0.1 | 3.51 | 2.27 | 3.32 |
| **EBITDA interest coverage (x)** | 25.3 | 16.9 | 8.5 | 5.4 | 3.2 | 1.7 | 0.7 | 8.16 | 4.21 | 6.17 |
| **EBITDA/sales (%)** | 23.4 | 24 | 18.1 | 15.5 | 15.4 | 14.7 | 8.8 | 3.1 | 4.4 | 4.4 |
| **Total debt/capital (%)** | 5.0 | 35.9 | 42.6 | 47.0 | 57.7 | 75.1 | 91.7 | 43.1 | 66.7 | 46.0 |

Given the fact that the Kratos stock was considered as trading below fair value, issuing new stock to finance the transaction would be considered 'dilutive.' If the acquisition were to generate positive cash flows relatively early, the stock price would benefit, producing a much better position to issue new equity based on higher valuation levels. That is exactly what happened when the acquisition was announced – both the stock price of the buyer and the seller went up, which is exceptional.

The acquisition price was settled at US$840 million (of which US$700 million was in cash and US$140 million in Kratos shares, with a lockup period for the buyer to avoid undue selling pressure). The cash position was financed by public, private and bank debt and it also used the cash proceeds of a further rights issue for the amount of US$165 million. A few months after the deal was done, Kratos organized a second rights issue for an amount of US$55 million to reduce part of the acquisition debt (the junior portion).

The sources and uses of the transaction are listed below:

| Sources | In USD | Uses | In USD |
|---|---|---|---|
| 500 million revolver | 223 | Cash to buyer | 696 |
| Senior unsecured notes | 250 | Common stock to buyer | 140 |
| A/R facility | 125 | Fees & expenses | 40 |
| Common stock issuance | 165 | Refinancing existing debt | 27 |
| Common stock to seller | 140 | | |
| **Total** | **903** | | **903** |

A few words on the acquisition price – which, as noted, was US$840 million – although it is not directly instrumental in the mezzanine topic here. Taking into account the projections, the expected cost of integration and the projected synergies and the cost of funding details provided in the case, one arrives at a stand-alone valuation of approximately US$816 million for Odin and an integrated valuation (post-synergy) valuation of approximately US$1,243.2 million. Conservatively, only cost savings and margins were taken into account as drivers. For example, what has been ignored is Kratos's ability to increase sales with complementary product lines from Odin. Taking all this into account, the US$840 million was nicely negotiated by Kratos. It was Castor's main objective to free up capital to focus on high-margin innovative products rather than to maximize the valuation in this case. The alternative cost of capital was therefore different for Castor, leaving Kratos set for an attractive valuation proposition.

The key value drivers behind that with–without synergies valuation gap lie, to a large degree, in the cost savings which account for almost 65% of the valuation differential. Nevertheless, given what we know about the industry, the intrinsic risk in the deal can be qualified as 'medium' for the mezzanine providers. Their stake in the total portfolio mix was significant, also because the room for additional senior debt was limited given the balance sheet of Odin/Castor pre-integration. Senior lenders always have limited enthusiasm about financing share acquisitions, as they consider shares weaker collateral versus the normal PPE ('Plant property and equipment') collateral. That has made the share of mezzanine larger than in normal transactions. The fact that the senior debt would be repaid with the second rights issued a few months down the road, forces most of the LT industry and performance risk on the mezzanine lenders pretty much on par with the equity holders. Compensation in the ballpark of the (expected) ROE for the combined firm should be sought.

# JJ BARS & RESTAURANTS

This case deals with a traditional mezzanine investment with the exception that it serves the purpose of fueling a rather aggressive growth strategy. In that sense it can be compared with a growth equity investment.

To analyze the fundamental risk of such an investment, a preliminary strengths and weaknesses analysis can be performed, taking into account the intrinsic characteristics of the restaurant industry.

| Strengths (company specific) | Weaknesses |
|---|---|
| • Good relationship with and amongst existing shareholders | • Sober to negative free cash flows due to growth nature of the business |
| • Diversification plans | • Currently stores are concentrated in part of Europe (mainly The Netherlands) |
| • Plans for food cost controls | • Limited economies of scale in purchasing due to complicated menus |
| • Mechanisms to leverage fixed costs across lunch and dinner | • Relatively high labor costs (in The Netherlands but also other parts of Europe) |
| • Good reputation within industry | • Health incidents are a permanent issue in the resto-business |
| • Strong management team which holds quite some shareholding in the company | • Uncertainty where the current shareholders want to be in the longer term – are they looking to exit etc.? |
| • Strong store management and attractive opening hours | |
| • Relatively low average capex | |
| • Low pre-opening expenses relative to industry | |

| Strengths (industry specific) | Weaknesses |
|---|---|
| • Reasonable to good industry growth, at least for the casual dining segment of the market (baby boomers, rise of dual-income households, and increased willingness to pay for convenience food) | • Food safety issues |
| | • Public sentiment (sugar, obesity, horsemeat incident, labeling and info distribution etc.) |
| • The casual dining segment, although fragmented has experienced the entrance of chains | • No real proof that concept will thrive in other European countries with other cultural and gastronomical preferences |

A critical open question is really about whether the resto-concept will survive a roll-out to other European countries. And if so, can it happen in a financially sustainable way? Although there is an African revival going on in Europe it is unclear whether the firm can leverage on that, as patriotic sentiment can cancel that effect out. Also, casual dining is perceived somewhat differently in different European countries.

From a financial technical point of view, the fact that the company is considering mezzanine goes back to the fact that the existing shareholders, and in particular the founder, are unwilling to dilute their stake further in this next round of financing. But in risk terms, growth financing is something that carries an equity risk and should therefore to a large degree (50% or so of total financing need) be financed with equity. Mezzanine is temporary equity encapsulated in a debt instrument. Consequently, mezzanine lenders are more focused on capital preservation and return generation through interest payment than equitable upside. Although there is variation in risk appetite amongst mezzanine providers, the fact that there is significant equity risk absorbed by mezzanine products (there is already quite some senior debt on the books of the company) might encourage one to conclude that a pure interest component will not suffice to cover the risk embedded in the product. Hence the discussion with respect to the warrants to complement the interest income and enhance the total return on the investment. It should be clear that increasing the interest component can lead to default or breach of covenants by the firm in a high-growth or too-slow-growth scenario going forward.

It is very likely that the new store opening will not generate actual FCFs for quite some time. That implies that one has to rely on the FCFs generated by existing stores to help support the payments of interim interest due (hence the reason why normally these kinds of projects would be largely equity financed). The good news is that mezzanine instruments (and mezzanine investors in general as well) are very flexible – that shows in the conditions of the proposed structure which includes:

- 1% commitment fee due upfront and 1.5 % drawdown fee at the moment of each draw.
- The 10% coupon will be paid annually on the accumulated capital.
- The 4% PIK coupon suggested will enhance the overall return on the investment without burdening the cash flow position of the company.
- Capturing part of the upside through the 3% warrant (also without burdening the cash flow position of the firm).

This review triggers the question with respect to the total return on the investment. A few words upfront: Although the BS method to value options can be used in this case, often investors will value the warrants based on the value of the equity stake they will receive after conversion of the warrants (perceived exit value of the obtained equity stake). That is most likely to happen in very early stage companies or where there is no clear path to exit. In this case, using the BS method will not help the investor to achieve a target IRR where the exit valuation does. This all has to do with the fact that under the BS method the option is valued assuming an at-the-money option position. In this case that would mean that the stock price and the exercise price of the warrant would be equal (€2.5 per share). Since the strike price at exit will be assumed to be higher than the stock price at entry (factoring in a successful rollout of the new stores), it helps to enhance the returns on the instrument.

The exit multiple will normally be a function of the EBITDA multiple at exit (year 2017). In this case it is best to use the EBITDA before POE. The multiple is often market driven and in this case will hover around 11x. That will yield the enterprise value. Deducting total debt will provide the equity value on which the 3% warrant exposure can be applied. That will provide the warrant value after conversion in absolute Euro terms. That value combined with the repayment schedule for the loan will allow you to calculate the IRR and the cash-on-cash return (or time money back) on the investment. The fact that EBITDA after POE is used will imply that more borrowing is needed under the revolved facility to open the same number of stores. Lower earnings and higher revolver interest costs account for the difference in return between the management case and base-case scenario. It should be noted that when public multiples are used, a liquidity discount should/could be applied which, in this case, could be as high as 30% given the company characteristics and the industry it is operating in, and given the level of illiquidity and non-comparability of disclosure. The question can emerge of which multiples to use. It can be noted that there might be an issue arising here. On the one hand, a pure comparison with pan-European or global resto-chains lacks a fundamental justification. On the other hand, using national resto-chain multiples (if they exist and are listed) would fail to capture the essential dynamics of the investments, i.e., going European with the business.

# POLAND A2

There are two major issues in this case that can be addressed. The first embodies the identification and allocation of the different project risks. The second, which concerns us most here, is the financing issue and in particular the fact that the senior lenders are looking for €60–90 million in additional equity for them to feel comfortable continuing with the deal.

## 1. Identification and assessment of risk

Identification and assessment of risk is extremely important and interesting. Nevertheless it is of a secondary nature within the context of a mezzanine book. We therefore limit ourselves to the assessment methodology for risk and the classification of risks as they occurred in the case.

In terms of assessment of risks there are only two critical questions:

1. What is the probability of a certain risk occurring?
2. If that risk occurs, what is going to be the economic impact on the project and how will it emerge?

From that perspective, one could conclude in this case that the major risk categories are: construction risk (completion on schedule and on budget), political/sovereign risk (guarantee, currency devaluation, legal system ...), financial risk (interest and exchange rate), operating risk (revenue-generating formula risk) and force majeure.

Within this context, the traffic risk analysis is essential. In the analysis provided in the case both indicators (1) ability to pay toll and (2) growth of traffic volume are related to GDP growth. The financial model provided models the inputs in line with estimations of GDP growth in the coming 10 years and beyond. This is critical and in practice prone to many errors. The simple fact that we often need two post-readings to get right the GDP of the quarter just finished shows it can be easily understood that projecting GDP growth 5 and 10 years from now needs to happen with an understanding of implicit incorrectness even when based on past data.

The same is pretty much true for expected inflation as it is the plug variable between 'real' and 'nominal' GDP growth. This will, in its turn, have an impact on toll rates and expected volumes of traffic. It further explains the need for stress testing of these models, something that is unfortunately outside the scope of a mezzanine book.

The main risks per category can be classified (in summary) as:

| Operating risk | Political risk |
|---|---|
| Revenue and traffic volume assumptions (H) | Creeping expropriation through taxes, fees and other restrictions (H) |
| Acceptance of toll rate levels (H) | |
| Force majeure (L) | Reliability and stability of legal system (predictability) (H) |
| Cash leakage and toll enforcement/avoidance (L) | |
| Service and equipment maintenance (L) | Force majeure (M) |
| Major maintenance (L) | Direct expropriation through 'end of concession' (M) |
| | Trade restrictions (L) |
| | Competing toll roads etc. (L) |

(continued)

| Financial risk | Construction risk |
|---|---|
| Forex risk (Euro-Zloty) (H) | Delays and cost overruns when constructing (M) |
| Senior debt service (H) | Obtaining permits (M) |
| Refinancing risk (H) | Land acquisition issues (L) |
| Interest rate risk (M) | Ancillary construction (L) |
| Funding risk of (construction) (L) | Supply of raw materials and equipment (L) |
| Cash control (L) | Design risk (L) |
| Non-convertibility of Polish Zloty (L) | Environmental risk (L) |
| | Contractor default (L) |
| | Force majeure (L) |
| | Future capex levels (L) |

It is indicated in brackets whether the occurrence of the risk has a high (H), medium (M) or low (L) impact on the financial model assessed through the DSCR (Debt Service Coverage Ratio).

The DSCR, in this case, is the key financial ratio to assess how stretched the financing is versus the ambitious, normal and basic scenario models in terms of toll rates and volumes per category of traffic.

## 2. The financing mix for the project

There are essentially a number of technical options on the table to get out of the deadlock, but not all of them are realistic. Below are the options listed and, where necessary, discussed:

(a) Increase the guarantee of the Polish government

Increasing the government's guarantee is very unlikely to happen, because it would directly impact the country's sovereign rating and creditworthiness. The €800 million was put in place to cover the amounts due on the zero-coupon bonds at maturity. Replacing senior debt with junior debt will leave a certain amount of unsecured effectively 'exposed' which seems very unrealistic, although it would increase the coverage ratio in the early years but increase it significantly in later years. Also, interest rate increases could become problematic as the floating interest rate could, when increasing, make the total amount due exceed the €800 million of the government guarantee (or shorten the maturity on the bonds which will once again put pressure on the coverage ratios in earlier years).

(b) Inject the requested €60–90 million in additional equity

Bringing in additional equity (thereby replacing a certain portion of senior debt) is unlikely as well. Increasing the equity with €60 million would mean that the sponsors' equity accounts for 38% (from 24.4% initially) of the total funding, which is far beyond industry practices. The expected returns are already in single-digit territory and increasing equity would further deteriorate that position. On top of this, returns for shareholders are only expected to come in as of 2018, and with such a long waiting period before shareholders' distributions commence, it is very unlikely that the sponsors would be willing to put in some more up-front capital.

(c) Convince the bankers (senior lenders) to accept the deal as it is

    Good luck with that!

(d) Work something out with the European Investment Bank

    The European Investment Bank doesn't normally provide unsecured loans and is only willing to roll-up interests due during the construction period; it also requires *pari passu* treatment with the other senior lenders. What could be targeted, however, is a situation in which the EIB rolls over the interest due until after the senior lenders have been satisfied (17 years), which means that it takes a 'de facto' subordinated position without offering contractually a subordinated loan (which would essentially not be within its mandate).

(e) Extend the maturities on the unsecured loans

    Another option would be to extend the unsecured bonds (those that indirectly are guaranteed by the government). There are a number of complications here that make the option more unlikely than not:

1. Extending the maturity of the unsecured bonds pushes maturity beyond normal industry standards.
2. The government needs to be willing to carry forward the guarantee for such a long time.
3. One needs to convince the shareholders to extend the maturity of both shareholders' loans as well for the same period, if not the unsecured bonds would become inherently more subordinated (as the shareholders' loans would both mature before the unsecured bonds, which although being *pari passu* would make the unsecured bonds more deeply subordinated) and more risky, which they would never accept.

Although the solution can technically work, it is unlikely to arrange such a complex structure as this, involving so many parties in such a short time span. If one applied a DSCR to the toll revenue sheet in the case, one would observe that the range would hover between 1.5 and 1.7 depending on the period analyzed (that is obviously after deducting an appropriate amount of net working capital from the indicated operating profit). Although it was based on a 50% capture rate, it demonstrates the enormous sensitivity in the model, partly explaining the nervousness of the bankers involved in the deal.

P.S. Option (d) is what eventually happened in reality, partly due to the fact that the EIB was willing to play ball and the fact that the concession offer expiration was looming six weeks out, which forced a somewhat quick and dirty type of deal.

The crux in this case comes down to the fact that if a downside scenario (lower toll rates, lower traffic volume) emerges, the senior debt maturity needs to be extended from 13 to 17 years. Extending the maturity will then create issues vis-à-vis the junior (zero-coupon) debt. Either that means that the junior debt matures (after 13 years) before the senior debt, which is unacceptable to the bankers as that would make their claim de facto subordinated. Or the junior debt matures after the extended 17-year senior maturity (after 18 years), which is not feasible either as there is no real market for Zloty bonds with such maturities. The fact that interest rates in the market are rising puts additional pressure on the models as it reduces the DSCR, which can only be solved within the model by extending the maturities of both the senior loans and the junior debt.

It is clear that the senior lenders use the most downbeat scenario model, which demonstrates the stress there is cash flow wise on the senior debt repayment schedule.

The fact that the junior debt position was arranged with the EIB had many benefits to all parties involved. To begin with, the government, and although the EIB would consume the whole €800 million in guarantee as well, it is clear that the benefit for the government is that it doesn't interfere with the capital-raising and creditworthiness issues of the Polish government in the international capital markets (sovereign debt issuance program). Having a supranational lender involved provides credibility to the other lenders that the project is bankable. Also, the fact that even if there were to be a default on the project later down the road, the EIB would prioritize the LT development of Poland and its development objective over pure financial interest and that in contrast to pure Western bond investors in the international capital markets. The EIB loan of €275 million was structured with deferral of all interest with a maturity of 17 years (equivalent to a zero-coupon bond). The bond was not subordinated but had a clause included that it could not be repaid before the senior lenders were repaid.

Despite the EIB loans the senior lenders required an additional 60 million equity investment coming from the sponsors, of which they received 32 million in contingent equity. To counterbalance that, the senior lenders offered an extended 17 years' maturity, subject to a cash sweep provision.

The final funding portfolio became:

1. €235 million of equity and shareholder loans.
2. €235 million senior debt.
3. €275 million in mezzanine loans.

# BUILDING AND OPERATING A WIND PARK

The purpose when building a capital structure is to provide a robust LT structure that has the potential to take into account the variability of certain pre-determined variables, in this case being predominantly the wind speed (in operational terms). Obviously, the spectrum of risks is much wider, as discussed in the case.

The choice for a straightforward mezzanine subordinated loan is logical. The subordination implies additional risks, but there is no direct reason to believe that there is an equity or value upside to be captured. Pricing of energy is determined, projections for energy generation are pretty stable (overall in the industry as well) and the PPA agreement includes 3% growth per annum, so the upside is truly limited. Other mezzanine products are of no use in a setting as described in the case. Highly exceptionally a preferred equity position could be considered, but the fixed dividend payout could be problematic. I have experienced situations where the mezzanine lenders have been alternatively looking for an upside through an interest component (%) that was linked to EBITDA (profit participating loan), but which was outright rejected by the sponsors of the projects, as it would de-stabilize the repayment capacity, and also that of the senior lenders. The fixed pricing range here will be a function of the sovereign spread, the amortization period and on the inclusion of a bullet tranche or payment on top of the position of the mezzanine loan in the cash flow or project waterfall as described.

Critical in this case is the ability to reflect the sensitivities of the project in the cash flow waterfall. That is very critical in pretty much each project finance environment as it embodies how stable the repayment schedule is and under what set of assumptions. The straightforward mezzanine loan will be priced significantly higher than the senior lenders in this case (300–400 bps) despite the relatively large portion of equity contributed.

Further aspects that will provide a stabilized project are the set of contractual arrangements which invariably will include:

- Power purchasing agreement ('PPA').
- EPC-contract for the engineering, procurement and construction of the infrastructure required.
- Operation & maintenance agreement ('O&M').
- Warranty, maintenance and service agreement ('WMSA').
- Transmission agreement.
- Carbon emission reduction purchase agreement.
- Inter-creditor agreement.
- The accounts agreement spelling out the project waterfall (and the management of the debt service reserve account ('DSRA').
- Land lease agreement (in independent power projects).

This is all on top of the financial contracts, share pledge, share retention and insurance related agreements.

The covenants in a project environment tend to include, besides the typical positive and negative covenants, project reporting covenants and the environmental and social impact covenant and reporting.

# FINANCING A REAL ESTATE COMPANY IN THE CEE REGION

This case requires a significant level of discretionary judgment and is not really based on hard classifications. Nevertheless, the opening question is very clear: is the interest rate on the instrument of Euribor + 650 basis points sufficient to cover the implicit risk the instrument carries? A combined look at the current ratio, DSCR and the debt/EBITDA shows a picture that is improving but from a very low and distressed base. There are some verifiable arguments that can help cutting through the fog in terms of what the short-to-mid-term future will look like for the firm and the economies in the CEE region and in particular the countries in which they are active.

Facts include the diversification of the firm in terms of countries and sectors (residential, office, …) of the real estate market as well as the fact that they have been able to offload some of the historic portfolio or at least turn it into income-generating assets. The diversification over multiple countries in the wider CEE region was a good call, as, since the crisis, the divergence in economic performance has become more accentuated between those countries than was the case before the 2008 great recession.

The next question then becomes how stable are the projections provided by the company? It is fair to say, although it is in general terms only, that it is extremely sensitive to make predictions about how the real estate market will evolve from here onwards in the region. The

CEE region as a whole is still, to a large degree, dependent on the performance of the Euro-bloc and its exports to that region. Ukraine is a mixed bag, as the eastern part of the country is still economically and politically tilted towards Russia. Great unknowns in this respect will be how long it will take to clean up (the remaining part of) the excess inventory in the real estate market, and even more important, how much liquidity organically can be created in each of those countries that will partly replace the relentless flow of cheap credit inflows those countries experienced before 2008 and which had clearly contributed to the valuation bubble formation.

Another feature less highlighted in the case deals with the fact that a massive amount of real estate projects were halted in 2008–2009, which now are being completed or have just been completed. That often happened because now at least those projects could be sold and generate (some level of) cash inflow, whereas if they were not completed, downpayments already made would have to be reimbursed, which would put enormous stress on the RE companies and wipe out the equity the RE firms had in those projects as well as the fact that it would trigger a de-fault on the bank debt in those projects, in turn often triggering an acceleration of those loans and/or, worse, a cross-default holding on the total debt of the firm, and subsequently a cross-acceleration.

In short, it seems that the interest component, although high, does not offset some of the qualitative risks in the case. Consequently, the convertible loan option might be appropriate to take advantage of some of the upside, which there clearly is given the low valuations in place based on the economic fundamentals of the case. That value cannot be derived from a higher interest rate, as the CF projections clearly demonstrate that there is limited debt capacity available above the intended interest rate. A step-up rate loan could have worked well in this scenario, but raises the question about the over-reliance longer term on the distant cash flows which, as argued, are very difficult to predict in this case as they as they are not only dependent on multiple variables but also variables that interact. A convertible loan seems to be preferred over a step-up loan.

You can't really protect against some of the market risks intrinsic in this case. However, it is possible to protect against some of the financial implications caused by those market risks. The most straightforward is a debt-to-equity swap if certain ratios drop below certain levels, leaving the lender with control over the RE inventory. That is preferred over a pledge on the shares of the company or other related companies, as that requires execution time, uncertain valuation and potentially a locked-up market for those shares. It could well help as secondary collateral as well as a pledge on the shareholders' and intercompany loans to avoid further cash outflow.

As the convertible loan would be provided at HoldCo level, a dividend pusher, inter-company loan or otherwise is needed to ensure liquidity at HoldCo level for repayment. With respect to the convertible loan, some preliminary aspects for consideration are in which shares the loan is convertible (HoldCo, subsidiary,..), the conversion ratio and conversion period. A unitranche is less evident here, also because the requested funding is in Euro terms whereas the firm operates in multiple CEE currencies. Although a multi-currency unitranche is pos-sible, I've never observed it in reality (yet).

The convertibility option provides access to that upside of the firm, which in a positive sce-nario can be considerable, but in a worst-case scenario provides quite some downside (interest on convertible loan is lower and default a realistic option) as well as exit liquidity issues if no buy-back can be organized. Also in that case an equity-to-debt swap clause should be considered to create liquidity that way.

Other clauses for inclusion would be:

- Drag/Tag-along rights to ensure joint exit and protection of the minority investor after conversion. It is important to understand that during the exercise period, the convertibility can be automatic if the majority shareholders plan to sell their stake during that period. Either the conversion happens automatically or the majority shareholders need to notify the convertible loan holder so that he can convert and participate in the sale through tag-along rights. The change of control business is then only needed if the sale were to happen during the non-convertibility period of the bond.
- Tight financial covenants.
- Cross-default/cross-acceleration clauses and/or cash sweep clause.
- Share retention and right of first refusal clause to ensure there is no transfer of existing equity (or newly issued equity) to third parties/related parties.
- Prepayment/cancellation clause in case of change of control.
- Limitation of leverage used in new projects. Rather than on a project basis, as the questions in the case suggest, it would be better to have a limitations clause at company level, reducing the overall risk. It leaves the door open, however, for the use of offshore SPVs in which the projects can be leveraged, and whose balance sheets don't have to be consolidated with that of the subsidiaries and ultimately the holding. That risk can be contracted out though, but might make the projects more expensive from a 'cost of funding' point of view.

The option suggested in the questions, to include a clause that would determine the 'allocation on which projects and in which countries the available capital will have to be spent,' seems unrealistic as it forces the investors to spend large amounts of time and hold significant experience in each of those countries, ignores the fact that some expenditures are not project specific and takes away the discretionary opportunity for the management team to run the business. If one is not convinced about the management, one had better not invest. It is, however, perfectly possible to agree contractually how much capital will be allocated to which countries and to what type of real estate classes (office, leisure, residential etc.)

Corporate governance standards and professionalism with subcontractors are open-ended issues. However, standards can be included as qualifying conditions or can be combined with tranched financing as implementation progresses. Tranched finance can be problematic in this case though, as it might make it difficult for management to commit to projects and/or receive bank financing on committed but not drawdown capital (that is then contingent on certain criteria).

## BUYING ORANGINA – A TYPICAL LBO WITH SOME INTERESTING QUESTIONS AHEAD!

In this case there is essentially one central issue, i.e., the analysis of the debt capacity and the cash flow analysis given the acquisition finance package that was already provided in the case.

## Cost of financing package and debt capacity analysis

Let's re-take the chart in the case with respect to the acquisition finance package, which can now be completed with the actual cost per product group:

| | | | | | Interest | Interest in |
|---|---|---|---|---|---|---|
| | Millions of € | Maturity | xFY2005 EBITDA | % of total | compensation (%) | millions of € |
| **Debt** | | | | | | |
| Senior debt: Tranche A | 250 | 7 | 1.36 | 12.9 | 5.5 | 13.75 |
| Senior debt: Tranche B | 260 | 8 | 1.41 | 13.444 | 6.1 | 15.86 |
| Senior debt: Tranche C | 260 | 9 | 1.41 | 13.444 | 6.6 | 17.16 |
| Facility D | 150 | 2.5 | 0.813 | 7.73 | 5.4 | 8.100 |
| First lien facilities | 920 | | 5.10 | 47.4 | | |
| Second lien | 120 | 9.5 | 0.65 | 6.18 | 8.95 | 10.74 |
| Senior debt + second lien | 1,040 | | 5.64 | 53.6 | | |
| Mezz. bridge facility | 300 | 10 | 1.62 | 154.64 | 8.2 +PIK margin (6.5%) | 24.6 |
| Total debt facility | 1,340 | | 7.26 | 69.07 | | |
| **Equity** | 600 | | 3.25 | 30.92 | | |
| Lion Capital | 300 | | | | | |
| Blackstone | 300 | | | | | |
| Total sources | 1,940 | | 10.51 | 100 | | |

The weighted average annualized cost of the acquisition debt finance package therefore amounts to 7.75%.

The following step is then to consider the annualized impact of the payment due.

| € Millions | 2006 | 2007 | 2008 | 2009 | 2010 | 2011 | 2012 | 2013 |
|---|---|---|---|---|---|---|---|---|
| **Total net cash position** | <81.5> | <79.6> | <76.7> | <71.9> | <64.8> | <56.5> | <48.5> | <38.9> |
| **Net total debt** | 921.0 | 871.3 | 789.4 | 674.7 | 554.2 | 415.3 | 253.5 | 83.6 |
| **Net senior debt** | 739.2 | 697.4 | 623.7 | 500.1 | 384.4 | 241.4 | 88.4 | 0.0 |
| **Payments to retire debt** | | 1254.4 | 151.4 | 194.4 | 193.9 | 201.4 | 204.9 | 210.7 |
| **EBITDA** | 193.5 | 201.4 | 212.3 | 220.5 | 239.6 | | | |
| **Interest coverage** | | 1.606 | 1.402 | 1.1344 | 1.2356 | | | |

As becomes obvious from the numbers, the financing package is somewhat stretched in terms of its repayment capacity, particularly in 2009. It is doubtful, given the situation Orangina is in – in economic terms – and the additional investment needed after acquisition, whether Orangina can deliver upon additional cash flows over and above the ones reflected in the projection which are mentioned in the case and which don't factor in organic growth but only inflation-linked growth. The valuation, which was in the bandwidth €1.9 billion–2.2 billion, is only feasible at the lower end of the valuation bandwidth for Blackstone/Lion Capital. Beyond that, there will have to be more equity put in with lower returns to be expected, or a re-visitation of the projections to see whether some of them can be upgraded to facilitate a higher repayment capacity.

Please observe that the amount of total acquisition finance indicated (i.e., 1,340 million) does not correspond with the opening position in the repayment schedule (i.e., 921 million). That is for two reasons: (1) The bridge facility for sell-off businesses (150 million) would be repaid on a 2.5-year timeline and that would be done with the proceeds of a set of divestitures that would be immediately effected after acquisition, including the water brand Apollonaris. That indeed happened directly after acquisition, and consequently the sell-off facility was repaid. (2) The divestitures generated more revenues than expected (or at least more than needed to repay the sell-off facility), and consequently the remaining part was used to pay off additional non-senior debt.

# LYONDELL CHEMICAL COMPANY

In this particular case, there are two issues coming together in a somewhat perfect financial storm. Driven by a deteriorating market in terms of volume and margins (commoditized to a large degree) on the one hand and all that happening against the background of the LBO a few years ago, which has made the balance sheet more leveraged than is good for a cyclical business (in fact that business wasn't really a poster child for an LBO to begin with, if not for the low predictability of cash flows characterizing this sector). A quick look at the income statement tells us that performance has been deteriorating ever since 2006. The LBO leverage clearly magnified and accelerated the level of distress in 2008–2009. From Dataset 2, it becomes clear that there is US$12.6 billion in senior secured debt outstanding for that part of the organization covered by the Chapter 11 filing (that explains the difference with the slightly higher US$13 billion in senior secured debt outstanding as that covers the whole Lyondell-Basell organization). With about US$12.2 billion in property plant and equipment ('PPE') outstanding (BS 2008), the seniors will have to turn to the softer collateral (if there was a first lien on those assets as well). They will most likely turn to the cash and deposits available for respectively US$406 and 1,091 million to satisfy their claims. It can be questioned whether the deposits with related parties can be liquidated at short notice given the overall deteriorating performance of the group.

And then there is US$9.5 billion in second lien and unsecured debt listed in the filing. A quick calculation tells us that there is US$10.2 billion in softer accounts receivables and inventory. We assume here that all assets can be liquidated at book value, which is highly unrealistic. Taking a 30% discount on book value for PPE and about 40–50% for inventory and accounts receivables, the mezzanine providers as a group have a 50% effective exposure with respect to their total claim, on which they would have to take a haircut in case of an effective liquidation, if no consensus can be reached in a Chapter 11 filing. That effective exposure becomes larger when including the fact that there is US$557 and 3.402 million in deferred taxes which have a priority position in a Chapter 11 filing (above senior secured) as well as US$2,251 and 823 million in accounts payable and other liabilities (all data based on 2008 numbers) with whom the mezzanine lender will be *pari passu* in case of a liquidation. I also assume because of the lower liquidation value of the PPE that the second lien holders will not be in a position to effectuate their claim and will become effectively unsecured and rank *pari passu* with all other mezzanine unsecured lenders.

These elements together lead to the conclusion that in a worst-case scenario the mezzanine lenders will be wiped out for 80% or more of their values, which clearly allows us to conclude that the level of subordination for the mezzanine lenders in this case is very significant if no consensus can be reached.

When turning now to the DIP facility discussed, the question emerges whether the mezzanine lenders should participate, whether the deal as suggested for them is acceptable and to what extent they would be better off participating.

As can be observed from Dataset 3, the changing dynamic of a DIP facility is the fact that the providers of DIP finance get priority over all other unsecured lenders (but after the senior lenders). For non-existing lenders it implies bringing in new money (to be lent short term). For existing lenders who want to participate it means bringing in additional capital on top of the amounts already provided. From that perspective, participating can be considered as adding more risk to your portfolio. On the other hand, it will allow you to roll-up part or all of your current unsecured position and front-leap all other mezzanine lenders who do not participate in the DIP scheme. The case further indicates that more and more bankruptcy judges allow, under certain circumstances, super-priority to DIP lenders, which means that they can front-leap even the senior secured lenders in that case. Whether that is to be expected in this case is questionable as the senior lenders seem to be willing to play ball in the DIP facility, driven to a large degree by the fact that the DIP lending carries a higher yield, is shorter term and there is still a large PPE base which will hold up to its book value better when the firm will operate as a going concern when coming out of Chapter 11 (versus moving from Chapter 11 to Chapter 7 in case no consensus is reached, when the liquidation value will be considerably lower as discussed). In fact, the senior lenders will see their original position fully secured by the book value of all PPE plus the fact that the additional DIP financing is shorter term. On top of that, with the DIP facility, the RC and GP facility have priority over the roll-up facility (which is the existing lending that the lenders committed to the firm before going into the Chapter 11 filing).

Additionally, the RC facility shall be secured by (a) a perfected first lien on all now owned or hereafter acquired accounts receivables and inventory of the debtors and the proceeds thereof ('the RC collateral') and (b) a perfected second lien on all now owned or hereafter acquired other assets and property of the debtors, including real and personal property, plant and equipment, the intercompany facility and the proceeds thereof (the 'Term collateral'). The GP facility and the roll-up facility shall be secured by (c) a perfected first lien on the Term collateral and (d) a perfected second lien on the RC collateral. The liens securing the roll-up loans shall, in all cases, be junior to the liens securing the RC facility and the GP facility.

All obligations under the facilities will be unconditionally guaranteed as well by (a) each borrower (with respect to the obligations of the other borrowers), (b) each subsidiary of LyondellBasell Industries AF SCA that is a US entity currently a guarantor of the Interim Loan facility or the Senior Secured Credit facility, (c) Basell Germany Holdings GmbH, secured by a prime lien on the stock of its direct subsidiaries, and (d) on an unsecured basis, by LyondellBasell and each other non-US subsidiary of LyondellBasell that is currently a guarantor of the Interim Loan facility or the senior Secured Credit facility.

No wonder the DIP facility was fully taken by the existing senior and new lenders! As the DIP deal stands there will be US$4.790 million in new funding coming in (excluding the roll-up facility). That literally put the mezzanine lenders out there on a limb (even further than they already were). The facts in the case raise the question why the mezzanine lenders did not respond louder to participate in the DIP facility, as it was they who could improve their situation most of all lenders involved in the deal.

The reason why the mezzanine lenders did not participate in this case might have everything to do with the fact that most of the mezzanine in this case was provided by the LyondellBasell Finance company, the internal finance company of the LyondellBasell group. As the DIP financing ultimately is guaranteed by other LyondellBasell Group companies, companies that ultimately own the LyondellBasell Finance company, it might be the case that the bankruptcy judge has excluded them from participating in the DIP facility to avoid conflict of interest, or more simply that the senior secured lenders and new lenders have put it up as a demand that the internal bank facility cannot participate in the DIP facility as that would compromise some of the guarantees provided under the DIP facility. The consequence, however, is that the claim that the internal bank has pre-petition will be ever-further subordinated and will become 100% effectively exposed. That has been the faith of many mezzanine providers in the years following the start of the financial crisis in 2008. As discussed in Chapter 11, mezzanine providers have been playing a critical role in restructuring the balance sheet following the financial crisis when adjusting to the new economic reality. During that transition they have been securing some of their original positions as part of the deal. Nevertheless, in many cases that option was not available and the mezzanine lenders were literally wiped out altogether. As mentioned on several occasions in the book, mezzanine has a very high level of equity risk included on average when considering the level of (senior) debt that is on most balance sheets. The pricing needs to follow that dynamic accordingly, as it needs to take into account a probability of default just like an actual shareholder does.

# Index

Printed and bound by CPI Group (UK) Ltd, Croydon, CR0 4YY

16/04/2025

14658506-0004